Classical Period

c. 1750–c. 1815

Romantic Period

c. 1815–c. 1900

Twentieth Century

1900–

Development of String
  Quartet (c. 1750)
Period of Mannheim
  Orchestra's Greatest
  Influence (c. 1750s)
Haydn's First Symphonies
  (c. 1758)
Opening of La Scala Opera
  House in Milan (1778)
Mozart's *The Marriage of
  Figaro* (1786)
Beethoven's *Symphony No. 5*
  (1807)
Schubert's First Lieder
  (1811)

Berlioz' *Symphonie
  fantastique* (1829)
Founding of New York
  Philharmonic Society and
  Vienna Philharmonic (1839)
Liszt's *Les Préludes* (1848)
Wagner's *Tristan und Isolde*
  (1859)
Verdi's *Aida* (1871)
Bayreuth Theater Opens (1872)
Invention of Phonograph (1877)
Debussy's *Prélude à l'après-
  midi d'un faune* (1894)

Stravinsky's *The Rite of Spring*
  (1913)
First Recordings of Jazz (1917)
Schoenberg's Early Serial Works
  (1923)
Long-Playing Records Invented
  (1948)
Messiaen's *Modes* (1949)
Development of Aleatoric
  Music (1950s)
Founding of Columbia–
  Princeton Electronic Music
  Center (1959)
Beatles Become Popular
  in United States (1963)

First Volumes of French
  Encyclopédie (1751)
Seven Years' War (1756–1763)
Rousseau's *Social Contract*
  (1762)
Beginning of Excavations
  at Pompeii (1763)
Industrial Revolution (c. 1770)
American Declaration of
  Independence (1776)
Kant's *Critique of Pure
  Reason* (1781)
Beginning of French
  Revolution (1789)
Napoleon Defeated at
  Waterloo (1815)

First Railroad Built in
  England (1830)
Reign of Victoria (1837–1901)
Invention of Photography (1839)
Marx's *Communist Manifesto*
  (1848)
Darwin's *Origin of Species*
  (1859)
American Civil War
  (1861–1865)
Unification of Italy (1861)
Franco-Prussian War
  (1870–1871)
Unification of Germany (1871)
First Impressionist
  Exhibition (1874)

Wright Brothers' Flight (1903)
Cubist Exhibition in Paris (1907)
World War I (1914–1918)
Einstein's *General Theory
  of Relativity* (1915)
Russian Revolution (1917)
Collapse of New York Stock
  Exchange (1929)
Hitler Rises to Power in
  Germany (1933)
World War II (1939–1945)
United Nations Founded (1945)
People's Republic of China
  Established (1949)
Sputnik (1957)
First Human Lands on Moon
  (1969)
Vietnamese War Ends (1975)

Mark Sims

Music

Music

Second Edition

Daniel T. Politoske
University of Kansas

Art Essays by
Martin Werner
Temple University

PRENTICE-HALL, INC.
Englewood Cliffs, New Jersey

Library of Congress Cataloging in Publication Data

Politoske, Daniel T.
    Music.

    Includes discographies.
    1. Music—Analysis, appreciation.
MT6.P647M9   1979   780'.15   78-10974
ISBN 0-13-607556-8

Printed in the United States of America

2   4   6   8   10   9   7   5   3

Prentice-Hall International, Inc., London
Prentice-Hall of Australia Pty. Ltd., Sydney
Prentice-Hall of Canada, Ltd., Toronto
Prentice-Hall of India Private Limited, New Delhi
Prentice-Hall of Japan, Inc., Tokyo
Prentice-Hall of Southeast Asia Pte. Ltd., Singapore
Whitehall Books Limited, Wellington, New Zealand

Cover Photo: S. Neidorf/The Image Bank
Photo Researcher: Carol Berger

Permission for use of the photographs appearing on the part opening pages is acknowledged as follows: *Part One: Guitar and Flowers* by Juan Gris, 1912, Oil on canvas, 44¼" × 27⅝", Collection, The Museum of Modern Art, New York: Bequest of Anna Erickson Levene in memory of her husband, Dr. Phoebus Aaron Theodor Levene; *Part Two:* Japanese woodcut by Ichieisai Yoshitsuya, Nineteenth century, Collection of the National Museum, Prague; *Part Three:* Miniature from *L'Apocalypse* by Jean Audez, Thirteenth century, Bibliothèque Nationale, Paris; *Part Four: Interior of the Royal Theater* by Pietro Domenico Olivero, 1740, Museo Civico, Turin; *Part Five:* Detail of *Court Music at Ismanins* by P. J. Hormans, 1773, Bavarian National Museum, Munich; *Part Six: Die Symphonie* by M. von Schwind, Nineteenth century, Neue Pinakothek, Munich; *Part Seven: Three Musicians* by Fernand Léger, 1944, Oil on canvas, 68½" × 57¼", Collection, The Museum of Modern Art, New York: Mrs. Simon Guggenheim Fund; *Part Eight:* Bandstand at Congress Park, Saratoga, 1878, Picture Collection, New York Public Library: Astor, Tilden, and Lenox Foundations; *Part Nine: The Jazz Musicians* by Nicholas de Stael, 1952, Picture Collection, New York Public Library: Astor, Tilden, and Lenox Foundations.

Contents

CHAPTER **21**
Romantic Symphony and Concerto 265

CHAPTER **22**
Romantic Program Music 282

CHAPTER **23**
Romantic Opera and Choral Music 297

CHAPTER **24**
Nationalism, Late Romanticism, and Impressionism 317

PART
9
Contemporary Music

Special Features

Preface

The second edition of *Music* is intended for anyone who is seriously interested in learning how to listen to music with greater perception and understanding. Music forms a part of almost everyone's life today—so much so that it is easy to listen to it without giving it much thought. Yet by making some effort to listen carefully to what is heard and by gaining some knowledge of the many different musical styles and forms that have developed over the centuries, a person can hear more and can have a far greater enjoyment of what is heard.

With this goal in mind, the present text places primary emphasis on the listening experience, encouraging the development of listening skills through a historical survey of musical styles. Although social, political, and cultural influences are highlighted throughout, the focus of the discussion is music itself rather than things peripheral to it. Major styles and periods of music are considered, along with the principal types and forms of composition prominent in each period. Representative examples are discussed, and the major composers of each style and period are presented. The focus on listening is strengthened by an accompanying record set with works from all major periods.

Organization

Music has certain basic terms and concepts that are peculiar to it, and an understanding of them is helpful, if not absolutely necessary, to most discussions of music. For this reason, Part One of the book is devoted to a survey of the fundamentals of music—melody and rhythm, harmony and texture, timbre and dynamics, form, and notation. Part Two briefly examines the music of five non-Western cultures and points out some of the ways in which their music differs from that of the West. The remaining seven parts trace major developments in the music of the Western world from the Middle Ages to our own time. Special attention is given to the different styles of music developed in the United States in Part Eight.

The book is organized flexibly so that it can be used in several ways. Each of the major periods in the history of Western music is presented as a compact unit that can be studied with or without the periods immediately preceding or following it. Individual chapters or sections within each period can also be selected as time and interest permit. Finally, the parts on non-Western and American music can be studied in full, by section, or omitted entirely.

Features

The revision process has made it possible to add a wealth of new feature material, all directed toward enhancing the reader's understanding and enjoyment of the study of music. The development of material to strengthen the reader's aural perception of music has received the most attention, but the importance of aesthetic and pedagogical factors has in no way been overlooked. Essentially, the new features can be grouped under the three headings that follow.

New Listening Material

In keeping with the book's primary goal, a variety of new listening items have been added. Perhaps most important are the Listening Guides given for each work and in most cases for each movement of the works analyzed in the book. Organized in outline form, the Guides offer a systematic coverage of the elements in each work, describing major characteristics of the structure and content of a work and providing a solid foundation for the comparison of different compositions. Also new in the second edition are nine Listening Previews, located at the beginning of each of the nine parts of the book, and five Cross-Period Listening Exercises involving such things as the evolution of the opera, Mass, and symphony. The detailed Listening Suggestions found at the end of each chapter in the first edition have been retained and revised to assure the availability of the selections.

Art Essays, Maps, and Other New Illustrations

Just as words alone cannot equal the experience of listening to music, verbal references and black-and-white photographs cannot give a true picture of the fine art of the major periods in the history of music. For this reason, full-color art sections, with interpretative essays by art historian Martin Werner, have been added for each period in the second edition. Each period also features a map of major centers of musical activity. Finally, increased space has been given in the new edition to interesting scores, manuscripts, and programs from all of the major periods, as well as to the varied instrumental groups of each of the periods.

Expanded Coverage of Basic Material

Great care has been taken in the second edition to provide an especially firm introduction to the elements of music, with increased coverage of instruments, form, and style. This initial emphasis is carried throughout the text with the individual outlines of musical elements for each major work found in the

Listening Guides and with Cross-Period Comparison Charts for each major period. Understanding is also heightened through the restriction of content to the most important composers and genres of each period. Other basic material—chronology charts, a full glossary, and a detailed index—have been retained in the new edition, supplemented by a new index of important works.

Readability and the Use of Notation

For the introductory student, the beauty of a musical work can be easily obscured by the use of too many technical words and the introduction of too much additional detail. Throughout the second edition, care has been taken to focus on only the most important details of musical style, presenting them in a clear and interesting fashion, in terms that will be accessible to the student. New visual materials, Listening Guides, and charts have been added to make even the most difficult concepts easier to understand.

Readers who have not learned to read music need not be alarmed by the many short musical examples found in the text. The examples, all of which are clearly labeled, are intended to enhance the discussions of music for those who read music and to give a general visual representation of sounds for those who do not. Ability to read music is not important to understanding the text. The main goal of the book is to stimulate the reader to listen to music, not to look at it.

Supplements

Although not essential to the use of the text, the accompanying set of six records, directly keyed to the major analyses found in the text, can be an invaluable aid to both student and instructor. Full movements are given for all instrumental works, full sections for all vocal works. A *Study Guide and Workbook* and an *Instructor's Manual/Test Item File* are also available. The first contains study aids, self-tests, listening exercises, and a series of cumulative reviews designed to place the study of specific works within a much broader framework. The revised manual features a number of form diagrams that can be used in the classroom to clarify form in specific works and simplify the comparison of form in different works.

Acknowledgments

Kind acknowledgments and profound thanks are due to many friends and colleagues for countless suggestions and much active help. The published works of Rose Brandel and William P. Malm provided valuable insights in the preparation of the first edition. In the second edition, J. Bunker Clark was especially helpful with his comments on American music, and Richard Wright provided excellent ideas for the jazz section. I also wish to thank the many reviewers involved in the development of both the first and second editions.

Thanks are also due to the many people at Prentice-Hall involved in each of the editions. In the preparation of the first edition, I owe a special debt of gratitude to Project Editor Michael Feist and Production Editor Sarah Parker. In the preparation of the new edition, special thanks are due to Art Director Florence Silverman, Manufacturing Buyer Nancy Myers, Production Editor Eleanor Perz, and especially to the Project Editor, Stephanie Roby, whose help was invaluable.

INTRODUCTION

Listening to Music

Music, in all its variety, is one of our most constant companions. It is the sound from our dashboards, the background to our movies, the special gift of our stereo sets and concert halls. Nearly everyone responds to some kind of music. Most of us can identify at least one performer or musical style that moves us emotionally. Our choices today are without limit, for technology gives us instant access to more than ten centuries of music. Even so, most of us can readily summarize our musical tastes with a simple thought: we like what we know.

In essence, we appreciate only that music that we have come to understand. We can follow a familiar piece of music with expectation, welcoming its main melodies, participating in its moments of climax and repose. An unfamiliar work is not likely to affect us so strongly, før we can only guess what its unfolding melodic and rhythmic content will be.

For these reasons, one obvious way of coming to love music is through repeated exposure to specific works. Indeed, few sensual pleasures equal that of immersing oneself in an afternoon of "oldies," be they rock, jazz, or symphonic. But to restrict oneself to the familiar is to limit the possibilities for pleasure, and to limit them sharply. A more adventurous way of increasing musical enjoyment is to cultivate the art of listening—the special abilities that enable a person to perceive the patterns of musical movement, the uses of musical themes, and, ultimately, the creative intentions of the composer and performer. Such abilities can heighten the enjoyment of unfamiliar works as well as familiar. For the attentive listener, they can open entire new worlds of musical experience.

An enhanced ability to listen to music is also likely to lead one to a deeper understanding of the meaning of music. Music is unique as a form of expression. Unlike traditional painting or sculpture, it is nonrepresentational. A melody can bring to mind a seascape or the death of a loved one, but it cannot represent them in an obvious way. In this sense, music is an art without subject matter.

Perhaps this is why music has often been said to convey pure emotion. The effect of music on the attentive listener is, in fact, very similar to that of other emotional experiences. Music does not express emotions in any clearly

1

definable way. A given work may strike two listeners differently, or it may call forth different reactions from the same listener on different hearings. In this way, music closely parallels the way in which emotions are played out in our inner lives, leaving us with feelings ambiguous in content, fluid, and strongly felt.

In that wordless state in which we think and feel, there is movement and rest, tension and release, dissonance and harmony, acceleration and retardation, intensity and dissolution. With attentive listening, one can perceive how many of these effects are created in music. Often one can even come to understand why a particular musical technique creates the effect it does. Perceptive listening can increase the level of the intellectual experience of listening, and at the same time intensify the emotional experience. Both aspects are equally important. Both contribute greatly to the potential for enjoyment.

Gris, *Guitar and Flowers*, 1912

Listening Preview   One of the most important elements in musical composition is style, that of the individual composer and that of the period in which a work was written. Listen to movements from three concertos—one written by Handel during the Baroque period, one written by Mozart during the Classical period, and one written by Tchaikovsky during the Romantic period. (Selections can be found in the record set that accompanies the text—Side 3, Band 3; Side 6, Band 1; and Side 8, Band 1—or in the record library.) What stylistic differences do you find in the three works? What qualities would you expect to find in other music written during the same periods?

I
Melody and Rhythm

The Basic Ingredients of Music

An outpouring of thoughts or emotions is not in itself artistic. It must be organized, disciplined, and refined—in short, it must be made accessible to another person.

Sound and Time

A musical work is essentially a disciplined and refined organization of sounds. The sounds that are produced proceed chronologically—from one moment to the next. Thus, music itself may be defined very simply as *sound* organized within *time*. Indeed, the twentieth-century composer Igor Stravinsky once defined music as "a speculation in terms of sound and time."

Musical Sound

Musical Tones

Many a music critic has damned a new work by calling it "noise." The critic knows that we expect *musical tones* to differ from other sounds and that we are likely to be shocked or disappointed when they seem not to.

All sounds are caused by vibrations of objects, which in turn produce vibrations in the air. But whereas the vibrations that create noise are random and irregular, a musical tone consists of a series of regular, evenly timed vibrations, recurring in a pattern. On an oscillograph, a device that records fluctuations in vibration, it is possible to see the difference between a noise such as a human scream and a musical tone held by a trained soprano:

Scream

Musical Tone

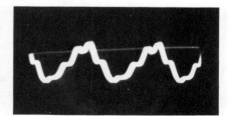

5

Pitch

**Notes and
Staff**

In a musical tone, the number of vibrations that occur per second determines a property called *pitch*. The greater the number of vibrations per second, the higher the pitch, and vice versa. Musical notation indicates pitch by *notes*, which are usually oval and arranged on a sort of linear ladder called a *staff*. The higher-pitched notes are placed higher on the staff:

High Pitches

Low Pitches

**Ascending and
Descending Tones**

It seems natural to think of pitch in spatial terms. We can, in fact, actually feel music ascend and descend in space. *Ascending tones* tend to produce a feeling of expansion or excitement. *Descending tones*, on the other hand, produce a downward pull that may be associated with rest, finality, or a preparation for another upward swell.

The beginning of Strauss's "Blue Danube" can be used to demonstrate how upward and downward movement is felt in music. A graphic representation of the passage would look something like this:

Graphic Representation

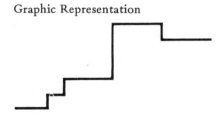

A notational representation of the same passage would look something like this:

Notational Representation

Melody

The notes on the staff shown immediately above represent a *melody*—a succession of tones used in a meaningful way. Melody is generally the first thing people listen for in a piece of music. It is also the "tune" that will be remembered long after the music is over.

**Disjunct and
Conjunct
Melodies**

Melodic lines may be characterized by upward or downward movement, by both, or by hardly any movement at all. A melody in which there are large distances between successive tones is called a *disjunct melody*. Such melodies often call for great dexterity in performance; consider the difficulty many

Memorable Melodies/Forgotten Melodies: *Why have certain melodies such as the "Habanera" and the "Toreador Song" from the opera* Carmen *become popular while others have been so largely forgotten? The answer can be found partly in the musical qualities of well-known melodies, partly in the nonmusical associations of the melodies, and partly in the subjective experiences of thousands of individual listeners.*

people have in singing "The Star-Spangled Banner." A melody that moves in small steps is called a *conjunct melody.* Such melodies are generally much easier to sing: "The First Noel," an extremely conjunct melody, is a familiar example. In a very general sense, disjunct melodies tend to impart drama and energy, while conjunct melodies are capable of sweeter, more lyrical effects.

Melodic Structure

As a complete artistic statement, a melody has a beginning, a middle, and an end. We are conscious of its structure much in the same way that we are conscious of the structure of a sentence. Just as the sentence's structure is understood in the reading, so is the structure of a melody understood in the listening.

Most of us actually have a very well developed understanding of music within our own culture. For example, nearly everyone can supply the last note of the following short melody, when it is sung or played:

MELODY AND RHYTHM

(As you have probably guessed, the last note of the melody is 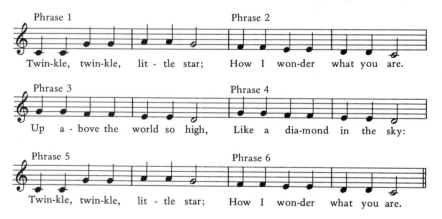 .) Moreover, most people can sense intuitively whether or not a musical work has ended. Few people, for example, would be satisfied with hearing the melody of "Yankee Doodle" without its final line.

Most people would also be dissatisfied if the second half of a melody began and ended just like the first. We expect melodies to change, to offer the *contrast* of new material. Try singing both sentences of "London Bridge" to the same melody. They begin the same but end differently. In cases where the first part of a melody *is* repeated from beginning to end, as in "The Star-Spangled Banner," the ear demands that it be followed by something new. In our national anthem, that something new is supplied by the lines beginning "And the rocket's red glare."

Although change is essential, the *repetition* found in "London Bridge" and "The Star-Spangled Banner" is just as important. In fact, without any conscious effort, most of us have learned to expect a fine balance between repeated elements, which give music its basic organization, and new elements, which provide dramatic impact. This is true with even the simplest, most repetitious melodies. The repetition at the beginning of the second sentence of "London Bridge" gives the piece a unity it would otherwise lack.

Clearly, we have strong expectations about melodies. We expect a melody to come to rest on a tone that conveys finality—and our ears can supply this tone. We expect melodies to change, to offer new and contrasting material. But at the same time, we want this contrast to be balanced by a unifying repetition. Almost intuitively, we understand some of the basic structural principles inherent in many melodies.

Think about the melodic structure of the following simple melody:

Contrast *(margin)*

Repetition *(margin)*

Phrase 1   Phrase 2
Twin-kle, twin-kle, lit - tle star;   How I won-der what you are.

Phrase 3   Phrase 4
Up   a - bove the   world so   high,   Like a   dia-mond in the   sky:

Phrase 5   Phrase 6
Twin-kle, twin-kle,   lit - tle star;   How I won-der what you are.

Phrases *(margin)*

Perhaps the first thing that is apparent about the melody is the fact that it is not heard all at once. Instead, we hear it in *phrases* that correspond to the lines of the poem. The ear structures the melodic material into six phrases, with the second seeming to answer the first, the fourth answering the third, and the sixth answering the fifth.

Another structural factor that is immediately evident to the ear is the repetition of certain *tonal* and *rhythmic patterns*. These are made obvious in this case by the repetition of words. The tonal pattern of Phrase 1, for example, is repeated exactly in Phrase 5. The rhythmic pattern of these two phrases is also identical. In fact, this rhythmic pattern is repeated, even when the tonal pattern itself is varied. Though some of the phrases move upward in pitch and some of the phrases move downward, all six of them are sung to the same rhythm. You will hear this constantly repeated rhythmic pattern even more clearly if you clap the song out.

Thus, when we listen for musical structure, we hear not only the upward and downward movements associated with pitch but rhythmic patterns as well. Music is, after all, organized within time. *Rhythm* is its organizing principle.

Rhythm

Historians have speculated that music originated in the beating of rhythms that were used to accompany ritual. In some cultures, music still focuses predominantly on rhythms, often very complicated ones. At times, in these cultures and even in our own, rhythmic patterns are played alone, with no accompanying melody. "Twinkle, Twinkle, Little Star," for example, can be clapped instead of sung. In most music, however, rhythmic patterns are wedded so closely to melody as to be nearly inseparable.

Consider the following example, a melody familiar to us as "America," but also the melody of "God Save the Queen," the national anthem of Great Britain:

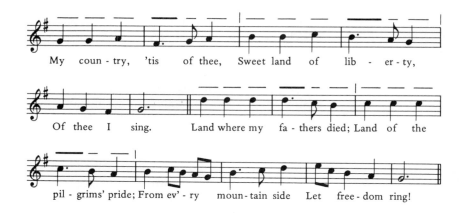

Certain patterns of long and short tones are immediately perceived by the ear. The pattern — — — — — — —, for example, is heard several times. In each case, the fourth note is longer than all the others, the fifth note shorter. In all, the — — — — — — — rhythm occurs four times in the song, creating a distinctive, repeated rhythmic pattern.

Meter

A regularly recurring pulse or *beat* underlies most rhythmic patterns. In "America," the beat is quite clear from the beginning. Also very clear is a recurring stress—or *accent*—on the first beat or every group of three beats. Sometimes this accent is very pronounced, sometimes less so, but it is always there. If the symbol / is used to indicate accented beats and the symbol ⌣ to show weaker beats, the pattern looks like this:

```
  /      ⌣    ⌣     /      ⌣    ⌣
  My    coun  try,  'tis       of thee,
  /      ⌣    ⌣     /      ⌣    ⌣
  Sweet land  of    li     ber  ty,
  /      ⌣    ⌣     /      ⌣    ⌣
  Of     thee I     sing ————.
```

The pattern for "Twinkle, Twinkle, Little Star" is quite different:

```
  /    ⌣    /    ⌣    /     ⌣    /     ⌣
  Twin kle, twin kle,  lit  tle  star ——— ;
  /    ⌣    /    ⌣    /     ⌣    /     ⌣
  How   I   won  der  what  you  are  ——— .
```

The pattern of accented and unaccented beats or pulses in music is called *meter.* "America" is said to be "in three," or in *triple meter,* because each accented beat begins a set of three equal beats. "Twinkle, Twinkle, Little Star" is "in two," or in *duple meter,* because each accented beat begins a set of two equal beats.

The ear perceives the beats in these songs in groups of three or two—that is, in *measures.* Having observed the formation of one measure, we expect that similar measures will follow, all in the same metrical pattern.

Everyone is acquainted with the metrical patterns used in special kinds of music. A person can easily fall into step to the meter of a march—ONE-two, ONE-two. Dances are also characterized by their meters—the waltz by its sweeping ONE-two-three and the polka by its vigorous ONE-two.

Other meters are formed from combinations of the basic duple or triple patterns. Especially within the last century, musicians have made unusual deviations from the traditional meters. Tchaikovsky, in the second movement of *Symphony No. 6* (the "Pathétique"), used a meter of ONE-two-THREE-four-five, while Béla Bartók, a Hungarian composer, used measures of seven beats. Igor Stravinsky, in *The Rite of Spring,* not only used unusual meters but also changed metrical patterns frequently to avoid a feeling of metric regularity.

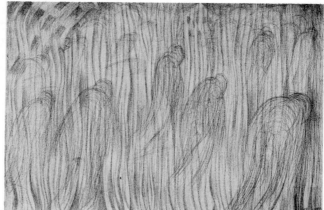

Collection, The Museum of Modern Art, New York: Gift of Vico Baer

Rhythm in Art: *Rhythm is found not only in music but in other art forms as well. The distinct pulses and accents found in Boccioni's* States of Mind I, II, *and* III *help to express the themes found in the subtitles of the works: "The Farewells," "Those Who Stay," and "Those Who Go." (1911, charcoal, each 23" × 34")*

One of the most delightfully surprising effects in music occurs when the meter of a work is deliberately upset for expressive purposes—that is, when an accent is placed on a normally weak beat. *Syncopation*, as this is called, can be obvious, as in Gershwin's "I've Got Rhythm," or it can be very subtle, as in certain seventeenth-century works of music. In dance music, syncopation creates a strong and distinctive rhythmic pattern. Syncopation can also be used to help propel music to the end of a phrase.

Rhythmic Motion

Meter organizes a composition into identical groups—measures—of strong and weak beats. Syncopation simply changes the expected placement of the strong beats. Aaron Copland, a modern American composer, has suggested that "we get the real rhythm only when we stress the notes according to the musical sense of the phrase."

The expressive impact of music is much diminished if music is played absolutely in meter, just as the beauty of poetry is lost if it is read in singsong fashion. In "America," for example, the amount of stress placed on notes changes from measure to measure. The strong beat in the second measure is stressed more than the strong beat in the first measure and, in the two measures that make up the line "Of thee I sing," there are four beats of nearly equal stress. The number of notes per measure and per beat also changes. In cases where there is more than one note per beat, the *rhythmic motion* seems much faster. Thus, in hearing music, we are conscious both of the meter and also of the way the rhythm plays against it for expressive purposes.

Tempo

A composer often provides a marking for *tempo*, or overall speed, to help convey the character of a composition. Several of the most common tempos, traditionally written in Italian, are given, with their translations, in the chart at the top of the next page. On a musical score tempos generally appear above the opening measure, while on concert programs they are often used to identify movements.

Other terms are sometimes added to show that the work is of a special nature. For example, the term *minuet*, or *menuetto*, indicates that a work or movement should be played in the manner of the traditional courtly dance of that name.

Within a composition the tempo may be varied for expressive purposes. An *accelerando*, or quickening, is often used to create excitement. A *ritardando*, or slowing down, suggests rest, deliberation, or other moods, depending on the context. Often such changes in tempo are part of a larger expressive scheme that may also include changes in melody and in the loudness or softness of the music.

Common Tempos		
largo (broad) *grave* (solemn)		very slow
lento (slow) *adagio* (leisurely)		slow
andante (at a walking pace) *andantino* (a little faster than andante) *moderato* (moderate)		moderate
allegretto (moderately fast) *allegro* (fast)		fast
vivace (vivacious) *presto* (very fast) *prestissimo* (as fast as possible)		very fast

Adjectives Often Used with Tempos

molto (very)
più (more)
meno (less)
poco (a little)
ma non troppo (but not too much)

Listening to Melody and Rhythm

Side 1, Band 1

The record set that accompanies the text gives aural examples of many of the points covered in Chapter 1. You may also want to listen to recordings of folk songs to find your own examples of the following: ascending and descending tones, disjunct and conjunct melodies, repetition and contrast, tonal and rhythmic patterns, duple and triple meter, syncopation, and tempo changes.

2

Harmony and Texture

Harmony

It is not surprising that people first approached music through the pulse of rhythm and the melodic medium of song. Melody and rhythm have been, from the earliest times, the natural materials of nearly all the world's music. *Harmony* is a more complex phenomenon and a relatively recent one. It involves the sounding together of two or more tones with the consequent effect of musical depth.

The effect of harmony is most evident in those works that have both a melody and an accompaniment. A vocalist sings a melody enriched by the harmonies of a guitar. A pianist produces a melody with the right hand while sounding great clusters of tones with the left. One is aware of enjoying a richer experience because the melody is supported by harmonic materials.

Harmony in written music is generally thought to have begun in the ninth century when monks added a second melodic line to the original melodic line in their chants. The second line was generally parallel to the first, producing a hollow sound that still evokes images of the Middle Ages. More sophisticated forms of harmony developed in the centuries that followed. It was soon discovered that two voices pulling in opposite directions could impart more drama and interest than parallel voices, and that three or more melodies could produce an even greater effect. In later centuries, after this polyphonic, or "many-voiced," style of music had been developed to a very high peak, some composers began to emphasize one voice or melodic line. What had been several layers of melody became a melody with harmonic support.

The Elements of Harmony

While melody refers to a single-line sequence of tones, harmony refers to tones that are sounded together. When two different pitches are sung together, we become less aware of their individual sounds. A composite, blended sound is heard. The nature of the sound depends on the relationship of the two tones—the distance, or *interval*, between them. When two tones are heard together, we speak of an interval; when three or more tones come together, the

Intervals and Chords

14

combination is called a *chord*. The study of harmony is, in effect, the study of tonal relationships found in intervals and chords and the way these groups of tones are organized within a musical composition.

It is clear to anyone who has ever experimented with a piano keyboard that different combinations of tones will produce different effects. When adjacent white keys are played together, the effect is somewhat harsh. In contrast, alternate white keys give a pleasing sound. Different harmonic effects are achieved as the interval between tones is increased. However, if two keys that are exactly eight white keys apart are sounded, there is little sense of harmony. The explanation behind the similar sounds in this eight-tone interval—which is called an *octave*—lies in the phenomenon of vibrations. The frequency of vibration of the higher tone in the octave is exactly twice that of the lower tone. This accounts for the similarity of sound.

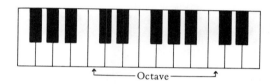

If we count all the keys—black and white—between and including those that produce the octave, they number thirteen. However, two of these thirteen keys, the first and the last, have the same pitch name. Thus, there are twelve different tones that can be used for harmonic purposes. When the twelve tones are played in order, the result is a progression known as the *chromatic scale*. Most of our music is based, not on this scale, but on scales that use only seven of these twelve tones.

Major Scale

Tonic Note and Related Intervals

The most widely used scale pattern in Western music is so familiar as to seem almost second nature. It is the *major scale* that we know as *do-re-mi-fa-sol-la-ti-do*. Any of the twelve tones of the chromatic scale may serve as *do*— the *tonic note*—of a major scale. The choice of the other six tones will depend on the choice of tonic because the pitch relationships—the intervals between tones—are the same in all major scales. If, for example, the note C is chosen as *do*, the note an interval of a *second* above it (*re*) will be D, the note an interval of a *third* above it (*mi*) will be E, and so on until the note an interval of an *eighth* above it (*do*, or C) is reached.

Minor Scale

Another seven-tone scale prominently used in much Western music is the *minor scale*. There are several versions of the minor scale, all of which differ from the major scale in the way the intervals are arranged. The pattern of one of the minor scales can be heard if you sing the syllables *la-ti-do-re-mi-fa-sol-la*. Music based on a minor scale often seems more serious and somber than music based on a major scale, as we will see later in numerous examples.

In any scale, the tonic note is that which conveys rest and finality. This is the tone that the ear supplies at the end of the incomplete example on page 7.

Chromatic Scale

Alinari/Scala

Harmony of Line: *In music, harmony refers to a very specific phenomenon. However, in a more general sense, all the arts deal with harmony. In sculpture, harmony of line is of major importance. The exquisite balance of figures and the flowing lines of Michelangelo's* Madonna with Child *amply illustrate the height of harmony in sculpture.*

Try singing the seven tones of the major scale (*do-re-mi-fa-sol-la-ti*) without the final tonic (*do*), and you will see how strongly the ear demands it. The seventh note pulls so strongly upward that you must supply the tonic mentally. By singing "Yankee Doodle" without the last two syllables, you can see the way the same effect operates in the realm of melody.

The tones or the major and minor scales thus have very specific relationships to each other. In melody these relationships are perceived as the music develops horizontally. With the addition of harmony, we feel the relationships both horizontally and vertically. Relationships are heard between simultaneous notes or chords as well as between consecutive notes.

Triads

If played together, the tones *do-mi-sol*—the first, third, and fifth notes of the major scale—produce a three-toned chord, or *triad*, that is very common in the music of our culture. Other triads can be formed by playing other alternate tones in the major scale. Thus, a triad can be made of the tones *re-fa-la* (2–4–6), *mi-sol-ti* (3–5–7), and so on.

Any of the tones in a triad can be duplicated in another octave, and although the chord will sound higher or lower, it will not be basically changed. In fact, the four-part harmony found in much of our music generally consists of triads with one of the tones duplicated (*do-mi-sol-do*, or 1–3–5–8, for example). The notes of a triad may also be arranged in different order (the inverted chord *sol-do-mi*, or 5–1–3, for example) without radically changing the nature of the chord.

What is important from a harmonic standpoint is that the different chords have different harmonic effects in a given piece of music. For convenience, chords are usually identified by the number of the tone on which they are based. Thus, a triad based on the first, or tonic, note of the scale is called the I chord or the *tonic chord*. Its notes are *do-mi-sol*, or 1–3–5. Just as the tonic note provides the gravitational center toward which the music returns, the chord beginning with this note is the harmonic center of a piece. All else in a composition happens in relation to the tonic and the tonic chord. Also important for the contrast they provide are the IV chord or *subdominant chord* (4–6–8) and the V chord or *dominant chord* (5–7–2).

Tonic Chord

Subdominant and Dominant Chords

These three chords, I, IV, and V, are enough to accompany many simple pieces of music. The harmonic scheme of "Yankee Doodle" is an example:

I		I	V	I		I	V
Yankee Doodle went to town/ Riding on a pony							
I		IV		V		I	
Stuck a feather in his hat/ And called it macaroni.							

Triads built on the other tones of the scale increase harmonic variety, but usually play less important roles than the I, IV, and V chords.

Cadences

The strongest chordal relationship in Western music is that between the tonic and dominant chords. When the V chord is played, the ear strives for and anticipates the I chord. It is the extended sounding of the V chord that makes the rock singer vibrate with energy and tension, only to go limp as the song reaches its final note—the first tone in the scale, accompanied in some way by the I chord.

Resolution

The *resolution* of the V chord to the I chord heard at the end of a rock song is a harmonic formula called a *cadence*. A cadence brings a musical composition, or part of it, to a strong, identifiable close. The V–I cadence, called the *authentic cadence*, almost invariably ends the main body of a composition. A less common cadence—and a weaker one—is found in the movement from the IV chord to the I chord. This weaker IV–I cadence, called the *plagal cadence*, is often sung to the word "Amen" at the end of hymns and, for that reason, is sometimes referred to as the "Amen" cadence. While the V–I cadence exerts a decisive pull from the dominant to the tonic, the IV–I cadence almost relaxes into the tonic, conveying a feeling of peace.

Authentic and Plagal Cadences

Courtesy of The Detroit Institute of Arts: The Dexter M. Ferry, Jr. Fund

The Relativity of Dissonance: *In the nineteenth century a famous art critic accused the painter of the art work shown here of "flinging a pot of paint in the public's face." In its own day,* Whisler's Nocturne in Black and Gold *seemed a very dissonant exception to the artistic rule. Yet the modern viewer is not likely to find the work the least bit outrageous.*

Consonance and Dissonance

Some chords, such as the triads already discussed, are pleasing and complete in themselves. Others may be so harsh that we sometimes erroneously feel they are not harmonious at all.

Music would be unnecessarily dull if restricted to pleasing or *consonant* sounds. It would be seriously limited in expressing inner realities if harsher, *dissonant* sounds were excluded. Who has not felt discordant tones ring in his or her own mind? Who has not experienced the interweaving of consonant and dissonant memories? Dissonance is as natural to music as to thought. Indeed, music is one of the few arts that can rival the mind in its power of expressing opposites almost at the same time.

Although some musical sounds may be displeasing in themselves, dissonance is usually more relative than absolute. Our judgment depends on our frame of reference. A series of dissonant chords will sound harsher than a single dissonant chord moving in transition toward the tonic. A series of dissonances will also be received differently in the twentieth century than it would have been in the seventeenth. It will be felt differently by a student of modern music than by people familiar only with the music of the Classical period.

In much of traditional music, dissonance is used cautiously. It serves to provide conflict and contrast with consonant sounds rather than as an entity in its own right. Dissonances strain to be resolved, and the traditional composer has usually treated them accordingly. But, as Igor Stravinsky once remarked, "Nothing forces us to be looking constantly for satisfaction that resides only in repose." Modern composers, seeking new means of musical expression, have learned to use dissonance for its own sake rather than simply as a foil to consonance.

That this development has caused some consternation is hardly surprising. Dissonances that are now taken for granted once provoked near revolutions in the musical world. Beethoven's *Symphony No. 3* (the "Eroica"), now a favorite Classical work, was in its own time considered unpleasantly dissonant.

Although the use of dissonance is greater today, composers in every age have countered consonance with dissonance. The late sixteenth-century Italian madrigalists, in particular, are noted for their occasional use of strikingly dissonant harmonies. Dissonance and consonance are equally important if music is to express the full range of human emotion. Each age must find the proper balance of the two for itself.

Changes in Tonality

Music based on a major or minor scale, or on any other scale that centers around a single tonic note, is said to be *tonal*. The *tonality* of a piece of music is defined by the note around which it revolves. If the tonic note is C, the tonality is C.

Accidentals and Modulations

Listening to music based on a major or minor scale, we expect to hear only the seven tones of that scale, and not the tones from some other scale. We expect the music to remain within the given tonality. When a note foreign to the scale—an *accidental*—is used, it creates a surprise. Even more surprising is a *modulation*—a shifting of the *do* or tonic and an acceptance, by the ear, of a new tonic and new harmonic relationships.

The explanations for accidentals and modulations are rather technical and demand more theoretical background than has been developed here. However, the ear is not bound to theoretical considerations. It clearly recognizes and understands surprises in tonality. In the Frank Sinatra recording of "Strangers in the Night," the entire melody, as it is sung for the final time, shifts upward to a different tonic. The Beatles' song "If I Fell in Love with You" also shows a very effective use of modulation. Generally, modulation results in greater intensity. The "Liebestod" (literally "love-death") from Richard Wagner's opera *Tristan und Isolde* derives much of its transcending power from the continuous upward shifting of the tonal center—that is, from modulation. Modulation is a vital force in creating harmonic interest in nearly all types and styles of music.

Texture

When a melody is accompanied by chords, the result is an interweaving of sound. Melody is the horizontal strand; the chordal harmonies are the vertical strands. This interweaving of sound is called *texture.* As fine or coarse threads in cloth are woven together with different techniques, so can melodies and harmonies be arranged to produce widely contrasting results.

Monophony

The simplest kind of musical texture—*monophonic* texture—consists of a single melodic line without accompaniment. Sing any melody you know and the result is *monophony.* Vocal solos, as well as solo works for such instruments as violin and flute, demonstrate the many artistic uses of monophony. So, too, does the music of China and Japan. It is almost entirely monophonic, consisting of finely articulated melodies, supported, if at all, by purely rhythmic accompaniments.

Polyphony or Counterpoint

In many cultures, especially in the Western world, a number of different ways of combining two or more voices or parts have been developed. Some Western music, particularly that of the fifteenth to eighteenth centuries, has a *polyphonic,* or *contrapuntal,* texture. Such music, known as *polyphony* or *counterpoint,* consists of several different voices, each of which is independent in its melodic structure. The result is several different layers of melody. The horizontal aspect of each voice is most important, but the several melodies do sound simultaneously, contributing to an overall vertical, or harmonic, effect.

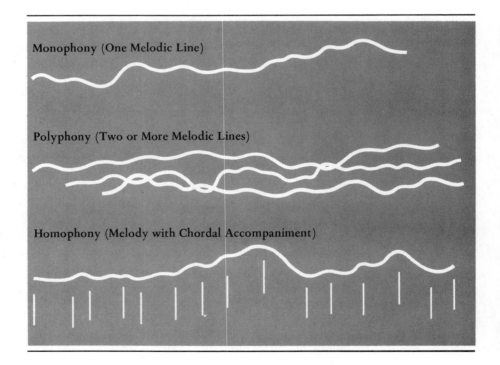

Monophony (One Melodic Line)

Polyphony (Two or More Melodic Lines)

Homophony (Melody with Chordal Accompaniment)

If you sing "Row, Row, Row Your Boat" as a round, you will note that while each voice moves independently, the interplay between voices produces a pleasant total sound. Not all songs can be treated in this way, however. While "Row, Row, Row Your Boat" works as a round, "America" will not. The writer of counterpoint uses special techniques to produce strong separate melodies and a harmonious whole. Listening to counterpoint also calls for special skills in that we must follow both the horizontal and the vertical elements. However, familiarity is all that is needed. Many people find counterpoint among the most stimulating elements in music.

Homophony

More common in our listening experience is *homophonic* texture, or melody accompanied by chords. In *homophony*, the melody is often heard in the highest voice, but it can appear in lower voices or be taken up by different voices in turn. While we tend to listen for the melody, the chordal activity in the nonmelodic voices is equally important.

A graphic representation of the three basic textures would look something like the examples given in the chart on page 20. The arrangement of polyphonic and homophonic textures, however, may take many forms other than the single examples given. In polyphony, the highest-pitched voice or part may enter first (as it does in the chart), or a lower-pitched voice may enter first, or all voices may begin together. In homophony, the arrangement of the chordal accompaniment may vary. Chords may be played with each note of melody, producing a firm vertical texture—something rather analogous to stripes in a painting. Or chords may be played only occasionally—just on the strong beats, for example—producing a texture that is lighter and more open.

Use of Arpeggios

Finally, the tones in a chord may be played as *arpeggios*—in succession rather than simultaneously—generally producing a more fluid texture. Even the untrained eye will notice the difference in these three examples from Schumann's *Album for the Young*, a collection of piano music:

Chord with Each
Note of Melody

Chords on
Strong Beats

Arpeggiated
Chords

In Western music, texture is not always constant throughout a composition. A solo voice may be joined in counterpoint by several other independent voices, bringing about a change from monophonic to polyphonic texture. Similarly, a homophonic piano work or symphony may make use of counterpoint for greater contrast or intensity.

Listening to Harmony and Texture

Side 1, Band 2 On the record set that accompanies the text, you will find aural examples of many of the points covered in Chapter 2. As musical examples are discussed in the following chapters, the characteristics of harmony and texture will be further amplified and clarified.

CHAPTER

3

Timbre and Dynamics

Timbre

A melody sung by Joan Baez will sound very different when performed by the operatic soprano Beverly Sills. Although both may sing the same pitches, the first produces a pure, clear sound and the second a richer sound. The explanation for these different qualities lies in tone color or timbre.

Timbre is a term used to describe the characteristic quality of the sound produced by a voice or instrument. The quality of the sound will be influenced by many factors. Among these are the material from which an instrument is made, the size and shape of an instrument or vocal mechanism, and the way in which an instrument or voice is used.

Voices

It is very likely that the first musical instruments people learned to use were their own voices. Like other music producers, people are equipped with strings or cords that vibrate to produce musical sound. These are, of course, the vocal cords, found within the larynx or "voice box." After sounds are produced in the larynx, they are amplified by sounding bodies—the throat, mouth, sinus, and nasal cavities.

That some voices are high in pitch and some low is common observation. Actually we are all able to produce a wide range of musical sounds by adjusting the muscles that affect our vocal cords. As muscular tension is increased, the vocal cords are shortened and a higher pitch is produced. As tension is decreased, the vocal cords are lengthened and a lower pitch is produced.

The overall range of sounds a person can make is determined largely by the size of the person's larynx. Just as a long string produces a lower sound than a short one, so does a large larynx produce a lower voice. Small larynxes and shorter strings produce higher pitches. These relationships also hold true in the orchestra: the double bass, a large, long-stringed instrument, produces a lower range of sounds than the much smaller violin. Among vocalists, the highest range belongs to the *soprano*. The other types of female voices, from relatively high to low, are *mezzo-soprano* and *contralto* (or simply *alto*). The three types of male voices, from highest to lowest, are *tenor*, *baritone*, and *bass*.

Voice Categories

23

Just as voices differ in the range of tones they can produce, so do they differ in style and quality. Sometimes this reflects cultural differences. Singing in the Western world is based largely on an Italian style—a relaxed, open-throated sound in which vowels are emphasized. In some non-Western countries, singing is based on entirely different artistic ideas. Chinese singers aim at a somewhat closed-throated sound, which seems strident or nasal to our ears. They may slide from one tone to another rather than come to rest on different tones as we do in singing Western melodies. Different cultures, then, have different methods of singing and different ways of judging the results.

String Instruments

Chordophones

Those instruments that produce sound through the vibration of strings, or chords, are *chordophones*. The modern Western orchestra features a large

Christian Steiner / Photo courtesy of New York Philharmonic

Orchestral Strings: *All four of the instruments of the violin family can be seen in this formal photograph of the New York Philharmonic: the violin at the left, the slightly larger viola in the middle, the cello at the right, and the double bass in the rear.*

section of these string instruments, the most prominent of which is the violin. The player draws a bow across the strings of this instrument or, at times, plucks the strings. The pitch of the tone produced depends on the length, thickness, tautness, and material of the string. Each string can be pressed down, or "stopped," at any point with the fingertip and thus lengthened or shortened to produce different pitches. Chordophones in the *violin family* are, from highest to lowest in pitch, the *violin*, *viola*, *violoncello* (or *cello*), and *double bass*. The first two are positioned on the shoulder. The cello rests on the floor and is held between the knees, while the double bass stands on the floor in front of the player.

Violin Family

All of the bowed instruments are noted for a smooth singing tone. When the player draws the bow over the string, vibrations are drawn forth, producing a nearly human tone in the high-pitched instruments and a warm, vibrant sound in the lower ones.

Plucked or Strummed Instruments

There are other chordophones that are specifically designed to be plucked or strummed. Several of these, such as the *guitar*, *banjo*, and *ukulele*, are familiar to us from folk music. All have frets, or ridges, on the fingerboard against which the musician presses the strings in order to produce a given tone or group of tones.

Harp Family

Another group of string instruments—one that seems to be represented in nearly every culture—is the *harp family*. The sizes and shapes of the many different *harps* vary considerably. However, they share one common characteristic: they are generally plucked.

Wind Instruments

Aerophones

While the string player produces sound by means of a vibrating string, the *aerophone* player does so by forcing breath through a tube and causing a column of air to vibrate. Aerophones are generally made of either wood or metal. In the Western orchestra, they are divided into two families—the woodwinds and the brasses.

Woodwind Family

Despite its name, the *woodwind family* includes both wood and metal aerophones. The woodwind tube is sometimes equipped with a flexible reed, such as the one found on the clarinet, which vibrates when the instrument is played. The air column vibrating within the instrument may be shortened or lengthened by means of finger holes or keys. By covering a hole through which air escapes, for example, the player can lengthen the column of air and produce a lower tone. This simple principle can be seen in the familiar song flute of elementary schools and no less in the archeological remains of the Stone Age. Aerophones were among the earliest melodic instruments. They are relatively simple to make, requiring only a piece of hollow reed, an animal horn, or a bone.

The Western orchestra includes a number of woodwinds. The *transverse flute*, held horizontally and played without a reed, has a high and brilliant tone. The *piccolo* is simply a shorter, and thus higher-sounding, flute. The *oboe*, similar to the flute in range, has a double-reed mouthpiece that gives it a reedy nasal tone—somewhat piercing, but yet sweet. Other double-reed instruments, all lower in pitch than the oboe, are the *English horn*, *bassoon*, and *contrabassoon*. In these instruments, sound is produced when the player blows between the mouthpiece's two very delicate, sensitive reeds. In the single-reed instruments, the *clarinet* and *saxophone*, sound is produced when the player makes the reed vibrate against the mouthpiece. The clarinet is especially impressive in the variety of its timbre. It is clear and sharp in the highest part of its range, warm and full in the lower.

Brass Family

The *brass family* includes, from highest to lowest in pitch, the *trumpet*, *horn*, *trombone*, and *tuba*. Structurally the brasses are quite similar. Each begins with a cup-shaped mouthpiece and ends in a flared bell. Air travels through a tube that is shorter or longer depending on the range of the instrument. The length of the tube in which the air column vibrates can be increased or decreased by means of valves (a nineteenth-century invention) or, in the case of the trombone, with a slide. However, changing the length of the

Christian Steiner/Photo courtesy of New York Philharmonic

Orchestral Winds: *The most prominent woodwind and brass instruments can be found in this photograph of a rehearsal of the New York Philharmonic. In the first row are piccolos, flutes, oboes, and an English horn. Behind them are clarinets, bassoons, and a contrabassoon. The brasses—horns, trombones, and tuba, with trumpets in the rear—are generally placed behind the woodwinds.*

MUSICAL ELEMENTS

tubing is not, by itself, enough to determine the pitch of a tone. To produce different tones with the same fingering, players must carefully adjust the muscles of their lips and the force of their breath.

The brasses can be bright or "brassy" in timbre, or they can be rich, mellow, and warm. They add considerable strength to the orchestral sound and are often used for special flourishes and symbolic effects. Each of the brasses may be muted to produce a nasal tone, either gentle or raucous, depending on how forcefully the instrument is played.

Percussion Instruments

The percussion instruments take advantage of two of our basic impulses—to bang objects together and to shake them. Percussion instruments include *idiophones* such as the *gong* or *cymbal*, in which the whole body of the instrument vibrates, as well as *membranophones* such as the *bass drum*, in which only a membrane vibrates.

Idiophones and Membranophones

Some percussion instruments can produce a series of definite pitches. The *xylophone*, for example, which is played by striking wooden bars with hammers, can produce a wide range of tones simultaneously or one at a time. The *timpani* (or *kettledrums*) can also produce tones of definite pitch, but no more than one tone at a time without being retuned—that is, without a readjustment of the tension of the drum head. Many percussion instruments produce tones of indefinite pitch and are used for rhythmic or dramatic purposes. These include *snare drums, cymbals, castanets, maracas,* and *gongs*.

Keyboard Instruments

Instruments with keyboards have been very popular for several hundred years. The *harpsichord* and *clavichord* were well known in the sixteenth century. On the harpsichord, a string is plucked when a key is depressed, while on the clavichord a string is struck. The sound of both instruments, especially that of the clavichord, is generally small and rather delicate. Another keyboard instrument, the *pipe organ*, reached a high point of development in the eighteenth century. It is capable of a very wide variety of sounds, which are produced by forcing air through the instrument's pipes. The *piano* was invented in the early eighteenth century and gradually replaced the harpsichord as the most popular keyboard instrument. Because sound is produced when hammers strike the strings within the instrument, the piano is often considered a percussion instrument.

The Evolution of Instruments

Musical instruments, like most other things, have changed in response to new technology. We have already mentioned the fact that the piano replaced the harpsichord in the eighteenth century. Many of the other instruments mentioned on the preceding pages have also descended from older and generally simpler forms. The modern transverse flute, for example, is the latest in a long line of simpler flutes, many of which still exist in other cultures and in

**Older
Instruments**

our own. One early type of flute, the *recorder*, is often played in ensembles that perform music of the Renaissance and Baroque, the periods in which this instrument was prominent. The *oboe d'amore*, an older version of the oboe, is sometimes used in late Baroque ensembles, where its sweet early eighteenth-century sound is much appreciated.

In most cases, the more modern instruments have extended the capacities of the earlier instruments. The modern metal flute can produce a much louder sound than the earlier wooden flutes, which might easily be overwhelmed in a large orchestra. The piano, unlike the harpsichord, can achieve many different levels of volume. A pianist can rapidly vary the level from very soft to very loud, while a harpsichordist must play each pitch in a passage at the same volume.

In each of these cases, the extension of the instrument's technical capabilities greatly influenced the kind of music that could be written for it. For example, after the piano appeared in the eighteenth century, composers found that they could use changes in volume to produce a much broader range of effects than were within the harpsichord's capacity.

Electronic Music

Naturally, composers today are in search of the same kinds of opportunities to extend musical language. One such opportunity is found in the use of electronics. In *musique concrète*, conventional sounds recorded on tape are altered electronically to produce new effects. The sound used may be music, human speech, or noises such as those heard on the street. The composer splices the tapes together and adjusts speed and volume to produce the desired effect. Even more innovative is music that is generated electronically rather than just altered by electronic means. With the use of *sound synthesizers*, entirely new and unconventional sounds can be created.

Electronic equipment offers the composer an infinite array of pitches and timbres that cannot be conveniently or accurately produced on other instruments. The uses of electronic sound are quite varied. In fact, in many compositions, natural and electronic music are combined.

The Orchestra

Most of the modern string, wind, and percussion instruments discussed earlier are used in the *symphony orchestra*. Some, such as the piano, are used only in certain pieces. Others, such as the violin and clarinet, are essential. In all, most symphony orchestras have about one hundred players playing from fifteen to twenty different instruments. The combination of sounds is, beyond question, impressive.

Just as individual instruments have changed over time, so has the orchestra. Up until about 1600, instrumental music was generally confined to individual performers or small groups of players. Small groups of listeners could assemble in one room—or chamber—to enjoy the refined, relatively soft sound

**Chamber
Ensemble**

of the *chamber ensemble*. Large ensembles were used only for festive or ceremonial occasions. But changes were in the air. Two Venetian composers, Giovanni Gabrieli and Claudio Monteverdi, were experimenting with the use

Symphony No. 1

in C Minor, Op. 68

An Orchestral Score: *The first page of the score of Brahms' Symphony No. 1 gives only a slight indication of the difficulty involved in writing symphonic music. Unless you are a musician or a student of German, you will probably be able to identify only about seven of the instruments listed. They are, in the order given, flute, oboe, clarinet, bassoon, contrabassoon, horn, trombone, timpani, first violin, second violin, viola, cello, and double bass.*

TIMBRE AND DYNAMICS

of large and varied instrumental ensembles to accompany their vocal compositions. Monteverdi, especially, was interested in creating orchestral effects by emphasizing the strings and combining the timbres of many different instruments.

Orchestration

During the eighteenth century, the size of the orchestra and the instruments in it became relatively standardized, although the orchestra itself was not yet as large or as inclusive as the modern orchestra. *Orchestration*, the art of writing instrumental music to achieve a variety of effects, developed greatly over the century as the size of the orchestra grew. In the nineteenth century, the orchestra was expanded to include many different percussion instruments as well as more wind and string players.

Today's symphony orchestra is divided into four sections: strings, woodwinds, brasses, and percussion. The strings are generally given the most important melodic parts, while the woodwinds provide special effects and reinforce the harmony. The brass instruments sometimes blend with the woodwinds in harmony. They can also be used strikingly in solo melodic parts, in climaxing passages, and in music of a military nature. The percussion section functions mainly as a source of rhythmic vitality and accent, but it may also be used to create special moods and effects. A wonderful example of the potential richness of orchestral music is found in Mussorgsky's *Pictures at an Exhibition*, as orchestrated by Ravel. In this piece, paintings hanging in an art gallery are repainted musically for the listener. Different sections of the orchestra are used in varied combinations, offering a full exploitation of the timbres of each instrument.

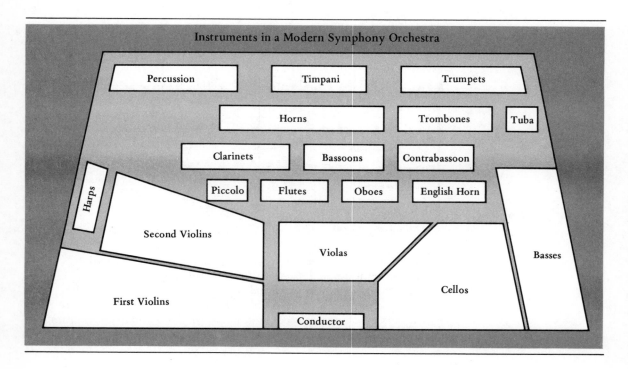

Instruments in a Modern Symphony Orchestra

The Growth of the Orchestra: *Although the photograph shows a modern orchestra, the work being performed is likely to be from the eighteenth century. The number of players is relatively small and the brass section is particularly limited.*

Dynamics

Intensity of sound, or *dynamics*, is basic to all musical expression. In traditional music, we often first become aware of the impact of dynamic effects upon hearing very sudden changes from soft to loud, or vice versa. For some of us, the first experience with musical dynamics is not at all subtle: the so-called "Surprise" Symphony of Haydn. Here, the surprise is a radical change in volume, a very loud chord coming on the heels of a gentle melody. Of course, dynamic effects can also be more subtle. In any case, the level of volume that a composer specifies for a given note, chord, or section of a work is an important indication of expressive intent.

Dynamic markings, like many other musical terms, are conventionally given in Italian. This is because Italian musicians around 1600 seem to have been the first to mark dynamics in their music. A list of the markings used most often is given in the chart on the next page.

The development of contrast in dynamic level is especially important in music. Ravel's famous *Bolero*, for example, would sound like a simple exercise in repetition were it not for its slow and steady increase in dynamic level and

Dynamic Markings

pp	*pianissimo*	very soft
p	*piano*	soft
mp	*mezzo piano*	moderately soft
mf	*mezzo forte*	moderately loud
f	*forte*	loud
ff	*fortissimo*	very loud
sf	*sforzando*	"forced," sudden stress on a single note or chord
fp	*forte-piano*	loud followed suddenly by soft

Crescendo

its changes in orchestration. Such building up of volume is called a *crescendo* and is indicated on a musical score by the mark <.

Of course, a crescendo can be realized on a much smaller scale than in *Bolero*. It may be heard in the single voice of the clarinet that introduces Gershwin's *Rhapsody in Blue* and in the so-called "Funeral March" of Chopin's *Sonata No. 2 in B♭ Minor*. One of the most thrilling of all crescendos occurs in Beethoven's *Symphony No. 5*, carrying the end of the third movement into the beginning of the fourth, ignoring the need for the traditional pause.

Decrescendo or Diminuendo

As might be expected, composers have also used a gradual softening effect, or *decrescendo*, for expressive purposes. Also called the *diminuendo*, this effect is indicated by the mark >, which very graphically shows a fading away of sound. The diminuendo may be found within a musical work or at its end. A well-loved symphony that virtually dies out at the close is Tchaikovsky's *Symphony No. 6* (the "Pathétique"). It was much criticized when first performed because at the time symphonies were expected to come to a loud and dramatic close.

Changes in volume are often closely related to changes in melody, tempo, and orchestration. If you listen closely to your own voice, you will soon discover that as you speak more loudly and more quickly, the pitch tends to rise. Conversely, lowering the pitch of your voice generally softens it and may slow it down as well. Of course, you can speak slowly in a high pitch and quickly in a low pitch, but the opposite combinations seem more natural. In music, as in speech, increases in tempo, volume, and pitch often work together to generate excitement and climax. The frenzied dance "In the Hall of the Mountain King" from Edvard Grieg's *Peer Gynt Suite* is an excellent example. Decreases in volume, speed, and pitch may also occur together. These decreases may be used to provide contrasts to the more exciting passages or to convey a variety of melancholy or restful moods. In orchestral works, the composer's choice of instruments is integral to the production of these effects.

Listening to Timbre and Dynamics

Side 1, Band 3

The record set that accompanies the text gives aural examples of the different voice categories and of many of the instruments discussed in Chapter 3. To develop a better understanding of orchestration and dynamics you may also want to listen to recordings of some of the pieces mentioned in the text. Finally, you may gain additional information by listening to one of the following records:

The Instruments of the Orchestra [Vanguard VSD 721–722]
The Orchestra and Its Instruments [Scholastic FT 3602]

4

Introduction to Musical Form and Style

Discovering Musical Form

When listening to music, we are conscious of movement—the succession of musical events. Unless we are familiar with a piece, we cannot anticipate the course of musical events any more than we can anticipate the plot of a drama after seeing the first act. Yet it is clear that in a musical work, as in a drama, the later action depends on or proceeds from the earlier action. We know that when the work is complete an overall design will be apparent.

The overall design of a piece of music is referred to as *form*. It is form that explains the choices of the composer—the conscious shaping of major ideas and the careful selection of detail. An awareness of form can make listening a more exciting, creative process.

Fundamental Principles: Repetition and Contrast

In music, the listener is confronted with an abstract, ever-changing flow of organized sound. It is difficult to say precisely what happens, as in a drama. Instead, most listeners simply try to describe "what it sounds like." And it is true that some music really does sound like something easily described—the singing of birds or the approach of footsteps. But in describing most music, we can only relate sounds, melodies, rhythms, and so on to other sounds, melodies, and rhythms in the composition. Thus, a melody may be identical to an earlier melody, similar to it, or quite different. These relationships can be made because as we listen, we become sensitive to the repetition of certain elements and the introduction of other, new material.

Repetition and contrast are the two most fundamental principles of musical form. This should not be surprising. Even simple examples such as "Twinkle, Twinkle, Little Star" show them to be the organizing principles.

Outlining Form

Form in music can be identified by giving a letter designation to each prominent musical idea and noting the order in which these ideas appear and are repeated. "Frère Jacques," for example, consists of four short musical ideas, or *motives*—the shortest units of melody. Each of the motives is presented and

Shortest Units: Motives

34

then repeated. The first motive, a, consists of only four notes. It is repeated before the second motive, b, is heard. After b is repeated, the third and fourth motives, c and d, are heard and repeated in turn.

a Are you sleeping,	c Morning bells are ringing;
a Are you sleeping,	c Morning bells are ringing;
b Brother John,	d Ding, ding, dong;
b Brother John?	d Ding, ding, dong.

The order of ideas here is aabbccdd, or more simply abcd. The form uses both of the fundamental principles—repetition and contrast.

Common Forms

Most forms can be outlined in a manner similar to that used for "Frère Jacques." Here we will consider a few of the most common forms.

Strophic Form

Phrases

Most songs are made up not of motives but of *phrases.* As noted in Chapter 1, these are longer melodic units, comparable to the lines of most poems.

The phrases of "The Star-Spangled Banner," like the motives of "Frère Jacques," show the clear use of repetition and contrast. The first four phrases, a, b, c, and d, are presented and then immediately repeated. Because of the repetition, *sections* can be perceived in the song. The first four lines of the song, the first section of the song, can be labeled Section A. The next four lines are a melodic repetition of Section A, and thus can also be labeled Section A. The six lines at the end, however, are different. These lines fall into two natural groups—four short lines and two longer lines—and can be labeled Section B and Section C. The resulting form is AABC.

Sections

Section A	a Oh, say can you see
	b By the dawn's early light
	c What so proudly we hailed
	d At the twilight's last gleaming?
Section A	a Whose broad stripes and bright stars,
	b Through the perilous fight,
	c O'er the ramparts we watched
	d Were so gallantly streaming?
Section B	e And the rocket's red glare,
	f The bombs bursting in air,
	g Gave proof through the night
	h That our flag was still there.
Section C	i Oh, say does that star-spangled banner yet wave
	j O'er the land of the free and the home of the brave?

These four sections make up "The Star-Spangled Banner" as we usually sing it. However, there are, as you may know, three other *stanzas*, all sung to the same music. If Roman numerals are used to symbolize each complete stanza, the form for the entire song can be written in this manner:

I A A B C	II A A B C	III A A B C	IV A A B C

This form is referred to as *strophic form*, in that the same music is repeated for each stanza—or strophe—of text. Many popular and folk songs are in strophic form.

Ternary Form

In music it is also common to find an organization of sections in a three-part or *ternary form*:

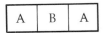

Here the middle section offers a contrast to the first and third sections. Nearly every march that a band plays is in ternary form, as are the minuets of Haydn and Mozart. The form provides a fine sense of balance and symmetry, leaving A for the novelty of B, then returning to the pleasurable familiarity of A.

Binary Form

Also important is two-part or *binary form*:

In this form, the second part often acts as an answer to the first. The AB form was very important during the seventeenth and eighteenth centuries and may readily be found in the works of Johann Sebastian Bach, Domenico Scarlatti, and other master composers of the period.

Theme and Variations Form

Repetition and contrast are opposing principles. The composer tries to make the best use of both of them. One way is to state a musical idea and then repeat it, varying it in such a way that it sounds at once familiar and new. If a number of such variations are put together, the result is a *theme and variations form*. A theme followed by four variations might be symbolized in this manner:

A	A^1	A^2	A^3	A^4

MUSICAL ELEMENTS

Form in Architecture: *Sectional organization, so prominent in music, is also found in many architectural designs. The three-part form, seen here in the facade of the church of Santa Agnese in Rome, has been chosen for numerous churches throughout the centuries, quite likely because of its obvious association with the trinity.*

Familiar examples of theme and variations form are Mozart's *Variations on the Theme "Ah, vous dirai-je, Maman"* (our "Twinkle, Twinkle, Little Star"), Brahms' *Variations on a Theme of Paganini*, and the second movement from Haydn's *Symphony No. 94* (the "Surprise" Symphony).

Other Forms

Virelai and Madrigal

Still other forms have been devised by composers in all ages. The music of fourteenth- and fifteenth-century French composers was influenced by poetry, and such poetic-musical forms as the *virelai* were popular. One of the most important forms in the sixteenth century was the *madrigal*—a form that tended to be based on continuous development rather than on sections. In the

Ritornello

Sonata and Rondo

seventeenth century, the *ritornello* form evolved, stressing a constant return to modified versions of the opening theme. By the late eighteenth century, the elaborate *sonata* and *rondo* forms had been developed. Throughout the nineteenth century, forms grew ever more elaborate, while, in our own century, much freer and looser forms have come into being, often involving a seemingly free flow of sound tied together by the barest of motives. These and other forms will be discussed as they are appropriate in chronological context.

Types of Compositions

The many different types of compositions that have been developed over the centuries can be categorized in several different ways. One obvious method is to categorize them by their use of form. Many works are based on a single form—on a theme and variations, a strophic, or a ternary form, for example. Included here are most *songs* and *marches* as well as many piano pieces. Other compositions are built up into larger, more complex structures, consisting of several relatively independent sections called *movements*, each of which is based on a different form. Perhaps the best known multi-movement work is the *symphony*.

Movements

Compositions may also be categorized by the use of different performing groups. There are *toccatas, études, nocturnes,* and *rhapsodies,* generally written for solo instruments. *Sonatas* may be intended for one instrument or for almost any combination of instruments. Works for small groups of instruments include *duets, trios, quartets, quintets,* and so forth. Compositions for orchestra include *symphonies, symphonic poems, concertos, suites,* and *overtures.* There are *Lieder* and *arias* for individual singers and *madrigals, motets,* and *Masses* for groups of singers. Numerous combinations of singers and instruments are possible in *cantatas, oratorios,* and *operas.*

New types of compositions have evolved in every age, just as the individual forms they are based on have evolved. We shall meet all of the compositional types mentioned above, and others, in their proper chronological context.

Musical Style

Music of any given time period has certain special characteristics. As fashions in clothing change, so do tastes and styles in music. Instruments and the manner in which they are used change, and new ways of using melody, harmony, and the other elements of music are devised by at least some of the composers in every period. Consequently, new musical styles emerge.

The musical style of any period is a kind of imprecise composite of the styles of all or most of the composers of the period. It is not always easy to determine which composers are typical of a period and which are behind or ahead of the time. Nor is it easy to give precise dates to any stylistic period, since styles of composition overlap from one period to the next. However, the approximate dates in the chart below can be used to outline stylistic periods in the history of Western music. These dates also serve as basic divisions of this text.

Period	Approximate Dates
Medieval	500–1400
Renaissance	1400–1600
Baroque	1600–1750
Classical	1750–1815
Romantic	1815–1900
Twentieth Century	1900–

INTRODUCTION TO MUSICAL FORM AND STYLE

5

Musical Notation

The Purpose of Musical Notation

Most people are familiar with the general appearance of musical notation, but many have never learned to "read music"—that is, to translate the written symbols into sound. Contrary to some popular opinion, however, there is no great hidden mystery about reading music. Fundamentally, musical notation is designed to indicate just two things—the pitch and the duration of the musical tones.

Pitch and Key

The pitch of a note is shown by its vertical location on a series of horizontal lines called a staff. The modern staff has five lines with four spaces in between. If you count the spaces above and below the top and bottom lines, this gives enough space for eleven notes. Higher and lower notes are placed on short *ledger lines* above or below the staff.

Use of Ledger Lines   High Pitches

Low Pitches

Clef
    The pitch of a given note depends on the *clef*, a sign that appears at the extreme left of the staff. Most familiar is the *treble clef*, which looks somewhat like a written capital G in reverse. In fact, it is also called the *G clef*, because the tail of the clef encircles the line on which the note G is written. When the treble clef is used, middle C—the C approximately at the center of the piano keyboard—is placed on the first ledger line below the staff. The notes of the other white keys go up the staff in order following it, as can be seen in the example at the top of the next page.

Treble Clef (G Clef)

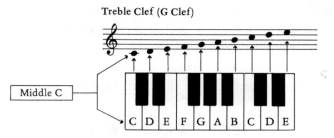

Middle C

C D E F G A B C D E

Notes below middle C can be written on additional ledger lines further below the staff. However, if the notes are considerably below middle C, the number of ledger lines soon becomes hard to read. So, for music that consists mainly of lower notes, another clef is generally chosen—the *bass clef*. When this clef is used, middle C is placed on the ledger line just above the staff:

Bass Clef (F Clef)

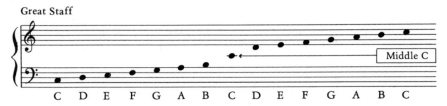

Middle C

C D E F G A B C

If you look closely at the bass clef, you will see that the two dots bracket the line on which the note F is written. Hence this clef is also called the *F clef*.

If the bass staff and the treble staff are placed one below the other, with an extra space between for the ledger line of middle C, the result is the *great staff*. All the white-key notes at the center of the piano keyboard can be written on this staff without a break.

Great Staff

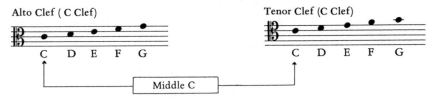

Middle C

C D E F G A B C D E F G A B C

Piano music is generally written on the great staff, with the space in the middle expanded somewhat for convenience.

Another, less common, clef—the *C clef*—is sometimes used for music with a range between those of the treble and bass clefs. The C clef can be moved around on the staff. If it is centered on the third line of the staff, it is known as the *alto clef*; if on the fourth line, the *tenor clef*. Wherever the clef appears, the line that passes through the middle of it is the location of middle C.

Alto Clef (C Clef)

C D E F G

Tenor Clef (C Clef)

C D E F G

Middle C

Sharps and Flats   The black keys on the piano are shown by the use of *sharp* (♯) and *flat* (♭) signs. These signs tell the performer to raise (sharp) or lower (flat) the pitch of a particular note by a half step:

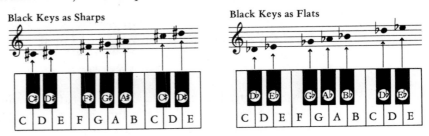

Notice that each of the black keys may represent either a sharp of the note below or a flat of the note above. A♯ is the same note as B♭, F♯ is the same as G♭, and so on. As you may have noticed, there are no black keys between B and C or E and F. Since the note one-half step above B is C, it follows that B♯ is the same as C. In like manner, C♭ is B, E♯ is F, and F♭ is E.

With the aid of either sharp or flat signs, the entire twelve-tone chromatic scale can be written. Using sharps the scale can be written this way:

Chromatic Scale

When a particular note is to be sharped or flatted throughout a piece of music, it would be inconvenient to mark it each time it appears. For this reason, signs to be used throughout are placed at the left side of the staff immediately after the clef. This group of signs is known as the *key signature*.

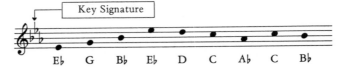

In addition to showing what notes should be sharped or flatted, the key signature also tells the performer the tonic note of the scale being used and hence what scale—or *key*—the music is built upon. In the example above, for instance, the tonic note is E♭ and the key is E♭ major.

The determination of key takes more technical knowledge than has been developed here. However, everyone can learn to recognize the key signatures of a few of the most commonly used keys.

Common Key Signatures

MUSICAL ELEMENTS

Major and Relative Minor Scales

As you can see, two scales, or keys, share each key signature. In each case, a *major scale* is paired with its *relative minor*. The key signatures are the same, but the tonic notes differ: the minor tonic is one and a half steps lower than the major tonic. This can be seen more clearly if we compare two specific scales:

Scale of F Major   Scale of D Minor

Major and Minor Modes

The most important difference between scales in the *major mode* and scales in the *minor mode* is the arrangement of half and whole steps. All major scales have half-step intervals after the third and seventh notes. Their relative minors have half-step intervals after the second and fifth notes.

After establishing a key, composers sometimes want to use a note that is not contained in the particular key, or scale, they have chosen. If they wish to add a sharp or flat, they write the sign to the left of that particular note. When used in this way, the sign—a sharp or a flat—is called an *accidental*. When composers wish to show that a note that would normally be sharped or flatted should be played without sharp or flat, they mark it with another sign, the *natural sign* (♮). This sign can be used either to cancel an accidental or to cancel a sharp or flat given in the key signature.

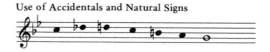

Use of Accidentals and Natural Signs

Duration and Meter

The appearance of a note tells the performer not only its pitch but also the length of time the note should be held. The different durations, or *note values*, are shown below:

Note Values

| Whole | Half | Quarter | Eighth | Sixteenth | Thirty-second | Sixty-fourth |

As the names suggest, each of these note values has a duration half as long as the preceding one. If a whole note represents four beats, a half note will represent two beats, a quarter note one beat, an eighth note half a beat, and so on.

Groups of notes of smaller value are often linked together with heavy *beams* to make them easier to read:

Use of Beams

If a composer wants to show a duration of another length—say three beats—there are two ways to do it. Two or more notes of smaller value can be linked together with a curved line called a *tie*. If, for example, three quarter notes equal to one beat each are linked together, the performer will play just one note for three beats. A composer may also use a *dot*. A dot added to any note increases its value by half the original length. If, for example, a half note equal to two beats is dotted, the note will be held for three beats.

Use of Ties and Dots

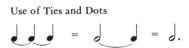

Periods of silence—or *rests*—in music must also be noted for duration. The standard rest signs are shown below:

Rests

| Whole | Half | Quarter | Eighth | Sixteenth | Thirty-second | Sixty-fourth |

Measures and Bar Lines

In most music of the Western world, the beats are arranged in regular groups of equal length, usually with an accent on the first beat of each group. These groups, as mentioned in Chapter 1, are called *measures*. They are divided on the written score by narrow vertical lines called *bar lines*. Sometimes the measures themselves are called bars.

A *time signature* is given next to the key signature at the beginning of the music. The time signature is a pair of numbers, one above the other. The lower number shows which note has a value of one beat. The upper number shows the number of beats in a measure. A time signature of $\frac{2}{4}$, for example, means that a quarter note gets one beat and that there are two beats in a measure. A time signature of $\frac{3}{8}$ means that an eighth note gets one beat and that there are three beats in a measure. Other possible time signatures include the following:

Time Signatures

Common time ($\frac{4}{4}$), is often shown by the sign **C**. A vertical line through the sign (¢) indicates *alla breve*, or *cut time* ($\frac{2}{2}$), which is often used for fast-moving music.

Common Time   Cut Time

Measures with any number of beats are theoretically possible. Traditional music is usually written in measures of two, three, four, or six beats. Modern composers, however, have experimented with other measures, such as those of five or seven beats.

Listening Preview   The treatment of musical elements varies greatly from culture to culture. Some non-Western groups, for example, share our interest in harmony, while others prefer an almost totally monophonic sound. Similarly striking differences can be found in the treatment of melody, rhythm, and all of the other elements of music. Listen to one of the four non-Western selections given on the record set that accompanies the text (Side 2, Bands 1–4) or choose a selection from among those listed at the end of Chapter 6. In what ways does the treatment of musical elements differ from that found in most Western music? Which aspects of the music make it possible to identify the work as distinctly non-Western?

6

Music in Other Cultures

Music as a Cultural Phenomenon

There are as many musical styles as there are cultures in the world. It is curious that the people of one culture prefer vocal music, those of another prefer dance, and those of still another prefer instrumental music. Why should there be such a wide range of musical specializations from one part of the globe to another? No single answer can be given. Both environmental conditions and group philosophies, however, help to determine, or at least to influence, the music developed by each cultural group.

In this chapter, we will survey several important musical traditions of the non-Western world. To describe any one of them completely would, of course, require a whole library of books and records. We can only suggest some of the main features of each tradition and, in some cases, the underlying attitudes that have caused the music of one culture to develop differently from that of another.

Music of Africa

In African societies, music is an essential part of daily life. Typically, there is special music for working in the fields, entertainment, news dissemination, gossip, and legal dealings. Each ceremony—celebrating birth, puberty, marriage, healing, the hunt, the new year, the new moon—has its own songs and dances. A god may be asked to aid a personal or communal project, to bring rain, or to give protection against fire and danger. Young people often learn the traditions of the culture and the "facts of life" through song. Thus, in many African cultures, music and dance serve as a unifying force, affecting nearly every aspect of life.

Bantu Music   The music of the Bantu-speaking peoples of central Africa is in many ways representative of the musical traditions of sub-Saharan Africa. The Bantu-speaking area is quite large, stretching from Kenya and Tanzania in the east to the Republic of the Congo in the west. Although there are many different Bantu languages and societies within the region, all share a similar cultural heritage.

Many Bantu rulers have traditionally had official orchestras, such as the royal drums of the Watutsi, which accompanied them wherever they went. The court bard, too, was and still is an important figure in many communities, composing and singing songs of the peoples' history. But music was in no way the exclusive privilege of the nobility. Nearly everyone participated in some way.

One of the distinctive aspects of Bantu music is related to the "tonal" nature of Bantu languages. The meaning of a word depends partly on the pitches at which the syllables of the word are spoken. This naturally has an effect on music. Melodies are apt to be greatly influenced by the speech tones of the words being sung. A song would sound ludicrous if, for example, a syllable meaning "dog" at a relatively low pitch were sung at a high pitch that changed the meaning to something entirely different. Another result of the tonal nature of Bantu languages is that instruments can be used to convey verbal meanings. This is the basis of the so-called talking drums, which send formulaic messages swiftly over long distances.

Responsorial Singing

Much of African music, and Bantu music in particular, is built on short melodic phrases, which are repeated, alternated, and varied to make up longer melodies. *Responsorial singing* is common: each phrase is sung by a leader, then answered by a chorus. Variations on the basic phrase are improvised.

"Work Song from Burundi"

One example of the responsorial style is found in a "Work Song from Burundi," sung while moving a heavy tree. Here the leader presents short phrases, repeating and varying them. The other workers respond with a short motive at the end of the leader's phrases.

Side 2, Band 1

Listening Guide for "Work Song from Burundi"

Timbre: male singers

Melody: based on motives or short phrases; largely descending; responsorial

Rhythm: patterns repeated

Texture: mainly monophonic, with a little overlap of leader and chorus

Form: derives from phrases sung and repeated by the leader; each phrase is answered by a motive sung by the chorus

Text: concerns the work of moving a large tree

Harmonic Techniques

A general similarity between European and Bantu music is found in the fact that both cultures make use of harmony. Bantu songs are sometimes sung in *parallel motion*, with the voices singing simultaneous notes that are always a steady, specific interval apart. There are also songs that make use of *imitation*: the second voice imitates the first, somewhat in the fashion of Western rounds. Another polyphonic texture is created when one voice holds a long *drone note* while the other sings a phrase. The first voice may then perform while the second holds the drone note, and so on in alternation. Counterpoint may also be performed by groups of singers and instrumentalists. In a song accompanied by harp or xylophone, the instrumentalists may repeat a

An Emphasis on Rhythm: *The Bantu emphasis on rhythm has led not only to the production of such elaborate and beautiful instruments as the one shown at the right but also to a number of works for percussion alone. Within the last century many important Western composers have begun to place similar emphasis on rhythm and have produced, like the Africans, a number of works just for percussion.*

short phrase over and over again, while the singers perform melodies based on the same short phrase.

To the Western ear, the most distinctive feature of central African music is probably its rhythm. We are familiar enough with its American offspring jazz, but the original is even more impressive. In ensemble playing, several different rhythmic patterns may be used at the same time. This creates a kind of *rhythmic polyphony*, with perhaps one drummer maintaining a duple meter, another a triple meter. Sometimes, in fact, a single performer will play one rhythmic pattern on a drum while singing another.

Rhythmic Polyphony

"Ibihubi"

Intense and contrasting rhythms can often be heard in the music of the Bantu peoples. In "Ibihubi," for example, five large drums and one smaller one are used. A basic pulse is clear throughout, while several different rhythmic patterns are played around it. The effect is both intricate and subtle.

Side 2, Band 2

Listening Guide for "Ibihubi"

Timbre: five large drums and one small drum

Melody: melodic patterns created by the drums

Rhythm: a basic beat with several complementary rhythmic patterns

Texture: several layers of different timbre, pitch, and rhythm

Form: free, with several different rhythmic patterns played around a basic beat

Music of the American Indian

A number of distinct geographical areas can be identified in the study of American Indian music. We will consider only two of the areas, and only two cultures within each area. The Plains-Pueblo region, including the entire central part of the United States and the Southwest, has been chosen because it is in some respects typical of early North American music. The Eskimo-Northwest Coast region has been chosen because it includes some of the most complex and imaginative music of the continent.

Music of the Plains

Among the peoples of the Plains are the Sioux, Comanche, Blackfoot, Crow, and Arapaho. Traditionally, these groups were buffalo hunters, following the migrating herds. During winter they lived in small family groups, but in summer larger groups joined together for a great hunt and for the social and religious celebrations that went with it. War, like the hunt, was highly esteemed. It was fought as much to win honor as to kill enemies. To "count coup"—that is, to touch an armed enemy in battle without trying to kill—earned a warrior the highest credit of all. Horses were the mark of wealth, and raiding parties were forever slipping into camps under cover of darkness to make off, if they could, with the enemies' mounts. Visions, dances, and spirits were of great importance in the religious and social life of the people.

In the traditional songs of the Plains, melodies cover a wide range, often beginning quite high and moving downward in a sort of terraced fashion. Rhythm is complex and changing. Voice quality is very tense and pulsating.

The songs are generally short. The text for the first half of each song is frequently made up of meaningless syllables. Singers may then vary the rest of the text—expanding or condensing it and changing words to bring it up to date or add a personal or topical reference. The musical form is often the kind known as *incomplete repetition:* ABCBC or AABCABC, for example.

Incomplete Repetition

"Sioux Sun Dance"

Ceremonial dances play an important part in the life of the Plains peoples. The sun dance is especially important. Among the Sioux, it is performed by four dancers, representing four different animals, around a tall pole that symbolizes the sun. The singers repeat melodic phrases in unison, mostly in descending motion. The music for the dance is divided into two sections. The first section is accompanied by a drum beating a quick rhythmic pattern. In the second section, the drum pattern is slower and the dancers blow whistles steadily.

Side 2, Band 3

Listening Guide for "Sioux Sun Dance"

Timbre: singers, drum, and whistles

Melody: motivic; motives and phrases are repeated, usually in descending motion

Rhythm: steady beat in drum, played under the freer voice part

Texture: largely monophonic

Form: two contrasting sections; motives and phrases repeated

Text: a tribute to the sun

Pueblo Music

Southwest of the Plains area live the Pueblos, settled farming people who speak a number of different languages. They include the Hopi, Zuñi, Taos, and several other groups, some of which have farmed the same land for centuries. The Hopi village of Oraibi, for example, is the oldest continuously lived-in settlement in the United States, dating at least from the early 1200s. As members of a basically peaceful group, most of the Pueblos have been willing to let the rest of the world go on its way undisturbed. In contrast to the Plains people, the Pueblos tend to be suspicious of aggressive individuality and, as a group, place greater value on moderation. Religious and ceremonial practices figure largely in their way of life. This is especially true among the Hopi, who regard themselves as a specially chosen, almost priestly people.

Pueblo songs are more complex than those of the Plains. They are longer and more varied, based on six- or seven-note scales. Although both groups share the same vocal tension and terraced, descending melodic style, Pueblo singers tend to favor the use of a low, growling voice, in contrast to the high-pitched voice of Plains singers. There are special songs for all the group ceremonies as well as for those of the many secret societies. Most complex, and perhaps best known to outsiders, are the Kachina dance songs, performed by masked dancers impersonating gods and ancestors.

Eskimo Music

To the north of the Plains-Pueblo region is the Eskimo-Northwest Coast region. While Eskimo living conditions have hardly encouraged an elaborate culture, Eskimo music is highly developed in many ways. It is rhythmically complex, with a variety of contrasting accents and meters. Melodies tend to undulate back and forth, generally moving in small intervals within a limited range. A declamatory or *recitative style* of singing is common. Eskimo music includes a number of dances, which vary from simple and relatively stationary solo dances to much livelier round dances with torches.

Recitative Style

Music of the Northwest

To the south, along the Pacific Northwest Coast, live a number of groups including the Kwakiutl, the Nootka, and the Sitka. These groups early enjoyed a highly developed culture. The sea provided abundant food; the land teemed with berries, nuts, and game for the taking. Consequently, the Northwest Coast peoples literally had wealth to throw away—and they did just that. The famous potlatch was an enormous feast at which powerful people tried to shame their rivals by giving away more wealth than anyone else did. When even giveaways were not spectacular enough, property was destroyed. Food, oil, robes of fur, and carved canoes went into the flames. Among some groups, slaves might be killed. The prestige gained by the winner of one of these consumption battles was great enough to make all the sacrifice worthwhile.

A custom grew up in some Northwest Coast groups whereby many songs and dances were owned by individuals. Only the owner of a song could perform it. Greatly valued, such a song could be bought or inherited. It could even be acquired by murder, if the murderer could validate the claim afterward with an impressive potlatch. Other songs belonged to secret societies. These, together with the privately owned ones, were performed during the ten holy days of the great winter feast. At more light-hearted moments, there were the usual everyday songs and dances, sometimes comic and satiric.

Northwest Coast music differs from all other American Indian music in one way: it includes rudimentary part singing. Either a drone or parallelism at various pitch intervals may be used. There are also intricate, percussive rhythms and clear, rhythmic swings in the melodies. The words of the songs are often bold, confident, even threatening:

> Do not think for a moment that you can defeat us, for we have slaves from all the other tribes, even from the coast tribes to the north.

Many different instruments are used among the Northwest Coast peoples, and the melodies and singing styles are, in general, bolder and more expressive than those of the Plains.

Music of India

Like many other ancient peoples, the people of India felt that music and religion were closely connected. The vibrations of musical sound were believed to be directly related to the laws of the universe. Therefore, correct performance helped bring harmony between people and the world around them and was even thought to contribute to the stability of the universe itself. Presumably, this idea was associated with the discovery of the octave and other intervals. About 510 B.C., the Greek theorist Pythagoras developed a similar idea, and it is quite possible that there was contact between the two civilizations in this period.

Ragas

Indian music is based on melodic formulas called *ragas*. Each raga offers a number of different melodic possibilities, which are explored and developed through improvisation. There are literally hundred of ragas, but most performers use only about fifty.

Talas

There is also a set of rhythmic formulas called *talas*. These are patterns of basic time units—units that are more or less equivalent to beats. The beats in a tala may number anywhere from three to over a hundred and are arranged in patterns of equal or unequal length. Talas and ragas together form the basis of the improvisational performance that is so important in Indian music.

Indian music makes little use of harmony in the Western sense. It does, however, use a drone note or chord. This may be the continuous sounding of either the tonic note, a 1–5–8 chord, or a 1–4–8 chord throughout the performance of a particular raga. To the untrained listener, this may sound monotonous. But in Indian musical theory, all notes are believed to take their meaning and effect from their relation to the tonic. Therefore, it seems logical to have this note constantly available for reference. Against the drone chord, the melody may be elaborately developed.

The voice is primary in Indian music, for it is thought to be the most perfect blending of the physical and the intellectual. The singer tries not so much to produce a rich tone quality as to obtain perfect accuracy of pitch. Here, again, we may see the influence of the metaphysical theory relating

The Granger Collection

A Classic Indian Ensemble: *Typical of northern Indian music is the ensemble seen here. The instruments are, from left to right, the tabla, the tambura, and the sitar, the last of which is played by Ravi Shankar, the person who has done perhaps the most to popularize Indian music in the West.*

music and the universe. Northern India has developed some purely instrumental music, but in the older tradition of southern India, all music is fundamentally based on song, with instruments functioning mainly as accompaniment.

Groups performing instrumental music, or vocal and instrumental music, are generally small. The instruments used may include strings, drums, flutes, and reed instruments similar to the oboe. One of the best-known Indian

Sitar

instruments is the *sitar,* a large, plucked string instrument.

The excitement of a performance is likely to derive in part from the contest that often develops among the participants. The drummer will introduce all kinds of complicated elaborations within the tala, while the singer or other leader does the same with the raga. Since the audience is quite aware of what is going on, a considerable amount of tension may be built up. When the performers finally, in perfect unison, reach the first note of the following tala, the sense of release is almost electric.

Music of China

Chinese music is at least as old as that of India. Because of the traditional Chinese passion for setting things in order and keeping records, we have a great deal of information about the theory and importance of music under the ancient dynasties. Confucius (551–479 B.C.) wrote extensively about music, since he considered it an essential part of moral life as well as a source of entertainment.

In China, as in India, music was believed to be related to the cosmos. Its function was to imitate and uphold the proper harmony between heaven and earth. Each note was thought to be associated with some natural element and some group in society. Correct pitch was so important that it was customary for each new emperor to order a rechecking of the pitches in use so that a true foundation note could be established. Use of the right note was considered important in keeping the land stable and prosperous. There was even a government office of music, set up to regulate and standardize pitch throughout the empire. The effect of all this on popular music was probably limited, but for the music at court, it was of great importance.

Ya-yueh and Su-yueh Music

Traditional Chinese music falls into two different categories. *Ya-yueh music* is refined, elegant, and polite. Historically, it has been the music of cultivated people and philosophers. The music is monosyllabic (one note to a syllable) and is not strongly rhythmic. *Su-yueh music*, on the other hand, was once considered vulgar and common, especially by educated people. It has many notes to a syllable, with complex melodies sliding from one note to another.

Pentatonic Scales

The *pentatonic*, or five-note, *scales* used in Chinese music are derived from a series of twelve notes that were traditionally produced by blowing on a series of bamboo pitch pipes, each precisely related in size to the preceding one. If middle C is used as the foundation note, the twelve notes fall into the following order:

Twelve-Note Series

Two of the scales derived from the twelve notes are shown below:

Pentatonic Scales

Quite early, the Chinese developed a system of musical notation, which may be why composed pieces are more important in China than in India. Composed pieces, in turn, made possible the use of large orchestras. But music for soloists and small ensembles has always been common as well.

Instruments have traditionally been grouped according to the material from which they are made—metal, stone, silk (that is, silk-stringed), bamboo, gourd, clay, skin, or wood. Each material was thought to have a characteristic sound, and all materials had to be represented in a full orchestra. Chinese music does not use chordal harmony. However, the Chinese ear is very sensitive to the interplay of timbre and overtone harmony that is heard when a melody is played in unison by all the different instruments.

In any history as long as China's, there are bound to be several stages in the development of musical tradition. After the early formative period, lasting more or less through the fourth century A.D., there were several centuries of political disunity. During this time, the music was greatly affected by foreign influences coming mainly along the great trade routes to the north and west. Eighth-century records show that at one time there were no less than ten different kinds of music, most of them foreign, being played by court-supported orchestras in the capital. The office of music is likely to have had a hard time maintaining the purity of ya-yueh in those years. Still, as long as the empire lasted—into our own century—the old music was used for religious and court ceremonies.

Chinese Opera

Through the centuries, the court lost much of its dominance over music. Regional and popular styles came to the fore, particularly the styles collectively known as *Chinese opera*. At least three hundred varieties of Chinese opera are known. Most of them are small and local, emphasizing folk drama; several, however, are highly developed art forms. The latter are generally associated with particular regions and named after a region's major city—Canton, Shanghai, or Peking. Peking opera is probably the best known to people in the West. Its stylized vocal conventions—the rasping voice of the hero and the high, thin singing of the heroine—take some getting used to but can be very effective. Instrumental accompaniment varies according to the scene. Battle and military scenes call for gongs, drums, cymbals, and a double-reed instrument called a *sona*. Civil and domestic scenes require a bowed lute and some sort of time beater as well as other instruments added according to the mood of the scene.

The musical life of mainland China changed dramatically after the formation of the People's Republic of China in 1949. Most of the traditional styles were modified to conform with the ideals of the revolutionary leaders. Music, it was believed, should serve the people rather than the elite, and it should be capable, through its emotional content, of teaching new values and discouraging old ones. Collective composition was favored over individual creativity, and a number of new works were signed by groups of composers. Interest was also revived in the many regional folk-song styles. During the Cultural Revolution beginning in 1966, artistic policies became increasingly severe. Much traditional Chinese music was ignored, and the playing of Western music was banned. In more recent years, these restrictions have been somewhat relaxed, but leaders still maintain considerable interest in musical performance and composition. Modern leaders seem to be following Confucius's belief that the value of music extends far beyond mere entertainment.

MUSIC IN OTHER CULTURES

Music of Japan

The foundations of Japanese music came mostly from abroad—from Korea, Manchuria, India, and especially China. In the centuries when China was growing into one of the world's greatest empires, Japan was still relatively undeveloped. Thus it was natural that much of Chinese culture was imported wholesale into Japan. Musically, this meant that the classical Chinese instruments, theory, and style largely supplanted the earlier music of Japan— Shinto chants and folk music. The other main musical import was Buddhist chant, which came with its religion from India, through China.

Gagaku

Gagaku, or "elegant music," is directly based on the Chinese ya-yueh and retains many of its principles. However, it has been reshaped by the Japanese and is far from a mere copy. Much of Japanese art centers on deriving the greatest effect from a deliberately restricted amount of material; this can easily be seen in Japanese flower arrangements. Often a piece of music concentrates on a few sounds in order to bring out their character. Ensembles also tend to be small. While a formal Chinese orchestra had to include instruments from all eight groups of materials, the gagaku ensemble generally includes only reeds, flutes, a mouth organ, drums, and gongs. In some types of gagaku, string

The Art of Delicacy: *In music as in all the other arts, the Japanese have tried to achieve the beauty of simplicity. A few carefully drawn lines serve to suggest an entire environment of lush foliage and misted skies in this detail from an eighteenth-century painting of a small ensemble of wind and string instruments. (Music by Shohaku, Post Ashikaga Idealistic School)*

instruments are never used. Even when the orchestra is larger, the music retains the chamber-music feel of a small group.

Another distinctively Japanese element is the use of elastic, or breath, rhythm. At some points in the music, especially at the beginning of a gagaku, there are passages in which it is impossible to "beat time" in any meter. The rhythm of the music sounds as if someone had taken a deep breath, held it, and then exhaled. This natural rhythm cannot be regulated but must be sensed in unison by the performers.

Theater Music

The most characteristic music in Japan is the music of the theater. The classical *noh drama* and the later, more popular *kabuki plays* developed their own musical styles, relatively independent of the Chinese opera. The *bunraku*, or puppet theater, also has its own music, performed by a singer-narrator who tells the story and speaks all the roles. Narrative songs similar to those of the bunraku are also performed separately, accompanied by either the *samisen* or the *biwa*, two popular Japanese string instruments. In the narrative songs, vocal and instrumental phrases alternate in standard patterns. These patterns are strictly regulated, but the singer may add almost unlimited elaborations. A virtuoso can create an effect as dramatic as that of any Italian opera singer.

Section of the Noh Drama *Hagaromo*

The vocal music of the Japanese theater often follows the structure of Japanese poetry. Generally, five- and seven-syllable lines are set against a structural framework of eight beats. The drumbeats and drummers' calls serve to mark the position of important beats in a phrase. They also act as a means of controlling the tempo in the vocal lines. Many of these features can be seen in the excerpt from the noh drama *Hagaromo* shown below:

Excerpt from *Hagaromo*

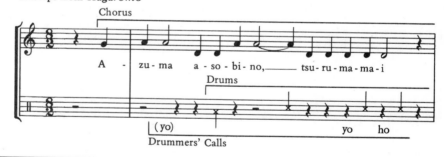

Listening Guide for a Section of the Noh Drama *Hagaromo*

Timbre: chorus, small drums, flute

Melody: declamatory, with many repeated notes

Rhythm: at times based on a clear beat; at times free

Texture: mainly monophonic; a little, incidental, improvised polyphony

Form: free, with repetitions of motives and phrases

Text: a tale about a fisher who finds a heavenly spirit's robe of feathers

MUSIC IN OTHER CULTURES

In 1868, when Japan began to accept trade with the West, foreign music was imported along with other Western things. However, Japanese students of music have tended to concentrate on either Western or Japanese music. There has been relatively little blending of the two. As East and West continue to exchange products and ideas, it will be interesting to see what future influence their music will have on each other.

Suggested Listening

Music of Africa

African Musical Instruments [Folkways 8460]
Music of Black Africa [Everest 3254]
Western Congo Folk Music [Folkways 4427]

Music of the American Indian

Authentic Music of the American Indian [Everest 3450]
Eskimos of Hudson Bay and Alaska [Folkways 4444]
Indian Music of the Southwest [Folkways 8850]
Music of the Pacific Northwest Coast [Folkways 4523]

Music of India

Classical Indian Music [Nonesuch 72014]
Indian Folk Music: Vol. 13 of *The Columbia World Library of Folk and Primitive Music* [Columbia 91 A02021]
Religious Music of India [Folkways 4431]
Traditional and Classical Music of India [Folkways 4422]

Music of China

China's Instrumental Heritage [Lyrichord 792]
Chinese Classical Masterpieces [Lyrichord 7182]
Exotic Music of Ancient China [Lyrichord 7122]

Music of Japan

Folk Music from Japan: Vol. 11 of *The Columbia World Library of Folk and Primitive Music* [Columbia 91 A02019]
Gagaku: Japanese Court Music [Lyrichord 7126]
Kabuki Music [Lyrichord 7134]
Masterpieces for the Koto [Lyrichord 7219]

Listening Preview   *Because the space devoted to Medieval and Renaissance music in a music appreciation textbook must be relatively brief, it is easy to overlook the fact that we are dealing with over one thousand years of musical changes. Listen to an early Medieval setting of the Mass (Side 2, Band 5, or the first selection at the end of Chapter 7). Then listen to a late Renaissance setting of the Mass by Palestrina (Side 2, Band 10, or a selection from the record library). What are the most distinctive differences between the two works? In what ways do these differences seem to reflect the increasing worldliness and sophistication of the people of western Europe?*

7
Medieval Music

The Medieval Period [c. 500–c. 1400]

The people of fifth-century Rome did not know their empire was dying. They only knew that money kept getting scarcer and life ever more dangerous. Survival was their main concern. How were peasants to prevent barbarian bands from raiding their livestock and burning their barns? How were travelers to reach their destinations without being murdered by brigands?

The best answer lay in finding a strong protector. The feudal system gradually evolved as vulnerable peasants gained protection from a few strong landowners in exchange for working their land. The most powerful shield of all, however, was the Church. In religion, people found an invincible savior who, in return for their devotion, promised to lead them from the miseries of life on earth to an eternity of bliss.

The feudal system and the Church remained important throughout the Medieval period. Only in the last few centuries of the Middle Ages were these two forces to be seriously challenged. As we shall see, the growth of trade and cities, the rise of strong rulers, and schisms in the Church all helped to usher in a new period.

General Characteristics of Medieval Music

The vast majority of the music that survives from the Middle Ages is religious. The music favored by the Church was vocal, incorporating most of the qualities that make any music singable. It was of limited range, mostly conjunct, and centered around a tonic note. The harmonic system that developed over the centuries was based on eight modes, or scales. These were loosely derived from ancient Greek modes and would eventually evolve into the major and minor modes so widely used in later centuries. Early Church music was monophonic, but in the later centuries of the Middle Ages the Church played an important part in the development of polyphony.

As might be expected, the same general characteristics were found in varying proportions in the secular music that developed during the Middle Ages. Although the words of the texts sung might differ considerably, the religious and secular music of the Middle Ages had many stylistic points in

Music and Medieval Society: *The social and economic developments that took place throughout the Medieval period had an inevitable effect on music. Composers, along with other western Europeans, were greatly influenced both by the gradual increase in the power of secular rulers and by the rise of urban centers. This detail from Lorenzetti's fresco* Good Government *presents a contemporary but somewhat idealistic view of urban life in the fourteenth century.*

common. Perhaps the most significant difference was the secular use of instruments to accompany songs. The use of musical instruments had been banned in the Church of the early Middle Ages, and only slowly did the Church come to accept anything but vocal music.

Music for the Church

By about the year 1000, the Church had codified its rituals into a standardized pattern of services. Services including psalms, prayers, and readings from scripture were held every day of the year. There were also a number of special days, often requiring much more elaborate services. Beginning with the great feast days of Easter and Pentecost, Church authorities later added hundreds of other feast days and saints' days to the Church calendar. For these many services, singers had to learn, often by ear, the music for innumerable psalms, responses, litanies, and antiphons.

The Office

In the monasteries, bells summoned the monks eight times a day to sing the Hours of the Divine Office, a round-the-clock series of services. The first was Matins, celebrated after midnight. Next came Lauds at "cock-crow," followed by Prime at sunrise. These were followed by Terce at midmorning, Sext at noon, None at midafternoon, Vespers before the evening meal, and, lastly, Compline at nightfall, just before the monks went to bed. Prayers, scripture readings, and the singing of hymns and psalms were all a part of the Hours of the Office.

The Mass

But the heart of the Church rite was the *Mass*, a reenactment of the Last Supper, when Christ offered his body and blood as a sacrifice. In the early centuries, Mass was celebrated only on Sundays and special days. Later, an elaborately sung High Mass often followed shortly after Terce every day of the week. The full celebration of the Mass was meant to capture the spirit of the people with the solemn movement of the celebrants before the altar, the glowing colors of embroidered vestments and altar cloths, the incense and candlelight, the bells tolling at the moment of the Elevation of the Host, and the chanting of the singers. Within the churches, people could thus find the beauty, drama, and promise of peace so often lacking in the rest of the Medieval world.

Proper and Ordinary Texts

The Mass consisted of two different kinds of texts. In the *Proper*, both the text and the music changed according to the particular rites of the day. In the *Ordinary*, the text was always the same although the music might vary. The Masses held on Christmas and Easter, for example, had different Proper texts, each appropriate to the particular feast day, but the Ordinary texts were the same on both days. The parts of the Mass that were most often set to music are shown below:

Proper	Ordinary
1. Introit	
	2. Kyrie eleison (Lord, have mercy)
	3. Gloria in excelsis Deo (Glory to God in the highest)
4. Gradual	
5. Alleluia or Tract; Sequence	
	6. Credo (I believe in one God)
7. Offertory	
	8. Sanctus (Holy, Holy, Holy, Lord God of Hosts); Benedictus (Blessed is he that cometh in the name of the Lord)
	9. Agnus Dei (Lamb of God)
10. Communion	

Plainchant or Gregorian Chant

The early music written for the Mass is known as *plainchant*, or *Gregorian chant*—after Gregory I, pope from 590 to 604. (No one is sure if Gregory himself really wrote plainchant. However, during his years as pope, many chants were collected and codified.) Each of the chants was made up of a single melodic line sung by a unison choir or a soloist without accompaniment.

Neumes

The chants were notated in symbols called *neumes*, a Greek word meaning "nod" or "sign." The earliest neumes were little marks resembling commas or Arabic curves. These were written without any staff immediately above the words in a musical manuscript. Possibly intended to depict the head and hand gestures of a lead singer, these neumes developed into a square notation that eventually came to represent specific pitches. A four-line staff was adopted, with a clef placed at the beginning to show the position of the note C or F. An example can be seen at the bottom of the page.

Chants were generally built on one of eight modes, which were loosely based on a system taken from the ancient Greeks. The eight modes make use of four different scale patterns. Each of these spans an octave in range and occurs in two versions. The first version, the *authentic*, begins on the scale's central note and extends to the note an octave above it. The second version, the *plagal*, has the same central note but begins four notes lower and thus has a lower range. The modern notation below shows the authentic *Dorian mode* and its related plagal mode, the *Hypodorian mode*. Both share the central note of D, but the Dorian mode has a range from D to D, while the Hypodorian mode has a range from A to A. Note that they use only the white keys of the piano keyboard.

Authentic and Plagal Modes

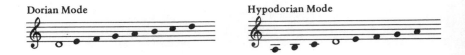

Dorian Mode   Hypodorian Mode

Melodic Styles

Plainchant melodies were written in a number of different styles. Some such as the Alleluias, were very *melismatic*—that is, with a large number of notes for each syllable of text. Other chants were *syllabic*, with only one note per syllable. Still others were *neumatic*, with several notes per syllable, but not as many as the melismatic chants.

Introit of the Requiem Mass

One example of neumatic chant is found in an early Introit of the Requiem Mass, or "Mass for the Dead." The first line of the chant is given below, first in Medieval notation and then in modern notation.

Early Medieval Art An emphasis on spirituality
arts of the early Medieval period, an impetus
declining centuries of Roman civilization. W
stressed the reality of physical existence in thi
thought of the world to come. It is remarkable i
tory of early Christian art paralleled this ch
reality. The general and persistent artistic te
dematerialization and abstraction. In the richl
apse mosaic, little sense of bodily weight or s
neath the conventionalized drapery. Christ a
seem to float in a golden, timeless void. The fl
temporal world is replaced by a world of sir
eternal order.

Fourteenth-Century Music Manuscript

y the end of the Medieval period, secularism
lly pleasure began to replace the early empha
t painting and sculpture, particularly in north
d to be permeated by religious feeling, now in
introspective, and mystical. The miniature o
re in a fourteenth-century music manuscrip
mannered style that was so typical of the pe
inted in a lovely decorative manner. Equa
utlining the figures in curving arabesques and
h bright, cheerful color. There is a curious and
mixture here of fact and fantasy: outlines o
und are carefully drawn, yet there seems to
n with relating the size of the figures to the
with consistent perspective. A sense of reli
beneath the surface of reality continues to be

The VI at the beginning of the chant indicates the mode or scale on which the music is based—in this case the Hypolydian mode. The clef at the beginning of the four-line staff shows on which line C will occur. Thus the chant begins on the note F, as can also be seen in the modern transcription.

The melodic motion in the Introit is almost always by steps—that is, in conjunct motion. The monophonic texture is characteristic of all chants. The form of the Introit is ABA. After the opening section, a contrasting section "Te decet hymnus" is chanted. Finally, the opening melody is repeated with the same words: "Requiem aeternam."

Side 2, Band 5

Listening Guide for Introit of the Requiem Mass

Timbre:	solo male voice intones first words; then unison male choir enters and sings chant unaccompanied
Melody:	mainly conjunct; limited range
Rhythm:	not indicated in original notation; notes probably of equal value most of the time
Harmony:	based on the Hypolydian mode
Texture:	monophonic
Form:	ABA

Text:

A Requiem aeternam dona eis, Domine; et lux perpetua luceat eis.
Rest eternal grant unto them, O Lord; and let light perpetual shine upon them.

B Te decet hymnus, Deus, in Sion, et tibi reddetur votum in Jerusalem; exaudi orationem meam, ad te omnis caro veniet.
You are praised, O God, in Zion, and unto you shall the vow be performed in Jerusalem; hear my prayer; unto you all flesh shall come.

A Requiem aeternam dona eis, Domine; et lux perpetua luceat eis.
Rest eternal grant unto them, O Lord; and let light perpetual shine upon them.

Hymns

In addition to plainchant, Church services throughout Medieval Europe included *hymns*. The hymn is one of the oldest types of music incorporated into Christian worship. Often based on folk melodies and set in strophic form, hymns were meant to be sung by the congregation.

Secular Music

Ventadorn

Courtly love bloomed first in the courts of Provence in southern France toward the end of the eleventh century. It was nourished by the mingling of Moorish, Oriental, and Spanish influences there, where the trade routes met. From Britain came the legends of King Arthur and of Tristan and Iseult to add their potent mystique. An early proponent of courtly love, Bernart de Ventadorn, once declared to Eleanor of Aquitaine that Tristan had never suffered for Iseult as he did for her.

Both erotic and spiritual, courtly love defied the monastic, ascetic emphasis of Christianity in other parts of Europe. It called upon men to seek

Troubadour

a form of temporal salvation through devotion to earthly, but highly idealized, women. Typically, the *troubadour* would sing of his adoring enslavement to an unattainable woman who was beauty and goodness incarnate. He would praise her loveliness, lament her disdain, vow to become more virtuous for her sake, and dedicate all his knightly deeds to her. Women also wrote and sang courtly love songs, with themes paralleling those of the male troubadours.

Troubadour songs were written in the southern vernacular tongue called the *langue d'oc*. Although the songs were written down as monophonic melodies, they may often have been sung to the accompaniment of harp, lute, or some other Medieval instrument. They were generally in triple meter and often in one of the Church modes.

Ventadorn: "Be m'an perdut"

"Be m'an perdut,"* by Bernart de Ventadorn, typifies the style of troubadour songs. The song is monophonic, with two stanzas. The form of the first stanza is AAB. In the second stanza, an additional B section is added at the end, resulting in an AABB form. The beginning of the first A section is shown below.

Beginning of First A Section

Be m'an per-dut lai en-ves Ven-ta-dorn tuih mei a-mic,

Side 2, Band 6

Listening Guide for Ventadorn's "Be m'an perdut"

Timbre:	solo baritone, unaccompanied
Melody:	mainly conjunct
Rhythm:	triple meter
Harmony:	based on a Church mode
Texture:	monophonic
Form:	strophic; AAB in first stanza; AABB in second stanza

Text:

I A Be m'an perdut lai enves Ventadorn tuih mei amic, pois ma domna no m'ama;

Now I am exiled from all my friends of Ventadorn, since my lady loves me not;

A et es be dreihz que jamais lai no torn, c'ades estai vas me salvatj'e grama.

wisest would I be never to return, for she has treated me with scorn and bitterness.

B Ve·us per que·m fai semblan irat e morn: car en s'amor me deleih e·m sojorn! ni de ren als no·s rancura ni·s clama.

And why, when she beholds me, is her face dark with anger? Only because I delight to dwell in her love— nothing else have I done to offend her.

*Notation reprinted from *A Treasury of Early Music*, compiled and edited by Carl Parrish, with the permission of W. W. Norton & Company, Inc. Copyright © 1958 by W. W. Norton & Company, Inc.

II A	Aissi c·ol peis qui s'eslaiss' el cadorn e no·n sap mot tro que s'es pres en l'ama,	Like the unwatchful fish that leaps to seize the bait, and finds himself hooked,
A	m'eslaissei eu vas trop amar un jorn, c'anc no·m gardei, tro fui en mei la flama	so did I plunge, unheeding, into too great a love, knowing not, till I was in the flame,
B	que m'ant plus fort, no·m feira focs de forn; e ges per so n·om posc partir un dorn, aissi·m te pres s'amors e m'aliama.	that it would burn me more cruelly than any furnace. Yet now I cannot make a move to escape, so close a prisoner does love hold me.
B	Mos Bels Vezers, per vos fai Deus vertutz tals c'om nous ve que no si' ereubutz dels bels plazers que sabetz dir e faire.	My beautiful one, God works such marvels through you that no one, seeing you, could fail to be taken captive, beholding the unequalled beauty of your words and ways.

Trouvères and Minnesingers

Flourishing a little later in northern France were the *trouvères*. They wrote in the *langue d'oïl* or northern dialect and continued the tradition of monophonic courtly love songs. In Germany there were *Minnesingers* who sang of courtly love and, at times, of the beauty of nature.

The Growth of Polyphony

Imagine a monk singing Matins for the two-hundredth time in a dark monastery chapel in the middle of the night. Fulfilling a creative urge, he impulsively invents an elaborate melody to adorn the familiar phrase of chant his brethren are singing. He is creating polyphony—in this case, the harmony of two melodies performed at the same time.

Organum

As long as it did not obscure the meaning of the text, polyphony—or *organum*, as it was called—was welcomed by the Church. In the earliest organum, which dates from the ninth century, a second voice duplicates the plainchant melody, running parallel to it, generally three or four notes above or below.

At first, the added voice moved only note-for-note with the original chant voice. Later, musicians created more decorative, flowing lines for the added voice, providing two or more notes for each note of the original voice. Contrary rather than parallel motion was often used so the voices could move more freely toward and away from each other. This style of organum flowered at the French monastery of Saint Martial of Limoges, a leading center for all the arts in the late eleventh and early twelfth centuries.

Tenor and Duplum

Musicians at Saint Martial sometimes extended the notes of the original chant line to great length. This line was often called the *tenor*, from the Latin *tenere* ("to hold"). The added line, now called the *duplum*, became the more important line, because of its melismatic use of many notes against each lengthy note of the tenor.

Medieval Architecture: *The towers of the cathedral at Chartres offer an illustration of two radically different phases of Medieval architecture. The tower on the right dates from the twelfth century and shows in its restrained lines the shading of the old Romanesque and Norman styles into the early Gothic. The tower on the left, erected three centuries later, is in a greatly embellished late Gothic style.*

Rapho Guillumette

Leonin

Polyphonic Styles

But it was in Paris in the late twelfth century that organum reached its peak of development. The great Leonin was choirmaster at Notre Dame when the new cathedral was being built. His music, collected in a volume called the *Magnus liber organi* ("Large Book of Organum"), is made up of two-voiced organa for the Propers of many Masses. The organa make use of two different styles of two-part polyphony—organum and discantus. Each work begins in *organum style*. The notes of the tenor line are extremely long, changing only when the duplum—a long, florid melody of many notes—changes syllables. The tenor notes thus set up a strong foundation for the melismatic upper part. Eventually, however, the music changes to *discantus style*, and the tenor notes begin to move in quicker rhythms, similar to the duplum rhythm.

Leonin: *Viderunt omnes*

Leonin's *Viderunt omnes* clearly shows both the organum and the discantus styles. The first section of the chant moves from the initial use of organum style to discantus, as is shown below. As the work continues, the organum style is heard again. Finally, at the very end, monophonic chant is heard.

Listening Guide for Leonin's *Viderunt omnes*

Timbre:	solo male voice sings top line; several male voices sing bottom line
Melody:	bottom line borrowed from Gregorian chant; top line conjunct
Rhythm:	triple meter
Harmony:	based on a Church mode
Texture:	mainly contrapuntal; monophonic at the end
Form:	first section changes from organum style to discantus style to organum style; last section is sung in monophonic chant
Text:	Viderunt omnes fines terrae salu- tare Dei nostri. All the ends of the earth have seen the salvation of our God.

While Leonin had preferred the organum style, his successor Perotin made more use of discantus. Although Perotin did write three- and four-part organa of his own, as well as hymns, he devoted much of his time to revising and shortening Leonin's works. He pruned long organum passages and often replaced them with new passages written in discantus style.

Perotin's successors continued to stress the use of discantus. They also followed Perotin in writing music with three and four parts. New words were sometimes added in the upper voices, often as a commentary on the original words retained in the tenor line. Out of this practice, a new type of composition was born. This was the *motet*, from the French *mot*, or "word." The motet soon attracted the interest of the aristocracy by the possibilities it offered for combining sacred and secular music. Over time, the voices in the motet became more and more independent. Each had its own melody, its own words, and at times its own rhythmic mode.

Motet

As the thirteenth century closed, the motet became freer in structure. Tenor and upper lines were borrowed from secular songs as well as from plainchant. Two French secular texts often appeared together over a tenor from plainchant. The evolution of the motet reveals in miniature what was happening to society in general. With the growth of cities and the increasing power of regional and national secular leaders, Church musicians began to look beyond the confines of the Church. They began to think that they might find something of value in the temporal world.

Music of the Fourteenth Century

In 1324, while the papacy was in its "Babylonian captivity" at Avignon, Pope John XXII issued a major bull. In it he expressed his concern over the growing elaboration of Church music. Things had gone so far, he said, that excitement was replacing devotion as the object of the singing. Worship was hindered rather than helped. Therefore he directed that, at least in the Divine Office and the Mass, modern decorations such as polyphony and secular melodies must be eliminated. Plainchant was the only proper music for the Church's worship.

But this proclamation went largely unheeded. The Church had lost a great deal of its earlier power. Amid such calamities as the Hundred Years' War, peasant uprisings, and the Black Death, the divisions within the Church were increasing. Furthermore, the new style was too popular to be suppressed.

Ars Nova

Vitry

Rhythmic Innovations

The term *ars nova* ("new art") was used by Philippe de Vitry (1290–1361) in the title of his treatise describing new characteristics of style in music of the fourteenth century. Among them was an important development in rhythm. Until the late thirteenth century, almost all measured music was in triple meter, the *tempus perfectum*, or "perfect time." Three was a number widely revered for mystical reasons. Duple meter was viewed as imperfect. Vitry observed, however, that triple and duple meters had now become equally acceptable. Another rhythmic innovation of the time was *isorhythm*. Composers began with a rhythmic pattern and a pitch sequence of the same or different length, which they combined into a single melody. When either the

Medieval Instruments: *This fourteenth-century Italian manuscript shows a number of the instruments popular in the late Medieval period. Perhaps most interesting is the early organ in the center. The other instruments, clockwise from the upper left, are a viol, a psaltery, a mandola, clappers, trumpets, kettledrums, a shawm, a bagpipe, and a jingle drum.*

rhythmic pattern or the pitch sequence ended, it was repeated. In cases where the two elements were of different lengths, the result was an extremely complex mixture of rhythm and melody.

The fourteenth century also saw a general increase in rhythmic complexity. Composers of motets began to change rhythms frequently. Musicians, following the directions given by time signatures, had to be ready to change from a pulse of two beats to a pulse of three while holding their own against the other lines, which were making similar shifts at different times.

Polyphonic settings of the Mass—the Ordinary rather than the Proper—also occupied composers in the fourteenth century. They made use of new as well as older styles. Kyries, Glorias, and other parts of the Ordinary seem as a rule to have been written independently of one another. The earliest complete polyphonic Ordinary known to have been written by one composer is the *Messe de Nostre Dame* ("Mass of Our Lady") by Guillaume de Machaut (c. 1300–1377).

Machaut

Machaut, a priest, poet, and civil servant, was also an important French composer. He was born in Champagne of a noble family. After ordination as a priest, he became secretary to King John of Bohemia and followed him on his military campaigns. At the same time, he also held honorary positions with churches at home in France. Throughout his life, Machaut maintained close connections with several royal families, writing poetry and music for them when his secretarial duties allowed. His secular music was generally written in one of four popular musical forms—*rondeau, virelai, ballade,* and *lai*—all based on poetic forms. Many of these works were written as vocal solos to be accompanied by two or three instruments. Others were monophonic, possibly with improvised accompaniment.

14th-Century French Forms

Machaut: "Douce dame jolie"

Virelai

The lovely *virelai* "Douce dame jolie" shows Machaut's monophonic vocal style to best advantage. The song includes a mixture of conjunct and disjunct motion, giving the melody a strong character. The meter is duple, and the rhythms are quite engaging. The musical form of the virelai falls into an ABBAA pattern.

Listening Guide for Machaut's "Douce dame jolie"

Timbre: solo male voice and recorder; drum part improvised, not a part of the original notation

Melody: largely conjunct, with some disjunct motion

Rhythm: duple meter

Harmony: based on a Church mode

Texture: monophonic (recorder doubles vocal part)

Form: virelai (ABBAA)

Text:

A Douce dame jolie,
pour Dieu ne penses mie
que nulle ait signourie
seur moy fors vous seulement.

Sweet lady of my delight,
I pray you, never dream
that anyone rules over me
save only you.

B Qu'ades sans tricherie
chierie
vous ay et humblement

For without deceit
would I cherish you
and humbly

B tous les jours de ma vie
servie
sans vilein pensement.

serve you all my
life without evil
thought.

A Helas! et je mendie
d'esperance et d'aie;
dont ma joie est fenie,
se pite ne vous en prent.

But alas! Here I am, a beggar,
pleading for hope and help;
for my joy is all ended
unless you have pity on me.

A Douce dame jolie,
pour Dieu ne penses mie
que nulle ait signourie
seur moy fors vous seulement.

Sweet lady of my delight,
I pray you, never dream
that anyone rules over me
save only you.

14th-Century Italian Forms

During the fourteenth century, Italy was torn by the same disasters as the rest of Europe. But Italian musicians reacted by making joyful, serenely sensuous music. In this age of Dante, Giotto, Petrarch, and Boccaccio, people seemed to regard art as a refuge of sanity in a world gone mad. Everyone, gifted amateurs as well as professionals, played and sang to make leisure hours more lovely. Three poetic-musical forms were especially popular: the *madrigal*, the *caccia*, and the *ballata*.

The *madrigal* was originally a rustic form from the north, having two or three parts in AAB form. The texts often involved the love of shepherds and shepherdesses or the beauty of nature. The upper voices provided melodic material while the slow-moving lowest voice laid a foundation for them. The melodies seemed to invite the listeners to bask in the beauty of the singers' voices.

Exact Imitation

The *caccia* was a work in which two upper voices entered separately singing the same melody in *exact imitation* of each other—in the same way that rounds are sung today. These voices were heard over another, slow-moving lower voice. Texts included hunting calls, shouts, and birdcalls, all set to elaborate melodies.

Landini

Toward the end of the fourteenth century, the *ballata*, similar to the French virelai, was also much heard in Italy. The works of Francesco Landini (1325–1397), the best-known Italian composer of the period, include several fine examples of the ballata.

Suggested Listening

Masses

Requiem Mass: Dies irae ("Day of Wrath") [Peters PLE-012]. This famous Sequence is made up of eighteen three-line stanzas, grouped in three patterns of AABBCC, each with its own rhyme, and a conclusion with a somewhat different verse and melody.

Machaut: *La Messe de Nostre Dame:* Kyrie, Gloria [Vanguard HM-1]. Machaut's "Mass of Our Lady" is the earliest-known complete polyphonic setting of the Ordinary by a single composer. Melodic unity binds the work together, while the sections vary in formal structure.

Motets

Anonymous thirteenth-century motet: "Povre secors/Gaude, chorus omnium" ("Little Help/Rejoice with Singing") [Experience Anonymes 35]. In this early motet, two voices, one singing a secular love song and the other a hymn of praise to the Virgin Mary, are heard above a viol tenor line derived from plainchant.

Vitry: "Tribum/Quoniam/Merito hec patimur" ("Afflicted/Since/Deservedly We Suffer") [Telefunken 6-41230]. Almost all of Vitry's motets make use of isorhythm. The present work begins with two upper voices. Then the tenor enters, setting up the isorhythmic pattern. There are six presentations of the rhythmic pattern for each sequence of pitches.

Songs

Ventadorn: "Can vei la lauzeta" ("When I See the Lark") [Telefunken 6-41126]. This tenor solo is a "lark song"—that is, a love song of despair. The form is free, based on one of the most beautiful of Provençal poems.

Landini: "Cosi pensoso" ("Thus Thoughtful") [Peters/EMI IC063-30113]. This is Landini's only known caccia. In the first section, the two upper voices sing in exact imitation, while the slower tenor adds a supporting foundation. The second section is made up of contrasting solo and group parts. The song is descriptive program music, bustling with activity.

8
Renaissance Music

The Renaissance Period [c. 1400–c. 1600]

The Renaissance marked a transition from a style of life that was predominantly religious to one predominantly secular. No longer were the people of western Europe guided solely by a mystical acceptance of divine authority. Instead, they turned to reason and scientific inquiry. To learn, to measure, to understand the structure of reality was the passion of the Renaissance. The modern sciences of astronomy and anatomy began. Voyages were launched to explore new oceans and new lands. New techniques and instruments for navigating and mapping were developed. Printing was invented. Artists concerned themselves with proportion and perspective. The age of anonymity was at an end. Individual creation, epitomized by the prophetic science and artistry of Leonardo da Vinci, was glorified.

The times were changing in political and economic ways as well. After the Hundred Years' War (1337–1453), the Church lost much of its grip on the people's purses and imaginations. Money and political power were now held by merchants, princes, and monarchs as well as by the Church.

The Renaissance came early to Italy, whose people, at home on the soil of the ancient Romans, set out to recapture the "golden age" of classical antiquity. The rulers of Italian city-states, such as the Medici of Florence and the Sforzas of Milan, and the powerful dukes of Burgundy in eastern France sought to show off their wealth by building splendid palaces that reflected the balance and proportion of the classical style. Renaissance princes gathered huge entourages to attend them at home and to travel with them wherever they went.

General Characteristics of Renaissance Music

Music was skillfully woven into nearly every aspect of court life. Private religious services, meals, processions through the city, leavetakings, and homecomings all called for accompaniment by elegantly dressed performers. Special occasions, such as weddings, jousts, hunts, masquerades, funerals, and wars, called for larger forces. All the trumpeters in the area would hurry to welcome a visiting prince or noble bride.

Music was thus an important part of daily life in the Renaissance. Instrumental music was widely heard, but vocal music is much more important in the notated music that has survived. Melodies, generally very singable ones, were often written in counterpoint. Four different voice parts became standard, and the use of imitation became increasingly popular. Harmony was still based on the Church modes, which were used with increasing ingenuity and freedom. While some of the forms used in the Middle Ages continued to prevail, a number of new forms evolved as composers sought new ways to express themselves.

New Developments in Polyphony

Medieval polyphony was most often performed by soloists, each singing a different vocal part. The number of parts was generally two or three, and they were confined to a fairly narrow range of pitches. Within this range, the melodic lines often crossed. Thus it was necessary to make the different parts contrast as much as possible. The parts were given contrasting melodies, rhythms, and sometimes texts, so that the listener could tell them apart. Voices or instruments were often chosen for their contrasting timbres, again to make it easier to hear the different parts.

In the early fifteenth century, however, each part of a polyphonic work was generally sung by several voices. This added greater depth and evenness to

An Age of Pageantry: *Gentile Bellini's late fifteenth-century painting* Procession in Saint Mark's Square *helps illustrate the splendor and sheer magnitude of Renaissance pageantry. Music invariably played a part on such occasions, as exemplified by the choir at the left.*

Alinari/Scala

**Wide Use of
Four-Part
Polyphony**

the sound of polyphony. By the mid-Renaissance, four parts became the normal number for a polyphonic work, resulting in very full-sounding harmonies. With these changes came an expansion of the overall range of the vocal parts. Melodic lines crossed much less often, making it no longer necessary for each part to be so distinctive. The same thematic material was frequently assigned to all the voices, so that a piece was more like a conversation among equals.

Plainchant continued to be used as a basis for experiment. A phrase of chant might still be used in the tenor, with the note values lengthened. However, the phrase might appear in the top voice as well or even wander from line to line, taking on new rhythmic identities in each line.

The use of imitation became very prominent. A theme would be stated first by one voice, then repeated, either exactly or with modification, by the other voices. Even when it underwent numerous changes, the theme acted to unify the piece.

**Careful Use of
Dissonance**

The attitude toward dissonance changed greatly during the Renaissance. Since Medieval part music relied so heavily on contrasting timbres, composers treated dissonance rather casually. Dissonance generally occurred on weak beats. Since most Medieval music was in triple time, which has twice as many weak beats as strong ones, there were ample opportunities for dissonance. Much of the dissonance in Medieval music resulted from the fact that compositions were often built up in layers. A composer began with one complete line, usually a tenor taken from plainchant, and wrote another line, a duplum, to go with it. Later the same composer or someone else would add a third line, relating it to the tenor according to certain rules, but paying little attention to the duplum. This process caused some extraordinary dissonance. In the fifteenth century, however, composers began to treat dissonance more systematically. Renaissance composers generally worked out all the lines at once and thus had greater control over all of them. For most composers, consonance became the norm. Dissonance became a special effect, to be used before cadences and at dramatic moments. It could occur on strong beats, but only with careful preparation followed by resolution. Thus, dissonance became both less common and more important.

The relationship of music to words changed greatly during the Renaissance. In the Middle Ages, texts were generally fitted to music with little or no regard for the meaning of the words. In contrast, a Renaissance composer was usually very alert to the general spirit and mood of a text, choosing a mode, melodic materials, and rhythms as appropriate to the text as possible. Words or phrases were often sensitively developed with *text painting*. The phrase "rise up," for example, might be set to an ascending scale. The word "death" might be sung to a dissonant chord.

Text Painting

This new concern for words also helped free rhythm from the repeated designs of the Middle Ages. The trend seems to have begun with the music of the fourteenth century. During the next hundred years, rhythm became more varied and spontaneous. Duple meter became very popular. Syncopation and other complex rhythms were freely mixed with simpler patterns.

Comparison of Medieval and Renaissance Music

Elements	Medieval Music c. 500–c. 1400	Renaissance Music c. 1400–c. 1600
Melody	Generally conjunct and singable Limited range	Generally conjunct and singable Wider range
Rhythm	Chant rhythm presumably free Triple meter in 13th century with duple meter accepted in 14th century Isorhythm and other complex rhythms in 14th century	Metric patterns not emphasized in religious vocal music but clear in many secular works Generally less complex than in 14th century Use of bar lines in 16th century
Harmony	Based on 8 Church modes	Church modes expanded to 12 Careful use of dissonance
Texture	Monophony very important Polyphony for 2, 3, and 4 voices by end of period Use of imitation in 14th century	Polyphonic music for 4 voices standard; 5 or more voices often used in 16th century Wide use of imitation Some homophony
Timbre	Notated music mainly vocal Small choirs sang monophonic chants Polyphonic music generally sung by soloists Instrumental music generally improvised	Notated vocal music still most important Small choirs sang polyphonic religious music Secular music for soloists and small ensembles More music written specifically for instruments
Important Forms	Free vocal chant forms Free and fixed poetic forms for secular music Strophic songs and hymns	Fixed poetic forms gradually replaced by imitative forms Strophic songs and hymns
Important Types of Compositions	Plainchant settings of parts of the Mass Motet (mainly secular) Secular songs Instrumental dances	Polyphonic settings of parts of the Mass Motet (mainly religious) Secular songs Instrumental dances Instrumental pieces such as the ricercar

Religious Music

In the fifteenth century, the motet changed gradually from a work that had both secular and religious aspects to one that was mainly religious. The Mass and the fifteenth-century motet, both of which shared a common musical style, were by far the most important types of religious music during the Renaissance. With the Reformation in the early sixteenth century, hymns became very important in the newly Protestant areas of Europe.

Religious Music of the Early and Mid-Renaissance

The lives of Renaissance composers reflected both the new glorification of the individual and the large variety of activities open to the talented. The career of Guillaume Dufay is in a number of ways typical. Born about 1400, Dufay began as a choirboy at the cathedral of Cambrai in northern France. As a young man, he appears to have gone to Italy to spend a few years at the Malatesta court; a number of his early works are dedicated to the family. After a year of study at the University of Bologna, he joined the papal choir, where he stayed nine years, except for visits to the Duke of Savoy's court. Afterward, his travels are hard to trace. He may have sung at the Burgundian court. We know he undertook at least one diplomatic mission. In his later years, he spent more and more time at home in Cambrai, where he died in 1474, internationally respected and loved.

Dufay wrote a number of Ordinaries of the Mass, each set as a complete cycle. In his Masses, he generally used plainchant for the tenor, writing two lines of polyphony above it and one line below it. The two lower lines, with longer note values, were probably played on instruments. Dufay chose melodies from a number of sources. He was among the first to use secular tunes in his Masses, borrowing melodies from *chansons*—secular songs with French texts.

Ockeghem

The brightest star of the next generation was Johannes Ockeghem (c. 1430–c. 1495). He was born in Burgundy, trained at the cathedral of Antwerp, and began his career in the service of Charles VII of France. Ockeghem stayed at the French court all of his life, except for one diplomatic mission to Spain. He had a splendid bass voice, and the long, expressive lines of his polyphony suggest a singer's self-gratification. Carried by a firm rhythmic energy, phrases extend and overlap one another, frequently avoiding cadences. He is known to have written at least ten Masses. In his Masses and in other works, he was fascinated by the use of *canon*—that is, of exact imitation, similar to that found in the rounds sung today. Canon could be used to create very elaborate textures. Any theme could be stated in a number of ways: in *augmentation* (lengthened note values), in *diminution* (shortened note values), in *inversion* (upside down), in *retrograde* (backward), and in different meters. The result could be very intricate indeed.

Josquin

Josquin des Prez (c. 1450–1521) was a choirboy under Ockeghem. His adult career took him all over Europe. In Italy, he served at the Sforza court in Milan, possibly at Ferrara, and with the papal choir in Rome. In France, he visited Cambrai and the court of Louis XII. He also spent time in the Netherlands and retired finally to the collegiate church of Condé. Josquin's early works show a rather academic mastery of Ockeghem's style. It was after he went to Italy that his technique became more facile and eloquent, and he began to write Masses, motets, and chansons that represent a high point of each genre. He used imitation to unify his music more thoroughly than anyone had before, passing the material from voice to voice so that each one had an equal part in the musical conversation.

Josquin: Kyrie of the *Missa pange lingua*

For his *Missa pange lingua*, Josquin borrowed the melody of the Gregorian chant *Pange lingua* ("Sing, My Tongue"), which he used imitatively in all four parts of the Kyrie. In writing an elaboration of an existing melody, he was making use of the so-called *paraphrase technique*. The technique can be seen by comparing the chant with the beginning of Josquin's Kyrie.

Paraphrase Technique

Gregorian Chant: *Pange lingua*

Josquin: Kyrie from *Missa pange lingua*

EARLY MUSIC

The Renaissance Sense of Beauty

Individual Creativity For both composers and artists, the Renaissance brought a glorification of individual creativity. Geniuses such as Michelangelo restlessly drove themselves toward heroic, often unattainable goals. Two concepts central to much of Michelangelo's work are embodied in the statue *David*: titanic yet human energy driven by divine inspiration. The work is enormous in size, approximately eighteen feet high. The subject, sternly aware of the approaching enemy, face and muscles tense with defiance, represents not only the biblical David but also the ideal of freedom for the Italian city of Florence. Renaissance artist and historian Vasari compared the statue to ancient sculptures of gods and athletes, saying it had "stolen the thunder of all statues, whether modern or ancient, Greek or Latin."

Michelangelo: *David* (1501–1504)

The Italian Renaissance In the Italian cities where the Renaissance began, great emphasis was placed on humanism—on human values and the ideals of Classical Greece and Rome. Raphael's *School of Athens* is probably the most complete and perfect pictorial statement of humanistic ideals achieved during the High Renaissance. All the compositional elements—the majestic architectural setting, the effortless sense of three-dimensional space, the massive yet active figures and their balanced symmetrical placement—achieve that quality of severe harmony ever since associated with the Renaissance.

Raphael: *School of Athens* (1508–1513)

The Renaissance in the North In the painting and sculpture of northern Europe, Renaissance humanism was fused with theology. Grünewald's *Incarnation* makes use of many of the lessons of Italian art, but the vision remains essentially Medieval. Intense light fills the panel, and the colors are iridescent, almost unearthly. The possibilities of color and light as an expressive force are explored in the service of the presentation of the timeless and enduring truths of Christianity.

Grünewald: *Incarnation* from the *Isenheim Altarpiece* (1510–1515)

Listening Guide for Josquin's Kyrie of the *Missa pange lingua*

Timbre:	small four-part choir, unaccompanied
Melody:	conjunct; based on the melody of the *Pange lingua* chant
Rhythm:	triple meter
Harmony:	based on a Church mode
Texture:	contrapuntal and imitative
Form:	ABC

Text:

A	Kyrie eleison; Kyrie eleison; Kyrie eleison.	Lord, have mercy; Lord, have mercy; Lord, have mercy.
B	Christe eleison; Christe eleison; Christe eleison.	Christ, have mercy; Christ, have mercy; Christ, have mercy.
C	Kyrie eleison; Kyrie eleison; Kyrie eleison.	Lord, have mercy; Lord, have mercy; Lord, have mercy.

Isaac

Heinrich Isaac (c. 1450–c. 1517) had a more colorful career than Josquin. It began at the court of Lorenzo de' Medici in Florence, where he made a name for himself as a composer and music master. With the death of Lorenzo in 1492, Isaac left Florence and eventually went to the court of Emperor Maximilian I in Vienna. In 1497 he was appointed imperial court composer, a post that left him free to travel and take other positions. He later returned to Florence, working partly as a secret agent for Maximilian, and eventually recovered his former job at the Medici court. Isaac's greatest work was the *Choralis Constantinus*, which includes polyphonic settings of Mass Propers for Sundays and certain feast days. Isaac also composed numerous Mass Ordinaries, motets, instrumental pieces, and secular part songs in the languages and styles of four different countries.

Music of the Reformation

The Reformation, which aroused sixteenth-century Europe to such bloody strife, was an attempt to end corruption in the Catholic Church. Leaders of the Reformation proclaimed that each person had a right to confront God directly in an essentially private act of worship. These same leaders believed that Latin should no longer be the sole language of worship. Protestants in each country developed their own forms of church service making use of the language of the country.

Luther

Martin Luther (1483–1546), one of the key figures at the beginning of the religious revolution, had a great love of music. He was very familiar with the music of the Catholic Church. He also sang, played instruments, and admired Josquin des Prez above all other composers.

Luther knew the power of music to sway souls. To him music was an invaluable part of Christian education and of daily life, for, he said, "The devil hates and fears music . . . and flees [it] as much as he does theology." Luther wanted his congregations to have music they could sing themselves, and thus

Chorale

the hymn—or *chorale*—became very important in his services.

Luther himself may have written some of the most famous chorales of the Lutheran church. Among the most famous is the adaptation of Psalm 46, "Ein' feste Burg ist unser Gott" ("A Mighty Fortress Is Our God"). Music for the Lutheran services was also adapted from Latin chants, which were translated into German and arranged for the congregation to sing.

Other Protestant leaders were less enthusiastic about the use of music in church services. John Calvin, for instance, subscribed to Saint Augustine's suspicion that music was not altogether wholesome. He barred polyphony and instruments from his church services, as had the early Catholic Church. Congregational singing of psalms was, however, greatly encouraged.

Council of Trent

The Catholic Church, in turn, initiated a number of counterreforms designed to reawaken religious fervor and purify Rome's spiritual leadership. At the Council of Trent (1545–1563), some attempts were made to control polyphony. One faction wanted such "scandalous noise" banned from the services on the grounds that it obscured the sacred texts. But princely music patrons objected. Special performances of polyphonic masterpieces finally persuaded the council that polyphony should remain as long as the text was clearly presented.

Religious Music of the Late Renaissance

The new awareness of words found among Renaissance composers had a major effect upon the motet and the Mass as well as upon secular music. The motets

Lassus

of Roland de Lassus (1532–1594) are almost a compendium of expressive devices used to display words with great feeling. Lassus also wrote Masses and a number of secular songs. Flemish by birth and training, he was one of the most popular composers of the age, and his career was glamorous. As a choirboy, he had such a beautiful voice that he was kidnapped three times, ending up at age twelve in the court of Ferdinando Gonzaga, Viceroy of Sicily. He spent his youth in various Italian households. After a brief stay in Antwerp, he went in 1556 to the court of Albert V of Bavaria, in Munich. A few years later, he was made *Kapellmeister* (chapel master), and he stayed there for the rest of his life.

Palestrina

Lassus' great Italian contemporary Giovanni Pierluigi da Palestrina (c. 1524–1594) was more conservative. His music was written for the Catholic Church, and expresses the ideals of the Council of Trent. Palestrina spent his career in the churches of Rome. From 1571 until his death, he led the Cappella Guilia of Saint Peter's and bore the honorary title of *maestro compositore* (master composer) of the papal chapel. His Masses and motets are models of beautifully conceived counterpoint. He handled dissonance carefully and sculpted his lines so that rising and descending curves balanced each other. His music represents a classical peak of Renaissance style.

Palestrina: Kyrie of the *Missa brevis*

The Kyrie of Palestrina's *Missa brevis* ("Short Mass") provides a good example of many aspects of his music. At the beginning, imitation of the opening theme by all voices is prominent. Throughout, we can hear the overlapping of phrases, the infrequent use of cadences, and the sublime sense of balance and proportion so characteristic of Palestrina's work.

Opening Theme in Four-Part Imitation

Side 2, Band 10

Listening Guide for Palestrina's Kyrie of the _Missa brevis_

Timbre:	small four-part choir, unaccompanied
Melody:	largely conjunct
Rhythm:	duple meter in the first two sections; triple meter in the last section
Harmony:	based on a Church mode
Texture:	contrapuntal and imitative
Form:	ABC
Text:	same text as in Josquin's Kyrie, page 81

Although Palestrina's Rome was a major center for composers of music for the Catholic Church in the years after the Reformation, other areas developed styles of their own. Venice, in particular, developed a style that reflected the city's love of ceremony, grandeur, and colorful display. The

RENAISSANCE MUSIC

The Gabrielis

Venetian style of music, which had its origins in the music written for services at Saint Mark's Basilica, used groups of singers and instruments. High, middle, and low voices, strings, and wind instruments might all be used together to create contrasting masses of sound. This style was the specialty of the Gabrielis, Andrea (c. 1520–1586) and his nephew Giovanni (c. 1557–1612). By the end of the century, the Venetian style was adopted in other European courts and cathedrals where the facilities were large enough.

Byrd

The English counterpart of Lassus and Palestrina was William Byrd (1543–1623). He wrote easily in any style he chose, but he was conservative by nature, primarily a composer of church music. Although a devoted Catholic, he was loyal politically to the Protestant queen. He thus wrote church music in both English and Latin. His English services are rich in texture and rhythmic play. Some are quite long and elaborate, as if to indulge the queen's fondness for pageantry. His three Latin Masses are brief but superbly constructed, with long lines unwinding over a subtle but powerful pulse.

Secular Music

Music as Entertainment

During the late fifteenth century, music making occupied much of the same time and energy that we today spend on radio, television, films, newspapers, and magazines. People in the upper and middle classes were expected to develop a considerable amount of musical skill. Music helped fulfill their need to do something well, to communicate, and to express themselves. After dinner a family and their guests would tune their instruments, get out part books, and read through the latest madrigals or chansons. A banker or politician could size up adversaries quickly after making music with them. In the evening hours a lonely boy or girl could find solace by quietly singing through some of John Dowland's lute songs.

Music Printing

The art of music printing both encouraged and chronicled this state of affairs. It began in 1501 when Ottaviano dei Petrucci of Venice issued the *Odhecaton* ("Hundred Songs"), the first of his almost sixty books of music. His books were exquisite, but his printing technique was complicated and expensive. Over the years, printing methods improved. Soon publishers were supplying, not only expensive editions for churches and private collectors, but also part books and anthologies for the growing middle class.

At first the demand was mostly for vocal music. Secular forms evolved rapidly with the new excitement over music's poetic expressiveness. In the sixteenth century, during the reign of French king Francis I, there was a fruitful intermixture of French and Italian music. French poets were turning to a simpler, more colloquial verse form that went well with the chordal, syllabic Italian part song called the *frottola*. A new style of French chanson also evolved in the sixteenth century. The new chansons were shaped by the stanzas and rhyme schemes of the poems on which they were based. They were thus in strophic form, using imitation and a number of other devices.

Frottola

Italian music came into its own at a time when sense of national identity was beginning to affect musical styles. Two trends—one literary and the other

**16th-Century
Italian Madrigal**

musical—culminated in the sixteenth-century Italian madrigal. The frottola became less popular, while the older lyric forms found in the poems of Dante and Petrarch were restored as the poetic ideal. The musical settings of the new poems were called madrigals in conscious archaism. They had nothing in common with the fourteenth-century pieces of the same name. In their earliest form, the sixteenth-century madrigals were, like the chansons of the same period, shaped by the stanzas and rhymes of the poems on which they were based. Later composers, however, rejected this reliance on poetic form and used more creative devices to shape their madrigals.

By the middle of the sixteenth century, the madrigal was fast becoming the most popular type of secular music in Italy. It was generally written for five voices, all sharing equally in the work. The texts concerned love—intense, erotic, and painfully ecstatic—or, sometimes, philosophical quandaries, and great use was made of text painting.

**Marenzio and
Gesualdo**

The madrigals of Luca Marenzio (1553–1599) and Carlo Gesualdo (1560–1613) represent a high point in the genre of the late sixteenth century. Their works are highly expressive because of their effective use of text painting and harmonic innovation. Gesualdo was perhaps the most unorthodox of Renaissance composers, juxtaposing chords that seemed completely unrelated to each other. His madrigals possess power and a strange beauty.

Renaissance Architecture: *The classical architectural styles of early Greece and Rome captured the European imagination during the Renaissance and again during the second half of the eighteenth century. The use of the classical temple portico can be seen here in Palladio's Villa Rotundo, a building dating from the late sixteenth century.*

Alinari/Scala

The madrigals of Claudio Monteverdi (1567–1643) both epitomize the genre and point beyond it. Monteverdi was later to write some of the first operas. Even in his early books of madrigals, which are in the conventional style, his dramatic flair is evident.

Monteverdi: "Si ch'io vorrei morire"

Monteverdi's madrigal "Si ch'io vorrei morire" reflects his skill in setting an impassioned love text. Each phrase is set uniquely so as to match each thought with the appropriate music. Text painting can be found in the opening phrase, which speaks of death ("morire") in descending melodic lines:

Opening Phrases

Listening Guide for Monteverdi's "Si ch'io vorrei morire"

Timbre:	five-part mixed vocal ensemble, unaccompanied
Melody:	largely conjunct
Rhythm:	basically duple meter but quite free
Harmony:	based on a Church mode
Texture:	homophonic and contrapuntal; some use of imitation
Form:	free, with repetition of first phrase at end

Text:

Si ch'io vorrei morire	Now would I gladly die,
hora ch'io bacio amore	now that, at last, O Love,
la bella bocca del mio amato core.	I kiss the lovely mouth of her whom my heart desires.
Ahi car'e doice lingua	Ah, dearest, sweetest tongue,
datemi tant' humore	give me such humors of thine
che di dolcezz' in questo sen m'estingua.	that on this breast I may perish for very sweetness and cease to be.
Ahi vita mia, a questo bianco seno	Life of my life, against thy white breast
deh stringetemi fin ch'io venga meno.	press me, crush me, make me nothing.
Ahi bocca, ahi baci, ahi lingua torn' a dire	Ah, mouth—ah, kisses—ah, tongue, come back to me
si ch'io vorrei morire.	that I may say, "Now would I gladly die,"

Eventually, Monteverdi's experiments carried him away from madrigals written in the Renaissance style to madrigals for one or two voices with instrumental accompaniment.

English Madrigal

While, in Italy, the madrigal was beginning to give way to different forms, in England it reached a new peak. Both music and literature were included in the vogue for things Italian during the reign of Elizabeth I. Italian madrigals began to circulate among the gentry about 1560. Madrigal singing became enormously popular, and English composers began to write their own. William

Morley

Byrd and Thomas Morley (1557–1602) were among the most popular composers of English madrigals.

The English were influenced by Italian styles but found in them a way to honor their own language. During Elizabeth's reign, the literary coffers overflowed and English poetry of high quality was readily available to composers. English madrigals are at times more tuneful and lighter than their Italian counterparts. Their texts express the widest range of moods, from pastoral gaiety and bawdy mirth, through the sorrow of unrequited love, to despair and the longing for death. The words are illustrated through the use of every contrapuntal, chordal, rhythmic, and harmonic device available at the time.

Ballett

Other related forms were also developed. One was the *ballett*, a rhythmically regular composition, simpler than the madrigal and usually homophonic. Most balletts can easily be recognized by their "fa-la-la" refrains. Morley wrote a number of balletts, including "Now Is the Month of Maying."

Morley: "Now Is the Month of Maying"

Morley's ballett is written in typical chordal style. The music for each of the three stanzas is the same, making the piece strophic in form. The stanzas themselves are in AABB form, giving the following overall form:

I	II	III
A A B B	A A B B	A A B B

There are five voice parts. The top line—the highest voice part—of the first A section shows the sprightly character of the text and music.

First A Section

Now is the month of May - ing, When mer - ry lads are play - ing, Fa la la la la la la la la, Fa la la la la la la.

Side 2, Band 12

Listening Guide for Morley's "Now Is the Month of Maying"

Timbre:	five-part mixed vocal ensemble, unaccompanied
Melody:	largely conjunct
Rhythm:	duple meter
Harmony:	major mode
Texture:	homophonic
Form:	strophic, with each stanza in AABB form

Text:

I A Now is the month of Maying,
      When merry lads are playing,
      Fa-la-la . . .

   B Each with his bonny lass
      Upon the greeny grass,
      Fa-la-la . . .

II A The spring, clad all in gladness,
       Doth laugh at winter's sadness,
       Fa-la-la . . .

    B And to the bagpipes' sound
       The nymphs tread out their ground.
       Fa-la-la . . .

III A Fie then, why sit we musing,
        Youth's sweet delight refusing?
        Fa-la-la . . .

     B Say, dainty nymphs, and speak,
        Shall we play barley-break?
        Fa-la-la . . .

EARLY MUSIC

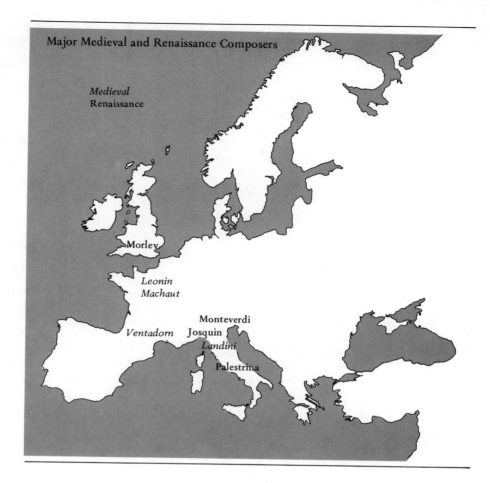

Major Medieval and Renaissance Composers

Medieval
Renaissance

Morley

Leonin
Machaut

Monteverdi
Ventadorn Josquin
Landini
Palestrina

Ayre

Solo songs or *ayres* with lute accompaniment were also fashionable in England. The *lute*, an early stringed instrument, was the most important and perhaps the only instrument in many English homes. Generally it was used, not to support vocal music, but as an equal partner with the voice. Lute songs were often very emotional. Some by John Dowland (1562–1626) might appear morbid if they were not so beautiful. His famous "Lachrymae" ("Flow, My Tears") opens with a four-note descending motive associated with death.

Dowland

Instruments and Instrumental Music

Consort

Renaissance instruments were classified as *haut* (loud) and *bas* (soft), and were grouped in families, or *consorts*. Flutes were often used, both in the transverse and recorder forms. The recorders came in several sizes from the tiny *sopranino* to the giant *contrabass*, which an adult had to play standing up. Other wind instruments included the *cornetto*, *shawm*, *trumpet*, and *sackbut*.

The Evolution of the Secular Song

To a large extent the secular song offers a means of gauging the temper of an era. It will become popular only if it offers something of value to the people of the period.

Listen to the secular songs of four different periods—either those listed below from the record set that accompanies the text, or others selected from the lists at the end of Chapters 7, 8, and 19.

Medieval:	Ventadorn's "Be m'an perdut"	Side 2, Band 6
Renaissance:	Monteverdi's "Si ch'io vorrei morire"	Side 2, Band 11
Romantic:	Schubert's "Gute Nacht"	Side 7, Band 3
Modern:	Beatles—any selection	Record Library

What musical qualities make it possible to identify the first two selections as Medieval and Renaissance? What musical qualities establish the latter two selections as more recent works?

In what ways can each of the four selections be seen as a reflection of the social and historical setting in which they were created?

String instruments used were *viols, lutes, guitars,* and other instruments of similar form. *Drums, bells,* and *cymbals* of different sizes added percussive color. A polyphonic piece could be played either by instruments of the same consort—just recorders or just viols, for example. Or a piece could be played by a *broken consort*—a mixture of recorders, viols and lutes, for example.

Pavane and Galliard

Dance music was very important for instruments. A favorite dance of the period was the *pavane*. A slow, stately processional dance, it was generally paired with the *galliard*, a quick, leaping dance in triple meter. Dancing the galliard called for great skill. Musically, the pavane and the galliard were often rhythmic variations of the same tune. Dances typically were made up of two or three sections, each repeated.

Many early instrumental works were simply transcriptions of vocal music. Madrigals, for example, were often played on the lute or on whatever instruments might be at hand. Byrd published some of his solo songs with accompaniments for viol consort. Lute music and lute songs were especially popular over all of western Europe.

It was natural, when adapting a vocal piece to keyboard or lute, to replace the long notes, which these instruments could not sustain, with groups of shorter notes. In this way, instrumental music gained independence from its vocal models. The *ricercar* was an imitative, contrapuntal piece patterned on the motet. The *fantasia* also used imitation, but in a freer style, as its name suggests. The *canzona*, originally a chanson for instruments, kept the rhythmic style and sectional structure of the chanson.

Though these pieces were often played by lute or consort, they were perhaps most prominent as works for keyboard instruments. Both the *organ* and the *harpsichord* were important in Renaissance music. Organ music, especially in Germany, became more and more elaborate. The harpsichord was the instrument for amateurs, and the music written for it remained somewhat simpler. Both the organ and the harpsichord, and the music written for them, were much more extensively developed in the Baroque period.

A Renaissance Ensemble: *The setting in this sixteenth-century Italian painting is likely to have been somewhat fanciful, but the instruments are those that were found in upper-class households throughout western Europe: a small harpsichord, a lute, an early flute, and a bass viol.*

Culver

Suggested Listening

Masses

Dufay: *Missa l'homme armé* ("Armed Man Mass") [Lyrichord 7150]. Dufay's Mass uses a very popular chanson as its tenor line. New melodies in the other three lines are woven around the tenor in counterpoint.

Ockeghem: *Missa fors seulement* ("'Except for' Mass") [MHS 1003]. The Kyrie of this Mass uses the top voice of Ockeghem's rondeau "Fors seulement l'attente" ("Except for the anticipation [of my death]") as the tenor. At the beginning of the Mass, the two upper voices answer the tenor in imitative fashion.

Motets

Lassus: *Resonet in laudibus* ("Let Praise Resound") [MHS 624]. An old German tune forms the basis of this joyous five-voiced Christmas motet. Its several sections differ mainly in their contrasting melodies and rhythms. Imitative counterpoint and homophonic writing alternate throughout the work.

Giovanni Gabrieli: *In ecclesiis* ("In the Congregations") [Angel S-36443]. This Venetian motet shows the transition from Renaissance to Baroque style in its use of contrasting groups of instruments and voices, both choral and solo. The Alleluia section, repeated many times, gives a sense of unity to the work.

Madrigals

Marenzio: "Zefiro torna" ("West Wind Return") [Springboard International MAC-9062]. This four-voice madrigal, based on a poem by Petrarch, presents the story of a lover who laments the return of spring without the return of his sweetheart, Laura, who has died. Text painting is especially evident with the words "l'aria, l'acqua e la terra" ("air, water, and earth") and "e cantar augelletti" ("and sing like a bird").

Morley: "Say Love" [Nonesuch 71097]. Morley's four-voice madrigal poses a question of a nature often found in Elizabethan love poetry: Can the one I love be faithful? There are two stanzas, the first of which is repeated at the end.

Instrumental Music

Byrd: "Go from My Windoe" [MHS 1071]. This setting is typical of adaptations made from popular songs for the small English harpsichord, the virginal.

P A R T

*Baroque
Music*

Listening Preview   Although some would argue a strong case for Handel, the Baroque composer best known and most revered today is almost certainly Bach. As an introduction to Baroque music, listen to one of Bach's fugues (Side 3, Band 4, or a selection in the record library). What musical qualities seem to be stressed in the work? What clues does the work offer about the spirit of the age in which it was written?

9

Introduction to Baroque Music

The Baroque Period [c. 1600–c. 1750]

The word "Baroque" is used today to refer to a historical period extending roughly from 1600 to 1750 and to the new styles of art and music that developed during the period. As is true of most historical periods, there are really no specific dates marking the beginning and the end of the Baroque period. Renaissance styles continued well into the seventeenth century. The beginnings of the Classical style can be found in some works created before the middle of the eighteenth century. But for general study, these dates will serve.

The Term "Baroque"

The origin of the term "Baroque" is uncertain. Possibly it derives from the Portuguese word *barroco*, an irregularly shaped pearl. Or it may have come from the Italian word *baroco*, a far-fetched syllogistic argument. Or perhaps it came from the name of a sixteenth-century Italian painter, Federigo Barocci.

Whatever its origins, when first applied to the art and music of the seventeenth and early eighteenth centuries, it was not intended as a compliment. "Baroque" was used as a word of scorn through most of the nineteenth century. It was not until the end of the century that people began to see the Baroque age as something other than a period of artistic decadence following the Renaissance. In 1888 German art critic Heinrich Wölfflin, in a paper on Roman architecture, wrote positively about the art of the seventeenth century. Other critics in turn took up the idea that there might be something good in the Baroque. Since then there has been a major reevaluation of the period, and today the works of Baroque artists and composers are thought to be among the finest in the history of the Western world.

Life in the Baroque Period

Europe in the seventeenth century was deeply affected by the aftermath of the Reformation. Politically, socially, and intellectually, both the Protestant Reformation and the Catholic Counter-Reformation left their mark. In a sense, the Reformation can be seen as the culmination of a long struggle between church and state. Through the Middle Ages, the Catholic Church had helped unify Europe. It had also served at times as a check on the power of secular rulers. During the Renaissance, however, the secular rulers grew stronger and the authority of the Catholic Church weakened. With Luther's call to reform, secular rulers all over Europe saw their chance to weaken papal power even further. By becoming Protestants, they could gain control over the churches within their lands. By remaining faithful to Rome, they could bargain with the pope, receive concessions for their support, and thus also gain greater control. Many of the bitter religious battles fought in the sixteenth and seventeenth centuries were motivated as much by politics as by theology.

The seventeenth century also brought major increases in commercial activity and in the power of the middle class. Throughout the sixteenth century, European trade networks had expanded. Spain and Portugal had begun the exploitation of the wealth of the New World. They were joined, in the seventeenth century, by the other nations of western Europe. Merchants and bankers, of course, figured largely in all of this and prospered by it. It was no accident that the two countries that came to dominate European trade—the Netherlands and England—were also those in which the commercial middle class was strongest.

Yet perhaps the most striking feature of the Baroque age was the growth of absolute monarchy. While asserting their right to rule unhampered by religious authority, national and regional rulers also tried to get rid of the traditional "liberties" of the nobles and the free towns. In their desire to gain control over all aspects of government, they did their best to put an end to the customary prerogatives of council and popular assembly. Sometimes they failed. In England, for example, the absolutist policies of Charles I led to the revolution of the 1640s and the execution of the king. But the rulers rarely failed completely.

The absolutist state par excellence was France. The French monarchy acquired an unprecedented amount of control over national life. France became the model for absolutists everywhere. Louis XIV, the Sun King who ruled from 1643 to 1715, was the symbol of monarchy for over half a century. French became the language of culture and diplomacy, and the French court at Versailles became the literary and artistic center of Europe.

Finally, the Baroque years were a time of greatly expanding horizons. As colonization of the New World increased, the scientific exploration begun in the Renaissance also reached a peak. Kepler and Galileo confirmed and extended earlier findings in astronomy. Leeuwenhoek with his microscope probed worlds too small for the naked eye. Newton formulated the law of gravity.

Art and Music in the Baroque Period

Art and music also reflected the Baroque search for knowledge and understanding. The period saw the work of several masterful painters, including such disparate artists as El Greco, with his strange, distorted figures, and Rembrandt, with his intense, dramatic presentation of a commonplace world. Architects exchanged the balanced, straight lines of the Renaissance for

The Age of Absolutism: *Absolute monarchs such as Louis XIV delighted in fêtes, spectacles, and royal balls, all of which called for special music composed to suit the tastes of the ruler. In France, music became virtually a state monopoly with the Sun King's establishment of a Royal Academy of Music and a Royal Academy of Dancing.*

massive, curved shapes with a multiplication of detail. In music, earlier rules of rhythm and harmony were ignored as composers tried to create a new style.

People today, viewing the art of the Baroque age, are often struck by the overt emotionalism found in many of the works. One explanation for this lies in the *doctrine of the affections*. In the seventeenth century, it was widely believed that various emotions—fear, anger, love, joy, and others—were caused by an imbalance of fluids in the human body. Both internal and external sensations were thought capable of stimulating the flow of these fluids and bringing about changes in a person's emotional state. The resultant emotions were known as affections, and the theory was thus called the doctrine of the affections. Works of art and music were expected to "move the affections" and stimulate one mood or another.

The Baroque period did not begin everywhere at once, nor did it develop in the same way in all countries. In music the theories that gave birth to the new style were shaped in Italy around the beginning of the seventeenth century. The creative center remained there for many decades, but France and Germany also made major contributions and eventually took over the

Doctrine of the Affections

INTRODUCTION TO BAROQUE MUSIC

leadership. Music in countries such as France and Spain, where the fashions of the court were dominant, differed in some ways from the music in countries such as England, where the middle class was strong. The church music in Roman Catholic countries differed in some ways from the church music in the Protestant states to the north. Nevertheless, the spirit of the times gave music a common style that distinguished it from the music of the Renaissance and the music of the Classical age that was to follow. To understand the Baroque style, we must first consider certain theoretical changes made early in the period.

Baroque Melody and Rhythm

In the late sixteenth century, a group unofficially known as the *Camerata* used to meet at the home of Giovanni de' Bardi, a wealthy gentleman of Florence. The members of the group were mainly interested in the revival of ancient Greek drama. In the course of their research, they came to the conclusion that the Greeks had not merely recited the words of their plays but had sung them as well. Obviously, the elaborate polyphony of the late Renaissance, with its interplay of melodic lines, could not be used in the revival of the Greek plays. The audience would scarcely be able to distinguish the words, let alone the emotions of the characters. What was needed was a style in which the music would be subordinate to the expression of ideas and emotions. From this need

Stile Rappresentativo

grew the *stile rappresentativo*—the representative, or theatrical, style.

Monody

The most important characteristic of this style was *monody*—that is, the homophonic use of one principal melody, with a simple chordal accompaniment. In the Renaissance, the ideal had been a large number of voices, all singing different melodies of equal importance. The new approach concentrated melodic interest in one voice, the highest. Monteverdi called this new technique the *secunda prattica* ("second practice"), in contrast to the older *prima prattica* ("first practice").

The earliest music written in the stile rappresentativo called for a musical declamation of the text in accordance with the natural rhythm of the words. The melody would be fairly simple, but in places where greater affective

Ornamentation

expression seemed to be needed, the singer could add *ornamentation*—elaborate melodic embellishments.

Many of the ornamental devices developed in the Baroque age are still used today. One is the *trill*, generally shown by the symbol ∿ or the abbreviation *tr* placed above a note. This shows that the note is to be played in rapid alternation with the note just above it. A *turn*, shown by the sign ∾, is slightly more complicated. It consists of a group of notes that "turn around" the main note. An *arpeggio*, shown by the sign ⌠ at the left of a chord, indicates that the notes are to be played one after another rather than all together.

Trill   Turn   Arpeggio

Written Performed   Written Performed   Written Performed

Because of the wide use of ornamentation, the basic beat of the music was sometimes interrupted. To accommodate a flurry of extra notes, the beat would have to slow down, speeding up again only when the singer returned to the basic melody. Herein lay another important departure from the prima prattica. In Renaissance music, an even rhythmic flow was fundamental. Some adherents of the old style claimed that this new music had no rhythm at all. It had, but people who were used to the old style often had difficulty in finding it.

With the stile rappresentativo came a growing interest in individual performance. The solo singer was becoming popular even before the advent of monodic music, but the importance of expression in the new style made soloists especially valuable. And the new music gave these soloists full opportunity to display their skill. Every kind of ornamental flourish was added to the melody. Sometimes these flourishes were indicated by the composer. More often, however, they were simply added by the performer.

Recitative and Aria

Gradually the stile rappresentativo developed into two different kinds of vocal compositions. The first, the *recitative*, kept the early emphasis on musical declamation, free rhythm, and fairly simple melody. The second, the *aria*, was a more elaborate composition with much more ornamentation.

Bel Canto Style

Soon after 1630, the stile rappresentativo itself was further reshaped into the *bel canto style*. In this style, the use of ornamentation in the aria decreased. The result was a simplification of harmony and rhythm leading to a smooth, flowing melody, generally in triple meter. A third type of vocal composition, the *arioso*, was also introduced. More melodic than the recitative, it was less rhythmically regular than the aria.

Arioso

Harmony and Texture in Baroque Music

Major-Minor Harmony

The early Baroque interest in the monodic style was paralleled by the development of *major-minor harmony*. Renaissance harmony had been based on the relationship of intervals within the Church modes. Certain intervals were recognized as giving consonant sounds, while others were noted for their dissonance. Composers made use of these consonant and dissonant sounds to get the harmonic effect they wanted. Toward the end of the Renaissance, however, the modern concept of key and scale began to emerge. The new concept stressed the importance of one basic note, the tonic, and its relationship to the other notes in a scale.

Chordal Progression

One result was the idea of *chordal progression*—the sense of one chord leading on to the next. As already noted, a dominant chord creates a pull toward the tonic. Other chords have other effects. They may serve to begin, lift, suspend, or close a piece of music. Major-minor harmony thus gives music a much stronger sense of inner dynamism than did the older modal harmony.

The use of the new harmony also added richness through the process of modulation—the changing of the tonal center of a piece. Once a particular note was established as the tonal center, new interest could be created by changing the center. Modulation was a basic compositional tool in the Baroque age and

Baroque Architecture: *The Baroque preference for curved lines and elaborate ornamentation can readily be found in the early eighteenth-century Austrian Monastery of Melk. An earlier example of Baroque architecture, one that seems more closely tied to the Renaissance heritage, can be found in Chapter 4, in the Italian church of Santa Agnese.*

has remained so ever since. It is valuable because it makes it relatively easy to change mood while keeping the unity of a basic theme. A motive first stated in the key of C major, for example, will sound more melancholy when restated in the related key of C minor. It will gain added sparkle if heard briefly in the key of G major. Modulation also makes longer compositions possible because changes of key help sustain the interest of the audience.

Equal Temperament

With the use of modulation came the introduction of *equal temperament*. The early Greek modes that formed the basis for the Church modes were based on intervals discovered by Pythagoras. The steps and half steps in the modes were not, in most cases, of precisely equal length. This unevenness caused problems when performers wanted to shift keys. The problem was especially acute with keyboard instruments, where the steps and half steps are of predetermined length. Thus, there was a move to equalize the steps so that all instruments could play as well in one key as in another. This tampering with tradition met with heated opposition from many quarters, but eventually the equal-tempered, or well-tempered, scale proved so useful that it became standard. Bach's *Well-Tempered Clavier*, a series of keyboard pieces in all keys, was written partly to show the advantages of the new tuning.

The use of dissonance also changed in the seventeenth century. Renaissance composers had been very careful about dissonance. Too much of it could easily have upset their delicately balanced modal harmony. But Baroque composers, with the security of a strong tonal center, could be more adventurous. Harmonic experimentation was thus an important feature of the early Baroque.

The musical texture that resulted from the emphasis on monody, tonal harmony, and affective expression was quite different from that of the Renaissance. As indicated, the monodic style, a distinctly homophonic style, stressed one principal melody with supporting harmony in the other parts. The harmonic support was generally supplied by two instruments. One—usually a harpsichord or an organ—played a chordal accompaniment, while the other—a low melodic instrument such as the viol, cello, or bassoon—reinforced the bass line of the chords. This type of harmonic support, played continuously under **Basso Continuo** the melody, came to be known as *basso continuo.*

The chords needed to supply harmonic support take a long time to write out, and Baroque composers were often working against tight deadlines. Furthermore, the chords suitable for one instrument might be awkward for another. So composers adopted a form of shorthand notation that came to be known as *figured bass.* The chords were not written out. Instead, composers wrote out only the melody and the bass line, placing over or under the bass notes numbers that indicated the type of chord to be played.

Figured Bass

The keyboard accompanist "realized" the bass by adding the appropriate notes. In the example above, the 6 under the note E calls for a chord made up of the note E and the note a sixth above it; counting the note E as the first note, the sixth note is C. The form of the chord to be used was left up to the performer.

The use of figured bass saved time for the composer. It also let the performers share in the creative process, giving the music a greater sense of spontaneity than would have been possible if all the parts had been set. The effect in this respect must have been similar to that of good jazz or rock improvisation, even though the kind of music was of course very different.

Homophony was a feature of much Baroque music, instrumental and vocal. But while in vocal music homophony almost completely took over the field, in instrumental music polyphony remained very important. There were at least two reasons for this. Instruments can handle more complex music than can the human voice; they generally have a wider pitch range, can change notes faster, and can jump wide intervals more easily. Also in purely instrumental music, there is no need to keep the melody simple so that words can be understood. Baroque composers soon realized that affective expression in instrumental music need not be merely copied from vocal styles.

Imitative
Counterpoint

A number of existing polyphonic techniques were further developed at this time. One of the most important was *imitative counterpoint*, in which the same theme is repeated by different voices, either exactly or with variations. Imitative counterpoint, already common in the Renaissance, was important in some of the major compositional forms, such as the fugue, that arose in the Baroque period.

Baroque Timbre

A major development in the Baroque period was the raising of instrumental music to equal status with vocal music for the first time in Western history. This was made possible in part by technical improvements in the instruments. It was also encouraged by the desire to stimulate the affections. The search for emotional expression led to a growing awareness of the potential of different instruments. It was realized that each instrument had its own characteristic tone, timbre, range, and flexibility. One was better suited to a certain purpose or mood than the others. Thus in the seventeenth century, composers started

Instrumentation

to write music with specific *instrumentation*—that is, with parts assigned to particular instruments.

Major
Instruments

While some instruments were being improved, other new instruments were being developed. The *violin*, for example, was developed in northern Italy after long experimentation. With its wide range and variety of dynamic possibilities, it offered a perfect medium for the Baroque spirit. It was often used by Italian composers such as Antonio Vivaldi and Arcangelo Corelli, whose works still form an important part of the violin repertory. Some of the violins produced in the Baroque age are still regarded as the finest in the world. Bearing the names of makers such as Antonio Stradivari, or of the Guarneri or Amati families, they sell for thousands of dollars and are the treasured possessions of the world's great violinists.

Like the violin, the *organ* was well suited to Baroque taste. It had great sonority, a wide range, and a huge capacity for dynamic contrast. Composers in many countries wrote music for the organ, but the heights of the genre were reached in Germany, where the instrument acquired a full set of pedals. This made possible the combination of powerful bass notes and vigorous upper-register sound that we associate with such composers as Dietrich Buxtehude and Johann Sebastian Bach. Organs, because they were so expensive to build, were generally public instruments and were, then as now, associated with church music.

Other major keyboard instruments of the Baroque age were the *harpsichord* and the *clavichord*. The harpsichord, a plucked-string instrument, lacked the sustained tone of the organ, but it had a precision and brilliance greatly suited to the music of the time. In France it replaced the lute as the most popular solo instrument. In Germany it was favored for fast-moving compositional forms such as the fugue. The clavichord, an ancestor of the modern piano, was much softer in volume than the harpsichord and was more of a chamber instrument.

Other Instruments

Other common instruments, which began to assume their modern form during this time, were the *viola, violoncello, flute, oboe, bassoon, trumpet, horn,* and *trombone.*

With the concern for specific instrumentation came a greater standardization of ensembles. No longer was it enough to gather a number of players and pass out parts. The instruments had to be the right ones for the music. Thus, the makeup of ensembles was closely related to the types of compositions that developed during the period. Orchestras, too, began to take shape, though they were used mostly as a supporting element in operas. Monteverdi's opera *Orfeo,* produced in 1607, called for an orchestra of thirty-six pieces, mostly strings.

Beginning of the Orchestra

Types of Compositions and Form in the Baroque Age

While some types of Renaissance compositions, such as the Mass and the motet, continued to be used in the Baroque period, a number of new types of vocal and instrumental music were developed. *Operas, cantatas,* and *oratorios* were important new vocal works. *Sonatas, concertos, suites,* and *fugues* were major new instrumental works.

Multi-Movement Works

Many of these works were divided into movements, with similar or different forms for each movement. A multiplicity of forms were used in the Baroque age, the most important of which can be seen in the chart on page 104. The simplest of these forms—*binary* and *ternary*—were discussed in Chapter 4. Two forms especially characteristic of the Baroque period—*ritornello* and *fugue*—will be considered in Chapter 10.

Ritornello and Fugal Forms

Contrast and the Concertato Style

As we have seen, the homophonic, basso-continuo texture of Baroque music was already quite distinct from the interwoven, equal-voice texture of Renaissance polyphony. Another important element in Baroque music was supplied by the idea of *contrast.* Contrast of different sounds was a device with obvious potential for affective expression. Composers explored it with ingenuity and enthusiasm. This led to the development of the *concertato style,* one of the most typical creations of the seventeenth century.

The word *concertato* seems to be derived from the verb *concertare,* which originally meant "to compete" and later "to collaborate." These meanings are both implicit in the concertato style, in which performing groups played or sang in alternation with one another. The alternating sounds might be those of large ensemble against small, chorus against chorus, single performer against ensemble, or chorus against ensemble.

Comparison of Renaissance and Baroque Music

Elements	Renaissance Music c. 1400–c. 1600	Baroque Music c. 1600–c. 1750
Melody	Generally conjunct and singable	Conjunct and disjunct Frequent ornamentation Much use of sequence
Rhythm	Even rhythmic flow Metric patterns not emphasized in religious vocal music but clear in many secular works	Free rhythm in recitative Steady, driving rhythms and clear meters in many vocal and instrumental works
Harmony	Based on 12 Church modes Careful use of dissonance	Based on major-minor system Greater use of dissonance
Texture	Polyphony, often imitative, for 4 or more voices Some homophony	Polyphony, often imitative, important in vocal and instrumental works Homophony also used frequently
Timbre	Notated music mainly vocal but some instrumental works Small choral groups Small instrumental ensembles	Instrumental music much more important than before Small choral groups Small orchestra of strings, winds, and continuo Soloists important in vocal and instrumental works
Important Forms	Imitative forms Strophic songs and hymns	Binary, ternary, ritornello, and fugue Development of many multi-movement works
Important Types of Compositions	Mass and motet Secular songs Instrumental dances Instrumental pieces such as the ricercar	Mass and motet, often with instrumental accompaniment Opera, cantata, and oratorio Sonata, concerto, fugue, and suite

We have seen the beginning of this style in the music of Venice in the sixteenth century. The Gabrielis experimented with a variety of possible contrasts, such as choruses of different overall ranges, or a full chorus against a solo quartet. Giovanni Gabrieli, in his works written for Saint Mark's, sometimes used as many as seven or eight choruses. Later composers imitated him where they had the space and resources to do so. Writers of the day commented with awe on the intensely emotional and dramatic effects created by such music.

Terraced Dynamics

The use of contrast appears also in the *terraced dynamics* of the Baroque age. These were sudden sharp changes in dynamic level. Terraced dynamics formed a natural part of the concertato style, but also owed something to the limitations of keyboard instruments. Neither the harpsichord nor the organ was capable of the kind of gradual dynamic shading found in the piano.

Two Masters of Baroque Music

All of these new developments in Baroque music culminated in the works of two great composers, Johann Sebastian Bach (1685–1750) and Georg Friedrich Handel (1685–1759).

Bach

Bach came from a musical family, and several of his own sons became composers in turn. Born in the small town of Eisenach, Bach lived in Germany all his life, holding various posts as violinist, organist, and music director. In 1723 he settled in Leipzig, where he served as director of the choir at Saint Thomas as well as a teacher of singing and Latin in the church's school.

The Master of Leipzig: *This artist's impression shows the Bach family at morning prayers, with Bach himself playing the clavichord, accompanied by one of his sons on the violin. The tradition of passing the craft of music from one generation to another has always been strong in Europe but perhaps never so impressive as in the Bach family.*

INTRODUCTION TO BAROQUE MUSIC

Married twice, he had twenty children, only ten of whom survived infancy. In his own lifetime he was much admired for his exceptional talents as an organist and improviser, but his compositions failed to achieve wide acclaim. Most of his works were written to fill specific needs. He wrote instrumental music for the court functions at Cöthen, choral music for the services at Leipzig, and keyboard works for the instruction of his own children. The neglect of most of his works for more than a century after his death would probably not have surprised Bach, though their later revival might have. Yet, as later generations have seen, the quality of even his most routine compositions is astounding. Indeed, Bach wrote masterpieces in almost all the different types of Baroque music. So effectively did he sum up the achievements of his age that the year of his death is now conveniently used to mark the end of the Baroque period in music.

Handel

Handel, born in the same year as Bach, was more cosmopolitan than his German compatriot. Early in his composing career, he spent a few years in Italy, where he learned to appreciate the melodic and homophonic styles then current. This influence can be seen in his many operas, written in the Italian style. After a brief return to Germany, he visited England and, on his second visit in 1712, decided to settle there. While he continued to write operas, Handel came more and more under the influence of English choral music. Conceding to English taste, he wrote a number of oratorios, which added greatly to his popularity in England both with the court and with the general public. Although best known, in his own time and today, for his vocal music, Handel also wrote many instrumental works. He went blind in 1753 but remained active musically to within days of his death.

Baroque Instrumental Music

The Rise of Instrumental Music

Italy was the main source of musical ideas during the early Baroque. We have already noted the rise of the stile rappresentativo, with its emphasis on textual clarity and expressiveness. Also Italian were the increasing use of dissonance and the rejection of counterpoint typical of those early years.

In the middle Baroque, from about 1640 to 1690, the influence of France became almost as important as that of Italy. This was the high period of French royal absolutism, and music, like the other arts, was closely bound to the state and the interests of the court. This was the age, too, when major-minor harmony became fully established. Dissonance was somewhat reduced, and in Italy the exuberance of the stile rappresentativo was being refined into the bel canto style. The first excesses of experimentation were past, counterpoint reappeared, and, for the first time, instrumental music began to emerge from its long subordination to vocal music.

By the late Baroque, from about 1690 to 1750, the main theoretical developments were complete and a number of important new types of compositions had taken shape. Instrumental music was now clearly as important as vocal. Italian and French influence spread to other countries, notably Germany, where some of the greatest keyboard music was written. The affections tended to be intellectualized—thanks, perhaps, to French rationality and systematization. The rules and standards evolved during the earlier years of the period were thoroughly accepted. In Germany, as we have seen, Bach wrote masterpieces in almost all the different types of Baroque music. But even during Bach's lifetime, some composers were seeking newer styles. Before the end of the Baroque period, elements of the Classical style could be seen.

The charge leveled against the Baroque by eighteenth- and nineteenth-century critics—that the period represented only a final, decadent stage of the Renaissance—can be clearly refuted. The Baroque is one of the most important eras in musical history, especially in terms of the contribution it made to the development of diverse types of instrumental music, perfecting those it inherited from the Renaissance and giving birth to new ones.

The Baroque Orchestra

The development of the Baroque orchestra, like that of Baroque theory, took place gradually. In 1600 it was uncommon for a composer to give specific instrumentation. By 1750 most composers did give specific instrumentation. The years in between were filled with experimentation and the exploration of new musical ideas about the use of different instruments.

The concertato style, with its stress on contrasting timbres, encouraged the writing of music suited to the characteristics of particular instruments. The trend became more marked as the concertato style evolved toward the true concerto styles of the late Baroque. Solo instruments also began to acquire their own music. This was true not only for the keyboard instruments but also for the violin and various wind instruments. The solo music undoubtedly influenced the way these instruments were used in ensembles as well.

Lully

The creation of professional orchestras also encouraged composers to write for specific instruments. Now the composers could be sure that the instruments they wanted would be present. One of the earliest of the professional orchestras was *Les Vingt-quatre violons du roi* ("The Twenty-four Strings of the King"). It was established by Jean-Baptiste Lully (1632–1687) at the French court in the mid-seventeenth century. As the name indicates, this was at first mainly a string ensemble. By the end of the century, however, a number of wind instruments had been added—flutes, oboes, and horns.

A Baroque Orchestra: *The small orchestra in this mid-eighteenth-century German engraving is in many ways typical. In the foreground are two instruments often found in the basso continuo—the cello and the harpsichord. The other performers are positioned, in common fashion, along the side of the harpsichord.*

The Bettmann Archive

Similar orchestras were soon organized throughout western Europe. Since French styles of the middle Baroque were widely imitated, Louis XIV's orchestra was bound to have had an influence on orchestras and orchestral writing elsewhere.

By the middle of the eighteenth century, the small Baroque orchestra was fairly standardized. The string section and the basso continuo were frequently joined by two flutes, two horns, two oboes, and two bassoons. The basso continuo was generally made up of a harpsichord, organ, or lute—playing the harmony as indicated by a figured bass—and a low, melodic instrument such as the viola da gamba, cello, or bass—reinforcing the bass line. It was not yet the Classical concert orchestra, but casual instrumentation had definitely been left behind.

Baroque Sonatas

The gradual development of instrumental music from its vocal roots is well illustrated by the *sonata*. The Baroque sonata can be traced back to the *canzon da sonar* ("sounded song"), an instrumental song of the late Renaissance, and beyond that to the early French part song, the *chanson*. At first the canzon da sonar simply imitated the contrapuntal texture of the chanson, with as many different parts as the composer wanted. But with the new monodic style came a

Trio and Solo Sonatas

preference for canzone of only a few parts. This led eventually to the *trio sonata*, which despite its name was a work for four instruments: two melody instruments playing over a basso continuo. Also popular was the *solo sonata*, a work for three instruments: one melody instrument and basso continuo.

At first the term "sonata" meant only that the music was wholly instrumental. It did not signify any particular compositional form. Some of the early canzone da sonar had ten or more sections of music. These were generally set in contrasting style with long sections in imitative counterpoint alternating with shorter homophonic sections. In time, the number of sections decreased, and the remaining sections grew longer, taking on the character of full-scale movements. It was with this later type of composition that the term "sonata" came to be most often associated.

Early Composers of Sonatas

Important composers in the early evolution of the sonata from the canzona were Salomone Rossi (1570–1630) and Biagio Marini (1595–1665). Rossi, a colleague of Monteverdi, is credited with having developed the trio sonata, which was later used extensively by Marini and others. The work of Marini, himself a virtuoso violinist, reflects the evolution of instrumental music toward its own independent compositions. His first works, published in 1617, were *madrigali* and *arie*, styled after the vocal madrigals and arias of the late Renaissance and early Baroque. His last works, in 1655, were *sonate da chiesa* and *sonate da camera*—sonatas for church and for chamber.

Church and Chamber Sonatas

At this time, the musical term *da camera* had a much broader meaning than it does today. Music "of the chamber" was not yet limited to ensemble music in which each part is played by a single instrument. Rather, the term *da camera* referred to any music written for neither the church nor the theater. Naturally, though, since camera music tended to be played in private homes rather than public halls, a small ensemble was generally used. Thus, the term "chamber music" acquired its present meaning. The sonata da chiesa, on the other hand, performed in church, often called for a larger ensemble, two or more instruments doubling each part to give the necessary volume.

Corelli

Both church and chamber sonatas were widely popular throughout the middle Baroque. It was Arcangelo Corelli (1653–1713) of Bologna who brought the compositional form to perfection. Widely traveled, Corelli achieved great fame as a violin virtuoso. As might be expected, most of his published works, including his sonatas, contain prominent parts for violin. From 1681 to 1707, he published four sets of trio sonatas—two for church and two for chamber. At the same time, he published one set of solo sonatas, equally divided between church and chamber. His church sonatas were usually written in four movements, alternating from slow to fast. The first two movements were generally contrapuntal, while the last two resembled dance forms, most often the *sarabande* and the *gigue*. The chamber sonatas were generally made up of two or three dance pieces. The music for these sonatas was usually homophonic with touches of counterpoint and a more contrapuntal prelude. The alternation from slow to fast was also kept in this type of sonata.

Other Composers of Sonatas

In addition to being used by virtually every Italian composer of the late Baroque, the trio sonata was also popular elsewhere in Europe. Henry Purcell (c. 1659–1695) in England, François Couperin (1668–1733) in France, and Dietrich Buxtehude (c. 1637–1707) in Germany all wrote notable trio sonatas.

Sonatas for One Instrument

A number of Baroque composers were also writing sonatas for a single, unaccompanied instrument. This type of composition, first used by Marini, was brought to perfection in the sonatas written by Bach for unaccompanied violin and unaccompanied cello. However, the most prolific writer of sonatas for solo instrument was undoubtedly Domenico Scarlatti (1685–1757). Scarlatti wrote over six hundred sonatas for the harpsichord, an unmatched display of creativity. He himself was a harpsichord virtuoso and helped lay the foundation for modern piano technique. His sonatas were written in the character of exercises, using a wide variety of techniques, one at a time. Each is a one-movement work, although they seem to have been intended to be played in pairs.

Domenico Scarlatti

Scarlatti: *Sonata in C Major,* K. 159

The *Sonata in C Major,* K. 159 offers a vivacious example of Scarlatti's sonatas for harpsichord. (K. stands for Kirkpatrick, a cataloguer of Scarlatti's works.) As is typical of Scarlatti's sonatas, the work is divided into two sections. Each section is repeated, so the form is AABB.

Section A

The brisk opening theme clearly establishes the key of C major in $\frac{6}{8}$ meter:

Opening Theme

This theme and its continuation are the melodic and harmonic basis for Section A. During the section, however, a modulation to the key of G major takes place. After the section ends, in the key of G major, the section is repeated.

Section B

Typically Section B should start in G major. But Scarlatti departs from the usual here and suggests C minor without firmly establishing it. The section begins with a variant of the opening theme. Later in the section, the opening theme itself returns firmly in C major and, with its continuation, brings the section to a close. Like Section A, Section B is then repeated.

Side 3, Band 1

Listening Guide for Scarlatti's *Sonata in C Major*, K. 159

Timbre:	harpsichord
Melody:	mainly conjunct; use of descending motives with many repeated notes
Rhythm:	$\frac{6}{8}$ meter; tempo Allegro (fast)
Harmony:	mainly major mode; first section begins in C major, modulates to G major; second section begins in C minor, modulates to C major
Texture:	homophonic
Form:	binary (AABB)

Although trio and solo sonatas were most common, sonatas were also written for three or more melody instruments over a basso continuo throughout the Baroque period. Toward the end of the period, the solo sonata became decidedly the most popular, heralding the transition to the solo and duo sonatas of the Classical age—works for one or two instruments. The Baroque sonata was also the ancestor of several other types of compositions developed in the Classical age, including the symphony.

Baroque Concertos

One of the most important types of instrumental work to emerge during the Baroque was the *concerto*. It first appeared in the late seventeenth century, in the works of composers such as Corelli. It was carried to its highest development during the first half of the eighteenth century.

A number of characteristics of Baroque music merged in the concerto. One was the idea of contrast between large and small groups. In large churches during special occasions, small professional ensembles were often supplemented by larger, less-skilled groups of players. The idea of writing music to take advantage of the different technical skills must have occurred fairly early to the composers associated with these churches. The use of homophony was also important in the development of the concerto and was in fact one of its early distinctions. Finally, the combination of several short sections in a single composition, already encountered in the sonata, achieved a new unity and power in the concerto.

Concerto Grosso

The *concerto grosso* ("large concerto"), the earliest true concerto, seems to have been the creation of Corelli. In a group of works published in 1714, but probably written around 1682, Corelli set a small group of performers against a much larger ensemble. The small group, known as the *concertino*, was generally made up of two violins and continuo—a group that could easily have played a trio sonata. The larger group, known as the *ripieno* ("full"), also had a basso continuo as well as additional string instruments and occasional wind instruments. The term *tutti* ("all") was used to refer to all of the instruments in the two ensembles combined.

Corelli's concerti grossi were often little more than sonatas divided between large and small groups. He made little effort to differentiate between the music written for the two groups and even kept the sonata nomenclature, calling his concertos da chiesa or da camera. He also used the structural forms that had been developed for the church and chamber sonatas. His church concertos were especially conservative, with five or more movements, much like the many sections of the older sonatas. However, the slow movements in these concertos were often very short, acting as transitions between the more important fast movements. The final effect was a four-movement structure.

Torelli

More important than Corelli in the perfection of the concerto's compositional form was Giuseppe Torelli (1658–1709) of Bologna. His earliest concertos, published in 1692, were orchestral works of several movements with occasional solo passages for violin. Pursuing this innovation, he soon evolved the *solo concerto*, in which a single instrument, rather than a small group of instruments, is set against the ripieno.

Solo Concerto

Ritornello Form

In his solo concertos, Torelli made a distinction between the music for the ripieno and the music for the solo parts, often using more contrapuntal material in the ripieno. He also began the use of the *ritornello* principle or form. Following this principle, the ripieno passages are a return—ritornello—to modified versions of the opening theme. The solo passages, on the other hand, offer changes or elaborations of the opening theme. Ritornello depends very much upon the use of major-minor harmony. The opening theme is first stated by the ripieno in one key. In the ritornelli, a variety of keys can be used, adding considerably to the possible modifications that can be made. This, in turn, makes it possible to have longer movements and a more complete working out of the musical idea. At the end of a movement, the final ritornello returns to the initial key, thus unifying the work. The simplified diagram below shows a typical ritornello pattern:

Ripieno	Solo	Ripieno	Solo	Ripieno	Solo	Ripieno
Initial Key ⟶		New Keys				⟶ Initial Key

Using longer, fuller movements, Torelli began to write concertos of just three movements: generally allegro—adagio—allegro, or fast—slow—fast. In keeping with Baroque tastes, the allegro movements were more important; the adagio movement was often much shorter than the other two. Torelli also

The Baroque Sense of Beauty

Bernini: *Ecstasy of Saint Theresa* **(1645–1652)**

Overt Emotionalism Baroque art, like Baroque music, began in Italy. As a definable style within the seventeenth century, it was the child of the Catholic Counter Reformation. The Catholic Church supported an art exciting, dramatic, dynamic, and sensuous—an art that would appeal not to the intellectual and cultivated few, as in the Renaissance, but to the broad masses of the people. Baroque artists succeeded in making transcendental events seem real, religious experiences direct, complete, and emotionally satisfying. A high point in Baroque emotionalism can be seen in Bernini's sculpture for the chapel of Santa Theresa in the church of Santa Maria della Vittoria. With amazing vividness, Bernini's work captures the delightful anguish of the nun's swoon in the presence of the angel, who is about to thrust the fire-tipped dart of Divine Love into her bosom. The saint's heavy drapery, the soft flesh of her face and that of the angel, the evanescent distentions of the clouds are interpreted so convincingly that the physical limitations of stone are overcome.

Opulent Interiors Opulent is perhaps the most descriptive word for the interior designs favored in both secular and religious buildings throughout the Baroque period. The Hall of Mirrors of Louis XIV's Palace of Versailles furnishes an outstanding example. The French tended to avoid the movement and emotion generally associated with Baroque art in favor of clarity, symmetry, and uniformity, qualities that in no way inhibited the splendid richness of effect achieved by the enormous paintings covering the vault, the green marble pilasters, and the arched mirrors they frame. In Germany, interior design was far less restrained than in France. Indeed, one finds an almost Medieval extravagance of feeling culminating in church interiors such as that of "Die Wies." In this late Baroque interior, powerful and dynamic Baroque curves have developed into more sprightly and delicate rhythms, and warm, rich Baroque colors have given way to even more evanescent color harmonies.

Rembrandt: *Self Portrait at the Easel* (1660)

The Dutch Bourgeois Style   In the Baroque age, Holland
guished from the rest of continental Europe by her li
geois institutions and Calvinist religion. To a degree
elsewhere, patronage rested with a large ascendant m
Rembrandt van Rijn, the giant of Dutch painting, shar
contemporaries their devotion to the middle-class do
around them, but while other Dutch painters were pri
cerned with the external physical aspects of their sub
brandt was interested in their inner spiritual expe
particular, Rembrandt found that the motion of lig
space and across physical forms could be used to express

Watteau: *Embarkation for Cythera* (1717)

Late Baroque and Rococo Styles In the eighteenth century, the Baroque style in both art and music developed into a style known as Rococo, the musical aspects of which will be discussed in Chapter 12. In painting and sculpture, there was no sharp break in continuity, but rather a shift in emphasis from the austere and ponderous to the relaxed, agreeable, and elegant. Rococo painters showed little interest in the Catholic Church's ecstatic visions of the saints. Instead they wished to delight the eye, to caress the senses. In the *Embarkation for Cythera,* Watteau transformed the heavy, dynamic figures of the Baroque into slender, graceful creatures. Small-scaled, delicate, and lyrical, Watteau's paintings present a vision of a world filled with beautiful ladies and devoted lovers gliding through wistfully atmospheric parks and woods, a world of silks and satins, a world devoid of pain and ugliness.

used certain internal devices that became standard in later concertos. These included a steady, driving rhythm, the use of strong patterns of triads to set the initial key, and the introduction of the ritornello by a series of three "hammerstrokes" on the tonic and dominant chords. This last device seems to have been borrowed from the fanfares of trumpet sonatas, which were very popular in Bologna at the time.

Vivaldi

All these elements, developed in the solo concerto, were transferred to the concerto grosso as well. They were also used by Antonio Vivaldi (c. 1675–1741) in the more than four hundred and fifty concertos he wrote in the first half of the eighteenth century. Vivaldi, a priest, taught music at a school for girls in Venice. Though a violinist himself, he wrote solo concertos for almost every available instrument and concerti grossi for many combinations of instruments. Vivaldi built on Torelli's structure but added some elements of his own. He made the adagio movements as important as the allegro movements. He liked programmatic music and often introduced such things as imitations of bird calls or rippling brooks in his solo passages. This, of course, gave him a chance to make use of the marvelous virtuosity in which he excelled, both as a composer and as a performer. But all of these flights of fancy

The Craftsmen Behind the Virtuosos: *Several of the major composers of the Baroque period, Corelli and Vivaldi among them, were violin virtuosos whose works added greatly to the development of the instrument. Much of the credit for the rising prominence of the violin, however, is also due to Stradivarius and the other master craftsmen who brought the physical construction of the instrument to perfection.*

ANTONIVS STRADIVARIVS

The Bettmann Archive

were held together by a firm adherence to the ritornello principle. He also used precise themes and a vigorous rhythm derived from a driving, mechanical beat.

Vivaldi's *Four Seasons, Op. 8, No. 1–4* is an outstanding collection of four solo concertos for violin, works that clearly show his mature skill. Accompanying the solo violin in each work is a chamber orchestra (the ripieno) made up of two violin parts, viola, and continuo. Vivaldi tried to associate the concertos—*Spring, Summer, Autumn,* and *Winter*—with the general and specific moods of each season.

Vivaldi: *Winter Concerto, Op. 8, No. 4, in F Minor*

In the *Winter Concerto,* Vivaldi's attempt to associate music and season can clearly be heard. At times, the music seems to suggest whirling wind and, at other times, the chattering of teeth. The work also shows many other characteristics of Vivaldi's concerto writing. It consists of three movements— Allegro non molto, Largo, and Allegro. The keys of the movements are F minor, E♭ major, and F minor. The brighter major mode and unusual key relationship of the second movement offer sharp contrast with the first and third movements.

First Movement: Allegro non molto; in Ritornello Form

The first movement of the *Winter Concerto* opens quietly with the ripieno instruments entering one at a time. Repeated notes gradually build into a dissonant chord progression that creates great tension. After the ripieno chordal statement, the solo violin enters with a quick theme based on arpeggios, repeated notes, and scales:

First Solo Passage

The ends of the phrases in the solo violin part are twice punctuated by the opening chordal material of the ripieno. Then solo violin and orchestra join in repeated notes, which suddenly quicken with greater intensity. The solo violin proceeds with the continuo in fast rhythmic motion, presenting several motives and scales. A longer solo for the violin follows. It is made up of a

Use of Sequence lengthy phrase played three times in descending *sequence* (a repetition of melodic material at increasingly higher or, in this case, lower pitches). After this the orchestra returns with quickly repeated notes. Soloist and orchestra briefly continue a rapid dialogue. Then the repeated notes return in the orchestra, building to a dissonant chord progression before the resolution. This last orchestral part is a modified, more elaborate version of the first orchestral part. The entire movement is in ritornello form.

Listening Guide for Vivaldi's *Winter Concerto,* First Movement

Timbre:	solo violin; ripieno made up of string orchestra with continuo
Melody:	conjunct and disjunct motion; ripieno theme uses many repeated notes; solo passages use arpeggios, repeated notes, scales, and sequence
Rhythm:	duple meter; tempo Allegro non molto (fast, but not too fast); slow rhythmic motion at first, then faster
Harmony:	mainly minor mode; begins in F minor, modulates to C minor and E♭ major, ends in F minor
Texture:	mainly homophonic
Form:	ritornello

Second Movement: Largo; in Binary Form

Use of Pizzicato

The slow second movement in the major mode is, in effect, an exquisite aria for solo violin, accompanied by orchestra. The violins in the orchestra are played *pizzicato*—that is, with the notes produced by plucking rather than by bowing.

Listening Guide for Vivaldi's *Winter Concerto,* Second Movement

Timbre:	solo violin; ripieno made up of string orchestra with continuo
Melody:	first theme largely conjunct with much use of sequence; second theme very lyrical
Rhythm:	duple meter; tempo Largo (very slow)
Harmony:	entirely major mode; begins in E♭ major, modulates to B♭ major, ends in E♭ major
Texture:	mainly homophonic
Form:	binary (AA¹)

Third Movement: Allegro; in Ritornello Form

The last movement returns to the fast tempo of the first movement. It begins with an extended violin solo before the orchestra enters. Throughout the movement the soloist and orchestra present and develop material alternately and simultaneously.

Listening Guide for Vivaldi's *Winter Concerto,* Third Movement

Timbre:	solo violin; ripieno made up of string orchestra with continuo
Melody:	conjunct and disjunct motion; use of scales and sequence; ripieno passages use many repeated notes
Rhythm:	triple meter; tempo Allegro (fast)
Harmony:	mainly minor mode; begins in F minor, modulates to C minor and E♭ major, ends in F minor
Texture:	mainly homophonic
Form:	ritornello

Bach's Concertos

Vivaldi's influence on eighteenth-century music, even into the Classical period, was enormous. Bach, in particular, was much taken with his work and transcribed a number of Vivaldi's concertos so that they could be played on keyboard instruments, either alone or with orchestral accompaniment. Bach's own concertos, both the famous *Brandenburg Concertos* and the solo violin concertos, show Vivaldi's influence, albeit transformed and deepened by Bach's own genius. One interesting variation in Bach's concertos is the use of wind instruments as well as string instruments in the concertino of the concerto grosso. His *Brandenburg Concerto No. 2*, for example, uses a concertino of trumpet, flute, oboe, and violin.

Handel's Concerti Grossi

Handel also wrote a number of notable concertos. The twelve concerti grossi of his *Op. 6* are splendid examples. Each uses two violins and a cello in the concertino. The six concerti grossi of his *Op. 3* are more varied, in that, like Bach, Handel used wind instruments as well as string instruments in the concertino.

Handel: *Concerto in B♭ Major, Op. 3, No. 1*

Handel's *Concerto in B♭ Major, Op. 3, No. 1* is in three movements: Allegro, Largo, and Allegro. The first and third movements use two oboes and one violin as the concertino. The solo instruments in the second movement are two flutes, one oboe, and two violins. In this concerto, two bassoons join the continuo, as is typical in Baroque music when high-pitched wind instruments are used.

First Movement: Allegro; in Ritornello Form

The first movement of the *Concerto in B♭ Major* is in ritornello form. The first theme, presented by the ripieno of violins, violas, and continuo, returns in partial form and once in nearly complete form during the movement. This strong theme opens with two descending arpeggios, followed by a motive in descending sequence, and closes with a scale:

Opening Ripieno Theme

The return of the ripieno theme is clearly heard each time because of the descending arpeggios. The solo oboes and violin of the concertino present the second and third themes, both of which offer contrast to the opening ripieno theme.

Listening Guide for Handel's *Concerto in B♭ Major,* First Movement

Timbre:	concertino of two oboes and one violin; ripieno made up of string orchestra and continuo with two bassoons
Melody:	first theme (by ripieno) made up of descending arpeggios followed by motive in descending sequence; second theme (by oboes) more conjunct; third theme (by solo violin) conjunct and disjunct
Rhythm:	duple meter; tempo Allegro (fast)
Harmony:	mainly major mode; begins in B♭ major, modulates most significantly to F major, ends in B♭ major
Texture:	mainly homophonic
Form:	ritornello

Second Movement: Largo; in Ternary Form

The second movement moves to the key of G minor and a slow tempo. The contemplative mood of the movement contrasts well with the brighter tone of the first movement. Contrast is also found in the fact that the concertino now contains two flutes as well as one oboe and two violins.

Listening Guide for Handel's *Concerto in B♭ Major,* Second Movement

Timbre:	concertino of two flutes, one oboe, and two violins; ripieno made up of string orchestra and continuo with two bassoons
Melody:	several themes; some characterized by arpeggios and repeated notes contrasted with others characterized by scales and conjunct motion
Rhythm:	triple meter; tempo Largo (very slow)
Harmony:	mainly minor mode; begins in G minor, modulates to D minor and B♭ major, ends in G minor
Texture:	mainly homophonic
Form:	ternary (ABA[1]) followed by a transition to the third movement

Third Movement: Allegro; in Ternary Form

The last movement features the original concertino of solo oboes and violin. There is also a return to the quicker tempo of the first movement. The final movement does not, however, return to the major key of the first movement; rather, it is in the minor key of G minor—the predominant key of the second movement.

Listening Guide for Handel's *Concerto in B♭ Major,* Third Movement

Timbre:	concertino of two oboes and one violin; ripieno made up of string orchestra and continuo with two bassoons
Melody:	ripieno passages feature arpeggios and scales; concertino passages feature groups of repeated notes and sequence

Rhythm:	duple meter; tempo Allegro (fast)
Harmony:	mainly minor mode; begins in G minor, modulates to B♭ major and D minor, ends in G minor
Texture:	mainly homophonic
Form:	ternary (ABA)

As a whole, the *Concerto in B♭ Major* offers a fine example of Handel's fresh, vivacious style.

The Fugue

Subject

The *fugue* represents the most mature form of imitative counterpoint, having eclipsed, by the end of the seventeenth century, the ricercar from which it evolved. The basis of a fugue is a melody called the *subject*. This melody is stated in the beginning by a single voice, then taken up in succession by the other voices. Statements of the subject may be separated by sections of freely invented counterpoint called *episodes*. These are often built upon a motive from the subject and elaborated with scale passages. The form of the fugue is based essentially on the alternation of statements of the subject and episodic passages.

Episodes

The supreme master of the fugue was Johann Sebastian Bach. Both of the two volumes of his *Well-Tempered Clavier* contain a prelude and fugue in each of the twelve major and twelve minor keys. The works represent a skillful probing of the potential of the fugue, while demonstrating Bach's limitless imagination.

Bach: *Fugue in G Minor*

Bach's *Fugue in G Minor*, written for organ, is a classic example of fugal structure—perhaps too classic to be typical. No two fugues by Bach or by any other composer are structured exactly alike. The *Fugue in G Minor*, however, is a fine model of most characteristics of Bach's keyboard fugues.

Exposition

In the first part, the *exposition*, the subject begins with an outlining of the G minor triad. The subject itself is divided into two parts. The first part, in two measures, begins and ends with relatively long notes. The second part changes to quicker rhythmic motion.

There are four voices in the fugue. Each of the voices presents the subject—the highest voice entering first, the lowest last—all in exact imitation. These four statements of the subject, which make up the exposition, begin alternately on the tonic G and the dominant D. After presenting the subject, each voice continues with a *countersubject*, or secondary melody, which is characterized in this fugue by a trill. The structure of the exposition is perhaps clarified by the following diagram. Note that the exposition is broken by a short episode.

Countersubject

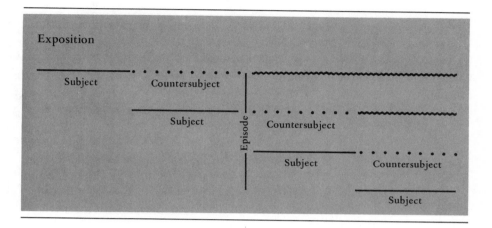

When the exposition is completed, an episode follows, briefly developing a motive from the subject. In the middle part of the fugue, the subject appears again four times, each time preceded and followed by an episode. The most prominent keys in this section are the contrasting ones of B♭ major and C minor.

Near the end, there is a modulation back to G minor. The subject is then presented for the ninth and final time, in the tonic key by the lowest voice.

Side 3, Band 4

Listening Guide for Bach's *Fugue in G Minor*

Timbre: organ

Melody: begins disjunct, then becomes more conjunct; the subject is in two parts followed by a countersubject; episodes characterized by use of sequence

Rhythm: duple meter; moderate to moderately fast tempo

Harmony: mainly minor mode; begins in G minor, modulates to B♭ major and C minor, returns to G minor, ends with G major chord

Texture: monophonic at beginning, then contrapuntal; homophonic in the final cadence

Form: fugue

BAROQUE INSTRUMENTAL MUSIC

Original Score of Bach's Fugue in E Minor: *The tenth fugue in the second volume of Bach's* Well-Tempered Clavier *has only three voices. The highest voice enters first, the second highest enters at the very end of the first line, and the lowest enters at the beginning of the third line, all of which can be clearly seen in Bach's manuscript. (MS. 35021)*

The Art of the Fugue, Bach's last work, is made up of eighteen canons and fugues. All are based on the same subject and arranged in order of increasing complexity. Included in the music is a four-note motive that, in German notation, spells out the composer's name:

The Suite

A *suite* is made up of a number of movements, each like a dance and all in the same key or related keys. Its history offers a good example of Baroque internationalism. The characteristic style of the individual dances was established in France, but the formal organization of the dances into a musical entity, the suite, was a German contribution.

The French dances were written for solo instruments, at first the lute and then the harpsichord. They were published in sets that included an *allemande*, a *courante*, a *sarabande*, and a random variety of other dances. Each set was thus a collection of short pieces, many of them separately titled and generally unified only by being written in the same key. Couperin wrote a large number of *ordres*, or suites, for harpsichord. Each was made up of several loosely connected short pieces, sometimes more than twenty. These were highly stylized, very graceful compositions, with delicate melodies, rich embellishments, and touches of wit.

The light, delicate style of the French suite owed much to the fact that it was originally played by lute. The harpsichordists of the late seventeenth century took over many technical devices from this most favored of Renaissance instruments. In particular they adopted the *style brisé*, or "broken style," a rapid alternation between high and low notes. It had originally been used to create a suggestion of sustained melody and harmony in the quickly fading plucked notes of the lute. Transferred to the brighter, more resonant tone of the harpsichord, the style brisé was carried to heights of perfection not imagined by the lutenists who had first devised it.

**Suites for
Ensembles**

Schein

Initially departing from the French preference for solo composition, German composers at the beginning of the seventeenth century wrote suites for ensembles. An important collection of suites was published in 1617 by Johann Hermann Schein (1586–1630). Entitled *Banchetto musicale* ("Musical Banquet"), it contained twenty suites written in five parts for viols. Schein, unlike his French contemporaries, limited the number of dances in his suites. Each suite has a combination of slow and fast dances: a *padouana (pavane)*, a *gagliarda*, a *courante*, and an *allemande*. In some of the suites, a single melody is used, with variation, for all the dances; in others, different melodies are added. All, however, are distinctly more unified than the loose French suites, giving the impression of one composition in several movements instead of a succession of separate pieces.

Later German composers replaced the padouana with the French overture (see page 122). They also introduced wind instruments to supplement the string ensemble. Both of these innovations came to be regarded as typically German. The German composers also made more use of counterpoint, enriching and deepening the harmonic texture of the movements. The opening movement gained in importance and, in later years, whole suites were often referred to as overtures.

**Bach's Suites and
Partitas**

The power and expressiveness of German suites, for ensemble and later for solo instrument, surpassed that of their French models. There are few compositions that can rival the "Air" from Bach's *Suite No. 3 in D Major* in somber, profound beauty of theme and texture. Bach also wrote three *partitas* (another name for the suite) for violin. These are among the most magnificent solo works ever created for that instrument. The complexity and grandeur of the "Chaconne" of the *Partita No. 2* is unparalleled.

By the mid-seventeenth century, the solo keyboard suite was also becoming popular in Germany and had achieved a fairly standardized

Froberger's Suites

structure. Those written by Johann Jakob Froberger (1616–1667) were written in three movements, using the dances of the early French suite: *allemande, courante,* and *sarabande.* By the end of the century, a *gigue* had been added as the concluding fourth movement.

Structure of Solo Keyboard Suites

By the late Baroque, the solo keyboard suite had become relatively standardized. The first movement, the *allemande,* was written in moderately fast duple meter. Beginning with a short upbeat, it made use of short running figures. The second movement, the *courante,* was often based on the theme of the first movement. The French version was generally in moderate $\frac{6}{4}$ time. The Italian version—the *corrente*—was a faster, more homophonic dance in $\frac{3}{4}$ time. The third movement, the *sarabande,* was a slow movement in triple meter, written in a dignified style, and often more homophonic than the earlier movements. It was sometimes followed by an ornamented version of the same dance called a *double.* The final movement, the *gigue,* was a lively, quick-paced dance in $\frac{6}{8}$ time, often written in imitative counterpoint. Occasional variants of this scheme might include an opening movement or other dances inserted between the standard movements. The form of most of the dance movements was binary, similar to the structure of Scarlatti's sonatas.

Suites by Purcell and Handel

The keyboard suite was also quite popular in England. Purcell was the most important English composer of harpsichord suites. Handel is also noted for his keyboard suites as well as for his famous *Water Music,* a large collection of dances and abstract movements for orchestra.

By the end of the Baroque era, the suite had reached its highest development. Like the sonata, it contributed significantly to the development of the Classical symphony.

Other Types of Compositions

Besides the sonata, concerto, fugue, and suite, a number of other important instrumental compositions were developed during the Baroque age. Prominent among them were compositions that were, like the fugue, primarily for solo keyboard instrument. Our discussion of these additional types of compositions, however, will begin with the sinfonia, and the overture that developed from it—both works for orchestra.

The Sinfonia and the Overture

Rather than implying any particular style, the term *sinfonia* was generally used to refer to the orchestral introductions or interludes written for vocal works such as operas or cantatas. Monteverdi wrote a sinfonia for his opera *Orfeo.* Rossi used the name for the introduction to an orchestral suite. Bach prefaced a number of his cantatas with sinfonias.

French Overture and Lully

Over the course of the seventeenth century, two distinct compositional forms emerged—one in Italy, the other in France. The *French overture* was largely the creation of Lully, whose influential position at the court of Versailles made him a major arbiter of musical taste. The earliest example of its use was in Lully's ballet *Alcidiane*, written in 1658. The French overture had two sections. The first section was slow, homophonic, and majestic in style, with an emphasis on uneven rhythms. The second section was fast moving, although still serious in character, and frequently began with some form of imitative counterpoint. This section often ended with an *allargando*, or slowing down, which might contain a repetition of the rhythm or theme of the first section. In later compositions, this closing passage was sometimes expanded into a third section.

Italian Overture and Alessandro Scarlatti

The development of the *Italian overture* was a major contribution of Alessandro Scarlatti (1660–1725), the father of Domenico. It had three sections: fast—slow—fast. The first section made some use of imitative counterpoint. The second and third sections, however, were in simpler homophonic style. In many parts of Italy, especially in Venice, overtures were often written for operas, with music based on the thematic material found in the operas' main scenes. The Italian overture, with its three sections, was still another progenitor of the Classical symphony.

The Toccata

The *toccata*, a form of prelude, dates back to the lute music of the early sixteenth century. In the Baroque period, it became a vehicle for keyboard instruments, particularly the organ. Extremely powerful works, toccatas are meant to convey a sense of improvisation. They are marked by irregular rhythms, sudden sharp changes of texture, and a relentless drive of scalelike passages, turns, trills, and other ornamentation. With its exuberant, dramatic nature, the toccata is a wonderful example of the Baroque spirit.

Frescobaldi

Girolamo Frescobaldi (1583–1643) was an early composer of toccatas. His pieces are made up of loosely connected sections that are rich in musical ideas and allow for great display of virtuosity. Since the toccata was clearly intended to be a performer's showcase, it is not surprising that it reached the height of its development in Germany, where composers could take full advantage of the advanced state of organ construction. Froberger created toccatas that were somewhat more controlled than Frescobaldi's. His works served as models for Buxtehude and Bach, whose toccatas, written in a freer and more elaborate style, were often coupled with fugues. Bach's *Toccata and Fugue in D Minor*, with its brilliant scales and sequential patterns, is one of the most famous works of this type.

The Fantasia

Like toccatas, most *fantasias* were written for keyboard instruments, although some, especially in England, were also written for ensemble. Nonsectional pieces in imitative counterpoint, they were initially indistinguishable from Renaissance ricercari. In the early seventeenth century, they became somewhat longer and took on a more complex formal organization, while retaining their earlier improvisatory character. In spite of the early Baroque interest in monody, the fantasia remained rich in contrapuntal material.

Suggested Listening

The Sonata

Vivaldi: *Sonata No. 1 in F* [Philips 9500-396]. This solo sonata for violin and continuo is a chamber work and, like a suite, consists of dance movements. The tempos are in a typical fast—slow—fast—slow pattern.

Buxtehude: *Sonata for Violin, Viola da Gamba, and Continuo, Op. 1, No. 7* [Nonesuch H-71119]. The North German style is quite evident in this trio sonata, which is made up of a series or chain of interconnected sections. In all, there are eight sections of varying tempos.

The Concerto

Bach: *Concerto for Harpsichord in D Major* [Telefunken 6-41037]. This solo concerto, a transcription of Bach's earlier *Concerto for Violin in E Major*, calls for considerable virtuosity on the part of the soloist. The use of the ritornello principle is particularly marked in the last of the three movements.

A. Scarlatti: *Concerto in G Minor* [Archive 198-442]. This concerto grosso has a concertino of two violins and cello and a ripieno of strings and continuo. The three movements are fast—slow—fast.

The Fugue

Bach: *Fugue No. 1 in C Major*, from *The Well-Tempered Clavier*, Vol. 1 [Piano: Columbia MS-6408; Harpsichord: Everest 3134]. In this fugue Bach displays his contrapuntal mastery by presenting the subject in its entirety throughout the work rather than creating contrast through juxtaposition of a countersubject.

Other Types of Compositions

Bach: *The Goldberg Variations* [Vanguard S-175]. This work represents the height of the use of theme and variations form in the Baroque period. Thirty sections follow the opening theme. They are arranged in groups of three: two free variations and one variation in canon, each canon written at a successively greater interval.

Handel: *Water Music* [MHS 553]. Scored for strings, continuo, horns, bassoons, and trumpets, this is no doubt Handel's most famous instrumental work. It is a large collection of dances and abstract movements, with a French overture for introduction. The instrumentation varies colorfully from one movement to the next.

C H A P T E R

II

Baroque Vocal Music

General Trends in Vocal Music

As we have seen, the Baroque style of vocal music began with the Italian interest in monody—that is, an emphasis on one principal melody rather than on the contrapuntal interweaving of several melodies characteristic of the Renaissance. Since the monodic style grew out of an interest in the revival of ancient drama, it is not surprising that it was soon used in Baroque dramas.

Early Composers of Monody

One of the earliest Baroque composers of monody was Giulio Caccini (1546–1618). In his *Euridice* (1600), produced in collaboration with Jacopo Peri, the stile rappresentativo crystallized. In fact, *Euridice* is commonly regarded as the first surviving opera. It contains airs, choruses, dances, and recitatives upon which later operas and other Baroque vocal compositions were to be built.

As a member of Giovanni de' Bardi's Camerata in Florence, Caccini felt it important to explain to his contemporaries the theory underlying his new style. This he did in the foreword of *Le Nuove musiche* ("New Music"), published in 1602; his treatise soon became a veritable handbook on monody. The technique, as Caccini saw it, called for a solo voice supported by instrumental accompaniment only loosely connected to the vocal part. Over a basso continuo, often made up of sustained low tones, the melodic line proceeded through both consonances and dissonances. Dissonance was vital to a vocal style that tried to approximate speech. It was subject to only one restriction: that each new bass note be consonant with the first melodic note sounded with it. The following notes of the melody could be dissonant to the bass note, until the bass note changed. Thus, in the monodic style, composers found a way to blend the rhythms, melodies, and harmonies of speech with those of music. Caccini used his new technique particularly in the dialogues of his operas.

The use of the monodic style and the compositional devices that it involved had an effect on many of the vocal works of the period. The eight books of madrigals written by Claudio Monteverdi between 1587 and 1638 neatly illustrate the progression from Renaissance to Baroque music. In attempting to present the text of his madrigals more convincingly, Monteverdi

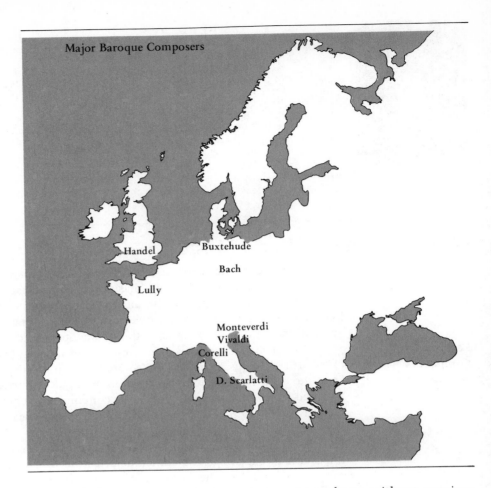

Major Baroque Composers

permitted dissonance to appear even on strong beats without previous preparation—if the emotive quality of the work called for it. He reduced the number of vocal parts from five to three or fewer and added a basso continuo. In these madrigals for few voices, the polarization of bass and soprano began to occur. This novel style, with free dissonance and accompaniment, was called the *continuo madrigal*. In time it evolved into the vocal-instrumental chamber works characteristic of the Baroque period.

Continuo Madrigal

Other types of vocal music were also vitally affected by the rise of the monodic style and the transformation of the madrigal. Monteverdi's innovations were part of a general shift from the four- and five-part polyphonic works of the Renaissance toward the vocal styles of the seventeenth century. Baroque vocal music tended to use the solo voice freely, often in contrast to passages of ensemble singing. Melodies were arranged more and more into long, unified lines. Restrictions on the use of harmony and dissonance were increasingly observed. Baroque vocal compositions were generally longer than their Renaissance ancestors, relying on major-minor tonal organization for greater variety and continuity. Monodies and other types of chamber music, such as the secular cantata, gradually took over the popularity that had once belonged to the madrigal. Even the Mass declined in importance, while the oratorio and the sacred cantata, which permitted greater freedom in musical and poetic organization, became prominent.

Baroque Opera

One of the most important inventions of the early seventeenth century was the special combination of music and drama that came to be known as *opera*. It was at least partly derived from certain secular dramatic amusements of the sixteenth century. Its staging, for example, was borrowed from contemporary theater and its poetry from the Italian pastorale.

Early Development

The earliest Florentine operas, among them *Euridice* and Jacopo Peri's *Dafne* (1597), were largely monodic. Instrumentation and melody were both subordinated to a clear rendering of natural speech. Counterpoint was neglected. Only at the end of crucial scenes did early composers of opera vary their monody by introducing songs or choruses, with more elaborate music, and often with dancing.

Monteverdi: *Orfeo*

The enrichment of the early operatic style was left to Monteverdi, whose madrigals already displayed his interest in monody. His *Orfeo* (1607) followed the general outlines of earlier operas. The story upon which the opera was based was one used in many early works. Taken from Greek mythology, it concerns Orfeo's descent into hell to rescue his beloved Euridice. Although the story was a common one, Monteverdi's opera was dramatically and musically far more sophisticated than any of the earlier operas. His score called for a large orchestra with a variety of instruments, many of which were specifically designated. He also included some purely instrumental passages for variety and color. The monodic vocal passages were enhanced by considerable variety in melodic writing. Monteverdi's expressive melodies and complex harmonies indicated great concern for all aspects of musical organization. He even wrote out the ornaments and variations for some of the solo parts. So complex was Monteverdi's score, so unlike any of its predecessors, that each of the six stanzas of one aria in the third act had a different orchestral accompaniment. Opera had indeed begun to mature.

"Tu se' morta"

An excellent example of Monteverdi's expressive monody is Orfeo's lament "Tu se' morta," an aria in the opera's second act. Having just learned that Euridice has died of a snakebite, Orfeo at first despairs. He then summons his courage and resolves to travel to the land of the dead to retrieve her, or failing that, to stay there with her. Monteverdi's music mirrors these emotions faithfully. Orfeo's despair is captured in the somber accompaniment and in the faltering rhythm of the opening phrases. Then the music moves ahead with greater assurance, reflecting Orfeo's decision to follow Euridice.

Chromaticism

Throughout the aria, Monteverdi made use of unsettling *chromaticism*, introducing notes that were not part of the scale. In the last phrase, the chromaticism becomes particularly jarring, conveying the idea of departure.

Monteverdi also used a considerable amount of text painting in Orfeo's lament. In the last phrase, note the melodic descent to *terra* ("earth"), and the melodic ascent to *cielo* ("heaven"), continuing even higher to *sole* ("sun"). Thus the melody as well as the rhythm is tied as closely as possible to the text.

Side 3, Band 5

Listening Guide for Monteverdi's "Tu se' morta,"* from *Orfeo*

Timbre:	tenor voice accompanied by basso continuo of organ and lute
Melody:	mainly conjunct; use of expressive leaps and chromaticism; some use of sequence
Rhythm:	duple meter; slow tempo; closely tied to text; expressive interruptions
Harmony:	mainly minor mode; begins in G minor, modulates to D minor at the end
Texture:	monodic homophony (melody with chordal accompaniment)
Form:	free, continuous unfolding of text with no clear sectional divisions

Text:

Tu se' morta, mia vita, ed io respiro?	You are dead, my life, and I breathe?
Tu se' da me partita	You have left me,
Per mai piu, mai piu non tornare, ed io rimango?	Never, never more to return, and I remain?
No, no, che se i versi alcuna cosa ponno	No, no, for if my songs can take effect
N'andro sicuro a piu profondi abissi,	I shall go surely to the deepest abysses,
E intenerito il cor del Re de l'ombre	And having softened the heart of the dreaded king
Meco trarrotti a riveder le stelle:	I'll bring you back again to see the stars;
O se cio negherammi empio destino	Or if this is denied me by cruel destiny,
Rimarro teco in compagnia di morte.	I shall stay with you in the company of death.
Addio, terra; addio cielo, e sole, addio.	Farewell earth; farewell sun and heaven.

*English translation by Denis Stevens, Professor of Music, Columbia University, President Accademia Monteverdiana, for Musical Heritage Society. Copyright 1968, Accademia Monteverdiana.

BAROQUE MUSIC

Orfeo started a movement that led to the creation of the bel canto style in the mid-seventeenth century. Bel canto arose in opposition to the dominance of poetry and musical virtuosity in early operas. It exerted a century-long influence on Baroque music. Composers writing in the bel canto style rejected most of the virtuoso effects of earlier writers. They preferred light, lyrical melodies and smoother rhythms interspersed with only a few more flamboyant passages. The bass grew to be nearly as important as the melody, leading to the reintroduction of contrapuntal techniques. Yet, despite the greater sophistication of melodic lines, the harmony of the bel canto style became almost exclusively triadic and quite simple.

By the middle of the seventeenth century, a clear distinction between recitative and aria had developed. In recitative the melodies were usually simple with many repeated notes, while the rhythm tended to follow the flow of the words. Music in the recitatives was generally subordinate to the text, which was used mainly for dialogue and descriptions of the action taking place in the plot. In arias the melodies were much more elaborate and interesting. A clear meter prevailed, and emphasis was placed on the music instead of the text, which usually commented repeatedly on action that had taken place or was about to take place.

Types of Recitatives

Baroque composers made use of two different types of recitatives. The first, accompanied only by continuo, was called *recitativo secco* ("dry recitative"). The second, accompanied by a larger instrumental ensemble, was called *recitativo accompagnato* ("accompanied recitative"). The second type was usually used for more dramatic moments.

Types of Arias

Arias generally belonged to one of three types. The earliest, the *strophic-bass aria*, was predominant in the years before 1630. It had a number of consecutive stanzas, the melodies of which were varied over a repeated bass line. In the 1630s a second type, the *ostinato aria*, appeared and was subsequently used for many years by Purcell and other composers. The ostinato aria set a lengthy melody over a short, constantly repeating bass, the *basso ostinato* ("obstinate" or "stubborn" bass), in the accompaniment. The third variety, the *da capo aria*, became the favorite of most composers between 1650 and 1750. It was made up of three sections. After the second section, the words *da capo* ("from the beginning") or *d.c.* were written in the score, indicating that the first section should be repeated. This repeat was often embellished with improvisations. The ABA form that resulted was used by such diverse composers as Bach, Alessandro Scarlatti, and Handel.

Most of these formative developments began in Florence. By 1630, however, Rome had become a center of opera. The Roman school expanded the subject matter of operas beyond the rather stereotyped pastoral themes of the early operas to include other serious subjects and even comedy. Choral singing was briefly popular in Rome, while the instrumental ensemble, structured around violins and continuo, began to suggest the modern orchestra.

Venetian Opera

From Florence and Rome, opera spread to other Italian cities, and later to other countries. The world's first public opera house opened in Venice in 1637, marking the emergence of this genre as entertainment for a broad audience. Monteverdi was the first important composer of operas in Venice. He wrote many of his finest operas, including *Il Ritorno d'Ulisse in patria* ("The Return of Ulysses to His Native Land") (1641) and *L'Incoronazione di Poppea* ("The Coronation of Poppea") (1642), after becoming music director at Saint Mark's. The expressive recitatives in these later works were the culmination of the original monodic style, while the arias were distinguished by their lovely melodies.

The Neapolitan Style

In Naples a new style of opera was arising in the late seventeenth century. While the mature Venetian style made use of counterpoint and often treated the orchestra as almost equal to the singers in importance, the Neapolitan composers adopted a much more homophonic style in which the vocal melody was clearly dominant. During the early eighteenth century, the Neapolitan style superseded the Venetian. It soon dominated not only Italian opera but that of all Europe except France.

A Neapolitan opera was generally divided into a series of structurally similar scenes, each of which was devoted to a particular mood or "affect." In each scene, a short recitative set forth the narrative action. The main character of the scene then sang an aria describing the emotions he or she was feeling. The music was difficult and called for considerable virtuosity on the part of the singer. Choruses were rarely used, and there were almost no instrumental movements after the overture.

Scarlatti's Operas   The person generally regarded as the founder of Neapolitan opera was Alessandro Scarlatti. His early works were very much derived from Venetian composers, but by 1700 he had moved toward the pre-Classical melodic style with its strongly supporting homophony. Scarlatti played an important part in the standardization of the instrumental overture into three sections: a fast opening section, a slow middle section, and a quick two-part final section in dance rhythm. This three-section work came to be known as the Italian overture. Scarlatti's operas vary greatly but are perhaps best distinguished by their da capo arias, lilting and virtuosic Italian melodies, and general elegance.

Opera Buffa   Because the early comic episodes were soon eliminated from serious Neapolitan opera, it is not surprising that an entirely independent form, *opera buffa*, or "comic opera," appeared in Italy soon after 1700. In the early eighteenth century, the two types existed side by side with little influence on each other. Opera buffa generally presented humorous or farcical subjects, often about the everyday lives of common people. Its music was simple, and performances were usually given by untrained singers and semiskilled actors. Not surprisingly, opera buffa was, in its early stages, regarded as low-class entertainment. Later, however, it was gradually transformed into a highly regarded art form in the works of Mozart and other composers. The tradition of comic opera, as a low-class entertainment and later as a higher form, was also developed in other European countries during the eighteenth century.

The French Style

Long before the spread of comic opera to countries outside Italy, serious opera had reached the rest of Europe. Only in France, however, did it develop a distinctly non-Italian style. The French opera was largely the creation of Lully. In his royal patron's service, he set out to make opera a dramatic medium of as much dignity as the contemporary theater of Corneille, Racine, and Molière.

Lully's Operas

Since Lully's operas were designed first of all to please the king, nearly all of their music was refined, stately, and somewhat pompous. The two-part French overture opened with a slow, majestic section and was followed by a quicker section in imitative counterpoint. Arias were shorter, simpler, and less numerous than their Italian counterparts and avoided virtuosic effects. A number of scenes involved such things as processions, pastoral interludes, dances, triumphs, funerals, and combats. Many of these were barely relevant to the rest of the action and served mainly as eye-pleasing spectacles. Orchestration was more colorful than in the Neapolitan opera. Considerable use was

Early Nationalism in Opera: *Following Louis XIV's tastes, Lully and other French composers developed an operatic style quite different from earlier styles developed by Italian composers. This contemporary engraving shows a scene from Lully's first opera,* Les Fêtes de l'amour et de Bacchus, *performed in an outdoor theater at Versailles.*

made of strings and continuo, along with some of the wind and percussion instruments of the day.

Rameau

The French operatic style, as first conceived by Lully, lasted with few changes through the eighteenth century. One composer who did add certain techniques was Jean-Philippe Rameau (1683–1764). Rameau was unusual among major composers in that he worked almost exclusively with opera. He modeled his music on Lully's but altered some of the details. In particular, he favored the Neapolitan da capo aria and used the orchestra more contrapuntally.

Opera in England

Purcell's Opera

Opera developed in England during the seventeenth century, influenced largely by earlier court entertainments such as the masque, which included dialogue, songs, dances, and instrumental music. It was Purcell who perhaps did the most to bring English opera to a level of greatness. Purcell wrote music for plays such as *King Arthur* and *The Fairy Queen* and one real opera, *Dido and Aeneas*. Many aspects of *Dido and Aeneas* are worthy of comment, including the sensitive setting of the English text and the emphasis placed on choral music and dance. Influence from the continent can be seen in the use of the French overture and the fact that the dialogue is sung in recitative. The arias present intense ideas, both textually and musically, as in Dido's famous lament, "When I am laid in earth." The chorus is featured prominently in the opera and is given delightfully surprising rhythms and charming moments of text painting. Purcell's dramatic genius reached its greatest heights in this brief masterpiece.

Handel's Operas

Handel was also an important composer of English operas. Born in Germany, educated in Italy, and widely traveled, he assimilated a variety of styles into his own works. Between 1712 and 1741, he wrote thirty-six operas, which show a thorough mastery of the Neapolitan style. Handel conceived of opera as a succession of alternating recitatives and da capo arias, with each two-part scene devoted to the expression of a single affect. His use of the *castrato singer*—a male soprano or alto—in such operas as *Julius Caesar* was a continuation of an Italian practice. However, he did depart now and then from standard Neapolitan procedure by using French overtures and beginning scenes with brief orchestral introductions. In effect, Handel added international touches to a thoroughly Italian art form.

Castrato Singer

The Cantata

Opera was by no means the only important Baroque contribution to vocal music. As monodic music became more and more popular in the early seventeenth century, Italian composers began to use the new style in other types of compositions. Many of these shorter monodic pieces with varying formats were called *cantatas*. The word was first used to indicate, not that the pieces had any particular structure or content, but simply that they were to be sung.

Italian Secular Cantata

By the middle of the seventeenth century, the Italian secular cantata had become more or less standardized. It consisted of recitative and aria sections for one, two, or possibly three voices and continuo. The works were designed largely for virtuoso display in a chamber setting. Their lyrics generally described a single situation or recounted a brief, uncomplicated narrative.

Throughout the seventeenth century, the evolution of the Italian cantata closely paralleled that of opera, especially because many composers were writing both types of compositions. The importance of the recitative declined somewhat, and, particularly in the cantata, the length of arias increased while their number declined. Also, as the music grew in expressive power, it came to rely much less on the text for emotional intensity.

Early Composers

The first of many important cantata composers during the middle part of the century were the Romans Luigi Rossi (1597–1653) and Giacomo Carissimi (1605–1674). Both were extremely prolific: three hundred and seventy-five cantatas by Rossi and one hundred and fifty-five by Carissimi survive. Rossi's cantatas freely combined recitatives, ariosos, and arias into as many as fourteen sections. His early arias were quite short and strophic in form; the later ones were innovative precursors of the da capo style. The arias and recitatives in his works were not yet organized into any stylized sequence. Carissimi's cantatas tended more toward the melodic bel canto style, but on the whole resembled Rossi's mature works. Later practitioners of the Venetian operatic style brought more counterpoint, more complex instrumentation, and stricter alternation of recitative and aria to the Italian cantata.

Scarlatti's Cantatas

Among those composers who continued the tradition of the Italian cantata in the eighteenth century, by far the most important was Alessandro Scarlatti, who wrote more than six hundred such works. By Scarlatti's time the cantata had been standardized. It now consisted of an introductory sinfonia followed by a pattern of alternating recitatives and arias. The Neapolitan style, which Scarlatti perfected, called for precise declamation in the recitatives, lyricism in the arias, and great virtuosity.

German Sacred Cantata

Schütz

The German sacred cantata resulted from a blending of the Italian monodic style and polyphonic vocal styles. Heinrich Schütz (1585–1672), a pupil of Monteverdi, is generally thought to have been the first to use Italian techniques to transpose the madrigal into a cantata suitable for the Lutheran service. Schütz's study of recitative enabled him to unite German texts with appropriate music in such works as *Psalmen Davids* ("Psalms of David"). From the Italians, he also learned the use of basso continuo, the idea of contrasting sections, and the value of melodic invention. Although he used the monodic style in many of his works, including *Kleine geistliche Konzerte* ("Small Spiritual Concertos") (1636), much of his writing was highly contrapuntal. His *Cantiones sacrae* ("Sacred Motets") (1625), for example, are for four voices and continuo. This happy union of counterpoint and Italian monodic methods, initiated by Schütz, greatly influenced the vocal works of later composers.

Buxtehude's Cantatas

Dietrich Buxtehude's cantatas make use of a variety of texts and musical styles. In many of his works, Buxtehude used a distinctive chorale-variation scheme, in which each stanza of a chorale, or congregational hymn, served as

Performance of a German Cantata: *The orchestra played an important part in the German sacred cantata, just as it did in most other vocal works of the Baroque period. The engraving at the left shows the orchestra required for one early eighteenth-century cantata. The conductor is standing in a key position between the basso continuo instruments, facing the chorus.*

the basis for elaboration by voices and instruments. The use of chorales in Buxtehude's cantatas was part of a traditional Lutheran concern for the words in the religious services.

Bach's Cantatas

Bach was the acknowledged master of the German cantata. He wrote nearly three hundred cantatas between 1723 and 1750. The works included both religious cantatas and secular cantatas, for soloists and chorus accompanied by a small orchestra.

Most of Bach's religious cantatas had both solo and choral movements. The choral movements were generally performed by a group of eight to twelve singers and an orchestral ensemble of eighteen to twenty-four instruments—string instruments, wind instruments, timpani, and continuo. Bach's unsurpassed melodic and harmonic abilities are very apparent in his cantatas, with their expressive recitatives, profound solos, and superb counterpoint. He generally began with a chorus, which sometimes incorporated an instrumental sinfonia. This was followed by five or six movements of alternating recitatives and arias. The cantatas usually ended with a harmonized chorale. Many of the works, despite their technical diversity and complex structure, were based on a single chorale text and melody.

Bach: *Cantata No. 80*

The *Cantata No. 80*, "Ein' feste Burg ist unser Gott" ("A Mighty Fortress Is Our God"), is a fine example of Bach's religious cantatas. It dates from 1715 and was written to commemorate the Reformation. The music calls for soloists, chorus, and an orchestra of violins, violas, cellos, trumpets, oboes, timpani, and continuo with the organ used as the keyboard instrument. The work has eight movements:

1. Opening movement for chorus and orchestra
2. Aria for soprano and bass accompanied by oboe, violins, viola, and continuo
3. Recitative for bass and continuo
4. Aria for soprano and continuo
5. Chorale for unison chorus accompanied by orchestra
6. Recitative for tenor and continuo
7. Duet for alto and tenor accompanied by oboe, violin, and continuo
8. Closing four-part harmonization of the chorale for chorus

The congregation may, at times, have joined in the last movement, singing the melody.

First Movement

The opening movement of *Cantata No. 80* shows Bach's mature contrapuntal style to great advantage. The phrases of the chorale melody are the basis for nearly all the melodic material. The first phrase is introduced by the tenors and violas and then imitated by the other voices of the chorus in succession. These voices, like the tenor, are doubled by instruments of the orchestra. The source of Bach's opening melody is clear if we compare it with the first phrase of the chorale:

First Phrase of Chorale

Ein'   fe - ste Burg   ist   un - ser Gott

Opening Tenor Phrase of Cantata

Ein' fe — — — ste Burg ist un - ser Gott

The following phrases of the chorale are presented in a similar elaborated fashion. Bach's genius as a composer can be seen in the brilliant imitative counterpoint used in each of the phrases. The result is a grand imitative work for chorus and orchestra.

Side 3, Band 6

Listening Guide for Bach's *Cantata No. 80*, First Movement

Timbre: four-part choir, small orchestra of violins, violas, cellos, trumpets, oboes, timpani, and organ continuo

Melody: largely conjunct, based on chorale melody

Rhythm: duple meter; moderate tempo

Harmony: mainly major mode; begins in D major, modulates most significantly through the keys of A major and B minor, ends in D major

Texture: imitative counterpoint

Form: based on chorale melody

Text:

Ein' feste Burg ist unser Gott,	A mighty fortress is our God,
ein' gute Wehr und Waffen;	a bulwark never failing;
er hilft uns frei aus aller Not,	our helper he amid the flood
die uns jetzt hat betroffen.	of mortal ills prevailing.
Der alte boese Feind	For still our ancient foe
mit Ernst er's jetzt meint,	doth seek to work us woe;
gross Macht und viel List	his craft and power are great,
sein grausam Ruestung ist,	and, armed with cruel hate,
auf Erd' ist nicht seinsgleichen.	on earth is not his equal.

The Oratorio

Laude

Cavalieri

Early Oratorios

The term *oratorio* (literally "place of prayer") was first used for a chapel in Rome where, during the late sixteenth century, popular religious services were often held. A common feature of these services was the singing of *laude*—allegorical "conversations" between God and the soul, heaven and hell, or other similar participants. Some laude were very simple, while others were more elaborate, amounting almost to sacred operas. The earliest major work that has survived is the *Rappresentazione di anima e di corpo* ("Representation of Soul and Body") (1600), by Emilio del Cavalieri (c.1550–1602). Closely resembling the contemporary operas of Caccini in its elaborate staging, the *Rappresentazione* is often considered more an opera than an oratorio. Similar compositions enjoyed modest popularity until the middle of the century, when Carissimi produced the first works that were indisputably oratorios.

Italian oratorios such as Carissimi's *Jepthe* (c.1649) were sacred works with long narrative texts in Latin or Italian. They were generally presented without scenery, costumes, or action. A narrator's part was often included to outline the dramatic action. As in operas and cantatas, structure was derived from the juxtaposition of recitatives, arias, and choruses. Instrumental accompaniments were also used. The oratorio differed from the opera not only in that it was generally not intended to be staged but also in its greater use of the chorus for narrative and dramatic purposes.

Performance of an English Oratorio: *This eighteenth-century English engraving has been labeled in a number of ways over the centuries, and no one is really sure whether or not Handel is the person shown conducting from the harpsichord. In any case, the work being performed is likely to have been one of his. As in the contemporary engraving of the German cantata shown earlier, the singers are missing, located beyond the print next to the orchestra.*

Handel's Oratorios

In Germany the most important composers of oratorios included Schütz, best known for *Die sieben Worte Jesu Christi am Kreuz* ("The Seven Last Words of Christ"), and Bach. But probably the greatest of all oratorio composers was Handel, whose works include *Israel in Egypt, Judas Maccabaeus, Saul*, and *Messiah*, his most famous work.

In all of his oratorios, *Messiah* among them, Handel followed the general structure of the Italian prototype. His works began with instrumental overtures and then proceeded with recitatives, arias, ariosos, and choruses. The somewhat limited use of modulation in his harmonies and the melodic emphasis in his arias were inspired by the Italian style. Yet his choral technique, which incorporated elements from a number of different vocal styles, departed considerably from the Italian practice in the use of imitation with occasional homophony.

Handel's oratorios, and his other vocal works as well, frequently demand great virtuosity from both singers and instrumentalists. His melodic phrases are often long ones based on scales and arpeggios. There is also a liberal use of melodic sequence. A fine balance is maintained between contrapuntal and homophonic textures. Imitation is generally very important in his choruses, but important words and climaxes are often set homophonically.

Handel: *Messiah*

Handel's *Messiah* was written in 1741, in the amazingly short period of twenty-four days, and was first performed the following year in Dublin. It is divided into three parts: the first dealing with the birth of Jesus, the second with his death and resurrection, and the third with the redemption of humanity. The music consists of a French overture, recitatives, arias, and choruses. It was first performed by a small chorus and a small orchestra made up of string instruments, wind instruments, timpani, and continuo.

Musical styles in Handel's *Messiah* range from the conventional da capo aria to freer structures using the ritornello technique. In these later movements, a main theme returns throughout, either in complete or shortened versions. The choruses of the work include some of Handel's best choral writing and are widely known and loved throughout the world. Few pieces of music surpass the "Hallelujah Chorus" in musical and dramatic intensity, or in popularity. Its strong homophonic opening creates a profound effect, while its judicious mixture of contrapuntal and homophonic textures gives it great contrast and interest.

"For Unto Us a Child Is Born"

The chorus "For Unto Us a Child Is Born" begins somewhat differently from the "Hallelujah Chorus." In both choruses, the orchestra first presents the opening theme. In the present work, however, the voices then enter imitatively, beginning with the sopranos. The result is a superb contrapuntal section based on the opening theme:

First Theme

For un-to us a child is born; un-to us a son is giv-en, un-to us a son is giv-en,

A new theme is introduced with the next phrase of text:

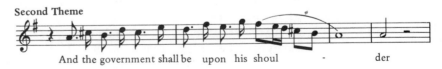

Second Theme

And the government shall be upon his shoul - der

The music then builds to a climax with the text "and his name shall be called Wonderful! Counselor!"—the last words of which are set chordally for emphasis. During the remainder of the chorus, the two themes are alternately and simultaneously developed in brilliant fashion. The chordal setting of "Wonderful! Counselor!" returns three times, each time creating an impressive climax. The orchestra brings the movement to a close with a ritornello of the first theme, in the original key.

Listening Guide for Handel's "For Unto Us a Child Is Born," from *Messiah*

Timbre:	four-part choir, small orchestra of string instruments, wind instruments, timpani, and continuo
Melody:	first theme largely conjunct; second theme begins with disjunct motion
Rhythm:	duple meter; moderately fast tempo
Harmony:	major mode; begins in G major, modulates to D major and C major, ends in G major
Texture:	alternating imitative and homophonic sections
Form:	ritornello, with alternating imitative and homophonic sections
Text:	For unto us a child is born; unto us a son is given; And the government shall be upon his shoulder, And his name shall be called Wonderful! Counselor! The Mighty God! The Everlasting Father! The Prince of Peace!

The Baroque Mass

With the growing interest in secular compositions and the fact that much of the new religious music was designed for use in Protestant churches, the Mass became a relatively less important type of music. Those composers who worked for the Roman Catholic Church still produced unaccompanied polyphonic works much in the style of the late Renaissance Mass. Often, however, they sought ways to achieve new color in their work, some by writing Masses for very large numbers of different vocal parts. Others, especially in Germany, began to use orchestral accompaniment in their Masses.

Like many other musical works, settings of the Mass became longer and more elaborate in the Baroque period. Composers often divided the music for the longer parts of the Ordinary into contrasting sections or movements. The texts of the Gloria and Credo were particularly subject to such division. In many cases, chorus and soloists alternated in the various sections. Mood, tempo, key, and other musical characteristics changed as well.

Missa Brevis

The Lutheran Church in Germany continued to use parts of the Latin Ordinary, but polyphonic choral settings were generally written only for the Kyrie and Gloria. This kind of shortened setting was called a *Missa brevis* ("short Mass"). (The Baroque Missa brevis should be distinguished from the Roman Catholic Missa brevis of the late Renaissance, which was a relatively short and simple setting of all five parts of the Ordinary.) In Bach's Masses, we find the culmination of the Baroque Mass: four settings entitled *Missa brevis* and one setting of the complete Ordinary, the *Mass in B Minor*.

Bach's Masses

Bach: *Mass in B Minor*

Bach's *Mass in B Minor* is one of his greatest accomplishments. It presents a rich variety of musical ideas that combine to form a sublimely convincing, cohesive whole.

The score of the Mass calls for a relatively small orchestra of violins, violas, flutes, oboes, trumpets, timpani, and continuo. Single instruments and small groups of instruments are often used in a solo capacity. Solo voices are also featured from time to time.

The five parts of Bach's Mass—the Kyrie, the Gloria, the Credo, the Sanctus, and the Agnus Dei—cover a wide range of moods, making use of a number of different techniques. The Kyrie, for example, uses imitative counterpoint and a strong rhythmic flow to express the supplication of the words "Kyrie eleison" ("Lord, have mercy"). The section of the Credo dealing with Christ's crucifixion uses extreme chromaticism to suggest agony. Because of the grand scope and wealth of ideas in the *Mass in B Minor*, a thorough study of it is time-consuming but very rewarding. Here, however, we will examine only the Sanctus. Although only a part of the entire work, it offers an excellent example of many of the characteristics of the work as a whole.

Sanctus

Bach divided the text of the Sanctus into several large musical sections:

A Sanctus: six-part chorus and orchestra
B Pleni sunt coeli: six-part chorus and orchestra
C Hosanna: eight-part chorus and orchestra
D Benedictus: tenor solo and orchestra
C Hosanna: eight-part chorus and orchestra

Section A

Use of Triplets

The first section of the Sanctus opens with all voices proclaiming the text chordally in $\frac{4}{4}$ meter. Most of the beats in the section are subdivided into three parts—or *triplets*—as seen in the opening theme:

Opening in First-Soprano Part

Sanc - tus, sanc -   - tus, sanc -   - tus

Several voices present basically conjunct lines together in triplet rhythm, moving contrapuntally within the basic homophonic texture.

Section B

With the text "Pleni sunt coeli," a contrasting section begins. The meter changes from duple to triple, and an important new theme is presented by the tenors. This theme has a distinct character because of the repeated notes at the beginning, the large rising interval that follows, and the use of sixteenth notes for the word "gloria." These rapidly sung notes emphasize the word, while contributing to the strong sense of constant rhythmic motion:

Second Theme in Tenor Part

Ple - ni sunt coe - li et ter - ra glo - - - - - - -

- ri - a   tu - - a

The Evolution of the Mass

Through the centuries, musical settings of the Mass have continued to play an important part in religious services. There has, however, been a trend, most notably in the last two centuries, to write Masses for performance in the concert hall as well as in the church.

Listen to musical settings of the Mass from five different periods—either those listed below from the record set that accompanies the text, or other selections from the record library.

Medieval:	Introit of the Requiem Mass	Side 2, Band 5
Renaissance:	Josquin's Kyrie of the *Missa pange lingua*	Side 2, Band 9
Baroque:	Bach's Sanctus of the *Mass in B Minor*, First Section	Side 3, Band 8
Romantic:	Verdi's *Requiem*	Record Library
Modern:	Bernstein's *Mass*	Record Library

What musical qualities make it possible to identify the first three selections as Medieval, Renaissance, and Baroque? What musical qualities establish the latter two selections as more recent works?

In what ways can each of the selections be seen as a reflection of the religious spirit of the period in which it was composed?

After the tenors complete the theme, the other voices in turn imitate it, entering alternately on the tonic and the dominant. All voices continue the imitative development of the theme throughout this fugal section.

Sections C and D

The Hosanna that follows is quick and vivacious, very appropriate to the spirit of the text. The Benedictus, by contrast, shows Bach in one of his most lyrical and contemplative styles. The closing Hosanna is an exact repeat of the first Hosanna.

Side 3, Band 8 (First Section only)

Listening Guide for Bach's Sanctus of the *Mass in B Minor*

Timbre: six- and eight-part chorus; small orchestra of string instruments, wind instruments, timpani, and continuo

Melody: different themes for each of the four sections

Rhythm: Section A—duple meter, slow tempo, beats subdivided into triplets; Sections B and C—triple meter, moderately quick tempo; Section D—triple meter, slow tempo

BAROQUE VOCAL MUSIC

Harmony:	Sections A, B, and C predominantly in D major; Section D predominantly in B minor		
Texture:	Section A contrapuntal within basically homophonic texture; Sections B and C contrapuntal; Section D contrapuntal and homophonic		
Form:	ABCDC		
Text:	A	Sanctus, sanctus, sanctus Dominus Deus Sabaoth,	Holy, holy, holy Lord God of hosts,
	B	Pleni sunt coeli et terra gloria tua.	Heaven and earth are full of your glory.
	C	Hosanna in excelsis.	Hosanna in the highest.
	D	Benedictus qui venit in nomine Domini.	Blessed is he who comes in the name of the Lord.
	C	Hosanna in excelsis.	Hosanna in the highest.

Suggested Listening

Opera

Monteverdi: "Pur ti miro" ("I Gaze on You"), from *L'Incoronazione di Poppea* ("The Coronation of Poppea") [Vox SOPBX 5113]. This famous duet, an aria for two voices, comes at the end of Monteverdi's opera. Its form is ABA. Both sections make use of short melodic imitations between the two voices. The duet in the A section is set over a descending motive in the continuo. A quicker pace is found in the B section.

Lully: "Dans ce jour" ("On This Day"), from *Alceste* [Columbia M334580]. In this scene two lovers, Cephise and Straton, sing a duet in which Cephise is accused of infidelity. She sings "Il faut changer" ("It is necessary to change"), while Straton sings "Il faut aimer" ("It is necessary to love"). Notice the clarity of the text setting and the strong rhythmic patterns, both typically French.

The Cantata

Bach: *Cantata No. 4*, "Christ lag in Todesbanden" ("Christ Lay in the Bonds of Death") [Vanguard HM-20]. All eight movements of this cantata are based on the chorale "Christ lag in Todesbanden," the melody of which was borrowed from a Gregorian chant. The sinfonia that opens the cantata is followed by a chorus. The other six movements feature a variety of solo and choral parts.

The Oratorio

Schütz: *Historia von der Geburt Jesu Christi* ("Story of the Birth of Jesus Christ") [Argo ZRG-671]. This Christmas oratorio is made up of recitatives, various ensembles, and choruses, all bound together by unity of key. The free-flowing recitatives provide dramatic description and are more complex than Schütz's earlier monodies.

Other Vocal Music

Handel: *Coronation Anthem No. 1: Zadok the Priest* [Angel S-36741]. The first of four anthems that Handel wrote for the coronation of George II in 1727, this has been sung at every English coronation since. A work of majestic effect, it is scored for a large orchestra—featuring strings, trumpets, timpani, and continuo—as well as a seven-part chorus.

Listening Preview   The symphony was by far the most important new type of composition to develop during the Classical period. Listen to the first movements of three symphonies by the three most important composers of the period: Haydn, Mozart, and Beethoven. (See Sides 4 and 5 of the record set that accompanies the text or choose similar selections in the record library.) What aspects of the music tell you that this is not Baroque music? What similarities do you find in all three pieces? What differences do you find in the styles of the three composers?

12

Introduction to Classical Music

The Classical Period [c.1750–c.1815]

The Classical period brought the repudiation of the complicated, highly mannered style of music heard in the Baroque age. Instead there was a demand for simpler music that could speak directly to the human mind and soul. Different ages, of course, have different sensitivities and, consequently, different ideas about human nature. The musical language that developed in the mid-eighteenth century is capable of addressing itself to many aspects of human nature, but it was grounded in the sensitivities of its own time. In order to understand the music of the Classical period more fully, we must know something of the age itself.

Life in the Classical Period

The early decades of the Classical era correspond roughly with what has been called the Age of Reason. The period was marked by a new interest in the improvement of the human condition, through natural science, technology, and social philosophy. Benjamin Franklin stands as a symbol of a generation that concerned itself with the practical fulfillment of the individual and with the individual's relationship to the social state. No longer was it simply taken for granted that the church or monarch would determine the course of history.

The middle class grew stronger throughout the Classical era, as technology laid the basis for the Industrial Revolution. The age of Haydn, Mozart, and Beethoven was also that which produced the first steam engine, the cotton gin, and the spinning jenny. Armed with the Newtonian laws of physics, people began to feel themselves increasingly in control of their universe—the explorers of their own immense capacities. Immanuel Kant attempted nothing less than a definition of the possible limits of human knowledge in his *Critique of Pure Reason* (1781). Diderot and other French philosophers worked to assemble this diverse knowledge in the ambitious *Encyclopédie*. In 1776 Adam Smith published *The Wealth of Nations*, the first systematic treatment of political economy. Political theorists on both sides of the Atlantic began to address themselves to the problem of monarchy: the growth of individualism had brought a strong challenge to the idea that monarchs ruled by divine right. The American Declaration of Independence proposed that all people were equal in the eyes of their Creator. Everywhere people seemed to glimpse the possibility of social improvement.

The Age of Reason soon passed into the Age of Revolution. As early as 1762, the French philosopher Jean Jacques Rousseau wrote that "Man is born free but everywhere is in chains." And, indeed, a reasoned examination of eighteenth-century society often seemed to lead to a rejection of that society in all its inequities and to a glorification of life in a more natural state—or at least to the belief that people did have certain "natural rights." The breakdown of traditional authority and the growing confidence in human abilities presaged the late eighteenth-century revolutions in America and France. It also heralded an individualism that could not be contained within the rational limits of the Classical world.

Art and Music in the Classical Period

In the middle of the eighteenth century, a preference for classic simplicity in both art and music emerged. In part, this indicated a revolt against Baroque

A Period of Transition: *The Classical period was one of transition, in music and in society. The French Revolution, falling roughly in the middle of the period, upset traditional social expectations and inspired thoughts of political and artistic freedom throughout Europe. The engraving of a French salon in the years just before the Revolution shows a leisured, elegant way of life that was soon to pass forever.*

The Bettmann Archive

styles. But it also reflected other influences, among them the archeological excavations at Pompeii and Herculaneum. With the excavations came a revival of interest in Greek and Roman art forms, outstanding for their symmetry and simple grandeur.

Since the arts of ancient Greece and Rome are termed "Classical," the eighteenth-century interest in these art forms is sometimes called "Neoclassicism" ("new" or revived Classicism). Architects, painters, and sculptors made direct use of Classical ideas. Buildings resembling those of ancient Greece and Rome sprang up in England and France, and even in the American colonies. Thomas Jefferson, when ambassador to France, traveled through Italy, gaining from Classical models inspiration that he would later use in the designs of Monticello and the University of Virginia. The architect Jacques Gabriel Ange made Classical additions to the palace of Versailles. The painter Jacques Louis David chose Greek philosopher Socrates and Roman statesman Brutus as subjects. The classic ideals of reason and proportion were the ideals of the age.

In music, however, there was little to revive. Although our knowledge of Greek music theory is extensive, few examples of actual music have survived, and we have no idea how even these few pieces sounded in their own time. For this reason, the musical style that coincided with the Neoclassic revival is today called Classical rather than Neoclassical. The music is related only in spirit to ancient art. "Serenity, repose, grace, the characteristics of the antique works of art, are also those of Mozart's school," wrote Robert Schumann, a nineteenth-century composer who admired the Classical style.

In both the art and the music of the Classical age, a high degree of order and symmetry is readily seen. This order and relative predictability says much about the taste of the people in the second half of the eighteenth century. However, the Neoclassical revival was a brief one—almost a fad. And the rational order of the period was in many ways illusory. The industrial and political revolutions of the time were soon to belie the social and cultural tenets of the Age of Reason.

The Emergence of the Classical Style in Music

Bach's Sons

Every so often a generation inherits an art form so fully developed, a style so richly articulated, that it seems as if nothing new need be said. A predicament very like this faced the sons of Johann Sebastian Bach, three of whom were composers in their own right. Wilhelm Friedemann Bach, Carl Philipp Emanuel Bach, and Johann Christian Bach had seen in their father's works the fullest achievement of the Baroque. They might also have recognized elements in the work of less-gifted contemporaries that were inevitably to bring the style to its demise. In fact, by the middle of the eighteenth century, the mature Baroque style had begun to fall from popularity. It was criticized for its extravagance and for its self-serving sophistication. Even the elder Bach was criticized at times for not having written in a simpler, more natural idiom. There had been a general change in sensibility, and with it came a demand for a new means of expression.

Rococo Style

This change was not confined to musical taste but, rather, represented a growing rejection of court society and the arts that it had favored. The late Baroque, especially that part of it known as the Rococo, had gloried in the ornamental, the pretty, the pleasantly artificial. Artisans carved innumerable scrolls on the arms and legs of ordinary furniture. Painters put cherubs in the corners of ceilings and sea-shell designs in the moldings. So, too, did musicians improvise decorations at every performance. Many composers left their melodic lines bare to accommodate these playful ornamentations. Music, like the other arts of the period, sought to imitate and entertain. The audience was to be charmed rather than moved deeply. In some ways, the Rococo music of the early eighteenth century can be seen as a transitional stage. Based on Baroque principles, the music departed from the Baroque in its extreme emphasis on elegant ornamentation. The works of French composer Couperin provide numerous examples of the style.

C. P. E. Bach

Empfindsamer Stil

Around the middle of the eighteenth century, Carl Philipp Emanuel Bach (1714–1788) played an important part in the creation of a new style, which came to be known as the "expressive style," or *Empfindsamer Stil*. The new style rejected the polyphonic complexities of the Baroque in an attempt to present emotions more freely. It permitted the expression of a variety of moods within a single movement, introducing different themes with corresponding harmonic and rhythmic changes. Thus there evolved a series of changes in the musical language of the mid-eighteenth century.

The music that developed from the Empfindsamer Stil, the music of the early Classical period, was simple and disarmingly original. Composers found themselves with new expressive tools and considerable freedom to use them in new ways. They were encouraged to use dynamic effects as never before. They were free to experiment with rhythmic contrasts and develop highly original melodies. Yet, even with all these new freedoms, the aim was to write simple, well-proportioned works. Composers recognized the fact that they must discipline their material and shape each work into an ordered, unified whole.

Attitudes toward the new music varied greatly. By some the composers in the new style were hailed as "romantics," people of great and noble sentiment. By others they were taunted for the easy tears their melodies provoked and for the part they were playing in the breakdown of the old Baroque order. Haydn, the first great figure of the new age, was described by one of his elders as a mere "scribbler of songs." It seemed to some that romantic musing was replacing three hundred years of solid polyphonic tradition.

When we listen to the works of the new composers—C. P. E. Bach, Haydn, and Mozart—we cannot help but feel historically removed from their audiences. To us the music sounds like the epitome of reason, not of sentiment. It is full of wit, grace, and balance. The composers are not those whom we would call "romantic." In fact, the term "Romantic" is now used to refer to a later generation—composers such as Chopin and Liszt, who seemingly rebelled against the very style now under discussion. What this suggests is that the terms used to describe music are historical rather than absolute. In order to understand them, we must know the history behind the terms.

As has been noted, the musical style that succeeded the Baroque, the style now called Classical, began to emerge in the middle of the eighteenth century. But it was not called Classical until the nineteenth century when it, too, was replaced by a movement more romantic than itself. Suddenly composers such as Haydn and Mozart had to be distinguished from those who continued their tradition in a more passionate vein. Over the years, there had been a gradual increase in experimentation. Composers began to use musical language in increasingly personal ways. By the nineteenth century, the Classical style had become more flexible, intense, and "romantic." The style that finally emerged—the Romantic style—was not a revolt against the Classical style but

Classical-Romantic Continuum

rather an expansion of it. It is thus possible to speak of a *Classical-Romantic continuum*, with order at one end and subjectivism at the other:

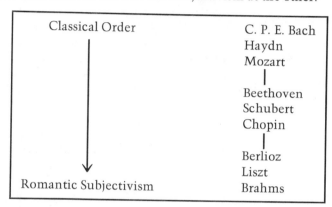

Classical Order

C. P. E. Bach
Haydn
Mozart

Beethoven
Schubert
Chopin

Berlioz
Liszt
Brahms

Romantic Subjectivism

Only after the Classical style had been superseded by the Romantic did it become common to speak of a "classic" beauty, an earlier standard of excellence against which the art of music could be measured. This standard is found in the works of Haydn, Mozart, and the early works of Beethoven.

Melody and Rhythm in Classical Music

In the Classical age, melody took on a dominant role in both instrumental and vocal music. When we recall a Classical work, it is usually the main melody—or theme—that we remember first. New emphasis came to be placed on the originality and expressive nature of melody. Composers often used melody as a means of conveying mood. They might use a disjunct melody to enhance the dramatic sense of a fast movement. A conjunct melody might be used to bring a sweet composure to the slow movement that followed. The emotional potential of melody was widely explored.

The significance of this change may be seen by comparing the Classical and Baroque styles. Many Baroque melodies were made up of the repetition of small melodic patterns or motives. The challenge to the composer, particularly in polyphonic instrumental music, lay not simply in the creation of a melodic line but as much in the arrangement of several lines, layer upon layer. The horizontal independence of the different parts meant that each part had its own upward and downward movements. The melodic climaxes of the several parts did not always coincide. In the music of the Classical period, however, there was much more likely to be a single melodic line that could clearly be felt to rise and fall.

Classical music also differed from that of the Baroque in its linear organization of melodic material. One of the forces that gives a Classical work its sense of unity is, oddly enough, the way it is divided. The polyphonic works of the Baroque age strove for continuous momentum—for a smooth, uninterrupted flow. In many cases, the music seemed to lack a clear articulation into phrases, partly because as one vocal or instrumental part came to the end of a melodic line another would often begin the same line or a similar line. With Classical music, however, regular phrases appear, and a fine sense of proportion is cultivated. In Classical music, as in simple folk songs, melody is organized into regularly recurring phrases.

Phrase Structure

A phrase is a short segment of melody (comparable to a line of poetry) that progresses toward a temporary pause or conclusion. "Twinkle, Twinkle, Little Star," which was well known in the late eighteenth century as "Ah, vous dirais-je, Maman," begins with two phrases that exactly balance one another:

The first movement of Mozart's *Symphony No. 40 in G Minor* also begins with two balanced phrases, the second of which complements or answers the first:

Moreover, each phrase is made up of three presentations of the same rhythmic motive.

The organization of music into phrases that are clearly heard is one of the chief characteristics of the Classical style. At the beginning of the period, phrases were often patterned closely on folk songs. They were generally four measures long, following the typical folk-song pattern. As compositions became more sophisticated, the length was varied. Mozart's phrases are often irregular, but they are carefully proportioned to the needs of the composition.

The changes in the use of melody and phrase structure in the Classical period could hardly fail to bring about changes in the use of rhythm. Baroque music seemed almost to propel itself, evenly and continuously. Seldom were there any marked changes in the overall rhythmic pattern. In a Classical work, however, the phrase structure punctuates the melody, resulting in a rhythmic variety much greater than that found in Baroque music.

Rhythmic Variety

CLASSICAL MUSIC

Classical Architecture: *The early nineteenth-century church of La Madeleine in Paris bears a remarkable yet somewhat superficial resemblance to the Parthenon in Athens. The number of exterior columns in the two buildings is exactly the same, but the style is different. The Parisian church, commissioned by Napoleon, is also almost half again as large as its Greek model.*

In addition, the new prominence of melody encouraged a reassignment of rhythmic chores. While all the different parts in the polyphonic music of the Baroque age helped to generate the rhythmic impulse, Classical music could afford the luxury of one part that was primarily melodic. Thus, in the music of the Classical period, we hear a melodic line in which the rhythm is variable, often supported by a more regular accompaniment. The rhythms of the melody could play against the more steady metrical accompaniment, adding to the expressiveness of the piece. An example of this kind of interplay can be heard in a song from a later period: "When Johnny Comes Marching Home." The rhythms of the melody can easily be distinguished from the regular march meter beneath it.

The use of rhythm in Classical music was also influenced by the tendency to show contrasting moods within a work or movement. Often more than one type of rhythmic activity would be used. There might, for example, be a change in tempo or contrasts between active and calm passages.

Despite this rhythmic variety, the music of the Classical period is generally characterized by steady meter and a regularly recurring pulse. At the

INTRODUCTION TO CLASSICAL MUSIC

same time, however, a gradual trend toward more varied and complex rhythms and more experiments in meter can be seen.

Classical Harmony and Texture

Harmony is the structural basis of Classical music. While specific harmonic relationships had become increasingly important in the Baroque period, they took on even greater importance in the Classical period. In the latter period, the structural use of harmony was a fundamental part of almost all long works.

An earlier discussion concerned the harmonic uses of three important triads: the I, V, and IV chords, based respectively on the first, fifth, and fourth tones of the scale. Of these the I and V chords are the most important. The V chord, particularly when heard at the end of a composition, produces in the listener a strong anticipation of the I chord. In the musical language of the Baroque and Classical periods, this was seen as an expressive struggle between the I and V chords. The V chord introduces tension, which the I chord resolves.

This pattern can be seen in numerous Classical melodies. However, for purposes of illustration, it is perhaps best seen in popular songs such as the American folk song below. The I and V chords alone are enough to provide harmonic accompaniment.

> I   I I   I   V
> Down in the val-ley, the valley so low————
>
> V   V V V   I
> Hear the wind whis-per, hear the wind blow————

Note that the I and V chords are balanced or organized in what appears to be a pattern. The song begins and ends with the I chord; the music in the middle is accompanied by the V chord. This harmonic organization helps give the piece a feeling of beginning, middle, and end.

If, in singing "Down in the Valley," we were to choose the note C for our tonic, we would be singing in the key of C major. A move from the I chord to the V chord in this key is simply a move from the triad beginning on C to the triad beginning on G:

I and V Chords in C Major

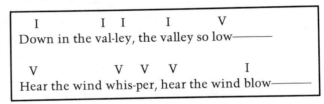

1   2   3   4   5   6   7   8

Within the composition, the move from the I to the V chord will be perceived as a movement from a stable "home" position to a position of conflict or insecurity.

The feeling of stability or conflict produced by individual triads depends on the key. Suppose, for example, that we had chosen not C but G as our tonic, in order to sing the melody at a higher pitch. We would be in the key of G major. The I chord would begin on G, and the V chord would begin on D:

I and V Chords in G Major

In this case, the triad beginning on G would give a feeling of stable home position. The triad beginning on D would introduce conflict.

Use of Modulation

The I–V–I pattern is often enough to provide harmonic structure for a brief song such as "Down in the Valley." However, it would soon prove boring in a longer work. Imagine instead that the music moved from the key of C major to the key of G major and then back to the key of C major. In many longer compositions of the Classical period, there is just such a movement. If the beginning of a composition is in the key of C major, the middle part is likely to be in the key of G major. The final part will generally return to the key of C major just as a melodic line generally returns to the tonic. The effect is much the same—a feeling of finality. The use of key changes, or modulation, already seen in the Baroque period when major-minor harmony was developing, was of prime importance to the Classical composer.

A question that logically arises upon first consideration of key change is this: how do we know that the music has really modulated to a different key? How do we know, for example, that it has modulated all the way from the key of C major to the key of G major rather than simply moved from the I chord to the V chord of the key of C?

The answer is that when the music modulates from one key to another, new tones are introduced. The seven notes in the key of C major are not exactly the same as the seven notes in the key of G major. Different keys select different tones from the twelve tones that exist in Western music—the twelve tones of the chromatic scale.

We can see why this is so by examining the scales of C major and G major on the piano keyboard. First, look at the scale of C major:

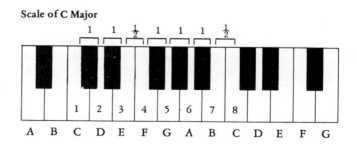

Scale of C Major

Each of the keys on the piano, whether black or white, is exactly one half tone higher than the key on its left. Thus, it is a half step from C to C♯, from C♯ to D, and from E to F. It's a whole step from C to D and from E to F♯. In the scale of C major, there are whole steps between most of the notes. Half steps fall between tones 3 and 4 and between tones 7 and 8.

Every major scale has the same pattern of whole and half steps. The half steps always fall after the third and seventh notes. The piano is basically "in the key of C," which means that it is built to play the C major scale without any black keys. In all other major scales the pattern of whole and half steps can be followed only if one or more black keys are used. In the G major scale, for example, a black key will be needed for the seventh note of the scale:

Scale of G Major

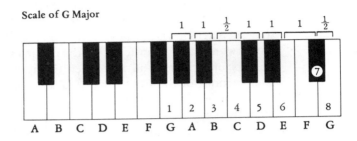

As noted in Chapter 5, the use of black keys is shown by the sharp or flat signs in the key signature:

Related Keys

Clearly the key of G major, with only one sharp, is more similar to the key of C major than is the key of E major, which has four sharps, or the key of D♭ major, which has five flats, or any other key with more than one note change. The notes of the closely related keys of C and G major are exactly alike except for the F♯. Thus, when music modulates from C major to G major, only one note changes. If, however, the music were to move from the key of C major to that of E major, more than half the notes would be new. It would present somewhat of a shock to our ears if a composer did this directly. Generally such a change will not be direct. Instead it will be made by passing through a series of related keys.

In Classical music, modulation from the original or home key to a key based on the dominant tone of the original key becomes an ever-present dramatic force. Often the modulation is gradual, beginning with the first phrase but not firmly established until the end of a movement. Sometimes it is abrupt and witty, as in some of Haydn's surprise effects. Like rhythm, modulation became more daring and experimental in the later Classical period, with more striking and more frequent changes, often between unrelated keys.

Minor Keys

The patterns of whole and half steps in the keys of C and G major are exactly the same. The same pattern is used for all the keys of the major mode. A different arrangement of half and whole steps is used in the minor mode. The character of the major mode, and of music based on it, is generally considered "bright," while that of the minor mode is ordinarily thought more somber. The minor keys thus offer composers additional choices for modulation and tonal contrast.

In actuality there are several forms of the minor mode. All of them begin the same, with a half step between tones 2 and 3 rather than between tones 3 and 4 as in the major mode. In the key of C minor, for example, the third tone is E♭ rather than E. (*Minor*, Latin for "smaller," refers to the fact that the distance between the first and third tones is shorter in the minor scale than in the major.) A minor scale may also have a half step between tones 5 and 6 and a whole step between tones 7 and 8, depending on melodic context.

At most, the C minor scale can have three flats:

C Minor

Relative Majors and Minors

Its key signature is also the key signature for the key of E♭ major. For this reason E♭ major is said to be the *relative major* of C minor. Likewise, C minor is the *relative minor* of E♭ major. This means that the two keys are closely related and that their relationship can be exploited through modulation. A work might begin in C minor, modulate to E♭ major, and return to C minor. This often happens in Classical music. If a movement opens in a major key, it is likely to modulate to a major key based on its dominant. But if it opens in a minor key, it is likely to modulate to the relative major. In the latter case, there may be a change of mood since the minor has a characteristically sad or wistful effect that can be effectively contrasted with the brighter major key.

Changes in Texture

Along with the increasing use of modulation came changes in musical texture. As the Classical style emerged in the mid-eighteenth century, the texture of music tended to be homophonic and less complex than before. In the late eighteenth and early nineteenth centuries, however, when musical forms grew longer and more elaborate, counterpoint began to be used somewhat more often, although music remained basically homophonic. In many cases, homophonic and contrapuntal textures were used in the same composition or movement. The juxtaposition was important in achieving contrast and variety. While sparse textures were often characteristic of music for solo instruments, the expanding orchestra was capable of producing increasingly dense textures.

Classical Timbre and Dynamics

Classical Orchestra

The Classical period saw the standardization of the orchestra as we know it today. The usually modest instrumental groups of the Baroque age were surpassed by orchestras of ever-increasing size. By the late eighteenth century, orchestras generally had between thirty and fifty players. The orchestra was dominated by the string section. The woodwind section usually included two flutes, two oboes, two bassoons, and, by the end of the century, the newly developed clarinet. The brass section was generally made up of two trumpets

A Classical Orchestra: *Not all Classical orchestras were as large as the one at Mannheim. The late eighteenth-century orchestra above has only about twenty performers. The predominance of strings, however, is typical, as is the fact that the conductor is leading the group from a keyboard instrument.*

and two horns, and the percussion section generally had two timpani. The basso continuo of Baroque times gradually passed out of use.

Stamitz

One of the largest and most famous of the early Classical orchestras developed at the German court of Mannheim, under the leadership of Johann Stamitz (1717–1757), a talented violinist and composer. All who heard the orchestra were awed by its size and discipline. Especially impressive was its mastery of dynamic effects. The Mannheim orchestra is sometimes credited with having created the crescendo, but it can more accurately be described as the first group to have shown what a strong effect a controlled increase of volume could have on an audience. Equally fine, if less spectacular, was the orchestra's performance of both sudden and sustained decrescendos. The ensemble playing of the Mannheim orchestra impressed many, including Mozart.

The modern symphony orchestra is somewhat larger than that of the Classical age, but the balance of instrumentation is very similar to that found in the earlier orchestra. The plan on page 157 shows the arrangement that would likely be used by a modern orchestra playing a symphony by Haydn or Mozart. The same instruments, although fewer of them, would have been used in a late eighteenth-century performance.

Coincident with the development of the Classical orchestra was the rise in prominence of the piano. Invented in 1709 in Italy, it was originally called

CLASSICAL MUSIC

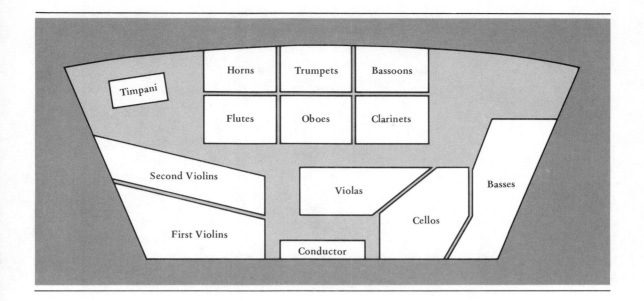

Pianoforte

the *pianoforte*. The pianist, unlike the harpsichordist, could vary the dynamic level of individual notes and chords. Thus sforzandos, crescendos, and decrescendos could be produced at will. The piano gradually replaced the harpsichord as the favorite keyboard instrument.

Vocal music continued to be important in the late eighteenth century, though instrumental music seems generally to have received greater attention from composers. Music for solo voices and choirs was written by nearly all composers of the period.

Types of Compositions and Form in the Classical Age

In the Classical period, a number of highly stylized types of music developed. Instrumental music became even more prominent than it had been in the Baroque age. *Sonatas* were written for all available instruments. Other types of chamber music were written for many different combinations of instruments, with the *string quartet* by far the most popular work for chamber ensemble. The *solo concerto* was very popular, as was a new type of composition, the *symphony*. Vocal music of the period included *songs, operas, Masses,* and *oratorios.*

Sonata Cycle

Particularly characteristic of Classical instrumental music was the so-called *sonata cycle*, a sequence of three or four movements, each cast in a specific form. A number of important Classical works are sonata cycles: the sonata for piano, the symphony for orchestra, the concerto for soloist and orchestra, and many small ensemble works such as the string quartet. All have the typical three or four movements cast in a variety of similar or different forms.

Comparison of Baroque and Classical Music

Elements	Baroque Music c.1600–c.1750	Classical Music c.1750–c.1815
Melody	Frequent ornamentation Much use of sequence Phrase structure not always clear	Melodies built on motives and short phrases Phrases often very regular in length
Rhythm	Free rhythm in recitative Steady, driving rhythms and clear meters in many works	Continued use of free rhythm in recitative Clear meters Greater rhythmic variety
Harmony	Major-minor system Use of modulation	Major-minor system Increased use of modulation as structural basis
Texture	Polyphony, often imitative, important in many works Homophony also used frequently	Homophony most important but continued use of polyphony, often within basically homophonic works Imitative counterpoint less important than before
Timbre	Instrumental and vocal music both important Small orchestra, with continuo	Instrumental music more prominent than vocal Larger, more standardized orchestra, without continuo
Important Forms	Binary, ternary, ritornello, and fugue Development of many multi-movement works	Sonata, rondo, theme and variations, ternary, and binary Many multi-movement works
Important Types of Compositions	Older types such as the Mass and motet New types such as opera, cantata, oratorio, sonata, concerto, fugue, and suite	Older types such as the Mass, oratorio, opera, solo concerto, and un-accompanied sonata Many instrumental works based on sonata cycle: symphony, concerto, sonata, and string quartet

Sonata Form

The sonata cycle should not be confused with the sonata, a work for one or a few instruments, or with the *sonata form*, a newly developed musical form. Sometimes called the *sonata-allegro form*, the sonata form provides an elaborate and lively structure for individual movements of sonata-cycle works. It was generally used as the form of the first movement and sometimes for other movements as well. The sonata form is divided into three basic sections: the exposition, the development, and the recapitulation.

Exposition

Bridge

The *exposition*, or opening section, of a movement written in the sonata form "exposes" the first theme in the home key. After the listener becomes familiar with this primary material, a harmonic transition, or *bridge* passage, takes place. The music modulates to a contrasting key—generally to the key of the dominant or, if the first theme is in a minor key, to the relative major. In the contrasting key, new material may be presented—perhaps several themes, unified mainly by the fact that they are cast in the same key. In some cases, however, the first theme reappears immediately after the bridge and is then followed by a second theme. The exposition closes with a cadence in the second key. Generally the entire exposition is repeated so that the initial musical ideas are heard again. The repetition is indicated by the sign :‖ at the end of the section.

Development

In the *development* section, the thematic material of the exposition undergoes a number of changes and musical excitement increases. New and sometimes distant keys are explored with frequent modulations. The themes of the exposition are presented in new ways. They may be broken into motives and recombined, with alterations in timbre, harmony, rhythm, or dynamics. Momentum and intensity generally increase throughout the section.

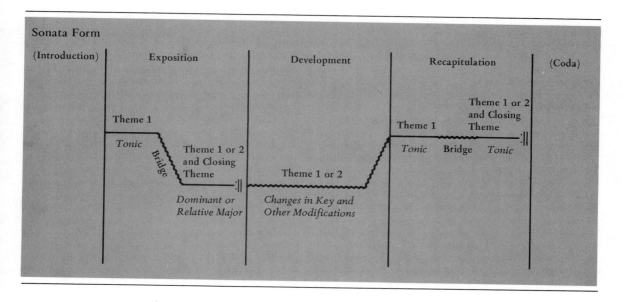

Sonata Form

INTRODUCTION TO CLASSICAL MUSIC

Recapitulation

Tension is pleasurably resolved in the final section, the *recapitulation*, with a return to the home key and the first theme. Although the section does present a thematic rerun, or recapitulation, of the exposition, it is not identical to the exposition. While the same thematic material is presented, the recapitulation lacks the excitement of a key change. In this final section, no contrasting key is firmly established. Though brief excursions to another key may take place, all themes from the exposition are usually played in the home key. At the end of the recapitulation, the development and recapitulation are sometimes played a second time, as a unit.

Coda

Some movements in the sonata form are preceded by a slow introduction of contrasting character. And some are concluded with a *coda* that affirms or reaffirms the ending.

Any description of the sonata form is a result of generalizations about compositions already written. Descriptions can merely attempt to capture in words the characteristics of this important Classical form. Individual composers naturally deviated from the model, being more concerned with the immediate expression of musical ideas than with matters of form. Although a general pattern was followed, no two works are exactly alike in form. The form grew out of the material, as is always the case in a living, changing style.

Rondo Form

The *rondo form* was also much used by Classical composers. In the rondo form, a primary theme, which always appears in the tonic, alternates with two or more themes of secondary importance, which are in different keys. Thus, a typical rondo form might be diagramed in this fashion:

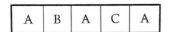

The rondo form differs from the Baroque ritornello form in a number of ways. Perhaps most important is the fact that in the rondo form the first theme always reappears in the tonic, while in the ritornello form it may return in other keys. Partly for this reason, the contrasting sections are more obvious in the rondo form.

Other Forms

Two other forms used in many Classical works are the theme and variations form and the ternary form. Both are somewhat simpler than either the sonata form or the rondo form.

The binary form was also used upon occasion. The ritornello and fugal forms of the Baroque age, however, gradually faded from the importance they had once held.

13

The Classical Symphony: Haydn and Mozart

Development of the Classical Symphony

Antecedents of the Symphony

The *symphony* of the late eighteenth century drew upon, and was influenced by, a number of earlier musical developments. The three-part Italian overture of the Baroque age suggested the overall fast—slow—fast plan of movements. The Baroque suite provided the concept of independent movements within a large work, as well as the minuet, a compositional form often chosen for the symphony's third movement. The binary form, which had been used in many Baroque sonatas, played an important part in the development of the sonata form of the Classical age—the form on which the first movement of most symphonies was based. These and other subtler influences were important in the development of the Classical symphony—a sonata cycle for orchestra.

Haydn

The orchestra and the symphony were both undergoing significant development in many different parts of mid-eighteenth-century Europe; Mannheim, Berlin, and Vienna were among the most prominent centers of activity. But it is in the works of Franz Josef Haydn (1732–1809), a major pioneer of the Classical style, that the growth of the symphony from a short work of simple style to a longer, more sophisticated work can most clearly be seen. Many of his symphonies are quite light and simple in style; others are considerably more serious. Many were written for the diversion of a small circle of aristocrats rather than for the general public. What is perhaps more surprising is the great number of Haydn's symphonies—he wrote more than one hundred and four. Most later composers wrote fewer than ten.

Structure of the Symphony

While some of Haydn's early symphonies have only three movements, four movements soon became the standard number. The tempos of the four movements were generally fast, slow, moderate, and fast. The first movement of Haydn's mature works, and of symphonies written by his contemporaries, was in sonata form, sometimes preceded by a slow introduction. The second movement was generally in binary or sonata form but sometimes in theme and variations form. The third movement was usually a stylized *minuet and trio* in

Minuet and Trio

ternary form. The last movement was generally in sonata or rondo form but sometimes in a sonata-rondo form that combined features of both forms.

Haydn's Symphonies

In 1761 Haydn became assistant music director at the Esterházy estate in Hungary. He served first under the patronage of Prince Paul Anton Esterházy and later under that of his brother Prince Nikolaus. Because the principal music director was old, Haydn took over the direction of his patron's orchestra. His duties were broad and varied, including the administration of the musicians' salaries and wardrobes as well as the supervision of their moral behavior. But, more important, Haydn was expected to write music—a great deal of music—for the many social events at the Esterházy palace.

The Patronage System

In eighteenth-century society, Haydn's position was really no more prestigious than that of a gardener, housekeeper, or other skilled servant. And yet it offered a number of real advantages. Haydn had at his command an excellent group of singers and players. He had the use of fine musical facilities, including an opera house. Because of the patronage system, he enjoyed economic security in a time when the financial position of the artist was otherwise precarious. Of course, the advantages could be outweighed by disadvantages if patron and composer had incompatible ideas about music. In

The First Great Master of Classical Music: *Haydn is shown here, at the keyboard, conducting the Esterházy orchestra. The Esterházys were among the most influential families in the Austrian Empire, and their position is likely to have played a large role in the dissemination of Haydn's music and stylistic innovations.*

The Bettmann Archive

this regard, Haydn was in many ways quite fortunate to be working for the Esterházy family—patrons who expected him to compose works in the latest style.

The compositions Haydn wrote for the Esterházys were quite original. He was a champion of new forms, an innovator in modulation, the acknowledged master of surprise, and yet his music was both logical and coherent. Early attempts at fresh melody, harmony, and phrasing developed under Haydn into the perfect balance of the Classical style.

Haydn's music drew on the folk songs of his native Austria and on the dance music of the Baroque. He was one of the first composers to develop themes in the Classical sense and to exploit the enormous power of modulation and changes of tonality for dramatic purposes. Perhaps his greatest contribution to the history of music was, as Classical-music scholar Charles Rosen has suggested, his recognition that "the dramatic course of a work . . . can be found latent in the material, that musical material can be made to release its charged force, so that music no longer unfolds as in the Baroque, but is literally impelled from within." Haydn and his contemporaries were somehow able to imply the dramatic development of an entire work in the musical relationships of its opening phrases.

The London Symphonies

The height of Haydn's symphonic art is nowhere more apparent than in his *Symphonies No. 92–104*, written not for the Esterházys but for British impresario Johann Peter Salomon. In 1791 Haydn, already well known throughout Europe, was commissioned by Salomon to write and conduct a series of "London Symphonies." At this point in his career, Haydn had gained a degree of freedom from the Esterházys and had moved to Vienna. There he had been in contact with Mozart and the young Beethoven. Clearly he was the master of an important new style of music, a status that accounted for Salomon's gratifying offer. And yet Haydn was not insensible to the beauty of Baroque music. Upon hearing the London orchestra (the orchestra that was to present his new works to the world) in a performance of the works of past masters, he was deeply moved. "Handel is the master of us all," he is reported to have said. It was not by chance that after he left London he devoted his last years to sacred music, notably *The Creation*, an oratorio that is still frequently performed. The English visits were as important to Haydn's later development as the Esterházy experience was to his middle years.

Haydn: *Symphony No. 94 in G Major* ("Surprise" Symphony)

Haydn's *Symphony No. 94 in G Major* was first performed in London, on March 23, 1792. It was an immediate success—especially the second movement, which included the "surprise" that gave the work its name. The *London Diary* called it "simple and profound," the highest kind of praise for a work in the Classical spirit. In our own time, the symphony continues to be widely appreciated and often performed.

First Movement: Adagio cantabile; Vivace assai; in Sonata Form

Introduction

The first movement opens with an introduction that readily evokes a pastoral setting—a sense of peaceful countryside that is never long absent from Haydn's music. The introduction is marked Adagio cantabile (slow, in a singing style) and is scored for woodwinds and violins.

Exposition

The sunny tone of the introduction turns thoughtful just before the exposition, which is in the home key of G major. The first theme, marked Vivace assai (very, very fast), is a vivacious, folklike melody introduced by the first violins.

First Theme

The final note in the theme is marked *forte* ("loud"). At this point the violins are joined by the full orchestra, which presents a loud rhythmic pattern in the lower register: /‿ ‿/‿ ‿/. This rhythmic pattern, accompanied by a whirling figure in the violins, has a generally rousing effect.

The music moves toward a repeat of the first theme with a delightful prefatory phrase that will be heard many times in the movement:

Prefatory Phrase

First Theme

After this phrase, just before the return of the first theme, the orchestra comes to a full stop.

When the first theme reappears in the violins, it is again followed by the full orchestra. But this time the triple rhythmic pattern and the theme are somewhat different. They are part of a bridge passage by which the music modulates to a new key—that of the dominant, D major.

After the new key is established, a quick series of scale passages is played by the violins and flutes. The second theme is then heard. It is marked *dolce* ("sweet") and is somewhat more lyrical than the first. The large-interval dips in the later measures have an especially pleasing effect.

Second Theme

CLASSICAL MUSIC

The exposition closes with a short scale figure and repeated notes. Haydn indicated that the exposition should then be repeated.

Development

The development section opens with a variation of the first theme:

Variation of First Theme

A series of modulations and dynamic changes help to create the dramatic tension so characteristic of development sections. Scales, arpeggios, and repeated notes are all heard in turn as familiar musical ideas reappear in a new context.

Recapitulation

The recapitulation begins with the first theme returning clearly in the home key. After a bridge passage based largely on scales, the first theme returns again and is momentarily developed. The second theme then returns briefly, also in the home key. The movement comes to a close with a short scale passage and a strong, repeated cadence.

Side 4, Band 1

Listening Guide for Haydn's *Symphony No. 94,* First Movement

Timbre:	orchestra of moderate size: string instruments, wind instruments, and timpani
Melody:	first theme largely conjunct; second theme more lyrical but less distinctive
Rhythm:	introduction in duple meter, tempo Adagio cantabile (slow, singing style); rest of movement in $\frac{6}{8}$ meter, tempo Vivace assai (very, very fast)
Harmony:	mainly major mode; begins in G major, modulates most significantly to D major, ends in G major
Texture:	mainly homophonic with some counterpoint
Form:	sonata form preceded by slow introduction

Second Movement: Andante; in Theme and Variations Form

The second movement of the "Surprise" Symphony is marked Andante (moderate) in contrast to the very quick tempo of the first movement. There is also a dynamic contrast between the vigorous final chords of the first movement and the first notes of the second movement, which are marked *piano* ("soft"). Finally, the second movement is in C major, providing a tonal contrast to the first movement in G major.

Theme

It was the second movement that immediately charmed London audiences with its use of a beautifully simple theme in a masterful theme and variations form. The first phrase of the theme is built mainly of triads. The first

THE CLASSICAL SYMPHONY: HAYDN AND MOZART

motive, in fact, uses nothing but the I chord (1–3–5) of the key of C. The second motive is based, as might be expected, on a version of the V chord (5–7–2).

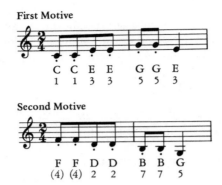

First Motive

C	C	E	E		G	G	E
1	1	3	3		5	5	3

Second Motive

F	F	D	D		B	B	G
(4)	(4)	2	2		7	7	5

The rest of the theme is nearly as simple. The first two phrases, each four measures long, are shown below. Note that the second phrase begins like the first but ends differently. The last note of each phrase, however, is the same —the dominant. The phrases are labeled a^1 and a^2 because they begin so similarly.

Phrases a^1 and a^2

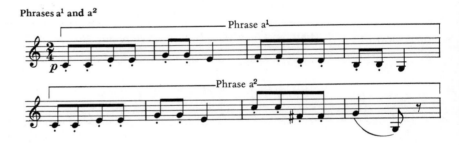

Phrase a^1

Phrase a^2

These phrases are first played softly by the violins. They are then repeated, even more softly. It is at the end of this repetition that the famous *ff* chord is heard. The chord is a V chord that needs to be resolved or answered, and it is indeed answered, in perfect balance, by another sixteen measures. Like the first sixteen measures, these are made up of two four-measure phrases played twice. The answering phrases are shown below, slightly simplified.

Phrases b and c

Phrase b

Phrase c

Note that the last phrase ends on the tonic note C, conveying a sense of finality and rest.

The theme then is made up of eight phrases arranged in the following order:

a^1	a^2	a^1	a^2	b	c	b	c
16 measures ending on the dominant				16 measures ending on the tonic			

Variations

From this simple material, Haydn created a series of delightful variations. In the first variation, the second violins play the theme. After they complete the first motive, the first violins enter lightly with a countermelody. The quick, conjunct notes of the countermelody are full of Classical charm and grace.

This part of the variation, the first half of the theme, is repeated. Then phrases b and c, the second half of the theme, are presented, also with a countermelody in the first violins.

In the second variation, the music moves to the key of C minor. The theme is boldly presented by the woodwinds and strings without any harmony or elaboration. The use of the minor adds greatly to the dramatic effect.

THE CLASSICAL SYMPHONY: HAYDN AND MOZART

As the variation unfolds, the first half of the theme undergoes substantial change, including modulation to a major key. It is then repeated. The second half of the theme does not appear at all in this variation. Instead, there is additional development of the first phrase. A unison passage then leads to the next variation without pause.

The major mode is firmly reestablished at the beginning of the third variation. This variation presents the theme in a new 2:1 rhythm—two notes are played for every one note in the original theme.

Variation 3

The repeat of Phrase a¹ is accompanied by a countermelody in the flute and oboe. Sometimes paralleling the movement of the theme, sometimes departing from it, this countermelody has a colorful, lilting effect. The second half of the theme then appears in varied form and is repeated.

In the fourth variation, the music generates an excitement that propels the movement to its close. The variation starts with a 3:1 rhythm, with three notes for every one note of the original theme. If you think "ONE-two-three" for every note of the theme, you can reproduce this rhythmic effect for yourself:

Variation 4

1-2-3 1-2-3 1-2-3 1-2-3   1-2-3 1-2-3 1-2-3 1-2-3

As the theme is played to this rhythm, it undergoes additional changes. Most notably in the opening phrase of the variation, *ff* chords are sounded on normally weak beats. Then, suddenly, a new variation of the first part of the theme is heard. The original melody is recast in an uneven *dotted rhythm* to produce an interesting new effect.

Use of Dotted Rhythm

Additional Variation of Theme in Variation 4

p dolce

What were formerly two notes of the same pitch and duration have become two notes of different pitch and unequal duration, and yet the theme remains recognizable. The second half of the theme is presented more dramatically, first with a 2:1 rhythm and then with a 3:1 rhythm.

Coda

The movement ends with a coda that is a work of art in itself. It consists of an extension of the fourth variation and a phrase from the theme. The treatment of this material produces a feeling of considerable suspense followed by resolution.

Side 4, Band 2

Listening Guide for Haydn's *Symphony No. 94,* Second Movement

Timbre:	orchestra of moderate size: string instruments, wind instruments, and timpani
Melody:	disjunct; phrase structure very symmetrical
Rhythm:	duple meter; tempo Andante (moderate); use of 2:1, 3:1, and dotted rhythms
Harmony:	mainly major mode; C major through most of the movement, C minor in the second variation
Texture:	mainly homophonic with some counterpoint
Form:	theme and variations (A - A^1 - A^2 - A^3 - A^4) followed by a coda

---

Third Movement: Allegro molto; Minuet and Trio in Ternary Form

Minuet

The third movement of the "Surprise" Symphony opens with a minuet that reflects the folk dances of the Austrian countryside. The music is strongly metrical, as is typical of most dances. The opening theme, in G major, is played by full orchestra:

Opening Theme

The triple meter and moderate to quick tempo are characteristic of the minuet.

The opening theme is followed by a short motive, first played by flute and violins. Then the motive is repeated, growing in volume as other instruments join in. The minuet is marked throughout by a great deal of playfulness and high spirits.

Trio

The minuet is followed by a short trio. Though the trio involves more than three instruments, it is not so fully orchestrated as the rest of the movement. Bassoon and violin share the presentation of a new theme.

Minuet

After the trio is completed, the minuet returns. Thus the movement is in typical minuet and trio form—a clear example of ternary form:

Section A	Section B	Section A
Minuet	Trio	Minuet

THE CLASSICAL SYMPHONY: HAYDN AND MOZART

Here and in the works of later composers, the court or country dance is transcended. It becomes idealized, not meant for actual dancing, except perhaps for that which takes place in the imagination of the listener.

Listening Guide for Haydn's *Symphony No. 94,* Third Movement

Timbre:	orchestra of moderate size: string instruments, wind instruments, and timpani
Melody:	minuet theme characterized by disjunct motion; trio theme more conjunct
Rhythm:	triple meter; tempo Allegro molto (very fast)
Harmony:	major mode; minuet and trio both begin in G major, modulate to D major, end in G major
Texture:	homophonic
Form:	ternary (ABA)

Fourth Movement: Allegro molto; in Sonata-Rondo form

Sonata-Rondo Form

The fourth movement, in G major, has characteristics of both the sonata and the rondo forms. Although the movement is basically in sonata form, the music frequently returns to the first theme in the tonic key—a return typical of works in rondo form. Haydn and his contemporaries are noted for combining aspects of sonata and rondo forms, particularly in the last movements of their symphonies.

Exposition

The tempo of the fourth movement is very fast, and the rhythm is at first quite dancelike in spirit. The first theme is full of impetuous energy. It is introduced by the first violins and then repeated by the first violins and the flutes:

First Theme

The passage that follows is more dramatic than melodic in character. A three-note motive is rapidly repeated and altered, with a resulting buildup of energy. The first part of the theme is then repeated with a different ending. After this, there is a bridge made up of a rapid scale passage in the violins accompanied by detached chords and repetition of the three-note motive heard earlier. The bridge establishes the contrasting key of D major. A lively second theme appears briefly in this new key, followed by excited scales and arpeggios in the violin.

Development

At the beginning of the development section, the first theme returns in the original key, thus suggesting the rondo form. The theme is then broken into motives, some of which recall motives that figured in the first movement of the symphony. Modulation, including changes from major to minor modes, occurs throughout the section. Development continues as the first theme returns again in G major, followed by a repetition in G minor:

First Theme in G Minor

Recapitulation

Coda

After the development section closes, a recapitulation of the first and second themes is heard in the home key. The movement ends with a brilliant coda. Its last measures offer yet one more surprise—a stark change in dynamic level, from soft to very loud.

Listening Guide for Haydn's *Symphony No. 94,* Fourth Movement

Timbre:	orchestra of moderate size: string instruments, wind instruments, and timpani
Melody:	first theme disjunct and conjunct, featuring repeated notes; second theme disjunct
Rhythm:	duple meter; tempo Allegro molto (very fast)
Harmony:	mainly major mode; begins in G major, modulates most significantly to D major, ends in G major
Texture:	mainly homophonic with some counterpoint
Form:	sonata-rondo followed by a coda

Mozart's Symphonies

It was probably in 1781, eleven years before the performance of the "Surprise" Symphony, that Haydn first met the young musician whom he later acknowledged as the greatest composer of his time: Wolfgang Amadeus Mozart (1756–1791). Though Mozart was quite young when they met, he had already done much to command the attention of serious musicians. He had been in the public eye since the age of six, when he performed with his father and sister at the court of Empress Maria Theresa of Austria. The career of this "boy genius" and his development in the later years of his short life represent another great chapter in the history of the Classical style.

Mozart was born into a very musical Austrian family. Like the young Bachs, he had a brilliant teacher in his father, Leopold Mozart, a court musician who devoted much of his time to the musical education of his son.

Early in his career, Mozart accepted a position as a court music director, and it seemed that he was destined to follow the path laid out by both his father and Haydn. However, the patronage system was ultimately to prove unbearable to him. This was partly because of his temperament and partly because historical changes created alternatives to this relationship.

From Child Prodigy to Acknowledged Master: *Although he failed to gain financial security and his works were not uniformly successful with the public, Mozart was acknowledged as a master of the Classical style by composers all over Europe. In this artist's impression, he is shown presiding over the performance of young Beethoven who in 1787 visited Vienna and sought out Mozart, to learn from him whatever he could.*

The Musician as a Public Artist

The Classical period coincided with the rise of a strong middle-class culture. No longer was music restricted to the Church or reserved for the aristocracy. By the end of the eighteenth century, it was possible for impresarios such as Salomon to arrange public concerts. It was at least theoretically possible for well-known composers to support themselves by giving concerts, teaching, accepting commissions, and publishing some of their own works. The commercial world could not, however, offer the security of the patronage system. Mozart's years as an independent artist—years in which he wrote several operas, a number of symphonies and concertos, and a great variety of chamber works—were marked by financial insecurity.

Mozart's earliest symphonies were, like Haydn's earliest symphonies, relatively short and simple. His later symphonies were much longer and more complex. It was during the summer of 1788, under great financial stress, that Mozart completed his last three symphonies, all of which have come to be regarded as masterpieces. They are generally referred to as *Symphony No. 39 in Eb Major, Symphony No. 40 in G Minor,* and *Symphony No. 41 in C Major.*

The last is also known as the "Jupiter" Symphony. These three symphonies show Mozart at the height of his achievement. All, especially *Symphony No. 40 in G Minor*, speak with an emotional urgency that is highly romantic. In fact, in Mozart's last works, the beginning of the movement toward the Romantic style can already be seen. The works have the order and control of the Classical age, but they seem to reach out with the passionate yearning of the Romantic style for what is beyond them.

Köchel

When Mozart died at the age of thirty-five, the scope of his work was neither known nor fully appreciated. It remained for a later musicographer, Ludwig von Köchel, to draw up a chronological list of Mozart's works so that later audiences could make reference to them. (Similar lists have been drawn up for other composers. After all, there may be a number of "Symphonies in C" written by any one composer.) Each of Mozart's compositions now bears a number from the Köchel list. The *Symphony No. 40*, for example, bears the designation "K. 550," or Köchel Number 550.

Mozart: *Symphony No. 40 in G Minor*, K. 550

The style of Mozart's mature symphonies, and indeed that of the late eighteenth century in general, is exemplified in the *Symphony No. 40 in G Minor*. No one work can be typical of all the work done by any one composer. Yet a number of general and specific characteristics of Mozart's late symphonies are beautifully evident in this work.

First Movement: Allegro molto; in Sonata Form

This symphony, the second of the three that Mozart wrote during the summer of 1788, is perhaps the most "romantic" of all of Mozart's symphonies. Nevertheless it is strictly Classical in its form and development. The drama of the entire symphony is somehow latent in the three-note motive at the beginning of the exposition:

Exposition

Opening Motive

Both the pitch and the rhythm of the motive are significant. The change in pitch—the interval between the first two notes—is very small. There is just the half step fall from E♭ to D. The rhythm also contributes to the sense of an abrupt fall. The short-short-long rhythm of two eighth notes followed by a quarter note combines with the tonal pattern to give a sense of a rapid fall onto the third note. In all its simplicity, this motive is the basis for the first theme and for much of the movement that follows.

The first theme is played by the violins above a soft, chordal accompaniment played by the lower strings. The accompaniment establishes the home key of G minor, while the theme itself hovers around the dominant and subdominant, never once coming to rest on the tonic. This accounts in part for the sense of mysterious agitation evoked by the music at the opening of the movement:

Phrases a and b

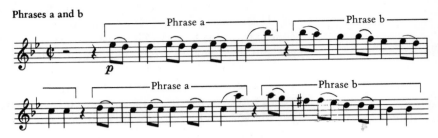

An examination of the phrases at the beginning of the movement shows that the third and fourth phrases repeat the first two—in sequence, one step lower. After this, a new, answering phrase is heard:

Phrase c

It, too, is repeated. The theme ends with the strings playing a series of emphatic chords that end in an abrupt halt.

The beginning of the theme is then repeated. A bridge follows, and after the modulation is complete, the second theme appears in the key of B♭ major, the relative major of G minor. The theme begins with a descending phrase played by the violins. It is answered by a woodwind phrase that draws the melodic line down even farther. The rhythmic motion in this theme is slower than it was in the first, giving the music a more lyrical feeling. The theme is repeated by flute, clarinet, and violins, almost as if in conversation. In an extension of this repetition, tension builds with a crescendo that leads to the closing section.

The closing section of the exposition begins with the clarinet playing the opening motive. The motive is passed back and forth between clarinet and bassoon, and then played forte by the first violins. The exposition ends with the first motive, followed by a strong, clear cadence. Mozart indicated that the exposition should be repeated.

Development　　In the development the opening motive and the first theme undergo substantial transformation. After a feeling of suspense has been established in the opening chords, the first theme is repeated in descending sequence by the high strings. The end of the theme is slightly changed to produce an unstable falling effect. Repetitions of the theme are altered in a number of other ways. The theme is, for example, played in the low register of the basses. At one point, the theme is reduced to insistent, obsessive repetitions of the opening motive:

Repetition of Opening Motive

In some of the alterations, the rhythm of the opening motive is retained while the tonal pattern is varied, sometimes inverted—that is, turned upside down. Toward the end of the development, the theme is passed imitatively between the strings and the woodwinds as tension builds. The section ends with a descending line played by flute and clarinets, a modulation that returns beautifully to the home key of G minor.

Recapitulation

The recapitulation begins with the first theme in the home key. This section differs from the exposition in two important ways. The bridge is extended, and the second theme is played in the home key of G minor rather than in the relative major—B♭ major. Because the second theme is now heard in the minor instead of the major key of the exposition, it takes on a new and more tragic character. The movement ends with a closing section built on the familiar first theme.

Side 4, Band 3

Listening Guide for Mozart's *Symphony No. 40*, First Movement

Timbre:	orchestra of moderate size: string instruments, wind instruments, and timpani
Melody:	first theme, and especially its conjunct three-note motive, dominates much of the movement; second theme conjunct and more lyrical
Rhythm:	duple meter; tempo Allegro molto (very fast)
Harmony:	mainly minor mode; begins in G minor, modulates most significantly to B♭ major, ends in G minor
Texture:	mainly homophonic with some counterpoint
Form:	sonata form

Second Movement: Andante; in Sonata Form

As in most sonata cycles, the second movement presents an emotional contrast to the first. It is marked Andante and set in the key of E♭ major, a key only distantly related to the G minor of the first movement. In this particular symphony, the second movement is written in the same form as the first —in sonata form. However, the movement still has a strikingly individual personality.

The two contrasting aspects of Mozart's mature works—Classicism and Romanticism—are readily apparent in the second movement. The work is the epitome of Viennese grace; the polite voices of flute, clarinet, and strings play well-turned phrases, giving the music an air of sophisticated charm. Yet at times a sense of urgency seems to take over, and the music becomes more dissonant and more forceful.

Exposition

The expressive contrast is suggested even in the opening bars of the movement. The first motive is played sweetly and evenly by the violas. The second violins join in, then the first violins, and at each joining the sweet melody becomes more overcast with tension. At the end of the first phrase, the calm, even motion turns into a hesitant dotted rhythm that foreshadows things to come. A rising two-note figure is played assertively here and later. The second theme, in B♭ major, then enters, with a sweet question-and-answer

THE CLASSICAL SYMPHONY: HAYDN AND MOZART

sound, returning the music and the listener momentarily to the world of Viennese grace.

Development and Recapitulation

The development begins with the first theme heard now in a more somber and intense form. It is followed by material from the second theme. The recapitulation is particularly creative in its subtle review of the earlier material.

Listening Guide for Mozart's *Symphony No. 40*, Second Movement

Timbre:	orchestra of moderate size: string instruments, wind instruments, and timpani
Melody:	first theme emphasizes repeated notes; second theme based on a question-and-answer phrase structure
Rhythm:	mainly $\frac{6}{8}$ meter; tempo Andante (moderate)
Harmony:	mainly major mode; begins in E♭ major, modulates most significantly to B♭ major, ends in E♭ major
Texture:	mainly homophonic with some counterpoint
Form:	sonata form

Third Movement: Menuetto Allegretto; Minuet and Trio in Ternary Form

The third movement is a minuet and trio in ternary form—ABA, or minuet-trio-minuet. The minuet, which opens the movement, is in the key of G minor, while the trio is in G major.

Minuet

The opening theme lacks the clear and dominant triple meter of the Haydn minuet, featuring instead a very prominent use of syncopation. A clear triple meter *is* played in the accompaniment, but attention is naturally directed to the more rhythmically active melody. The first two phrases of the theme are shown below, with x's to mark the syncopation.

Phrases a and b

The phrase structure of the opening theme is asymmetrical. Two phrases of three measures each are followed by one phrase of five measures and another of three. The unpredictability of the melodic structure adds considerable interest. Interest is also added by the change from minor to major mode at the beginning of the second section of the minuet. Both sections are based on the same thematic material and both are repeated.

Trio

The trio, set in G major, features a smooth lyrical melody that offers contrast to the more abrupt opening theme. Like most other trios, it is thinly orchestrated. Solos are scored for flute, violins, and horns, and in some phrases

Minuet

wind instruments appear in duet. After the trio, the minuet is repeated, as usual.

Side 4, Band 4

Listening Guide for Mozart's *Symphony No. 40*, Third Movement

Timbre:	orchestra of moderate size: string instruments, wind instruments, and timpani
Melody:	disjunct and conjunct motion in both themes; second theme more lyrical
Rhythm:	triple meter (duple meter suggested momentarily by syncopation in first theme); tempo Allegretto (moderately fast)
Harmony:	minor and major modes; G minor dominates in minuet; G major in trio
Texture:	homophonic
Form:	ternary (ABA)

Fourth Movement: Allegro assai; in Sonata Form

Finale

The fourth movement, or *finale*, is in sonata form. It is cast in the home key of G minor and played Allegro assai (very fast).

Exposition

The movement opens with a G minor arpeggio—that is, the notes of the tonic chord, played one by one. This rising pattern, sometimes called the "rocket" motive, is played softly by the first violins and answered loudly by the full orchestra:

The first phrase of the theme is heard four times before the second phrase enters. The latter starts with a descending motive but ends with a version of the first phrase. It is then repeated. After the theme has been presented, a bridge including rapid scales leads to the contrasting key of B♭ major and the second theme. The exposition comes to a close with material from the second phrase of the first theme.

Development

The rapid-fire development section is particularly appropriate in a finale. The dramatic rocket motive of the first theme is developed extensively, with the different instruments of the orchestra repeating it in turn in a complex contrapuntal dialogue. Frequent modulations at a rapid tempo add to the increasing excitement.

Recapitulation

Coda

At the beginning of the recapitulation, the exhilarating first theme is heard again. The second theme, now in the home key, also returns. This time it has a wistful, even tragic, sound. A powerful coda brings the symphony to an end.

177　　THE CLASSICAL SYMPHONY: HAYDN AND MOZART

Listening Guide for Mozart's *Symphony No. 40*, Fourth Movement

Timbre:	orchestra of moderate size: string instruments, wind instruments, and timpani
Melody:	first theme opens with disjunct ''rocket'' motive; second theme more conjunct
Rhythm:	duple meter; tempo Allegro assai (very fast)
Harmony:	mainly minor mode; begins in G minor, modulates most significantly to B♭ major, ends in G minor
Texture:	mainly homophonic with some counterpoint
Form:	sonata form followed by a coda

Suggested Listening

C. P. E. Bach's Symphonies

C. P. E. Bach: *Symphony No. 2 in D Major* [MHS 3390F]. In C. P. E. Bach's time, the symphony was still in a developmental stage. Generally it was in three movements (fast—slow—fast) and revolved around tonic-dominant chord and key relationships. Although this symphony retains the Baroque continuo, Bach introduced a number of new characteristics including a greater use of homophony, an emphasis on melody, and a wide range of dynamic effects. Scoring is for flute, oboes, bassoons, horns, strings, and continuo.

Haydn's Symphonies

Haydn: *Symphony No. 7 in C Major* (''Le Midi'') [Turnabout 34150]. Subtitled ''Le Midi'' (''Noon''), this symphony is the second of a group of three, the other two entitled ''Le Matin'' (''Morning'') and ''Le Soir'' (''Evening''). It is an early work, in four movements, and shows some use of counterpoint. Solo instruments are prominently featured.

Haydn: *Symphony No. 101 in D Major* (''Clock'' Symphony) [Angel S-36868]. Haydn's ''Clock'' Symphony has, as do many of his symphonies, a subtitle suggested by characteristics of the music. The subtitle of the present work comes from the very regular, repeated pattern of music played by the bassoons and pizzicato strings in the second movement. The first movement is typical of Haydn in that it opens with a slow introduction—in this case, a very somber adagio in D minor—and then breaks suddenly into a bold presto in D major.

Mozart's Symphonies

Mozart: *Symphony No. 35 in D Major* (''Haffner'' Symphony), K. 385 [Columbia MS-7066]. This work was originally a serenade written to celebrate some personal good fortune. It had a march and two minuets in addition to the movements expected in a symphony. The extra movements were later dropped.

Mozart: *Symphony No. 41 in C Major* (''Jupiter'' Symphony), K. 551 [London 6369]. The ''Jupiter'' Symphony is Mozart's last and perhaps his most brilliant. The basic material comes from rather mundane sources, such as counterpoint exercises and comic-opera themes. But Mozart's treatment raises the music far above the ordinary. A number of very stormy passages are heard, contrasted with many brighter passages.

14

The Classical Symphony: Beethoven

Beethoven's Symphonies

Ludwig van Beethoven (1770–1827) grew up in the German city of Bonn. His father, a court singer under the patronage of Elector Maximilian Friedrich, was a man of artistic temperament but no great talent.

Young Beethoven received little general education. He began his musical career as assistant organist at the Elector's court, where he immersed himself in performance and composition. When the Elector decided to establish an orchestra, Beethoven was quick to see possibilities in this new medium.

By 1792 Bonn had grown too small for Beethoven's ambition. In that year he left for Vienna to study with the masters. Although Mozart was now dead, Haydn was not. Count Waldstein, one of Beethoven's early sponsors, paid tribute to the masters in a letter to Beethoven: "You are going to Vienna in fulfillment of your long frustrated wishes . . . you will receive the spirit of Mozart from the hands of Haydn."

The Musician in an Age of Revolution   Beethoven took up residence in Vienna during the aftermath of the French Revolution. The French king, Louis XVI, had been taken into custody, and the Elector of Bonn would soon lose a sister, Marie Antoinette, to the guillotine. Austria and Prussia, the oldest of enemies, were united in a struggle against the new French Republic—a struggle that they were, at least in the short run, to lose. French troops were soon to march through Austria. Aristocrats would stream like refugees into Vienna. The old social order was weakening to the point of chaos. It was natural in such an environment that there would be changes in the aspirations of young composers such as Beethoven. It was also natural that social attitudes toward these people would change. No longer could they be considered simply the servants of the upper class.

Beethoven was the first musician of common background to mix with the aristocracy on his own terms. Talent was his nobility, he often said, and it was credential enough. Though intermittently sponsored by various princes, Beethoven deferred to no one. He seems to have had absolute confidence in his own standards, social and musical. Although he studied with Haydn, he later said that he gained little from his lessons. Beethoven was fierce in his insistence on originality as the mark of the true artist.

Beethoven's nine symphonies are far fewer in number than those of Haydn or Mozart. Yet they are as lengthy or longer than the later works of both of his famous predecessors. Beethoven's first symphonies reflect the Classical spirit perfectly. His Third, Fifth, and Sixth symphonies, however, while still Classical in their basic orientation and structure, have an unprecedented vitality and intensity. They play an important part in the gradual transition from the Classical style to the Romantic. Differences in Beethoven's earlier and later symphonies are sometimes attributed, in part, to his emotional despair and triumph over his increasing deafness.

In his later symphonies, Beethoven generally included more melodic material than he had in his earlier, shorter symphonies. Sections within movements often take on new significance. The development of motives and themes becomes more intense. In movements written in sonata form, development often takes place, not just in the development section, but in other sections as well. In fact, codas often serve as second development sections.

Beethoven also added new elements to the timbre of the symphonic orchestra. The trombone, for example, makes its symphonic debut in his Fifth Symphony. Solo and choral voices are heard in the last movement of the Ninth Symphony. Strings remain basic in Beethoven's orchestra, but wind instruments take on ever more important melodic roles.

The Symphony as an Emotional Program

The Sixth Symphony

In his desire to make the symphony accommodate vast emotional schemes, Beethoven greatly expanded Classical forms. Yet at the same time, he brought a new unity to the work as a whole. He was the first to write symphonies in which a single motivic idea reappeared in each movement. What had been a cycle of contrasting movements now became a unified emotional program— somewhat similar to the kind of chronological progression found in literature. An extreme example, Beethoven's *Symphony No. 6* (the "Pastoral"), has movement titles that sound like chapter titles in a novel:

1. Awakening of Pleasant Feelings upon Arriving in the Country; Allegro ma non troppo
2. Scene by the Brook; Andante molto mosso
3. Peasants' Merrymaking; Allegro
4. The Storm; Allegro
5. Shepherd's Hymn of Thanksgiving after the Storm; Allegretto

The Third Symphony

Scherzo

While the "Pastoral" draws quite clearly on the imagery of the countryside, a different kind of inspiration may be seen in *Symphony No. 3* (the "Eroica"). Originally conceived as a tribute to Napoleon, the work is generally associated with the concept of heroism. The monumental first movement is followed by the traditional slow movement, in this case a funeral march. The third movement is a lively *scherzo*—a light, quickly moving compositional form that gradually replaced the traditional third-movement minuet. The

A Composer Both Classical and Romantic: *While Beethoven built upon the work of Haydn and Mozart he often went beyond them, developing new ideas that were to be used by the Romantic composers of the era to come. His way of life also foreshadowed the coming age. He lived many years in self-imposed exile, devoted almost single-mindedly to his art, thus fulfilling the Romantic notion of the artist as a tragic figure of heroic proportions.*

finale is frankly exuberant, as if the hero has come full circle to victory. The four movements thus convey a succession of emotions. They do not literally trace the career of any one person but instead express Beethoven's feelings about any person of great and heroic nature. Napoleon, as it happened, was not to prove worthy of the tribute. When news came that the great hope of the French Revolution had crowned himself Emperor, Beethoven angrily scratched out the dedication. The man he had seen as a hero had become, it seemed, just another despot.

Beethoven: *Symphony No. 5 in C Minor*

Beethoven's *Symphony No. 5*, possibly the most popular of all symphonies, first began to appear in the composer's musical sketchbooks during the years 1801 and 1802, soon after the completion of the "Eroica." *Symphony No. 4*, in a lighter, more idyllic vein, was finished before the Fifth. It stands as an emotional relief between the Third and the Fifth symphonies. Schumann described it as "a slim Greek maiden between two Norse giants." The Third and the Fifth symphonies were conceived during a period of great inner conflict, after Beethoven first learned that he was going deaf. His own great personal loss seemed to have given him a greater understanding of the enormity of human suffering.

The emotional power of the Fifth Symphony is thus in some ways a reflection of the strength of Beethoven's own spirit. That Beethoven should have gradually lost the one sense that he had possessed "in highest perfection" has always seemed one of the cruelest ironies in the history of music. It also seems almost miraculous that his compositions did not cease when his hearing did. Beethoven's genius, however, does not lie in the fact that he was a deaf composer. Musicians in all ages have claimed to compose music "in their heads." Few, if any, have had orchestras at their elbows, and all have had to generate sound on paper. For Beethoven deafness did not present so great a problem to his art as it did to his spirit and to his relationship with the world. "My affliction causes me the least trouble in playing and composing, the most in association with others," he wrote in a letter dated 1801. In another document, a will or testament to his brothers, he wrote, "I must live like an exile; if I venture into company a burning dread falls on me, the dreadful risk of letting my condition be perceived." For this reason, and on the advice of a physician, Beethoven retired in 1802 to the quiet village of Heiligenstadt. From his letters at this time, we know that he succumbed to periods of intense misery, but the creative force within him was coupled with his will to live. "I will take Fate by the throat," he wrote. "It shall not wholly overcome me." Such was the determination that gave birth to the Fifth Symphony.

First Movement: Allegro con brio; in Sonata Form

Exposition

The symphony opens authoritatively, with a motive that is undoubtedly the most famous in all symphonic literature. The basic, unifying rhythm of the first four notes immediately establishes the mood of the entire work:

Opening Motive

When asked for an explanation of this compelling motive, Beethoven answered, "Fate knocking at the door." It is unlikely that he meant that the music literally reproduced such a sound. He was more likely to have been using the words figuratively—making reference to the energy conveyed by the motive, a force similar to the remorseless energy that to him seemed the essence of fate. Beethoven used the motive with a single-mindedness appropriate to such an interpretation. In the course of the first movement, the motive is stated, restated, and infinitely changed. It is heard in the other movements as well, bringing new unity to symphonic writing. Yet even with this constant reassertion of the initial motive, the symphony is characterized by frequent emotional changes. In fact, the opening motive itself is transformed into a statement of heroic defiance and finally into a celebration of strength. It is singularly appropriate that this motive was used as the theme of BBC radio in London during the Second World War: its four notes spoke of a commitment to victory.

The most significant characteristic of the opening motive is its rhythm
—three short notes of equal duration followed by a much longer note. The
relative length of the fourth note is varied even at the outset. In the second
statement of the motive, presented in descending sequence, the final note is
held for two measures rather than one:

First Two Statements of Opening Motive

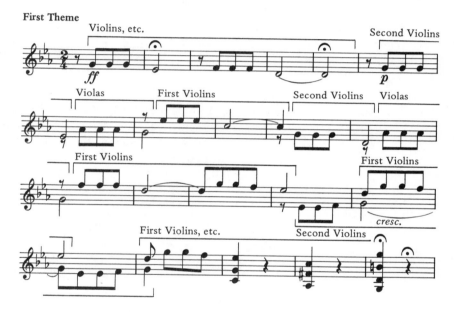

The entire first theme is based upon the opening motive. As the theme
unfolds, the motive is tossed quickly from one section of instruments to
another:

First Theme

Note that it is primarily the rhythm of the motive that is stated and
restated. The tonal pattern is varied for dramatic purposes. When the violas
enter, the motive is played in sequence one tone higher. However, the interval
between the last two notes of the motive has been shortened. In other places
the interval is larger. Sometimes the third note of the motive is lowered on its
way to the fourth note. In the answering phrase, the pattern is inverted.

Out of the simple rhythm of the opening motive, Beethoven was thus
able to create a very dramatic first theme. Repetition, sequence, and tonal
variation all play important parts. The material is so perfectly ordered, the
alterations so integral to the dramatic structure, that we may not even be
conscious that the motive has been altered.

After the first theme comes to a loud and abrupt end, the opening motive is immediately taken up again. The entire orchestra enters with the initial statement. Then the string instruments, one by one, carry the motive downward into the range of the cellos and the double basses. The melody returns to the violins, and once again the motive is carried to the lower register. When the melody again returns to the violins, they begin a driving upward passage marked with sforzandos. The music alternately rises and descends as momentum and tension build.

At the end of this energetic passage, there is a bridge. The music modulates to the key of E♭ major, the relative major, in preparation for the second theme. Now that a major key has been introduced, we might expect some change in emotional coloring. Significantly, the change of key is underscored with a variation of the original motive. The variation appears as a sort of introductory fanfare to the second theme:

Variation of Opening Motive

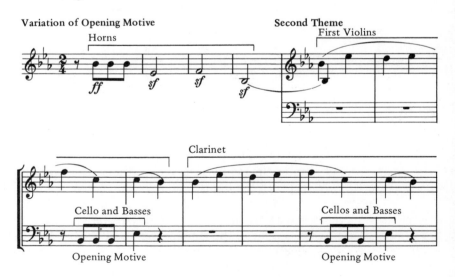

The altered motive, sounded by the horns, does indeed seem brighter than the original motive. It is also extended to include two additional notes.

The second theme is a gentle, lyrical statement of only four measures. It is shown below, immediately following the altered motive of the bridge passage. The rhythm of the original motive is heard in the accompaniment played by the lower strings.

The lyrical second theme takes on a new urgency when it is repeated by the clarinet and the flute. It is then extended by the violins in rising sequence. As

184   CLASSICAL MUSIC

the rhythm of the basic motive reasserts itself again and again, the music rises to a crescendo.

A strong closing theme then emerges:

Closing Theme

This theme is immediately repeated, reinforcing its closing function. The rhythm of the basic motive then returns, and the exposition ends with a feeling of victory. Beethoven indicated that the exposition should be repeated.

Development

The development begins with the first motive played by horns and clarinets. The strings answer, this time reducing the motive to the very smallest of intervals. After this, different groups of instruments play the first motive imitatively in rising sequence. They are accompanied by the lower strings playing in descending sequence.

At the climax of the development section, the rhythm of the basic motive is pounded out by the full orchestra. The fanfare that preceded the second theme is then heard, answered by an impatient staccato passage. The latter part of the development is remarkable for a number of reasons—the suspense created by its harmonies, the momentary absence of the motive, and the slower rhythmic motion. In the final measures of the development, Beethoven has succeeded, perhaps better than any other Classical composer, in making us anticipate the return of the first theme. An almost physical participation is demanded. We feel the music braking and then straining through a series of eighth notes to the fourth note of the opening motive. When the goal is reached, the relief is overwhelming:

End of Development

Recapitulation

The recapitulation begins at the end of the passage shown above, with the sounding of the opening motive. It goes on to review the earlier material but is interrupted after the first statement of the theme by an oboe solo. Momentarily, we are released from the driving rhythms that characterize the rest of the movement. However, the opening motive soon returns followed by the second theme, which is introduced this time by the bassoons. The closing theme follows, as expected, and the recapitulation ends with the return of the first

THE CLASSICAL SYMPHONY: BEETHOVEN

motive. The movement, however, continues with an extensive coda. In its varied presentations of the opening motive, the coda equals the intensity and scope of the development section. The movement ends with very loud and powerful chords.

Listening Guide for Beethoven's *Symphony No. 5,* First Movement

Timbre:	moderately large orchestra of string instruments, wind instruments, and timpani
Melody:	opening motive of primary importance; first theme built upon variations of opening motive; second theme more lyrical; closing theme begins with conjunct motion, becoming more disjunct
Rhythm:	duple meter; tempo Allegro con brio (fast with spirit); rhythm of opening motive is heard repeatedly
Harmony:	mainly minor mode; begins in C minor, modulates most significantly to E♭ major, ends in C minor
Texture:	homophonic and contrapuntal
Form:	sonata form followed by a coda

Second Movement: Andante con moto; in Theme and Variations Form

The second movement is slower and is set in the contrasting key of A♭ major. Although basically in theme and variations form, it bears little resemblance to the theme and variations movement in Haydn's "Surprise" Symphony. Beethoven's work is more complex and lacks the clearly sectionalized series of variations found in the earlier work.

There are two important themes in the movement, each of which undergoes considerable development. The first, marked dolce, is reflective in spirit. It is played by the cellos and violas, accompanied by basses playing pizzicato:

First Theme

The first theme continues with woodwinds playing longer notes. The full orchestra then brings the first theme to a close.

The second theme has the familiar rhythm of the first movement's opening motive:

Second Theme with Rhythm of Opening Motive

Variations

Throughout the movement both themes undergo changes in dynamics, tempo, and harmony. Each is played to a variety of accompaniments and by different groups of instruments. Most of the variations center on the first theme. The theme is broken into smaller and smaller units, as if a more careful reflection on the matter would reveal greater complexity. There is also a sense of growing mastery as the lilting rhythm of the original theme becomes more even and secure. The opening measures of the first two variations of the first theme illustrate these changes:

First Theme: Variation 1
Cellos and Violas

First Theme: Variation 2
Cellos and Violas

Coda

The third variation of the first theme is followed by a coda played at a slightly faster tempo. It is based on motives heard earlier in the movement and ends with a cadence played by the full orchestra.

Side 5, Band 2

Listening Guide for Beethoven's *Symphony No. 5*, Second Movement

Timbre:	moderately large orchestra of string instruments, wind instruments, and timpani
Melody:	two themes, both subject to variation; first theme disjunct with dotted rhythm; second theme more conjunct with more even rhythm
Rhythm:	triple meter; tempo Andante con moto (moderate with motion); rhythm of first movement's opening motive recurs in the second theme
Harmony:	mainly major mode; begins in A♭ major, modulates to C major and A♭ minor, ends in A♭ major
Texture:	mainly homophonic
Form:	theme and variations followed by a coda

Third Movement: Allegro; Scherzo in Ternary Form

One of the important changes made in the Classical symphony in Beethoven's time was the replacement of the third movement minuet with a scherzo. A scherzo ("joke" or "trifle" in Italian) is generally in the triple meter of the minuet. It tends, however, to be lighter and quicker than the earlier dance movement. Although Beethoven did not use the term scherzo for the third movement of *Symphony No. 5* and the movement does differ in several respects from a typical scherzo, it is often called a scherzo. The organization is that of the typical scherzo—ternary, or ABA—but only the B section has some

THE CLASSICAL SYMPHONY: BEETHOVEN

of the lighter spirit of the scherzo. This can be seen, in part, in the choice of keys. The A section is in the home key of C minor, while the B section is in C major.

Section A

The movement opens with an ominous dialogue between low- and high-register strings. Cellos and double basses enter first, playing the opening phrase of the first theme, a phrase that begins with a rising arpeggio. This phrase is balanced by an answering phrase played by the first violins. The minor key and the very soft dynamics contribute to the foreboding mood of the theme:

First Theme

After the first theme is developed in a second exchange, the short-short-short-long rhythm of the first movement's opening motive suddenly recurs. Technically, it is now the second theme of the third movement. Confined largely to a single tone, it is more insistent than ever. It thus offers an extreme contrast to the hesitant theme that opened the movement. The second theme is played very loudly by the horns and is then taken up by the full orchestra and expanded:

Second Theme

The rest of the A section alternates between the two contrasting themes. It ends with a burst of violin activity, accompanied by offbeat chords in the woodwinds.

Section B

The B section that follows is much more in the spirit of the typical scherzo. It begins with double basses and cellos lumbering away at the bottom of the orchestra in the key of C major. A delightful imitative passage follows as the theme moves upward. Violas, second violins, and first violins are heard in turn. The mood is one of exuberant playfulness. The first half of the section is then repeated, after which cellos and basses hesitantly present the theme again for another round of imitation. This half is also repeated, softly and with

Vienna, the Center of Classical Music: *The imperial capital of Vienna gained a predominant position in European music in the late eighteenth century and has remained highly influential ever since. The engraving shows the city as it was in the time of Haydn, Mozart, and Beethoven.*

changes. Pizzicato cellos and basses lead back to the minor key with an air of quiet mystery.

Section A

 The A section is then repeated. But this time the second theme is hushed and its rhythm is much less insistent than it was at the beginning of the movement. This creates a feeling of suspense and anxiety, as does the sound of the violins, played pizzicato or at times softly bowed. Suspense is further heightened by a quiet tapping of the timpani, played under the final statement of the first theme. The timpani part begins with the rhythm of the second theme, which soon turns into continuously repeated notes. Above these the violins present a lengthy passage that finally resolves to the tonic as the music moves without pause to the triumphant opening of the finale.

Side 5, Band 3

Listening Guide for Beethoven's *Symphony No. 5*, Third Movement

Timbre:	moderately large orchestra of string instruments, wind instruments, and timpani
Melody:	first theme begins with rising arpeggio; second theme stresses repeated notes; third theme is lighter and quicker than the first two
Rhythm:	triple meter; tempo Allegro (fast); rhythm of the first movement's opening motive recurs in the second theme
Harmony:	mainly minor mode; C minor in Section A; C major in Section B
Texture:	monophonic, homophonic, and contrapuntal
Form:	ternary (ABA[1])

THE CLASSICAL SYMPHONY: BEETHOVEN

Fourth Movement: Allegro; Presto; in Sonata Form

With the opening chord of the finale, Beethoven establishes the brilliant key of C major and, incidentally, the symphonic debut of the trombone. The opening is joyful, suggesting a kind of spiritual rebirth. Perhaps it was for the sake of this effect that Beethoven chose to end the symphony in C major rather than in the original key of C minor. Note that the first three notes of the opening theme are simply the tonic chord of C major. This conveys an immediate feeling of security and strength:

First Theme
Full Orchestra

The orchestration of the first theme, and of the movement as a whole, is especially colorful. Two other newcomers to the symphony orchestra, the piccolo and the contrabassoon, are used for special dramatic purposes. The contrabassoon provides harmonic support along with the cellos and basses, while the piccolo adds brilliance at the top of the orchestral range.

The first theme is followed by a second, also in C major:

Second Theme
Horns

After the second theme, there is a modulation to the key of the dominant, G major. Another theme then appears in the new key. In this theme, the rhythm of the symphony's opening motive adds to the general feeling of exhilaration.

Third Theme
Violins

Following a repetition of the third theme, scale passages signal the beginning of the closing section. In this section, a final theme is presented and repeated.

Closing Theme
Violas

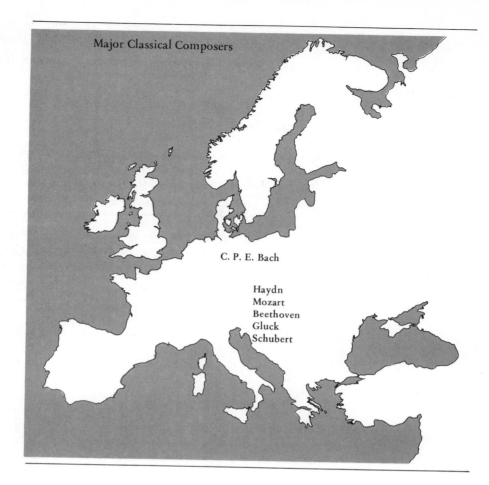

Major Classical Composers

C. P. E. Bach

Haydn
Mozart
Beethoven
Gluck
Schubert

The exposition ends with a strong cadence. As in the first movement, Beethoven indicated that the exposition should be repeated.

Development

The development is a virtuoso display characterized by dynamic contrasts, rapid modulation, and the fragmentation and recombination of earlier motives. There is also an unprecedented return to material from the third movement. The second theme of the preceding movement, one of the many themes based on the rhythm of the symphony's opening motive, is heard once again, stated as it was last heard in the final portion of the third movement—the portion that resolved into the first theme of the finale. This time the resolution signals the beginning of the recapitulation.

Recapitulation and Coda

The recapitulation reviews the material from the exposition in the expected order. A long coda follows, integrally fashioned from the thematic materials of the movement; the second, third, and closing themes are extensively developed. The conclusion of the symphony is marked Presto (as fast as possible), and it moves with powerful and inevitable pressure to the final C major chord

THE CLASSICAL SYMPHONY: BEETHOVEN

Listening Guide for Beethoven's *Symphony No. 5,* Fourth Movement

Timbre:	moderately large orchestra of string instruments, wind instruments, and timpani
Melody:	four themes, as illustrated above
Rhythm:	duple meter; tempo Allegro (fast) through most of the movement, Presto (very fast) at end of movement; rhythm of the first movement's opening motive recurs in different forms
Harmony:	mainly major mode; begins in C major, modulates most significantly to G major, ends in C major
Texture:	mainly homophonic with some counterpoint
Form:	sonata form followed by coda

Beethoven wrote only four more symphonies after the Fifth Symphony. *Symphony No. 6* is a celebration of the pleasures of country life. *Symphony No. 7* is a powerful, romantic work on a large scale; *Symphony No. 8* is a complement to it—relaxed, joyful, and strong. *Symphony No. 9,* like *No. 3* and *No. 5,* is an artistic milestone. A colossal work, it ends with a finale in which the words of Schiller's "Ode to Joy" are sung by soloists and choir. It is one of the strongest statements of serenity and strength that a composer has ever made.

Suggested Listening

Beethoven's Symphonies

Beethoven: *Symphony No. 1 in C Major, Op. 21* [DG 138801]. This symphony is very Classical both in style and in spirit. Beethoven's own imagination and energy are clearly apparent in its fine balance and proportion.

Beethoven: *Symphony No. 3 in E♭ Major, Op. 55* (the "Eroica") [DG 138802]. While Classical forms were still the basis for this symphony, Beethoven added a number of new ideas. The first movement is made up of a wide variety of thematic materials. The second movement is a somber funeral march, and the third a lively, yet at times contemplative, scherzo. These and other characteristics foreshadow many later innovations made by Beethoven and his successors.

Beethoven: *Symphony No. 6 in F Major, Op. 68* (the "Pastoral") [DG 138805]. The five movements, and the programmatic titles for them, make this work unique among Beethoven's symphonies. Classical in structure but Romantic in spirit, it represents a new facet of Beethoven's creativity.

Beethoven: *Symphony No. 7 in A Major, Op. 92* [DG 138806]. This vivacious work shows Beethoven's respect for the past as well as his desire for fresh expression. The first movement begins with a slow introduction. The rest of the first movement, in sonata form, is strongly unified by a repeated motive. The second movement is in theme and variations form, but it includes a contrasting middle section. The brilliance and energy of the scherzo and the finale show Beethoven's creative genius at its best.

Beethoven: *Symphony No. 9 in D Minor, Op. 125* [DG 2707013]. This is one of Beethoven's most monumental works. Classical forms become simply the supporting framework for a wealth of different materials. The famous final movement, with its powerful, dramatic setting of Schiller's "Ode to Joy," is strongly Romantic in style.

C H A P T E R

15

The Classical Concerto

Development of the Classical Concerto

The Classical concerto, a work of several movements, is essentially a musical confrontation between solo instrument and orchestra. A violin concerto, for example, contrasts the sound of the solo violin with the larger sound of the orchestra as a whole. A small number of Classical concertos do include more than one solo instrument. Mozart wrote a concerto for two pianos, and Beethoven, a "triple concerto" for violin, cello, and piano. However, most works call for a single solo instrument playing in alternation with the entire orchestra.

In the Classical concerto, the soloist enters like the hero of a drama. The opposition of one against many is a familiar theme in all the arts. In music the concept is never more prominent than in the concerto.

Origins of the Concerto

The solo concerto of the Classical period developed from the Baroque concerto. As we have seen, the concerto grosso of the Baroque age contrasted a small group of instruments—the concertino—with a larger group—the ripieno. It was not very long before a number of Baroque composers, Torelli and Vivaldi among them, were also writing concertos for solo instrument and orchestra. Ambition may well have played a part in this. The earliest of the Baroque solo concertos were for violin, written by virtuoso violinists. Bach and Handel also wrote solo concertos, for harpsichord and for organ. These Baroque works naturally had a major influence on the solo concertos of the Classical age.

The concerto, like the Classical style itself, was also influenced by Italian opera. In the Italian aria, one singer emerged from the larger company to present a melody. The solo aria thus lent a certain dramatic force to opera. Classical composers were quick to apply this principle to instrumental works, particularly to the concerto. It is no coincidence that Mozart, the most prolific and accomplished of Classical concerto writers, was also the most successful composer of Classical operas.

Relationship Between Soloist and Orchestra

Cadenza

Although the Classical concerto opposes a single instrument to many, it nevertheless sets up a fair and equal contest. The orchestra can attain a greater dynamic level as well as a greater variety of texture. Soloists, on the other hand, can dazzle the audience with their virtuosity. Indeed, concertos offer soloists special opportunities to do just that. During certain passages, generally toward the end of a movement, the orchestra remains silent while the soloist indulges in what sounds like a spontaneous expression—the *cadenza*. This difficult-sounding, usually fast-moving passage was at first meant to be improvised by the performer, who was in many cases the composer of the work. Mozart and Beethoven were famous for the cadenzas they improvised during performances of their piano concertos. Many such cadenzas are lost to us, but some were written down for the benefit of students and other performers. Gradually, it became the custom to compose, rather than improvise, the cadenza. Yet the passages still retain a spirit of free improvisation and exuberant breaking away from the orchestra in pursuit of personal expression.

Yet as noted above, even the most virtuosic soloist does not draw all the attention. The orchestra provides much more then mere accompaniment. In fact, it is often the dominating force—announcing the first theme, for example, or interrupting the end of the cadenza to give a final, affirmative musical statement. Sometimes the soloist accompanies the orchestra or enters into the fullness of the orchestral sound, momentarily giving up individuality. More often there is give-and-take as soloist and orchestra engage in musical dialogue, presenting countermelodies or imitation of one another and exchanging parts. The one and the many are of equal musical importance.

Structure of the Classical Concerto

A Classical concerto is almost always made up of three movements. Like the symphony, the concerto is basically a sonata cycle. And, as in the symphony, there is a contrast in tempo between the different movements. The most common tempo pattern is fast—slow—fast.

Double Exposition

The first movement of the Classical concerto is generally in sonata form, modified to include two separate expositions—technically, a *double exposition*. The first is for the orchestra alone, the second for the soloist with the orchestra. The soloist tends to present more elaborate versions of the themes stated during the orchestral exposition and generally adds at least one new theme as well. The usual development and recapitulation sections follow, with both soloist and orchestra taking part in each.

The second movement of the Classical concerto may take one of several different forms. It is generally slow, lyrical, and spacious, permitting a great deal of elaboration on the part of the soloist.

The third movement is often in rondo form, occasionally in theme and variations form. It tends to be lively and dancelike in character. The minuet or scherzo movement that appears in the Classical symphony is generally omitted.

The contrast between movements and the structural uses of theme and tonality are important in the Classical concerto. However, the overall design depends just as much on the creative interplay between soloist and orchestra.

Mozart's Concertos

Perhaps more than any other Classical composer, Mozart was remarkable for his great productivity of concertos, the composition of which interested him throughout his creative life. Supposedly, it was a piano concerto that Mozart presented to his father at the age of four. By the age of nine, he had written concerto arrangements for a number of J. C. Bach's works. The concerto continued to engage his energies in the few short decades left of his life. In all Mozart wrote more than forty concertos.

Mozart: *Piano Concerto No. 17 in G Major*, K. 453

More than half of Mozart's concertos are for piano. He is known to have written at least twenty-five concertos for the instrument. The piano of Mozart's time was more limited in dynamic capacity, and finer and more crystalline in tone, than the modern piano. These qualities undoubtedly influenced the way he used the instrument.

One of his best piano works is the *Piano Concerto No. 17 in G Major*, K. 453, written in 1784. It is scored for an orchestra of moderate size, including strings, flute, two oboes, two horns, and two bassoons. (Later concertos would include parts for clarinets, trumpets, and timpani as well.)

First Movement: Allegro; in Sonata Form

The first movement of Mozart's *Piano Concerto No. 17* includes an orchestral exposition and a piano exposition followed by development and recapitulation sections. It is characterized by a lively marchlike rhythm.

The orchestral exposition opens with a lilting theme in the first violins, reinforced by the woodwinds:

This is followed by a second theme, played forcefully by the full orchestra:

In a symphony, we would now expect to hear a bridge to the dominant key followed by the restatement of the first theme or the presentation of another theme. In the first exposition of the Classical concerto, however, another pattern is generally followed. A third theme is presented in the home key—in this case, the key of G major. After some preparatory scales and arpeggios, we hear this theme, a restless, thoughtful statement played by the strings:

Third Theme

The third theme is repeated with slight variation by the woodwinds. Then a modulatory passage leads to the closing theme:

Closing Theme

The orchestral exposition draws to a close with forceful chords played by the entire orchestra.

Solo Exposition At the beginning of the solo exposition, the piano enters easily with a rising passage that flows into the first theme. As is typical in the Classical concerto, this theme, heard before in the first violins, is now elaborated by the soloist. The woodwinds participate in the first theme, just as they did at the beginning of the movement when it was played by the violins. The second theme is then played by the orchestra, with the piano adding a decorative passage of its own. After modulating to the dominant key of D major, the piano introduces a new theme, here called the *piano theme:*

Piano Theme

This playful melody is first played by the piano alone. A rhythmic string accompaniment is then added, and finally the theme is taken over by the woodwinds. The third theme from the first exposition follows the piano theme. It is first played by the piano with a light, rhythmic accompaniment in the strings. Then the woodwinds present the theme, while the piano plays an accompaniment. The solo exposition comes to an end with a review of some of the earlier material, including the second theme.

Development The development begins with a lengthy passage of piano arpeggios played against the woodwinds. A motive from the piano theme is then developed, mainly by the piano in dialogue with itself. The section is only lightly accompanied.

Recapitulation The recapitulation returns to the first theme, played, as in the opening, by the first violins. This time, however, the piano enters quite early, before the

Cadenza

second theme. The recapitulation also includes the piano theme and the third theme, played in that order by the soloist. The cadenza at the end of the movement was written out by Mozart. It is followed by a final statement of the closing theme by the orchestra.

Side 6, Band 1

Listening Guide for Mozart's *Piano Concerto No. 17*, First Movement

Timbre:	solo piano; orchestra of moderate size: string and wind instruments
Melody:	five themes, as illustrated above
Rhythm:	duple meter; tempo Allegro (fast)
Harmony:	mainly major mode; begins in G major, modulates most significantly to D major, ends in G major
Texture:	mainly homophonic
Form:	sonata form with two expositions

Second Movement: Andante; in Free Rondo Form

First Theme

The lyrical quality of the themes and the modulations to remote keys contribute to the sensitive, sentimental mood of this movement. The first theme is played by the strings. (This, incidentally, represents the strings' only major contribution to the movement.)

First Theme

Note that the theme closely resembles the third theme of the first movement. Thus it already seems somewhat familiar. The first theme is immediately followed by new material in the woodwinds. A lightly scored dialogue ensues.

Second Theme

After a melancholy second theme has been presented, the piano enters very simply with the first theme. As is customary, the soloist elaborates upon the theme. In the course of the movement, the first theme returns three more times.

Other Themes

A number of new themes are also heard, as well as elaboration of previous material. The music modulates through numerous keys—sometimes quite suddenly—with a consequent heightening of Romantic feeling. The

Cadenza

cadenza for this movement, played just before the final statement of the first theme, is a masterpiece in itself.

Listening Guide for Mozart's *Piano Concerto No. 17*, Second Movement

Timbre:	solo piano; orchestra of moderate size: string and wind instruments
Melody:	main theme conjunct and lyrical; other themes more disjunct
Rhythm:	triple meter; tempo Andante (moderate)
Harmony:	mainly major mode; begins in C major, modulates most significantly to G major, ends in C major
Texture:	homophonic
Form:	free rondo

Third Movement: Allegretto; Presto; in Theme and Variations Form

The finale is a delightful theme and variations with a Presto coda. In this movement Mozart used the usual means of variation—that which we encountered in the second movement of Haydn's "Surprise" Symphony. At the same time, the music presents the concerto's characteristic interplay between soloist and orchestra.

Theme

The theme is divided into two equal parts. It is presented by flute and violins accompanied by the lower strings:

Part 1

Part 2

Both parts of the theme are repeated, as indicated by the repeat sign :‖ . Thus the theme has the following organization:

a	b	a	b	c	d	c	d
Part 1				Part 2			

Variations

As noted above, the theme is first stated by the orchestra. The piano enters in the first variation. Indeed, it dominates Part 1 of the first variation, generally playing two notes for every one in the string accompaniment. In Part 2 the piano part is imitated by the violins.

In the second variation, solo and orchestral parts are more equally balanced. In the first statement of Part 1, the piano accompanies the woodwinds, now playing three notes to every one of theirs. The piano part thus moves faster than the orchestra, gaining speed as the movement becomes more intense. Piano and violins take up the melody as Part 1 is repeated. The repetitions of Parts 1 and 2 no longer simply repeat the earlier material. Instead they offer new

Frederick the Great as Soloist: *Like many other rulers of his day and of earlier centuries, Frederick the Great of Prussia was an accomplished amateur musician. Here he is shown playing the solo part in a flute concerto, possibly of his own composition.*

materials. During Part 2 the piano maintains the 3:1 accompaniment. The melody is first stated by the woodwinds, with imitation in flute and bassoon. In the repetition of Part 2 that follows, the melody is played by the piano and the violins.

The third variation opens with a woodwind dialogue. The piano takes over as Part 1 is repeated. The soloist supplies the melody with the right hand and a 4:1 accompaniment with the left hand. Part 2 begins with an imitative passage in the woodwinds. The variation ends with the piano dominating once again.

The fourth variation is in the minor mode. Syncopation is heard, first in the winds and then, as Part 1 is repeated, in the piano. A similar pattern emerges in Part 2, which ends with an exciting forte.

The major mode returns in the fifth variation. The section begins with the orchestra playing vigorous descending scales. The piano enters as Part 1 is repeated. The melody is played by the left hand under an exhilarating trill played by the right hand. In Part 2, the orchestra returns with loud ascending scales. The piano joins in as Part 2 is repeated. Its chromatic scales add greatly to the dramatic energy.

Coda

The movement ends with a long coda, marked Presto, written in comic-opera style. This rousing section develops new material while returning several times to the original theme. The music ends good-naturedly by reclaiming the original theme in the final measures.

Listening Guide for Mozart's *Piano Concerto No. 17*, Third Movement

Timbre:	solo piano; orchestra of moderate size: string and wind instruments
Melody:	theme mainly conjunct with repeated notes and sequence
Rhythm:	duple meter; tempo in main part of movement Allegretto (moderately fast); tempo in coda Presto (very fast)
Harmony:	mainly major mode; begins in G major, with repeated modulations to D major; fourth variation in G minor; ends in G major
Texture:	homophonic
Form:	theme and variations followed by a coda

Other Composers of Classical Concertos

Haydn's Concertos

Haydn and other Classical composers, including Haydn's brother Michael, also wrote a number of important concertos. The works were for a variety of instruments—violin, cello, flute, oboe, trumpet, horn, harpsichord, and piano. Most often they were written for a single solo instrument, but occasionally two instruments were featured, as in Haydn's *Concerto in F Major for Harpsichord, Violin, and Strings.* Haydn's concertos, along with Mozart's, played an important part in bringing the Classical concerto to its mature compositional form.

Beethoven's Concertos

Beethoven later took over the reins and infused the concerto with the even greater drama and expressiveness of the Romantic style. In his concertos as in his symphonies, the existence of the Classical-Romantic continuum can clearly be seen. His early concertos are very close in style to those of Mozart and Haydn; his later concertos, however, are developed far beyond the works of the earlier composers.

Beethoven's most significant concertos are the five he wrote for piano and the one he wrote for violin. Classical clarity and precision are especially characteristic of the early piano concertos. The works maintain the compositional form of earlier concertos, including the double exposition in the first movement. The last piano concertos and the violin concerto, while still in three movements, are much freer in structure.

Suggested Listening

Concertos by Josef and Michael Haydn

J. Haydn: *Horn Concerto No. 2 in D Major* [Turnabout 34031]. Haydn's concerto opens with full orchestra, followed by solo horn. Then orchestra and horn play the first theme together. A horn concerto was particularly difficult to write in Haydn's time. The instrument had no valves and could therefore play only certain notes in the specific key in which it was built. It was also very difficult to keep in tune. Thus, a horn concerto was both a composer's and a performer's tour de force.

M. Haydn: *Trumpet Concerto in D Major* [DG ARC 198415]. The Baroque age was the great era of the trumpet, even limited as the instrument was at that time without valves. This concerto harks back in some ways to that period. The solo part is very demanding and provides brilliant contrast to the orchestra. Baroque in sound, Classical in spirit, this trumpet concerto is one of the last major works of its type.

Mozart's Concertos

Mozart: *Clarinet Concerto in A Major*, K. 622 [Seraphim S-60193]. Mozart was particularly fond of woodwind instruments and was extremely sensitive to the delicate but penetrating sound of the clarinet. The present concerto has the typical three movements. The instrumentation is suitably light, giving the clarinet support without overcoming it. The exquisite melodies in the solo part and the expressive interplay between soloist and orchestra are among the finest features of the work.

Mozart: *Piano Concerto in B♭ Major*, K. 595 [Columbia MS-6839]. This is a late and thus very mature work in the typical three-movement format. It includes some wonderful melodies, especially in the piano part. Lyrical themes are effectively contrasted with more brilliant themes.

Beethoven's Concertos

Beethoven: *Violin Concerto in D Major, Op. 61* [Angel S-35780]. Beethoven's only concerto for the violin is one of his finest concertos, even one of the best in the entire nineteenth century. It is in three movements and calls for great virtuosity from the soloist. Though it is rooted in the Classical style, its great dramatic power strongly foreshadows the Romantic tendencies of the later nineteenth century.

Beethoven: *Piano Concerto No. 5 in E♭ Major, Op. 73* ("Emperor") [Philips 839600]. This, Beethoven's last piano concerto, was first performed in 1812 by the same Carl Czerny whose piano exercises later became familiar to generations of students. Cast in the traditional three-movement format, it is an expansive work with wide contrasts in all elements of style. Difficult to perform, it is one of Beethoven's masterpieces.

16

Classical Chamber Music: The Sonata and the String Quartet

The Nature of Classical Chamber Music

The Classical period, which saw the mighty achievement of the symphony, was no less distinguished in its perfection of works for very small groups of musicians. Amateur and sometimes professional musicians gathered in middle-class homes and the drawing rooms of the well-to-do. Small groups also performed out-of-doors—in the gardens of summer estates, in the streets, and even in the gondolas that traveled the waterways of Venice. Large repertoires of music were written for a variety of small instrumental groups.

Chamber music is generally defined as music written for a small group of performers with only one player to a part and without a conductor. In a broad sense, the definition of chamber music also includes music written for one or two performers. Orchestral music, by contrast, involves whole sections of instruments that play in unison except during rare solo passages.

Classical Sonatas

The piano played a major role in much of Classical chamber music, especially in the development of the sonata. *Classical sonatas* were generally written for one instrument—the piano—or for piano and one other instrument.

String Ensembles

Also popular were works for small groups of string instruments. The most common type of composition was the *string quartet*, a work for four instruments—first violin, second violin, viola, and cello. *String trios, string quintets, string sextets,* and so on, were also written, but they were considerably less popular than the quartet. At times another instrument, such as the piano, was added to a string trio or quartet, resulting in a *piano quartet* or *piano quintet.* Such an ensemble was named for the unusual instrument in it.

As has been noted, chamber music differs from orchestral music in two obvious ways—in the small number of players involved and in the separate voices of the instruments. More important, however, are the differences in conception and effect. A symphonic orchestra is capable of grand and impressive sound as well as great contrast in timbre and dynamics. A chamber work, on the other hand, is economical in its means of expression. In a string quartet, the listener can follow the voices of the different instruments simultaneously. The resulting texture is clear and transparent. Limited in variety of timbre and texture, the work achieves its effect through the ever-changing dialogue of its instruments.

Development of the Classical Sonata

The sonata of the Classical period, a work for one or two instruments, is in some ways a composite of the many different types of sonatas popular in the Baroque age. At the same time, it is not completely like any of the earlier works. Like the trio and solo sonatas of the Baroque age, it is a work of several movements of contrasting character. Like Scarlatti's sonatas for unaccompanied harpsichord, it stresses the sound of a keyboard instrument. Not surprisingly the popularity of the Classical sonata paralleled the growing importance of the piano as a solo instrument. By the late eighteenth century, the sonata for piano or for piano and another instrument, generally the violin, had become a very popular form of home entertainment. Baroque influences were important in shaping the Classical sonata, but the work had been molded into something completely new by the late eighteenth century.

A Grand Piano from the Late Eighteenth Century: *Although the first pianofortes were produced at the beginning of the eighteenth century, the piano did not truly begin to replace the harpsichord as the most popular keyboard instrument until the Classical age. A number of Beethoven's early keyboard works were in fact published for "harpsichord or pianoforte." The piano shown here was built in Salzburg in 1788.*

The Granger Collection

Structure of the Classical Sonata

Just as the Classical symphony is a sonata cycle for orchestra, the Classical sonata is a sonata cycle for piano, or for piano and another instrument. The number of movements in the cycle varies from three to four. The first movement is always in sonata form, although it is sometimes preceded by a slow introduction. The second movement may be in sonata, ternary, or theme and variations form. In a four-movement work, the third movement is generally a minuet and trio, while the last movement is in rondo or sonata form. Sonatas with only three movements omit the minuet.

Major Composers of Classical Sonatas

Schubert

Haydn's most important works for piano are sonatas. Mozart too wrote sonatas for solo piano and sonatas for piano and violin. In the early years of the nineteenth century, Franz Schubert (1797–1828) also emerged as a major composer of solo piano sonatas. While many of their works are of fine quality, it is in the sonatas of Beethoven that the epitome of the genre is reached. His works form a bridge between Classical and Romantic styles and foreshadow many later nineteenth-century developments.

Beethoven: *Piano Sonata in C Minor, Op. 13*

One of Beethoven's finest and best-loved works is the *Piano Sonata in C Minor, Op. 13* (the "Pathétique"), which was published in 1799, quite early in his career. The work is in three movements.

First Movement: Grave; Allegro di molto e con brio; in Sonata Form

Introduction

Main Part of Movement

The first movement begins with a slow, ominous introduction. This contrasts dramatically with the main part of the movement, which is marked Allegro and cast in sonata form. The structure of the sonata form is clear, but it is further clarified by the return of the slow introductory material between the exposition and the development, and again after the recapitulation. Dramatic contrasts of theme, key, and dynamics are much greater here than in piano works written earlier in the Classical period.

Listening Guide for Beethoven's *Piano Sonata in C Minor*, First Movement

Timbre:	piano
Melody:	dotted motive prominent in introduction; first theme stresses rising motion; second theme more lyrical
Rhythm:	duple meter; tempo of introduction Grave (very slow); main tempo of movement Allegro di molto e con brio (very fast, with spirit)
Harmony:	mainly minor mode; begins in C minor, modulates most significantly to E♭ major, ends in C minor
Texture:	mainly homophonic
Form:	sonata form preceded by slow introduction

Second Movement: Adagio cantabile; in Rondo Form

The second movement is marked Adagio cantabile and placed in the contrasting key of A♭ major. The first theme is one of Beethoven's most lyrical:

First Theme

Second and Third Themes

The melody is repeated immediately with a new accompaniment.

Later in the movement, two other themes are presented in contrasting keys. Each of these is preceded and followed by the first theme in the movement's tonic, or home, key—A♭. The movement is thus in rondo form. An outline of the arrangement of themes is shown below:

A	A	B	A	C	C	A	A

Listening Guide for Beethoven's *Piano Sonata in C Minor,* Second Movement

Timbre:	piano
Melody:	first theme lyrical and flowing, with lilting accompaniment; second theme disjunct and restless; third theme conjunct, with agitated accompaniment
Rhythm:	duple meter; tempo Adagio cantabile (slow, in singing style)
Harmony:	mainly major mode; A sections in A♭ major; B section modulates through minor mode to E♭ major; C sections modulate to A♭ minor and E major
Texture:	mainly homophonic
Form:	rondo (AABACCAA)

Third Movement: Allegro; in Rondo Form

The third movement is in the sonata's home key of C minor. It opens with a vivacious theme in duple meter:

First Theme

Second and Third Themes

Two other themes are later heard in different keys. Each presentation of a new theme is followed by a return to the first theme in the tonic key. Thus the third movement, like the second, is in rondo form, this time a more extended form with a repetition of the second theme toward the end.

A	B	A	C	A	B	A

CLASSICAL CHAMBER MUSIC: THE SONATA AND THE STRING QUARTET

The Evolution of Keyboard Music

The music written for keyboard instruments has been affected perhaps as much by changes in technology as by changes in musical style. The compositions that were written for the harpsichord of the Renaissance and Baroque ages differed significantly from those that were written for the piano of the Classical age, in large part because of the technical differences in the instruments. Virtuosic possibilities continued to increase with the perfection of the piano in the early nineteenth century, and the twentieth century brought even more options with the use of electronics and other new technological devices.

Listen to works written for keyboard instruments in four different periods—those listed below from the record set that accompanies the text, or other selections from the record library.

Baroque:	Scarlatti's *Sonata in C Major*, K.159 (for harpsichord)	Side 3, Band 1
Classical/ Romantic:	Beethoven's *Sonata in C Minor, Op. 13*, Third Movement (for piano)	Side 6, Band 2
Romantic:	Liszt's *Hungarian Rhapsody No. 6 in D♭ Major* (for piano)	Side 7, Band 2
Modern:	Selection from Cage's *Sixteen Sonatas and Four Interludes* (for prepared piano)	Record Library

What are the most notable differences in the musical qualities of the various instruments? In what ways do the composers seem to have taken advantage of the different technical capacities of their instruments?

Side 6, Band 2

Listening Guide for Beethoven's *Piano Sonata in C Minor,* Third Movement

Timbre:	piano
Melody:	first theme characterized by sequence and repeated notes; second theme features flowing scale passages; third theme features disjunct, syncopated passage
Rhythm:	duple meter; tempo Allegro (fast)
Harmony:	mainly minor mode; A sections in C minor; first B section in E♭ major; C section in A♭ major; second B section in C major
Texture:	mainly homophonic
Form:	rondo (ABACABA)

CLASSICAL MUSIC

Development of the String Quartet

The earliest standardized chamber groups were those that played the Baroque trio and solo sonatas (described in Chapter 10). As music became more melodic in the Classical sense, the use of harpsichord continuo declined. The hole that would have been left in the musical fabric was filled by more active middle string instruments. What developed was a string quartet, made up of two violins, one viola, and one cello.

At first the lower strings were limited to accompaniment, in deference to the Classical taste for homophony. The violin was invariably the melody instrument. All parts were kept simple enough to be played by amateurs. Indeed, the earliest quartets were written more for the enjoyment of the players than for any audience.

Structure of the String Quartet

The overall structure of the string quartet, and of most other works for small string ensemble, is very similar to that of the symphony. All of the works are based on the concept of the sonata cycle, and all eventually came to have four movements. The forms of the individual movements in the string quartet are usually the same as those found in the symphony.

The similarities found between the symphony and the string quartet are not surprising when we consider the history of both compositional forms. Haydn wrote a number of short "symphonies" for the small group he directed at the Esterházy palace. At the time, no one thought it necessary to define these works as either symphonies or chamber works since neither type of composition had yet been fully developed. Nevertheless, it was under Haydn that the string quartet, the most important type of chamber music, took definite form. The symphony itself, as we have seen, grew into a work for a larger, well-defined group of players.

Major Composers of String Quartets

Haydn's String Quartets

Many of the early string quartets, including some of Haydn's, were called *divertimenti*—music for entertainment. Gradually, however, Haydn's string quartets, and those of other composers as well, came to serve more serious musical purposes. Haydn developed the lower voices, making them more independent and interesting. In fact, he sometimes used contrapuntal textures within an essentially homophonic framework. In this way music for the string quartet was able to derive strength not only from Classical use of melody and harmony but also from the independence of voices so typical of earlier times.

Mozart's String Quartets

Mozart's string quartets built upon the traditions established by Haydn. His mature works gave more equal emphasis to all four instruments. The parts written for viola and cello became more demanding. The works as a whole gradually became longer and more complex.

Beethoven's String Quartets

Beethoven chose the string quartet for the expression of some of his most profound and difficult musical ideas. With Beethoven the work became less and less a medium for the amateur. As in his sonatas and symphonies,

An Early String Quartet: *In this artist's impression, Haydn is shown leading the rehearsal of a string quartet. Works for small groups of string players had been popular in earlier ages, but they were largely superseded by the trio sonata with its basso continuo during the Baroque age. Thus the string quartet was very much the invention of the Classical age.*

Beethoven approached the quartet with little concession to the limitations of players or audience. Especially in his last quartets, the demands on both are extraordinary. Beethoven tended to use the quartet as a medium for experimentation. The result was often confusing to his audiences. In some ways, his quartets were too modern for their time. Since Beethoven's day, a number of other composers have also chosen to introduce their most experimental ideas in quartets and other chamber works. Small ensemble pieces lend themselves well to such experimentation. The tonal relationships are especially clear and the musical ideas may be closely followed.

The Classical Sense of Beauty

Neoclassicism In art, as in music, a desire for a new means of expression arose toward the middle of the eighteenth century. This yearning for a new and "pure" style, coinciding as it did with the excavations at Herculaneum and Pompeii, culminated in a style based on Classical Greek and Roman models. Philosophers and revolutionaries sought precedents in the republics of ancient Athens and Rome, and it was almost inevitable that Classical art, with its sobriety, its idealization of and obedience to rational rules, would also strike a responsive chord. Based in part on early republican fervor, Neoclassical styles outlived the French Revolution and provided the basis for the Empire style of Napoleon Bonaparte's reign. This late style can be seen in Canova's statue of Napoleon's sister Pauline Borghese. Following a Greek prototype, Canova presented his subject as Venus Victorious. Head and body are idealized, while the clear, cold outline imparts the character of ancient relief.

Canova: *Pauline Borghese* (1808)

David: *Distribution of the Standards* (1810)

The Work of David Jacques Louis David was one of the first painters to use Classical themes as metaphors of modern life. An ardent republican, he became the virtual dictator of French art in the years after Napoleon's rise to power. In his heroic *Distribution of the Standards*, Rococo lightness and evanescence are displaced by austere configurations intended to evoke lofty thoughts—thoughts of self-sacrifice and moral elevation. Each of the figures is carefully set apart from his neighbor by David's sharp, icy, relief-like drawing and restricted, uniform colors. Elements of dress and setting are treated, however, with an almost scientific exactitude. David's attempt to create a synthesis of Classical idealism and direct observation had a major influence on early nineteenth-century art.

than by the growing power and wealth of both the English nobility and merchant class, a wealth that created a great demand for portraiture. The seventeenth-century Flemish painter Van Dyck had established a standard of refined portrait painting in England that subsequent English painters sought to emulate. Sitters expected to be flattered and shown at their very best. They wished to look both elegant and aristocratic. Gainsborough, in his *The Honourable Mrs. Graham*, preserved the Vandyckian tradition. Posed full-length in rich brocade beside a column and before a landscape background, the young woman is the very model of grace and breeding. Because of his feeling for color and quiet sensitivity to personality, Gainsborough was able to elevate the rather pedestrian art of portraiture as it was practiced in eighteenth-century England to the level of high art.

Gainsborough: *The Honourable Mrs. Graham* **(1775)**

Frederic Lewis

Goya: *Saturn Devouring His Children* (1819–1823)

Romantic Tendencies One of the great individualists of nineteenth-century art, Spanish master Francisco Goya did most of his work some years before the Romantic movement coalesced around French painter Delacroix in the 1820s. Goya saw his country ravaged by Napoleon's soldiers and witnessed the growing poverty and moral decay following the withdrawal of the French forces. During these years he withdrew from the confusions of Madrid to a small house across the river. Its walls he covered with his "black paintings." To paint them he employed the materials he could still find in a ravaged land—lamp black, earth brown and white—yet these nightmare visions of subhuman, devil-worshiping monsters glow with an eerie, almost unnatural light. *Saturn Devouring His Children* is particularly hypnotic. Glorying in mindless fury, Saturn cannibalizes the horribly mangled body of a tiny man. Outlines are rough and colors dominated by a deathly black. It is an art wrenched from the depths of the subconscious.

Beethoven: *String Quartet No. 7 in F Major* ("Razumovsky")

Beethoven wrote a total of seventeen string quartets. The first six were published as a set in 1801. *Quartet No. 7* was published in 1806, after Beethoven's great spiritual crisis and the writing of the Fifth Symphony. The seventh quartet—*Op. 59, No. 1*—is one of a set of three commissioned by the Russian Count Razumovsky. While the Count probably expected his set of quartets to contain the usual six works, each of the three he received was much longer than any of the quartets written by Haydn or Mozart. Beethoven's quartets, like his symphonies, were generally longer and more challenging than those of earlier Classical composers.

The Razumovsky quartets, as they were later called, were greeted with some consternation. One critic described them as "patchwork by a madman," though conceding at the same time that the music was well constructed and "deep in thought." Performers of the works were greatly taken aback. Thayer, the noted Beethoven biographer, reports that a cellist flung down his score in the middle of a performance and trampled it. Today, however, the quartets seem more accessible. Their lyric and dramatic qualities are perhaps more appealing to people who have inherited the Romantic tradition of nineteenth-century music.

Quartet No. 7, the first of the three Razumovsky quartets, is in four movements, each of which is in sonata form or in modified sonata form. Yet even with the similarity of organization, each movement has a distinctly different emotional coloring.

First Movement: Allegro; in Sonata Form

The first movement opens unconventionally with a quiet lyric melody played by the cello:

This is unusual because most such works reserve the opening statement for the violin. They also avoid using a lyrical theme so early in the work.

After the opening theme a short chromatic passage leads to a continuation of the theme, played by the two violins, imitated by viola and cello. Another chromatic passage helps to establish a new key. A second theme is then stated:

After some interplay among all four instruments, the rhythmic motion slows down to bring the exposition to a close.

Development

The development section follows without a pause. It begins with the first theme, again played by the cello. The theme is presented in several different keys, accompanied by chords and quickly moving notes. Midway through the development, the rhythmic motion slows again, and the first violin begins the opening theme, suggesting that the recapitulation is about to follow. But instead the development continues for several measures.

Recapitulation

The recapitulation is unusual in that when the original key returns at the beginning of the section we hear, not the first half of the opening theme, but the second half. The two parts of the opening theme are in fact reversed, since the first half immediately follows the second. After this the second theme appears as expected. The movement closes with a coda, preceded by several measures of long notes that further develop the first theme.

Coda

Side 6, Band 3

Listening Guide for Beethoven's *String Quartet No. 7*, First Movement

Timbre:	string quartet: two violins, viola, and cello
Melody:	first theme very lyrical; second theme also lyrical and much more conjunct
Rhythm:	duple meter; tempo Allegro (fast)
Harmony:	mainly major mode; begins in F major, modulates most significantly to C major, ends in F major
Texture:	homophonic and contrapuntal
Form:	sonata form followed by a coda

Second Movement: Allegretto vivace e sempre scherzando; in Sonata Form

Exposition

The second movement offers an immediate contrast to the first. While the first movement seems to unfold from a basically lyrical impulse, the spirit of the second movement derives mainly from the lively rhythm of its opening motive. The music has a scherzolike quality generated by this hesitant yet active motive, which is played first in *staccato* fashion—in short, clipped notes—by the cellos. After the opening motive has been expanded into the first theme and the first theme itself has been greatly expanded, the second theme enters in a minor mode. In a number of the passages that follow, the music seems to generate a sort of nervous irritability.

Use of Staccato

Development, Recapitulation, and Coda

The development section reworks melodic and rhythmic aspects of the first theme. The recapitulation is followed by a coda that further develops the opening theme.

This movement, like the first, is basically in sonata form, but the form is perhaps not as easily heard here as it was in the earlier movement. Most clearly recognizable are the repetition and development of the opening motive and the first theme.

CLASSICAL MUSIC

Listening Guide for Beethoven's *String Quartet No. 7,* Second Movement

Timbre: string quartet: two violins, viola, and cello

Melody: first theme characterized by short staccato notes; second theme conjunct and more lyrical

Rhythm: triple meter; tempo Allegretto vivace e sempre scherzando (fast, lively, and playful throughout); several rhythmic patterns recur, especially that of the opening motive

Harmony: mainly major mode; begins in B♭ major, modulates most significantly to F minor, ends in B♭ major

Texture: monophonic, homophonic, and contrapuntal

Form: sonata form followed by a coda

Third Movement: Adagio molte e mesto; in Sonata Form

In most quartets as in most symphonies, the second movement is the slowest in tempo. In the present work, however, Beethoven chose to make the third movement the slowest. The tempo marking for the movement means "very slowly and sadly," indicating the deeply Romantic feeling of this portion of the work.

In addition to the Romantic tempo marking, Beethoven wrote the following description of the movement: "A weeping willow or acacia tree over my brother's grave." Only one of Beethoven's brothers had died, an infant Beethoven had never known. Thus it is probable that this movement, like the "Eroica," expresses not so much a biographical statement as a poetic feeling with its own reality.

The music proceeds with a great deal of tension among the different instrumental parts. The relationship is generally one of conflict. Melodies and rhythms of great contrast are played, sometimes at the same time by different instruments. The movement is, like the others in this quartet, in sonata form.

Listening Guide for Beethoven's *String Quartet No. 7,* Third Movement

Timbre: string quartet: two violins, viola, and cello

Melody: first theme disjunct; second theme more lyrical

Rhythm: duple meter; tempo Adagio molto e mesto (very slowly and sadly)

Harmony: mainly minor mode; begins in F minor, modulates most significantly to C minor, ends on dominant chord of F minor

Texture: homophonic and contrapuntal

Form: sonata form followed by a rather lengthy coda

Fourth Movement: Allegro; in Sonata Form

The third movement continues into the final movement without a break. Along with the tempo marking for this movement, Beethoven included the

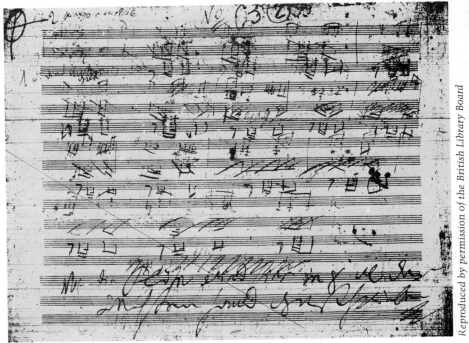

Sketchbook Page for Beethoven's *String Quartet No. 7: Beethoven generally began his compositions by sketching out a number of different musical possibilities. For his seventh quartet, he is known to have produced several sketches, possibly as many as thirteen. The page above shows a series of early ideas for the finale, ideas that were largely rejected, as can be seen in the multitude of slash marks.* (MS. 47852)

words *Thème russe* ("Russian theme"). True to this marking, the movement does make use of a melody from a Russian folk song, in the first theme:

The theme was drawn from a collection of songs presumably given to Beethoven by Count Razumovsky.

The movement continues in the fashion typical of works in sonata form. The recapitulation is followed by a substantial coda.

Listening Guide for Beethoven's *String Quartet No. 7*, Fourth Movement

Timbre:	string quartet: two violins, viola, and cello
Melody:	first theme based on Russian folk song; second theme conjunct and lyrical
Rhythm:	duple meter; tempo Allegro (fast)
Harmony:	mainly major mode; begins in F major, modulates most significantly to C major, ends in F major
Texture:	homophonic and contrapuntal
Form:	sonata form followed by a coda

Suggested Listening

The Classical Sonata

Mozart: *Piano Sonata in F Major*, K. 332 [DG 138949]. The three movements of this work show many different facets of Mozart's style. The virtuosic style of the last movement is especially impressive.

Beethoven: *Sonata for Violin and Piano in A Major, Op. 47* ("Kreutzer" Sonata) [DG 2530135]. Dedicated to the violinist Rodolphe Kreutzer, this sonata is probably the best known of Beethoven's two-instrument sonatas. The energy and drama of Beethoven's mature style are clearly evident in the work.

The String Quartet

Haydn: *String Quartet in E♭ Major, Op. 33, No. 2* (the "Joke") [London 6385]. The six string quartets of *Op. 33* mark a turning point in the works Haydn wrote for string ensemble. Thematic development is considerably more extensive than in his earlier quartets. All four instruments have more or less equal importance. Finally, Haydn uses a scherzo instead of the expected minuet in these four-movement works. The "joke" of the second quartet is found in several amusing musical effects that vividly display Haydn's keen sense of humor.

Mozart: *String Quartet in G Major*, K. 387 [RCA ARL 1-0760]. This quartet, one of a series dedicated to Haydn as a mark of the strong friendship between the two composers, makes thematic references to Haydn's *Op. 33, No. 5*. Although the work is basically in G major, it opens in D minor, the poignancy of which is made even stronger by the use of chromaticism. The texture remains light in spite of the very expressive harmonies. The nature and development of melodic material is quintessentially Classical.

Other Chamber Music

Mozart: *Serenade in G Major*, K. 525 ("Eine kleine Nachtmusik"—"A Little Night Music") [Vanguard 2126]. This serenade, Mozart's most famous and beloved, includes five movements. The music is generally somewhat lighter in mood than that found in many of Mozart's symphonies. Written for a small string orchestra, the work represents Mozart's most elegant and charming style.

Schubert: *Piano Quintet in A Major, Op. 114* (the "Trout") [Vanguard 71145]. This quintet in five movements at times places the piano in opposition to the strings and at other times blends it with them. Melodic and harmonic materials are dramatically expressive.

17

Classical Vocal Music

Opera in the Classical Period

While instrumental works are perhaps the most important legacy of Classical music, vocal music also received considerable attention from the major composers of the period. The types of vocal music developed in the Baroque period continued in use, and no important new types were devised. Operas, Masses, and oratorios were all popular, but it is probably in opera that the freshest and most vital creations are to be found.

Gluck

Haydn, Mozart, and Beethoven all wrote operas—Beethoven only one. Another German composer, Christoph Willibald Gluck (1714–1787), also wrote a number of operas, some of which are still performed today. The works of the four composers brought new direction to both the serious and comic opera traditions of the Baroque age.

Before we enter into a discussion of the changes wrought by Classical composers, however, there is something to be gained from a consideration of the very special and unusual nature of opera in any period. An understanding of the conventions and materials of opera can add greatly to the appreciation of the individual works produced in the Classical period.

The Special Nature of Opera

Opera has long enjoyed a reputation as the grandest and most glamorous of musical compositions. It is entertainment on a large scale. A combination of music and theater, opera draws upon the resources of an orchestra, vocal soloists, a chorus, and in some cases a ballet company as well. As a mixture of different musical media, opera appeals to an audience on a number of different levels.

The Conventions of Opera

In order to enjoy opera, a person must be willing to accept its imaginative aspects as well as a number of conventions that have developed to suit the particular needs of the art form. Every art form has certain customary ways of representing the real world. These often grow out of the natural limitations of the medium. Most of us find it easy to accept the portrayal of a boundless, rolling landscape on the flat surface of a painting. Movie audiences have no difficulty in accepting the insertion of sentimental music during even the most private of cinema love scenes. Few of us would criticize Molière for casting his dialogue in rhymed couplets. It would also be difficult to criticize Shakespeare for giving his characters long soliloquies quite beyond the inclinations of normal people. In short, most of us are willing to grant each of these art forms its own necessary methods.

The conventions of opera can be accepted in much the same way if they are recognized and understood. Most important is the fact that much or all of the text is sung rather than spoken. This is only one of many ways in which opera differs from spoken drama. In a play the author has ample opportunity to reveal the complexities of the plot, develop characters, and depict action on all levels. In an opera, where music is the main means of expression, the plot and the characters are often condensed and stylized. The texts of most operas are rather short and sketchy. When Beaumarchais' play *La Folle journée* ("A Day of Folly"), for example, was made into an opera (Mozart's *Le Nozze di Figaro*, or "The Marriage of Figaro"), many of the comic complications had to be left out. In some operas strenuous physical actions must be limited because singers cannot perform them and sing beautifully at the same time. Even with these limitations, however, the opera is a fully realized work. Words and actions are amply conveyed, reinforced, and elaborated in the musical score. Music provides the context in which the plot and characters must be judged.

If the conventions of opera are understood, some of the unnatural happenings in opera may seem more reasonable. It is clearly unnatural for a woman to sing loudly while she lies on her deathbed. This kind of action would be difficult to accept in a play. But in an opera, it may be necessary for the singer to complete certain climactic phrases if the aria is to make sense as music. She must do this even if the drama itself is not thereby improved. The audience accepts it as a convention of opera. Similarly it accepts the fact that characters who are called upon to take swift action will nevertheless repeat their thoughts four or five times if the music demands it. Some conventions of plot are accepted purely for reasons of expediency. It is difficult to believe that superficial disguises will prevent sworn lovers from recognizing one another. But this occurs time and again in the plots of Classical comic operas. None of these unrealistic devices need detract from the enjoyment of opera. Opera, through its music, introduces an entirely different dimension of reality.

Because it is a musical medium, opera is able to reach expressive depths that are beyond the scope of ordinary drama. Music intensifies the portrayal of the plot and characters, thus compensating for the often sketchy text. Few spoken words of love can bear comparison with the great love arias of opera. Nor can the terror and suspense conveyed by music be easily duplicated by words alone. It is music's unique expressiveness that explains the impact of opera as theater.

A Wedding of Music and Theater: In the final scene of The Magic Flute, *Mozart's last opera, hero and heroine are united at the feet of the high priest and surrounded by full chorus. The work ends in triumph, with a splendor both musical and visual.*

The Materials of Opera

Opera's basic appeal seems to lie in the expressive intensity of the music. Much additional interest, however, derives from the relationships among opera's many different elements: solo voices, ensembles, choruses, orchestra, text, and visual staging. The composer must reconcile and integrate all of these competing elements into an artistic whole.

Solo Voices

The operatic heroine is almost always a soprano, the highest voice. There are several different types of soprano voice, ranging in timbre and style from the light and lyrical to the full bodied and dramatic. Perhaps the most exciting voice is that of the *coloratura soprano,* whose part calls for a virtuosic display of high notes, trills, and arpeggios—a part similar to that of the instrumental soloist in a concerto. A soprano is often a heroine offstage as well as on—the famous *prima donna* ("first lady") traditionally adored by the opera-going public. Famous sopranos of our time include Joan Sutherland, Beverly Sills, Renata Tebaldi, and Birgit Nilsson.

If all women in opera were sopranos, there would be little contrast in the upper range. Some female parts are written for the slightly lower and heavier voice of the *mezzo-soprano* or for the even lower voice of the *contralto*. A soprano's servant, rival, or older relative is often cast in a lower range to provide contrast. In operas where all female parts are scored for sopranos, composers generally differentiate among them in style of composition.

Male roles generally fall into three ranges—*tenor, baritone,* or *bass.* At times, however, parts for young men, especially aspiring young suitors, may be cast as soprano parts and played by women in disguise—a convention often difficult for modern opera-goers to accept. The tenor is the highest of the usual masculine ranges and is often the protagonist or lover. Important male parts may also fall to the lower-voiced baritone. The bass, the very lowest of voices, may be cast as an older man, an authority figure such as a king or a priest, or a villain. The composer of opera has wide latitude in the choice of male roles and ranges. As in the choice of female voices, the main objective is to provide dramatic variety.

The soloists sing both arias and recitatives. In arias the action generally stops while the singer comments upon it. The music is of central interest. In recitatives, however, the action is likely to continue. *Recitativo secco* is heard most often, while *recitativo accompagnato* is generally reserved for more dramatic moments.

Choruses and Ensembles

In opera the composer uses not only soloists but also choruses and small ensembles that perform duets, trios, quartets, and so on. In an ensemble two or more characters may join in a single melodic line, expressing shared feelings. Or they may sing back and forth, completing the melody between them. In some cases several characters will sing different melodies expressing different emotions. This increase in musical activity generally coincides with a dramatic crisis. There are also ensembles in which different characters harmonize a single melody.

In some operas a chorus is used to present a larger mass of vocal sound. During a wedding party or a military scene, for example, a large number of singers may be brought on stage to form the chorus in front of which the principal soloists appear. The chorus may participate in the action or may simply comment upon it in the manner of ancient Greek drama. Choral scenes are often accompanied by dancing or other colorful effects.

Orchestra

Soloists, ensembles, and choruses are accompanied by an orchestra located in the pit, the area just in front of the stage. The composer varies the orchestration in accordance with the mood and action on the stage. A large military scene may call for a full symphonic effect, a bedroom scene for the lighter instrumentation of a chamber work. In addition to accompanying the singers, the orchestra may be called upon to support the dramatic action with various sound effects—thunder and lightning, bird songs, trumpet calls, the music of a shepherd's pipes. The orchestra also performs independently, opening the opera with an overture and in some cases presenting preludes to individual acts. Other orchestral passages may function as interludes or as accompaniment to dance. The size of the opera orchestra has varied from one period to another. In the Baroque period, it was quite small, in the Classical period, a little larger, and in the Romantic period, larger still.

Libretto

The text or script of an opera is called the *libretto* ("little book"). Generally it is poetic in form. In most cases the author, or librettist, derives the material from a play, a story, or a historical account. The material must then be structured to meet the special demands of opera.

The libretto is clearly an important component of opera, second only to the musical score—some would say, equal to it. And yet English-speaking audiences cannot always rely on the libretto for an understanding of the action, for it is likely to be in another language—usually Italian, German, or French. Many librettos published in English-speaking countries, however, include English translations, which may be read before seeing the performance. And even without a translation, an opera can usually be understood through its

Synopsis

music and visual action, especially with the aid of the *synopsis* of the plot that is usually included in the program.

Scenery and Staging

Although opera can give pleasure through its libretto and music alone, the full theatrical experience is not complete without the visual elements—the scenery and the staging. Opera is, after all, theater. It draws on the theatrical arts of costume, scenic design, lighting, and choreography. The importance of the visual element can be seen in the budget of the Metropolitan Opera of New York. A typical production costs thousands of dollars for the staging alone.

To an audience that does not understand the language of the libretto, clarity of staging can be especially important. Characters may use gesture and visual effect to convey the plot. Some of the finest moments in opera are produced by a powerful combination of visual and musical effects. In Gounod's *Faust*, for example, the heroine rises toward heaven to the accompaniment of an invisible chorus of angels. In Mozart's *Don Giovanni*, the protagonist goes down to hell as flames and smoke envelop the stage and voices from the underworld promise eternal torture. Staging is of critical importance to the theatrical art of opera.

The Serious and Comic Operas of the Classical Period

German-speaking composers were the leading masters of opera in the Classical period. Their works generally fall into two categories, *opera seria* and comic opera, the latter including *opera buffa* and *Singspiel*.

Opera Seria

Opera seria ("serious opera" in Italian) was inherited from Baroque composers. It found its earliest Classical expression in the late eighteenth century in the works of Gluck and Haydn. The operas tended to be highly stylized, with subjects that were almost always heroic, generally concerning the gods and heroes of ancient times.

As the Classical spirit took hold, reformers attempted to make the opera seria simpler and more emotionally direct. Gluck sought to abolish "useless and superficial ornament," and expended his efforts "in the search for simple beauty instead." Gluck's works enjoyed considerable success with Classical audiences, and the ideas they contained had great influence on serious opera.

Mozart wrote two major serious operas, *Idomeneo* at the beginning of his career and *La Clemenza di Tito* ("The Mercy of Titus") at the end. But it is for his comic operas that he is remembered today and for these same operas that he was honored in his own time.

Opera Buffa

Opera buffa ("comic opera" in Italian) is fast paced and humorous, full of frivolity, practical jokes, and comic confusion. The very term *buffa* suggests the buffoonery that characterizes it. But opera buffa is also capable of great melodic beauty. Especially in the works of Mozart, the music begins to admit an underlying seriousness and sensuality, at least in certain arias and scenes. *The Marriage of Figaro* and *Don Giovanni* are notable for their fusion of comic and serious elements.

Singspiel

Singspiel ("song play" in German) was also a popular form of comic opera in the Classical period. In it the dialogue is spoken rather than sung in recitative, resulting in a simpler presentation closer to our own musical comedies.

As has been noted, all the major Classical composers wrote at least one opera. Haydn wrote a number of them, but they were produced on a small scale and were not generally performed outside the Esterházy court. Beethoven wrote only one, a serious moral drama entitled *Fidelio*. Mozart was the most successful operatic composer of the three. It is to him that we turn for a greater understanding of the comic opera of the period.

Mozart: *The Marriage of Figaro*

Two of Mozart's most important operas are comic operas in the opera buffa style: *Le Nozze di Figaro* (1786), which translates into "The Marriage of Figaro," and *Così fan tutte* (1790), which may be loosely translated as "They All Do It." He also wrote two operas in Singspiel style: *Die Entführung aus dem Serail* (1782), or "The Abduction from the Seraglio," and *Die Zauberflöte* (1791), or "The Magic Flute." Mozart's *Don Giovanni* is in a special category of its own, since it prominently combines both buffa and seria traits.

Mozart's first opera buffa was based on a play by the French writer Beaumarchais, a work entitled *La Folle journée*, or *Le Mariage de Figaro*. The play was the second of a trilogy, following *Le Barbier de Seville* ("The Barber of Seville"), which was the basis for another opera written thirty years later by Gioacchino Rossini. Both *The Barber of Seville* and *The Marriage of Figaro* focus on the adventures of Figaro, the servant or valet of a Spanish noble, Count Almaviva.

Da Ponte's Libretto

The librettist for *The Marriage of Figaro* was Lorenzo da Ponte, a theater poet at the court of Emperor Joseph II in Vienna. In converting Beaumarchais' play into a workable opera, he reduced the number of characters from sixteen to eleven and did some rather significant editing of content. Beaumarchais' play had satirized the upper classes and their relationship to the servant class—a topic particularly threatening to German aristocrats at a time when

LE

MARIAGE DE FIGARO

OU

LA FOLLE JOURNÉE

COMÉDIE EN CINQ ACTES

PAR

BEAUMARCHAIS

REPRÉSENTÉE POUR LA PREMIÈRE FOIS, A PARIS, EN 1784

From Play to Opera: *Beaumarchais' play about the marriage of a Spanish valet was first presented, with its original French text, in Paris in 1784. Two years later it was presented as an opera, with Italian text and music by Austrian composer Mozart. The opening page of the original program shows a scene that Mozart turned into a rousing trio.*

revolutionaries were just about to overthrow the government of France. To get clearance for Mozart's opera, da Ponte had to assure the Emperor that he had "cut anything that might offend good taste or public decency at a performance over which the sovereign majesty might preside." And to a great extent he had. Mozart's opera takes full advantage of the cleverness of Beaumarchais' plot, but it largely discards the play's political implications.

Plot Synopsis

The opera concerns the impending marriage of Count Almaviva's valet Figaro to the Countess's maid Susanna. The plot revolves around a series of comical confusions—suspected lovers jumping out of windows, hiding in closets, and so forth. But essentially there are three major dramatic conflicts. First, the Count is bent on making love to Susanna, if possible before her wedding takes place. Second, a former rival of the Count, Bartolo, has an old grudge against Figaro and so wishes to prevent his marriage. Bartolo is in league with the Count's housekeeper, Marcellina, who has loaned Figaro money and has a contract stating that Figaro shall either repay her or marry her. Thus the Count, Bartolo, and Marcellina all wish to postpone or prevent Figaro's marriage for personal reasons. The third conflict involves the young page Cherubino. Seemingly in love with love itself, Cherubino especially adores the Countess, whom he woos with original love songs and other attentions, all of which enrage the Count.

Jealousies lead to a number of comic deceptions. However, at the end, all major problems are pleasantly resolved. Figaro, who had been separated from his parents at birth, proves to be the son of Marcellina and Bartolo. Upon learning that she is Figaro's mother, Marcellina drops her demands, embraces her long-lost child, and determines to marry Bartolo at this late date. Susanna and the Countess ultimately thwart the Count in his amorous designs. Susanna arranges to meet him in the garden, but it is the Countess, disguised as Susanna, who keeps the rendezvous. Figaro, however, has not been told of the deception planned by Susanna and the Countess. Seeing the woman he believes to be his sweetheart with the Count, he is so angered that he seeks out the Countess to tell her of her husband's infidelity. But the "Countess" is, of course, Susanna in disguise. When Figaro recognizes this, he proceeds to make advances to his disguised bride-to-be, feigning infidelity. For this he is boxed on the ears and thus reassured of Susanna's love and purged of his jealousy. The Count and the Countess are similarly reconciled. As for Cherubino, everyone seems to be in a good-natured conspiracy to protect him from the Count's wrath. Early in the opera, the Count dispatches him to the army, but he returns in secret. He reappears toward the end of the play disguised as a young girl, in the company of his new beloved, Barbarina. The opera ends with the ringing of wedding bells. A day of torment and folly has been resolved in the happiness of love.

Overture

The overture to *The Marriage of Figaro* sets the mood for the entire opera. It is in abridged sonata form, without any real development section. Like most other operatic overtures, it is fairly short and dramatic. As the overture proceeds, the music becomes rhythmically faster, building to a higher pitch and bigger sound as if in anticipation of the opening curtain.

Listening Guide for Mozart's *The Marriage of Figaro*, Overture

Timbre:	orchestra of moderate size: string instruments, wind instruments, and timpani
Melody:	several themes; first theme largely conjunct with quick rhythmic motion; others characterized by strong accents and syncopation
Rhythm:	duple meter; very fast tempo
Harmony:	major mode; begins in D major, modulates most significantly to A major
Texture:	homophonic
Form:	abridged sonata form with no development section

Act I

Duet: Figaro and Susanna

Act I begins with a short orchestral introduction, followed by a duet, "Cinque, dieci." Figaro, a baritone, is heard first, singing a series of very deliberate motives as he measures the bedroom that he will soon share with Susanna. We hear him call out the measurements, "cinque" ("five"), "dieci" ("ten"), and so on.

First Theme

Susanna, a soprano, enters, trying on a hat and contributing a new melodic idea, a cheery, quickly moving melody that contrasts with Figaro's straightforward presentation.

Second Theme

After a few moments, Figaro notices Susanna and her hat and joins in her melody. Here, as before, the music offers a perfect reflection of the actions of the characters.

Side 6, Band 4

Listening Guide for Mozart's *The Marriage of Figaro,* Act I, First Duet

Timbre:	soprano and baritone; orchestra of moderate size: string and wind instruments
Melody:	first theme (Figaro's) built on short motives; second theme (Susanna's) more lyrical
Rhythm:	duple meter; fast tempo
Harmony:	major mode; begins in G major, modulates most significantly to D major, ends in G major
Texture:	homophonic and contrapuntal
Form:	free form based upon the alternation of two themes

Text:

Figaro (misurando):
Cinque . . . dieci . . . venti
. . . trenta . . . trentasei
. . . quarantatre . . .

Figaro (measuring):
Five . . . ten . . . twenty
. . . thirty . . . thirty-six
. . . forty-three . . .

Susanna (guardandosi nello specchio):
Ora sì ch'io son contenta; sembra fatto in ver per me.
Guarda un po', mio caro Figaro,
guarda adesso il mio capello.

Susanna (inspecting herself in the mirror):
Now I'm really satisfied with it; it looks quite as if it were made for me.
Look here a moment, Figaro darling,
just look at this cap of mine.

Figaro:	Figaro:
Sì, mio core, or è più bello; sembra fatto in ver per te.	Yes, sweetheart, it's much prettier now; it really does look made for you.
Figaro e Susanna:	Figaro and Susanna:
Ah, il mattino alle nozze vicino quanto è dolce al tuo/ mio tenero sposo, questo bel capellino vezzoso che Susanna ella stessa si fè'!	Ah, with the day of our wedding so near how sweet to you my tender husband is this darling little cap that Susanna made herself!

The first duet is followed by a recitative passage in which Susanna and Figaro discuss their prospective bedroom. Susanna does not like the room, though Figaro is proud of his new quarters. It is nearly the best room in the house—situated right between those of the Count and Countess. He points out how convenient it will be in the next duet.

Duet: Figaro and Susanna

The second duet, "Se a caso madama la notte ti chiama," begins with Figaro explaining to Susanna, "If at night your mistress should ring, you would quickly answer the call; and if the Count should ring for me, it would be equally convenient." Figaro expounds these advantages in the bright key of B♭ major. Susanna switches to the minor mode, expressing her fears that Figaro might be sent on some errand and the Count appear at her door. Repeatedly Figaro tries to hush this line of thought, but he is finally caught by Susanna's mood. Figaro and Susanna share the same melodic material in this duet. The orchestral accompaniment is simple but effective.

The duet is followed by a recitative in which Susanna tells Figaro of the Count's designs as they have been conveyed to her by her singing teacher, Don Basilio, the Count's mouthpiece. The Countess then rings for Susanna, and she leaves Figaro alone and angry on the stage.

Cavatina: Figaro

In the *cavatina*—or short lyrical song—that follows, "Se vuol ballare" ("If You Feel Like Dancing"), Figaro voices his belief that "two can play at this game": he can deceive and outwit the Count. As Figaro gains in aggressive spirit, the meter changes from the moderate ¾ of the opening to a quick ²⁄₄. Thus the A and B sections of the cavatina are differentiated for dramatic purposes. The song ends with a restatement of the A section followed by a vigorous coda in the ²⁄₄ tempo. Figaro is determined to protect his interests.

As Figaro leaves, Bartolo and Marcellina enter. In recitative they discuss their plot to force Figaro to marry Marcellina. Bartolo wants revenge against Figaro, the man who had once spoiled Bartolo's own chances of marrying the Countess.

Aria: Bartolo

After Marcellina exits, Bartolo, a bass, explains his motives in a strong aria, "La Vendetta," that immediately characterizes the man. The aria is marked Allegro con spirito and alternates between a number of different melodic ideas, much as a man in Bartolo's situation might alternate between rage at his past failures and visions of future revenge. At the end of the aria, the music returns to the opening melody, which is heard this time with a dramatic orchestral accompaniment that adds greatly to its final intensity.

As Bartolo leaves the stage, Marcellina and Susanna enter. Each shares with the audience some cutting remarks about the other, in recitative, before they face each other, in a duet.

Duet: Marcellina and Susanna

At the beginning of the duet, "Via resti servita," the two women engage in sarcastic politeness. Marcellina is heard first, saying to Susanna, "To greet you, my lady, I'm honored supremely." The allegro interchange soon degenerates into a kind of name calling. Each woman imitates the other musically and quite possibly in gestures as well. The orchestra adds to the fiery exchange, playing a triplet accompaniment against the duple meter of the vocal parts. At the end, Marcellina exits angrily, leaving a laughing Susanna as the apparent victor.

Susanna comments again on Marcellina, in recitative, as Cherubino enters. The page is upset because the Count, finding him with the gardener's daughter Barbarina, has dismissed him. Cherubino, who believes he is in love with the Countess, takes one of her gloves from Susanna and covers it with kisses. He then offers to sing Susanna a love song of his own composition.

Aria: Cherubino

In his aria, "Non so più," Cherubino, a soprano, comments on his love for women in general. "I can't give you a good explanation," he says of his state of mind, and then he proceeds to describe the daydreams of beauty that absorb him. The aria begins at an allegro tempo, moving from a quick melody made up of short motives (Section A) to a more lyrical melody (Section B) and then returning to the original melody (Section A). This is followed by a more thoughtful lyrical melody (Section C), which slows to a dejected adagio as Cherubino concludes that if no one else will listen he will talk to himself about love.

Much comic activity takes place during the recitative that follows. The Count knocks at the door, whereupon Cherubino hides behind a chair. The Count begins to make advances to Susanna but is interrupted by the approach of the singing teacher, Basilio. Not wanting to be discovered alone with Susanna, the Count hides behind the chair just as Cherubino nimbly jumps into its seat. Susanna covers Cherubino with a dressing gown as Basilio enters. Basilio, it turns out, is looking for the Count in order to tell him of Cherubino's attentions to the Countess. Upon hearing this, the Count leaps into view, and all three join in a trio.

Trio: Count, Basilio, and Susanna

The trio, "Cosa sento? Tosto andate" ("What's That? Go at Once!"), is marked Allegro assai and involves the quick interplay of three different voices: baritone, tenor, and soprano. Susanna's part is the most rhythmically active. At one point, she becomes faint but recovers abruptly when the men rush to seat her in the chair where Cherubino is hiding. In the course of the trio, the Count and Basilio assure Susanna that they mean no harm. Basilio apologizes for spreading the rumor about Cherubino, but the Count is still annoyed on this score. While telling the story of Cherubino and the gardener's daughter, he accidentally uncovers the hidden Cherubino. The trio ends with the wily Basilio singing quick eighth notes against the dotted rhythms of the frightened Susanna and the angry Count.

After a short recitative, Figaro enters carrying a white veil and accompanied by peasants strewing flowers. During the chorus that follows, Figaro praises the Count for having earlier abolished the feudal custom that would have given him sexual rights to his female servants before their marriages. The presentation is a mixture of choral singing and recitative, humorously ironic in tone.

In the recitative that follows the chorus, Cherubino is saved from disgrace. But he is told that he must leave nevertheless. The Count makes him a captain and dispatches him to a regiment in Seville.

Aria: Figaro

In the rousing final aria of the first act, "Non più andrai" ("No More"), Figaro tells Cherubino that he must now put aside his romantic ideas and court finery. He must get on with the business of being a soldier. The music is appropriate to Figaro's advice—a $\frac{4}{4}$ march theme, embellished with trumpets and other military effects. The aria is in rondo form—ABACA. The invigorating thematic material of the A section closes the first act.

Acts II, III, and IV

The acts that follow continue to develop and then resolve the complex plot. Mozart's music seems to match each dramatic situation and nuance. The Countess, for example, is given music very appropriate to her nobility in her famous aria "Dove sono?" ("Where Am I?"), with its moderate rhythms and soaring lyrical melody. The vocal ensembles in the last three acts are exceptionally sensitive. The characters are given rhythms and themes particularly indicative of their moods or actions. Throughout the opera, the music adds meaning to the text in ways both obvious and subtle.

Other Types of Classical Vocal Music

Oratorios and Masses

Classical composers were also attracted to sacred vocal music, particularly the oratorio and the Mass. Haydn wrote two important oratorios that are still frequently performed—*The Creation* and *The Seasons*. In addition, he wrote a number of Masses, the most famous of which is the *Missa in angustiis* ("Mass in Time of Fear," or the "Lord Nelson" Mass.)

Mozart's Masses are among his most dramatic works. They range from short, simple works to several that are very lengthy and ornate, the latter group including the well-known *Requiem Mass*, upon which he was working when he died.

Beethoven's sacred vocal works include two Masses and an oratorio. The *Missa solemnis in D Major* is generally thought to be one of his greatest achievements. A work of grand symphonic proportions, it was intended to be played as concert music rather than as liturgical music.

During the Classical period, sacred vocal works took on some of the structural and stylistic characteristics of the symphony. Generally large works, they were usually written for a chorus of moderate size, soloists, and an orchestra of small or moderate size. The liturgical sections of the Mass became longer and were usually subdivided into musical sections of considerable length. Solos became as elaborate as those found in Classical operas. Choral sections were also, at times, very elaborate and demanding. The Mass and the oratorio were truly the religious counterparts of the opera, symphony, and concerto of the period.

Suggested Listening

Classical Opera

Mozart: *Die Entführung aus dem Serail:* "Erst geköpft, dann gehangen" ("First Beheaded, Then Hanged") [Angel S-3555]. Osmin's aria, one of rage and threats of vengeance, is a thorough self-characterization. Osmin is one of Mozart's most successful creations, not only as a *basso buffo* ("comic bass"), but also as a fully developed figure of the coarse ruffian. He is spiteful, sensual, and dangerous. The opera is a Singspiel with German text and spoken dialogue.

Mozart: *Don Giovanni:* "Là ci darem la mano" ("Give Me Your Hand") [DG 2711006]. In this duet Zerlina is about to give in to the advances of Don Giovanni. She is a simple peasant girl, so her music is uncomplicated. Zerlina and Don Giovanni are representative of the two different types of characters found in the work: she is a buffa character, he is seria. Mozart was skilled at contrasting these types, achieving effects that have been compared to those found in Shakespeare's dramas.

Beethoven: *Fidelio:* "Jetzt, Alter, hat es Eile" ("Now, Jailer, I Need You") [Angel S-3625]. In this duet Pizarro tries to bribe Rocco, the jailer, to murder the imprisoned Florestan. It is an excellent composition that was slighted in the first drafts of the opera. The work as a whole is a fine example of a "rescue opera."

The Classical Oratorio

Haydn: *The Creation:* Introduction: "Representation of Chaos" [DG 2707044]. Haydn was already familiar with the works of J. S. Bach and Handel when he wrote *The Creation*. The orchestral introduction to this oratorio recalls programmatic qualities of the Baroque period. However, the Enlightenment's conception of God and nature, well blended with reason and benevolence, required a certain simplicity of style that is readily found here.

The Classical Mass

Mozart: *Mass in C Major* ("Coronation" Mass), K. 317: Dona nobis pacem ("Grant Us Peace") [Philips 6500234]. The music for the Dona nobis is a repetition of part of the Kyrie with a gradual increase in tempo. This repetition underscores the emotional link between the Kyrie and the Dona nobis. Soloists, chorus, and orchestra are all used in a splendid example of the very elaborate Mass music typical of the Classical period.

Beethoven: *Missa solemnis in D Major, Op. 123:* Credo [Angel S-3679]. This is an impressive setting, divided into contrasting sections. The use of instruments, chorus, and soloists varies from one section to the next in order to represent changing moods in the text. "Et resurrexit" ("And He Rose Again"), for example, is a joyous section for chorus and orchestra, celebrating the risen Christ.

Listening Preview   In many ways, the music of the Romantic period was built upon trends already quite evident at the end of the Classical period—in particular, the increasing desire for subjectivity and emotional release. However, the period also saw a number of new developments, especially in the use of harmony. Listen to two Romantic works: Chopin's Nocturne in E♭ Major, written quite early in the period, and Strauss's Till Eulenspiegel, written toward the end of the period. (See Sides 7 and 8 of the record set that accompanies the text or find selections in the record library.) In what ways does Chopin's work seem to support the notion of increasing subjectivity? What new musical qualities are found in Strauss's work?

Introduction to Romantic Music

The Romantic Period [c.1815–c.1900]

Romanticism is not so much a style of art as a way of perceiving and dealing with the world. Its outstanding characteristic is its stress on the individual and on subjective feeling. Because of this subjective emphasis, the Romantic movement is difficult to define in general terms. While some Romantic artists placed faith in utopias to come, others saw the past as the ideal age. Some sought truth in the life of the common people, while others sought escape in exotic dreams and fantasy. Although most gloried in the beauty of nature, others feared its awesome power. These many impulses, all a part of the Romantic spirit, exerted a major influence on the minds and imaginations of the people of the nineteenth century.

The movement developed partly out of the upheavals of the preceding era. By the end of the eighteenth century, during the lifetimes of Haydn, Mozart, and Beethoven, revolutionary social and political events had changed the whole of Europe. With these changes came a slow and gradual evolution in artistic sensibilities. In literature the winds of change appeared much earlier than in music. As early as 1774, with Classicism in music not yet at its peak, Johann Wolfgang von Goethe wrote his morbidly introspective novel *The Sorrows of Young Werther*. Such blatant emotionalism would not appear in music for another half century. Its seeds, however, were increasingly evident by about 1815.

Life in the Romantic Period

Romanticism originated in a desire to change the world for the better—to build upon the debris of the old Europe a structure that would reflect the beauty of the natural world and the nobility of humanity. Among the earliest expressions of Romanticism were the writings of Jean Jacques Rousseau, who stressed individual enjoyment as the highest goal in life. Well before Rousseau's *Social Contract*, eighteenth-century rationalism had challenged the two great bastions of traditional authority, the divine right of the monarchy and the church that had upheld it. Where years of enlightened skepticism had provided revolutionary tinder, early Romantic impulses furnished the spark. Revolution followed.

The relatively quick success of the American Revolution found no parallel in Europe. There the French Revolution was merely the dawn of a seemingly endless cycle of democratic revolutions and repressive reactions. Nevertheless, with each swing of the pendulum, with each additional shock to the old order, the middle class gained new power and confidence. It became increasingly clear that, despite repeated setbacks, a new order had indeed begun.

Equally important to the rise of the middle class was the Industrial Revolution, which gathered momentum throughout the nineteenth century. Wealth, for so long a matter of privilege, now became more closely tied to productivity and thus more widely distributed. What the middle class was progressively gaining in the various democratic revolutions, it was consolidating in the economic and social spheres as well.

These new social alignments inspired a great deal of study and theorizing. The early socialists hoped to be able to shape revolutionary events to bring about utopia. A few of these theorists held notions as whimsical and fantastic as the wildest creations of Romantic art. Karl Marx was more sober in his blueprint for a working-class revolution, *The Communist Manifesto* (1848). The novels of Charles Dickens, though laced with humor, also took a hard look at Europe's social ills in the industrial age. All of this interest in the workings of middle-class society eventually led to the science of sociology.

Other scientific advances opened new frontiers as well. Archeological and historical investigations fed the Romantic fascination with the past. Charles Darwin tied this interest in the past to the Romantic love of nature in his *Origin of Species* (1859), which set evolutionary theory upon firm footing. Meanwhile, horizons were expanding everywhere. The colonization by industrial Europe of large parts of the world had introduced products, works of art, and previously unexplored modes of feeling. The Romantic century was one of accelerating change and ceaseless novelty.

Literature, Art, and Music in the Romantic Period

Position of the Artist

As society changed in the early nineteenth century, so did the role of the artist and the relationship of art to society. Without commissions and patronage, Romantic artists became severe critics of society and its institutions. As a result, art seemed to oppose what it had once served—the class structure. The artist of the Romantic period achieved unprecedented artistic and social independence, rejecting the limitations of patronage and substituting the ideals of social conscience and individualism. Meanwhile an audience for the new style was slowly forming. It was no longer a refined aristocracy or a religious congregation using art and music to intensify devotion but was now an unsophisticated, sentimental public that valued art primarily as entertainment.

The Romantic Hero

To the Romantic era we owe the still popular idea of the artist as hero. The Romantic hero, and thus the Romantic artist, often appeared as a prophetic loner, weighed down by a burden of sensitivity and individualism. Misunderstanding, loneliness, and suffering were the lot of Romantic heroes.

They not only tolerated isolation but gloried in it, hoping to expose by their own eccentric and sometimes shocking behavior the moral hypocrisy of the age. Endowed with an intrinsic nobility, idealism, and honesty, they seemed to transcend the conventional ideas of good and evil that bound the average person.

This highly charged atmosphere of individualism produced art with heavily subjective qualities. Emotional forces predominated. States of feeling were accorded great importance, even though they were sometimes difficult to convey in a clear and straightforward manner. Mystery and ambiguity, fantasy and fear were all integral parts of Romantic expression. While the Classical period had emphasized somewhat anonymous qualities—wit, manners, balance, clarity, and reason—the Romantic period emphasized purely personal forces. Even love was conceived more as a state of the individual than as a relationship between two people. Romantics tended to describe their own infinite longing for a loved one rather than the attainment of any real partnership. Artists sought to overwhelm and be overwhelmed rather than to establish a pleasant equilibrium between themselves and their audiences.

Second only perhaps to the theme of Romantic individualism was the theme of nature. The Romantics saw nature, not merely as a passive background, but increasingly as an animate thing that, in its many different moods, symbolized human emotions. It could be gentle and soothing or mysterious and violent. To many Romantics, nature represented an ideal of freedom, an environment in which people could act naturally and give free rein to their impulses, where their liberated imaginations could develop limitless possibilities.

Romantic artists also showed keen interest in exotic themes, places, and ideas. They found inspiration in Oriental and African work and in foreign legend and mythology. The nineteenth century's fondness for the strange and different—Coleridge's use of opium and his poetic ecstasies about faraway and ancient happenings, for example—is sometimes regarded as an attempt to avoid the harsh realities of a Europe in turmoil. However, it must also be understood as part of the general Romantic tendency to emphasize the fanciful, to exalt the workings of the imagination, and to belittle the products of reason so universally admired during the greater part of the eighteenth century.

The Romantic era was marked, too, by a general curiosity about the supernatural. There developed, especially among the German transcendentalists, an interest in mysticism that, in its attempt to transcend the limits of time and space, was not unlike the exoticism found in Coleridge's works.

Romantic Literature

As has been noted, literature was the first of the arts to fully embrace the Romantic movement. In Germany the poet who most strongly exemplified Romanticism was Goethe. In *The Sorrows of Young Werther* and later in *Faust*, Goethe embodied for his age the ideal of the melancholy hero. Werther, a passionate aesthete, pursues his own ruin in an impossible love affair. Faust, an erudite scholar and a symbol of Classical learning, finds beauty in horror and pain. He sells his soul for youth, knowledge, and power, with tragic consequences.

The Romantic Hero in Literature: *In "Childe Harold," Byron embodied all the melancholy and disillusionment of the Romantic hero caught up in an age not of his choosing. The poem follows the hero's travels through Europe, recounting tales of earlier ages.*

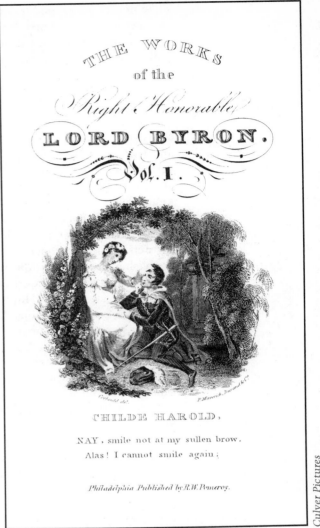

In England the Romantic movement produced an important group of poets, among them Blake, Byron, Wordsworth, Coleridge, Keats, and Shelley. Byron himself was almost an archetypal Romantic hero—captivating, benevolent, ridden by passion and guilt. In Byron we also find the wittier side of Romanticism. His *Don Juan* is a brilliant satire of eighteenth-century attitudes and manners. The Romantic absorption with nature is nowhere better shown than in the work of Wordsworth, to whom "the meanest flower that blows can give/Thoughts that do often lie too deep for tears." The Romantic attraction to the supernatural is perhaps most powerfully expressed in Coleridge's *Rime of the Ancient Mariner.*

The poet who most typified French Romanticism was Charles Baudelaire, who in *Les Fleurs du mal* ("The Flowers of Evil") described the mystery and grace he saw in the coarsest of things. His cherished melancholy was perhaps the epitome of Romanticism, leading him to rely on imagination to re-create the world according to his own personal feelings.

Romantic Painting

Romantic painters derived many of their themes from Romantic literature as well as from the more general Romantic impulses that influenced all the arts of the period. Many Romantic painters saw their work as a reaction against "Classical artificiality" and took great interest in "nature." Landscape paintings copied natural settings as the ideal. The use of simple peasants as subjects, rather than refined aristocrats, reflected the growing interest in the common people.

Painters, sculptors, and architects sought inspiration where they could find it—in the revival of older styles, especially the distant Gothic style, and in innovation. A number of new subjects and techniques were tried. The bizarre, the horrible, and the supernatural particularly fascinated some painters, as can be seen in John Fuseli's *The Nightmare.* New techniques, such as broader brushstrokes, generally lent themselves less to the representation of objective reality than to the expression of subjective emotion. Artists also displayed a developing social conscience, as seen in the late works of Goya.

The chief exponent of Romanticism in painting was Eugène Delacroix, whose close friendship with Chopin and Baudelaire strongly influenced his work. Aiming at an emotional "poetic truth" instead of simple accuracy of detail, Delacroix's paintings throb with sensuality, cruelty, and a splendor that seems at variance with his declared intention to be "natural."

Romantic Music

Music of the Romantic period was inspired, to an unprecedented degree, by painting and poetry. Yet at the same time, it contributed certain qualities to Romanticism that were unobtainable in any other medium. Music is perhaps the most Romantic of all the arts. Alone, without words or pictures, music can suggest the mystery and ambiguity of human emotion. The poet Sidney Lanier wrote that "Music is love in search of a word." And, indeed, music does go forth in search of the inexpressible. In the Romantic period, music was an especially appropriate medium for the artist who wished to express a longing for love, for beauty, for the infinite.

The music of the Romantic period is marked by new purposes and new drives, but the style itself was created with the basic tools inherited from the Classical age. The Romantic style in music was, not one of revolution against what had preceded it, but instead a continuation and extension of the Classical style—thus, the Classical-Romantic continuum. Composers devised little that was really new in a musical sense, but rather they continued to develop the melodic, rhythmic, and harmonic materials of an earlier age.

Although certain Romantic traits in music can be seen in the late eighteenth century, it was not until the second and third decades of the nineteenth century that Romantic characteristics became truly dominant. They were to remain the musical ideal until they were largely rejected and replaced with new ideas around the turn of the twentieth century.

Romantic Melody and Rhythm

Lyrical Melodies

Romantic composers emphasized melody to an even greater extent than their predecessors. The music of the Romantic period favors inspired lyrical melodies rather than those logically developed out of small motives. Melodic phrases are generally longer and more irregular than those of the Classical period, while cadences are less frequent.

Many Romantic melodies are songlike in character. Folk melodies were widely used, and German song became a virtual showplace for melody. In instrumental music, melody with accompaniment often served to express the infinite yearning of the Romantic. Many Romantic works, both vocal and instrumental, are characterized by a melody that begins haltingly and then slowly builds to great fervor, a technique that we have already seen in the third movement of Beethoven's Fifth Symphony.

While many Romantic melodies are rather simple, others are quite complex—filled with chromaticism, disjunct motion, and ornamentation. Melodies calling for great virtuosity abound in the operas and concertos of the period.

Rhythmic Experimentation

Romantic rhythm, like Romantic melody, varies from the simple to the complex. In much of the music, the rhythm conforms to an established meter and to regular four- or eight-measure phrases. However, Romantic composers also experimented with new meters and rhythmic patterns. Thus, as a whole, the rhythm of the Romantic period is more varied and complex than that of the eighteenth century. In a desire to suggest emotional conflict, Romantic composers often played one kind of rhythmic pattern against another—a steady duple rhythm against a triple, for example. Changes of rhythmic pattern and meter within a movement became increasingly common during the nineteenth century.

Harmony and Texture in Romantic Music

Harmonic practices of the nineteenth century evolved directly from those of the Classical period. Techniques found in Classical works, especially in the later works of Beethoven, were extensively explored by Romantic composers and were often transformed to meet the specific needs of the new period.

Harmonic Experimentation

In Romantic music, tonality becomes not only a means of logical structure but also a way of achieving striking emotional effects. The rich possibilities offered by changes to remote keys are fully exploited. Minor and major keys are strongly juxtaposed, and seldom-used keys are brought to new prominence, in part as a result of the improved technology of instruments. Key changes occur ever more rapidly until finally, in the work of Wagner, we find a continuous modulation that is a perfect metaphor for the endless ardor of the Romantic period.

Romantic music also makes increasing use of chromaticism—that is, of tones (or accidentals) that are not in the scale upon which a passage is based. In Classical music, at least before Beethoven, accidentals tend to appear as surprising touches or as part of a predictable change of key. In the music of the

Romantic period, chromaticism takes on increasing importance. Frequent accidentals disrupt our expectation of key, introducing a kind of uncertainty that seems to reflect the character of the period as well as the passions of the Romantic composers. A comparison of the first theme from Mozart's *Symphony No. 40* and a highly chromatic passage from Chopin's *Nocturne in E♭ Major, Op. 9, No. 2* helps to illustrate this change in musical language. Note the many accidentals in the latter example, compared to the complete lack of them in the former:

As chords were increasingly embellished with accidentals and modified in the course of key changes, music became more dissonant. Ultimately dissonance became not only a means to final resolution but an integral part of Romantic expression. Certain chords once used simply to facilitate key changes became more and more useful to composers and gradually more acceptable to Romantic audiences. One suspects that the very discovery of new dissonances—always a shocking matter in music—must have gratified the rebellious Romantics.

By the end of the Romantic period, the great use of chromaticism and dissonance had seemingly exhausted the possibilities of the major-minor system of harmony and thus opened the way for the development of new harmonic systems. Within these new systems, twentieth-century composers have continued to explore and expand the use of dissonance.

Changes in Texture

Romantic texture was not subject to the amount of experimentation that Romantic harmony was, yet some changes can be seen. In the music of the period, harmony and melody often work closely together to convey the primary emotional idea of the work, leading to a basically chordal texture. Many Romantic composers, however, looked with special interest at the works of J. S. Bach, and contrapuntal passages or sections are not uncommon in their work. In general, the availability of an enlarged orchestra and more complex harmonies contributed to a denser, more complicated texture in Romantic music.

Romantic Timbre and Dynamics

In the Romantic period, music was most often written for very small or very large groups. The proliferation of solo works, especially for the piano, was in many ways an expression of the individualism of the age. So too was the enthusiasm for virtuoso performance. Duets and chamber ensembles were also common.

Romantic Architecture: *The architects of the Romantic age followed as many disparate paths as Romantic poets and painters did. The Paris Opera, shown above, is highly representative of the Neo-Baroque flourishes favored by many in the middle years of the nineteenth century. Other Romantic architects found inspiration in Gothic, Renaissance, or Classical models, and some looked even farther afield to the exotic architecture of the East.*

Larger Orchestra

The composer of instrumental music was able to rely on a larger orchestra, enriched by a number of instruments that were either newly developed or newly added to the orchestra: piccolo, clarinet, trombone, tuba, English horn, contrabassoon, and harp. Several new percussion instruments were introduced for dramatic purposes, and every part of the orchestra was enlarged. Berlioz and others helped to expand the techniques of orchestration, making possible broad, kaleidoscopic effects and rapid changes of timbre.

Choruses likewise grew greatly in number and size in the Romantic period. Choral societies with hundreds of members appeared in Europe and the United States. The Handel and Haydn Society of Boston was founded as early as 1815.

Although military and town bands of wind and percussion instruments had existed in previous centuries, there was a major increase in the number of bands in the nineteenth century. This was due in part to improved technology in wind instruments. Of great importance was the fact that valves were added to brass instruments, allowing them to play chromatically and in every key. Until the twentieth century, however, few composers wrote serious works for bands.

Greater Use of Dynamics

Technical improvements also brought greater dynamic flexibility, and with the expansion of the orchestra the dynamic range increased as well. Not surprisingly, dynamic changes became a very important part of Romantic music. In all types of Romantic music, both gradual and sudden changes are used, with effects ranging from very subtle to very dramatic.

Types of Compositions and Form in Romantic Music

Romantic composers developed a number of new types of compositions, almost all of which were marked by the emotional qualities of the period. They also made use of most of the types of compositions popular in the Classical period, altering them to suit the needs of their own age. Virtually no new forms were developed by Romantic composers; instead they altered Classical forms to fit the Romantic mood.

Short Compositions

Piano Pieces

Many of the new types of compositions developed during the Romantic age were intended specifically as vehicles for lyric and dramatic expression. Among them were several short piano works, including *nocturnes* ("night pieces"), *études* ("studies"), *impromptus, ballades,* and a variety of stylized dances. Such works generally focused upon the presentation of a single mood, or possibly a change of mood, ranging from pure whimsy to despair. The piano became increasingly popular in the Romantic age, and the amount and variety of music written for it grew greatly throughout the century.

Lieder

On a comparable scale in the vocal field was the *Lied* (pl. *Lieder*), developed most beautifully by Schubert and Schumann. Like the short piano work, the Lied reflected the Romantic's desire to convey intense lyric emotion. It also reflected the deep interest of the Romantic in the literature of the time. Lieder were often organized into *song cycles*, with one unifying theme.

Long Compositions

The sonata cycle was still the basis for the symphony, concerto, string quartet, and sonata of the Romantic period, but it differed in many ways from the sonata cycle of the Classical period. Composers often varied the number and order of movements, while compositions themselves became longer and more grandiose. Themes were often used more for their melodic effect than for their logical placement within a movement.

The symphony continued as a major work for orchestra, although composers sometimes added extramusical associations to it, making it programmatic. The solo concerto, often for piano or violin and orchestra, generally

Comparison of Classical and Romantic Music

Elements	Classical Music c. 1750–c. 1815	Romantic Music c. 1815–c. 1900
Melody	Often built on motives and short phrases Phrases often very regular in length	Often very lyrical Phrases often longer and less regular in length
Rhythm	Clear meters except in recitative Considerable rhythmic variety within movements	Meters sometimes changed within movements Greater variety of meters and rhythmic patterns
Harmony	Major-minor system Great use of modulation as structural basis	Major-minor system Expanded use of both modulation and chromaticism
Texture	Homophony most important but continued use of polyphony, often within basically homophonic works	Homophony and counterpoint both used Texture often quite dense in works for large groups
Timbre	Large, standardized orchestra, without continuo Small instrumental ensembles, especially string quartet, also prominent	Continued growth of orchestra Large choirs and bands Small ensembles still prominent
Important Forms	Sonata, rondo, theme and variations, ternary, and binary Many multi-movement works	Forms of Classical period used and expanded in a variety of ways Many multi-movement works
Important Types of Compositions	Older types such as the Mass, oratorio, opera, solo concerto, and sonata Many instrumental works based on sonata cycle: symphony, concerto, sonata, and string quartet	Types of compositions from Classical period, often expanded Newly developed symphonic poem and solo song cycle

retained its basic Classical structure and often called for virtuosic display. Chamber music for various ensembles, especially the string quartet, continued to be written, and the sonata for solo piano, or for piano and one other instrument, remained popular. Like the symphony and the concerto, chamber works generally were based on Classical models freely altered to suit the needs of the new style.

Program Music

Program Symphonies and Symphonic Poems

The integration of different arts is strongly apparent in the *program symphony* and the *symphonic poem* of the Romantic period. Such compositions were generally related to extramusical elements such as poetry or painting through a verbal description or program. While the program symphony falls loosely into a sonata-cycle form, the symphonic poem, or tone poem, is a one-movement work. Among the most famous examples of program symphonies are two of Berlioz' works, the *Symphonie fantastique* and *Harold in Italy*, a work based on Byron's famous poem. Well-known symphonic poems are Liszt's *Les Préludes* and Richard Strauss's *Don Quixote*.

Overtures and Incidental Music

At times the *overture* also became a type of program music. Generally serving as an introduction to an opera or play, it was sometimes conceived independently. Overtures such as Tchaikovsky's *Romeo and Juliet* reflect the dramatic work with which they are associated much in the same way that a cinema theme—another type of program music—does today. A considerable amount of *incidental music*, meant to be performed during the course of a play or other entertainment, was also written during the Romantic period. The triumphant march to which so many newlyweds leave the alter was originally written by Mendelssohn as incidental music for Shakespeare's *A Midsummer Night's Dream*.

Choral Music and Opera

Religious music and opera were also important during the Romantic period. The Mass, beginning in the Classical period, took on symphonic dimensions. Both the Mass and the oratorio became somewhat more secular, longer, and more imaginative. Opera flourished as never before under the genius of such composers as Wagner, Verdi, and Puccini. Romantic composers intensified opera, gradually deleting the recitative in favor of more elaborate music and adding new spectacle and splendor.

Form

Romantic composers trusted more to the validity of emotion than to any rules of form. They tended to value spontaneity and were not averse to presenting their compositions as products of fleeting inspiration. Compositions of the period bear such titles as "Musical Moment," "Fantasy Pieces," and "Reverie," directing attention to the supposedly spontaneous nature of their composition.

Spontaneous composition had, of course, been appreciated in the Classical period. Part of what impressed the early audiences of Mozart and

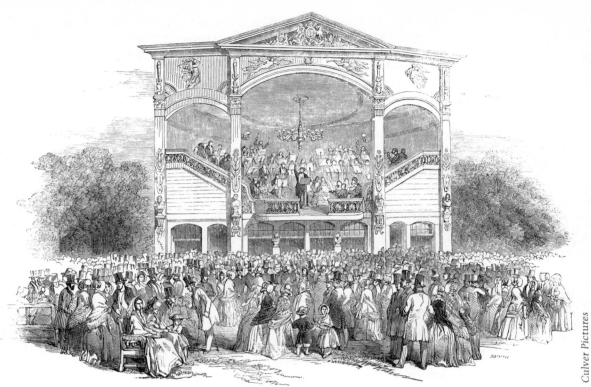

A Concert in the Park: *The nineteenth century brought the establishment of innumerable orchestral societies and a phenomenal growth in the number of public concerts given. The midcentury engraving above of a well-attended outdoor concert at Surrey Zoological Gardens accompanied an article that praised the establishment of yet another orchestra, noting that it was "indicative of the good taste and enterprise" of the Gardens' proprietors.*

Beethoven was their ability to improvise on a theme. This kind of improvisation depended upon an understanding of formal principles and a creativity in using them. To Romantic composers, however, spontaneity seemed to demand a release from principles and a relaxation of Classical forms.

The late works of Mozart and Beethoven clearly demonstrated that Classical forms could be used for effective Romantic statement. New forms were thus not essential, and as has been noted, Romantic composers developed virtually none. Instead they based their works on Classical forms, putting them to new uses.

Use of Classical Forms

Short compositions for piano were generally sectional, often binary or ternary in form, while songs were frequently strophic. As the century progressed, freer, less traditional structures were sometimes used, but the early reliance was upon Classical forms.

For sonata-cycle works, the forms of the Classical era also continued to be used—theme and variations, ternary, rondo, and sonata forms. But Romantic composers seemed more interested in lyrical content and timbre than in form. Increasingly, form developed from the composer's use of musical ideas, whereas previously the use of ideas had been, to a much larger extent, governed by form. In many instances the sonata form became an argument between contrasting themes or motives as well as between different tonalities. Thematic development was somewhat less rigorous than before. The very expressiveness of Romantic melodies worked against any attempt to break them down, recombine them, or otherwise alter them in development. Romantic melodies begged not so much for development as for repetition. Recapitulation sections were often used, not to recap the initial material, but to give a new and more tragic presentation.

In the hands of Romantic composers, Classical forms became looser so that greater scope might be given to melody and the play of emotion. Clarity of form thus became less and less important, losing ground to the emotional intensity of the period as a whole.

INTRODUCTION TO ROMANTIC MUSIC

19

Romantic Piano Music

Directions in Piano Music

In the nineteenth century, music for the piano developed into a brilliant, dramatic, and lyrical showcase for virtuoso performance. While Classical composers for solo piano had devoted themselves largely to the sonata, Romantic composers often preferred shorter pieces. Nocturnes, études, impromptus, ballades, and a variety of dances all lent themselves to the capturing of a definite mood. Romantic composers were also likely to choose descriptive titles and programmatic associations for their works rather than the simple key designations that had been used by earlier composers.

Classical Piano Music

These changes took place gradually, falling readily within the artistic framework of the Classical-Romantic continuum. Haydn's piano works were sonatas, denoted only by chronology and key signature—*Sonata No. 1 in C Minor*, for example. Mozart's major piano compositions were also sonatas, with titles similar to those used by Haydn. Beethoven's sonatas, however, were occasionally given subtitles such as "Tempest," "Appassionata," or "Moonlight," and he wrote a number of other piano works as well, including bagatelles (literally "trifles"). The piano music of Beethoven thus forms a bridge between Classical and Romantic styles, foreshadowing many developments in the later nineteenth century.

Early Romantic Works

By the time of Robert Schumann (1810–1856) and Felix Mendelssohn (1809–1847), the sonata no longer dominated solo piano literature. With Schumann we encounter collections of short "character" pieces with descriptive, even fanciful, names: *Carnaval*, *Fantasiestücke* ("Fantasy Pieces"), *Kinderscenen* ("Scenes from Childhood"), and *Waldscenen* ("Forest Scenes"). Individual pieces bear even more explicit titles. In *Waldscenen*, for example, we find pieces whose German titles can be translated as "Hunter on the Watch," "Solitary Flowers," and "Bird as Prophet."

Late Romantic Works

Composers in the late nineteenth century continued the work of the early Romantics. Johannes Brahms (1833–1897) wrote short pieces and sonatas that rank among the finest in musical literature for piano. Others such as Edvard Grieg (1843–1907) in Norway, Isaac Albéniz (1860–1909) in Spain, and Sergei Rachmaninoff (1873–1943) in Russia demonstrated by their outstanding works that the piano was the most international and admired instrument of the age.

Thus although Romantic composers continued to write piano sonatas and to draw upon an inheritance of fugue, variation, rondo, and dance, they also developed a new literature for piano—a literature featuring short lyric or dramatic pieces. Today the Romantic piano piece remains the basis of study for nearly all piano students.

Chopin's Piano Music

Perhaps more than any other composer, Frédéric Chopin (1810–1849) established the piano as a voice of Romanticism. He wrote almost exclusively for solo piano, learning to exploit its expressive resources to great advantage.

Chopin was born in Poland in 1810. Although he was passionately attached to his native land and drew heavily from its musical traditions, he spent most of his life in self-imposed exile. When Russian troops overran Warsaw in 1831, Chopin, then on tour in Austria, decided not to return. He lived the greater part of his adult life in Paris, though his will specified that his heart be returned to Poland for burial.

Paris was a music-loving city, and in 1831, when Chopin arrived there, piano music was at an all-time fashionable high. Competition between leading pianists and teachers was widespread and very spirited. Social events were often organized around piano performance, with the solo concert becoming ever more popular. The pianist became the star of the salon, and the theatrics of piano playing often caused women in the audience to swoon. Celebrated performers were greeted with the hero worship and hysteria that have more recently been associated with rock idols.

Into this environment came twenty-one-year-old Chopin, a former child prodigy who had already written numerous works and performed with much success in Warsaw and Vienna. He immediately impressed Parisian society with his original style of performance and composition. He appeared regularly in the salons of intellectuals and artists. However, he seldom performed in public concert, in part because he had not the physical strength to play loudly and forcefully. His technique was delicate and sensitive, filled with fine nuances and melodic shadings.

Legato

Chopin treated the piano as a singing instrument. His melodies are often characterized by a smoothly connected—or *legato*—style. Such a style had always been natural to song but could not be achieved in piano music until the development of the sustaining pedal (often mistakenly called the "loud" pedal).

Rubato

Chopin made extensive explorations of the uses of pedal and legato playing. He also used *rubato*, a technique in which small displacements in rhythm are introduced for expressive purposes. Rubato literally means "robbing"—in music, robbing time value from one note and giving it to another. The technique allows the pianist to linger on a chosen note, perhaps the high climactic note of a phrase, and then make up the time lost by playing the notes that follow more quickly. Pianists today learn to sense where rubato should be applied in Chopin's works through careful interpretation of each score.

Repetition of theme is an important means of organization in Chopin's music. Even in short pieces such as nocturnes, waltzes, and mazurkas, the main theme appears several times, alternating with one or more secondary themes. With every repetition, the main theme gains in intensity—in part because of the repetition and in part because the theme is varied. The variations may include such things as increased ornamentation, dynamic change, rubato, and syncopation.

In listening to music of the Classical period, we expect to hear a logical development of themes and an opposition of large tonal areas. In listening to Chopin, we are more likely to hear a repetition of melody and accompaniment, with intensity achieved through subtle variation and surprise. Modulations tend to be either abrupt and passionate or wondrously fluid as one tonality seemingly dissolves into another.

Nocturnes

Field

Among Chopin's most celebrated works are his *nocturnes*, or night pieces. The nocturne, one of the earliest of the new solo piano pieces, was conceived by Irish pianist John Field (1782–1837). Basically it is mood music, reflecting the subjective feelings of an artist at night. Most of Chopin's nocturnes are ardent works characterized by a long, lyrical melody set over a chordal or arpeggiated accompaniment. Fantasy, agitation, melancholy—all the feelings of the night are represented. The nocturne was apparently well suited to Chopin's own needs. Karasowski, his biographer, notes that he "generally improvised in the dark, frequently at night. . . . Then would he bury himself in the theme heart and soul, and develop from it tone-pictures full of lofty inspiration and . . . poetry."

Chopin: *Nocturne in E♭ Major, Op. 9, No. 2*

The second of Chopin's nocturnes, the *Nocturne in E♭ Major*, is one of the best known. It was written in 1833 when the composer was twenty-three years old. Like most of the other nocturnes in *Op. 9*, it is made up of a number of sections. A main theme alternates with a secondary theme until both are superseded by a third theme. The main theme, heard at the opening of the work, is a slow, graceful melody played over fluid chordal accompaniment:

Main Theme

The accompaniment is very steady, with a bass note at the beginning of each measure followed by two successively higher chords. This pattern ceases only during the brief cadenza at the end of the work.

Second Theme

After the first presentation, the main theme is immediately repeated, this time with ornamentation. A second theme follows, characterized by a lack of stable key. The instability, caused by modulations, is in this case most attractive. A colorful chromatic passage then leads back to the main theme, now more highly ornamented. This time the notes of the melody are approached chromatically by half steps. The opening of the main theme, which was at first conveyed by means of only six notes, now requires fourteen. After a repetition of the second theme, the main theme reappears, even more intensely ornamented. We can see Chopin's artistry by comparing the climactic last measure of the main theme as it undergoes progressive ornamentation:

Changes in Last Measure of Main Theme:
First Presentation

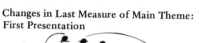

Second Presentation

Ornament Added

Third Presentation

Sixteenth Notes Changed to Thirty-second Notes

Fourth Presentation

Syncopation Added

Third Theme

After the fourth presentation of the main theme, a third theme is presented and repeated with ornamentation. It functions somewhat as a coda. The form of the entire piece can be outlined in the following manner:

A	A	B	A	B	A	C	C

A short cadenza follows, played in the upper register by the unaccompanied right hand. It builds to a crescendo and then subsides to pianissimo as the accompaniment returns for the final quiet measures.

Listening Guide for Chopin's *Nocturne in E♭ Major*

Timbre:	piano
Melody:	three themes, one in each section; the first theme, the most prominent and important, is very lyrical; the other two themes are conjunct and closely related to the first in rhythm and overall contour
Rhythm:	$\frac{12}{8}$ meter; tempo Andante (moderate)
Harmony:	mainly major mode; begins and ends in E♭ major, with several modulations
Texture:	homophonic
Form:	AABABACC

Études and Preludes

Among Chopin's earliest works are two important collections of *études*, or studies. Each was written to illustrate and develop a specific technical skill. The first, *Étude in C Major, Op. 10, No. 1*, for example, involves the playing of arpeggios over a wide span in the right hand. It is a brilliant piece that calls for great virtuosity. The constant arpeggios in the right hand are accompanied by a slowly moving bass line that supports the chords and helps in modulation to related keys.

Taken as a whole, the études cover a large part of nineteenth-century piano technique. Though written partly as exercises, they are musical masterpieces and have become popular concert works.

In addition to his collection of études, Chopin also wrote a series of twenty-four short *preludes*, each with its own idea or mood. Briefer than the études, the preludes show Chopin's pianistic art in miniature.

Dances

Mazurkas

Particularly brilliant was Chopin's use of the dance forms of his native Poland. Among his works are more than fifty examples of the *mazurka*, a Slavic dance in $\frac{3}{4}$ meter, with exotic rhythmic touches of Eastern Europe. The works range in spirit from exultation to lament. In them Chopin conveys both pride in his homeland and passionate sorrow for Poland's loss of freedom. The *polonaise*, a heroic dance of ceremonial importance, was also the basis for several of Chopin's works. The *Polonaise in A♭* and the *Polonaise-Fantasie* are grand patriotic statements on a virtuoso scale. Chopin also wrote fourteen *waltzes*, which remain concert favorites today.

Polonaises

Waltzes

Ballades, Sonatas, and Scherzos

Among Chopin's other works for piano, perhaps the most important are his ballades, sonatas, and scherzos. The *ballade* is essentially a narrative piece for piano, though the literary narrative or epic on which it is based need not be indicated by the composer. Chopin, in fact, did not indicate the inspirational

A Salon Performance by Chopin: *In this artist's impression, Chopin is shown performing as he did most often, for a small and select group of artistically inclined Parisians.*

sources of his ballades. Particularly popular is his *Ballade No. 1 in G Minor.* Of the *sonatas*, the *Sonata in B♭ Minor* is best known.

The *scherzo*, originally a movement of the sonata cycle, was treated by Chopin as a work in itself. His four scherzos are the first Romantic examples of the work as a full-scale piano composition. Like most other works by Chopin, the scherzos have a spontaneity and improvisatory quality about them, due in part to the free ornamentation added to repeated themes.

Chopin's Legacy

When Chopin died of tuberculosis at the age of thirty-nine, he was one of the most revered of Romantic artists. Nearly all of his works are still performed regularly today. The term "piano music" is for many people nearly synonymous with "Chopin."

Aurore Dudevant, the cigar-smoking feminist better known by her pen name George Sand, lived with Chopin for many years. She summarized his gift particularly well: "No musical genius has appeared so full of deep poetic feeling as Chopin. Under his hand the piano spoke an immortal longing. A short piece of scarcely half a page will contain the most sublime poetry." Chopin did not need large forms to express this longing. He found the perfect creative medium in the short piece and in the lyric voice of the piano.

Liszt's Piano Music

Of very different talent and temperament was Franz Liszt (1811–1886), another great performer and composer of piano music in the Romantic period. Liszt was blessed with great physical strength and a fiery, egotistical disposition. His piano technique was the talk of Europe, as were his many flamboyant love affairs. Throughout his long career, Liszt was pursued by women and surrounded by a veritable cult of students intent on learning the style of their great master. Characteristically he refused to accept payment for teaching because "neither God nor the Emperor accepts gifts." As teacher, composer, pianist, lover, and individualist, Liszt had a powerful influence on the music and the Romantic imagination of his time.

Liszt was born in Hungary to a family in the service of the Esterházys. Like Chopin, he gained early recognition in Vienna and then settled in Paris. Although apparently not a child prodigy, he early developed a great facility for sight reading and improvisation. His memory was phenomenal. After hearing a piece of music only once, he could generally reproduce all or most of it at the keyboard. These gifts helped him become one of the foremost arrangers of

Manuscript Page from Liszt's *Soirées de Vienne: Even the untrained eye can recognize the difficulty of the music Liszt wrote for his* Soirées de Vienne *("Evenings of Vienna"). The passage shown is marked Vivace—that is, very fast—and requires considerable agility in the right hand.*

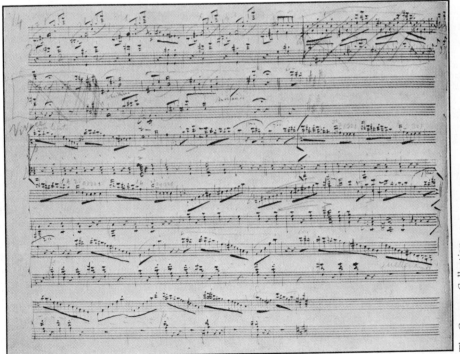

orchestral scores for piano. And his insatiable appetite for literature of all kinds contributed to his success as a composer of program music.

It was at the piano, however, that Liszt made his reputation. Much of his style as a composer can be explained by his playing technique. Liszt was above all a virtuoso pianist—and, some would add, a showman. An important

Paganini's Influence

influence on his life was the great violin virtuoso Niccolò Paganini (1782–1840), whom Liszt heard in concert in 1831. He saw no reason why the piano could not attain the virtuosic heights of Paganini's violin. He therefore wrote, and played, works of dazzling difficulty—works that demanded a certain theatricality of performance or, in the words of one observer, a "great tossing of the hands." Liszt's performances were unquestionably marked by theatrics but also by incomparable finesse and power.

While Chopin generally wrote in an economical fashion, drawing on the very special resources of the piano, Liszt composed in a resplendent orchestral manner. His works, on the average, take in a larger part of the keyboard than the works written by his contemporaries do. More notes sound simultaneously. Ornamentation occurs on many levels. Liszt made piano transcriptions of a number of orchestral works, including Beethoven's symphonies, and was thus experienced in creating the various orchestral sounds, loud and soft, on the piano. This writing of transcriptions, however, did much more than encourage experiments in piano timbre. Long before the advent of recordings, it made symphonies and other orchestral works accessible to audiences in places that could not sustain a full orchestra.

Liszt wrote a wide variety of works for solo piano, including the *Mephisto Waltz, Liebestraum* ("Love Dream"), several collections of études, and the renowned *Sonata in B Minor*. He is probably best known, though, for his

Rhapsodies

rhapsodies. The *rhapsody* is one of the most romantic of musical works. It has no set form, aside from the free use of sections, relying instead primarily on the artist's subjective organization. Generally the rhapsody is dramatic or heroic in tone and rich in emotional color. It is usually scored to achieve a large sound and is commonly written for piano or orchestra.

Liszt's *Hungarian Rhapsodies* were written after the composer's trip to Hungary in 1838. Receiving news of severe flooding in his native land, Liszt crossed the Danube and was received as in triumph by his fellow Hungarians. In appreciation and patriotic pride, he wrote a series of fifteen rhapsodies through which he hoped to convey "certain states of mind in which are condensed the ideals of a nation."

The rhapsodies were based on the gypsy music that was commonly heard in the towns and countryside of Hungary. All of the works make use of dance and folk material. One, the *Hungarian Rhapsody No. 15 in A Minor*, is based on a traditional march tune of the Hungarian army, the *Rákoczy March*. In places Liszt attempted to imitate gypsy instruments, particularly the *cimbalom*, a string instrument played with hammers.

Most of the rhapsodies are technically very difficult to play. They are characterized by extreme dynamic contrasts and luxuriant ornamentation. Typical are the repetition of difficult melodic figures, the use of octaves, rapid scales and arpeggios, and other colorful effects for which Liszt was famous. The variation and development of themes provide much occasion for virtuosity—wonderful technical displays that have all the feeling of true improvisation.

Liszt: *Hungarian Rhapsody No. 6 in D♭ Major*

Changes of mood and texture are frequent in Liszt's rhapsodies. In most of the works, quick dancelike material is contrasted with melancholy gypsy airs. Such a contrast can readily be found in the *Hungarian Rhapsody No. 6 in D♭ Major*, along with contrasts of tempo and key. The four large sections that make up the piece can be outlined thus:

Section A	Section B	Section C	Section D
Tempo giusto (At a fitting tempo)	Presto (Very fast)	Andante (Moderate)	Allegro (Fast)
D♭ Major	C♯ Major	B♭ Minor	B♭ Major

Section A

In the first section, pounding chords in the left hand accompany a hesitant dancelike melody in the right. Syncopation is strongly apparent throughout, and the section ends with a brief flourish that travels quickly up and down the keyboard.

Section B

The quickly moving second section also makes use of syncopation. Its tempo provides bright contrast to the slow motion of the preceding section.

Section C

The third section is set in the key of B♭ minor, the relative minor of the key used in the first section. Marked *Quasi improvisato* (somewhat improvised), this section evokes the slow, haunting quality of a gypsy violin. Its improvisatory character stems from its slow tempo, expressive melody, unusual rhythmic patterns, and apparent lack of clear meter.

Cadenza and Section D

A brief, clashing cadenza links the third section to the final section, which offers a vehicle for Liszt's dazzling virtuosity. The section begins with a rather simple conjunct melody that is presented several times with ever increasing complexity. Toward the end, scale passages, arpeggios, great chords, and a presto tempo make one feel that the limits of technical virtuosity and showmanship have been reached.

Side 7, Band 2

Listening Guide for Liszt's *Hungarian Rhapsody No.6 in D♭ Major*

Timbre:	piano
Melody:	different themes in each of the four sections; all marked by a folklike quality
Rhythm:	duple meter; tempos in four sections are slow—fast—slow—fast; specific tempos are shown above
Harmony:	mainly major mode, with third section in minor mode; specific keys are shown above
Texture:	homophonic
Form:	ABCD

Suggested Listening

Early Romantic Piano Music

Liszt: *Transcendental Études* [Columbia M-30488]. These études range from the quiet and lyrical to the symphonic. They are of almost insuperable difficulty to the performer and were influenced strongly by the great violinist Paganini. The music is at times very chromatic, with many unresolved dissonances.

Mendelssohn: *Variations sérieuses, Op. 54* [London 6676]. A Classicist in spirit and training, Mendelssohn developed his style considerably beyond that of the earlier generation. The variation structure in this work is quite clear, but the melodic and harmonic language are adventuresome for the time. The variations require extensive virtuosity of the pianist.

Schumann: *Carnaval* [Philips 802746]. This collection of character pieces portrays two contrasting aspects of Romantic style. Schumann personifies them in the fiery, impulsive piece entitled "Florestan" and in the quiet, dreamlike piece entitled "Eusebius." His style, while rooted in Classical technique, expanded broadly into new means of expression.

Late Romantic Piano Music

Brahms: *Variations and Fugue on a Theme by Handel, Op. 24* [London 6474]. Brahms often turned to the past for assistance and inspiration, as he did in choosing the theme for this set of variations. The theme is well suited for variation because of its neatly divided phrases and its tonic-dominant orientation.

Rachmaninoff: *Preludes, Op. 23* [DG 138076]. Rachmaninoff's piano writing was influenced by the work of Chopin and Schumann, as well as by the music of his native Russia and the Orient. The preludes in *Op. 23* have a certain exotic quality and a considerable amount of chromaticism. With one or two popular exceptions, the works are technically very difficult.

Romantic Song

The Growth of Lieder

Art Songs

In the Romantic period, an abundant new literature developed for the solo voice with piano. The new works were known, in a general sense, as *art songs.* In German-speaking countries, where songs are known as *Lieder*, the development was particularly intense. The compositional form of Lieder allowed for a variety of lyric expression on a dramatic, if limited, scale. Like most other songs, the Lied combined a poetic text with music, but it derived its special characteristics from the German Romantic movement of the early nineteenth century.

Schubert's Influence

The Lied found its first major champion in Austrian composer Franz Schubert, one of the earliest Romantic composers. Although Mozart and Haydn had written many attractive songs, most of their works had resembled either arias or folk songs. Beethoven also wrote songs, most notably his song cycle *An die ferne Geliebte* ("To the Distant Beloved"), but his larger vocal and instrumental works are of much greater significance. It was Schubert who first treated the Lied as a major vehicle of musical expression.

Improvements in the Piano

There are several reasons for the sudden, immense development of the Lied at the beginning of the Romantic period. One important factor was the continued improvement of the piano. Compared with earlier pianos, the instrument for which Schubert composed was quite rich and warm in tone. The early nineteenth-century piano was capable of a lovely singing tone sustained by a new pedal technique. Able to perform a variety of tasks—to blend in with and complement the voice, to add lyrical and dramatic support to it—the piano provided an ideal accompaniment to the voice. Romantic composers were quick to make use of this happy combination. So were the many middle-class families who, having acquired a piano, wanted songs with piano accompaniment. This new role of the piano as the center of amateur vocal performance did much to promote the nineteenth-century emphasis on song.

Outburst of German Poetry

The growth of Lieder was also encouraged by the outburst of lyric poetry that occurred in Germany just before the Romantic period in music. Not until the time of Beethoven could the Germans boast of a poetic literature equal to that which had long existed in England and Italy. But in the latter part of the eighteenth century, a number of important writers came to the fore—most notably Johann Wolfgang von Goethe and Friedrich von Schiller. Heinrich Heine, another great lyric poet, was born in 1797, the same year as Schubert. Poetry and music thus flourished together in the climate of early German Romanticism. Goethe, Schiller, Heine, and the many other German poets of the early nineteenth century were nearly as important to the development of the Lied as the composers whom their work inspired.

Characteristics of the Lied

Structure

Lieder are truly compound art forms. Literary nuances deeply influence the music, while the music enhances, and more fully "realizes," the emotional implications of the poetic lines. Lieder thus vary in structure according to the emotional requirements of the poems on which they are based. Some, such as Schubert's "Erlkönig" ("The Elf King"), are freely structured. Others, such as Schubert's "Gute Nacht" ("Good Night") or "Die Forelle" ("The Trout"), are in modified strophic form: the same basic melody and accompaniment are repeated, with some modification, in each stanza.

Piano and Voice

Just as the Lied is a partnership between poetry and music, so also is it a partnership between piano and voice. The melody, of course, is presented mainly by the singer. But the pianist provides much more than accompaniment. Many Lieder begin with a piano introduction that sets the mood and establishes the basic rhythm and thematic idea. As the song progresses, the piano may contribute solo passages that are integral to the artistic design. And finally, the last lines of the Lied, often a very expressive element of the work, are generally played by the piano alone. Although the piano sometimes simply duplicates the melodic line, it usually has a part that is different from the melody and of equal significance. In most cases, the piano provides, in the words of critic Paul Henry Lang, "the soil from which the vocal flower grows."

Schubert's Lieder

The Romantic concept of the hero was virtually incarnated in Franz Schubert (1797–1828). His life was marked by almost unbelievable creativity but also by much suffering—poverty, ill health, and loneliness. He was apparently subject to great extremes of emotion, and though he was undoubtedly a disciplined craftsman, there are numerous anecdotes attesting to the almost spontaneous creation of his greatest works. He is said to have written as many as seven songs in a single day. And he is thought to have been a composer by instinct, a natural talent who chose to sing of natural things—the brook, the field, the moonlit countryside, the experience of love. Like the Romantic poets Byron, Keats, and Shelley, he died a young man. But his genius seems to have been that of youth. He had completed more than half his songs by the time he was nineteen.

Romantic Themes: *Schubert's Lieder almost invariably deal with themes of love, heroism, or death—themes particularly suited to the tastes of the Romantic audience. The French edition of* Espérance *shown above further capitalized on current tastes with the melodrama of its cover illustration.*

The Use of Symbolism in Schubert's Lieder

Schubert's Lieder are filled with symbolism—with musical sounds that are meant to represent the sounds and feelings of life itself. Such symbolic content generally appears in the piano part. A river, for example, might be indicated by a gently flowing arpeggio or a lover's despair by dissonant chords in the minor mode. In "Gretchen am Spinnrade" ("Margaret at the Spinning Wheel"), the sound of the wheel is suggested by a revolving, rapid treble part played over a heavier punctuating rhythm that represents the treadle. The song, based on a scene from Goethe's *Faust*, expresses Margaret's deeply disturbed feelings over

Gretchen am Spinnrade

Faust's "unholy courtship." As her thoughts become more erotic, the wheel speeds faster, then comes to an abrupt stop at the memory of Faust's kiss. The revolving treble part is then heard again as Margaret returns to her work. Throughout, the piano part contributes greatly to the force of the song.

The symbolic uses of the piano part vary from work to work, ranging from obvious imitation of natural sounds to very subtle interpretive effects. The sound of horses' hooves is reproduced to great dramatic effect in a number of Lieder. The wind, the music of an organ grinder, the falling of rain or teardrops—all lend themselves to imitation in the Lied. At times the effects are even subtler. In the song cycle *Die schöne Müllerin* ("The Fair Maid of the Mill"), the piano part may be equated with the brook that the young miller follows in search of his beloved. Beside it he confides his feelings, and here he finally drowns himself after his love is rejected.

In Schubert's works, and in other German Lieder, the melody generally works with the accompaniment, helping to convey the story and the emotional changes involved. Schubert's "Erlkönig" offers a good example. The song, in free form with some repetition, is based on a ballade by Goethe that deals with the legend that anyone who sees the elf king inevitably dies. The piano introduction suggests hoofbeats as a father and child ride through a dark forest. Vocal line and accompaniment differentiate the four voices of the poem—narrator, father, child, and elf king. The fright of the child, who sees the elf king, and the reassurances of the father, who does not, are vividly portrayed in the minor mode. The child's terror is further conveyed through the dramatic use of dissonance and the rising pitch of the child's cries. The voice of the elf king is smooth and seductive. At the end of the song, the galloping piano figure slows as the father arrives home with the boy dead in his arms. The "Erlkönig," written when Schubert was only eighteen years old, is a powerful demonstration of the way in which text and music can work together to enhance a work of poetry.

Schubert: *Die Winterreise*

It was in 1827, a year before his death, that Schubert conceived of a song cycle based on Wilhelm Müller's poem *Die Winterreise* ("The Winter Journey"). This was a time of great emotional stress for Schubert, one in which he felt himself "utterly unfit for any society," alone and isolated from the world. His few companions were a melancholy assortment of second-rate poets who did little to lift his spirits. And his physical state was rapidly deteriorating.

It is not surprising that Schubert in this state was immediately attracted to the imagery of Müller's poetry. As one of Schubert's friends wrote, "Life had lost its summer, winter was upon him." And yet it would be wrong to assume that the music he wrote for *Die Winterreise* was simply a record of Schubert's state of mind. In the last years of his life, he also wrote the *Symphony in C Major* as well as a number of piano sonatas, a Mass, and a quintet—none of which suggests the despair of *Die Winterreise*.

The texts of the twenty-four songs that make up *Die Winterreise* concern a lover who has been utterly rejected by his only beloved. The cycle expresses

Die Schöne Müllerin

Erlkönig

his despair as he leaves the young woman's house to wander endlessly through a dark winter landscape. The organization of the cycle differs from that of the original poem, and there is no real narrative thread. Instead each song develops a particular kind of heartbreak—a mood, a memory, or an image in the lover's journey.

"Gute Nacht"

"Gute Nacht," the first song in the cycle, marks the beginning of the journey. The disappointed lover leaves the house where his beloved lies sleeping. He sets out on a road "veiled with snow" with only a "moon shadow" as his companion. Müller's poem, with English translation, is given in the Listening Guide on the next page.

As you can see, each stanza of the poem is eight lines long. Schubert, however, chose to use a twelve-line stanza for the musical setting. This means that in each stanza, some of the poetic lines are sung more than once. In the first two stanzas, Lines 5 and 6 are repeated as a unit, as are Lines 7 and 8. The third stanza has a more complicated pattern, repeating one line several times as a kind of refrain. In the final stanza, the last four lines are repeated as a unit. The musical form is modified strophic.

Introduction and First Stanza

The song begins in the minor mode, in a $\frac{2}{4}$ meter of moderate tempo that suggests the lover's trudging through the snow. Like most other Lieder, it opens with a piano introduction—in this case, a six-measure phrase that reappears between stanzas. Then the vocal part enters:

Opening Melody

Fremd bin ich ein - ge - zo - gen, Fremd
zieh ich wie - der aus

The minor mode is appropriate, since the lover realizes that he is departing as he arrived, a stranger. When he recalls the hopes of the past in Lines 5 and 6, the mode changes to the relative major. These lines are then emphasized by repetition at a higher pitch in another key. It is almost as if the very recollection has transported the lover. With Lines 7 and 8, which suggest a return of despair, the music returns to the minor mode. The return is announced by a stabbing, uneven rhythm played in octaves on the piano. The rhythm, so threatening here, is repeated in each stanza of the song.

Second Stanza

The second stanza, which speaks of the journey to be made, is sung to exactly the same music. The first two stanzas of the music are thus in a strict strophic form.

Third Stanza

In the third stanza, however, there are a number of expressive variations, mainly in the melody. Variety is achieved by small means—some of the intervals in the melody are altered, ornamental notes are added, and the melodic direction of some of the phrases is changed. In the opening line, for example, the melody is drawn upward to the tonic rather than downward as it was in the first two stanzas—perhaps because the line now voices a question. With such alteration, new interest is added to the now familiar melody.

Fourth Stanza

In the fourth stanza, the music changes from minor to major. In addition to providing modal contrast, the change brings a new poignancy, coming as it does with the lines "I wouldn't disturb your dream; It's a shame to spoil your rest." The music then modulates toward the dominant, and the uneven rhythm takes on a new tenderness. As the song draws to its final "Good Night," the mode returns to the sorrowful minor. The song ends with the piano playing steady, repeated chords.

Listening Guide for "Gute Nacht" from Schubert's *Die Winterreise*

Timbre: baritone and piano

Melody: predominantly disjunct melody with descending motion emphasized throughout

Rhythm: duple meter; tempo Moderato (moderate)

Harmony: mainly minor mode; first three stanzas begin and end in C minor; last stanza begins in C major and ends in C minor

Texture: homophonic

Form: modified strophic form, with four stanzas

Text:

I
Fremd bin ich eingezogen,
Fremd zieh ich wieder aus.
Der Mai war mir gewogen
Mit manchem Blumenstrauss.
Das Mädchen sprach von Liebe,
Die Mutter gar von Eh—
Nun ist die Welt so trübe,
Der Weg gehüllt in Schnee.

I came here as a stranger,
A stranger I depart.
The month of May was kind to me,
With many a bouquet of flowers.
The girl spoke of love,
Her mother even of marriage—
Now the world is so dreary,
The road veiled with snow.

II
Ich kann zu meiner Reisen
Nicht wählen mit der Zeit,
Muss selbst den Weg mir weisen
In dieser Dunkelheit.
Es zieht ein Mondenschatten
Als mein Gefährte mit,
Und auf den weissen Matten
Such ich des Wildes Tritt.

I cannot choose
The time for my journey;
I must find my own way
In the darkness.
A moon shadow wanders with me
As my companion,
And on the white fields
I seek the footprints of beasts.

III
Was soll ich länger weilen,
Dass man mich trieb hinaus?
Lass irre Hunde heulen
Vor ihres Herren Haus;
Die Liebe liebt das Wandern—
Gott hat sie so gemacht—
Von Einem zu dem Andern—
Fein Liebchen, gute Nacht!

Why should I tarry longer,
So they can drive me out?
Let mad dogs howl
Before their master's house.
Love loves to wander—
God made it so—
From one to the other—
My sweetheart, good night!

IV	Will dich im Traum nicht stören,	I wouldn't disturb your dream;
	Wär schad um deine Ruh,	It's a shame to spoil your rest;
	Sollst meinen Tritt nicht hören—	You shall not hear my
	Sacht, sacht, die Türe zu!	footstep—
	Schreib im Vorübergehen	Soft, softly, close the door!
	An's Tor dir: gute Nacht,	On the door I write to you,
	Damit du mögest sehen,	As I pass, "Good Night,"
	An dich hab ich gedacht.	So you may see
		That I was thinking of you.

Other Songs in Schubert's *Die Winterreise*

The other songs in *Die Winterreise* speak of many different moods. Some evoke melancholy images—the lover looking for the footsteps of his beloved in the snow or waiting for a love letter he knows will not come. But Schubert did include some relief from the general despair. In "Frühlingsträume" ("A Dream of Springtime"), the lover momentarily returns to his happier past, and in "Muth" ("Courage"), he voices a determination not found in the songs surrounding it. In the last song, "Der Leiermann" ("The Organ Grinder"), the lover comes upon an organ grinder, a beggar who wanders senselessly and alone. The two disappear together into the distance as the pathetic musician's tune is played to a fine diminuendo on the piano. The effect is one of intense sadness.

Schubert's Last Works

After completing *Die Winterreise*, Schubert wrote a number of songs that were later collected in a volume entitled *Schwanengesang* ("Swan Song"). The collection, however, is not as Schubert intended it to be, for he died before it was completed. In fulfillment of a last wish, he was buried at the side of Beethoven. He left more than six hundred songs as well as numerous instrumental works, many of which remained either unknown or unperformed for half a century after his death.

Schumann's Lieder

A second great composer of Lieder, Robert Schumann (1810–1856), was born in Germany about thirteen years after Schubert. In many ways, Schumann, like Schubert, lived the legend of the Romantic artist. His career was marked by great creativity and emotional torment.

The young Schumann had an irrepressible passion for literature, music, and all things beautiful and expensive. His activities were somewhat of a trial to his widowed mother, who hoped that he would eventually practice law. Schumann did study law, but the discipline does not seem to have suited his temperament. He was, in his mother's words, "a young and inexperienced man who lives but in a higher sphere and will have nothing to do with practical life." After a long inward battle, Schumann abandoned his legal studies and committed himself totally to music. For instruction he went to a leading piano teacher in Leipzig, Friedrich Wieck.

A Gifted Couple: *Clara Schumann, who inspired numerous works by her husband, Robert, and her friend Brahms, was not only a gifted pianist but also a talented composer in her own right. She is shown here with her husband in an early daguerreotype.*

Wieck was apparently under no illusions about his pupil. Though perceiving that Schumann had considerable talent and imagination, he also noted his pupil's overconfidence and his impatience with "dry cold theory"— attitudes both typically Romantic. Wieck recommended as a model student his own daughter Clara, a prodigy at the piano whose accomplishments spoke well of her father's methods. Schumann, however, lacked Clara's patience with technique and soon turned from piano performance to composition. He also tried music criticism, becoming editor of the *Neue Leipziger Zeitschrift für*

Musik ("The New Leipzig Journal for Music"). As the son of a bookseller and an inveterate reader, he proved highly successful in his editorial role. Criticism and composition flowed readily in a period of feverish work.

In 1835, when Schumann was twenty-five years old, he became conscious of a profound love for Clara Wieck, now sixteen years old. She herself had apparently admired Schumann from the first time he set foot in her father's house. Wieck, however, objected to the proposed marriage between his daughter and his pupil. Although he liked Schumann, he saw in him a basic instability of temperament. He also wished his daughter to marry a man wealthy enough to sponsor her concert career. At this point, Clara was already becoming a well-known artist, and Schumann was but an enthusiastic young composer. For several years before their marriage, Schumann and Clara were kept apart by Wieck. It was during this period and in the early years of his marriage that Schumann wrote some of his greatest lyric works—both Lieder and piano compositions.

Schumann: "Widmung"

"Widmung," or in English, "Dedication," was written in 1840, the year of Schumann's marriage. It was, of course, a dedication to Clara. The song is based on a poem by Friedrich Rückert, a German poet who was a contemporary of Schubert. The text can be found in the Listening Guide on the next page.

The song is in $\frac{3}{2}$ meter and in the major mode. Its form is ternary, or ABA. *Section A* begins with a piano introduction, a rushing piano arpeggio that sets the emotional tone for the entire piece. This is followed by the opening melody, which rises as it enters. The first two phrases are shown below:

Opening Melody

Du mei - ne See - le, du mein Herz, du mei - ne

Wonn', o du mein Schmerz

The melody in the second phrase soars even higher than that in the first. The music then modulates briefly to the subdominant to produce an ardent new effect. Only at the end of Section A, the end of the first stanza of the poem, does the music return to the home key.

Section B   In Section B, the music jumps quickly to an unexpected key, effecting a sharp change of color. The piano arpeggios heard in Section A disappear, and in their place we hear a steady succession of chords in triplets. The melody is rhythmically slower, with notes of longer duration. The effect is one of almost religious awe, which accords well with the poetic text with its references to peace, heaven, and self-realization through love. Intensity is achieved through quietness, a means often used in small lyric works where symphonic impact is not possible.

Section A

The last A section begins like the first. The last part of the section, however, differs both in melody and in harmony. The work itself ends, as it began, with piano arpeggios.

Side 7, Band 4

Listening Guide for Schumann's "Widmung"

Timbre: tenor and piano

Melody: conjunct and disjunct motion in vocal part

Rhythm: triple meter; tempo Innig, lebhaft (fervently, lively)

Harmony: major mode; A sections in A♭ major, B section in E major

Texture: homophonic; arpeggiated piano accompaniment in A sections; chordal piano accompaniment in B section

Form: ternary (ABA¹)

Text:

A
Du meine Seele, du mein Herz, du meine Wonn', o du mein Schmerz, du meine Welt, in der ich lebe, mein Himmel du, darein ich schwebe, o du mein Grab, in das hinab ich ewig meinen Kummer gab!

You are my soul, you are my heart, You my delight, and you my pain; You are my world in which I live, And you my heaven in which I soar; You are my grave wherein I ever Buried all my grief!

B
Du bist die Ruh', du bist der Frieden; du bist vom Himmel mir beschieden. Dass du mich liebst, macht mich mir wert, dein Blick hat mich vor mir verklärt, du hebst mich liebend über mich, mein guter Geist, mein bess'res Ich!

You are my rest, you are my peace, You were allotted me by heaven; That you love me gives me my worth; Your glance transfigures me in my own eyes; You, loving, raise me up above myself, My good spirit, my better I.

A¹
Du meine Seele, du mein Herz, du meine Wonn', o du mein Schmerz, du meine Welt, in der ich lebe, mein Himmel du, darein ich schwebe, mein guter Geist, mein bess'res Ich!

You are my soul, you are my heart, You my delight, and you my pain; You are my world in which I live, And you my heaven in which I soar; My good spirit, my better I.

Other Works by Schumann

"Widmung" was written in the period of Schumann's most glorious musical outpouring. From these years date some of his greatest chamber music—notably the three string quartets in *Op. 41* and the *Piano Quintet, Op. 44.* The song cycle *Frauenliebe und Leben* ("Woman's Love and Life") was also written during this period. In eight songs, the cycle traces the experiences

261 ROMANTIC SONG

of a woman, from love at first sight through engagement, marriage, and childbirth to widowhood. The final song, describing bereavement, ends with a piano coda that brings back material from the first song. Another masterpiece, the cycle *Dichterliebe* ("The Poet's Love"), is also from this period.

Despite his accomplishments as a composer and the emotional and artistic partnership he enjoyed in his marriage, Schumann grew less and less able to deal with the world. In 1854 he attempted suicide and was taken to an asylum, where he died two years later.

Later Composers of Lieder

Brahms' Lieder   Johannes Brahms, a close friend of both Robert and Clara Schumann, was also a major composer of Lieder, as well as of other types of works. Among his most notable Lieder are his folk-song arrangements and a work entitled *Vier ernste Gesänge* ("Four Serious Songs"), which he wrote at the time of Clara Schumann's final illness.

Wagner   Although primarily a composer of operas, Richard Wagner (1813–1883) wrote one particularly notable song cycle, the *Wesendonck Lieder*. Composed to give expression to Wagner's love for Mathilde Wesendonck, the work presents many characteristics of Wagner's operatic writing on a smaller scale. Perhaps most prominent are the thought of submission to love and death and the use of chromatic harmony.

Wolf   Another, very innovative composer of German Lieder was Hugo Wolf (1860–1903), who wrote the bulk of his work in the late 1880s. Wolf's songs are generally thought to mark the culmination of the German Romantic Lied. As a composer, Wolf was noted for his highly expressive and frequently chromatic writing.

Mahler and Richard Strauss   In the works of later German composers, among them Gustav Mahler (1860–1911) and Richard Strauss (1864–1949), the Lied was carried beyond its original Romantic form and developed in a number of new and different directions.

Mahler: *Lieder eines fahrenden Gesellen*

One obvious expansion of the original Lieder style can be found in Mahler's song cycle *Lieder eines fahrenden Gesellen* ("Songs of a Wayfarer"). Instead of using the piano to accompany the singer, Mahler used a large orchestra. There are four songs in the cycle, each presenting one or more changes of mood.

First Song   The first of the four songs reflects sadly on the wedding of the singer's sweetheart to someone else. The text alludes frequently to elements in nature and closes in deep sorrow. The mood changes radically, though, with the second song of the cycle.

Second Song   "Ging heut Morgen" ("Walked This Morning"), the second song in the cycle, begins with a bright text about a morning walk through the fields. The lines ring with exuberance until, at the end, the intense sorrow of the preceding song returns.

Many characteristics of Mahler's style can be found in the song. The orchestra is used with great vitality in support of the solo voice. The form is modified strophic, with changes in the setting of each stanza of the text. Duple meter and the major mode characterize the lyrical melody that begins the first stanza:

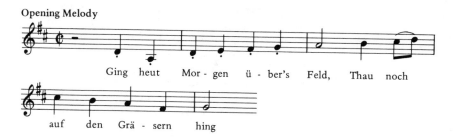

Opening Melody

Ging heut Mor - gen ü - ber's Feld, Thau noch auf den Grä - sern hing

While this theme also opens the second and third stanzas, the continuation is quite different each time. In addition, the third stanza is introduced by a marked change of key.

The last, very short stanza also emphasizes the beginning of the first theme. But the stanza closes in a melancholy mood that matches the sorrow of the text.

Third and Fourth Songs

The third and fourth songs in the cycle explore other aspects of unhappy love in ways both subtle and intense. Mahler, like many other composers in the latter part of the nineteenth century, was always very careful to match the mood of the text with appropriate musical ideas. Exact repetition of themes and sections is therefore rarely found.

The French Art Song

Berlioz, Fauré, Debussy, and Ravel

The art song also developed in France and other countries during the nineteenth and early twentieth centuries. France acquired a great literature of art songs by such composers as Hector Berlioz (1803–1869), Gabriel Fauré (1845–1924), Claude Debussy (1862–1918), and Maurice Ravel (1875–1937). The French poetry of the period is less intensely introspective than the German, and the musical style of these composers is consequently somewhat lighter and less consciously profound. Their works show the sensitivity and elegance so often found in French music.

Suggested Listening

German Lieder

Schumann: *Dichterliebe, Op. 48* ("The Poet's Love") [DG 139101]. This cycle is an indirect celebration of Schumann's love for Clara Wieck. In many of the songs Schumann has perfectly wedded voice to accompaniment, making the piano important melodically as well as harmonically. A rich variety of material and mood is apparent throughout.

Brahms: "Sapphic Ode" [Columbia M-34535]. The melody of this song emphasizes triads and long phrases. Rhythm is rendered important by the subtle syncopation always present in the accompaniment. Its fine lyrical quality and rich harmonies make the song one of Brahms' best loved.

Wolf: "Peregrina II" from the *Mörike Lieder* [DG 2530584]. Wolf wrote a major collection of songs using poems by the German poet and novelist Eduard Mörike. The poem upon which the present song is based lends itself well to declamation and a fragmentary presentation. Most of the musical interest is thus found in the piano part. Wolf's chromaticism, as shown here, stretches the bounds of tonality and sounds strikingly modern.

R. Strauss: *Vier letzte Lieder* ("Four Last Songs") [Angel S-36347]. Like Mahler, Strauss used an orchestra to accompany the singer in many of his songs. The great contrasts in style of expression heard in this work show Strauss to be a master orchestrator, very sensitive to the setting of a text and to the capabilities of the singer.

French Art Songs

Berlioz: *Les Nuits d'été, Op. 7* ("Summer Nights") [London 25821]. Berlioz' cycle *Les Nuits d'été* is considered a landmark in song literature because of its very early use of orchestral accompaniment. The colorful and subtle orchestration is quite appropriate to the texts of the songs, all of which differ greatly in mood and spirit.

Fauré: "Après un rêve" ("After a Dream") [RCA LSC-2279]. This song, like many others by Fauré, shows his mastery of lyric melody, fluid rhythms, and interesting harmonies. Fauré was also noted for his sensitivity in setting texts to music. The excellent French poetry with which he worked no doubt contributed to his inspiration.

CHAPTER

21

Romantic Symphony and Concerto

Trends in the Symphony

In their development of the short piano piece and the song, Romantic composers were very innovative. In fact, they created a new tradition. But innovation was not the sole characteristic of the period. In their symphonic works, most Romantic composers chose to follow earlier forms, building on the mighty achievements of the Classical past.

The roots of the Romantic symphony can be found in the late works of Mozart, in a number of the symphonies written by Beethoven, and in the **Schubert's** symphonic works of Schubert. Schubert as a composer of Lieder owed little to **Symphonies** his predecessors. In his symphonic writing, however, he was greatly influenced by Classical composers. He admired Beethoven and openly used certain of his works as models for composition. Like Beethoven, Schubert was a transitional figure whose works can be placed somewhere near the center of the Classical-Romantic continuum. His music shows certain Romantic tendencies—an emphasis on lyrical melody, for example, and a freer use of Classical forms—but his intentions were in many ways Classical.

Schubert's symphonies are an epilogue to the Classical era and a prologue to the Romantic. Eight complete works survive, the greater number written before he was nineteen years old. The last, the *Symphony in C Major*, is recognized as one of his finest. The most popular of his symphonies, however, is the so-called "Unfinished" Symphony, which he began in 1822 but never completed. We have only two full movements of the work. The first movement, marked Allegro moderato, is in sonata form. The second movement, marked Andante con moto (moderately with motion), is in modified sonata form with no development section. The third movement, of which we have only ten measures, was to have been a scherzo.

The value of Schubert's symphonic achievement was not recognized in his own time. As music critic Donald Tovey has remarked, "The tragedy of Beethoven's deafness needs no comment; but the history of the arts is full of tragedies not less pathetic and far less inspiring to the imagination. . . . Schubert, who was not deaf, never heard his own mature orchestral music at all."

**Program
Symphony**

**Abstract
Symphony**

**Characteristics
of the Abstract
Symphony**

In the years after Schubert's death, the symphony remained one of the major types of music for orchestra although it underwent many changes. Some composers, especially Liszt and Berlioz, sought a new basis for symphonic writing. The result was the program symphony. The works were based in a general way on the Classical symphony, but they derived much of their logic and form from literary or other artistic works rather than from purely musical ideas.

There was, however, another trend, characterized by a more traditional approach. Mendelssohn, Schumann, Brahms, and Tchaikovsky all wrote "abstract" symphonies, organized around purely musical ideas as the truly Classical symphony had been. These Romantic traditionalists believed that the Classical sonata cycle was capable of expressing the essence of Romanticism. Unlike the composers of program symphonies, they avoided subjective organization in their larger works, although their writing itself was often very subjective in spirit. In general, they retained Classical forms for typically Romantic ideas.

Although the composers of abstract symphonies still wrote themes based on motives, they gave increasing prominence to lyrical melodies emphasizing conjunct motion. They used a variety of rhythms; steady and very regular rhythmic patterns were often suddenly disrupted by irregular patterns. Major-minor harmony underwent great exploration; the system was so thoroughly and freely used that it in effect broke down by the end of the century. Chromaticism became more evident and remote key relationships were more often exploited. Composers made extensive use of certain chords with added tones—chords that soon became typical of Romantic harmony. One such chord is the dominant ninth (5–7–2–4–6), which is both dissonant and pleasing, suggesting a bittersweet quality. In the Classical period, such chords, when used at all, had been thoroughly integrated into the harmonic structure. In Romantic music, they were generally sounded conspicuously, to produce striking harmonic effects, and at times were not resolved as expected.

Texture in the abstract symphony of the Romantic age became increasingly dense, and the range of dynamics expanded greatly. Contrasts in timbre as well as contrasts in melody were frequently stressed. Classical forms, though respected, were treated more freely than before. Brahms, for example, in the last movement of his *Symphony No. 1*, omitted a formal development section and instead incorporated extensive development into the exposition and recapitulation. Occasional changes were also made in the overall sonata cycle. Schubert, like Beethoven, wrote a symphony of five movements rather than four. And Tchaikovsky ended his *Symphony No. 6* with an intense Adagio lamentoso instead of the traditional quick finale.

The changes Romantic composers made in the Classical symphony are in large part attributable to the dictates of the Romantic spirit. Romantic composers did not feel compelled to adhere to the Classical ideals of balance and proportion when to do so would prevent them from expressing the emotions and musical ideas they had in mind. Some emotions, after all, are disproportionate and unbalanced. In emphasizing the individuality of their

The Romantic Orchestra and Chorus: *The symphonic orchestra continued to grow in size throughout the nineteenth century. Its increasingly massive and powerful sound was further enhanced by the frequent addition of a large chorus as seen in this 1893 performance in a British concert hall.*

musical ideas, Romantic composers inevitably changed the Classical symphony.

Many characteristics of the abstract symphony of the Romantic age were, of course, already present to some degree in Beethoven's works. Among other things, his writing shows increasing chromaticism and modulation to remote keys as well as a tendency to alter form for expressive reasons. As we have observed, his *Symphony No. 6* has five movements, and his *Symphony No. 9* features a chorus and soloists. Moreover, Beethoven used a large orchestra, prefiguring the even larger ones that would be available to his successors.

The Romantic symphony was not, however, merely an extension of Beethoven's ideas. The intense thematic development found in Beethoven's works appears somewhat less frequently in Romantic symphonies. Melodies often undergo repetition and variation rather than development in the Classical sense. We hear a melody again and again in changing context— perhaps altered in harmony, timbre, and texture. Less often do we hear it broken down into its constituent motives, recombined, and inverted as we did in Beethoven's *Symphony No. 5*. The concentrated development process of the Classical age became, in a general sense, less essential in the symphonic works of the Romantic age.

Brahms' Symphonies

Of those Romantic composers who followed the tradition of Beethoven and Schubert, it was perhaps Johannes Brahms (1833–1897) who achieved the finest synthesis of Classical ideal and Romantic spirit. One of the most beloved of Romantic composers, he was born five years after Schubert's early death and spent his childhood in a run-down section of the north German city of Hamburg. His father was a musician who played a number of instruments in settings ranging from street and tavern to the city's philharmonic orchestra. He agreed to let his son play in a local orchestra, but the boy showed a strong preference for the piano instead and, ultimately, a talent much greater than his father's.

Under the guidance of an expert teacher, Johannes learned quickly. At the age of ten, he appeared publicly in an ensemble; at thirteen he played in tavern dance bands; at fifteen be began to give solo concerts. But Brahms was only a minor performer in a country rich with virtuosos. As a young man, he turned his attention to composition, producing among his first works a number of piano sonatas and songs.

Brahms' career was furthered by his association with several prominent musicians. Among them were, most notably, Eduard Reményi, the Hungarian violinist with whom Brahms toured in 1853, and Joseph Joachim, another violin virtuoso who, like Brahms, was much interested in composition. It was through Joachim that Brahms was introduced to Robert and Clara Schumann. Schumann was greatly impressed by Brahms' work and character. In his influential *New Leipzig Journal for Music*, he predicted that the young man would "give us the highest ideal expression of our time."Although Schumann's prediction was premature, it proved fairly accurate in the end.

Brahms' early works, mostly for the piano, were much influenced by the works of Schubert and Schumann. Many reflect the conflict that Brahms experienced as a guest in the Schumann household. Brahms developed a deep love for Clara, whom he admired both as a woman and as an artist. That she was fourteen years his senior hardly mattered, but that she was the wife of his friend and sponsor caused him an emotional anguish that is readily apparent in his letters and compositions. Nonetheless the two of them maintained a close and enduring friendship.

Brahms wrote only four symphonies, all late in life after having achieved recognition for his songs, chamber music, and choral writing. His other orchestral works include two overtures—the *Academic Festival Overture* and the *Tragic Overture*—a number of concertos, and the popular *Variations on a Theme by Haydn.*

Brahms: *Symphony No. 3 in F Major*

Symphony No. 3 in F Major may well be the most Romantic of Brahms' symphonies. The opening motive (F-A♭-F) is supposedly associated with his motto *frei aber froh* ("free but happy"). The symphony was written in 1882 and performed in Vienna and Berlin in the following year, evoking much praise and controversy.

First Movement: Allegro con brio; in Sonata Form

Exposition The symphony begins with the winds playing the opening motive: F-A♭-F.

Opening Motive

The A♭ is an accidental, for it does not occur in the key of F major. An A♭ does appear in the key of F minor, however, and its momentary presence here results in the kind of ambiguity that is common in Romantic music: Is the mode major or minor?

A firm sense of F major is established in the first phrase of the opening theme. The phrase, played in octaves by the violins, is made up almost entirely of the notes of the F major triad. Yet even here the minor tones of the opening motive are not completely lacking: the accompaniment, played by the bass instruments in notes of longer duration, is F-A♭-F. In the second phrase of the first theme, the tonal ambiguity once again becomes acute. The accidentals in the second phrase are an indication of shifting tonality:

First Theme

The fluctuation between major and minor and the marking *passionato* ("passionately") at once suggest the Romantic nature of the work.

After a new and brief theme that dissolves into quick arpeggios, the music modulates gently through the key of D♭ major to the key of A major, one key melting into another. The next important theme is in the key of A major, its lyricism offering effective contrast with the more abrupt first theme. The meter changes from $\frac{6}{4}$ to $\frac{9}{4}$ here, giving the melody an elusive rhythmic quality that helps distinguish it from earlier material. A change of tone color also enhances this theme. It is lightly orchestrated, with the melody in the clarinets and a pizzicato accompaniment in the lower strings.

Second Major Theme

The closing section of the exposition is introduced by a return to the opening motive and $\frac{6}{4}$ meter; scales and arpeggios are featured. Rising chromatic scales bring the exposition to a close. Following Classical tradition, Brahms indicated that the exposition be repeated.

Development

In the development, both of the major themes are heard, altered by new contexts and contrasting tone colors. The second theme, once a graceful, flowing melody, is now played in an agitated manner by cellos, violas, and bassoons. The first motive is reiterated by the horns in a succession of keys, and the first theme is played quietly and tentatively, leading into the recapitulation.

Recapitulation

The opening motive then boldly reappears in the original F-A♭-F pattern to announce the recapitulation. In this section the thematic materials from the exposition are restated and further developed. The recapitulation is followed by a coda based on the first theme. This theme finally vanished in diminuendo as the movement ends with a sustained chord.

Coda

Side 7, Band 5

Listening Guide for Brahms' *Symphony No. 3*, First Movement

Timbre:	large orchestra of string instruments, wind instruments, and timpani
Melody:	opening fanfare-like motive and two major themes as illustrated above
Rhythm:	$\frac{6}{4}$ meter (felt sometimes as triple and sometimes as duple) and $\frac{9}{4}$ meter; tempo Allegro con brio (fast with spirit)
Harmony:	fluctuates between minor and major modes, predominantly F major and F minor; frequent modulations; some chromaticism
Texture:	homophonic and contrapuntal
Form:	sonata form with lengthy coda

Second Movement: Andante; in Ternary Form

Section A

The second movement, in C major, begins with a lovely, songlike theme. It is played *semplice* ("simply") by the clarinets accompanied by the bassoons:

First Theme

The theme itself is completely within the key of C major, but chromatic harmonies soon intrude. After the clarinet has stated the theme, the entire orchestra repeats and elaborates on it, creating a joyous, pastoral effect.

Section B

A second theme, marked *espressivo dolce* ("sweetly expressive"), is announced by clarinet and bassoon at the beginning of the middle section. After an initial statement that suggests G major, it too becomes quite chromatic:

Second Theme

p espr. dolce

The woodwinds continue to be featured prominently throughout this section, with the strings sometimes doubling them or more often accompanying them.

Section A

The original key of C major reappears with the return of the first theme, which is now developed extensively with quadruplet and triplet rhythms. Finally the theme, played again by the clarinet, is reaffirmed in its original simplicity just before the movement ends with a series of quiet chords.

Listening Guide for Brahms' *Symphony No. 3*, Second Movement

Timbre:	orchestra somewhat reduced; wind instruments are emphasized, especially the clarinet at the beginning
Melody:	two very lyrical themes
Rhythm:	duple meter; tempo Andante (moderate)
Harmony:	major mode; predominantly C major in A sections and G major in B section; some chromaticism
Texture:	mainly homophonic
Form:	ternary (ABA)

Third Movement: Poco allegretto; in Ternary Form

Section A

The third movement, like the second, is ternary in form, following the Classical treatment of the third movement. The movement is in C minor and begins with a restless lyric melody played by the cellos:

First Theme

p espressivo

Like a number of other nineteenth-century symphonic themes, this theme has been used in our own times as the basis for a popular song.

ROMANTIC SYMPHONY AND CONCERTO

The middle section, in A♭ major, contains two themes, both of which lend themselves to chromatic harmonies. The opening section is then repeated, but it is reorchestrated to produce a new effect. The first theme, originally stated by the cellos, is now played in turn by horn, oboe, and violin. After a short coda, the movement ends quietly.

Listening Guide for Brahms' *Symphony No. 3*, Third Movement

Timbre:	orchestra somewhat reduced; cellos are emphasized at beginning
Melody:	several themes; first theme is very lyrical; second theme is based on three-note motives
Rhythm:	triple meter; tempo Poco allegretto (rather fast)
Harmony:	mainly minor mode; predominantly C minor in A sections and A♭ major in B section
Texture:	mainy homophonic
Form:	ternary (ABA) followed by a short coda

Fourth Movement: Allegro; in Modified Sonata Form

The finale begins in the key of F minor, the key suggested at the opening of the symphony. The sonata form of the movement is modified by the omission of a development section. Considerable development does, however, take place in the course of the exposition, recapitulation, and coda.

The first theme is a conjunct melody played *sotto voce* ("in an undertone") by strings and bassoons. It is then taken up in an expanded form by flute and clarinet.

First Theme

Contrast is provided by a stately second theme with chordal accompaniment, introduced by clarinets, bassoons, and strings.

Second Theme

After the second theme has been heard, a portion of the first theme reappears dramatically in the lower strings and bassoons. Then after a modulatory passage stressing dotted rhythms, another theme enters.

Third Theme

The Romantic Sense of Beauty

Middle-Class Values and the Art of Protest Essentially hardheaded and pragmatic in most spheres of life, the dominant middle class of the early Romantic period valued music and art that prettified and sentimentalized existence. Isabey, in his miniature portrait of Marie Louise, perfectly summarized the official taste of his time. We are shown a pretty, self-satisfied young woman assured of her wealth and position, but we learn nothing of the living human being within.

Isabey: *Marie Louise d'Orleans* (1832)

Daumier: *The Parisian Janitor* (1832–1835)

To many Romantic artists, however, art served as a means of protest. Daumier was one of many who devoted their art to social comment. Often biting and satirical, in *The Parisian Janitor* his compassion came to the fore. Here he proclaimed his belief in the common people and their essential dignity and worth. There is no dramatic incident, no anecdote—just a poor janitor at work. Yet by modeling the figure firmly in simple outline and by creating a stable design, Daumier imparted a kind of quiet grandeur to the scene.

Scala/Editorial Photocolor Archives

Delacroix: *Women of Algiers* (1834)

Exoticism   Early in the nineteenth century, the Newtonian idea of
rational universe began to yield to Wordsworth's vision of exis
tence as dark and inscrutable. The Romantic world was one i
which the mystery of nature and the primacy of feelings were dom
inant. Romantic painters were drawn to Rousseau's ideas abou
the beauty of nature and the goodness of humanity, corrupted no
by instinct but by institutions. Artists yearned for the faraway
the exotic and uncorrupted, the "primitive." In 1831, one of the grea
est of the Romantic painters, Delacroix, was overjoyed when pre
sented with the opportunity to travel in North Africa. Everywher
he went he made sketches and water colors. *Women of Algiers* is on
of a number of later paintings in which the artist recalled and ro
mantically transformed the images of his travels. Delacroix'
delight in the brilliance of natural light and color in many way

Landscape Painting Romanticism brought a strong emphasis on natural appearance. The more Romantic artists became enamored of nature, the more they were compelled to confront the problem of recording optical truth. This is nowhere more true than in the art of English painter Constable, whose fascination with nature's fugitive moods and phases transformed the character of landscape painting. Like Wordsworth, Constable saw a connection between intimacy with nature and oneness with God. He found great moral significance in nature, and in this regard and in the poetic feeling expressed in his canvases he was very much a Romantic. Yet his use of broken color and loose brushwork to capture the most subtle and transient aspects of nature—the movement of a cloud, the luminosity of a shaded path—are equally expressive of the nineteenth century's growing interest in unalloyed realism.

Constable: *Salisbury Cathedral from the Bishop's Garden* (c. 1826)

Turner: *The Slave Ship* (1839)

The Work of Turner Unlike Constable, Turner was interested not i
the normal or serene but in the dramatic, the titanic, the visionar
Rather than Wordsworthian, his imagination was Byronic. Thoug
The Slave Ship is rooted in the reality of the cruelties of the slav
trade, Turner here was essentially interested in using his unde
standing of natural phenomena to express the sublime. He mad
light the very essence of his painting. Details nearly disappea
There is only a dazzling radiance filling the work, obscuring form
with its pulsating movement. For Turner, men and women wer
only tiny specks in the face of the uncontrollable, incompreher

Played first in C major, this bright theme is soon carried into the minor mode. Such changes of mode are frequent in this particular movement and characteristic of the Romantic symphony in general.

A final theme brings the exposition to a climax.

Final Theme

Recapitulation and Coda

The first theme returns quietly in the tonic key of F minor at the beginning of the recapitulation. It is followed by considerable development of motives and themes from the exposition. The coda that follows begins in the key of B minor and features the first theme accompanied by triplet and quadruplet rhythms. The second theme then reappears, and the opening motive of the first movement is recalled. The symphony ends as it began with the use of both major and minor modes of the F scale. The cumulative effect is one of great emotional contrast unified by the genius of the composer.

Listening Guide for Brahms' *Symphony No. 3*, Fourth Movement

Timbre:	large orchestra of string instruments, wind instruments, and timpani
Melody:	several themes as illustrated above; opening motive from first movement returns at end
Rhythm:	duple meter; tempo Allegro (fast)
Harmony:	fluctuates between minor and major modes; begins in F minor, modulates most significantly to C major and B minor, ends in F major; some chromaticism
Texture:	homophonic and contrapuntal
Form:	modified sonata form, with no specific development section, followed by a coda

---

Brahms died ten years after the composition of *Symphony No. 3*. The population of Vienna lined the streets as his cortege passed by. And in his home city of Hamburg, where he had long been denied recognition, the flags were flown at half staff. Brahms has remained one of the most popular of all Romantic and post-Romantic composers. Today when schoolchildren learn the names of the great composers, they are told of the "three B's": Bach, Beethoven, and Brahms—the Baroque master, the Classical master, and the Romantic who was so profoundly inspired by both of them.

Tchaikovsky's Symphonies

The Russian Peter Ilyich Tchaikovsky (1840–1893) was a composer who revered the Classical tradition yet produced works that are in their deepest essence Romantic. Like Brahms, he based his symphonic works on Classical forms, altering and changing them to give expression to Romantic ideas.

Tchaikovsky's Ballets: *During the second half of the nineteenth century, ballet became one of the most popular of Russian art forms. Tchaikovsky contributed greatly to its prominence with works that still hold a central position in the repertory of ballet companies throughout the Western world. A scene from* Sleeping Beauty, *performed by London's famed Sadler Wells Ballet Company, is shown above.*

Rubinstein's Influence

Nationalistic Russian Composers

Tchaikovsky's life was roughly contemporary with that of Brahms. However, he was geographically far removed from the world of Brahms, Liszt, and their colleagues. The imperial city of Saint Petersburg, where Tchaikovsky spent his youth, was dominated by its own native virtuoso, the pianist Anton Rubinstein (1829–1894). It was at Rubinstein's conservatory that Tchaikovsky studied piano and composition and made contact, musically speaking, with the Western world. For although there was at this time a nationalistic Russian school—including among its members Alexander Borodin (1833–1887), Modest Mussorgsky (1839–1881), and Nikolai Rimsky-Korsakov (1844–1908) —the conservatory itself was distinctly international in spirit. As a student there, Tchaikovsky became familiar with Classical German symphonies, Italian opera, and song and dance styles from all over Europe. His own music, while it reflects a Russian folk heritage, is international in intent.

Tchaikovsky has always been widely admired for his melodic gift. The melodies from his ballet scores—*Swan Lake, The Sleeping Beauty,* and *The Nutcracker*—are dearly loved by many who have no knowledge of their source, who have heard them only as arranged and performed in popular format. Also well known are his piano concertos and his *Romeo and Juliet* and *1812* overtures. "None but the Lonely Heart," a perennial favorite, is one of his many songs.

As a composer, Tchaikovsky greatly admired Mozart and Beethoven. His

Symphony No. 4

own *Symphony No. 4* was modeled on Beethoven's *Symphony No. 5* and opens with a "fate" motive similar to that of the older work. However, in Tchaikovsky's work, the unfolding of long and often lyrical melodies takes precedence over the thorough development of the opening motive.

Tchaikovsky: *Symphony No. 6 in B Minor*

Symphony No. 6, generally regarded as Tchaikovsky's most important symphony, was written in his last year, after a highly successful American tour. It is scored for a large orchestra of string and wind instruments with timpani. The symphony opens with a somber Adagio followed by a tempestuous first movement marked Allegro non troppo and loosely based on sonata form. The second theme, a lyrical descending melody, is one of the most familiar in all symphonic literature:

First Movement

Second Movement

The second movement, marked Allegro con grazia, begins with a lilting tune in the unusual meter of $\frac{5}{4}$. So graceful in its opening, this movement gradually builds to a sense of pressing inner conflict.

Third and Fourth Movements

The third movement, Allegro molto vivace, is a brisk march that seems to express resolution or courage. The resolution of the third movement, however, is soon placed in tragic perspective by the Adagio lamentoso of the final movement. Thus instead of concluding triumphantly in the Classical manner, Tchaikovsky's last symphony ends in a despair that has seldom been equaled in literature, art, or music.

Other Composers of Romantic Symphonies

In many ways, the works of Brahms and Tchaikovsky represent a high point in the composition of Romantic symphonies. Yet a number of composers writing both before and after Brahms and Tchaikovsky also contributed greatly to the tradition of the abstract symphony.

In the early Romantic period, at a time when many composers were experimenting with program symphonies, Felix Mendelssohn and Robert Schumann were perhaps the most important upholders of tradition. Their works show the growing pains of the time—Classical forms are apparent, but fresh melodic and harmonic ideas strain against them. Of Mendelssohn's five

Mendelssohn and Schumann

symphonies, the three subtitled "Reformation," "Scottish," and "Italian" are still frequently heard today. Even though the works have descriptive titles, they are not programmatic in nature. The "Italian" Symphony is one of Mendelssohn's most outstanding works. Schumann's four symphonies are noted for their rather consistent use of the entire orchestra. There is little of the contrast of individual timbres heard in later Romantic works.

As the nineteenth century progressed, many other composers attempted to express Romantic ideas within the general framework of the Classical sonata cycle. The Belgian composer César Franck (1822–1890), for example, is remembered for his skillfully executed *Symphony in D Minor*. The symphonies of Anton Bruckner (1824–1896), an Austrian, are notable for their length and depth and for the large orchestra they require.

Franck and Bruckner

Mahler

Mahler, like fellow Austrian composer Bruckner, also composed on a large scale. One of his symphonies has seven movements. He was eclectic in style, drawing inspiration from many different periods and genres. Chamber elements, choruses, and vocal solos all appear in his symphonic works. As a late nineteenth-century composer and heir to much earlier experimentation with chromaticism, Mahler is sometimes regarded as post-Romantic.

Dvořák

Still another important Romantic composer is Antonin Dvořák (1841–1904), a Czech. His work will be discussed later in connection with the nineteenth-century nationalistic movement in music.

The Romantic Concerto

Like the symphony, the concerto underwent a transformation during the nineteenth century. Melody became more important. Chromaticism and movement between remotely related keys were heard more frequently. The orchestra was generally larger, and the works, though usually still in three movements, tended to be longer. As in the symphony, Classical forms were still used, but more freely. The balance between soloist and orchestra was often manipulated for dramatic effect. Mendelssohn, for example, omitted the orchestral exposition in the first movement of his *Violin Concerto in E Minor*, bringing in the soloist almost at once. Perhaps in response to Romantic individualism, virtuoso elements were increasingly emphasized.

Many composers of symphonies and piano music also wrote concertos. Chopin wrote two concertos for piano, in F minor and E minor. Schumann wrote three, one each for piano, cello, and violin. And Liszt wrote three for piano—the third, *Concerto Pathétique*, an arrangement of an earlier solo piece. Among Brahms' works we find two piano concertos, a *Double Concerto for Violin and Cello*, and the beautiful *Violin Concerto in D Major*, which remains one of the most popular of all concertos. Other important works include Tchaikovsky's *Piano Concerto No. 1 in B♭ Minor* and *Violin Concerto in D Major*, Grieg's *Piano Concerto in A Minor*, and Dvořák's *Cello Concerto in B Minor*.

Tchaikovsky: *Violin Concerto in D Major*

One of the most outstanding Romantic concertos for violin was written by Tchaikovsky in 1878. The work met with much criticism at the time. Several famous violinists complained that the soloist's part was so difficult that it was virtually unplayable. But the work later became very popular and today holds an important place in the violin repertory.

First Movement: Allegro moderato; in Sonata Form

Introduction and Exposition

The first movement is set in the key of D major and organized in loose sonata form. It opens with a brief introduction by the orchestra led by the first violins. The solo violin then enters and, after a few prefatory measures, presents the first theme:

First Theme

The theme is imitated briefly by the orchestral violins, and then it is extended and embellished by the soloist. A confrontation between orchestra and soloist follows, with terse orchestral chords opposing the solo violin's virtuoso scales and arpeggios. A second theme, marked Con molto espressione, is then announced by the soloist. In the material that follows, both themes are ornamented and broken up. The soloist occasionally plays two-note chords by

Double Stopping

double stopping—that is, by playing on two strings at a time.

Development

The development begins with a repetition of the first theme played by flutes and strings over a rousing rhythmic accompaniment by the wind instruments. The music is shown below in simplified form:

Repetition of First Theme

In the course of the development, the theme is set to new accompaniments, fragmented, and otherwise transformed. The development, which began in the key of A major, changes key frequently. At the climax of the movement, the

Cadenza

soloist plays an elaborate cadenza filled with double stops, arpeggios, and scales, and ending in the customary fashion with an extended trill.

Recapitulation and Coda

The orchestra then returns for the recapitulation. A coda, marked Allegro giusto, gives the soloist additional opportunity to display technical mastery.

Second Movement: Andante; in Ternary Form

Section A

The second movement, in G minor, is labeled Canzonetta to suggest its songlike quality. After an introductory passage by winds and horns, the soloist enters softly with a melancholy, folklike melody:

First Theme

The first theme is then imitated by flute and clarinet.

Section B

The second theme follows, introduced forte by the solo violin. It is repeated and extended, still by the soloist, with sparse accompaniment by the orchestra.

Section A

At this point the soloist reintroduces the first theme, now ornamented and developed against countermelodies in the flute and clarinet. The introductory material then reappears, suggesting repetition but leading instead, without a break, into the last movement.

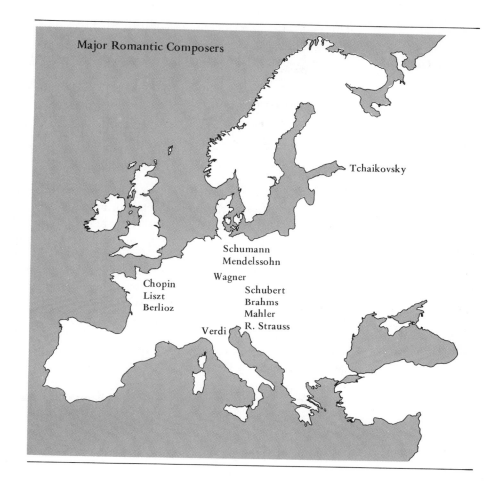

Major Romantic Composers

Tchaikovsky

Schumann
Mendelssohn

Wagner

Chopin
Liszt
Berlioz

Schubert
Brahms
Mahler
R. Strauss

Verdi

Third Movement: Allegro vivacissimo; in Modified Rondo Form

The finale, cast in a modified rondo form (ABCABCA), begins in A major, the dominant of D major—the home key of the concerto. To establish the new key, Tchaikovsky chose to open with a unison motive in A by the entire orchestra.

Introduction, Cadenza, and First Theme

After a brief orchestral introduction and a cadenza for the solo violin, the soloist presents the vivacious first theme in the key of D major. The theme is based on a short figure that Tchaikovsky took from a traditional Russian folk dance.

First Theme

ROMANTIC SYMPHONY AND CONCERTO

This energetic theme is spun out against a light accompaniment in strings and woodwinds.

Second Theme

A second theme is then introduced by the soloist in the key of A major. Like the first, it is based on Russian folk music.

Second Theme

The second theme is varied by strings and horns and by the soloist.

Third Theme

A third, slower theme in the minor mode is then presented in dialogue fashion by solo oboe and clarinet, which are later joined by cello and bassoon.

The third theme is followed by the reappearance of the first theme in the original key of D major, which is in turn followed by the second and third themes, now in new keys. Finally the opening theme is heard a third time, this time developed in a manner designed to bring out the virtuoso capacities of the soloist. After a final burst of virtuosity from the soloist, the orchestra brings the work to a close with a resounding cadence.

The full brilliance of the orchestra is displayed throughout the movement, both in solo exchanges and in more densely orchestrated passages. The tempo increases as the work progresses—an increase often found in a finale.

Side 8, Band 1

Listening Guide for Tchaikovsky's *Violin Concerto in D Major*, Third Movement

Timbre:	solo violin and large orchestra of string instruments, wind instruments, and timpani
Melody:	three themes; first two themes based on Russian folk music; third theme very lyrical
Rhythm:	duple meter; tempo Allegro vivacissimo (fast and very lively)
Harmony:	mainly major mode; begins in A major, modulates through several keys, ends in D major
Texture:	mainly homophonic
Form:	modified rondo (ABCABCA)

Suggested Listening

The Romantic Symphony

Schubert: *Symphony No. 9 in C Major* (the "Great") [Odyssey Y-30669]. This work was conceived on a grander scale than any of Schubert's previous symphonies. Each of the movements is quite long, but the use of thematic ideas is very tight and convincing. Thematic elements vary from the generously lyrical to the concise. Schubert's symphonic writing here shows considerable progress beyond earlier Classical symphonies in tonality and expanded format. Properly speaking, this is Schubert's tenth symphony. The ninth, the so-called "Gmunden-Gastein," has been lost.

Mendelssohn: *Symphony No. 4 in A Major, Op. 90* (the "Italian") [Columbia MS-6628]. The subtitle of this work was suggested by a trip to Italy. The symphony as a whole follows Classical models, but with a new vitality. The last movement, based on a sprightly Italian dance, the saltarello (from *saltare*, "to jump"), beautifully illustrates Mendelssohn's creativity within a very tightly knit structure.

Tchaikovsky: *Symphony No. 5 in E Minor, Op. 46* [Angel S-36885]. This symphony is one of Tchaikovsky's most popular, with its very lyrical themes and the strong sense of drama created by its stark contrasts of timbre, dynamics, and harmony. The third movement, a waltz instead of the traditional scherzo, provides bright relief from the more somber movements that surround it.

The Romantic Concerto

Schumann: *Piano Concerto in A Minor, Op. 54* [Odyssey Y-30668]. This work contains many difficult scales, arpeggios, and other figurations for the soloist. The chordal passage with which the piano solo begins reappears throughout the first and last movements. Generous use of syncopation yields a great many rhythmic surprises.

Brahms: *Piano Concerto No. 2 in B♭ Major, Op. 83* [RCA LSC-3253]. The second of Brahms' piano concertos is marked by great majesty and exaltation. The concerto has four movements: two fast movements and one slow movement followed by the traditional fast finale. Great technical virtuosity is demanded of the pianist.

Tchaikovsky: *Piano Concerto No. 1 in B♭ Minor, Op. 23* [RCA LSC-2252]. Of Tchaikovsky's three piano concertos, this is the best known and loved. It has been made especially popular in recent years by the American pianist Van Cliburn. Striking contrasts of mood and theme allow the soloist to explore widely the capabilities of the piano. Brilliant, technically difficult passages are countered by others more sustained and lyrical.

22

Romantic Program Music

The Development of Program Music

The Romantic period was a time of very close relationships between the arts. Poets, painters, and composers were drawn to the same themes and often to each other in a community of shared interests. In the time of Haydn and Mozart, musical composition was a craft to be exercised by relatively isolated specialists working for patrons. It was the patron, not the composer, who was assumed to be a person of culture. But in the Romantic era, the composer, like the artist in general, became a kind of cultural hero. The leading composers of the period were generally well educated, conversant with many different artistic media. Schumann, Liszt, Berlioz, and Wagner were all accomplished writers and critics as well as composers. Wagner and Berlioz even wrote some of their own librettos. Most Romantic composers worked and socialized with painters, poets, actors, and dramatists. Schubert spent his years of poverty in the company of poets. Chopin lived with one novelist, Liszt with another. And Berlioz, in love with the works of Shakespeare, married a leading Shakespearean actress of the time. In their art and in their lives, Romantic composers strongly identified with the literary movements of nineteenth-century Europe.

During the Romantic period, an increasing number of symphonies and other works were based on literary, or even pictorial, ideas. Composers often supplied verbal descriptions in concert programs indicating the origin of their works—perhaps describing the very feelings and actions to which the music alluded. The music, known as *program music*, was purely instrumental, yet it was closely associated with nonmusical ideas, which were generally described in the program given to the listener. An example can be found in Berlioz' symphony *Harold in Italy*. The title of the symphony indicates that the work is in some way related to Byron's famous poem *Childe Harold*. The titles of the individual movements call forth even more specific associations. The first movement, for example, is entitled "Harold in the Mountains: Scenes of Melancholy, Happiness, and Joy," and the second movement, "March of Pilgrims Singing Their Evening Hymn."

Characteristics of Program Music

The programs written for program music do not always refer to literary works. Some allude instead to some real or fancied experience of the composer. In the program for Beethoven's *Symphony No. 6,* a work that falls rather easily into the category of program music, reference is made in a general way to a succession of pastoral scenes that the composer apparently experienced or imagined—"Awakening of Pleasant Feelings upon Arriving in the Country," "Scene by the Brook," and so forth. A program may also relate music to the visual arts. Mussorgsky, in *Pictures at an Exhibition,* immortalized the work of a painter. Or, less concretely, a program may simply relate a work to the occasion it was written to commemorate. Brahms' *Academic Festival Overture* suggests, in content as well as title, the event at which it was performed; the work contains a number of allusions to old school songs. A more popular example, Tchaikovsky's *1812 Overture,* celebrates with musical imagery the Russian victory over Napoleon.

Whether or not a work is programmatic depends, in part, on the artistic inclinations of the composer—on how willing the composer was to specify the content of the work. Tchaikovsky's *Symphony No. 6* was originally to be titled "A Programmatic Symphony," but Tchaikovsky later decided not to specify the program. The absence of a program has never detracted from the work's accessibility. Conversely, Richard Strauss at first declined to give in detail the program of his symphonic poem *Till Eulenspiegel.* However, his public demanded a written guide to the work, and in listening we are very much influenced by the program Strauss eventually did supply.

Although programmatic works differ in the extent to which they rely on their association with nonmusical ideas, it is generally true that familiarity with these ideas helps the listener follow the musical design. One can certainly enjoy Tchaikovsky's *Romeo and Juliet* without being familiar with the Shakespearean plot, for the music itself is dramatic and very appealing. Yet if we know Shakespeare's play and the manner in which the overture relates to it, the listening experience is much richer. This is, in part, because the appearance of themes is governed not purely by musical organization but also by the ideas of the story. The opening theme in Tchaikovsky's *Romeo and Juliet,* for example, alludes to a specific character, Friar Lawrence; the theme reappears whenever Tchaikovsky wanted to evoke the idea of the friar. An examination of the musical structure alone will not tell us this. Similar examples of literary or pictorial influence on musical structure can be found throughout many works of program music. In most cases, however, these programmatic elements loosely coexist with traditional musical forms. While the Romantic composer found in program music alternatives to the strict and purely musical designs of the Classical period, the forms of the earlier age were seldom abandoned entirely.

Types of Program Music

The program music written during the Romantic era includes *program symphonies, symphonic poems, concert overtures,* and *incidental music* for theater as well as short piano works. Thus with the exception of the symphonic

283   ROMANTIC PROGRAM MUSIC

poem, which was a creation of the nineteenth century, Romantic composers were merely applying a new logic based on extramusical ideas to preexisting Classical structures.

The Program Symphony

Beethoven, in his *Symphony No. 6*, had already set the precedent for the program symphony. The notion was later taken up by the Romantic composers as a means of developing symphonic literature in a new direction. The most successful composers of the new program symphonies were Berlioz and Liszt. Berlioz is chiefly remembered for *Harold in Italy* and the *Symphonie fantastique*. Among Liszt's program symphonies are the *Faust Symphony* and *A Symphony after Dante's Divine Comedy*.

Berlioz: *Symphonie fantastique*

Hector Berlioz (1803–1869) was born in the French village of Meylan, near Grenoble. In the small mountainous village, there was not even a resident music teacher. A violinist from a neighboring town had to be imported to give instruction to the local youth. From this teacher, Berlioz learned to use his voice as well as to play the flute, the clarinet, and the guitar. In all of Meylan—and even in the neighboring village of La Côte—there was not a single piano available for young Berlioz' use.

Berlioz' relatively modest early musical education allowed him to see music differently from many of his contemporaries. To him, music was associated mainly with church services and local festivals—in other words, it belonged to public occasions, and essentially dramatic ones at that. Such music was almost always strengthened by its nonmusical associations. Berlioz also saw music as a product of diverse instruments, each with its decidedly individual character and sound. Forced to bypass the usual piano training, Berlioz came to understand much better than his peers the distinctive effects of different instruments. He was soon to use this understanding to achieve bold new sounds in orchestration.

At the age of eighteen, Berlioz settled in Paris, ostensibly to begin his education in medicine. But it was soon clear that music was his proper field. He was especially drawn to opera, and often, after attending a performance, he spent many hours studying the score in the library of the Royal Conservatory. By 1826 he had entered the conservatory as a student.

One of the passions of Berlioz' early Parisian career was Shakespeare, whose works he first encountered in 1827 at a performance of *Hamlet*. The power of the English drama impressed him deeply, as did the leading lady. Berlioz fell madly in love with the Ophelia of the company, an actress named Harriet Smithson. He pursued her for many years, at first in imagination and later in reality. In the early stage of his passion, he even arranged private concerts at his own expense, largely so that the woman he loved would hear of his "fame."

Contemporary Caricature of Berlioz: *Berlioz'
music with its early use of an enlarged orchestra and its daring exploitation of the
possibilities of tone color startled many of
the audiences of his day. Caricatures such as
the one here sought to cast his creativity
in an almost diabolical light.*

At this time, Berlioz was writing mainly Masses, cantatas, and overtures.
But he had also begun to conceive of a grand symphony to be entitled *Episode
de la vie d'un artiste* ("Episode from the Life of an Artist"). In it, he said, "the
development of my infernal passion is to be depicted." While working on his
symphony, he heard rumors of Harriet Smithson's supposed relationship with
her manager and fell into a great fit of agitation. It was in this mood that he
developed the plan of the symphony that has come to be known as the
Symphonie fantastique ("Fantastic Symphony"). He completed the work in
Rome, where he had gone to study, having won, after several failures, the
illustrious Prix de Rome. On his return to Paris, a series of romantic coin-
cidences led him straight to his beloved. Till then he had never even met
the actress he loved, but he deviously arranged for her to be present at a
performance of the new symphony. In due course the pair were married, only
to be separated after a few years.

The program of the *Symphonie fantastique* is quite detailed, so much so
that it offended many of Berlioz' musical contemporaries. However, it captured
the imagination of the public, acting, as historian Jacques Barzun has pointed
out, rather like a "promotional aid." The symphony is organized in five
movements, and Berlioz' notes relate quite readily to the music.

Program of Berlioz' *Symphonie fantastique**

Introduction: A young musician of extraordinary sensibility and abundant imagination, in the depths of despair because of hopeless love, has poisoned himself with opium. The drug is too feeble to kill him but plunges him into a heavy sleep accompanied by weird visions. His sensations, emotions, and memories, as they pass through his affected mind, are transformed into musical images and ideas. The beloved one herself becomes to him a melody, a recurrent theme [the *idée fixe*] which haunts him continually.

First Movement: *Reveries, passions:* First he remembers that weariness of the soul, that indefinable longing, that somber melancholia and those objectless joys which he experienced before meeting his beloved. Then, the volcanic love with which she at once inspired him [the *idée fixe*], his delirious suffering, his return to tenderness, his religious consolations.

Second Movement: *A ball:* At a ball, in the midst of a noisy, brilliant fête, he finds his beloved again [the *idée fixe*].

Third Movement: *In the country:* On a summer evening in the country he hears two herders calling each other with their shepherd melodies. The pastoral duet in such surroundings, the gentle rustle of the trees softly swayed by the wind, some reasons for hope which had come to his knowledge recently—all unite to fill his heart with a rare tranquility and lend brighter colors to his fancies. But his beloved appears anew [the *idée fixe*], spasms contract his heart, and he is filled with dark premonition. What if she proved faithless? Only one of the shepherds resumes his rustic tune. The sun sets. Far away there is rumbling thunder—solitude—silence.

Fourth Movement: *March to the scaffold:* He dreams he has killed his loved one, that he is condemned to death and led to his execution. A march, now gloomy and ferocious, now solemn and brilliant, accompanies the procession. Noisy outbursts are followed without pause by the heavy sound of measured footsteps. Finally, like a last thought of love the *idée fixe* appears for a moment, to be cut off by the fall of the axe.

Fifth Movement: *Dream of a witches' sabbath:* He sees himself at a Witches' Sabbath surrounded by a fearful crowd of specters, sorcerers, and monsters of every kind, united for his burial. Unearthly sounds, groans, shrieks of laughter, distant cries, to which others seem to respond! The melody of his beloved is heard [the *idée fixe*], but it has lost its character of nobility and reserve. Instead, it is now an ignoble dance tune, trivial and grotesque. It is she who comes to the Sabbath! A shout of joy greets her arrival. She joins the diabolical orgy. The funeral knell, burlesque of the Dies Irae. Dance of the Witches. The dance and the Dies Irae combined.

Symphonie fantastique by Hector Berlioz, program notes from Eulenburg Pocket Score (E 422). Reprinted by permission of Ernst Eulenburg, Ltd., London. Bracketed material added to show position of the *idée fixe*.

As you can see, the program develops a series of strongly Romantic contrasts. The hero, deep in an opium-inspired dream, has visions ranging from one extreme to another; his mind paints images both wild and poetic. Although the program centers on Berlioz' passion for Harriet Smithson, it presents an artistic rather than an autobiographical conception of the affair.

Use of the Idée Fixe

The work is filled with the association of musical ideas and extramusical images, the most basic of which is found in the *idée fixe* ("fixed idea," or recurrent theme). Berlioz' idée fixe represents the beloved throughout the symphony. First heard in the introduction, the theme recurs in various forms in all five movements, ending up as a disreputable dance tune in the last movement. The initial form of the idée fixe, played by flutes and violins, is shown below.

Idée fixe

Use of the Orchestra

The orchestra required for the *Symphonie fantastique* is unusually large. The orchestration, extraordinarily sensitive and colorful, impressed even the severest critics of the day. The score is filled with very specific directions about dynamics and other aspects of performance. Berlioz was widely recognized as a master of orchestration. His sensitivity and concern for the best use of different instruments are evident in an impressive treatise he wrote on the subject.

Formal Structure

Despite its originality in sound and conception, the *Symphonie fantastique* is formally based on Classical models. The first movement ("Reveries, passions"), preceded by a slow and lengthy introduction, is in a free and expanded sonata form. The second movement ("A ball") is a waltz organized in ternary form with an introduction and coda; the idée fixe, now in waltz meter, appears in the trio. The third and fourth movements ("In the country" and "March to the scaffold") are also in ternary form, again with introductions and codas. The last movement ("Dream of a witches' sabbath") is built freely in sections, with music based on a number of themes including the idée fixe in dance-hall style and the Medieval chant Dies Irae, traditionally played only at a Mass for the Dead. The work is thus in many ways based on Classical precedents, but Berlioz' use of irregular phrases, subtleties of timbre, and innovative harmonies obscures the clarity of form.

The *Symphonie fantastique*, first performed in 1830, was unique in its own time and somewhat disturbing to many members of the Parisian audience. One negative critic wrote that "the audience thought it was having a nightmare during the whole performance." The harmonies, at times very chromatic, were received with some surprise by early audiences. The wealth of orchestral sound may have seemed overwhelming to some of the people in the 1830 audience. And the use of the Dies Irae in a witches' sabbath was decidedly shocking at the time. Even today the work has a surprising freshness and originality of sound.

The Symphonic Poem

Tone Poem

Relatively few program symphonies were written in the Romantic period. Many composers were drawn instead to a new and shorter form, the symphonic poem, or as it is sometimes called, the *tone poem*. The symphonic poem is essentially a program symphony in one movement. Its relative shortness points to the fact that, during the Romantic period, the preference was frequently for shorter compositions. The short piano piece and the symphonic poem became in many ways the pride of Romantic music.

**Liszt's
Symphonic Poems**

The creator of the symphonic poem was Franz Liszt, who in 1848 completed *Les Préludes,* the first work of this type. It was originally intended as part of a larger work. After it was completed, however, Liszt decided to present it as an independent composition. Finding a similarity of mood and spirit between the music he had written and the poems in Lamartine's *Méditations poétiques,* Liszt produced his own version of one of the poems as a program for the work. The program begins with a question, "What is our life but a series of preludes to that unknown song of which the first solemn note is sounded by death?" It then goes on to describe the different emotional states of the human spirit.

Les Préludes is organized in sections, with different dramatic or emotional states portrayed musically in each. Expressive lyrical melodies allude to love. Blustering chromatic activity is used to represent a storm. And a relaxed pastoral melody portrays nature at its best. In the final sections, the love themes are transformed into exciting martial figures to portray self-realization. The work is based on solid musical principles. It is thematically unified, with much of the material spun out of the three-note motive presented in the introduction.

The symphonic poem proved a very effective vehicle for Liszt's ideas. He later wrote *Orpheus, Mazeppa, Hamlet, The Battle of the Huns,* and several other poems for orchestra. These works, however, have not remained as popular as *Les Préludes* and are seldom heard today.

**Strauss's
Symphonic Poems**

Liszt's disciples made wide use of the symphonic poem. Among the works heard most often today, though, are three by the late Romantic composer Richard Strauss: *Don Juan, Till Eulenspiegel,* and *Don Quixote.*

Strauss: *Till Eulenspiegels lustige Streiche*

One of the most successful composers of the symphonic poem was Richard Strauss (1864–1949). He was born in Munich at a time when Romanticism in music had come into full flower. Strauss's father was a professional musician, a well-known horn player who held rather conservative ideas about musical style. As a child, Strauss studied Classical works of his father's choosing. But as a young man, he turned, as young people often do, to a newer style. An important factor in this change was the influence of Hans Guido von Bülow (1830–1894), a leading conductor whom Strauss met when Strauss himself was

**Von Bülow's
Influence**

about twenty years old. Von Bülow was Liszt's son-in-law and a devoted follower of Wagner, who was soon to carry on a rather famous affair with von Bülow's wife. Through von Bülow, Strauss was able to have some of his early works performed, and he soon obtained a position as associate conductor in the German city of Meiningen. In this capacity he became familiar with much of the new music of the time, including the works of Mendelssohn and Brahms and the newer experiments of Wagner and Liszt. Eventually Strauss himself won a place among these masters, becoming a part of the new musical development that captured the German imagination in the late nineteenth century.

By 1885, the year Strauss took up his post at Meiningen, the symphonic poem had become immensely popular. The young conductor was very much attracted to this type of composition, which he consistently referred to as the tone poem. Three such tone poems are among his earliest works: *Macbeth*, *Don Juan*, and *Till Eulenspiegel*. In the composition of these early works, Strauss was much influenced by Wagner, particularly in the use of motives to suggest certain characters or actions. Other elements in Strauss's work—his use of chromaticism, the frequent ambiguities of key and mode, and the complexity of orchestration—also show the influence of Wagner. Strauss was generally able to achieve a very close relationship between literature and music. His works are, for this reason, much more meaningful with a knowledge of his detailed programs.

Wagner's Influence

One of the most popular of Strauss's tone poems is *Till Eulenspiegels lustige Streiche* ("Till Eulenspiegel's Merry Pranks"), written in 1895. Legend tells of the adventures of one Till Eulenspiegel (literally "Till Owl-Mirror"), a popular German folk hero who seems to have lived in the fourteenth century. Till was a lower-class rogue—a clownish fellow with a penchant for practical jokes directed mainly at his social superiors. His adventures have been variously recorded in German and in English. Strauss drew from the legend the basic ideas for his tone poem, altering and devising situations to suit his own needs.

Legend of Till Eulenspiegel

The form of such a work is, as one might imagine, determined to a considerable degree by the content of the tale. In fact, however, Strauss was able to make use of a Classical form that accorded well with Till's story. For his tone poem, he chose a rondo form—a form that composers since Haydn's time have often treated in humorous fashion. As used in *Till Eulenspiegel*, the rondo form allows for the alternation of themes portraying different espisodes of the tale and motives representing the rascally Till.

Structure

The work opens with a quiet motive in the violins, which introduces the hero Till:

Motives Representing Till

Opening Motive

ROMANTIC PROGRAM MUSIC

Another motive, associated with Till's roguish character, is then revealed by the horn. It is repeated and finally grows into a complete theme, played against a violin accompaniment:

Horn Motive and Theme

Till's playfulness is suggested by the quick staccato and lively syncopation of the horn motive. In both the Till motives, the chromatic intervals suggest Till's wily nature. As the first section proceeds, the two motives are presented in a variety of guises while Till is contemplating new pranks.

First Escapade

The beginning of the first escapade is then signaled by a cymbal crash, a rapidly rising scale in the clarinets, and triplet rhythms as Till gallops on horseback through the crowded marketplace. The rapid rhythmic motion and chromatic harmony evoke the confusion caused by the wild ride.

Second Escapade

In Till's next adventure, he masquerades as a priest. The tempo becomes slow and sedate as a quiet, restrained theme is played by violas and bassoons:

Theme of Till as a Priest

Till cannot long maintain his disguise, though, and as he begins to lose his composure, his first motive is heard again in the clarinet. The music turns somber for a moment, as if to suggest that Till has become somewhat apprehensive about his daring impersonation.

Third Escapade

The violin now presents Till as a lover. The theme is based on the horn motive, but its rhythm and character are quite changed. The German marking in the score means "ardently."

Theme of Till as a Lover

The theme is developed momentarily, but the music's mood becomes more somber when it becomes apparent that Till's amorous attentions are not succeeding. The horn motive is inverted and boldly expanded by the full orchestra. Till seems angry and eager for revenge.

Till's Critics   Till's critics are represented by a chromatic passage in the minor mode played chiefly by bassoons and cellos. Several exchanges between this theme and Till's impudent horn motive suggest a dialogue. Finally Till seems to win the debate, with the sounding of Till's first motive by strings and woodwinds.

Till's Character   As Till strolls away, he whistles a light tune, heard first in the clarinets and violins:

Departure Theme

The following section develops the horn motive and, briefly, the opening motive, presenting it in many different rhythms and timbres. Various aspects of the motive and the person it represents are explored.

Till's Execution   The theme of Till as a priest then returns. His moment to face justice has come. The snare drums roll, foretelling Till's execution, but even now Till's opening motive returns, suggesting that he has not wholly lost his jaunty spirit. This is followed, however, by an ominous slow section in the minor mode portraying Till's growing fear and eventual death.

Yet the work ends brightly with a return to the first two motives, reminding us that we have been concerned only with a story.

Side 8, Band 2

Listening Guide for Strauss's *Till Eulenspiegels lustige Streiche*

Timbre:	very large orchestra of string, wind, and percussion instruments
Melody:	several motives and themes; two motives at beginning represent Till
Rhythm:	great variety of different meters and tempos
Harmony:	mainly major mode; begins and ends in F major with frequent modulations; some chromaticism
Texture:	mainly homophonic, with some counterpoint
Form:	expanded, free rondo

Other Works by Strauss   After *Till Eulenspiegel* Strauss wrote the tone poems *Also sprach Zarathustra* ("Thus Spake Zarathustra") and *Tod und Verklärung* ("Death and Transfiguration"), both of which have highly philosophical programs. *Don Quixote*, another very popular tone poem, was completed in 1897. Strauss's later career was devoted to opera. Of his works in this genre, four remain important today: *Salome, Electra, Der Rosenkavalier* ("The Rose Cavalier"), and *Die Frau ohne Schatten* ("The Woman Without a Shadow").

Strauss ended his career as an official in the musical organization of Hitler's Third Reich. Though many other musicians had refused to cooperate with the Nazis, he did not. "My whole life belongs to German music and to an indefatigable effort to elevate German culture," he assured Adolf Hitler in 1935. He later became disillusioned with the Nazis but remained dedicated to his personal goal until his death in 1949.

Overtures and Incidental Music

One of the important inspirations for program music was the theater. It seemed natural to Romantic composers to base music on the plots and characters of drama. For this purpose, the overture proved eminently useful.

As we have seen, the overture was originally a one-movement orchestral work played before the first act of an opera or oratorio. Its function was to set the mood for the work to follow, either in a general way or by presenting some of the themes from the work. Although these overtures were thus, in their conception, closely tied to larger works, several of them later began to appear in the concert repertoire as independent works. Overtures by Mozart and Rossini were often performed independently. So was Beethoven's *Leonore Overture No. 3*, one of several versions of the overture to the opera *Fidelio*.

Concert Overtures

As opera overtures began to achieve independent concert status, composers in turn began to think of them as independent works, or as *concert overtures*. Such an overture could simply draw upon the imagery, plot, and characters of a dramatic work. It need not be performed as part of an opera or other theatrical event. Most of the independent concert overtures of the Romantic age were based on plays, but some were written to illustrate poems or to mark special occasions. Mendelssohn's *Calm Sea and Prosperous Voyage*, based on two of Goethe's poems, and Tchaikovsky's *1812 Overture* are examples of concert overtures that have no connection with theater.

The concert overture shares many characteristics with the symphonic poem. Both are one-movement orchestral works often based on literary ideas. In fact, some composers used the term overture for works that might just as well have been called symphonic poems. Mendelssohn, for example, designated as overtures some works that Liszt would have likely termed symphonic poems.

Despite the ambiguous distinction between the two types of compositions, however, a few general differences can be found in most of the works. The concert overture, generally cast in sonata form, is usually more tightly organized and more likely to be related to dramatic material. Prominent examples of such overtures, in addition to those already mentioned, are Beethoven's *Prometheus Overture*, Mendelssohn's *Fingal's Cave*, and Brahms' *Academic Festival Overture*.

Incidental Music

While the Romantic period saw the growth of the independent concert overture, it also encouraged the writing of music to accompany performed drama. Such music is called *incidental music* because it is incidental to the drama. It may appear between the acts, in ballroom scenes and chamber scenes, and in other stage situations in which music might realistically be heard.

Works by Bizet and Grieg

In concerts today, incidental music is generally performed as a suite for orchestra. Among the most popular of these suites are the two by Georges Bizet (1838–1875) for Daudet's play *L'Arlésienne* ("The Woman of Arles") and the two by Edvard Grieg (1843–1907) for Ibsen's *Peer Gynt*.

Composers have occasionally written both an overture and incidental music for a single drama. Beethoven did this for Goethe's *Egmont*, although

Images of a Midsummer Night: *Shakespeare's play of fairy creatures, supernatural happenings, and general enchantment offered very appropriate subject matter for the Romantic composer. The themes seem almost ready made for the spirit of the age.*

only the overture remains popular today. Perhaps the best-known overture with incidental music is that written by Mendelssohn for Shakespeare's *A Midsummer Night's Dream.*

Mendelssohn: *A Midsummer Night's Dream*

Felix Mendelssohn (1809–1847) was one of the most influential composers of the early Romantic period. Born to a wealthy and cultured family, he was raised in considerably more fortunate circumstances than many of his fellow Romantics. His grandfather was a noted Jewish philosopher, his father a banker. Felix and his sister were exposed to all the cultural and social advantages of nineteenth-century Germany—readings from the classics, visits to Goethe and other artists, and travels through Europe. Mendelssohn was physically attractive and socially irresistible. He was a kind of hero to a whole generation of struggling Romantics.

As an artist, Mendelssohn was incredibly versatile. He was a renowned conductor and administrator; in fact, he earned his early reputation by organizing a revival performance of Bach's *Saint Matthew Passion.* He was also a gifted pianist and critic and was responsible for furthering the careers of a number of young composers whose reputations eventually outshone his own. As a composer, he was a traditionalist aspiring to the Classical style in music. He nevertheless caught the growing spirit of Romanticism, as can be seen, for example, in his *Songs Without Words,* a collection of short piano pieces.

Romantic influences are also apparent in the overture and incidental music he wrote for *A Midsummer Night's Dream.* The overture was written in 1826, when Mendelssohn was only seventeen years old, a student at the University of Berlin. The incidental music was written later, when he was thirty-four, at the request of the King of Prussia, who was planning a production of Shakespeare's comedy. Although there are thirteen musical incidents, only three—the "Scherzo," "Nocturne," and "Wedding March"— have achieved any independent popularity. As might be expected, the overture and the three most popular incidental pieces are sometimes presented in concert as a suite. In some performances, the "Intermezzo" and "Finale" are also included. Yet even when performed independently of the play, Mendelssohn's music conveys much of the beauty and charm of Shakespeare's immortal comedy.

Overture

Exposition

Despite its strong programmatic basis, Mendelssohn's Overture is in sonata form. The music that opens the piece evokes the spirit of the forest fairyland with four sustained woodwind chords proclaiming the meeting of Oberon and Titania, king and queen of the fairies. This light music continues in a theme played by woodwinds and violins. A lyric second theme is then heard portraying the human lovers. A contrasting group, the comic tradesmen, are characterized by a theme in the violas. Finally there is a loud bray from the ophicleide, a deep-voiced precursor of the tuba: Bottom the Weaver has found his head transformed into that of an ass. The exposition is program music at its finest.

Development, Recapitulation, and Coda

The development, in its energetic, imaginative use of earlier material, captures the fantastic activity of the woodland elves and fairies. The recapitulation begins with the four sustained woodwind chords of the opening and ends with a coda integrally fashioned from the various themes. At the very end, we hear once again the four chords that began the work. In the words of one reviewer, these chords are "the magic formula which dissolves the dream it had before conjured up."

"Scherzo"

The incidental music that Mendelssohn wrote for *A Midsummer Night's Dream* builds upon the charm of the Overture. One of the most popular of the original thirteen pieces is the "Scherzo," written to be played before the opening of Act II. It begins with a high-pitched lively theme associated with Puck. The theme is presented by the woodwinds:

First Theme

"Nocturne"

Mendelssohn's "Nocturne" has also remained popular. The music is associated with the pairs of lovers who, bewitched by Puck's flowery potion, lie sleeping in the depths of the forest. When performed with the drama, the "Nocturne" is played between Acts III and IV. The horn presents the opening melody, a quiet theme both tender and heroic:

Horn Theme

"Wedding March"

By far the best known of all the incidental music Mendelssohn wrote for *A Midsummer Night's Dream* is the "Wedding March." It was conceived as an accompaniment to the several marriages that form the happy ending of the play, and today, outside the theater and the concert hall, it continues to be played at the conclusion of numerous traditional wedding ceremonies. The music begins with a trumpet fanfare followed by the jubilant main theme:

Main Theme

The "Wedding March" also includes contrasting sections suggestive of the different loves that are realized in the course of the play—mortal and immortal, royal and common. Brass and woodwind timbres are emphasized, adding greatly to the festive mood.

Suggested Listening

Program Symphonies

Berlioz: *Harold in Italy, Op. 16* [Columbia M-30116]. Related in subject to Byron's *Childe Harold*, Berlioz' *Harold in Italy* is a program symphony in four movements unified by a recurring theme. Classical forms are used, but in a very free manner. Although a solo viola is featured, the part is not sufficiently demanding or important enough to warrant calling the work a concerto.

Berlioz: *Romeo and Juliet Symphony, Op. 17* [Philips 839716/7]. This seven-movement work was written on a grand scale for soloists, chorus, and a very large orchestra that supplies a vast array of contrasts in color. The program follows the essential dramatic features of Shakespeare's play. Perhaps the most popular and appealing of the movements is the "Queen Mab Scherzo."

Liszt: *Faust Symphony* [Columbia M2S-699]. This, the first of Liszt's two program symphonies, is in three long movements. The large orchestra is augmented by tenor soloist and male chorus. Themes associated with the central characters of Goethe's *Faust*—Gretchen, Faust, and Mephistopheles—recur at appropriate places throughout the work. The very expressive use of musical elements makes this truly a Romantic composition.

Symphonic Poems

Mussorgsky: *Night on Bald Mountain* [Columbia MS-6943]. The program of this symphonic poem is based on a series of mysterious, frightful events, including a Black Mass. Melodic materials and very colorful orchestration are used to suggest unearthly voices and the god Chernobog. An expanded sonata form provides the structural basis for the work, which is one of Mussorgsky's most accessible and entertaining.

R. Strauss: *Also sprach Zarathustra, Op. 30* ("Thus Spake Zarathustra") [Angel S-35994]. This work, one of Strauss's best-known symphonic poems, was used in the film *2001: A Space Odyssey*. The opening motive—the tonic-dominant-tonic notes played by the brasses—is very arresting and acts as a strongly unifying element of the work. Also striking are the variety of rhythms and the way in which the horns are used.

Overtures and Incidental Music

Mendelssohn: *Hebrides Overture* (*Fingal's Cave*) [DG 2530126]. The *Hebrides Overture* was conceived not as an introduction to a dramatic work but as an independent one-movement piece that contains its own drama. The first theme, which opens and closes the work, depicts the bleakness of the seascape. The elements of dynamics and tempo contribute greatly in the musical buildup to the storm that plays a central part in the movement.

Bizet: *L'Arlésienne Suites No. 1 and 2* [Columbia M-31013]. Bizet's incidental music for Daudet's play was originally written for a small orchestra, but later rescored by Bizet himself for a much larger orchestra. Of the twenty-seven incidents written for the play, four have been included in each of the two suites. All of the pieces have a tuneful quality that is very engaging.

C H A P T E R

23

Romantic Opera and Choral Music

Opera in the Romantic Period

Opera flourished during the Romantic period. In opera, composers found yet another opportunity to associate words with music. Librettists and composers gave free rein to their imaginations and, as we will see, a number of exciting innovations took place.

Influence of Mozart and Beethoven

Two pre-Romantic operas, Mozart's *Don Giovanni* and Beethoven's *Fidelio*, were important precursors of the Romantic opera. *Don Giovanni*, written in 1787, two years before the fall of the Bastille, depicts one man's violent struggle with supernatural powers. Don Giovanni, the cruel deceiver and seducer of a long succession of women, is the prototype for a number of characters found in later Romantic operas. The emphasis on supernatural effects, the tremendous contrast between conflicting principles, and the dramatization of the conflict are all elements that were soon to be identified with the Romantic movement. The other major forerunner of Romantic opera, Beethoven's *Fidelio*, was written between 1805 and 1814, after the composer's thorough search for appropriate subject matter. The opera, based on an actual event that took place during the French Revolution, deals with the selflessness, bravery, fidelity, and heroic humanitarianism of the rebels. Many Romantics were inspired by Beethoven, seeing him as a nationalist and an enthusiastic rebel. The music in *Fidelio* is often explosive, and, in combination with the drama of good against evil, it creates an intense emotional effect. Beethoven's work thus broke away from the usual style of eighteenth-century opera and heralded the opera of the Romantic era.

In the following sections, discussion will focus on the three national styles of opera most prominent in the Romantic period—French, Italian, and German. All of the styles owe something to the works of Mozart and Beethoven, and all offer certain innovations.

French Opera

Since the days of Gluck, Paris had been the center of European opera, and it remained so through the first half of the nineteenth century. During the early years of the French Revolution, opera seemed especially suited to the propaganda needs of the new leaders. Huge public spectacles were held, with spectacular choral sections and "hymns" written to be sung by the audience as well as by performers. After the Revolution, operas with large numbers of singers remained popular, and the awakened appetite for spectacle contributed to the development of the style that came to be known as *grand opera*.

The Development of Grand Opera

Grand opera was essentially the creation of three people—Louis Veron, Eugène Scribe, and Giacomo Meyerbeer. Veron, a businessman, was the director of the Paris Opera during the early 1830s. Scribe wrote librettos, and Meyerbeer was the composer. The three wished to break away from dependence on early Greek and Roman subject matter and concentrate instead on the Middle Ages and on modern times. The operas they produced were serious, spectacular, and heroic, with events inevitably unfolding on a huge scale. Plots were often based on current events, and local settings were frequently used.

Meyerbeer's Operas

Giacomo Meyerbeer (1791–1864), perhaps more than any other composer, determined the direction in which grand opera would evolve. It was only fitting in cosmopolitan Paris that a German Jew who had gone to Venice to study the Italian style should create operas that would be regarded everywhere as eminently French. Meyerbeer's works are based on the extravagant romanticizing of history and call for an undisciplined profusion of scenery and effects. His *Robert le Diable* ("Robert the Devil"), first produced in 1831, was a smashing success—in part because it provided the shock effect demanded by the public. The work was described by Schumann as "a conglomeration of monstrosities." For *Les Huguenots* ("The Huguenots") Meyerbeer took his subject from the French religious wars of the late sixteenth century. The opera offers another example of the extravagant music and theatrical performances the French were flocking to at the time.

Berlioz' Les Troyens

Another important grand opera, indeed one of the foremost French operas of the entire century, was Berlioz' *Les Troyens* ("The Trojans"), written in the late 1850s. The story concerns, not the lives of individuals, but monumental events—the fall of Troy and the fate of the Trojans as a group. The many large choral and ballet scenes are very characteristic of grand opera. Other traits in *Les Troyens*, however, are not so typical. The melodies are well disciplined and closely related to the text. The orchestral interludes were obviously written with great care.

Comic and Lyric Styles

Offenbach's Operas

Opéra comique, with dialogue generally spoken, was also popular in nineteenth-century Paris. Of the many composers writing in this style, Jacques Offenbach (1819–1880) was one the most successful. His style, light yet satirical, was to influence the development of comic opera and operettas throughout Europe. Offenbach's tremendous popularity may be attributed in part to his revival of eighteenth-century vaudeville humor as well as to the lucidity and conciseness of his music. He satirized all that he disliked in grand opera. He also made fun of traditional opera themes, particularly in his *Orphée aux Enfers* ("Orpheus in the Underworld") and his *La Belle Hélène* ("Helen the Beautiful"). Elsewhere he parodied Medieval legend and satirized contemporary politics, common subject matters of grand opera. For Offenbach criticism was a sport, not a morally inspired mission. Incompetent rulers and generals, silly high-society types, and lusty clergymen were, in Offenbach's operas, more to be laughed at than condemned.

Operas by Thomas and Gounod

Toward the middle of the century, *lyric opera* developed as a compromise between serious, elaborate grand opera and the lighter opéra comique. Two major composers of lyric opera were Ambroise Thomas (1811–1896) and Charles Gounod (1818–1893). Thomas's *Mignon* displays the clarity, songlike quality, and controlled expression of the lyric style. Gounod's *Faust* (1859) remains the best-attended opera in French history. Its colorful plot and tuneful melodies have endeared it to countless listeners.

Bizet: *Carmen*

A peak of opera composition in France was reached by Georges Bizet (1838–1875) in his opera *Carmen*. This powerful work, written in the last year of the composer's life, differs from earlier Romantic opera in that much of its text is in prose rather than poetry. Oddly enough, despite the tragic love story that forms the plot, *Carmen* was originally designated as an opéra comique. Its Spanish setting and "exotic" music testify to the interest in foreign subjects that was widespread in France at the time. The scenes are quite realistic; the music is colorful and concise.

The story is set in Seville and revolves around the beautiful, sensuous gypsy Carmen, who works in a cigarette factory. Don José, a corporal, loves Carmen intensely, but she rejects his love and turns to Escamillo, a toreador. In the end, the heartbroken José stabs Carmen to death.

Bizet's music seems to capture the essence of the passionate tale and all of its nuances. The melodies vary from the disarmingly lyrical to the powerfully dramatic. Rhythms from Spanish dances appear occasionally, and there is some use of chromaticism. The moderately large orchestra plays an important role, providing the singers with colorful and vibrant support.

The Prélude hints at several of the arias to follow, principally the famous "Chanson du toréador" ("Toreador Song") and the theme heard just before Carmen's death. In the opera itself, Carmen sings several memorable arias, notably the "Habañera," the "Seguidille," and the "Chanson bohème" ("Gypsy Song").

"Chanson bohème"

The "Chanson bohème," which opens the second act of the opera, aptly portrays the heroine's personality. Carmen sings exuberantly of the pleasures of gypsy life while her friends dance with abandon. The tempo is moderately fast in triple meter, and the minor mode seems especially appropriate to the gypsy mood.

After a substantial orchestral introduction, featuring pizzicato strings and two flutes, Carmen sings the opening, and principal, melody of the aria:

Opening Melody

Les tring-les des sis-tres tin-taient ____ a-vec un é-clat mé-tal-li-que

The aria is strophic in form, with three stanzas of text. Each stanza ends with Carmen's friends joining her in a vivacious "Tra-la-la" in the major mode. The effect of the change from the minor to the major at the end of each stanza followed by the change back to the minor at the beginning of the next stanza is quite striking. Musically the second and third stanzas differ only slightly from the first.

Percussion instruments, particularly tambourine, triangle, and cymbals, are increasingly prominent as the aria proceeds. With the final "Tra-la-la," the tempo begins to increase, growing faster and faster until the orchestra closes with a repetition of the opening material in a breathless whirl of sound and dance.

Late Romantic Style

Operas by Saint-Saëns and Massenet

By the late nineteenth century, Paris was no longer the center of European operatic activity, but a number of French composers continued to write beautiful works, generally lyric in style. *Samson et Dalila* (1877), a biblical work by Camille Saint-Saëns (1835–1921), was very popular. Though Saint-Saëns was not noted for his work in opera, this particular work was a considerable success. The lyrical sentimentality of Jules Massenet (1842–1912) made him one of the most popular opera composers of his time. His great interest in sensual love poetry is shown clearly in *Manon*, an opera based on an eighteenth-century tale of romance. Massenet's work brings us to the close of the late Romantic style in French opera and into the twentieth century.

Italian Opera

In Italian opera of the early nineteenth century, music was strongly dominant over drama. Melody, supported by colorful instrumentation, harmony, and rhythm, formed the single most important aspect of opera. Recitatives and arias were still clearly separated in the traditional way, although recitatives were increasingly accompanied by the orchestra rather than by basso continuo. As the century progressed, Italian opera changed, becoming both more cosmopolitan and more national in character. The change began with the works of Rossini, continued with Donizetti and Bellini, and reached a climax in the works of Verdi.

Early Romantic Operas

Rossini's Operas

Although Romanticism was somewhat less evident in Italy than in France or Germany, some of its traits can be found in the operas of Gioacchino Rossini (1792–1868), whose life and influence spanned the first half of the nineteenth century. The texture of Rossini's music is light, and his melodies, often sung with coloratura ornamentation, are very appealing. He caught the public's imagination with happy tunes, lively rhythms, and his fine talent for building dramatic excitement.

Rossini presented his comic opera *Il Barbiere di Siviglia* ("The Barber of Seville") in 1816, and it was soon celebrated throughout Europe. His *Otello* (1816) was also popular until an opera of the same name was presented by Verdi in 1887, totally eclipsing Rossini's version. Rossini's last opera, *Guillaume Tell* ("William Tell"), first produced in 1829, established him as an important composer of grand opera. After the great success of *William Tell*, the thirty-seven-year-old Rossini retired. For the remaining thirty-nine years of his life, he wrote no more operas.

Donizetti's Operas

The most important figures in Italian opera between Rossini and Verdi were Donizetti and Bellini. Gaetano Donizetti (1797–1848) was a prolific extrovert who created operas that were both dynamic and exciting. He felt it was quite all right to interrupt an aria with dialogue in order to keep it in close touch with the plot. His melodies tended to be ostentatious, and he used a multiplicity of ensembles and choruses to build volume and color. Flamboyant vocal effects are common in his works, especially at the end of a scene or act. His *Don Pasquale*, an opera buffa, is one of the brightest operatic gems of the age. His *Lucrezia Borgia* and his *Lucia di Lammermoor* both display the more melodramatic and violent facets of Romantic art quite powerfully. *Lucia di Lammermoor*, based on a story by Sir Walter Scott, is the more tightly conceived work, with melodies and rhythms that the public could easily appreciate and remember. The heroine's "mad scene" includes some of Donizetti's most elaborate and difficult writing for solo voice.

Bellini's Operas

Vincenzo Bellini (1801–1835) leaned toward a quieter, more contemplative style. His melodies were more expressive and delicate than Donizetti's, his harmonies subtle and varied. He was a meticulous, painstaking perfectionist, which may be why we have fewer operas by Bellini than by Rossini or Donizetti. *Norma* (1831) exemplifies not only Bellini's insistence that the aria retain the central position in the opera but also his belief that strong dramatic scenes, carefully chosen, could be most effective. In *Norma* he also gave a somewhat more important role to the orchestra than was usual in Italian opera. Apart from *Norma*, Bellini's worthiest creations are *La Sonnambula* ("The Sleepwalker") of 1831 and *I Puritani* ("The Puritans") of 1835.

Verdi's Operas

The name of Giuseppe Verdi (1813–1901) has come to stand, not only for the career of a single composer, but for a whole type of opera. Verdi's music cannot be considered apart from his personality and situation in life. Verdi was a patriot, closely associated with Italy's midcentury struggle for nationhood, and his nationalism strongly influenced his work. Many of his operas have to do with revolutionary conspiracies. His singers voiced stirring appeals on behalf of freedom and democracy. For him nationalism could not help but express itself in music.

All of his works, with the exception of *Falstaff*, were serious in mood, since comedy was hardly appropriate for the kinds of questions he wished to raise. His desire for naturalness led him to stress believable characters and the human voice. Orchestra and scenery are nearly always secondary.

Verdi's operatic career developed in a careful, continuous fashion. *Nabucco* ("Nebuchadnezzar"), a biblical opera presented in 1842, was his first real success. *Macbeth* (1847) was the other important opera written early in his career. It seemed especially melodramatic to Italian audiences, for whom the mere portrayal of murder and witches on the stage was a shocking breach of custom.

The second phase in Verdi's development featured three major operas: *Rigoletto*, *Il Trovatore*, and *La Traviata*. Written between 1851 and 1853, all were inspired by well-known plays. The works are somewhat reminiscent of Donizetti in that they were written in the tradition of grand opera, but they are much more profound and more direct than the works of the earlier Italian composer.

Rigoletto (1851) was inspired by Victor Hugo's *Le Roi s'amuse* ("The King Is Enjoying Himself") and features a hunchbacked court jester in the title role of Rigoletto. Two of the arias from the opera have become especially well known: "Caro nome" ("Dear Name") and "La Donna è mobile' ("Woman Is Fickle").

Il Trovatore ("The Troubadour"), first presented in 1852, was based on a play by the Spanish author Antonio Garcia Gutiérrez. The great variety in the opera's plot and music can be attributed in part to the influence of Meyerbeer. Azucena, the gypsy mother, is one of the many exotic characters that intrigued Verdi's audiences.

Verdi: *La Traviata*

Verdi's *La Traviata* ("The Frail One"), which first appeared in 1853, was based on Alexandre Dumas' *La Dame aux camélias* ("The Lady of the Camellias") and, like the novel, is supremely sentimental. Violetta, a courtesan, falls in love with Alfredo, a young man of respectable family. Violetta and Alfredo live together for a time, but at his father's pleading she nobly leaves him to save the good name of his family. Her health, already frail, breaks under the strain, and Alfredo returns to her just as she dies of consumption in the last act of the opera.

The Height of Sentimentalism: *Both Verdi's opera* La Traviata *and Dumas' novel upon which it was based played upon the Romantic audience's desire for heartbreaking themes. The music seen here was scored for piano, giving the public a chance to re-create the opera's most moving moments in their own homes.*

"Ah, fors' è lui" and "Sempre libera"

Upon first realizing her love for Alfredo, Violetta sings one of the most famous arias from the opera: "Ah, fors' è lui" ("Ah, Perhaps It's He"). The aria is in two sections, the first beginning with the words "Ah, fors' è lui" and the second with the words "Sempre libera" ("Always Free"). Brief recitatives precede each of the sections.

In the recitative preceding the first section, Violetta muses on the possibility of finding true love. These thoughts carry her into the first section of the aria. Two themes are heard, both in triple meter at a moderate tempo. The first theme, in the minor mode, is halting and disjunct, as Violetta con-

ROMANTIC OPERA AND CHORAL MUSIC

templates the mystery of love. The second theme, in the major mode, is more lyrical and conjunct, as the thought of love overcomes her.

First Section: First Theme

First Section: Second Theme

The orchestra provides a light accompaniment throughout. In some performances the entire first section is repeated.

Then, suddenly, in a brief recitative, Violetta comes to her senses, realizing that she is committed to her life as a fashionable prostitute and cannot change. The recitative ends with very elaborate scale passages.

In the second section of the aria, "Sempre libera," Violetta enthusiastically anticipates the continuation of her life as a courtesan. The tempo is fast, the music in the mode major:

Second Section: First Theme

Over a simple, chordal accompaniment, the vocal fireworks multiply, abounding with scales, sequences, and high notes. At points of climax, the singer, following tradition, usually slows the tempo freely for expressive purposes. For a moment, Violetta hears Alfredo serenading her outside the window, but she is undaunted and repeats the section, vowing to remain free.

Side 8, Band 3

Listening Guide for "Ah, fors' è lui" and "Sempre libera" from Verdi's *La Traviata*

Timbre:	soprano; large orchestra of string and wind instruments
Melody:	first section begins with disjunct motion and becomes more conjunct; second section largely conjunct
Rhythm:	first section—triple meter, tempo Andantino (moderate); second section—⁶⁄₈ meter, tempo Allegro brillante (fast and spirited)
Harmony:	first section—F minor changing to F major; second section—begins and ends in A♭ major

Texture: homophonic

Form: binary (AB) with a recitative preceding each section

Text:

Violetta (sola):	Violetta (alone):
Recitativo:	Recitative:
È strano! È strano! In core	How strange! How strange! His words
Scolpiti ho quegli accenti!	
Saria per me sventura un serio amore?;	Are burned upon my heart!
Che risolvi, o turbata anima mia?	Would a real love be a tragedy for me?
Null'uomo ancora t'accendeva—O gioja	What decision are you taking, O my soul?
Ch'io non conobbi, esser amata amando!	No man has ever made me fall in love. O joy,
E sdegnaria poss'io	Which I have never known— loving, to be loved!
Per l'aride follie del viver mio?	And can I scorn it
	For the arid follies of my present life?
Aria:	Aria:
Ah, fors' è lui che l'anima	Ah, perhaps he is the one
Solinga ne' tumulti	Whom my soul,
Godea sovente pingere	Lonely in the tumult, loved
De' suoi colori occulti!	To imagine in secrecy!
Lui che modesto e vigile	Watchful though I never knew,
All'egre soglie ascese,	He came here while I lay sick,
E nuova febbre accese,	Awakening a new fever,
Destandomi all'amor.	The fever of love.
A quell'amor ch'è palpito	Of love which is the very breath
Dell'universo intero,	Of the universe itself—
Misterioso, altero,	Mysterious and noble,
Croce e delizia al cor.	Both cross and ecstasy of the heart.
Recitativo:	Recitative:
Follie! follie! Delirio vano è questo!	Folly! All is folly! This is mad delirium!
Povera donna, sola,	A poor woman, alone,
Abbandonata in questo	Lost in this
Popoloso deserto	Crowded desert
Che appellano Parigi,	Which is known to men as Paris,
Che spero or più? Che far degg'io! Gioire,	What can I hope for? What should I do? Die
Di voluttà ne' vortici perir.	In the whirlpool of earthly pleasures!
Aria:	Aria:
Sempre libera degg'io	Forever free, I must pass
Folleggiare di gioja in gioja.	Madly from joy to joy.
Vo' che scorra il viver mio	My life's course shall be
Pei sentieri del piacer.	Forever in the paths of pleasure.
Nasca il giorno, o il giorno muoia,	Whether it be dawn or dusk,
Sempre lieta ne' ritrovi.	I must always live
A diletti sempre nuovi	Gaily in the world's gay places,
Dee volare il mio pensier.	Ever seeking newer joys.

ROMANTIC OPERA AND CHORAL MUSIC

The Evolution of Opera

In the Classical and Romantic periods, opera reached its height as a form of public entertainment. To a great extent, the works of those eras were written not only to present fresh musical ideas but also to capture the public imagination and in many cases to achieve box-office success. This has been much less true in our own age, in part because of the competition of so many other forms of public entertainment.

Listen to selections from the operas of four different periods—those listed below from the record set that accompanies the text, or other selections from the record library.

Baroque:	Monteverdi's *Orfeo*, "Tu se' morta"	Side 3, Band 5
Classical:	Mozart's *The Marriage of Figaro*, "Cinque, dieci"	Side 6, Band 4
Romantic:	Verdi's *La Traviata*, "Sempre libera"	Side 8, Band 3
Modern:	Berg's *Wozzeck*, any selection	Record Library

What musical qualities make it possible to identify the first three selections as Baroque, Classical, and Romantic? What musical qualities suggest that the last selection is of a more recent era?

In what ways can each of the selections be seen as a reflection of the social and historical setting in which it was created?

After *La Traviata*, Verdi embarked on a brief and rather unsatisfactory association with Parisian opera. He was commissioned to write two operas in French, *Les Vêpres siciliennes* ("Sicilian Vespers") in 1855 and *Don Carlos* in 1867. The first opera was based on the 1282 massacre of the French invaders in Sicily. The second was loosely based on a drama by Schiller about the Spanish court. In it Verdi dealt very effectively with the emotional power of freedom, love, and misery.

In 1871, with the appearance of *Aïda*, Verdi reached the pinnacle of his career. The occasion was festive. Cairo had a new opera house, and Verdi had been commissioned to write an opera for the opening of the Suez Canal. He broke with tradition by creating most of the text himself. His worldwide fame and his vast experience allowed him to take such liberties with very good results. Single-handedly, he planned the scenes, wrote the dialogue in all its detail, clarified the plot, and composed the music. The result was an opera rendered unusually effective by its unity of drama and music. In the arias, choruses, ballets, processions, and marches of *Aïda*, Verdi combined the grand opera of France with the best of Italian opera. The arias "Celeste Aïda" ("Celestial Aïda"), sung by the hero Radames, and "Ritorna vincitor" ("Return Victorious"), sung by Aïda, are among Verdi's finest.

Verdi's *Otello* is one of the most outstanding works of opera seria produced in Italy during the nineteenth century. It appeared in 1887 after a long period of nonproductivity for Verdi. The libretto is, of course, based on Shakespeare's play. Music and drama are very thoroughly integrated; arias and ensembles flow smoothly together. In none of Verdi's earlier works were the various musical pieces so intimately connected with one another as in *Otello*. Chromaticism and a relatively free treatment of tonality are important harmonic features of the music.

Verdi's *Falstaff*, produced in 1893, had the same rejuvenating effect on opera buffa that *Otello* had on opera seria. Now approaching eighty, Verdi was growing cynical about the human condition, and he satirized it strongly in *Falstaff*. The work is one of the greatest comic operas of the century, a perfect wedding of text and music. It is a fine credit to Verdi's genius and an appropriate culmination of his great career.

Verismo and the Works of Puccini

Operas by Mascagni and Leoncavallo

Three important Italian composers who continued the Romantic tradition in the late nineteenth and early twentieth centuries were Mascagni, Leoncavallo, and Puccini. Many of their works belong to the movement known as *verismo*, or "realism," which made use of subject matter based on everyday events and the lives of the common people. Pietro Mascagni (1863–1945) is best known for his *Cavalleria rusticana* ("Rustic Chivalry"), a famous example of the verismo style. Ruggiero Leoncavallo (1858–1919) is also remembered for an opera in the realistic style, *I Pagliacci* ("The Clowns"). *Cavalleria rusticana* and *I Pagliacci*, both relatively short works, are often presented together.

The works of Giacomo Puccini (1858–1924) represent a variety of subjects and styles. His interest in exotic subjects can be seen in two of his most popular operas: the "Japanese" *Madama Butterfly* and the monumental "Chinese" *Turandot*. By comparison, *Tosca* is set in Verdi's own Italy. *La Bohème*, first presented in 1896, also has a European setting—the Latin Quarter of nineteenth-century Paris.

Puccini: *La Bohème*

The realism of the verismo style is especially strong in *La Bohème*. As a whole, the opera provides an excellent example of many aspects of Puccini's style.

The tale revolves around Mimi, a poor and pretty young seamstress, and Rudolfo, an equally poor young poet. The opera centers on various experiences in the Bohemian lives of the two young people and their friends. Mimi and Rudolfo soon fall in love, but in true Romantic fashion Mimi dies of consumption in the last scene, leaving Rudolfo heartbroken.

ROMANTIC OPERA AND CHORAL MUSIC

"Che gelida manina"

Soon after they meet, Rudolfo helps Mimi to look for a key she has dropped. Their hands touch in the search, and Rudolfo comments on the coldness of her hands. The aria "Che gelida manina" ("What a Cold Little Hand") is in duple meter and the major mode. It has two sections, the first of which starts with a simple series of repeated notes. The melody then becomes more active:

Opening Melody

Rudolfo
dolciss.
pp

Che ge - li - da ma - ni - na, Se la la - sci ri - scal -

dar. Cer - car che gio - va? Al bu - io non si tro - va.

In the course of the first section, Rudolfo asks Mimi to stay while they look for the key—which he has already found and slipped into his pocket.

In the second section, there is a modulation and a meter change as Rudolfo tells Mimi he is a poet. The section builds to a dynamic climax with the orchestra providing strong support.

In this aria and in others, Puccini's gift for writing beautiful, lyrical melodies can clearly be seen. His text settings are nearly always syllabic, without scales and arpeggios. His melodies and their supporting orchestration often evoke a strong emotional response in the listener. The music seems to capture the very essence of late Romantic Italian opera, with its superb melodies, chromatic harmony, and interest in the common people. Puccini's work helped to close an era.

German Opera

More than in any other country, Romanticism in Germany was ideological. Nationalism there was of such universal political significance that it could hardly but affect the whole of German culture. The violent potential in both Romanticism and nationalism found a fertile medium in German opera.

Patriotic and Medieval legends were a major source for Romantic artists, especially in Germany. Superstition, fantasy, and the supernatural were also frequently introduced. These themes were particularly evident in the librettos of German operas. Another Romantic trend, the glorification of the common people, was also very important in German operas during the Romantic period.

Weber's Der Freischütz

German Romantic opera had its first great flowering under the leadership of Carl Maria von Weber (1786–1826). Weber was already an experienced conductor by the time be began to write opera. His *Der Freischütz* ("The Marksman") was written in 1821 and proved a masterpiece. It is a story of good and evil, of Germanic Christianity versus barbaric paganism. The heroes seem to fit in naturally with the wonderfully merry villagers and bucolic setting,

The Master of Late German Romanticism: *Philosopher and poet as well as composer, Wagner became the idol of thousands and the cult hero of something like a new religion. One of his greatest admirers was Bavarian king Ludwig II, whom he inspired to finance many of his works. Wagner is shown here at the keyboard, surrounded by a circle of friends.*

while the villains ultimately find they have no place in the rural society. Among the most admirable scenes are the hunters' and bridesmaids' choruses, the songs and dances of the peasants, and the supernatural "Wolf's Glen" scene. The last features a very dramatic orchestral accompaniment played by a combination of strings, clarinets, flutes, and horns.

Wagnerian Opera

Nineteenth-century Romantic opera reached a climax in the work of Richard Wagner (1813–1883). He began writing opera at the age of twenty. In *Die Feen* ("The Fairies") and *Das Liebesverbot* ("The Ban on Love"), he seemed merely to be getting acquainted with the tasks facing him as a musician and dramatist. These were not particularly original works. It was not until he reached his late twenties that he wrote his first major opera, *Rienzi*, a grand opera in the Meyerbeer tradition.

ROMANTIC OPERA AND CHORAL MUSIC

A turning point in Wagner's evolution was reached in 1843 with *Der fliegende Holländer* ("The Flying Dutchman"). Heinrich Heine's version of a German legend supplied the plot, and the result was a truly German opera. The story concerns a Dutchman condemned to roam the seas forever. At last he is released from his bond with the devil through the love of a woman. The orchestration is very colorful, the melodies frequently tuneful, and the characters well conceived. The impact of the entire work is quite forceful.

In Wagner's *Tannhäuser* (1845), the grand opera trappings of *Rienzi* were combined with the idea of redemption, an idea already used successfully in *The Flying Dutchman*. The Medieval knight Tannhäuser enjoys a love affair with Venus and then unsuccessfully seeks forgiveness from the Church. The pure love of the heroine Elizabeth finally resolves the situation. The ensembles, choruses, ballets, and crowd scenes no doubt contributed to the opera's great popularity. There is a noticeable trend toward unity. The various arias and ensembles are still clearly separated from one another, but not as strictly as in Wagner's previous works. The music is also more chromatic than that in Wagner's earlier operas.

Lohengrin, Wagner's next major work, was first performed in Weimar in 1850 under the direction of Liszt. It was based on a tale taken from German folklore, but the emphasis was placed on questions of religion and philosophy. The knight Lohengrin is a symbol of divine love, while Elsa depicts that portion of humanity incapable of strong faith. Crucial to the plot is the "forbidden question": Elsa must never doubt Lohengrin by asking his name or country. Musically the work is fairly traditional in technique, but there are signs of Wagner's developing style. The use of recurring themes and motives, a technique he had used before and one that was to become one of his trademarks, is extended here. Particularly important are the motives for Lohengrin and for the "forbidden question." By this time, Wagner had abandoned the clear distinction between aria and recitative. Choruses are very prominent and often directly involved in the action. In order to achieve a more restrained and subtle instrumental effect, Wagner often chose to use sections of the orchestra in small mixed groups. Surprisingly in a work that followed *Tannhäuser*, there is relatively little chromaticism.

Wagner's Theoretical Writings

By 1849 Wagner had begun to formulate new theories about the integration of music and drama. He set forth his thoughts and opinions in several books. *Art and Revolution* (1849) and *Opera and Drama* (1851) explained his political philosophy and its relationship to his music, thus providing a rationale for his later compositions. He believed that drama and music should be more balanced, disagreeing with the traditional view that music was the end, drama merely the means. He also believed that the orchestra should carry a larger share of the musical burden than the human voice. Harmonic schemes should be conceived on a grand scale, he insisted, so that they might unify entire musical dramas and groups of musical dramas.

Leitmotivs

Wagner's philosophical writings also called for the extensive use of *Leitmotivs*—that is, of melodic and rhythmic motives associated with a particular person, thing, or idea that would be heard in the orchestral accompaniment.

The Ring Cycle

The second of Wagner's two major philosophical treatises, *Opera and Drama*, was primarily an apologia in advance for *Der Ring des Nibelungen* ("The Ring of the Nibelung"), a cycle of four operas written over a period of twenty-two years from 1852 to 1874. The four operas in the cycle are *Das Rheingold* ("The Rhine Gold"), *Die Walküre* ("The Valkyrie"), *Siegfried*, and *Die Götterdämmerung* ("The Twilight of the Gods"). Two separate tales from Nordic mythology are combined. The plot of the complete cycle is very complex, involving gods, humans, giants, and elves. All are involved in a struggle to rule the world, a struggle that revolves around the possession of a ring made from Rhine gold. Those who possess the ring are cursed by it and can never find love. Final redemption comes only when the ring is returned to the river at the end of the cycle.

Wagner: *Die Walküre*

The second opera in Wagner's Ring cycle, *Die Walküre*, represents most aspects of Wagner's mature style. The plot concerns Wotan, the chief god, and his children: nine daughters, the Valkyries, born to his goddess wife Erda; and a son and a daughter, Siegmund and Sieglinde, born to a mortal wife. The Valkyries are warriors whose main task in life is to take dead heroes to Valhalla, the hall of the gods. In the opera Siegmund and Sieglinde, separated as children, meet again as adults. They fall in love and run away from Hunding, Sieglinde's husband. Brünnhilde, leader of the Valkyries, tries to help them in their escape, much to the displeasure of Wotan. Siegmund is killed, and Sieglinde is hidden in the forest, where she will later bear a son, Siegfried, the hero of the next opera of the cycle.

The harmony in *Die Walküre* is rather chromatic, with frequent and sometimes rapid modulation from one tonality to another. Melodic phrases are often long and of irregular length. Form is quite free and fluid within an act. The old concept of recitative and aria is gone completely. For the most part, the music flows continuously without a clear separation into sections. The text is set syllabically and is seldom repeated. Virtuoso display rarely occurs in the singers' parts. Wagner wedded text and music carefully, never permitting the music to overwhelm the drama.

"Der Ritt der Walküren"

At the beginning of Act III, the famous "Der Ritt der Walküren" ("Ride of the Valkyries") is heard as the warrior goddesses assemble on a mountaintop after Siegmund's death. The very large orchestra is used in a most dramatic and flashing manner. The challenging Valkyrie Leitmotiv rings out boldly, played by horns and bass trumpets:

Valkyrie Leitmotiv

As the Valkyries assemble, one of them, Gerhilde, begins to sing their call, a very disjunct and dramatic motive:

Opening Melody
Gerhilde

Ho - jo - to - ho!   Ho - jo - to - ho!

Ho - jo - to - ho!   Ho - jo - to - ho!

The entire scene is very colorful—vocally, orchestrally, and visually. The structure of the music is quite free, based on repetitions of the above themes.

Side 9, Band 1

Listening Guide for "Der Ritt der Walküren" from Wagner's *Die Walküre*

Timbre:	soprano; large orchestra of string, wind, and percussion instruments
Melody:	largely disjunct; two motives prominent, one from orchestral introduction, one from vocal part
Rhythm:	triple meter; tempo Lebhaft (lively)
Harmony:	B minor moving to B major
Texture:	homophonic and contrapuntal
Form:	free, built largely on repetition of two motives

Text:	Gerhilde:	Gerhilde:
	Hojotoho! Hojotoho!	Hoyotoho! Hoyotoho!
	Heiaha! Heiaha!	Heyaha! Heyaha!
	Helmwige, hier!	Helmwige, come here!
	Hieher mit dem Ross!	Come here with your horse!

During the two decades in which he was concerned with the composition of the Ring Cycle, Wagner also wrote two other immensely powerful and successful operas: *Tristan und Isolde* and *Die Meistersinger von Nürnburg*. Vastly different in character, both works illustrate certain aspects of Wagner's mature style.

Wagner: *Tristan und Isolde*

Wagner's *Tristan und Isolde* is a tragic epic about love, despair, and death. It was written between 1857 and 1859, when Wagner was in love with Mathilde Wesendonk, the wife of a close friend. The Celtic legend of a faithful knight, magically enamored of his lord's wife, provided the basic material for the opera.

The dramatic significance of the plot is conveyed primarily through the music, which is in Wagner's most mature, richly chromatic style. Text and music are so well combined as to seem almost inseparable. Isolde's famous "Liebestod" ("Love-Death"), sung at the end just before she expires on her beloved Tristan's dead body, is a superb example. The entire work is

Ill-Fated Lovers: *The sketches above show the costumes for the characters Tristan and Isolde in the premiere performance of the opera in Munich. Tristan was played by Ludwig Schnorr von Carolsfeld, whose portly figure lacked the grace of the sketch.*

continuous and symmetrical, without division into distinct arias and ensembles.

Prelude

Wagner often used the term "prelude" instead of the term "overture" for the music that introduced his operas. The Prelude to *Tristan und Isolde* is one of his most famous compositions. Built largely on short motives, it is highly chromatic and moves so easily and quickly from one suggested key to another that traditional major-minor harmony seems to have disappeared. It is a well-organized work, with motives repeated, changed, and extended. Most important perhaps, it offers a brilliant preview of the drama to follow.

Side 9, Band 2

Listening Guide for the Prelude to Wagner's *Tristan und Isolde*

Timbre:	large orchestra of string, wind, and percussion instruments
Melody:	largely motivic; almost all motives very conjunct
Rhythm:	$\frac{6}{8}$ meter; tempo Langsam und schmachtend (slow and yearning)
Harmony:	very chromatic; suggests keys without strongly confirming them
Texture:	homophonic and contrapuntal
Form:	free, built from repetition of several motives

ROMANTIC OPERA AND CHORAL MUSIC

Wagner's only comedy, *Die Meistersinger von Nürnberg* ("The Master-singers of Nuremberg"), was staged in 1868 in Munich. The opera revolves around the conflict between conservative tradition, embodied by the master-singer guild of the story, and the modern creative attitude toward art. *Die Meistersinger* includes four main arias as well as ballets, choruses, and ensembles. Many of the melodies are derived from folk songs, which Wagner used as symbols of tradition. Typical of his very effective writing is the use of a kind of Baroque contrapuntal style to underscore the traditionalism of the guilds.

The staging of his operas was so important to Wagner that he designed a special theater for their presentation. The theater was built in Bayreuth, Germany, and is still in use today. The large orchestra needed for Wagner's operas—including for one opera eight horns, five tubas, four trumpets, and four trombones, plus strings, woodwinds, and percussion—sat in a huge orchestra pit extending far under the stage. This design made possible a better blend of orchestral sounds and a better balance of singers and orchestra.

Wagner's last opera, *Parsifal*, was completed and performed at Bayreuth the year before he died. The opera concerns the legend of the Holy Grail. The music displays strong emotional intensity, orchestral flair, complicated and subtle harmonies, and extreme chromaticism.

Wagner continued to compose until his death. The many Wagner cultists and, indeed, most of Europe mourned his passing. He had profoundly influenced the culture of his age and at the same time embodied its aspirations, values, and style.

Choral Music in the Romantic Age

The chorus in the nineteenth century, like the orchestra, grew to immense proportions, with some choruses including hundreds of singers. Its newest role was as a participant in works that were chiefly symphonic in nature. The chorus was, in effect, an added element in the timbre of the nineteenth-century symphonic orchestra. Beethoven, Berlioz, Liszt, and Mahler all made use of choruses in this way.

Short Choral Works

Shorter secular works for chorus—often accompanied by piano or small instrumental ensemble—also received a great deal of attention during the Romantic period. Works by Schubert and Brahms, among others, became a part of the growing choral repertoire. Brahms' folk songs are particularly charming.

Large Choral Works

Larger choral works were generally based on traditional types of compositions, mainly the Mass and the oratorio. Beethoven's two long Masses, with soloists, chorus, and orchestra, foreshadowed the later course of Mass composition in many ways. A number of composers followed his lead, writing for even larger groups of performers and expanding their works to ever greater lengths. Berlioz' *Messe des Morts* ("Mass of the Dead") is a monumental work in every way, with an enormous chorus and orchestra, four brass choirs, and many percussion instruments, including sixteen timpani. The music captures the many moods of the text in a very dramatic and colorful fashion.

Many of the Masses written in the nineteenth century were written for the concert hall rather than for the church. Many, in fact, are far too long for use in a church service. In the liturgical texts, particularly in those of the Requiem Mass, composers found a drama and excitement that inspired them to write music quite incompatible with liturgical uses.

The Requiem Mass

The Requiem Mass proved an especially attractive vehicle for a number of Romantic composers. Bruckner and Liszt each wrote one *Requiem*. Brahms wrote *Ein deutsches Requiem* ("A German Requiem"), a work that used not the traditional Latin text, but rather a sequence of psalm paraphrases in German arranged by the composer himself. Highly expressive yet controlled, it is one of the most sincerely hopeful, warmly Romantic religious compositions of the century. In his *Requiem*, Brahms did not resort to bombastic choral and orchestral techniques but relied instead on his mature melodic and harmonic style. Verdi's *Requiem*, unlike Brahms', does make use of the traditional Latin text. The work is very dramatic, filled with great contrasts. The musical style resembles that of the operas of his middle period and seems most fitting for the dramatic text. An especially impressive, highly lyrical *Requiem* was written by Fauré. His work avoids the dramatic mood of so many Romantic *Requiems* and instead offers a sense of contemplation and peace.

Hymns

Notable settings of the *Stabat Mater* text, a thirteenth-century hymn to the Virgin Mary, were also written during the Romantic period. Rossini and Verdi both set the hymn to music, employing soloists, chorus, and orchestra. The text of an even older hymn, *Te Deum laudamus* ("We Praise Thee, O God"), inspired a number of elaborate settings by such composers as Berlioz, Bruckner, and Verdi.

Oratorios

The oratorio found favor with many Romantic composers. Mendelssohn's two oratorios—*Saint Paul* and *Elijah*—are frequently performed today. Another important Romantic oratorio, Berlioz' *L'Enfance du Christ* ("The Childhood of Christ"), is a quietly engaging work that subtly and almost tenderly gives musical expression to the nativity theme.

The increased size of the nineteenth-century choruses and orchestra added greatly to the expressive potential of choral music. Early in the twentieth century, however, a reaction set in. Many composers made drastic reductions in the size of the performing group and in the length of their compositions.

Suggested Listening

French Opera

Berlioz: *Les Troyens à Carthage* ("The Trojans at Carthage") [Philips 6709002]. The subject of this opera is taken from the story of Dido and Aeneas in Virgil's *Aeneid*. The work represents the peak of Berlioz' operatic writing. It includes many of the spectacular elements of grand opera, yet it is tight and convincing, both musically and dramatically.

Italian Opera

Rossini: *Il Barbiere di Siviglia* ("The Barber of Seville") [DG2709041]. In this work Rossini masterfully combined comic drama with vital, appropriate music. The melodies are often highly embellished, and the rhythms are driving and exciting. Especially delightful are the many vocal ensembles presenting simultaneous contrasts of attitude and music.

Verdi: *Aïda* [London 1393]. Based on an Egyptian plot, *Aïda* is one of the finest operas of Verdi's middle years. Drama and music seem perfectly wedded in all the dramatic situations. The music itself ranges from the very tender to the powerfully intense.

Puccini: *Madama Butterfly* [RCA VICS 6100]. Puccini's superb talent for creating beautiful melodies is coupled here with an exotic but very human setting. The story is that of the ill-fated love between a Japanese woman and an American officer. The opera is deservedly one of the composer's most popular works.

German Opera

Weber: *Der Freischütz* ("The Marksman") [Angel S-3748]. This early example of German Romantic opera presents rather ordinary people in extraordinary supernatural circumstances. The melodies are at times suggestive of folk music, while the orchestra is used colorfully for strong, dramatic effects.

Wagner: *Die Meistersinger von Nürnberg* ("The Mastersingers of Nuremberg") [Angel S-3776]. This grand, colorful work is much lighter in spirit and somewhat less chromatic than most of Wagner's other mature operas. Outstanding solos, dramatic choruses, the use of Leitmotivs, and imaginative orchestration contribute to the attractiveness and continuing popularity of the work.

Choral Works

Brahms: *Ein deutsches Requiem* ("A German Requiem") [Angel S-3624] Brahms' use of his own arrangement of German psalm texts in place of the Latin texts makes this *Requiem* unique. The composer's sensitivity to the singing voice and his great skill in orchestral writing contribute much to the memorable quality of the work.

Verdi: *Requiem* [London 1275]. Verdi's fine sense of drama is very apparent in his *Requiem*, one of his most striking compositions. Lyrical and dramatic expression are combined in very effective proportions.

Mendelssohn: *Elijah* [Angel S-3738]. Mendelssohn's *Elijah* is probably the best known and most often performed of all nineteenth-century oratorios. The beautifully written solos and choruses and the interesting orchestral accompaniment have made the work a favorite of many listeners and performers.

CHAPTER

24

Nationalism, Late Romanticism, and Impressionism

Nationalistic Music

National styles of music became quite distinct during the Romantic period. It was a period that saw the unification of Italy and Germany, the spirit of which cannot be missed in the works of Verdi and Wagner. Yet in the operas of these two masters, nationalism is seen more in dramatic content than in the music itself. In other parts of Europe, however, a number of nineteenth-century composers wrote works that reflected their homelands musically as well.

Sources of Nationalistic Music

National contrasts in musical style began as early as 1600. Before that there had been little recognition of distinct, national musical traditions in written music. Most of the new techniques that were developed locally in the pre-Baroque era had tended to be adopted with reasonable speed by the other composers of western Europe.

After 1600, as the spirit of political nationalism grew stronger and more important, distinct national styles became increasingly prominent. The seventeenth-century Italian developments of monody and opera were strongly resisted in France. The French court countered with its own type of opera, a style based on the works of Lully and other French composers. An unprecedented duality arose in Baroque opera, based partly on national awareness. Before long, composers from other countries felt the need to choose between Italian and French methods. In particular, both the Spanish and the Germans tended to imitate the Italian method.

Throughout the seventeenth century, France and Italy were regarded as the primary sources for new music. In the eighteenth century, Germany moved into prominence. The works of the German Baroque composers were, however, still rather international in style, continuing to show certain French or Italian characteristics. It was not until the middle of the century, with the emergence of Haydn as a figure of international importance, that German music gained a strong identity of its own. Mozart and Beethoven soon reinforced the German leadership. By the end of the Classical period, Germany had become the predominant force, especially in instrumental music.

With the Romantic period came an unprecedented nationalism in musical styles. The trend continued into the twentieth century, with rivalries in music and the other arts paralleling political struggles. Nations possessing a strong musical tradition vied with one another for influence, while lesser countries, perhaps even more concerned with national identity, tried to develop their own musical styles. In addition, conflicting and uncertain allegiances led to the appearance of a number of local and regional styles.

Characteristics of Nationalistic Music

The nationalistic music of the Romantic period generally focused upon the presentation of particular sounds characteristic of a nation's or region's folk music. At times, this could be accomplished by stressing a single musical element—melody or rhythm, for example. More often, however, several musical elements were combined to create the particular national flavor desired.

Folk Melodies

As might be expected, the melodies of nationalistic music were commonly inspired by folk songs. The composers of earlier ages, especially the composers of the Baroque age, had generally ignored peasant music or at best had parodied it. Romantic composers, however, found that the once-slighted music possessed certain qualities that could readily be used to create national styles. Among the most significant of these qualities was the use of unusual intervals, short phrases, and a relatively narrow range. Brahms, Grieg, and Mussorgsky were only a few of the many composers who made liberal and adventurous use of the folk melodies of their respective lands.

Unusual Rhythms

Romantic composers also experimented with rhythm, foreshadowing the twentieth-century desire for rhythmic excitement. Intrigued by unusual folk-song rhythms, nineteenth-century composers sometimes wrote in highly irregular meters. Composers also tried to capture the infectious energy of many folk songs, especially those associated with dance music. The native music of Spain was particularly noted for its dancelike qualities.

Changes in Harmony

Harmony, already a major preoccupation of nineteenth-century composers, was greatly affected by the new interest in folk music. When scholars and composers began the serious study of peasant works, they soon found that the harmonies of many songs were far from simple. Scales and harmonic progressions often departed from accepted norms. Experimenting with these characteristics, a number of composers developed new scales quite different from the traditional scales of the major and minor modes. Throughout Europe the search for new national idioms led composers to cast aside many time-honored rules of progression and dissonance and to replace them with novel harmonic processes.

Nationalistic Music in Russia

The currents of nationalism flowed with peculiar strength in Russia. Long isolated from the rest of Europe by distance and the centuries of Tatar domination, Russia had developed quite differently from the West. Peter the

Great and some of his eighteenth-century successors, impressed by Western science and military power, tried to make up for lost time, imposing Western ways by imperial fiat. But in so doing, they sowed the seeds of deep division within Russia itself. A long ideological struggle began between those who believed that Russia's only hope lay in Westernization and those who rejected such Westernization as a betrayal of the nation's soul. In the nineteenth century, the conflict became acute. Music and literature were among the chief battlegrounds.

Glinka

Mikhail Glinka (1804–1857) was one of the earliest composers of Russian nationalist music. As a young man, he visited western Europe, where he heard the works of Mozart and Beethoven and became enthralled with Italian opera. Returning to Russia in 1834, he began a serious career as a composer. Although he wrote a number of orchestral pieces and chamber works, his best-known and most influential works were his two operas, *A Life for the Czar* and *Russlan and Ludmila*.

Glinka's *A Life for the Czar*, first presented in 1836, follows the grand opera of France very closely in style and development. Innovative aspects are found, however, in the choral numbers and dance scenes, both of which use Russian folk melodies and rhythms to portray peasant life. The introduction and the finale are folk choruses, suggesting that Glinka intended his first opera to express the heroism and devotion of all Russians rather than of a single hero.

Glinka's next opera, *Russlan and Ludmila*, was based on a fairy-tale romance by the Russian poet Alexander Pushkin. Like his preceding opera, *Russlan and Ludmila* is made up of a succession of fanciful and often disconnected scenes framed by two great folk choruses. However, the new opera differed from the preceding one in its even greater use of folk material, employing a wide variety of dances, melodies, and rhythms.

The Russian Five

After Glinka a group of younger composers, sometimes called "The Russian Five," tried to give musical expression to their intense national feelings. Mily Balakirev, César Cui, Alexander Borodin, Modest Mussorgsky, and Nikolai Rimsky-Korsakov were united more by their opposition to Western idioms than by any common style. Other Russian composers, Rubinstein and Tchaikovsky among them, had adopted the mainstream French, Italian, and German styles as their own. The Five saw this leaning to the West as a danger to be resisted.

Mussorgsky

In many ways the most important composer of the Five, and certainly the most original, was Modest Mussorgsky (1839–1881). The only one of the Five never to visit the West or even to leave Russia, Mussorgsky identified strongly with the peasants of his native land. He also took great interest in Russian folklore. In the course of a short, rather Bohemian life in Saint Petersburg, Mussorgsky wrote a number of different types of works, the most successful of which were his songs and operas. Striving for a realistic rendering of human speech in music, Mussorgsky wrote works of unprecedented dramatic quality. Through the use of complex phrasing and meters, he was able to represent character and feeling with unusual vividness. The result was a new musical language dominated by speech, declamatory rather than lyrical.

Music in Tsarist Russia: *Saint Petersburg, Russia's gateway to the West, was a major center of the music controversy between nationalists and Westernizers—a controversy that escalated with the establishment of Rubinstein's "international" conservatory in 1862.*

Of his *Boris Godunov*, one of the great operas of the nineteenth century, Mussorgsky wrote: "I explore human speech; thus I arrive at the melody created by this kind of speech, arrive at the embodiment of recitative in melody. . . . One might call this a melody justified by sense." Linking his melodies closely to character and situation, Mussorgsky constructed a work that is both a psychological drama of guilt and conscience and an epic of his nation's destiny. To his speechlike melody he added bold dissonances and adventurous harmonies. Another striking effect was the dramatic contrast created when sustained low tones were played under harmonically active passages in the upper register. Rimsky-Korsakov made an extensive revision of Mussorgsky's *Boris Godunov*, and for years his version was the one heard most often. Today, however, the merits of Mussorgsky's own work are once again recognized.

Mussorgsky: *Pictures at an Exhibition*

**Ravel's
Orchestration**

Structure

Pictures at an Exhibition was originally written for piano but is best known in a version orchestrated later by the French composer Maurice Ravel (1875–1937). The music is based on an exhibition of paintings by the Russian artist and architect Victor Hartmann, a friend of Mussorgsky. A kaleidoscope of piano colors, massive chords, and a wide range convey the many different emotions evoked by the paintings. The work, a succession of movements each relating to a specific painting, is an excellent example of program music inspired by the visual arts. At the beginning of the work and between a number of the movements, the "Promenade" is heard. Acting as a sort of musical excursion between paintings, it constitutes yet another programmatic aspect of the work.

"Promenade"

The "Promenade" is based on a theme that is typically Russian in its harmonic suggestions and frequent changes of meter:

Theme of the "Promenade"

The score is even marked Allegro giusto, nel modo russo ("at a fast but fitting tempo, in the Russian manner"). The theme is repeated and extended several times throughout the brief "Promenade." Texture varies considerably from the single voice that first presents the theme to the dense harmonization of it that is heard later and repeated several times.

Side 9, Band 3

Listening Guide for "Promenade" from Mussorgsky's *Pictures at an Exhibition*

Timbre:	very large orchestra of string, wind, and percussion instruments (the work was originally written for piano)
Melody:	main theme rather disjunct
Rhythm:	changing meter; tempo Allegro giusto (fast but fitting)
Harmony:	major mode; begins in B♭ major, modulates to F major, ends in B♭ major
Texture:	monophonic and homophonic
Form:	first theme evolves into other thematic material, then returns at the end

---

"Gnomus"

The first episode of Mussorgsky's *Pictures at an Exhibition* is a movement entitled "Gnomus," after a painting of a limping dwarf. The music is characterized by rapid changes in rhythmic motion, chromatic harmony, ambiguity of key, and the minor mode. The opening seven-note motive, with its abrupt, wide-interval skips, is suggestive of the dwarf's jerky gait. The motive returns several times during the movement and is contrasted with a number of secondary motives and themes.

NATIONALISM, LATE ROMANTICISM, AND IMPRESSIONISM

Listening Guide for "Gnomus" from Mussorgsky's *Pictures at an Exhibition*

Timbre:	very large orchestra of string, wind, and percussion instruments
Melody:	several different motives and themes; the first motive is very disjunct; other motives vary from conjunct to disjunct
Rhythm:	triple and duple meters; tempo Allegro vivo (fast and lively), slowing down in some sections
Harmony:	minor mode; basically E♭ minor with much chromaticism
Texture:	mainly homophonic
Form:	free rondo, with the opening motive returning several times

Other Movements

A wide variety of images are suggested in the titles of the remaining movements: "The Old Castle," "Tuileries," "Bydlo" (a Polish oxcart), "Ballet of the Unhatched Chicks," "Two Polish Jews, One Rich, One Poor," "The Market at Limoges," "Catacombs," "The Hut on Fowl's Legs," and "The Great Gate of Kiev." The final movement, based on Hartmann's design for the city gates of the ancient capital of the Ukraine, is the most grandiose of all. Its music seems to capture the spirit of Russian tradition.

Use of the Orchestra

Ravel's orchestration of Mussorgsky's piano work was particularly brilliant. He used an extremely large orchestra in order to capture the contrasts in the original score. The woodwind section alone is made up of a piccolo, two flutes, two oboes, an English horn, two clarinets, a bass clarinet, two bassoons, and a contrabassoon. Such an orchestra allows a range of dynamics, timbres, and textures that is strikingly impressive.

Nationalistic Music in Other Parts of Europe

Russia was not the only country to seek a musical language for its national aspirations. Here we will examine nationalistic movements in four other parts of Europe—Bohemia, Spain, England, and Scandinavia.

The Music of Bohemia

Bohemia, a predominantly Czech region, had once been an independent kingdom but in the nineteenth century was merely a province of the great Austro-Hungarian Empire. Restive under what they increasingly regarded as foreign domination, the Czechs began to take an interest in their native music as a form of artistic expression. The first collection of Czech folk songs was published in the 1820s, and the earliest Czech opera was presented in 1826.

Czech peasant music was somewhat more like conventional Western music in rhythm and harmony than were the folk songs of Russia. Nevertheless, the music offered definite possibilities as the basis for a distinctive art music. The composer who first perfected the union of native Czech music with the traditional art music of western Europe was Bedřich Smetana (1824–1884). Many of his works are, like Wagner's and Verdi's, nationalistic in choice of

Smetana

subject matter rather than in the use of peasant materials. His comic opera *The Bartered Bride* (1866), which later became the Czech national opera, does not include any folk songs at all. The opera does, however, deal with village characters and peasant life. It contains numerous choral and dance numbers, such as polkas and furiants, with a pronounced Czech flavor, but the rhythmic, harmonic, and melodic style is largely Western.

Smetana's early symphonic works were very much influenced by Liszt, but late in his career, he wrote an original cycle of six symphonic poems called *Má Vlast* ("My Native Land"). Like his operas, these six works applied traditional methods of construction to the goal of creating a truly national music. The cycle, most famous for the second poem "Vltava" ("The Moldau"), named for one of the country's main rivers, was conceived as an epic of the Czech people.

Dvořák

Another Czech composer, Antonin Dvořák (1841–1904), made much greater use of native folk music. Influenced in many ways by Brahms, Dvořák blended the traditional rhythms and colors of Western music with those of Slavic dances and songs. His *Quartet, Op. 96*, for example, makes use of the pentatonic, or five-note, scale he discovered in folk music. His first set of *Slavonic Dances* (1878) aroused a general European interest in the peasant tradition even though all the melodies were in fact his own. His second set of *Slavonic Dances* (1886) is particularly distinguished for its countermelodies and colorful orchestration. In his *Gypsy Songs, Op. 55*, Dvořák produced yet another work based on folk music, with many of the melodies held together by dancelike rhythms. The fourth song in *Op. 55* is the familiar "Songs My Mother Taught Me."

The Music of Spain

Toward the end of the nineteenth century, there was a revival of interest in traditional Spanish music, again associated with a renewed interest in national folk songs and dances. Isaac Albéniz (1860–1909), the first important figure in the movement, began as a composer of light Romantic music. However, a period of residence in Paris heightened his awareness of the music of his native land. Between 1906 and 1909, he wrote a collection of twelve piano pieces called *Iberia* that achieved remarkable effects in their idealization of traditional Spanish dances. Each of the pieces alternates a dance rhythm with a vocal refrain to evoke the spirit of a particular place in Spain. *Iberia* does show the influence of non-Spanish composers. Yet some aspects of the music are so reminiscent of that quintessentially Spanish instrument, the guitar, as to leave no doubt where Albéniz' heart really lay.

Albéniz

Falla

Another composer who looked to the Spanish musical heritage was Manuel de Falla (1876–1946). In his *Nights in the Gardens of Spain*, a composition for piano and orchestra, Falla endeavored to evoke the very spirit of his native land. Much of the music is derived from the rhythms, modes, and ornamentations of Andalusian Spain. The work is often considered to be a group of tone poems although the movements have no program beyond their brief titles. In a later work, a concerto, Falla mixed Spanish folk songs, Medieval liturgical music, Renaissance polyphony, and eighteenth-century popular music in order to represent the musical history of Spain. Of all his works, though, perhaps the best known to Americans is *The Three-Cornered Hat*, a ballet based on a witty tale of a philandering official and a virtuous peasant wife.

The Music of England

Elgar

In the late nineteenth century, a number of English composers, most notably Edward Elgar (1857–1934), brought their country back to a degree of importance in musical composition. They did not at first achieve a clearly defined English style. Elgar's *Enigma Variations* and his famous *Pomp and Circumstance March* closely resemble the Romantic German compositions of Richard Strauss.

Vaughan Williams

With the early twentieth-century works of Ralph Vaughan Williams (1872–1958), however, England could finally boast of a serious composer who tried to shape native materials into a contemporary style. In a book called *National Music* (1934), Vaughan Williams wrote: "Art, like charity, should begin at home. If it is to be of any value it must grow out of the very life of [the composer] himself, the community in which he lives, the nation to which he belongs." Thus Vaughan Williams sought in English folk music a source of inspiration for his own music. He worked as both a collector and a harmonizer of folk tunes, often building entire movements out of melodic lines rooted in folk song. He did this by avoiding the use of counterpoint, traditional modulations, and motivic development. Instead he used unusual and parallel chord progressions and a basically homophonic texture.

Among the works by Vaughan Williams that depend most clearly on folk elements is the *English Folk Song Suite*, written for band and later arranged for orchestra. The composition differs from most such works in that it avoids dance tunes entirely. Another popular work by Vaughan Williams is *Fantasia on Greensleeves*. Based on the well-known English melody, it was originally an interlude in the opera *Sir John in Love*.

The Music of Scandinavia

Grieg

The Norwegian composer Edvard Grieg (1843–1907), after early attempts at writing in the German symphonic style, became a leading figure of the nationalistic movement in Scandinavia. His interest in creating truly Norwegian music is very much apparent in his two *Peer Gynt Suites* (1876), which were originally presented as incidental music for Ibsen's drama about the adventures of a young Norwegian peasant. The well-known section "In the Hall of the Mountain King" dramatically exemplifies the energy of Grieg's music.

Grieg was also a master of songs and short piano pieces. In both types of compositions, he used techniques characteristic of Norwegian peasant music.

His scales often waver between major and minor, with frequent pentatonic tendencies—qualities clearly derived from Norwegian folk music. His *Lyric Pieces*, a series of short works for piano, demonstrate his ability to create typical "Norwegian" effects through the use of folklike tunes and harmonies. The subject matter of many of his works also reflects his love for his native culture.

Sibelius

One of the most important nationalist composers of the late nineteenth and early twentieth centuries was Jean Sibelius (1865–1957) of Finland. In his earliest works, Sibelius adopted a Scandinavian rather than a specifically Finnish outlook. Encouraged by a group of artists around him, however, Sibelius developed an intense interest in the *Kalevala*, the main body of Finnish myth and folklore. It was folklore, not folk music, that was to prove the main inspiration for his nationalistic works. In the years that followed, he made very little direct use of the techniques or melodies of Finnish folk music in his own compositions. Yet the *Kalevala* myths inspired him to create his own unique mythological-romantic style—a style that incorporated much of the color and ambiance of Finnish folk music.

Sibelius's symphonic poems probably reveal, better than any of his other works, his deep commitment to Finnish mythology. At the age of twenty-seven, he presented his first major symphonic poem, *Kullervo*, for soloists, chorus, and orchestra. A long work in five sections, rich in contrasting moods and timbres, it is patterned rather roughly on the life of Kullervo, one of the *Kalevala* heroes. Another symphonic poem, *En Saga*, was presented in its final revised form in 1901. Without a program and intended merely to suggest the atmosphere of Nordic sagas, *En Saga* mixed melodic diversity with an unusual harmonic liberty. Although, like many of Sibelius's other works, *En Saga* was not clearly set in any standard form, it does suggest certain aspects of sonata form and is distinguished for the variety of its orchestration.

Sibelius: *Finlandia*

In 1899, when Finland was still under the domination of the Russian Empire, the Finns undertook a great patriotic celebration to support the freedom of their press, which they felt to be endangered. Included in the festival was a series of "Tableaux from the Past" depicting six crucial scenes in the history of the Finnish people. Sibelius provided an extensive musical accompaniment, the finale of which received no special attention at the time but later achieved fame under the title *Finlandia*. Probably his most popular composition, *Finlandia* is a work of great fervor, power, and energy. Contrasts of theme, rhythm, and key distinguish the various sections. The first section seems to express the unrest of Finland under a hated foreign rule. The last section, notable for its hymnlike melody, became a rallying song for the nationalistic aspirations of the Finnish people.

Beginning of Last Section:

NATIONALISM, LATE ROMANTICISM, AND IMPRESSIONISM

Late Romanticism

Musically the late nineteenth century was marked by a number of conflicting tendencies. As we have seen, there were composers in all parts of Europe who were seeking particularly nationalistic styles. The nationalistic aspirations, in and of themselves, were not contrary to Romanticism. But much of the music created was an abandonment of the true Romantic style. And, as we shall soon see, a number of other composers were also seeking new styles, not for nationalistic reasons, but rather because they believed new means of expression were needed.

Not all composers, however, were ready to forsake the Romantic style. As the nineteenth century drew to an end and the twentieth began, characteristics recognized as Romantic remained prominent in the works of many composers, especially in the works of German composers. This late Romantic, or post-Romantic, style can be traced, to some degree, down to our own day.

Late Romanticism in Germany

In the works of the late Romantic composers of Germany—Wagner, Mahler, and Richard Strauss—the Romantic impulse became intensified and exaggerated. For some time subjective expressiveness, freed from many Classical restraints, had been leading to the expansion of orchestral size and variety and consequently to a denser texture. Also prominent in the late Romantic style were innovative harmony and the lengthening of traditional types of compositions such as the symphony. Lyrical melody and rhythmic variety remained important, as did the early Romantic custom of looking to literature and the visual arts for inspiration.

Influence of Wagner

A number of German composers continued to build extensively on mid-nineteenth-century harmonic practices. Many followed Wagner in placing particular stress on chromaticism. Some, in fact, saw the use of chromaticism as the only way to develop fresh sounds in musical language.

Mahler's Symphonies

Gustav Mahler, whose Lieder with orchestral accompaniment were discussed in Chapter 20, is perhaps best known for his nine symphonies. The symphonies were written for an orchestra that was large even by Romantic standards. Wind instruments are numerous and prominent in Mahler's symphonies, while solo voices and choruses often add interest and variety in timbre. In Mahler's *Symphony No. 8 in E♭ Major* (the "Symphony of a Thousand"), a work written in 1906 and 1907, two choruses and eight soloists augment the extremely large orchestra. The symphony is in two long movements, the first based on the Medieval hymn "Veni creator spiritus" ("Come, Holy Spirit") and the second on the ending of Goethe's *Faust*. A vast array of themes and timbres create effects ranging from subtle to bombastic. Simple songlike passages written in a single key are often juxtaposed with others that are extremely chromatic.

Strauss's Operas

Richard Strauss, noted not only for his symphonic poems but also for his operas, followed in the tradition of Wagner. His works show a familiarity with

Classical and earlier Romantic techniques, but his writing, like Mahler's, expands in all directions beyond them. In opera, particularly in *Salome* (1905), he wrote luxurious, chromatic counterpoint for a very large orchestra. His mixture of chromatic and nonchromatic harmony produced spectacular effects. In some of his later works, he expanded chromaticism almost to the point of denying the major-minor system entirely.

Schoenberg

The early works of Arnold Schoenberg (1874–1951) belong very much to the late Romantic movement. Schoenberg wrote in a contrapuntal, chromatic style and easily rivaled Wagner and Strauss in his expressive ambition. His *Gurrelieder* ("Songs of Gurre"), for example, calls for a huge orchestra, six soloists, and four choruses. The prominence of chromaticism in the *Gurrelieder* points toward Schoenberg's later efforts to develop an entirely new harmonic system—the twelve-tone serial technique, which will be discussed in Chapter 27.

Late Romanticism Outside of Germany

Fauré

Romantic styles continued to be developed by composers in other countries as well. In France the works of Gabriel Fauré (1845–1924), though somewhat more restrained than the works of the late Romantic composers in Germany, nevertheless seemed to embody the spirit of French Romanticism. His songs, his *Requiem Mass*, and his instrumental works all show his great skill in creating lovely, singable melodies accompanied by subtle chromatic harmony.

Rachmaninoff and Scriabin

Composers in Russia, including some already discussed as nationalists, were also part of the late Romantic tradition. Sergei Rachmaninoff (1873–1943) continued a strongly Romantic style, especially in his piano concertos. Alexander Scriabin (1872–1915), on the other hand, was among the most progressive of late nineteenth-century Russian composers. His compositions blend earlier Romantic forms and techniques with a harmony that often forsakes triadic and major-minor structures.

Sibelius and MacDowell

Composers in many other countries also espoused a late Romantic style. Sibelius's symphonies and his *Finlandia* are prominent instances. In the United States, Edward MacDowell (1861–1908) was perhaps the most important of a group of late Romantic composers. His *Woodland Sketches* are still known to many piano students, and his piano concertos are occasionally heard in concert.

Beyond Romanticism

As we have seen, chromaticism, used with ever greater freedom within the major-minor system of harmony, was one of the most important aspects of style among late Romantic composers. Two general lines of development from it can be observed in music about 1900. Many composers continued, even down to the present, to use some type of major-minor harmony in free and imaginative ways. Others, beginning in the last decades of the nineteenth century, rejected the system and worked out new means of harmonic expression. One of the earliest and most influential of the composers who rejected previous tradition was Debussy, the main figure in the development of the Impressionist style of music.

Impressionism

Impressionist Paintings

The term *Impressionism*, now a respectable label for one of the most significant artistic movements of modern times, was first applied in derision to the work of a group of avant-garde painters. The revolutionary style of painting found in the works of Monet, Manet, Renoir, and others emphasized the play of light on a subject, using diffused outlines and subtly interwoven colors to suggest sentiments and moods. This fascination with light led to a preference for outdoor themes shaped and shaded by the changing sunlight at different seasons and different times of day.

Symbolist Poetry

The literary counterpart of Impressionist painting was the Symbolist movement in French poetry. Led by Mallarmé, Verlaine, Rimbaud, and the Belgian Maeterlinck, it repudiated the moralism, sentimentality, and literalness it found in late Romanticism. Advocating a kind of return to nature, Symbolist poets delighted in atmosphere and nuance, shading their landscapes indistinctly in the manner of the Impressionist painters. They wanted readers to sense the emotion in their poetry, not be told about it. Their verses deliver their meaning subtly and with only the vaguest of assertions, relying on sound and metaphor rather than on definable meaning. Using words and phrases designed to arouse subconscious feelings, the Symbolists allowed no technical restrictions to interfere with the achievement of their goals. Traditional poetic forms and styles were often sketched, broken, or replaced by ambiguous, irregular structures.

Impressionism in Music

Debussy

The composer who above all epitomizes Impressionism in music is Claude Debussy (1862–1918). It was one of his early works—a cantata entitled *La Damoiselle élue* ("The Blessed Damoiselle")—that first drew the label of Impressionism to music. It was Debussy's mature work, however, that not only demonstrated but largely determined the very nature of Impressionism in music.

Debussy himself disliked the label "Impressionist" for his music, since he was not trying to imitate the Impressionist painters. Instead he was attempting to set French music free from the heaviness and formalism he perceived in the dominant German tradition. He wanted to return French music to its fundamental sources in nature—to allow it to find once again its own lighter, freer genius and express what he felt it was best fitted to express. In this sense he could almost be called a nationalist. And indeed he learned a great deal from the Russian nationalists who were his contemporaries, though he rejected their strongly folk-oriented style. His most immediate associations were perhaps with the Symbolist poets, whose subject matter he often used.

Nonetheless, Debussy and the composers he influenced had much in

The Master of Impressionism: *Like the early Romantics, Debussy was fascinated by the interrelationship of all the arts and found inspiration in both poetry and painting as well as in nature, earlier French masterpieces, and the exotic music of the East. He is shown here at the keyboard.*

common with the Impressionist painters. Like the painters, they sought to appeal to the senses rather than the intellect of their audiences. While Romantic music had generally tried to express well-defined emotions or ideas, the style developed by Debussy was more understated and less specific. Although Debussy used many Romantic devices—suggestive titles, colorful and changing timbres, motivic melodies—he used them in more subtle ways. The result was a diffused sense of musical color and motion analogous to the luminous outlines and the play of light and color in Impressionist painting. In fact, some of the favorite images of the new painters—moving water, rustling leaves—lent themselves readily to Impressionist treatment in music.

Impressionist music is in many ways more difficult to define than earlier styles of music. Although Debussy himself had a clear goal in view, he deliberately tried to avoid falling into any predictable patterns. Above all he insisted on the freedom to use whatever compositional devices might best serve the needs of his current subject. Not all of Debussy's music is considered Impressionist. And those qualities that are considered Impressionist change significantly from piece to piece because the composer never ceased experimenting with new material and absorbing new influences.

Influence of Nature

Certainly one major influence on Debussy's music was his great love of nature. The relationship he saw between nature and music is perhaps best expressed in his own words:

> I can imagine a music specially designed for the open air, all on big lines, with daring instrumental and vocal effects which would have full play in the open and soar joyfully to the treetops. Certain harmonic progressions which sound abnormal within the four walls of a concert hall would surely find their true value in the open air. Perhaps this might be a means of doing away with these little affectations of over-precision in form and tonality which so encumber music.

In a way, this sounds very close to some aspects of the early Romantic ideal. But the direction Romanticism had taken in its later years was as unacceptable to Debussy as was the passionate, often unlovely realism that had grown from it. Rejecting the overt realism of novelists such as Flaubert and Zola and their direct identification of art with life, he rejected also the programmatic explicitness and overpowering sound of Berlioz and Wagner. He created instead an evanescent world of suggestion, delicately hinted at rather than boldly portrayed.

Debussy's melodies differ markedly from the strong, broadly articulated themes of his immediate predecessors. Instead, his melodies are generally built from short motives of narrow range freely combined and often repeated.

The beat in Debussy's music is often veiled by the use of syncopation and irregular subdivisions of measures. Rhythms thus seem to flow across metrical boundaries. This indistinctness of meter contributes greatly to the desired effect of understatement and suggestiveness. In other works, however, Debussy used a clear, pulsing beat or, at times, the rhythm of some exotic dance.

Harmonic Innovation

Harmony, though, was the chief means by which Debussy achieved his effects. His use of harmony was perhaps his most revolutionary departure from traditional practice. While Classical and earlier Romantic composers had treated chords as functional elements in a harmonic progression, Debussy and the Impressionists came to regard the expressiveness of a chord as separate from its context. The effect of a chord became an end in itself. If a certain chord seemed particularly striking, it might be repeated up and down the staff in the kind of parallel motion that had been specifically forbidden in the harmony of the previous centuries. The *gliding chords* that became typical in Impressionist harmony can be seen below in a passage from Debussy's *Soirée dans Grenade* ("Evening in Grenada"):

Gliding Chords

By use of the gliding chord and other similar techniques, Debussy weakened the traditional pull to the tonic note. He also introduced a number of other daring new combinations of tones—chords spanning intervals of nine, eleven, and even thirteen notes—which added greatly to the sense of dissonance. Debussy's opera *Pelléas et Mélisande* made such great use of ninth chords that it has been called the "land of the ninths."

Debussy's harmony is also distinguished by the variety of scales he used. He is particularly identified with the *whole-tone scale*, which he found in the works of some of his predecessors and contemporaries and in the music of the Far East and made peculiarly his own. The scale divides the octave into six whole-step intervals rather than the seven half- and whole-step intervals of the conventional Western scale:

Whole-Tone Scale

Lacking the half steps of the conventional scale, the whole-tone scale is limited in expressive scope. But it is especially suitable if the composer is seeking to escape from the dramatic pull of major-minor tonality. Whole-tone harmony has a muted, ambiguous quality that greatly suited Debussy's purposes. He employed it often and quite imaginatively.

Debussy also used the old Medieval Church modes and the pentatonic, or five-note, scale common in Chinese music and in some Western folk music. The chromaticism that had already become widespread in late Romantic music is likewise important in his work. In his desire to avoid predictability, however, he seldom depended completely on any one of these scales. In many of his works, he shifted back and forth among different scales in order to get just the tonal color he wanted.

The effect of Debussy's harmonic practice was not to destroy the concept of key but to expand it. In his works a new standard of consonance and dissonance evolved. Dissonance often went unresolved, and even a final cadence might be merely less dissonant than the chords that preceded it. A key was no longer a defined area in harmonic space with clearly identifiable boundaries. Instead it became an elusive entity, sensed as just a little bit out of reach but still somehow exerting an influence on the music.

Debussy's music is seldom explicitly contrapuntal, though occasional countermelodies do rise briefly out of the underlying chords. His fondness for parallel motion and gliding chords make for a generally homophonic style. At times, however, broken chords and other techniques are used to create a complex and lively polyphony. And at other times monophonic passages are heard, focusing the music temporarily into a clear, pure line.

*Changes in
Timbre*

Debussy and his followers often composed for large orchestras, but they rarely sought the powerful, overwhelming effects of late Romanticism. Rather, the orchestral sound was veiled, and individual timbres were made to stand out delicately against it—the somber lower-register tones of flute and clarinet, the clear high notes of the violin, the muted voices of horn and trumpet. There were numerous solo passages for flute, oboe, and English horn. The harp was often featured, alone or with other instruments. And diverse percussion instruments—timpani, cymbals, glockenspiel, celesta, xylophone, and so on—added color to the orchestral sound. Debussy was also a highly accomplished pianist. His writing for piano makes sensitive use of the instrument's broad range of colors and effects.

Freer Forms

Debussy disliked being bound by traditional forms and sought new, more flexible patterns. He believed that form should arise out of the subject matter of a work instead of being, in the older fashion, imposed upon it. In his larger works, he sometimes made general use of Classical structures, but always with much freedom, introducing motives and returning to them in obedience to the flow of musical ideas rather than according to preset patterns. While it is possible to discern the presence of contrasting sections in these works, the beginnings and endings of sections often overlap. Thus, in form as in all other elements of his music, Debussy tried to replace sharp definition and conclusive statement with suggestion and ambiguity. He wished to leave his listeners not with an answer but with an impression.

Debussy: *Prélude à l'après-midi d'un faune*

In 1892 Debussy began work on a composition inspired by Stéphane Mallarmé's long poem *L'Après-midi d'un faune* ("The Afternoon of a Faun"). Although Debussy intended to make his composition a full-length work, only the prelude was completed. The opening lines of the poem set the mood as the faun, light-footed and magical in his human shape with tiny horns and small goat feet, contemplates the airy nymphs:

Ces nymphes, je les veux perpétuer.
  Si clair,
 Leur incarnat léger, qu'il voltige
  dans l'air
 Assoupi de sommeils touffus.
  Aimai-je un rêve?
 Mon doute, amas de nuit ancienne,
  s'achève
 En maint rameau subtil, qui,
  de meuré les vrais
 Bois mêmes, prouve, hélas! que bien
  seul je m'offrais
 Pour triomphe la faute idéale de
  roses
 Réfléchissons . . .
  ou si les femmes dont tu
 gloses
 Figurent un souhait de tas sens
  fabuleux!
 Faune, l'illusion s'échappe des yeux
  bleus
	These nymphs I would perpetuate.
	  So light
	 their gossamer embodiment, floating
	  on the air
	 inert with heavy slumber.
	  Was it a dream I loved?
	 My doubting, harvest of the bygone
	  night, concludes
	 in countless tiny branches; together
	  remaining
	 a whole forest they prove, alas, that
	  since I am alone,
	 my fancied triumph was but the
	  ideal imperfection of roses.
	 Let us reflect . . .
	  or suppose those women that
	 you idolize
	 were but imaginings of your
	  fantastic lust!
	 Faun, the illusion flows from the
	  blue eyes,

Et froids, comme une source en pleurs, de la plus chaste:	icy as a spring of tears, of the one more chaste.
Mais, l'autre tout soupirs, dis-tu qu'elle contraste	But that other one, all sighs, do you say she is different,
Comme brise du jour chaude dans ta toison?	like a warm day's breeze ruffling in your fleece?
Que non! par l'immobile et lasse pâmoison	Ah, no! Through the motionless, oppressive swoon
Suffoquant de chaleurs le matin frais s'il lutte,	that chokes with heat the cool morning if it struggles
Ne murmure point d'eau que ne verse ma flûte	no water flows save that which spills from my flute
Au bosquet arrosé d'accords; et le seul vent	onto the harmony-sprinkled thicket; and the only wind,
Hors des deux tuyaux prompt à s'exhaler avant	quick to breathe out through the twin pipes before
Qu'il disperse le son dans une pluie aride,	scattering the sound in a dry rain,
C'est, à l'horizon pas remué d'une ride,	appears on the still horizon like the seen, serene, and artificial breath
Le visible et serein souffle artificiel	
De l'inspiration, qui regagne le ciel.	of inspiration, returning heavenward.

First Section Debussy's *Prélude* is scored for three flutes, two oboes, an English horn, two clarinets, four horns, cymbals, two harps, and strings. A solo flute presents the first theme—a theme made up of several juxtaposed motives:

First Theme

p *douce et expressif*

Harps, wind instruments, and muted strings enter to mark the end of the flute theme. The theme is then repeated and ornamented with irregular subdivisions of beats. This rhythmic irregularity, coupled with rather frequent changes in meter, creates a vague sense of beat and an easy, fluid rhythmic flow. Through much of the work, the strings are divided—the viola section, for example, is given two lines to play at the same time rather than just one. This division helps create a dense texture, but the dynamic level is generally low and the strings are often muted, so the effect is never overpowering. The prominence of flute and harp aptly reinforces the summery, rural quality of the work.

Harmony is quite chromatic, as can be seen in the accidentals of the first theme. The listener, however, is not strongly aware of dissonance because of the subtle nature of the music. While Debussy has clearly tried to avoid strong commitment to a particular key, there is nevertheless an emphasis on one note as the tonal center most of the time.

Middle Section

A contrasting middle section is introduced by a new theme in the woodwinds supported by a syncopated chordal accompaniment in the strings:

Second Theme

expressif et très soutenu

The theme is extended with numerous changing and conflicting rhythms.

Last Section

The first theme then returns in a completely new setting. Its extension is also different from what it was when first heard.

While the work fits into a generally ternary pattern, the listener is much more aware of the use of timbre, motive, and rhythm than of any formal structure. In all, the *Prélude* is a masterpiece of nuance and subtle understatement.

Side 9, Band 4

Listening Guide for Debussy's *Prélude à l'après-midi d'un faune*

Timbre:	large orchestra of string instruments, wind instruments, and cymbals
Melody:	opening theme, which is built from several motives, is most prominent; second theme features descending motion
Rhythm:	basic 8 meter with some changes; moderately slow tempo
Harmony:	very chromatic with no strong feeling of tonal center
Texture:	homophonic
Form:	free ternary (ABA¹)

Debussy's innovative *Prélude* later provided inspiration for an equally innovative ballet. The work was first choreographed by the great Russian dancer Waslaw Nijinsky, who substituted stylized, two-dimensional movements reminiscent of a Greek frieze in place of the ordinary ballet steps. Like the music, the ballet was received with mixed feelings. Nijinsky's more conservative fellow choreographer Michel Fokine could scarcely bear to watch it.

Other Works by Debussy

Among Debussy's other Impressionist works are the *Suite bergamasque* (which includes his famous "Clair de lune") and a number of preludes for piano, three nocturnes and *La Mer* ("The Sea") for orchestra, the opera *Pelléas et Mélisande*, a string quartet, and several songs.

Debussy died in 1918, a victim of cancer. In his own lifetime, he was recognized as a composer of singular importance. He was admired throughout Europe for his almost Classical restraint and sense of proportion—qualities not always shared by the many composers who imitated his style. He probably did more than anyone else to shift the center of musical attention away from Germany and Austria. His work may readily be said to mark the end of the Romantic style and the opening of a new age.

Other Impressionist Composers

Many of Debussy's contemporaries were also experimenting with the elements of music. It is in fact not always easy to decide which of them were influenced by Debussy and which were making their own independent discoveries. Debussy certainly exercised great influence over the music of his day and, for that matter, over that of succeeding generations. But few other leading composers were simply followers of Debussy. Rather they learned from him, incorporated elements of his style, and made their own syntheses.

Ravel, Respighi, Delius, and Scriabin

Maurice Ravel (1875–1937), Debussy's younger French contemporary, used an Impressionist style in his ballet *Daphnis et Chloé*. Composers elsewhere used many of the same techniques, as did, for example, the Italian composer Ottorino Respighi (1879–1936) in his *Fountains of Rome*. Frederick Delius (1862–1934) in England and Alexander Scriabin (1872–1915) in Russia were among the many others who at times shared the Impressionist spirit.

Suggested Listening

Nationalistic Music

Mussorgsky: "Coronation Scene" from *Boris Godunov* [Melodiya/Angel S-40049]. The splendor and pageantry of early seventeenth-century Russia are magnificently portrayed in this scene, as Boris is crowned Czar of All the Russias. The brilliant use of chorus and orchestra, the vibrant bass voice of Boris, and the colorful costumes and scenery make this one of the most spectacular scenes in opera.

Dvořák: *Slavonic Dances* [DG 138080]. Dvořák's dances use a variety of characteristically Slavic dance rhythms and are imbued with the spirit of old Bohemia. The influence of Classical style on Dvořák can be heard in the clear, contrasting sections of the dances.

Albéniz: "Triana" from *Iberia* [Piano: London 2235; orchestra: Nonesuch 71189]. The music Albéniz wrote for *Iberia* is typical of the folk music of Spain in its rhythms, its harmony, and the evident influence of the guitar. "Triana" depicts the town of Triana in southern Spain, across the river from Seville.

Vaughan Williams: *English Folk Song Suite* [Westminster Gold 8111]. The melodies of English folk songs are clearly heard in these imaginative arrangements. Vaughan Williams' use of harmony in these works is rather conservatively Romantic and thus fits well with the nonchromatic sound of the folk songs.

Grieg: *Peer Gynt Suite No. 1* [Columbia MS-6196]. Grieg's music includes both haunting, lyrical melodies and moments of great drama. In this suite written for Ibsen's play, the melodies and harmony are quite Romantic in style yet strongly suggestive of the native music of Norway.

Late Romantic Music

Mahler: *Symphony No. 3 in D Minor* [London 2223]. The large orchestra required for Mahler's Third Symphony is used very sensitively, providing both color contrast and at times dynamic power. The fifth movement includes an alto solo and women's chorus, with melody and text from Mahler's own earlier collection of songs *Des Knaben Wunderhorn* ("The Youth's Magic Horn").

Rachmaninoff: *Rhapsody on a Theme of Paganini* [Columbia M-31813]. The *Rhapsody on a Theme of Paganini* is probably Rachmaninoff's best-known work for piano and orchestra. The pianist is given many chances to show great virtuosity. The basic clarity of Paganini's theme permits wide exploration of both theme and harmony.

Sibelius: *Symphony No. 2 in D Major* [London STS-15098]. This symphony, probably Sibelius's most popular, represents the abstract side of his writing very well. Filled with the spirit of his native Finland, the work uses Classical forms in expanded and innovative ways.

Impressionist Music

Debussy: *Nocturnes* [London 6023]. The three sections of this work are called "Nuages" ("Clouds"), "Fêtes" ("Festivals"), and "Sirènes" ("Sirens"). Many of the composer's characteristic techniques are apparent, especially the use of the whole-tone scale and the sensitive orchestration. Even the vague titles are appropriate to his subtle, nondescriptive approach.

Debussy: *La Cathédrale engloutie* ("The Sunken Cathedral") [Orion 73112]. This prelude, the tenth in Debussy's first book of twelve, is technically less difficult than some of his others, but musically it is one of the finest. Its inspiration was a Breton legend of a mysterious cathedral that sometimes, on clear mornings, rose up out of the sea. The thick, sustained chords create blurred harmonic progressions suggesting the engulfing waves.

Ravel: *Daphnis et Chloé Suites No. 1 and 2* [Philips 6500311]. These suites were arranged from music Ravel had written for a ballet. They include many Impressionist elements such as colorful orchestration and unorthodox harmonies. Ravel's use of classical Greek characters gives the action of the ballet and the music of the suites a timeless quality.

Impressionism Impressionism in painting, a precursor of Impressionism in music, was an attempt to present only that which was
subjectively visible at a given moment in time. Impressionist artists
tried to exclude references to the past as well as any moralization
or idealization. The result, in the works of Monet and his followers,
was a new manner of portraying nature. Canvases were covered with
contiguous and overlapping strokes of pure or nearly pure color
quickly applied in an attempt to find the equivalent of sunlight,
glare and transparent shadow. In Monet's *Pool of the Water Lilies* the
broad brushstrokes blur and soften the clarity of objects, and the
dazzling brilliance of the hues disallows any convincing sense of
depth.

Seurat: *A Sunday Afternoon on the Island of La Grande Jatte* (1884–1886)

Post-Impressionism   A number of artists soon became disenchanted with what they perceived as Impressionism's shallow objectivity and ephemeral nature. In seeking a more solid and durable style Seurat made use of a new technique of paint application that has generally come to be known as Pointillism. In *A Sunday Afternoon on the Island of La Grande Jatte*, the confetti-like application of paint preserves Impressionism's freshness and brilliance of color within a structure of formal, nearly abstract beauty.

Cézanne also sought an aesthetic vision beyond that of Impressionism. In works such as *Mont Sainte-Victoire*, he concerned himself with what might be called the architecture of picture making, the creation of a balanced and unified universe. He relinquished all effort to capture changing atmospheric conditions. Instead light becomes a generalized brightness. The landscape takes on the character of a serene, austere, balanced mathematical equation.

Where Cézanne searched for structure, Van Gogh explored art's ability to communicate heightened states of emotion. In *The Ravine*, he demonstrated his special gift, using color and directional brushstrokes to express human passions. Exaggerating optical reality, he made paint reveal his exaltation before nature.

Cézanne: *Mont Sainte-Victoire Seen from Bibemus Q*

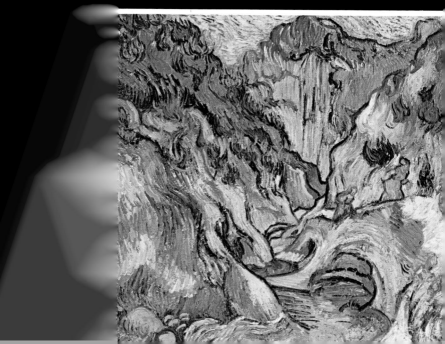

re in the Impressionist period. A sculptor of great g...
red toward the close of the nineteenth century—Auguste
. Like the Impressionists, he explored the reality of nature as
revealed by light falling upon surfaces. A modeler of pliable
ials more than a carver of resistant stone, Rodin worked his
es with a touch alive to the most delicate nuances of plane
ng the ephemeral alterations of the body as it shifted in the
As seen in his bronze bust of Balzac, his art is one of emphatic
eration. Features are suggested in an almost sketchlike
er, yet the force and vigor of the great novelist emerge over
ingly.

Rodin. Half...

Léger, *Three Musicians*, 1944

Listening Preview   *Among the most notable developments in the music of the early twentieth century were changes in the traditional use of rhythm and a parallel increase in the use of percussive sounds. Listen to the "Danse sacrale" from Stravinsky's The Rite of Spring (Side 10, Band 3, or a recording from the record library). What rhythmic innovations do you hear? In what ways does the work differ from orchestral music of earlier periods?*

25

Introduction to Early Twentieth-Century Music

The Early Twentieth Century [1900–1950]

Material Progress   In terms of material progress, the world began moving at a breathless pace at the beginning of the twentieth century. Practical inventions began multiplying late in the nineteenth century, and their discovery has not yet ceased. Telephones, radios, electric lights, and automobiles were familiar to most Americans and many Europeans by the 1920s. Television, rocketry, and electronic computers followed soon after. In medicine, research opened the way to organ transplants, the discovery of hidden genetic factors, and cures for diseases that had once ravaged whole populations. Freud, Adler, Jung, and their successors explored the depths of the human psyche. The science of astronomy grew so rapidly that a mere decade or two into the second half of the century astronomers were probing the secrets of Mars and Venus, listening seriously for possible radio communications from nonhuman races in other solar systems, and finding hints that they might be looking at objects close to the edge of the universe.

World Wars   Still, scientific progress was hardly able to give the people of the first half of the twentieth century the peaceful paradise of which their ancestors had dreamed. World War I, the Russian Revolution, the Spanish Civil War, World War II, and the Chinese Revolution all took place in the years between 1914 and 1949. So did the development of the atomic bomb. After a half century of preparation for and fighting of world wars, humans had finally advanced to the point where they could destroy the entire planet.

Artistic Movements   The visual arts sharply mirrored these developments. In 1907 Pablo Picasso painted the first Cubist work, *Les Demoiselles d'Avignon* ("The Young Ladies of Avignon"). Another repudiation of ordinary reality was found early in the century in the paintings of Henri Matisse and his followers, a group called the Fauves (from the French word for wild animals). In Paris, Surrealist painters such as Joan Miró, Salvador Dali, and Max Ernst created endless images of anxiety and torment populating strange and fantastic landscapes. The Abstract Expressionist works of the midcentury carried the process still further, avoiding all semblance of a recognizable image. Similar trends could be seen in sculpture in the works of such artists as Henry Moore, who sought to portray the cosmic forces he found implicit in natural objects such as trees, bones, shells, and rocks.

Many of the artistic works of the early twentieth century were specifically created in rebellion against the crippling alienation artists felt in the newly technological world. Yet technology itself provided new means of artistic expression, most notably photography. Amid the welter of stock westerns, crime thrillers, and cheap romances, directors such as D. W. Griffith, Fritz Lang, Sergei Eisenstein, and Ingmar Bergman saw the artistic potential of the cinema and developed it brilliantly.

Architecture and the applied arts took another route. The doctrine that "form follows function" was established at Walter Gropius's new art school in Germany, the Bauhaus, which started in 1919. The influence of the Bauhaus school extended not only to architecture but to industrial and advertising art, to interior design, and to the styling of everything from automobile tires to

A Half-Century of World Wars: *The military devastation that wracked Europe twice during the first half of the twentieth century had a unavoidable effect on art, literature, and music. The result was often an increased sense of alienation and a desire to create statements of protest or detachment.*

perfume bottles. Other architects who pioneered in functional design included Alvar Aalto in Finland, Le Corbusier in France, and Frank Lloyd Wright in the United States.

In literature a multitude of new techniques were attempted. The experimental writing of Gertrude Stein and James Joyce's stream-of-consciousness narration in *Ulysses* influenced the writers of an entire generation. T. S. Eliot's *The Love Song of J. Alfred Prufrock*, *The Wasteland*, and *The Four Quartets* remain major landmarks of modern poetry. *The Trial*, Franz Kafka's novel of 1925, introduced readers to a nightmarish bureaucratic labyrinth that has come to seem disquietingly familiar to the present generation.

Playwrights also drew upon and sometimes satirized the temper of the time. George Bernard Shaw, Eugene O'Neill, and Jean-Paul Sartre were only a few of the dramatists who tried to use the theater as a pulpit to expose the meaninglessness or insanity they found in the real world. At times literature and music collaborated to produce such philosophical statements, as seen in Bertolt Brecht and Kurt Weill's *Threepenny Opera*, first produced in Berlin in 1928.

Dance, one of the oldest arts, also showed new vitality in the early years of the twentieth century. The interpretive power of traditional ballet received great stimulus from the entrepreneur Sergei Diaghilev. At the same time, a few pioneers, rejecting traditional ballet entirely, sought to return to the basic sources of movement and build a wholly new type of dance better suited to the modern spirit. Drawing upon ancient myth, folk custom, and modern psychology for insights, Martha Graham choreographed dances of rare dramatic power. She also made great use of music written for her by contemporary composers.

Both alone and in conjunction with the other arts, music participated in this early twentieth-century upheaval. Like the rest of the arts, it went in many directions and proclaimed many different ideas about its own role. Some of the paths taken have already seemingly turned out to be dead ends. Others are still, and will probably continue to be, of lasting importance.

Trends in Early Twentieth-Century Music

Like the rest of society, composers were profoundly affected by the calamity of World War I. In the decades before the war, a great sense of optimism, based largely on the improving material standard of living, had pervaded much of the Western world. But after 1918 the remembered carnage and futility of the war encouraged a widespread feeling of hopelessness. Not only did the prospects for a peaceful world seem bleak, but the tendency of industrial society to automatize the lives of individuals was increasing. Mass production, mass movements, even mass entertainment seemed to make personal creative efforts superfluous or impossible. People were increasingly divorced from the products of their labor and from their own inner lives.

As a result, composers, like other artists, felt themselves deprived of any real social or economic role in society. This feeling prompted many of them to disassociate themselves from the music of the nineteenth century. The late Romantic passion of Wagner and his followers was rejected as pompous. The Impressionist concern for nature and sensuality was held to be overly subjective. A number of composers set out to rid their work of past encumbrances and to create a means of expression so new that their works might not even be recognized as music by earlier standards. The pursuance of these goals by a number of major composers contributed to an unprecedented turmoil in musical style.

Objectivity

One of the most important new trends among composers in the years after World War I was an emphasis on objectivity. The trend was not peculiar to music. Artists in all fields began to aspire to a kind of detachment from their own works. It was as if aesthetic objects had gained an existence separate from the character and emotions of the people who gave them life. To the Romantic artist, art had been above all a projection of the artist's own creative imagination. To the twentieth-century objective artist, art was governed by rules inherent in the art form and in the techniques used to create it. In the latter case, the role of the artist involved a kind of service to the artistic medium—a shaping of the ideas at hand according to certain abstract rules. The Romantic concern with the expression of emotion was replaced by a new concern for structure, organization, and formal restraint.

Primitivism

Another artistic trend in the years after World War I was an interest in "primitive" art as a source of inspiration. Perhaps influenced by anthropological studies of non-Western societies, many artists came to associate what they considered primitive life with the freedom and spontaneity that Western civilization seemed to deny them. A number of composers began to regard the late nineteenth-century works of Debussy and the other Impressionists as overly refined. Hoping to reinvigorate Western music, they turned to folk traditions outside the European mainstream. The energetic rhythms of Africa had a great influence on postwar composers, as did the songs and dances of peasants in Asiatic Russia, the Balkans, and the Near East.

Nationalism

A new version of nationalism was espoused by some twentieth-century composers. Earlier composers motivated by nationalism had for the most part tried to incorporate individual folk idioms into their music. Their twentieth-century successors were more likely to use folk elements to expand tonal possibilities and create entirely new styles. Composers such as Bartók, Stravinsky, Prokofiev, and Shostakovich all made such experiments, although none of them can be classified simply as a nationalist.

Futurism

Futurism also made its appearance in the early twentieth century. Declaring that art needed a revolutionary aesthetic to make it compatible with the new world, the Futurists proclaimed that motion in the visual arts and noise in the auditory forms were the true objects of modern art. In an important 1913 manifesto, one Futurist composer, Luigi Russolo, wrote, "We must break out of this narrow circle of pure musical sounds, and conquer the infinite variety of noise-sounds." Some Futurists experimented with *microtonal composition*—music that uses an octave divided into more than the twelve half tones of the traditional scales. The French-American composer Edgard Varèse was one of the outstanding adherents of this movement.

Early Twentieth-Century Architecture: *The most striking architectural innovation of the late nineteenth and early twentieth centuries was undoubtedly the American skyscraper. More subtle, yet in many ways equally important, was the German Bauhaus movement with its insistence that form follow function. The shop block of the Bauhaus shown here exemplifies the school's credo in its totally austere yet beautiful lines.*

Gebrauchsmusik

Gebrauchsmusik, or functional music, espoused by Paul Hindemith, was another important development. Reacting to what he considered "esoteric isolationism in music," Hindemith and several other German composers tried to write works that would be more easily understood by the general public. Hindemith also took into account the need that amateur performers had for an expanded repertoire. Thus, Gebrauchsmusik represented a conscious attempt to meet the needs of all segments of society.

Light and Satirical Styles

Some composers reacted to the devastation of the war and the decline of Romanticism by writing light and even satirical music. Largely a French movement, it centered around Erik Satie and a group of younger composers known as "The Six." The turning toward irony and humor was felt to be a necessary antidote to both Impressionist obscurity and Romantic bombast. The artistic philosophy it implied was similar to that of French court composers of the seventeenth and eighteenth centuries. Like the earlier composers, Satie and "The Six" attempted to write clear, neatly constructed

INTRODUCTION TO EARLY TWENTIETH-CENTURY MUSIC

pieces that would entertain and bring pleasure to their audiences. Aided by new dissonant harmonies, some of them wrote witty parodies of the highly passionate favorites of the past. Comic works served a dual function. They helped to purge certain antiquated musical techniques. They also helped to express the frustration and discontent of the new age.

Music of a Machine Culture

Since the composers of the twentieth century could no longer regard as their own the sources of imagery that Romantics had discovered in nature, many of them began to look instead to the products of industrialization as the symbols most relevant to the age. In particular, aspects of the accelerating process of urbanization found their way into the music of the 1920s. At the same time, machine culture itself became a subject for art. The machine offered a powerful symbol of dynamic energy and motion—qualities that were sought by a number of early twentieth-century composers. Prokofiev's *Age of Steel* was just one of many works written in praise of engines and industry. Such works were often intentionally "dehumanized" in order to mirror what artists felt to be the depersonalizing features of modern life.

Jazz

The early years of the twentieth century also saw the evolution of jazz. Born not in Europe but in the United States, jazz was to become a major force in the music written on both sides of the Atlantic. Once it had become well established in America, European composers such as Hindemith, Weill, and Stravinsky began to take notice of it, borrowing both its techniques and its inspiration. The European interest in jazz peaked during the 1920s, with many composers adding elements of jazz in even their most serious works.

Interest in folk and popular music also reached a new peak, due largely to wide dissemination through recordings. New popular styles developed every few years—blues, swing, and, in the second half of the century, rock.

Neoclassicism

One post-World War I movement seen in some of the works of Stravinsky and Hindemith can be described rather loosely as *Neoclassicism*. The Neoclassicists were influenced by the techniques of earlier ages, especially by the Baroque emphasis on counterpoint and the Classical ideals of order and clarity of form. Many Neoclassical works combine such early techniques and forms with new aspects of twentieth-century style.

Atonality

The composers of the early twentieth century introduced a number of new techniques that would have been unthinkable just a few decades earlier. One of the most important was *atonality*. The technique can best be defined as a tendency to avoid referring to or creating any specific tonal center in a work. In order to achieve this, music has to abstain from harmonic and melodic patterns or phrases implying them.

Serialism

Interest in atonal technique led to the invention in 1923 of the twelve-tone, or serial, system of composition. As developed by Schoenberg and later refined and elaborated by his followers, *serialism* called for an equal emphasis on all twelve notes of the chromatic scale. The notes were to be used in a very systematic way following predetermined formulas. The new system was basically an attempt to rescue music from what was regarded by many as the great chaos of modern composition. Although serialism's formulas were revolutionary, the system nevertheless involved a clear structure. A set of harmonic principles served as a blueprint for composition, much as the harmonic theory of the nineteenth century had served.

Still other composers turned to electronic machinery as a new means of expression. In the late 1940s in Paris, Pierre Schaeffer made experimental changes in musical sounds and noise by means of a tape recorder and other electronic devices. His work developed into a movement known as *musique concrète* ("concrete music"). Even greater advances in electronic music have been made since 1950.

Early Twentieth-Century Melody and Rhythm

Melodic Variety

The variety of melodic styles that developed in the music of the early twentieth century is enormous. Working from such models as plainchant and Oriental music, a number of composers sought to obtain tighter melodic lines, free of extraneous adornments. Many composers, Stravinsky and Schoenberg among them, chose to build their melodies upon motives and phrases of irregular length, avoiding the highly structured quality and symmetrical phrases of earlier eras. Such melodies often featured large jumps through a broad pitch range. At other times, melodies were restricted to small movements in a narrow range. The latter choice was often used to create a very chromatic effect. Many twentieth-century melodies show a complete lack of tonal center. Others are vaguely or even strongly tonal. A wide variety of scales were used to form the basis of melody and harmony, among them the major, minor, chromatic, whole-tone, and pentatonic scales, as well as the Medieval Church modes.

Rhythmic Innovations

Rhythm, certainly one of the most outstanding features of early twentieth-century music, showed a departure from previous practices at least equal to that of melody. Nineteenth-century composers were very much interested in rhythmic variety and complexity, but their successors went much further. Inspiration for new rhythms came from a number of non-European sources. Great use was also made of rhythmic *ostinato*—a short, stubbornly repeated pattern, which was often used as a unifying force. Still other composers rediscovered and applied older European rhythmic techniques. Among these were the rhythms of Medieval and Renaissance polyphony—rhythms that often avoided a strong constant beat in order to allow the greatest possible latitude to the voice or voices involved.

Ostinato

The renewal of old techniques and the invention of new ones made it possible for twentieth-century composers to create tense and powerful rhythms—irregular, unpredictable, and demandingly alive. Much of the power of the new rhythms was attributable to changes in the use of meter. In the Classical and Romantic periods, one meter ordinarily prevailed for a complete movement or section. In the twentieth century, however, this stability was renounced, and composers seeking a more pliant rhythm began to vary their meters frequently. In many of Stravinsky's works, for example, the meter shifts at almost every measure—a procedure that contributes much to the dynamic energy of the music. In a situation of this kind, it becomes almost misleading to

Frequent Changes in Meter

Transition to a New Age: *Of all the composers of the early twentieth century, it was perhaps Igor Stravinsky who had the greatest impact on the public mind. He is shown here, seated, with another revolutionary—Claude Debussy—standing at his side.*

speak of meter. Instead, the individual beat often becomes the basis of rhythm, generating short motives that multiply and combine to create exciting new patterns. Such formulas must necessarily avoid the traditional four-measure phrases and symmetrical rhythms of earlier music. Not all composers of early twentieth-century music were quite so innovative in rhythm. Yet many of the composers who continued to make use of more stable meters experimented with untraditional phrasing and unusual meters. Five, seven, nine, eleven, and thirteen beats to a measure became common, with the beats themselves frequently subdivided in a variety of ways. In many cases the irregularity of the overall rhythmic pattern tended to counteract any regularizing effect of the nominal division into measures.

Early Twentieth-Century Harmony and Texture

New Harmonic Techniques

The harmonic structure of early twentieth-century music was also quite unlike that of any preceding era. One of the new harmonic systems developed early in the century, *pandiatonicism*, involved the use of a style that was essentially free of chromaticism and did not have the restrictions on chord progression usually found in major-minor harmony. At the same time, Stravinsky, Copland, and others often achieved a dissonant effect by sounding two different chords together. The practice of superimposing two different tonalities was known as *bitonality*. *Polytonality*, a technique involving the superimposition of more than two tonalities, was found to be less useful because the human ear cannot easily distinguish several tonalities played simultaneously. Another technique, *bimodality*, involved the superimposition of the major and minor modes.

A number of other early twentieth-century composers chose not to experiment with different tonalities but instead to reject tonality entirely. Different methods of achieving atonality, or the lack of tonality, will be discussed in Chapter 27.

Renewed Interest in Counterpoint

The music of the early twentieth century was also very much influenced by a renewed interest in counterpoint. A variety of contrapuntal textures were used, ranging from the rather traditional styles of the Baroque period to new textures that were very sparse and economical. Sometimes single notes or short motives were presented in rapidly contrasting registers.

Homophony and monophony, and various combinations of all textures, were used as well. While a number of composers continued to use the dense textures of late Romanticism, many others favored clearer and simpler textures. In a general sense, the most notable characteristic of early twentieth-century texture was probably its great variety.

Early Twentieth-Century Timbre

A number of circumstances contributed to modifications of timbre in the early years of the twentieth century. One of the most important was the new feeling that sounds need not be pleasing to the ear in order to serve musical functions. This made possible the addition of previously unthinkable instruments such as wind machines and airplane engines.

Stress on Percussive Sounds

Another important influence on timbre was the increased interest in rhythm, which led composers to stress percussive sounds at the expense of the lyric string sounds of the nineteenth century. At times this was done by using traditional instruments in untraditional ways. In Bartók's *Allegro barbaro*, for example, the piano is used almost entirely as a percussive instrument, and in several other works violinists are expected to play with the wood of the bow, to tap the body of the violin with the bow, and to hit it with the hand. Composers also achieved a more percussive sound by adding such new instruments as the xylophone and the wood block to orchestras and chamber groups. In some cases even wilder and more innovative sounds were sought through the use of

Comparison of Romantic Music and Early Twentieth-Century Music

Elements	Romantic Music c. 1815–c. 1900	Early Twentieth-Century Music 1900–1950
Melody	Often very lyrical Phrases long and often irregular in length	Wide variety of styles and characteristics
Rhythm	Meters sometimes changed within movements Great variety of meters and rhythmic patterns	Meters often changed within movements Even greater variety of meters and rhythmic patterns
Harmony	Major-minor system greatly expanded	Major-minor system used by some Experimentation with new methods of creating tonal harmony Atonal styles
Texture	Homophony and counterpoint both used Texture often quite dense in works for large groups	Homophony, counterpoint, and new textures such as pointillistic all used Range of textures from sparse to very dense
Timbre	Large orchestras, choirs, and bands Small ensembles also prominent	Earlier performing groups continued to be used Bands grew in popularity Increasing stress on percussive sounds
Important Forms	Forms of Classical period used and expanded in a variety of ways	Forms of all previous periods used, though changed in many ways Freer forms developed
Important Types of Compositions	Types of compositions from Classical period, often expanded Newly developed symphonic poem and solo song cycle	Types of compositions from all periods used and expanded

rattles, thundersticks, and garbage cans. And a few composers wrote chamber pieces for ensembles made up exclusively of percussion instruments.

Use of Electronic Instruments

Changes in timbre were also brought about by technical advances. Electronic instruments were first devised in the 1920s and quickly put to use by the more progressive composers. These and other electronic instruments developed later in the century added greatly to the composer's repertoire of possible tone colors.

Early Twentieth-Century Types of Compositions and Form

New Types of Compositions

The composers of the early twentieth century continued to make use of many of the types of compositions developed in earlier centuries—symphonies, Masses, operas, and string quartets, among others. New types of compositions also evolved at a rapid pace. Some were similar to older works but had new names that were in many cases programmatically descriptive. Others, as we shall see in succeeding chapters, were quite new. A number of these new works were for particularly innovative combinations of instruments, including purely percussion ensembles.

Types of compositions were dictated to some degree by commissions from foundations, performing groups, and soloists. These commissions—the modern continuation of the patronage system—were sometimes specific, as when a pianist would ask a composer to write a sonata, but more often general, as when a foundation would ask for some sort of work for orchestra.

The twentieth century brought much more striking changes in form. With the early twentieth-century rejection of so many traditional musical techniques, form became a major problem. Classical forms had depended heavily on the major-minor system of harmony—a system that had been so largely abandoned. Much of the music of the twentieth century also involved totally new key relationships, distorted motives, and a general avoidance of complete restatements. Thus, although traditional forms continued to be used in many works, they were often so changed as to become in most instances unrecognizable.

New Forms

A number of composers chose to avoid traditional forms and developed new and freer forms. Compositions were often made up of a continuing series of ideas with brief recapitulations from time to time. Other works involved constantly changing themes or motives held together only by a repeated ostinato. No generally settled pattern emerged, and wide experimentation has continued up to the present day.

26

New Styles of Tonality

Experiments with Tonality

Two main lines of development can be perceived in the music of the early twentieth century. While some composers experimented with radically new ways of using tonality, others chose to produce atonal works that avoided tonality entirely. For people familiar with the traditional musical styles of the Western world, the works of the first group of composers are generally easier to comprehend.

Different Styles of Tonality

Many of the early twentieth-century composers felt that their music had to be based on some concept of tonality. A few continued to use the major-minor system of harmony to create tonal sounds. Others explored new harmonic systems, while retaining the emphasis on tonal centers.

Among the most important composers of tonal music were Bartók, Hindemith, and Stravinsky. None of them can be easily categorized. Each explored, digressed, and experimented too much to fit under any single label. Stravinsky's works are especially varied, liberally mixing many different styles, rhythms, harmonies, and forms. Bartók's works have a distinctive individual quality that makes them difficult to compare with other music. And Hindemith's works, although somewhat more systematic and consistent than those of Stravinsky and Bartók, show significant changes over the years. Nevertheless the three composers do share a number of characteristics that set their works apart from those of the more sharply revolutionary atonalists—the most obvious, of course, being their adherence to tonality.

The Music of Bartók

Influence of Folk Music

Several different influences can be seen in the work of Béla Bartók (1881–1945). In his youth he was caught up in the nationalist movement in his native Hungary, and he shared the typical nationalist interest in folk and peasant music. Most of his early works were based on folk melodies, some of which he had collected himself during lengthy field trips. Like a number of his contemporaries, he found in such melodies a key to new avenues of melodic and harmonic development.

His interest in folk music was not limited to Hungarian melodies but encompassed a wide range of different European and Near Eastern styles. Romanian, Slovak, Arabian, Turkish, and Serbo-Croatian melodies can all be found in his early works. A certain Oriental quality is often heard, reflecting the Asiatic origins and affinities of many of the peoples of southeastern Europe. In this respect, Bartók's work can be considered a link between the music of the East and West.

Bartók also drew, indirectly, on the work of other composers. His string quartets have a textural richness reminiscent of Beethoven. His style of harmony and his orchestration both seem to have been influenced in minor ways by the works of Liszt and Richard Strauss. However, it was the music of Debussy that most influenced his mature compositions. From a study of the works of the French Impressionist master, Bartók learned a great deal about modern orchestration and the effectiveness of transparent texture. He was surprised and delighted to find that Debussy used the pentatonic scale that he himself had earlier championed. He attributed the coincidence to their mutual interest in Russian folk music.

Finally, though perhaps less profoundly, Bartók was influenced by nature, the sounds of which sometimes provided him with both material and inspiration. In the five piano pieces of his *Out of Doors Suite*, he tried to re-create the ambiance of the night and its creatures. One of the movements, "The Night's Music," shows his unusual sensitivity to the sounds of the countryside. Against a pianissimo background of thick, dissonant chords, he set a melody that approximates the chirping and croaking of frogs and other nocturnal creatures. In other works, however, Bartók's ideas were much more abstract. In his early *Improvisations on Hungarian Folksongs*, for example, he used sounds that were probably derived more from his imagination than from close observation or imitation of real events.

Drawing on these influences, Bartók developed a number of original compositional techniques, many of which have become standard practice among twentieth-century composers. For this reason, and also because Bartók's music is of consistently high quality, a study of his works can serve as a useful introduction to contemporary music.

Bartók's melodies tend to be fairly simple. They are often largely defined by the scales he used. These include not only the pentatonic, whole-tone, and various European folk scales but also three- and four-note scales derived from Arabic music, which contribute a certain exotic effect to his works. Occasional melodies make use of all twelve chromatic tones.

Octave Displacement

One interesting melodic practice that Bartók often used is *octave displacement*—that is, the placing of successive notes of a melody in different octaves. Although the device is also used in the works of many of Bartók's contemporaries, he himself apparently learned it from peasant music. "Hungarian peasants do not devote much care to selecting a suitable pitch," he wrote. "Whenever a note is too high or too low for them, they transpose it by an octave, regardless of design and rhythmic conditions."

Bartók rarely ornamented his melodies, preferring to expand them by other means. One such means was harmony. His simplest melodies are often accompanied by especially exotic and complicated harmonies, as can be seen in his collection of folk-song arrangements *For Children*.

Rhythm assumes a special importance in Bartók's music. Other musical elements are often subordinated to it, and many of his works generate an overwhelming rhythmic energy. Sometimes this energy is the result of an insistent repetition of groups of notes accented by chords. At other times, energy is created through the use of asymmetrical and changing meters, dance and speech rhythms, or irregular subdivisions of beats. Most of these techniques are used in his *Mikrokosmos*, a collection of graded piano pieces that can almost serve as an inventory of Bartók's compositional techniques.

Polyrhythms

Bartók also made much use of *polyrhythms*—a type of rhythmic counterpoint in which several different rhythms proceed simultaneously.

Many different harmonic techniques can be found in Bartók's works. The wide variety of scales he used made it possible for him to achieve new and complex effects without wholly abandoning the relationship to a tonal center. The tonal relationships in his works are, however, often quite ambiguous. Even in passages suggesting traditional harmony, he systematically avoided any distinction between major and minor modes. In his more innovative works, he went considerably further, often introducing some degree of bitonality while remaining fundamentally concerned with the relationship of all the notes to a single tonality. He also made much use of *tone clusters*—very dissonant chords made up of several adjacent notes.

Tone Clusters

Much of Bartók's music is contrapuntal. There are frequent passages of stunning richness, with each of the independent lines adding color and density to the sound. He also believed that the physical positioning of the different instruments on the stage played an important part in the proper rendering of texture. In *Music for Strings, Percussion, and Celesta*, for example, he stipulated that the two string orchestras involved should be separated by the other instruments.

Bartók's timbres are typical of twentieth-century music, with the range of tone colors extended in almost every possible direction. In his *Concerto for Orchestra*, the use of a wide variety of solo and group sounds was one of his central goals. His *Music for Strings, Percussion, and Celesta* calls for a double string orchestra with celesta, piano, harp, xylophone, timpani, and a number of other percussion instruments. (The *celesta*, invented in 1886, is a small keyboard instrument with steel bars that are struck to produce sound.) Because of his interest in rhythm, Bartók placed special emphasis on percussion instruments. He also used a number of other instruments in a very percussive manner.

Bartók was least innovative in his use of form. Throughout his career he made use of the structural principles of earlier music, following at least the general outlines of such Classical forms as the sonata and rondo. In a general sense, he remained committed to traditional patterns of thematic contrast, development, variation, and recapitulation.

Form in much of Bartók's music depends greatly on his method of motivic development. He often built entire movements or entire works from motives or the smallest of phrases. A motive of perhaps only two or three notes is varied, developed, extended, and transformed continually in the course of a work. Thus a movement or composition seems to grow organically into its final shape and form, emerging out of material introduced at the beginning. In his *Quartet No. 1*, a single four-note motive, which first appears at the beginning of the second movement, develops into the theme of the finale. Each movement of his *Quartet No. 3* develops from its first few notes. The very difficult *Quartet No. 4* has one simple motive that serves as the basis for the extremely complex first and last movements.

Bartók: *Music for Strings, Percussion, and Celesta*

Bartók's *Music for Strings, Percussion, and Celesta** is one of his best-known works. It can also be used to illustrate many aspects of his style. First performed in 1937, it was written in honor of the tenth anniversary of the Basel Chamber Orchestra. Bartók specified in the score how the orchestra was to be arranged:

	Double Bass I	Double Bass II	
Violoncello I	Timpani	Bass Drum	Violoncello II
Viola I	Side Drums	Cymbals	Viola II
Violin II	Celesta	Xylophone	Violin IV
Violin I	Pianoforte	Harp	Violin III
	Conductor		

The work is in four movements of contrasting tempos and moods. A central tonality is clearly stressed in each movement, although little reference is made to traditional harmony.

First Movement: Andante tranquillo; in Fugal Form

The first movement is a neatly structured fugue. The subject, presented by the violas, immediately sets the character of the movement by its chromaticism and constantly changing meters:

Subject

con sord.

The dashed lines indicate subdivisions of measures, added to help performers in counting.

The subject is restated a number of times in different ways. The texture gradually becomes denser until eight parts are finally heard in the strings and celesta. At the climax of the movement, the subject is presented in inverted form.

Listening Guide for Bartók's *Music for Strings, Percussion, and Celesta,* **First Movement**

Timbre:	orchestra of moderate size with string instruments, percussion instruments, and celesta
Melody:	fugue subject, very chromatic and disjunct, serves as basis for almost all melodies
Rhythm:	complex, frequently shifting meters; tempo Andante tranquillo (moderately slow and peaceful)
Harmony:	basically tonal; begins and ends with tonality centered on A
Texture:	almost entirely contrapuntal, except at climax
Form:	fugue

Second Movement: Allegro; in Sonata Form

The second movement is cast in a rather straightforward sonata form. The main theme is introduced at once. It begins with a two-note motive that recurs throughout much of the movement.

Main Theme

Glissando

The line between the first two notes indicates a *glissando*—an extremely rapid and sequential playing of all the tones between the two notes.

All of the other themes in the second movement seem to grow from some element of this first theme so that the structure is very tightly knit. The main theme of the first movement is briefly heard as well.

Bartók takes full advantage of instrumental color throughout the movement. The strings, for example, are played with a great variety of techniques—at times pizzicato, sometimes with a mute, occasionally close to the bridge at the center of the instrument to produce a dry and harsh sound, and at other times with a partial depressing of the strings to produce a light and feathery sound. Although the strings introduce much of the important thematic material, they sometimes seem to function almost as percussion instruments, presenting short motives in a dry, staccato manner. Bartók's unusual arrangement of the orchestra also adds to the effect. When the two groups of strings play in dialogue together, the percussion instruments are heard, not behind them, but between them.

Side 10, Band 1

Listening Guide for Bartók's *Music for Strings, Percussion, and Celesta,* **Second Movement**

Timbre:	orchestra of moderate size with string instruments, percussion instruments, and celesta
Melody:	several themes built from motives; disjunct motion favored; main theme features chromatic upward sweep
Rhythm:	mainly $\frac{2}{4}$ meter with some other meters used as well; tempo Allegro (fast)
Harmony:	tonal but somewhat dissonant at times; begins and ends with tonality centered on C
Texture:	contrapuntal and homophonic
Form:	sonata

Third Movement: Adagio; in Rondo Form

Tremolo

The third movement quietly explores the sounds of the individual instruments. The xylophone is heard at the beginning, soon joined by the timpani. Then a number of small groups of instruments are contrasted with each other. Notes are played glissando by strings and harp, and a muted string *tremolo*—a rapid repetition of a single note—creates one of the many unusual effects. The movement is in rondo form—ABCBA—made somewhat untraditional by the fact that the main theme of the first movement is heard between the sections.

Listening Guide for Bartók's *Music for Strings, Percussion, and Celesta,* **Third Movement**

Timbre:	orchestra of moderate size with string instruments, percussion instruments, and celesta
Melody:	main theme made up of chromatic, rather conjunct fragments; other themes very chromatic and largely disjunct
Rhythm:	basically duple meter; tempo Adagio (slow)
Harmony:	tonal, with no clear or steady central note
Texture:	homophonic with some counterpoint
Form:	rondo (ABCBA), with sections divided by material from first movement

---

Fourth Movement: Allegro molto; in Free Rondo Form

The final movement opens with a brief passage of sweeping pizzicato chords in the strings. The main theme is asymmetrical and syncopated, with a dancelike quality. It alternates with contrasting secondary themes in a free rondolike structure. Just before the end of the movement, the first-movement theme makes one final appearance, effectively unifying the whole work.

NEW STYLES OF TONALITY

Timbre:	orchestra of moderate size with string instruments, percussion instruments, and celesta
Melody:	main theme dancelike and very conjunct; other themes largely conjunct and fairly chromatic; fugue subject from first movement appears toward end
Rhythm:	basically duple meter; tempo Allegro molto (very fast)
Harmony:	tonal, begins and ends with tonality centered on A
Texture:	homophonic with some counterpoint
Form:	free rondo (ABACDEDFGA)

Bartók achieved a unique synthesis of old and new in his music. As his style developed, his works became more and more complex in rhythm, texture, and harmony. But he never completely abandoned tonality. Throughout his career he devoted himself to writing in a clean, compressed, and economical style—a style that drives continuously forward with an especially dynamic vitality.

The Music of Hindemith

The German composer Paul Hindemith (1895–1963) was one of the leaders of the twentieth-century attempt to make serious music more accessible to the general public. He felt that modern music, especially the atonal styles, had become so doctrinaire that it ignored the listener's desire for simplicity, directness, and personal sympathy. Composers, Hindemith believed, had stressed virtuosity for its own sake and had proceeded without regard for any principles of beauty. In doing so they had abdicated one of their basic responsibilities to their audience. They had failed to communicate. As a result, Hindemith asserted, they could not expect their work to be of any true and lasting value.

Involvement with Gebrauchsmusik

It was Hindemith's intention in the late 1920s to replace this compositional self-indulgence in "music for music's sake" with what he called *Gebrauchsmusik*, or "music for use." Following Gebrauchsmusik principles, a composer had to organize music according to the needs and level of understanding of the audience. Composers also had to bear in mind other factors, such as the place where the music was to be played and the abilities of the performers. Furthermore, Hindemith strongly suggested that to achieve a proper Gebrauchsmusik, composers had to adopt a rational, logical approach and base their music upon certain primary principles of order. To Hindemith, this insistence on logic and order in no way conflicted with the creative process.

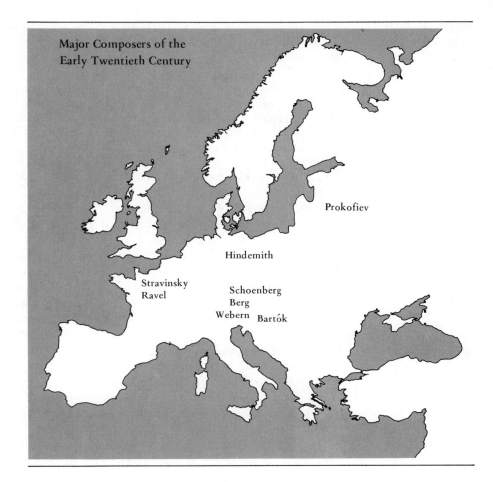

Major Composers of the Early Twentieth Century

While never abandoning his emphasis on order and logic, Hindemith did, as he grew older, become somewhat less rigorous in his adherence to the stern principles of his youth. The harsh demands that he placed on himself and his music softened, and his work grew in expressive power and lyricism. This mellowing process had the effect of introducing into his music certain Romantic elements that he had earlier rejected. After 1940 he gave increasing thought to the symbolic qualities of his music. He believed, along with the philosophers and mystics of many cultures, that the relationships of the elements in music were symbolic of a higher order in the spiritual universe. Thus in his song cycle *Das Marienleben* ("The Life of Mary"), the various tonalities are given symbolic values. The basic key of E is associated with Christ, the dominant key of B is identified with Christ's earthly being, and the other keys are linked with spiritual ideas of greater or lesser importance, depending on how close they are to the key of E.

Opposition to
Extreme
Harmonic
Innovation

Hindemith, with his Classical bent for system and order, objected strenuously to the harmonic experiments of some of his contemporaries. In his fifties he wrote:

> If anything seems to be of little reward, it is the search for originality in harmony. After a thousand years of research, experiment, and application, harmony has become thoroughly known; no undiscovered chord can be found. If we have to depend on novelty in harmony, we might as well write our last funeral march for the death of our own music. . . . There is only a limited number of harmonic and tonal combinations, and no matter how big this number is, it will be exhausted after centuries of continuous use.

That is, Hindemith claimed, harmonic possibilities are of necessity limited. The obsessive quest for new harmonies at the expense of traditional methods was, he insisted, doomed to fail.

Hindemith also accused his most important antagonists, the serialists, of violating the "natural" laws of sound. He likewise attacked other modern composers and in general objected strongly to new avant-garde systems.

Hindemith's own music, including works for large orchestras, small ensembles, and solo instruments, is noted for its lean, uncompromising style. It can be overwhelming with its sometimes complex textures and yet at the same time remarkably clean in its clear phrasing. A calm but powerful insistence on order propels each work toward a logical conclusion.

Hindemith's treatment of melody is founded partly on his training in the music of the German Reformation and Baroque period but even more on the songs of Medieval Germany. The influence of Brahms and Richard Strauss can also be heard in his works.

In rhythm Hindemith again modeled his own style on Renaissance and Baroque techniques. He thus abstained from the sense of overriding force sought by many twentieth-century composers. Much of his music moves along with steady rhythms. Elsewhere, however, he made use of polyrhythms. In such passages, where rhythmic energy seems to burst through Hindemith's basic sense of restraint, there is a strong feeling of rhythmic nervousness and power.

Harmony, as Hindemith himself recognized, was the point on which he differed most profoundly with other twentieth-century composers. In his *Craft of Musical Composition* (1937), he elaborated his theories, maintaining among other things the absolute necessity of tonality. He stated that since there were only a limited number of harmonic possibilities, they could readily be fit into an all-inclusive system. The system that he developed was based on a threefold premise. First, there exists only a finite number of possible combinations for the intervals of the twelve-tone scale. Second, each interval has a natural, unchangeable relationship with all the others and with the central tonalities. Third, if these relationships are not preserved, music must necessarily descend into chaos.

Hindemith's critics have pointed out that his assertion about the limited number of harmonic possibilities ignores certain elementary truths of composition. They maintain that the values and meanings of chords and intervals are not fixed but vary constantly according to the context in which they are used.

Hindemith's own harmony, the result of the practical application of his theories, makes use of the twelve tones of the chromatic scale but avoids atonality, in that the twelve tones are organized around a tonal center. In general, he sought to achieve a mood of uncluttered serenity, one of the most characteristic aspects of his music. Often this was done by the use of simple triads. Other passages seem modal in design, harking back to older scales—an element probably derived from his conservative training. Especially typical was **Polyharmony and** his use of a kind of *polyharmony*. This was a counterpoint, not of note against **Polychords** note in the older fashion, but of chord against chord. Such counterpoint produces *polychords*—very dense chords made up of two or more triads.

Hindemith's deep involvement with the early music of Germany had an influence on all aspects of his style, including his use of timbre. Like the Classical composers he admired, Hindemith chose timbres with care and economy. His orchestral works display a rather consistent fabric throughout, with solo parts heard very rarely.

For the forms of his compositions, Hindemith again turned to the German musical heritage, making use of both Baroque and Classical models. He resurrected the concerto grosso, the toccata, and the fugue as well as the balanced structure of the Classical sonata. His *Ludus tonalis* ("Tonal Game") for solo piano includes excellent fugal writing. He also wrote solo and duo sonatas for a number of different instruments. He developed a particular fondness for dance forms and was also one of the first European composers to become interested in jazz. All of his music, regardless of its inspiration or form, is classical in the widest sense. It has a logic of design and makes clear use of the basic principles of repetition and contrast.

Hindemith: *Mathis der Maler Symphony*

Hindemith's most famous work, and possibly his most successful, is *Mathis der Maler** ("Matthias the Painter"), written in 1934. First presented as an opera, it is perhaps best known as a symphony excerpted from the original. The full-length opera dramatizes the life and art of Renaissance painter Matthias Grünewald. Against the background of the Reformation and a peasant revolt, Matthias engages in a personal and moral struggle. Repudiating both his deep commitment to painting and the favor of a powerful patron, he decides to join the peasants. When the peasants are defeated, he flees with his newfound love, the daughter of the peasant leader, and endures trial, uncertainty, and disillusionment. At last, having relived in a vision the temptation of Saint Anthony, a subject from his greatest altarpiece, he devotes himself again to his art.

The opera centers on the question of how an artist can go quietly about his work while people are struggling and suffering all around him. For what

NEW STYLES OF TONALITY

reason does the artist create art that it should be pursued under such circumstances? The question is as relevant today as it was during the Reformation or in Hindemith's own time. It should be noted that the opera dates from the early years of the Hitler era.

The *Mathis der Maler Symphony* is scored for an orchestra of moderate size. Included are pairs of flutes, oboes, clarinets, bassoons, and trumpets, four horns, three trombones, tuba, timpani, percussion, and strings. Apart from the trombones, tuba, and percussion, the orchestra is like one from the late Classical era. The melodies and harmonies of the symphony, and of the opera, were influenced by Medieval modes, Gregorian chants, and popular religious songs of the Reformation.

The symphony has three movements. Each is derived from the opera score and named after one of the three panels in Grünewald's great Isenheim altarpiece at Colmar in France, one panel of which can be seen on the color insert in Part 3.

First Movement: Ruhig bewegt; Ziemlich lebhaft; in Sonata Form

The first movement, the overture of the opera, is entitled "Angelic Concert," in reference to the panel that shows angels singing a hymn at the birth of Christ.

Introduction

In the introduction that precedes the movement itself, Hindemith features an early German chorale, *Es sungen drei Engel* ("There Sang Three Angels"). The melody of the chorale is first presented in moderate tempo by the trombones:

Introductory Theme Based on Chorale

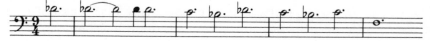

An active countermelody in the strings is woven around it.

Exposition

After the chorale tune is heard twice more, the sonata form begins with a quick theme in duple meter:

First Theme

Two other themes follow—one quiet and stately, the other more nervous and quick moving. The opening motive of the movement's first theme then returns to close the exposition.

Development

The development opens briefly with the first theme followed by the second. The two themes and motives from them are juxtaposed and tightly interwoven. The "Three Angels" chorale then returns broadly in triple meter in the trombones. Its triple meter is played against a duple meter in the rest of the orchestra, producing a general feeling of metric fluidity. The opening motive of the first theme is then heard again, and the rhythmic motion slows, finally stopping for an instant.

Recapitulation

What seems to be a recapitulation opens, not with the first theme, but with the quick-moving third theme. It is then followed by the first and second themes. Thus while Hindemith's use of the Classical sonata form is basically quite clear, he was obviously not bound by any predetermined order of theme and structure.

Side 10, Band 2

Listening Guide for Hindemith's *Mathis der Maler Symphony,* First Movement

Timbre:	orchestra of moderate size with string, wind, and percussion instruments
Melody:	German chorale melody used in introduction; three main themes in main body of movement
Rhythm:	introduction in $\frac{9}{4}$ meter, tempo Ruhig bewegt (at a restful pace); main body of movement in duple meter, tempo Ziemlich lebhaft (rather lively)
Harmony:	tonal harmony expanded beyond major-minor system
Texture:	largely homophonic with some counterpoint
Form:	sonata preceded by introduction

Second Movement: Sehr langsam; ABAC

The second movement, "Entombment," comes from the last scene of the opera and calls to mind the scene of Christ's burial. The mood is intense and restrained. Dissonant harmonies and changing meters contribute to the movement's great expressiveness.

Listening Guide for Hindemith's *Mathis der Maler Symphony,* Second Movement

Timbre:	orchestra of moderate size with string, wind, and percussion instruments
Melody:	main theme rises haltingly, using repeated notes and conjunct motion; other themes begin with disjunct upward leaps
Rhythm:	duple meter; tempo Sehr langsam (very slow)
Harmony:	tonal harmony expanded beyond major-minor system
Texture:	homophonic with some counterpoint
Form:	series of sections: ABAC

Third Movement: Sehr langsam; Sehr lebhaft; in Ternary Form

The final movement, "The Temptation of Saint Anthony," begins with a slow, dramatic introduction. But soon the excitement of the subject is mirrored in a fast $\frac{9}{8}$ meter. After a dynamic climax is reached, a slow, quiet contrasting section begins. A final section returns to a quicker tempo and broader dynamics with several different thematic elements. Prominent toward the end of the movement is the Gregorian hymn *Lauda Sion salvatorem* ("Sion,

Praise Thy Savior") played by the winds over a fast-moving accompaniment in the strings:

Theme Based on Gregorian Hymn

The final measures, preceded by a pause, are marked Alleluia in the score and provide a dramatic climax of broad chords. The ending seems to rejoice over both the saint's triumph and the painter's renewal of faith.

Listening Guide for Hindemith's *Mathis der Maler Symphony*, Third Movement

Timbre:	orchestra of moderate size with string, wind, and percussion instruments
Melody:	main theme swings broadly up and down in both conjunct and disjunct motion; great variety of other themes; closing theme taken from Gregorian hymn
Rhythm:	introduction in duple meter, tempo Sehr langsam (very slow); main body of movement in ⅞ meter, tempo Sehr lebhaft (very lively)
Harmony:	tonal harmony expanded beyond major-minor system
Texture:	homophonic with considerable counterpoint
Form:	ternary (ABA¹) preceded by introduction

Hindemith's career was further linked to German art by his friendship with the painter Max Beckmann. The two men seem, like Picasso and Stravinsky, to have shared a common spirit. Both belonged to the northern tradition of humanism, recognizing their responsibilities to others as well as to their art. Partly because of their political sympathies, their work was declared "degenerate" by the Nazis, and they were both forced to leave Germany. Later each taught in the United States, where they received high acclaim for their achievements.

It was Hindemith's lifelong goal to reorient contemporary music in directions he thought consistent with historical traditions and the natural laws of music. Although his influence has varied from one decade to another and his harmonic system has been rejected by many composers, Hindemith is still regarded as one of the most important composers of the twentieth century.

The Music of Stravinsky

The works of Igor Stravinsky (1882–1971) are so varied that any summary of his contribution to music must necessarily be incomplete. Never content to repeat past successes and always eager to continue the search for new techniques and styles, Stravinsky moved from style to style throughout his life. His early pieces show many traces of the style of his first teacher, Rimsky-Korsakov. Especially attributable to Rimsky-Korsakov are Stravinsky's early use of Russian and Oriental melodies within a basically German-Romantic harmonic system. Other formative influences included Debussy and Scriabin. However, Stravinsky soon discarded most of these derivative traits along with his early technique.

Early Use of Folk Music

In the writings of his later years, Stravinsky linked his knowledge of Russian folk melodies with his youthful nationalist enthusiasm. Early in his career, he studied several collections of peasant music, including one prepared by Rimsky-Korsakov. Although he did not as a rule base his work explicitly on folk sources, many of his earlier pieces display undeniable folk characteristics. Three melodies in the *Firebird*, one in *Les Noces* ("The Wedding"), and one in *Petrouchka* were all intentionally taken from folk music. But in general, Stravinsky's works, like Bartók's, contain more exotic tendencies than overt folk elements, as is particularly evident in *Petrouchka* and the *Firebird*. Nationalism affected Stravinsky in much the same way that it did Bartók. It influenced his early works but soon diminished greatly as a source of inspiration.

Early Ballets

The early years of Stravinsky's career were spent mainly in Russia. During this "Russian period," Sergei Diaghilev commissioned him to write a number of ballets, some of which are now among his best-known works. The *Firebird* (1910) was his first major success. Its initial performance in Paris made him an instant musical celebrity, and he received the acclaim of Debussy and other composers all over Europe. A year later he added to his success with *Petrouchka*. And two years later, in 1913, he produced a third ballet, *Le Sacre du printemps* ("The Rite of Spring"). This last had a sensational impact. Now regarded as one of the most important works of the twentieth century, it roused the first-night audience to such violent reactions that the music could barely be heard.

The *Firebird Suite*, taken from the ballet, is distinguished by its brilliant use of timbre, orchestration, and texture. In place of the Romantic ideal of blended timbres, Stravinsky followed Rimsky-Korsakov and emphasized the contrast and opposition of timbres. Each instrument or group retains its unique sound, making the entire fabric of the orchestration seem transparent. In Stravinsky's later works, this tendency toward separation of timbres became even more pronounced.

Other musical elements in the *Firebird Suite* are also typical of Stravinsky's early work. His great interest in rhythm is apparent in the "Dance of Kastchei." The section displays an almost frenzied rhythmic force, which Stravinsky characteristically dared to follow with one of the most lyrical sections of the entire work. Clashing and unusual harmonies abound, with frequent contrasts of chromatic and nonchromatic effects.

Stravinsky: *The Rite of Spring*

Stravinsky's third major ballet, *Le Sacre du printemps*, or *The Rite of Spring*,* describes a pagan fertility ritual in which a young girl dances herself to death to

---

*Igor Stravinsky, *Rite of Spring*. Copyright 1921 by Edition Russe de Musique. Copyright assigned 1947 to Boosey & Hawkes, Inc. Excerpts reprinted by permission.

appease the god of spring. The ballet is in two parts and includes the following movements:

Part 1   The Fertility of the Earth
         Introduction
         Dance of the Youths and Maidens
         Dance of Abduction
         Spring Rounds
         Games of the Rival Towns
         Entrance of the Celebrant
         The Kiss of the Earth
         Dance to the Earth

Part 2   The Sacrifice
         Introduction (The Pagan Night)
         Mystic Circle of the Adolescents
         Dance to the Glorified One
         Evocation of Ancestors
         Ritual Performance of the Ancestors
         Sacrificial Dance

Stravinsky's score, with a melodic, harmonic, and rhythmic inventiveness that surpassed even the boldness of his own earlier works, seemed to push music to the brink of anarchy. Stravinsky had long been willing to experiment with every compositional element to reach his expressive goals. In *The Rite of Spring*, his previous stylistic innovations crystallized.

Rhythmic Innovations

Melodies in *The Rite of Spring* are very motivic, with each motive treated as part of a process of constant variation. But it is probably in the rhythm that the most startling innovations are found. Early in the work, Stravinsky introduced a new rhythmic device that soon became a favorite of many composers. It is based on the use of two quick beats that occur continuously, in no predictable pattern, often syncopated to their accompaniment. The result is a rhythm that generates surprising energy. Additional rhythmic devices used in *The Rite of Spring* include driving ostinato rhythms, frequent changes of meter, polyrhythms, and syncopation. Another of Stravinsky's typical procedures, one that astonished listeners at the time, involves the rhythmic transposition of motives to different beats. A motive that originally began on, say, the first beat of a measure might, when repeated, begin on the second beat or on any other later beat.

Unusual harmonies abound in *The Rite of Spring*. A variety of scales are used along with uncommon intervals and pandiatonicism. Frequent clashes of harmony are made possible by Stravinsky's clear definition of each tonality within the multitonal whole.

Texture in the work varies greatly, ranging from very sparse to extremely dense. A huge orchestra is needed to render it. The brasses alone include eight

A 1930s Production of *The Rite of Spring: The striking rhythms of Stravinsky's*
The Rite of Spring *offered choreographers a difficult yet rewarding task—one very*
much in accord with the spirit of modern dance. The scene above is from Martha
Graham's production at the Metropolitan Opera House in New York.

horns, five trumpets, three trombones, and two tubas. The woodwind and percussion sections are even larger.

Intricate Score

Like many other modern composers, Stravinsky included meticulous directions to the performers in the score. Dynamic and tempo markings abound. Rather than depend on words such as allegro and adagio to indicate tempo, Stravinsky often used metronome markings. The direction $\mathord{\downarrow} = 160$, for example, was used to show that the music should be played at a rate of 160 quarter notes per minute. Stravinsky provided other helpful advice as well. In a note at the beginning of the score, for example, he explained that at least five timpani would be needed and suggested ways in which the timpani players could divide their labors.

The music requires highly skilled players. Individual parts are very demanding; even counting beats is difficult since the meter changes so often.

Form in *The Rite of Spring* is largely determined, not according to any traditional design, but rather by the content and structure of the ballet. Musical form seems to grow out of the variation and evolution of motives and rhythms.

NEW STYLES OF TONALITY

"Danse sacrale" from Stravinsky's *The Rite of Spring*

Stravinsky's love of rhythmic invention is most apparent in the climactic last movement, the "Danse sacrale" ("Sacrificial Dance"). The metrical pattern of the first twelve measures is shown below:

$\frac{3}{16}$	$\frac{2}{16}$	$\frac{3}{16}$	$\frac{3}{16}$	$\frac{2}{8}$	$\frac{2}{16}$	$\frac{3}{16}$	$\frac{3}{16}$	$\frac{2}{8}$	$\frac{3}{16}$	$\frac{3}{16}$	$\frac{5}{16}$

The rhythm continues to be unpredictable and driving throughout the dance.

Several different motives are explored. Two of the most important are heard near the beginning:

Prominent Motives

All of the instruments are used percussively in the dance. Indeed, the orchestra seems at times to function as one large percussion instrument. Even the strings, so often noted for their lyrical qualities, play short motives in a percussive manner.

The music is tonal in that certain tones are stressed through repetition or through frequent reappearance. The harmony is generally quite dissonant when compared with earlier music, but it seems most appropriate to Stravinsky's goals.

Form in the dance is quite free. It evolves from the presentation and repetition of the various motivic materials.

Side 10, Band 3

Listening Guide for the "Danse sacrale" from Stravinsky's *The Rite of Spring*

Timbre:	very large orchestra of string, wind, and percussion instruments
Melody:	short repeated motives emphasized
Rhythm:	meter changes frequently, often every measure; quick tempo
Harmony:	tonal centers emphasized through repetition of central notes
Texture:	mainly homophonic; often very dense
Form:	free, evolving from the presentation and repetition of motives

---

After World War I and the Russian Revolution, Stravinsky lived in Paris for fifteen years. Still associated with Diaghilev's Ballets Russes, he was called upon to orchestrate some eighteenth-century music by Pergolesi for a ballet called *Pulcinella*. At first reluctant and entirely uninterested in Pergolesi, Stravinsky soon became deeply involved in the project. He later recalled, "*Pulcinella* was my discovery of the past, the epiphany through which the whole of my late work became possible. It was a backward look, of course—the first of many love affairs in that direction—but it was a look in the mirror, too." Stravinsky had entered his Neoclassical phase.

Neoclassicism

The orchestra required for *Pulcinella* and for the suite derived from it is much smaller than that needed for *The Rite of Spring*. Stravinsky specified a number of solo string players, a small group of orchestral strings, and a small section of wind instruments. He also stipulated that the entire orchestra should consist of thirty-three players. While Stravinsky used much of Pergolesi's harmony, which today seems very consonant, he did inject occasional dissonances of his own. He also made use of eighteenth-century forms in *Pulcinella*.

Abstract principles of structure seemed to dominate Stravinsky's works thereafter. Neoclassical works such as *Oedipus Rex* abound with references to other ages and styles, notably those of the Baroque and Classical periods. They also make use of some Renaissance techniques. Responding to criticism that his music had become derivative and reactionary, Stravinsky wrote, "A real tradition is not the relic of a past irretrievably gone; it is a living force that animates and informs the present." The real purpose of Stravinsky's Neoclassicism seems to have been the establishment of discipline—not of form but of style.

Although not entirely a Neoclassical work, Stravinsky's *L'Histoire du soldat* ("The Soldier's Tale") marks, according to Stravinsky himself, his final break with the Russian orchestral school. A brief stage work with a small ensemble, it resounds with angular, unblended timbres and percussive rhythms. Stravinsky's choice of instruments was influenced by his recent discovery of jazz, and the work seems to have been designed as a showpiece for unusual timbres. Throughout, Stravinsky pushed the instruments to the extreme limits of their ranges, emphasizing wide leaps and other virtuoso effects. We find characteristically complex rhythms with a driving ostinato as well as the increased use of counterpoint that became common in Stravinsky's Neoclassical period.

Oedipus Rex, an opera-oratorio with a text by Cocteau, offers a fine example of Stravinsky's fully developed Neoclassical style. In the work, he used lyrics and melody sparingly, mainly to support other elements of the work. The music is developed in such a way that each passage seems to unfold into the next. This type of construction contrasts with the basically Romantic structure of his early works, in which the music seemed to move in blocks or sections of form, timbre, and tonality. Finally, the work shows the repeated superimposition of contrasting harmonic materials and the resulting polychords and polytonality so highly favored by Hindemith.

In sum, Stravinsky stands out among twentieth-century composers as one of the most versatile and certainly the least predictable. He explored a multitude of possibilities, from the paganism of *The Rite of Spring* to the solemnity of the *Symphony of Psalms*. For each work he established a unique harmonic and rhythmic framework. Many of his works confounded both his critics and his admirers. It seemed that his daring knew no limits, yet most of the techniques he adopted were in fact derived in some way from some previous composer or style. For a long time, it appeared that Stravinsky's approach to music was irrevocably opposed to serialism. But toward the end of his life, he surprised his audiences with a group of serial compositions. His works of this type will be considered, along with other modern serial works, in the final chapter of the text.

French Composers Experimenting with Tonality

Satie

Many other composers also chose to work within the tonal framework. In France several composers developed outstanding styles. Among them was Erik Satie (1866–1925), a younger friend of Debussy with a keen sense of humor. Satire and whimsicality are apparent even in the titles of some of his works. An obvious example can be found in his *Trois morceaux en forme de poire* ("Three Pieces in the Shape of a Pear"). In another work, the lighthearted ballet *Parade*, his style is especially concise and reserved.

Poulenc

In the next generation, Francis Poulenc (1899–1963) also developed a highly individual style. Usually writing in the economical fashion so common in French works, he created music that was tonal but often quite dissonant. Many of his works are of conventional types—sonatas, concertos, songs, and operas—but with a fresh harmonic language. Two late works are his *Gloria*, for soprano, chorus, and orchestra, and the opera *Les Dialogues des Carmélites* ("Dialogues of the Carmelites"), which is about a group of nuns martyred during the French Revolution. His many chamber works possess the charm and control so typical of French music in general.

Ravel

Perhaps the best known of all twentieth-century French composers, however, was Maurice Ravel (1875–1937). His music ranges from Impressionist to Neoclassical. His *Sonatine* for piano uses Classical forms, but with melodies and harmonies that have little relationship to the major-minor system. No doubt his ballet *Boléro* is his best-known work, with its brilliant orchestration and its single rhythmic pattern repeated throughout. Two piano concertos exemplify his mature abstract style. The *Concerto for the Left Hand*, written for the one-armed pianist Paul Wittgenstein, is an unusual and vibrant virtuoso work. The second piano concerto, the *Concerto in G*, is a very attractive, rather concise composition that makes apparent Ravel's knowledge and love of the instrument for which it was written.

Ravel: *Concerto in G*

Ravel's *Concerto in G** is in three movements and is scored for piano and a large orchestra with many percussion instruments as well as a harp. The harmony is tonal, but dissonance is both frequent and prominent.

First Movement

The first movement is in sonata form with no development section. The movement begins with a quick tempo and agitated arpeggios in the piano supporting the first theme in the piccolo. Here the piano is clearly used as part of the orchestra, accompanying another solo instrument. The tempo then slows somewhat as the piano becomes the solo instrument. The second theme, played by the piano, is lyrical and at first rather slow moving. The bassoon repeats the theme, supported quietly by the rest of the orchestra and the piano. The quick tempo then returns with the closing material of the exposition, throughout which the piano nimbly plays chordal and arpeggiated patterns. A brief scale passage for the solo piano functions as a transition to the

*Ravel, Piano Concerto in G. Copyright 1932, Durand et Cie. Excerpts used by permission of the publisher. Elkan-Vogel, Inc. Sole representative, United States.

The Early Twentieth-Century Sense of Beauty

Cubism In both art and music, the early years of the twentieth century brought a multiplicity of different movements. Perhaps most important in the visual arts was the Cubist movement. Cubist artists sought to produce a new synthesis of mass and space, a vision of prismatic planes fluctuating in equivocal spatial relation. In part, they were seeking an artistic re-

Picasso: *Accordionist* **(1911)**

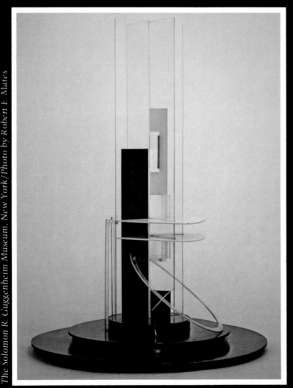

The Solomon R. Guggenheim Museum, New York/Photo by Robert E. Mates

Gabo, *Column* **(1923)**

alization of new concepts of physics, of the twentieth-century discovery that solids and voids are always in ambiguous relation, never definitely one or the other. In Picasso's *Accordionist*, forms have become faceted and seem to hover–spider-web fashion–in front of the picture plane. In Gabo's *Column*, space is made to flow through and around transparent, hovering planes.

Futurism The Cubist construction of a new reality was taken up and treated with special verve by artists of the Futurist movement in Italy. The Futurists optimistically, if intemperately, found a kind of salvation in modern physics and its discovery that the underlying reality of nature is energy. Futurist painters employed the shifting facets and multiple views of Cubism in works that attempted to represent the changing sensations, the frenzied tempo and pulse of modern life. Even within the circle of French Cubism itself, Futurist impulses were felt. In Duchamp's *Nude Descending a Staircase*, Cubist simultaneity is made to serve a more dynamic intent. Described are not the elements and relationships of the parts of the human body but its extension through space. The figure itself does not clearly appear; instead we see the "shock waves" it causes as it

Duchamp: *Nude Descending a Staircase, No. 2* (1912)

Expressionism Humanity's central role in the old Christian universe, challenged by the physical scientists of earlier ages, was struck a death blow by modern physics. Another assault on traditional beliefs came with the advent of modern psychology and its image of human beings fundamentally and irrevocably irrational. Freud's revelations of the subconscious world struck a responsive chord in Germany in the early years of the century. There Expressionist painters were eager to plumb the hidden depths of human emotion. They proceeded to create pictures whose subjects were psychological rather than physical, intangible instead of clearly apparent. In his *Blue Mountain*, Kandinsky, a Russian who became associated with the German Expressionists, employed expressive distortion, saturated colors, and passionate brushwork to express feelings of inner compulsion.

Kandinsky: *Blue Mountain* (1908)

De Chirico: *The Delights of a Poet* (1913)

Metaphysical and Surrealistic Art In the "metaphysical" art of de Chirico, a longing for a golden age and a desire for classic beauty are set against modern anxiety—the ideal and the everyday are juxtaposed in disturbing opposition. "Everything," said de Chirico, "has two aspects: the current aspect, which we see nearly always and which ordinary men see, and the ghostly and metaphysical aspect, which only rare individuals may see in moments of clairvoyance and metaphysical abstraction." De Chirico's *Delights of a Poet* is a visually disturbing reverie, combining the fantastic and familiar—incongruous locomotive and traditional buildings, deep space and ominous shadow. Such painting laid the groundwork for the psychic speculations of Surrealism, in which, as Max Ernst wrote, we feel "the fortuitous encounter upon a non-suitable plane of two mutually distant realities."

recapitulation. Then the themes are repeated and developed in expected order. A unique characteristic of the recapitulation is that the piano plays the second theme as part of a solo cadenza, ornamented throughout with trills. A vivacious closing section follows, and the movement ends with a crisp descending scale for the orchestra and piano.

Second Movement

The slow second movement provides melancholy contrast to the first. Its form is ternary. The first section features the piano by itself for many measures playing a hauntingly lovely melody in triple meter:

But while the theme is clearly in triple meter, its accompaniment in the left hand seems to be constantly straining toward a $\frac{6}{8}$ meter. The result is a very subtle rhythmic tension. The shorter middle section of the movement emphasizes arpeggios and scales in the piano. This leads to the final section, which begins with a repeat of the first theme played by the English horn and accompanied by the piano and other instruments.

Third Movement

The third movement, cast in sonata form, returns to a fast tempo. The tempo is so quick, and the themes appear so rapidly, that it seems likely that Ravel was more interested in the virtuoso effect of the whole sound than in the listener's perception of form. Several themes appear in the exposition, each heralded by four sharply accented chords. The piano prepares for the first theme by playing a whirlwind pattern of chords alternating between left and right hands. Then the theme itself is introduced by the clarinet:

The rhythmically surprising second theme is then played by the piano:

The third theme is played by the horns, then by the trumpets, in $\frac{6}{8}$ meter.

Third Theme

The closing section of the exposition features a flashing succession of scales and arpeggios played by the piano.

A long crescendo builds throughout the development section. The sound begins quietly in the cellos and basses. Bassoons, harp, and other instruments are gradually added, playing parts of the first three themes. The recapitulation comes without pause or warning, as the piano suddenly begins the opening theme, which the clarinet had presented before. The other themes follow in the expected order, rising to a brilliant ending with the four accented chords from the opening of the movement.

Tonal Music in England and Russia

Britten

In England the work begun by Elgar and Vaughan Williams was continued by a younger generation including such composers as Benjamin Britten (1913–1976). Britten's music is in an attractively fresh tonal style. In works such as his opera *Peter Grimes* and his *Simple Symphony*, he has shown a particular ability to create very appealing melodic lines.

Prokofiev and Shostakovich

The production of tonal music continued in Russia as well. Those composers writing after the Revolution were very much affected by the Communist Party's opposition to "formalism"—that is, very progressive traits of style such as atonality. Composers were expected to adjust their styles so as to make them more accessible to the general public. Sergei Prokofiev (1891–1953) and Dmitri Shostakovich (1906–1975) were perhaps the most important of the many composers who had to contend with the wishes of the Communist Party while developing their own styles. Prokofiev, in particular, is remembered for a number of highly successful works, principally the *Classical Symphony*, the opera *Love for Three Oranges*, *Peter and the Wolf*, and his piano sonatas. The *Classical Symphony*, written in 1917, offers a fine example of Prokofiev's work in general and of his Neoclassical style.

Prokofiev: *Classical Symphony*

Prokofiev's *Classical Symphony** was written for an orchestra of moderate size with the instrumentation of a late eighteenth-century orchestra. The symphony is in four movements, all of which are quite concise—again much in the spirit of a late eighteenth-century work.

*Prokofiev, *Classical Symphony*. © Copyright 1925 by Breitkopf and Haertel, agents for Edition Koussevitzky; Renewed 1952. Copyright and renewal assigned to Boosey & Hawkes, Inc. Excerpts reprinted by permission.

Manuscript Page from Prokofiev's Opera *The Flaming Angel: Among the early twentieth-century composers, Prokofiev was one of the most versatile, writing operas, oratorios, cantatas, ballets, and music for films, as well as abstract instrumental works. On the manuscript page above, note the constant use of accidentals and the many changes of meter.*

NEW STYLES OF TONALITY

First Movement

The first movement, cast in sonata form, shows Prokofiev's skill in combining an older form and instrumentation with fresh melodic and harmonic ideas. The first theme grows from a rising D major arpeggio:

First Theme

The immediate repetition of part of the theme a step lower, beginning on C, offers an unexpected shift in harmony. The music soon returns to D major for the presentation of the second theme. Then after a modulation to A major, the third theme is heard:

Third Theme

But it is an A major that is almost immediately destroyed by the use of chords not belonging to the key. A brief closing section in the key of A major features arpeggios and scales.

A measure of rest separates the exposition and development sections. Parts of all the thematic materials from the exposition are developed at a variety of tonal levels. The recapitulation then begins with a return of the opening theme, but it is in C major rather than D major. The original key of D returns, however, with the second theme. The third theme is also in D, followed by the closing section, again based on arpeggios and scales.

Last Three Movements

In the last three movements, Prokofiev again combined traditional styles with harmonic innovation. The second movement is in ternary form, at the traditional slow tempo. The third movement is a gavotte, also in ternary form. And finally, the fourth movement is, as might be expected in the most traditional of works, in sonata form.

Suggested Listening

The Works of Bartók

Bartók: *Concerto for Orchestra* [Angel S-36035]. Bartók's *Concerto for Orchestra*, in five movements, is particularly interesting because of the way in which Bartók used the whole orchestra in the role of the soloist. Individual instruments are featured as well. There are a number of unusual effects, such as the "Bartók pizzicato," achieved by slapping the strings against the fingerboard. Much of the music suggests folklike melodies.

Bartók: *Mikrokosmos* [Telefunken 6-35369]. This extensive series of piano pieces begins with very elementary works and progresses to those of intermediate difficulty. A variety of modern rhythmic and harmonic styles are explored, many of them based on folk material. The last three dances, for example, are founded on Bulgarian rhythms and melodies.

The Works of Hindemith

Hindemith: *Symphony in B♭ for Concert Band* [Seraphim S-60005]. Music for the concert band began to flourish only in the twentieth century. This work by Hindemith was an important contribution to the literature. It is in three movements, all of which explore the band's distinctive capabilities. Hindemith's love of counterpoint is seen in the fugal form he chose for the last movement.

Hindemith: *When Lilacs Last in the Dooryard Bloom'd* (*A Requiem for Those We Love*) [Odyssey 4-33821]. Written in 1945 at the end of World War II, this work for soloists, chorus, and orchestra uses Walt Whitman's famous poem for text and title. It is marked by the Classical restraint and order characteristic of Hindemith, but it also manifests great feeling.

The Works of Stravinsky

Stravinsky: *L'Histoire du soldat* ("The Soldier's Tale") [Columbia MS-7093]. The plot of this ballet, written in 1918, revolves around a bargain made by a soldier with the devil. The music incorporates the rhythms of popular dances as well as those of ragtime and jazz. There is a Neoclassical quality about the contrapuntal textures and the emphasis on clarity of instrumental timbres. As originally conceived, the work includes narration, but it is often performed simply as a ballet.

Stravinsky: *Symphony in C* [Columbia MS-6548]. Stravinsky's *Symphony in C* is a Neoclassical work in four movements. It is scored for an orchestra of eighteenth-century size and instrumentation. Classical forms are used, but with freshly conceived melodies, rhythms, and harmonies.

27

Atonality and Serialism

Experiments with Atonality

The growing interest in chromaticism during the late nineteenth century turned out to be more than just a passing fashion. It had started with the free use of tones alien to a given key—a technique that created new tension while keeping the security of a recognizable tonal center. By the twentieth century, however, even before 1913, the year in which Stravinsky's *The Rite of Spring* caused such a furor in the musical world, some composers were deliberately abandoning the security of a tonal center. At first the avoidance of tonality—*atonality*—was tried only in short passages. Later it was expanded to movements and entire works. A number of the more venturesome composers believed that such a path was the only one open for truly contemporary musical expression, and they undertook to create a radically new style. Important leaders in the endeavor were Arnold Schoenberg, Alban Berg, and Anton von Webern, the three composers whose works we will consider in this chapter.

The Music of Schoenberg

The Austrian-born Arnold Schoenberg (1874–1951) was perhaps the most important pioneer of the atonal music style. His atonal works were the product of years of difficult labor on his part and at the same time a logical result of the development and transformation of harmony in the late nineteenth century. The music of Brahms and Wagner exerted a very powerful influence on Schoenberg. From Brahms he learned the important technique of using a motive for continuous development, with each new theme evolving almost imperceptibly from the previous one. From Wagner he derived an increasingly dissonant, chromatic harmony, as can be seen in his string sextet *Verklärte Nacht* ("Transfigured Night") of 1899. Schoenberg's early works are in the late Romantic style—chromatic but still basically tonal. Yet his approach left him dissatisfied. Over the years, his chromatic style changed, with a continual weakening of the old emphasis on a central tone. The last movement of the *String Quartet No. 2, Op. 10* (1908) was his first strongly atonal work, and from 1910 on virtually all of the compositions that Schoenberg produced were atonal works.

Kokoschka's Vision of Schoenberg: *In his portraits, Expressionist painter Oscar Kokoschka tried to show not the surface image of a person but the inner depths, the workings of the person's mind and emotions. However, it has often been suggested that his works show more of his own personality than that of the people he painted.*

Influence of Expressionist Painting

Schoenberg was closely associated with the Expressionist movement in German painting, and this undoubtedly figured in his shift away from the late Romantic style. Expressionism, like the Fauvism from which it was partly derived, discarded photographic realism and created intensely charged, highly introspective works that were meant to speak directly to the inner spirit. Sometimes the paintings were abstract; sometimes the objects in them were recognizable but distorted. The subjective reality of Expressionist paintings was seldom a happy one. Oskar Kokoschka's *Self-Portrait* shows a man hollow-eyed, hypersensitive, and haunted. Max Beckmann's much later *Departure* inspired something of the uncomprehending horror of Kafka's writings. Schoenberg himself produced some Expressionist paintings, and the direction his music took was greatly influenced by the works of Expressionist painter Emil Nolde. In addition, he was a good friend of Wassily Kandinsky, one of the most daring members of the Expressionist school. It is interesting to observe that Schoenberg abandoned the tonal system at almost the same time that Kandinsky abandoned the representation of any sort of recognizable concrete objects. The artist was no longer to be the reporter or even the interpreter of reality. Instead he became the creator of a new reality.

Early Atonal Works

Atonality literally means "without tonality," and it implies that all twelve tones of the chromatic scale are to be treated rather equally, without special emphasis on any one of them. In most of his early atonal works, Schoenberg relied on a combination of vocal texts with music to create meaning and continuity within the atonal framework. The texts tended to be brief descriptions of psychological states and were often intensely expressive, as in Schoenberg's song cycle *Das Buch der hängenden Gärten, Op. 15* ("The Book of the Hanging Gardens"). The music generally shows great changes of mood, with contrasts of tension and relaxation, loudness and softness, dense and sparse sounds.

Sprechstimme

Aside from the use of atonality, Schoenberg's early works also show other innovations. One of the more important is the use of the *Sprechstimme* ("speaking voice") technique. This is a melodic style in which the singer does not sustain pitches but slides from one to another. The result is a highly inflected type of recitation rather than song in the usual sense. Another innovation was the *Klangfarbenmelodie* ("tone-color melody") technique, in which each note of a melody is given to a different instrument. This technique was used in a very obvious way in Schoenberg's *Five Orchestral Pieces, Op. 16.*

Klangfarben-melodie

Schoenberg: *Pierrot lunaire*

Pierrot lunaire, Op. 21* ("Pierrot of the Moon"), written in 1912, offers a good example of Schoenberg's Expressionist atonal style. It is a rather melodramatic cycle of twenty-one movements based on poems by the Belgian poet Albert Giraud. The work is scored for solo voice accompanied by piano, piccolo, flute, clarinet, bass clarinet, violin, viola, and cello. The instruments are never used all together but instead are grouped in different combinations in each movement.

"Mondestrunken"

Orchestral Introduction

The first movement, "Mondestrunken" ("Moon-drunk"), is written for voice, flute, violin, cello, and piano. The piano begins quietly at a moderate tempo with a motive that is stated four times:

Piano Motive

The violin plays a simpler motive against the piano motive.

First Stanza

The vocalist then enters performing in Sprechstimme, the technique that is used throughout the work.

EARLY TWENTIETH-CENTURY MUSIC

First Line of Vocal Part

Den Wein, den man mit Au - gen trinkt

(The x's in the score are simply an indication that the notes are to be performed in Sprechstimme.) The vocal part generally moves in small intervals but occasionally jumps very large ones. There is some repetition of motives, but more often one motive grows into the next.

The three stanzas of text are all separated by short instrumental interludes, but otherwise the music seems to flow steadily without obvious sections. The overall form is quite free. Meters and rhythmic patterns change continually, avoiding any sense of beat and regularity. The dynamic level is very low, except for a sudden change to forte near the end.

Side 10, Band 4

Listening Guide for "Mondestrunken" from Schoenberg's *Pierrot lunaire*

Timbre: ensemble of solo voice, flute, violin, cello, and piano

Melody: instrumental themes mostly disjunct; vocal themes more conjunct; sung in Sprechstimme throughout

Rhythm: meter alternates irregularly between $\frac{2}{4}$ and $\frac{3}{4}$, although not clear or important to the listener; tempo Bewegt (restful)

Harmony: atonal

Texture: contrapuntal and homophonic

Form: free, with repetition of some motives

Text:

I Den Wein, den man mit Augen
  trinkt,
  Giesst Nachts der Mond in
  Wogen nieder,
  Und eine Springflut über-
  schwemmt
  Den stillen Horizont.

The wine one drinks with the
  eyes
The moon pours down in waves
  at night,
And a spring tide submerges
The still horizon.

II Gelüste, schauerlich and süss,
  Durchschwimmen ohne Zahl
  die Fluten!
  Den Wein, den man mit Augen
  trinkt,
  Giesst Nachts der Mond in
  Wogen nieder.

Longings, terrible and sweet,
Unnumbered, swim the flood!
The wine one drinks with the
  eyes
The moon pours down in waves
  at night.

III Der Dichter, den die Andacht
  treibt
  Berauscht sich an dem heilgen
  tranke,
  Gen Himmel wendet er
  verzückt
  Das Haupt und taumelnd saugt
  und schlürft er
  Den Wein, den man mit Augen
  trinkt.

The poet, constrained by
  devotion,
Drunken with the holy drink,
Enraptured, lifts heavenward
His head and, reeling, sucks
  and gulps
The wine one drinks with the
  eyes.

"Columbine"

The text of "Columbine," the second movement, is also in three stanzas, as can be seen in the Listening Guide. The vocal part again uses a variety of intervals, with an overall emphasis on small intervals. Flute, clarinet, violin, and piano accompany the soloist. Parallel dissonant chords stand out in several passages, but the overall dynamic level is quiet throughout. The form is quite free even though there is brief repetition of some motives.

Listening Guide for "Columbine" from Schoenberg's *Pierrot lunaire*

Timbre:	ensemble of solo voice, flute, clarinet, violin, and piano
Melody:	conjunct and disjunct; sung in Sprechstimme throughout
Rhythm:	triple meter, not clear or important to the listener; tempo Fliessende (flowing)
Harmony:	atonal
Texture:	contrapuntal and homophonic
Form:	free, with repetition of some motives

Text:

I Des Mondlichts bleiche Blüten,
Die weissen Wunderrosen,
Blühn in den Julinächten—
O bräch ich eine nur!

The moonlight's pale blossoms,
The white wonder-roses,
Bloom in the July nights—
Ah, could I pick but one!

II Mein banges Leid zu lindern,
Such ich am dunklen Strome
Des Mondlichts bleiche Blüten
Die weissen Wunderrosen.

To ease my anxious mourning
I search by the dark stream
For the moonlight's pale blossoms,
The white wonder-roses.

III Gestillt wär all mein Sehnen,
Dürft ich so märchenheimlich,
So selig leis—entblättern
Auf deine braunen Haare
Des Mondlichts bleiche Blüten!

Stilled then were all my yearnings,
Could I, with fairy stealth,
In silent wonder—let fall
Over your brown hair
The moonlight's pale blossoms!

Other Movements of Schoenberg's *Pierrot lunaire*

In the remaining nineteen movements, a wide variety of instrumentation and effects are explored. Schoenberg was obviously trying to capture the spirit of each poem in a subjective and dramatically appropriate manner. The results are very arresting—the work seems to speak to us in a new musical language.

Use of the Serial Technique

Schoenberg was convinced that the possibilities of tonal music had been exhausted. But he recognized that atonal techniques were not yet sufficiently developed to take its place. This situation led him into a ten-year period of reevaluation and experimentation during which he worked out a new method of organizing atonal harmony called *serialism* (or *dodecaphony*). With this as a theoretical framework, he began to produce works that had a tremendous influence on later twentieth-century music.

Schoenberg's earliest compositions using the serial technique were written in 1923. All were quite brief, written for solo instruments or small groups. Later, as he gained confidence, he wrote longer works for larger ensembles, most notably the *Variations for Orchestra, Op. 31*, the *Violin Concerto, Op. 36*, and the *Piano Concerto, Op. 42*. The works had a radically new sound, and the audiences who first heard them were seldom pleased.

Twelve-Tone Row

The underlying structure of Schoenberg's serialism and the rules that articulate it are based upon the atonal principle that all twelve tones of the chromatic scale must be treated with equal emphasis. In order to achieve this equality, a serialist composer begins with a *twelve-tone row*, in which each chromatic tone appears exactly once. The twelve notes may be arranged in any order that the composer chooses. The only limitation, in the strict use of the system, is that all twelve notes must be played before any one is repeated.

Forms of the Tone Row

The composer may cast the notes of the row in any rhythmic pattern and in any register. Once the row is constructed, four different forms are possible: *original*, *retrograde*, *inversion*, and *retrograde inversion*. Examples of all four forms are given below.

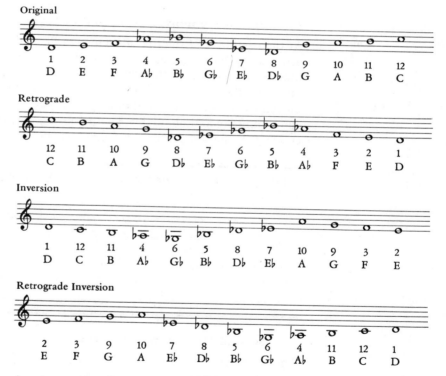

As you can see, the retrograde form is produced by reversing the order of the notes, starting with the last note and ending with the first. The inversion is made by turning the intervals of the original row upside down. If, as in the example, the first two notes are originally D and E, they will become D and C. The retrograde inversion is produced by reversing the order of the inverted notes.

ATONALITY AND SERIALISM

All four forms of the row can also be transposed so that they begin on any of the eleven other pitch levels. Thus there is a possible total of forty-eight forms for any tone row. The many different forms may be used melodically, contrapuntally, or to build chords, perhaps in support of a melody also derived from the row.

Schoenberg: *Suite for Piano, Op. 25*

Schoenberg's use of the tone row in the first two movements of his *Suite for Piano** is very imaginative. The original tone row, on which the entire work is based, is shown below.

Original Form of Tone Row

1	2	3	4	5	6	7 8	9	10	11	12
E	F	G	D♭	G♭	E♭	A♭ D	B	C	A	B♭

First Movement: Rasch; in Free Form

At the beginning of the first movement, "Praeludium," the pianist plays the original row with the right hand. At the third tone, the left hand begins to imitate the right in a transposed form of the original row. The texture is momentarily contrapuntal, followed very soon by chords. Throughout the movement various forms and transpositions of the original row are used, both contrapuntally and chordally. The meter is ⁶⁄₈, but rhythmic patterns vary so greatly that the sense of beat and meter is obscured.

Side 10, Band 5

Listening Guide for Schoenberg's *Suite for Piano*, First Movement

Timbre:	piano
Melody:	conjunct and disjunct; derived from tone row
Rhythm:	mostly ⁶⁄₈ meter with major change near the end, but not necessarily clear to the listener; tempo Rasch (quick)
Harmony:	atonal, derived from tone row
Texture:	contrapuntal and homophonic
Form:	derived from the use of various forms of the row

Second Movement: Etwas langsam; in Free Form

The second movement, "Gavotte," is played in duple meter. As in the first movement, rhythms change regularly, so that the characteristics of the old dance form—the gavotte—are not always apparent. The original form of the

*Excerpts used by permission of Belmont Music Publishers, Los Angeles, California 90049. *Suite für Klavier, Op. 25:* Copyright 1925 by Universal Edition. Copyright renewed 1952 by Gertrude Schoenberg.

first-movement row is used, but the fragmented rhythms give it a completely different character:

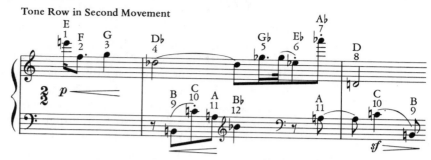

Tone Row in Second Movement

Notice how Schoenberg split the row into three segments: tones 1 2 3 4 in one segment, tones 5 6 7 8 in another, and tones 9 10 11 12 in still another. Having divided the row in such a fashion, he then proceeded to use the last four tones before the middle four.

Listening Guide for Schoenberg's *Suite for Piano*, Second Movement

Timbre:	piano
Melody:	conjunct and disjunct; derived from tone row
Rhythm:	mostly duple meter as typical of a gavotte but other meters occasionally interrupt; tempo Etwas langsam (somewhat slow)
Harmony:	atonal, derived from tone row
Texture:	contrapuntal and homophonic
Form:	derived from the use of various forms of the row

Other Movements in Schoenberg's *Suite for Piano*

The remaining movements in the suite are entitled "Musette," "Intermezzo," "Menuett," and "Gigue." The "Musette" features the repetition of the note G throughout, producing a sound reminiscent of the bagpipe. ("Musette" is the French word for bagpipe.) The "Menuett" is classically structured with a minuet, a trio, and a repetition of the minuet. Schoenberg's use of such a traditional form represents a very skillful blending of the old and the new.

Serialism as an Art Form

The concept of the twelve-tone row was not completely new with Schoenberg. Several composers before him had written chromatic melodies using all twelve tones in a systematic way. The great significance of Schoenberg's work lies in his development of the different forms of the tone row and the use of the row within a coherent system.

In the serial technique, we meet a completely new musical language—a radically different treatment of all aspects of music. Listening to serial music for the first time is much like hearing an unfamiliar language. At first the words make no sense whatsoever, but if we study the language for a time, we begin to grasp its meaning and become more and more comfortable with it. So it is with any new style of music. The more we hear it and study it, the more accessible it becomes. It simply takes time for people who are so much conditioned by the tonal music of the eighteenth and nineteenth centuries to become comfortable with the atonal sounds of serialism.

It is important to remember that although serialism is strongly associated with atonality, the one may exist without the other. Music can be atonal, as we have seen, without using the serial technique. Schoenberg's *Pierrot lunaire* is an obvious example. And conversely, a composer may construct a tone row that sounds quite tonal—one with prominent triads, for example.

It should also be noted that it is virtually impossible to tell simply by listening whether or not a work is based on a serial technique. Even if listeners know that a work is based on a tone row, they will have difficulty in hearing more than the most obvious characteristics of the row and its various forms.

The serial technique is rather like a set of tools. It is primarily a method that a composer uses to organize the twelve tones and bring order to a basically dissonant style. Every serial composer has used the technique in different ways —a fact that will become evident when we consider the works of two of Schoenberg's early students, Berg and Webern. Together these two composers were largely responsible for the early propagation and further development of serialism.

The work of Schoenberg and his immediate successors has had far-reaching influence. Nearly every composer of our time has at least experimented with serialism. Many have extended the principles of the system to govern other aspects of composition, using it strictly or freely and combining it with other techniques. The serial technique has thus proved a stimulus and a valuable asset, even though it has not become the almost universal musical language that major-minor harmony was in the past.

The Music of Berg

Stress on Lyricism

The Austrian composer Alban Berg (1885–1935) was an ardent disciple and a close friend of Schoenberg. Berg's style of composition was largely based on the serial technique, but it was tempered with a strong sense of lyricism. His works thus seem less removed than Schoenberg's from the late Romantic style.

Berg's greatest masterpiece is probably his Expressionist opera *Wozzeck*. First performed in 1925, it raised a storm of protest from the public. The libretto was based on a play of the same name by an early nineteenth-century dramatist, Georg Büchner. The plot concerns a pathetic soldier whose life is almost totally determined by his political and social environment. Such a story was in many ways uncomfortably appropriate not only in a nineteenth-century play but also in an early twentieth-century opera. The music incorporates serial technique only sparingly, but the style is usually atonal. Berg's interest in past traditions is revealed in his use of Classical forms to provide a

A Very Modern Opera: Berg's Wozzeck *struck the public in much the same way that Stravinsky's* The Rite of Spring *did. Largely atonal, the work makes use of both Sprechstimme and Leitmotivs.*

structural basis for the work. These forms function behind the scenes for the most part and are now usually perceived by the listener.

Two other outstanding works by Berg are his *Violin Concerto* and a second opera, *Lulu*, left unfinished at his death. Both make great use of serial technique, but the *Violin Concerto* includes tonal writing as well. Throughout his works, Berg used both tonal and atonal harmony, choosing one or the other according to the dramatic purpose of the individual work. In this way he achieved a style that he found personally valid and convincing.

Berg: *Lyric Suite*

Berg's *Lyric Suite** clearly shows many characteristics of his music. The work is a string quartet with six movements alternating between fast and slow tempos. It is rather freely based on several different tone rows.

*Lyric Suite by Alban Berg. Copyright 1927, Universal Edition. Excerpts used by permission of the publisher. Theodore Presser Company, sole representative United States, Canada and Mexico.

First Movement: Allegretto gioviale; in Binary Form

The opening movement begins with a brief chordal introduction. This is followed by the first tone row, which is presented as the main theme by the first violin:

First Tone Row

*Hauptstimme
and Nebenstimme*

In the usual manner of serialist composers, Berg indicated this phrase and certain others with the symbol H⌐, meaning *Hauptstimme*, or principal part. He also used the symbol N⌐, meaning *Nebenstimme*, or secondary part. These marks were added to help performers see more quickly and easily which parts to emphasize.

While the use of the tone row is sometimes obvious in the first movement, it is more often hidden in contrapuntal and chordal passages. Both conjunct and disjunct motion are heard, with greater stress on the latter. Rhythmic patterns are quite varied and changing, and the meter alternates rather frequently between $\frac{4}{4}$ and $\frac{2}{4}$. The texture is largely contrapuntal, with the four instruments of the string quartet often moving independently of one another. A wealth of performance directions are given in the score, with special attention paid to dynamics.

Side 10, Band 6

Listening Guide for Berg's *Lyric Suite,* First Movement

Timbre:	string quartet
Melody:	largely disjunct; derived from tone row
Rhythm:	duple meter alternating between $\frac{4}{4}$ and $\frac{2}{4}$; tempo Allegretto gioviale (rather fast and jovial)
Harmony:	atonal, derived from tone row
Texture:	largely contrapuntal
Form:	binary (AB)

Other Movements in Berg's *Lyric Suite*

The other five movements are entitled "Andante amoroso," "Allegro misterioso," "Adagio appassionato," "Presto delirando," and "Largo desolato." The descriptive movement markings reflect the very expressive qualities of the music. While the movements are organized rather clearly and traditionally in sections, melody and harmony are organized serially in a fresh, at times very dramatic, manner.

EARLY TWENTIETH-CENTURY MUSIC

The Music of Webern

Anton von Webern (1883–1945), who like Schoenberg and Berg was born in Austria, was trained as a musicologist, composer, and conductor. He was a devoted student of Schoenberg, and he avidly explored the possibilities of serialism. While Berg injected serial music with a somewhat Romantic spirit, Webern's style was much more Classical in its careful organization and economy of means.

Webern's music does not use many notes. He usually wrote for solo instruments or small ensembles, and his style was particularly lean and sparse. Some claim that melody simply ceased to exist with Webern—that it became completely merged with harmony. Certainly there is little relation to any traditional melodic style in most of his works. His melodies are characterized by very small and very wide leaps, and he frequently used octave displacement. The rhythms in his works vary. Some are quite steady, while others are very irregular and so syncopated that they completely hide any feeling of the basic beat.

Pointillistic Texture

Webern's use of a tone row was usually quite strict, though he sometimes repeated a note within the row or divided the notes of the row into parts that were used rather independently. His textures are, like his melodies, quite sparse, often made up of a single note or a very short motive followed immediately by one in another part and in a higher or lower register. This type of texture has often been compared with the paintings of the Pointillists—paintings in which images are built up out of innumerable tiny, distinct points of unblended color. Webern often used the outlines of Classical forms, but he effectively concealed them from the listener by his highly novel style. All of his works are quite brief. One movement of his *Five Pieces for Orchestra* lasts only nineteen seconds.

Although most of Webern's compositions were for small ensembles, he also wrote a few orchestral works, several sets of songs, and two cantatas. The title of his *Symphony, Op. 21* is somewhat misleading. The expected orchestra is only a small chamber group.

Webern: *Symphony, Op. 21*

Webern's *Symphony, Op. 21** displays many of his most characteristic techniques. It was written for a small chamber ensemble made up of clarinet, bass clarinet, two horns, harp, first and second violins, viola, and cello. The work has only two movements and takes only ten minutes to perform. In effect, the *Symphony* is a skillful miniature—a study in contrast and exploitation of timbre and in control over pitch through the use of the row in its various forms.

**Symphony, Op. 21* by Anton Von Webern. Copyright 1929, Universal Edition. Excerpts used by permission of the publisher. Theodore Presser Company, sole representative United States, Canada, and Mexico.

First Movement: Ruhig schreitend; in Sonata Form

Almost from the beginning of the first movement, several different forms of the tone row are used. We clearly hear the first four notes of the original and inverted forms in the horns:

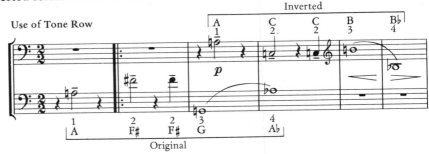

Another form of the row is then started in the other instruments, and from this point on the various forms are constantly intertwined. Webern was not interested in having the forms heard individually; instead he used them to create a general effect.

The wide leaps within and between parts contribute to the characteristic pointillistic texture. In most cases, an instrument plays only one note, or two at the most, before another instrument takes over. The $\frac{2}{2}$ meter remains constant throughout the first movement, but no steady sense of beat is set up, and thus the duple meter is not apparent. Nor is the form obvious. It is definitely a miniature sonata form, but this becomes clear only with thorough knowledge of the music.

Side 11, Band 1

Listening Guide for Webern's *Symphony, Op. 21,* First Movement

Timbre:	small chamber ensemble of string and wind instruments
Melody:	merged with harmony
Rhythm:	duple meter, but not clear to listener; tempo Ruhig schreitend (at a serene pace)
Harmony:	atonal, derived from the use of several forms of the tone row
Texture:	sparse and pointillistic
Form:	sonata form, but not readily apparent to listener

Second Movement: Sehr ruhig; in Theme and Variations Form

The second movement is made up of a theme and seven variations. The theme, which is a variation of the tone row of the first movement, is presented by the clarinet and then split up into less continuous groupings of notes, which are played by other instruments.

Theme

EARLY TWENTIETH-CENTURY MUSIC

The Evolution of the Symphony

Up until the end of the nineteenth century, the history of the symphony was one of ever-increasing magnitude. Over the years, new instruments were added, parts were written for choral groups, texture became denser, and dynamic range expanded to enormous proportions. The twentieth century brought an end to the general expansion, with composers writing symphonies for groups of varied sizes, often with very untraditional instrumentation.

Listen to selections from symphonies of four different periods—those listed below from the record set that accompanies the text, or other selections from the record library.

Classical:	Mozart's *Symphony No. 40 in G Minor*, First Movement	Side 4, Band 3
Romantic:	Brahms' *Symphony No. 3 in F Major*, First Movement	Side 7, Band 5
Late Romantic:	Mahler, any symphony, first movement	Record Library
Modern:	Webern, *Symphony, Op. 21*, First Movement	Side 11, Band 1

What musical qualities make it possible to identify the periods in which the symphonies were written? In what ways does each work reflect the spirit of its time?

Notice how Webern repeats most of the tones in the theme to give them greater emphasis.

The variations tend to flow rhythmically, one into the next. No emphasis is placed on recognition of the tone row, although it is always present. The variations are most easily distinguished by changes of instrumentation:

Variation 1: strings
Variation 2: wind instruments and harp
Variation 3: entire ensemble
Variation 4: entire ensemble
Variation 5: strings and harp
Variation 6: wind instruments
Variation 7: entire ensemble

ATONALITY AND SERIALISM

Listening Guide for Webern's *Symphony, Op. 21,* Second Movement

Timbre: small chamber ensemble of string and wind instruments

Melody: theme is inverted form of original tone row

Rhythm: duple meter, but not clear to listener; tempo Sehr ruhig (very serenely)

Harmony: atonal, derived from the use of several forms of the tone row

Texture: usually sparse; somewhat pointillistic

Form: theme and variations

Suggested Listening

The Works of Schoenberg

Schoenberg: *Erwartung, Op. 17* ("Expectation") [Columbia M2S-679]. *Erwartung* is a miniature opera, written for one female singer and a large orchestra. The singer portrays a woman searching for her lover. Both text and music convey the intensity of her hope and anguish as she pursues the quest, only to learn, at the last, that he is dead. The music is atonal, and new material seems to evolve with every phrase. The effect is strongly emotional, even shocking.

Schoenberg: *Variations for Orchestra, Op. 31* [Columbia M2S-694]. This work contains an introduction, a theme, nine variations, and a finale, all built on a single tone row. The row is presented quite clearly as the theme, with prominent dotted rhythms. The complex use of the row in the variations results in a multiplicity of moods, textures, and harmonies.

The Works of Berg

Berg: *Wozzeck* [DG 2707023]. Each act of Berg's opera contains a number of sections freely built on earlier compositional forms such as the suite and the march. The music is generally atonal, with occasional references to a central tonality. The orchestra is large, used in a very colorful manner. Both conventional singing and Sprechstimme are employed to good effect.

Berg: *Orchestral Songs, Op. 4* [Columbia MS-7179]. These songs are often called the "Altenberg Lieder," in allusion to the fact that the text is based on the poetry of Peter Altenberg. The songs are early works, scored for vocal soloist and orchestra, and show the influence of both Schoenberg and Debussy. The expressive, chromatic writing anticipates the style and effects of serial music. The songs have great dramatic impact, yet often suggest a feeling of tenderness.

The Works of Webern

Webern: *String Quartet, Op. 28* [DG 2720029]. The tone row used in this quartet is extremely intricate. The work begins with the B-A-C-H motive used in Bach's *Art of the Fugue*, with the second half of the row a retrograde inversion of the first half. The work displays Webern's usual extreme economy of materials. The timbres of the various string instruments are skillfully utilized to bring out the well-organized, dissonant harmony.

Webern: *First Cantata, Op. 29* [Angel S-36480]. A text by Hildegarde Jone forms the basis of this intense and dissonant composition for soprano, chorus, and orchestra. Like many other atonal works, this one is very difficult for the singers, but strikingly effective when well performed. It is especially notable for its use of dynamic contrast.

Listening Preview   Through most of the nineteenth century, concert music in America was dominated by the European tradition. Popular music, on the other hand, became Americanized much more rapidly. Listen to two examples of twentieth-century American music—the first two sections of Aaron Copland's Appalachian Spring and Louis Armstrong's rendition of "West End Blues" (Side 11, Bands 2 and 4, or recordings from the record library). To what extent does the first selection resemble the early twentieth-century music of Europe? What factors seem to mark both works as American?

28

Main Currents in American Music

Colonial and Early American Music

Early Religious Music

When the Pilgrims and the Jamestown colonists came to America in the seventeenth century, English music came with them—hymns, psalms, ballads, dance tunes, and more. Early musical development was strongest in the New England colonies, where much of the music was religious. The fact that the music was considered religious did not, however, mean that it was always solemn. The *Ainsworth Psalter*, which the Pilgrims brought with them in 1620, contained a number of metrical versions of the psalms, some of which were set in the style of lively dances.

American religious music, isolated from steady contact with its English roots, developed in a fundamentally European but yet distinctive way. This specifically American quality was perhaps less perceptible in the growing urban centers of the East Coast than in the rural and western regions. In fact, by the end of the seventeenth century, religious music in America could be roughly divided into two parallel traditions—one urban, the other rural.

Urban churches generally followed what was considered the "regular" style of singing. A simple vocal technique was used with close adherence to a written score and good musical discipline among the four parts, whether sung by choir or by congregation. The music itself also tended to be fairly simple. A good example of the style—though it happens to be English rather than American—can be found in the hymn tune "O God, Our Help in Ages Past," which dates from the early eighteenth century. In typical fashion, it is based on a psalm and is in the so-called common meter, with four-line stanzas of eight, six, eight, and six syllables, respectively, set in a plain, steady, one-note-to-a-syllable style.

At the same time, a number of rural religious songs also took shape. These were less influenced by formal musical standards and were sung in what was called the "usual" style. This rural style was often more ornate and improvisational than the regular style and did not, in most cases, make use of musical notation.

Singing Schools

A very important development in early American music—the *singing school*—began around 1720. Itinerant singing masters traveled from town to town conducting series of weekly sessions and often making an additional profit by selling the necessary songbooks. The musical sessions generally climaxed in a public concert in which the local singers sang in parts. The music taught at the singing schools usually included psalms, hymn tunes, anthems, and fuging tunes, each with a short imitative section. Prominent among composers of music for the singing schools was William Billings (1746–1800). A self-taught composer, Billings conspicuously lacked technical sophistication and made no effort to acquire it.

Billings

Secular Folk Music

Meanwhile, a secular folk tradition also began to develop. Songs originally brought from England changed their contours a bit, picked up new words here and there, and soon became comfortably American. They were passed on informally from one singer or fiddler to another at barn raisings, on the trail, or around the fire on winter nights, changing as they went—sometimes greatly, sometimes scarcely at all. In some parts of the United States, notably the remote southern Appalachian region, many of these tunes have survived in common use up to the present day. Tracing their evolution from their English or Scottish origins is one of the fascinating elements in the study of American folklore.

European Influence

While folk music soon became part of the American tradition, composed music long remained fundamentally European in style. Throughout the colonial period, music outside of the folk tradition was dominated by European composers, European teachers, and European performers. This is not to say that Americans were uninterested in concert music. An influential group of amateurs, including Thomas Jefferson and Benjamin Franklin, had much to do with introducing the works of such European composers as Haydn and Mozart to the eastern seaboard. Jefferson hoped to create a cultural center at his Virginia home, Monticello. Franklin was not only a lover of music but an amateur composer and the inventor of a glass harmonica that inspired several works by Mozart.

In fact, the late eighteenth century was a time of increasing musical interest and activity throughout what would soon be the United States. Amateur composers studied European works, and books of music instruction were published. Public concerts grew in popularity, and impressive, expensive pipe organs were built in many city churches. Philadelphia and Charleston became the chief music centers of the era. By 1762, the Saint Cecilia Society, the first major musical society in the New World, had been established in Charleston.

Hopkinson

It was also in the eighteenth century that some Americans began to think that their country should be able to do more than echo the European style of music. Thus, Francis Hopkinson (1737–1791) announced himself as the first truly American composer. That he made such a claim indicates a rising awareness among Americans of their own potential. Hopkinson wrote several large works as well as a number of songs, the best known of which is "My Days Have Been So Wondrous Free," the first surviving song by an American.

Before leaving colonial and early American music, one curious development that found considerable favor in America and England in the seven-

Jefferson as Violinist: *In this artist's impression, Jefferson is shown playing a duet with a captured British officer during the American Revolution. The setting is Monticello, Jefferson's own adaptation of the Classical architectural style then favored in Europe.*

Fasola and Shape-Note Notation

teenth and eighteenth centuries should be mentioned. This was a system of sight singing known as *fasola* because it used principally those three syllables—fa, sol, and la. The fasola system led in the early nineteenth century to the development of *shape-note notation*, in which four notes of different shapes—generally triangular, round, oblong, and diamond-shaped—were used to show relative pitches in a melody. Shape-notes were much used in the rural South in the nineteenth century, largely in popular collections of hymns and anthems. Today shape-note singing is still avidly pursued by a number of small groups in the South.

Trends in Nineteenth-Century Music

Orchestras and Choral Societies

During the nineteenth century, the eighteenth-century trend toward musical sophistication accelerated. The first orchestras were founded, often in association with choral societies. One of these, the Handel and Haydn Society of Boston, was established in 1815, and another, the New York Philharmonic

Society, was established in 1839. The success of the new orchestras often depended on the flamboyance with which they were presented to the general public. "Monster" concerts, with hundreds of instrumentalists and singers, were attended by audiences numbering in the thousands. Extravagant displays of this sort were good publicity and helped to encourage the development of America's modern symphony orchestras.

Thomas

The person most responsible for the rise of the symphony orchestra in America was Theodore Thomas (1835–1905), who joined the New York Philharmonic Society as conductor in 1879. Until then, the Society had been a cooperative venture run by the players and generally performing only a very limited repertoire of familiar works. Under Thomas, business affairs were taken out of the hands of the musicians and given over to a full-time manager—an arrangement that was to become typical of the complex symphonic corporations of the twentieth century. At the same time, Thomas himself, as conductor, asserted more and more control over the music. He organized new types of concerts, sometimes featuring solo performers, and expanded the repertoire, adding new vocal, chamber, and orchestral works. In 1891 he accepted an invitation to go to Chicago. Citizens there were eager to have a symphony orchestra of their own—preferably bigger and better than that of their eastern rival. The money for salaries and a concert hall was raised by public subscription, and under Thomas's direction the Chicago Symphony became one of the nation's major orchestras.

Despite the growing American interest in serious music, the ruling style continued to be European throughout the nineteenth century. True, there were hints of a developing national style. But even with the growing number of music conservatories and performing groups at home, the majority of American composers continued to receive their training in Austria, Germany, or other European music centers. Such practice continued, in fact, up until World War I.

Mason

One of the most important figures in early nineteenth-century American music was Lowell Mason (1792–1872), a composer, conductor, and the creator of musical education in public schools in Boston and elsewhere. As much an entrepreneur as an artist, Mason used advertising techniques to attract audiences and quite frankly wrote his music to suit the current fashion. He introduced improved teaching methods and compiled a number of song collections including *The Boston Handel and Haydn Society Collection of Church Music*. Mason's greatest importance was in popularizing hymns based on music adapted from the standard European masters.

Foster

As the century progressed, nationalistic elements slowly began to make themselves felt in American music. Stephen Foster (1826–1864) wrote a number of sentimental ballads in the Romantic tradition, but he is far better remembered for his songs inspired by southern black spirituals. The works are not authentic black music. Foster visited the South only once, and that was after he had already written most of his songs. However, even if not ethnically correct, the songs had a freshness and an "American" quality that was appealing to many middle-class families. The songs also inspired, through their popularity, an interest in their sources.

Gottschalk

Another composer who made use of distinctively American elements was Louis Moreau Gottschalk (1829–1869), a virtuoso pianist from New Orleans. Gottschalk's music was written in a somewhat exotic Romantic style, a style that he managed well enough to achieve considerable success in Europe, making him virtually the only American of his day to do so. His works, although basically European in style, contain many traces of Caribbean rhythms and other rhythms learned in the lively intercultural crossroads of his native city.

Sousa

The marches of John Philip Sousa (1854–1932) show another aspect of the American character in music. Director of the Marine Band from 1880 to 1892, Sousa later organized his own band and toured the United States, Canada, and Europe, winning great acclaim for his stirring, inspired marches. Many of them, especially "Semper Fidelis" and "Stars and Stripes Forever," are still played by bands today.

MacDowell

Perhaps the prototypical American composer of the period was the German-trained Edward MacDowell (1861–1908), a man once regarded as America's greatest composer. At the age of fifteen, he left America to study in Europe and established himself there as a successful composer before returning to the United States in 1888. Throughout his career, he was a strong supporter of American nationalism, yet his music, in its lack of any folk, religious, or Afro-American elements, seems not to reflect this interest.

Following a style very much within the German-Austrian tradition, MacDowell wrote music for orchestra, chorus, piano, and solo voice. Among his early works are a number of program symphonies with highly personal content and two piano concertos with a Liszt-like breadth and power. As he grew older, his compositions became smaller and more precise. He abandoned orchestral music after 1896 and near the end of his short life devoted most of his time to writing quaint and lively piano pieces. These late works, including *Woodland Sketches* and *Fireside Tales*, were generally brief character pieces— miniatures of evocative delicacy.

Other American composers turned to very different styles. Some were attracted by French and Russian musical developments, particularly by Impressionism and Russian nationalism. Stimulated, perhaps, by the latter movement, a number of American composers undertook for the first time a serious study of the American folk tradition. A concern for contemporary affairs also made itself felt in a number of works.

Griffes

One of the most important of the composers influenced by the new trends was Charles Tomlinson Griffes (1884–1920). After four years' study in Germany, he returned to America at the age of twenty-three to begin a career as a composer and teacher in a boys' school. Griffes' eclectic temperament led him to study Oriental scales and themes, the new French Impressionism, and Scriabin's innovations in Russia. He was perhaps most strongly influenced by Debussy. In his works for piano, orchestra, and chorus, Griffes achieved an Impressionistic, neutral tonality, making use of unresolved dissonance, bitonal ostinatos, and augmented chords. His last and probably greatest work was his *Piano Sonata*. But perhaps his most enduring and most popular work was his symphonic poem *The Pleasure Dome of Kubla Khan*.

Trends in Twentieth-Century Music

World War I proved a watershed for many aspects of American art and life, and not least for music. During the heady, affluent decade that followed the war, many composers turned from the old German-dominated tradition to follow new paths and find new sources of inspiration in French music.

French Influence

The general fascination with all things French that characterized the attitude of young American artists in the 1920s was particularly liberating to music. The French tradition encouraged the absorption of new influences in a way that German late Romanticism did not. Griffes, as we have seen, had already been stirred by the Impressionism of Debussy. In the next generation, other young Americans were stimulated by their study of French music to become both more French and more American in their styles of composition. Having learned the new techniques, they set to work to apply them to indigenous American sources.

Influence of Nadia Boulanger

Many of the aspiring young American composers of the 1920s studied in Paris with Nadia Boulanger (b. 1887), whose influence as a teacher of composers, performers, and music scholars remains of considerable importance. From her the young composers acquired a grasp of the principles, not merely the surface appearance, of the new developments in French music. In particular they gained an understanding of the early work of Stravinsky. Many of them began to intermix exotic elements in their compositions. At the same time, a number of them discovered and made use of the melodic, harmonic, and rhythmic wealth contained in American folk and ethnic traditions. From Oriental music they learned the uses of unusual scales, and when they looked back across the Atlantic to their own American heritage, they found the rhythms of jazz, folk music, and religious tunes. The result of all this innovation was, not the founding of any one American school or sound, but rather the subsequent development among twentieth-century American composers of quite dissimilar styles. Music historian Otto Deri has divided these twentieth-century styles into four groups, with some overlapping among them: Nationalists, Traditionalists, Progressives, and Experimentalists.

Nationalism

Like the Nationalist composers in Europe, those in America attempted, in varying degrees, to base their work on native folk styles. For the Americans this meant especially jazz and religious music. One of many important Nationalist composers was George Gershwin (1898–1937). Skillful at handling both popular and more complex styles, Gershwin wrote numerous successful popular songs and musical comedies as well as concert works such as *Rhapsody in Blue* and the great folk opera *Porgy and Bess*. Perhaps more than any other composer, he possessed the ability to incorporate the techniques of jazz into music of all natures.

Copland

Indigenous American material has also been very important in the work of Aaron Copland (b. 1900). Copland, who was born in Brooklyn of immigrant

Gershwin

Russian-Jewish parents, early developed a strong desire to become a composer and in 1921 went to France to study with Nadia Boulanger. Upon his return three years later, he embarked on a career as a composer, as a proponent of new music, and as a concert organizer, lecturer, and conductor.

Copland's early works use jazzlike rhythms, bold dissonances, and occasional Jewish melodies for programmatic and evocative effect. Later he turned away from this style, regarding it as superficial, and produced a series of nonprogrammatic, abstract works including his *Piano Variations* (1930). His works in this middle period were generally quite difficult and seemed most concerned with the working out of purely musical ideas. After 1935 Copland began writing music for wider, less technically expert audiences. He wrote a number of ballets based on American themes as well as scores for films, including the film versions of John Steinbeck's *Of Mice and Men* and *The Red Pony*. Making frequent use of American folk and popular music, including cowboy tunes, jazz, ragtime, and hymns, Copland appeared at this stage to be concentrating on communication and not on theoretical problems.

The many different elements of Copland's ever-changing style, insofar as they can be identified, seem to be dominated by a desire for organization, clarity, and control. His melodies, flavored as they so often are with folk and religious tunes, are for the most part easily understood. They typically feature conjunct motion with occasional larger intervals. Copland believes that a long melodic line is indispensable and creates it by using repeated motives and adding new materials so that the melody seems to grow out of itself. His melodies have generally been both distinctive and very attractive.

Like most other twentieth-century composers, Copland has been much concerned with rhythmic vitality. Nearly all of his works have an unmistakable rhythmic drive. His earlier pieces are especially noteworthy for their use of percussive rhythms and ostinato. Various other contemporary devices, many of them introduced or made popular by Stravinsky, also appear in his works—among them the use of changing meters and the asymmetrical displacement of accents within the measure. By these and other means, he has achieved the syncopations that give his meters their characteristic unpredictability.

In harmony Copland has remained rather consistently tonal. Within this framework, he has used a number of now standard modern methods such as polytonality and the deliberate confusion of the major and minor modes. It is true that in some of his more recent works, such as the *Piano Fantasy* (1957), he has begun to make use of the serial technique. Yet in the vast majority of his work, he has retained the triad as the basis of harmony, using it regularly in order to suggest the simplicity and beauty of rural life. The texture of much of his music is rather transparent, with a stress on individual timbres, frequently in their upper ranges.

Copland's ballets, *Appalachian Spring*, *Billy the Kid*, and *Rodeo*, are among his most popular works. Here we will consider the first ballet, *Appalachian Spring*, a work for which he received the Pulitzer Prize in 1945.

A 1940s Production of *Appalachian Spring: Copland purposefully chose simple melodies for his ballet* Appalachian Spring, *partly to assure that the music would be accessible to the largest possible audience. The scene above is taken from an early Martha Graham production.*

Copland: *Appalachian Spring*

Copland's *Appalachian Spring** comes close to representing the very essence of pioneer America. The work was originally commissioned for Martha Graham and her dance company. Although the first score called for only thirteen instruments, in 1945 Copland orchestrated the ballet for a moderately large orchestra made up of pairs of wind instruments, timpani, ten other percussion instruments, harp, piano, and strings.

The preface to the score gives the basic story behind the ballet. The ballet opens with the spring celebration of a newly built farmhouse in the Appalachian hills in the early nineteenth century.

> The bride-to-be and the young farmer-husband enact the emotions, joyful and apprehensive, their new domestic partnership invites. An older neighbour suggests now and then the rocky confidence of experience. A revivalist and his followers remind the new householders of the strange and terrible aspects of human fate. At the end the couple are left quiet and strong in their new house.

The music written for *Appalachian Spring* falls into eight sections.

First Section

The first section is marked "Very slowly" and is based almost completely on a three-note motive that is repeated, changed, and expanded many times:

Opening Motive

Each of the characters taking part in the opening section is presented in turn, all in a very soft, understated manner.

Side 11, Band 2

Listening Guide for Copland's *Appalachian Spring,* First Section

Timbre:	orchestra of moderate size with string, wind, and percussion instruments and piano
Melody:	based largely on a three-note motive
Rhythm:	duple meter; very slow tempo
Harmony:	clearly tonal, in the key of A major
Texture:	homophonic and contrapuntal
Form:	one of a series of sections

Second Section

The second section offers great contrast to the softness and gentleness of the first section. The music is lively and exuberant with a number of descending and ascending arpeggios and scales. One very bright, conjunct theme stands out:

Main Theme

Side 11, Band 2 (Immediately following First Section)

Listening Guide for Copland's *Appalachian Spring,* Second Section

Timbre:	orchestra of moderate size with string, wind, and percussion instruments and piano
Melody:	basic theme is descending and conjunct
Rhythm:	duple meter; fast tempo
Harmony:	clearly tonal; begins in A major, modulates through C major, ends in F major
Texture:	homophonic and contrapuntal
Form:	one of a series of sections

MAIN CURRENTS IN AMERICAN MUSIC

Other Sections in Copland's *Appalachian Spring*

The third section is a duet for the bride and groom. The rhythm seems to express hesitation, with its changing meters and prominent syncopation. In the fourth section, the tempo is again lively as the revivalist and his followers appear. The music soon flows into a square dance in duple meter with generous use of syncopation. The fifth section, the bride's solo dance, is still faster, based on a version of the theme in the second section. Changes of meter and key suggest her mingled joy and apprehension. The sixth section is slower, bringing back the gentle, understated motive of the first section.

The seventh section is probably the best known. In it the lovely Shaker melody "Simple Gifts" is used as the basis for a series of five variations:

Theme of Seventh Section

As the dancers enact the daily tasks of wife and husband, more instruments join in, and the volume increases until the last, more quiet variation. The eighth and final section is then heard. The music has a slow tempo and a quiet dynamic level that recalls the first section once again both in mood and in motive.

Traditionalism

The composers of the Traditionalist group are generally identified by their devotion to the music of the past. They can be divided into two very different subgroups. The Neoromantics favor a style that has evolved out of the Romantic tradition. The Neoclassicists, on the other hand, tend to place greater value on universal means of expression presented within rather strictly circumscribed forms.

Neoromantics and Neoclassicists

Barber

A composer who in many respects typifies the Neoromantic style is Samuel Barber (b. 1910). His music is generally lyrical and tonal but with unusual harmonies. *Adagio for Strings* (1936) and the earlier *Dover Beach* (1931) for voice and string quartet are popular examples of his work. His *Concerto for Piano*, written in 1962, is a very engaging work featuring complex and driving rhythms. In 1966 his opera *Anthony and Cleopatra* was commissioned for the opening of the Metropolitan Opera House in New York.

Piston

The Neoclassical side of Traditionalism can be seen in the work of the New Englander Walter Piston (1894–1976). Piston studied with Nadia Boulanger in Paris and later taught music at Harvard, where he remained as an important instructor and writer of textbooks until he retired in 1960. Piston has composed almost exclusively for orchestra and chamber group. He did write one ballet, *The Incredible Flutist*, which is among his most highly praised works. His music is characterized by clearly defined melodies that display considerable variety of motion and mood. He often created unusual rhythmic effects with unequal subdivisions of the beat, yet he did not try to incorporate jazz or other consciously "American" elements in his music. His harmony relies on a tonal foundation with a rich contrapuntal texture. And, as one might expect, he particularly favored Classical forms.

Progressivism

Progressive composers have developed styles more modern than those preferred by the Traditionalists. Their techniques, however, have been largely those already developed to some extent by other composers—atonality, serialism, and new rhythmic devices, among others.

Sessions

One of the leading Progressives is the Brooklyn-born Roger Sessions (b. 1896). In 1925, after his early studies, he began a period of foreign travel that included trips to Italy and Germany. In 1933, he returned to the United States to teach. His compositions include operas and works for orchestra, piano, and chamber ensemble. Sessions' musical style has changed considerably through the years. Many of his early works exhibit extreme contrasts of mood, as can be seen in his incidental music for a play, *The Black Maskers* (1923), one of his best-known works. He moved from a very Classical approach in the *Symphony No. 1* (1927) to a more chromatic style in the *Piano Sonata No. 2* (1946), and then to a twelve-tone style in the *Quintet for Strings* (1958). Even his melodies underwent a sort of evolution, becoming longer after 1935 and acquiring greater importance. His harmonies have also changed strikingly in the course of his career. His early works have many features of traditional harmony, particularly the use of a well-defined tonal center. This gave way gradually to a dissonant, atonal style. In most cases, his atonal works have been a compromise between serial technique and freely structured chromaticism.

Experimentalism

The fourth general group of twentieth-century American composers, the Experimentalists, have taken diverse paths in search of new methods, techniques, and materials. One of the more important composers in this group was

Cowell

Henry Cowell (1897–1965), born in California, the son of impoverished parents. In childhood Cowell had little chance to hear European concert music, but he did hear Medieval Church modes played by a local organist, the Oriental melodies of his Chinese neighbors, and the Irish folk songs of his own relatives. As a young man he began to compose, following his own intuition, and though he later acquired some formal training, the eclectic influences of his youth stayed with him. He became a writer as well, producing or contributing to important works on twentieth-century music and making significant contributions to the study of non-Western music.

Cowell's compositions include works for orchestra, band, chorus, chamber group, piano, and voice. His melodies are based on a wide range of folk sources—American, Japanese, Indian, Persian, Celtic, and others. His harmonies include considerable dissonance, much of it unresolved. He was particularly fond of thick tone clusters.

Experimentalism in Painting: *The twentieth century has been marked by far-reaching experimentation in all the arts. One of the most important movements in American painting—Abstract Expressionism—developed in the years just after World War II. An early example can be seen in Jackson Pollock's* Number 1, 1948. (*Oil on canvas, 68" × 104"*)

Experiments with the Piano

However, it was in his expansion of the sound-producing capabilities of the piano that Cowell made his most fruitful contribution to modern music. Not content with the instrument's ordinary range of timbre, he began to experiment with direct manipulation of the strings and produced some startling new sounds. One of his works, *The Banshee*, for example, calls for two players—one at the keyboard and the other standing at the crook of the grand piano. The player at the keyboard merely holds down a pedal while the other player sweeps, plucks, slaps, and scrapes the open strings with hand and fingernails, following a specially devised and very precise system of notation. The result is a shrieking, wailing, eerie sound entirely appropriate to the title of the work. In other works, the keyboard is used along with the manipulation of the strings. Such a technique is common today, but Cowell seems to have been the first to make serious use of it.

Ives

Another very important Experimentalist was Charles Ives (1874–1954). Ives was fortunate in his father, a Connecticut bandmaster who combined an intelligent love of the classics with a passionate curiosity about all sorts of sounds. These enthusiasms he passed on to his son. At a time when polytonality had scarcely yet been thought of in Europe, Ives was learning to sing familiar songs in one key while his father accompanied him in another key. When chromaticism was still the furthest limit of daring for most American composers, Ives was hearing quarter-tone intervals on an instrument his father had invented.

Ives studied music at Yale but decided not to make it his career. He knew that the kind of music he wanted to write would never earn him a living in his own generation. As a successful life-insurance salesman, he made himself relatively secure against financial worries and was free to experiment musically as he would.

Early Innovative Work

Many of the works that resulted from Ives' combination of an experimental temperament and complete professional freedom were quite extraordinary. Ives anticipated by decades techniques that later became identified with Bartók, Hindemith, Stravinsky, and even Schoenberg—among them polytonality, atonality, and polyrhythms. He was, in fact, so far ahead of his time that most of the conductors and performers to whom he occasionally showed his work considered it unplayable. Indeed, the greater part of his music remained unknown until after World War I. One conductor who did express a willingness to present one of his symphonies was Gustav Mahler, but Mahler died before the project could be carried out.

That Ives' early role as a musical innovator went unrecognized can probably be attributed to two main factors. The first was that he did not demand recognition. He seemed content to leave his work unknown and unplayed if the musical public showed itself disinclined to hear it. The other reason was that, unlike such composers as Hindemith and Schoenberg, he never organized his innovations into a system. Instead he roamed widely over whole new musical continents, seeking out and using new technical devices as they served to express the ideas he had in mind rather than as techniques for their own sake.

Ives' treatment of melody was often surprising. He was very fond of quoting from hymns, popular songs, folk songs, or well-known classics in order to establish a desired emotional context. Once this was done, however, he might alter and develop the melodies in unexpected ways—inverting them, turning them around, or expanding or diminishing the intervals.

Ives' rhythmic techniques had a great deal to do with the fact that his work was considered "hopeless" by more conservative composers. He frequently used irregular meters such as $\frac{5}{8}$, $\frac{11}{8}$, or $\frac{7}{4}$, as Stravinsky was later to do. Occasionally he avoided metrical consistency altogether and instead simply added a bar line wherever he wanted an accented beat.

In harmony and texture, he was equally complex. In fact, he seemed to disregard all preconceptions about the structure and function of chords. His music is full of polytonal and occasionally atonal passages. He also made much use of free, dissonant counterpoint—sometimes so dense that the ear can scarcely distinguish the lines. Some of the tone clusters in his music written for piano were unplayable by ordinary means, so he specified that a piece of wood be used to press all the necessary keys at once.

The sum total of this extreme harmonic dissonance and rhythmic irregularity was more than many listeners of Ives' day could understand. Many heard only clashing chaos. But Ives had something to say with this dissonance. He seems to have felt that each line of music, like each human being, had a certain right to an independent existence. If the various independences sometimes clashed—well, that was acceptable. He believed, and wrote, that music should concern itself with life's ideas and experiences, dissonance and all.

Stereophonic Effects

One further device to which Ives' regard for musical independence led him was the creation of *stereophonic effects*—the use of several different performing groups, each with its own conductor, stationed in different parts of the performing area. Such a technique was used in a work written in 1908, *The Unanswered Question.*

In general, Ives' use of form was as free as his use of the other musical elements. Whether writing for orchestra, chorus, solo voice, piano, or chamber group, he used traditional forms only insofar as they served to express his ideas. He studiously avoided symmetrical and balanced construction, and within single movements he often allowed great disparity of mood and material. In his *Concord Sonata*, for example, passages of great difficulty and sophistication alternate with references to banal popular music. The unity found in Ives' works lies partly in his use of theme and structure and partly in his use of programmatic ideas.

Ives: "Fourth of July"

Ives' "Fourth of July"* is one of the four movements in his work entitled *A Symphony: Holidays.* This particular movement shows his adventurous style to good advantage. The other movements are "Washington's Birthday," "Decoration Day," and "Thanksgiving." The orchestra required for the symphony includes large sections of wind, string, and percussion instruments.

Ives prefaced the score for "Fourth of July" with the following brief description:

> It's a boy's "4th,"—no historical orations—no patriotic grandiloquences by "grown-ups"—no program in his yard! But he knows what he's celebrating—better than some of the county politicians. And he goes at it in his own way, with a patriotism, nearer kin to nature than jingoism. His festivities start in the quiet of the midnight before and grow raucous with the sun. Everybody knows what it's like. The day ends with the sky-rocket over the Church-steeple, just after the annual explosion sets the Town-Hall on fire.

The work opens with a sustained and muted F major chord in the low strings. At the same time, the first violins softly play the opening motive of

*Ives, "The Fourth of July." Copyright © 1959 by Associated Music Publishers, Inc. Excerpts used by permission.

"Columbia, the Gem of the Ocean" in the key of C♯ major. The music thus begins with a clear example of the use of bitonality.

Opening Motive and Chord

In the second measure, suggestions of a new key in the second violin make the sound even more dissonant. String basses and tuba in turn play the opening motive in different, slow rhythms while a dissonant counterpoint is begun in one of the violin parts. The meter changes frequently—$\frac{4}{2}$, $\frac{4}{4}$, $\frac{7}{8}$, $\frac{4}{4}$, and so forth. Dissonance continues to grow as other instruments enter and the tempo and dynamic level gradually increase. Motives from "Columbia, the Gem of the Ocean" are heard again and again.

A climax approaches as the violin plays a brief excerpt from the "Battle Hymn of the Republic," followed by a motive from "The Battle Cry of Freedom" in the horn. Soon the horns and then the trumpets play a short passage from "Reveille":

Theme Based on "Reveille"

The mood then changes as the steady rhythm of a dissonant march begins. The piccolo, however, subtly slips in a phrase of "The Girl I Left Behind Me." The march is finally interrupted by a sudden explosive burst of sound, with tone clusters in the strings: the fireworks have started. Here as in many other passages, several different rhythmic patterns occur simultaneously, creating great rhythmic conflict and confusion. After this brief outburst, the mood becomes very quiet. Chromatic dissonance continues, and an altered version of "Columbia, the Gem of the Ocean" returns in the trombone part:

Chromatic Trombone Line

After the tune has been completed, there is a brief pause. Then furious activity breaks out in the entire orchestra, with dissonant chords, tone clusters, and glissandi in the strings. The sky rocket has obviously gone over the church steeple. The excitement then subsides toward a quiet, dissonant ending.

Listening Guide for Ives' "Fourth of July"

Timbre:	large orchestra of string, wind, and percussion instruments and piano
Melody:	themes based on quotes from a number of popular tunes
Rhythm:	meter changes frequently; tempo slow at first, then faster
Harmony:	basically tonal, with chromaticism and dissonance; at times bitonal
Texture:	homophonic and contrapuntal
Form:	divided into freely formed sections

Suggested Listening

The Music of the Nationalists

Gershwin: *Porgy and Bess* [Columbia OS-2016]. This outstanding American opera caused a sensation when it appeared in 1935 and has continued popular to the present day. The plot deals with the lives of ordinary southern black people of the time in a rural setting. Elements of blues, jazz, and spirituals are appropriately incorporated. The musical style as a whole is very accessible, yet sophisticated. The opera itself is dramatically effective and thoroughly enjoyable.

Copland: *Rodeo* [Columbia MS-6175]. This ballet, first presented in 1942 and choreographed by Agnes de Mille, contains many folk elements. It is set in the Old West, and the plot concerns a young woman who longs to share the manly life of the cowboys on the ranch. Since the ballet was composed long before the women's liberation movement, she finds her happiness—and her true love—at the end when she abandons "unwomanly" ambitions and changes her blue jeans and riding boots for a party dress. Cowboy songs are skillfully worked into the score, and the orchestration brings out a succession of moods.

The Music of the Traditionalists

Barber: *Adagio for Strings* [Columbia MG-31155]. This work was first performed under the direction of the celebrated conductor Arturo Toscanini, who had heard some of Barber's early music and decided it was worth performing. Like many of Barber's other works, the *Adagio* is rather conservative in style but very convincing. The lovely lyrical melodies and the fresh tonal harmony clearly show the Neoromanticism of Barber's style.

Piston: *The Incredible Flutist* [Columbia MS-6943]. This ballet is one of Piston's most immediately attractive works. It shows his typically careful and disciplined style to excellent advantage. A wide variety of moods develop as the composition unfolds.

The Music of the Progressives

Sessions: *The Black Maskers* [Mercury 75049]. Sessions based this suite on the incidental music he had earlier written for Leonid Andreyev's play of the same name. There are four parts, corresponding to the four acts of the play. The horror and strangeness of the plot, involving a grotesque masquerade and a murder, are portrayed through the use of harsh dissonances and striking timbres.

The Music of the Experimentalists

Ives: *General William Booth Enters into Heaven* [Columbia MS-6921]. Ives pays tribute here to the founder of the Salvation Army, with an instrumental group that sounds like a marching band and quotations from several well-known Army hymns. A chorus adds another dimension of color, as it thunderously acclaims the victorious hero. Ives' technique is at its best in this work.

Ives: *Piano Sonata No. 2* (the "Concord" Sonata) [DG 2530215]. This generally programmatic sonata is subtitled "Concord, Mass., 1840–1860" and celebrates some of the town's more famous citizens: Emerson, Hawthorne, Thoreau, and the Alcotts. Parts of familiar tunes materialize unexpectedly, the meters change frequently, and conflicting rhythmic patterns are prominent. While the overall harmony is tonal, several passages are very dissonant and suggest atonality.

C H A P T E R

29

American Popular Music

Sources of Popular Music

Folk music, soul music, jazz, country, rock—whatever the style, popular music plays an important part in the daily lives of most Americans. Its origins are deep in the human spirit, and its history reaches back to the earliest ages.

Popular music in America has been influenced by folk traditions around the world. Over the years the millions of immigrants who came to this country brought with them the music they knew and loved. At times this music has been sustained virtually intact. Croatians still do round dances to traditional music in Detroit. German songs are heard in Milwaukee. And Chinese music abounds around Grant Street in San Francisco. Often, however, the music has changed in America, been blended and mixed with other traditions to create "American" folk and popular music. Often, too, folk traditions have served as a basis for distinctly new types of music. This can be seen most clearly in the black folk music roots of jazz and rock.

Because of the great importance of folk music both as a musical style in and of itself and as a source of other popular styles, we will begin our discussion of popular music in America with an examination of the two major folk traditions: Anglo-American folk music and black folk music.

Anglo-American Folk Music

Anglo-American folk music is strongly rooted in the English and Scottish styles brought to the New World in the seventeenth and eighteenth centuries. In these early centuries, singing and dancing were among the most popular forms of informal entertainment in the colonies. Folk songs were sung daily in homes, at work, and of course on festive occasions. Often unaccompanied they were at other times sung with the support of household instruments such as the guitar and the *dulcimer*—an early string instrument. Songs were devised by young and old and passed on orally from one generation to the next. Most remained unwritten and were thus prone to variation and easily responsive to outside influences.

General Characteristics

Stylistically, Anglo-American folk songs share a number of basic characteristics. The music is generally uncomplicated, in part because of the need to pass it on verbally from one person to another. Melodies are usually conjunct and organized into phrases of equal length. Rhythm and meter are derived to some extent from the words of the songs. Texture is generally homophonic, with the melodies supported by chordal accompaniment. Form is normally symmetrical and strophic. Repeated phrases occur, helping to delineate the structure more clearly. This simple and direct style, however, contrasts with the profound ideas that the lyrics often convey.

Ballads

Some of the most important characteristics of Anglo-American folk music come from the *English ballad*, or narrative song. The typical ballad is made up of several stanzas with a recurrent refrain. The themes are generally sentimental, social, or political. A large part of the folk heritage of the British Isles was transmitted through the years by ballads, and when the English, Scots, and Irish came to America, the ballads came with them.

The English ballad tradition remained strongest in New England and Appalachia. The ballads of these regions, like their antecedents, ordinarily recount the outlines of a tragic story, sometimes with refrains unrelated to the rest of the narrative. Their lyrics combine American colloquialisms and more refined literary English. Many New World ballads originally had no accompaniment or relied on the support of a single repeated chord strummed on a guitar or banjo.

Occupational Songs

Another type of Anglo-American folk music, derived more or less from the ballad, is the *occupational song*. The lyrics generally concern such things as the perils, loneliness, humor, or joys of mining, farming, cowherding, railroad building, and the many other jobs that went into building America. Some of the songs highlight serious accidents and tragedies. Others make a joke out of hardship. An example of the second type is found in the lyrics of a song about tarriers, or railroad laborers:

> . . . one day a premature blast went off;
> And a mile in the air went big Jim Goff;
> And drill, ye tarriers, drill. . . .
>
> Next week, when payday came around,
> Jim Goff a dollar short was found.
> When he asked what for, came this reply:
> "Yer docked fer the time you was up in the sky!"
> And drill, ye tarriers, drill. . . .

One special type of occupational song, the *sea chantey*, was at first borrowed from other countries, but was gradually remolded to reflect the spirit of American sailors.

Instrumental Music

Purely instrumental folk music supplied a background for dancing and marching. The *square dance*, patterned after the English rural jig, was a New World invention that required no more accompaniment than a lone fiddle and clapping hands. A number of *marching tunes* were also devised, generally for fife and drum. As in vocal music, economy of style was a basic factor. One or two instruments had to suffice, although more could be added if they were available.

Other Types of Folk Songs

A number of other types of folk songs were also patterned after British prototypes. *Patriotic songs* were widespread. During the Revolutionary War, many such songs were written to convey news of battles, celebrate victories, boost morale, bolster courage, and even to make jokes about the enemy. Children's *play songs* such as "Skip to My Lou" were abundant. *Love songs* such as "I Gave My Love an Apple" and *lullabies* were somewhat rarer.

One uniquely American type of folk song related *tall tales* about life in the New World. Although they were musically similar to English songs, their lyrics manifested the peculiarly American penchant for self-deprecating humor and exaggeration found perhaps most clearly in the Paul Bunyan legends. As we have seen, this penchant often carried over to occupational songs.

Relatively pure versions of English folk music are still found in the remoter regions of Appalachia and the southern hill country. Scattered inhabitants of these areas have entertained themselves for generations with songs handed down by memory. In other areas, marked by a steady influx of immigrants from Europe, Africa, and elsewhere, the prevailing Anglo-American folk style has incorporated many foreign elements—among them the folk styles of Germany, France, Poland, and Russia. Some foreign songs, such as the French "Alouette" and "Frère Jacques" and the German "O Tannenbaum," have survived intact, even retaining their original non-English lyrics. Others, especially children's songs, have been translated into English to become lasting favorites.

Use of Styles from Other Nations

In the hands of professional folk singers, the singing of Anglo-American folk songs has today become more of a self-conscious art. Singers are generally trained artists, such as Joan Baez and Judy Collins, who often present not the original folk songs but formally composed songs in folk style. However, many of these professional singers, Pete Seeger in particular, are very well acquainted with the history of their art. Although they regularly alter traditional songs to please their audiences, they also try to encourage public interest in authentic folk music and folklore.

Black Folk Music

Of all the ethnic influences that have gone into the creation of popular music in America, probably the most fruitful has been that of black Africa. As noted in an earlier chapter, West African music, though very different from European music in many respects, shared with it certain basic characteristics of harmony. Thus, when the two traditions were brought together in America by slavery, it was possible for them to blend. Black folk music was just the first of many important and widely influential results.

Generally pressed into slavery on the west coast of Africa, the blacks who began arriving in America in 1619 brought with them a highly developed musical tradition and a habit of incorporating music into virtually every activity of life. Much of their music came to America intact. Once here it was gradually assimilated to meet new needs.

American blacks developed a wide repertoire of songs, both secular and religious. One early type of secular song, perhaps the closest of all to African prototypes, was the *field holler* that slaves often sang while working. A field holler was the yearning cry of a slave working alone, a sound midway between a yell and a song, whose words determined the tone. It began with a high, long-drawn-out shout and then glided down to the lowest note the singer could reach. Such songs were characterized by falsetto tones, swoops and slides from note to note, complicated and unexpected changes of rhythm, and an occasional line of melody from Anglo-American ballads or hymns. They were heard not only in the fields but wherever a black man or woman worked at hard, lonely tasks. When slavery ended, the songs were taken onto the docks, into the railroad camps, and onto the Mississippi River.

Related to the field holler was the *group work song*. This too was close to African sources, for whenever Africans worked together at a task they found it natural to pace their labor with a song. Field hands sang as they hoed or picked the cotton. Rowing songs were used to time the strokes on the flat-bottomed boats of the South. Later on, work songs were chanted by chain gangs and by railroad workers, whose backbreaking, dangerous labor was regulated by the rhythmic chanting of the song leader. The leader played a very important part in the group work song, choosing the song to be sung, setting the pace, adjusting it to the feel of the work being done, and improvising catchy lyrics and musical byplay to fire the energies of the other workers. A good song made the work go faster and better and relieved the weary monotony of it.

Although there was great variety in their lyrics and uses, the earliest work songs were almost entirely African in sound and structure. They made use of the African call-and-response pattern, expressive African vocal techniques such as those used in the field holler, and occasional syncopated African rhythms built around a steady meter. Most work songs were sung with the leader and chorus responding to each other, but some were performed almost in unison, with incidental improvised ornamentation. Also typical of the early work songs was the use of tonic harmony, with little sense of the dominant or subdominant chords. Gradually, however, the songs picked up melodic and harmonic complexities from Anglo-American ballads and hymns and evolved toward a style that anticipated the blues.

Another musical style that closely resembled its African counterparts was the *ring shout*, a shuffling dance with chanting and handclapping. To an African, dancing was a natural part of worship, but as the Bible was thought to prohibit dancing in church, slaves had to be content with a short shuffling step executed counterclockwise in a ring. This circular movement was accompanied by excited clapping and a kind of *shout song* that provided more rhythm than melody. Biblical stories supplied the words for the shout songs, which were chanted in the customary leader-chorus fashion. Starting slowly, the music gathered speed and intensity with the hypnotic repetition of body movements and musical phrases.

Field Holler

Group Work Song

Ring Shout and Shout Song

Song Sermons

In many black religious services, the sermon also took on some of the qualities of a song, generally with a driving, hypnotic rhythm. Delivering such a *song sermon*, the preacher would at different times speak, chant, or sing, steadily increasing speed and passion as the song proceeded. The congregation, caught up in the pulse of the rhythm, would interject rhythmic cries or abbreviated lines of melody, using words such as "Amen!" or "Yes, my Lord!" Starting with a fixed text and then improvising, with a slow crescendo in the repeated phrases, an accomplished preacher could generate tremendous energy and fervor.

Lining Out

Lining out was a technique borrowed from white colonial churches. In many of these churches hymnbooks were in short supply; in others many of the people of the congregation were illiterate. Thus, it was common practice for the preacher to sing each line of a hymn or psalm and then wait for the congregation to repeat it. This technique adapted itself perfectly to the African call-and-response pattern. In their own use of lining out, blacks added the African repertoire of swoops, slides, shouts, and other ornaments to their responses, so that at times there was a splendid cacophony of multiple versions going on all at once.

The Blues

The invention of the *blues* represents a major contribution of black folk music to American popular music. The blues style is characterized by distinctive *blue notes* produced by slightly slurring the pitch of certain tones of the major scale, generally the third and seventh tones. The style was somehow right for plaintive songs of sadness. A whole repertoire of such songs grew up, created by prisoners, lonely people far from home, and thousands of others who needed to ease their pain by expressing it.

The usual blues song is based on the I, IV, and V chords. Generally the music is cast into twelve-measure units, divided into three lines of four measures each, resulting in an overall AAB form for each twelve-tone unit. The first half of each line is sung, while the second half is a *break*—a short musical passage played on one or more of the accompanying instruments. In the lyrics, the first two lines are always the same, made to rhyme with the third. Thus, the old African call-and-response pattern persists, now between singer and instrumentalists, and also between the lines of the text. The result is an easily identified, resilient structure open to multiple repetitions and variations. It was very adaptable to jazz styles and ultimately to other styles as well. The blues style itself reached a peak of popularity in the early years of the twentieth century. Two of the greatest blues singers of the era were the unforgettable Bessie Smith and Gertrude "Ma" Rainey.

Spirituals

In many respects, the religious counterpart of the blues was the *spiritual*. Developed largely in rural areas in the mid-nineteenth century, spirituals did not receive much public attention until they were made popular after the Civil War by groups such as the Fisk University Jubilee Singers. "Nobody Knows the Trouble I've Seen" and "Steal Away" are among the most familiar examples. The black spiritual was superficially similar to spirituals written early in the nineteenth century during the Protestant "Second Awakening." However, it is the black spiritual that has remained important to the present

Blues in the Twentieth Century: *Bessie Smith, widely known in the 1920s as the "Empress of the Blues," performed with most of the great jazz musicians of her era. Her songs had an earthy realism and honesty seldom found in the other popular songs of the time.*

day. The music of the black spiritual was in effect an extremely successful mixture of English melodies and harmonies and West African rhythms and styles of performance.

As originally performed, black spirituals underwent a great deal of improvisation. Practically all the elements of a spiritual—melody, rhythm, form, and text—were altered with each singing. The later written versions could only capture the text and the basic melodies. The spirit and embellishments added during the performances eluded transcription.

Nevertheless, certain aspects of the spiritual style remained constant in all the songs. As with the blues, the melodies were generously adorned with sliding pitches. Rhythm was enlivened liberally with syncopations: not only the now familiar shift of accent from the customary first and third beats in a $\frac{4}{4}$ meter to the second and fourth, but also more minute shifts within subdivisions of normal beats. Texture, which appears monophonic in transcribed versions of the spirituals, was in fact homophonic and even polyphonic in performance, when improvised parts were added. In form, spirituals often followed the call-and-response pattern.

Gospel Hymns

The *gospel hymn* rose to popularity after a Protestant revival movement in the 1850s. Gospel music is not strictly a part of the black or white folk tradition because it is generally written by songwriters, but the music written was quickly assimilated into black folk music. The hymns were first performed in huge tents during revival meetings. After World War I, they were introduced in black churches, where the congregations greatly embellished both the melody and rhythm of the songs. The result, as presented in recent years by such singers as Mahalia Jackson, is a joyous music with an insistent beat that contributes much to the overall flamboyant, pulsating effect.

Black folk music has unquestionably had a major influence on the popular music of twentieth-century America. Perhaps less well known is the very significant effect it had on the popular music of the nineteenth century. Stephen Foster, the composer of black-inspired songs for white Americans, has already been mentioned. His songs were sung in parlors in homes all over the country. They also became part of a typically American form of entertainment, the *minstrel show*. Based on the music and humor of blacks as understood by whites, the first minstrel shows featured white performers who masqueraded as blacks by darkening their faces with burnt cork. After the Civil War, however, blacks stepped in to play the roles themselves. The shows relied on a standard routine of jokes, slapstick, dancing, skits, and music, all presented by a group of performers who sat in a semicircle. The dancing featured the buck-and-wing, the ancestor of tap dancing, while the skits generally parodied a popular play such as *Uncle Tom's Cabin*. A grand cakewalk finale caricatured the courtly elegance of southern aristocracy. Minstrel shows also capitalized on patriotic, sentimental, and topical themes and ultimately provided the format for *vaudeville*, the variety show of the early twentieth century.

Minstrel Shows and Vaudeville

Jazz

Jazz, one of the few distinctly American art forms, was derived from a variety of sources. Its rhythms were strongly influenced by the rhythms of West Africa. Its basic harmonic structure was taken from the European tradition. And many aspects of its melody and harmony were adapted from nineteenth-century American folk music, especially from black folk music. Among its direct ancestors are black work songs, field hollers, the blues, military marches, dance tunes, and the popular songs and minstrel show music of the nineteenth century. Several types of religious music also contributed to its birth, most notably ring shouts, song sermons, and lining out. Other types of religious music, including variations of European church melodies and black spirituals, were also influential.

General Characteristics

In general, jazz is distinguished by its emphasis on rhythm, especially syncopation, and its use of improvisation. The performers usually begin by introducing a theme and its accompanying harmony. A meter is clearly established, and syncopated patterns are superimposed on it. The work as a whole takes form through a series of melodic and rhythmic improvisations on the theme and harmony. Each new section brings further elaboration. The result, especially in highly embellished pieces, is a theme obscured by variations. Eventually the variations appear to bear no relation at all to the original statement of the melody even though the underlying chords usually remain the same. Typical methods of variation include ornamenting a theme, replacing part of the theme with new melodic material, and embellishing the theme by means of contrapuntal techniques.

Ragtime

Joplin

The development of jazz depended to a large extent on a style of music that was developed in the 1890s. *Ragtime*, or "ragged time," was inspired by military marches and by the banjo tunes played to accompany jigs and cakewalks in the minstrel shows. Scott Joplin (1868–1917) played a large part in the development of ragtime and became one of its greatest composers. During its heyday, from about 1897 to 1917, ragtime became a national craze and was by far the most popular kind of music in America. Primarily piano music, ragtime adheres to a strict $\frac{2}{4}$ or $\frac{4}{4}$ meter and is clearly divided into sections. The left hand establishes the harmonies and maintains a rhythm that emphasizes accented beats. Meanwhile, the right hand ornaments this chordal foundation with syncopation, runs, and arpeggios.

Early Jazz Styles

The first important center for the new jazz style was the notorious red-light district of New Orleans called Storyville. There at the beginning of the twentieth century, musicians such as composer-pianist "Jelly Roll" Morton (1885–1941) worked together to transpose the ragtime style into what came to be known as jazz. Among the outstanding musicians heard in Storyville were players such as Buddy Bolden, Joe "King" Oliver, and the young Louis Armstrong.

Morton

When Storyville was closed down in 1917 by the federal government, the main center of activity in jazz shifted to Chicago. There the small New Orleans ensemble, often made up of only three featured instruments with percussion backup, grew larger. It was also in Chicago that white players first began to take any major part in jazz performances, beginning with the first great white soloist Bix Beiderbecke.

Jazz Combos

In both New Orleans and Chicago, jazz musicians generally performed in small ensembles, or *combos*. A front line of several solo instruments—a trombone, clarinet, one or two trumpets, and later a saxophone—improvised collectively on the melody while the rest of the group provided a background of harmony and rhythm. The rhythm section consisted of some combination of tuba, banjo, guitar, piano, string bass, washboard, and drums. A bass and a snare drum were always used, and tom-toms, cymbals, and other percussion instruments were often added.

The melodic and harmonic practices of the New Orleans and the early Chicago styles were generally similar. Thematic improvisations very often remained recognizably related to the original theme, with arpeggios and scalelike material commonly used to vary the theme. Methods of embellishing the melodies were influenced by the blues. Phrases were generally two and four measures in length, often followed by a break—a short improvised cadenza. Harmony tended to stay within the major mode, and chord progressions were

AMERICAN POPULAR MUSIC

made up chiefly of the I, IV, and V chords. There was some chromatic harmony, but it was rare.

The rhythms of early jazz were based on a rigidly steady $\frac{4}{4}$ meter, defined by the percussion instruments. Superimposed over this was a series of syncopations that accented normally weak beats of the measure. A twelve-bar blues progression or a thirty-two-bar popular song structure generally served as a framework, with breaks and longer solos added for variety and contrast.

Armstrong: "West End Blues"

Armstrong

Louis Armstrong (1900–1971) was one of the giants of jazz from the early decades of the century through the 1960s. In a 1928 recording of "West End Blues" his skill at improvising on the trumpet is very evident. The piece begins with an introductory trumpet solo by Armstrong and thereafter follows the blues form very closely, presenting five twelve-bar sections. Different instruments are featured in each of the sections: trumpet in the first, trombone in the second, clarinet and voice in the third, piano in the fourth, and all of the instruments in the last. The work, a classic in its own time, offers a good illustration of many of the characteristics of jazz in the 1920s.

Side 11, Band 4

Listening Guide for Armstrong's "West End Blues"

Timbre:	small combo featuring trumpet, trombone, clarinet, voice, and piano
Melody:	rather simple, singable tune; improvisation adds to it and replaces it
Rhythm:	duple meter; moderate tempo
Harmony:	major mode; much improvisation over repeated chord progression
Texture:	mainly homophonic
Form:	after opening trumpet solo, twelve-bar blues form presented five times

The Big Band Era

By the late 1920s, jazz was again on the move, with New York becoming the next great center of activity. This was due in part to the influence of Fletcher Henderson (1898–1952) and Duke Ellington (1899–1974)—the latter probably the greatest single figure in jazz history. New York saw the development of the "big band" or "swing" style, a style that rose to its greatest heights in the decade between 1935 and 1945.

Henderson and Ellington

In the early 1930s, Kansas City also became an important center for jazz, with bands such as the one headed by Count Basie. Basie's famous broadcasts from the Reno Club in Kansas City made it the heart of jazz for a time.

Written Arrangements

Big band music was for the most part written down, a major departure from the earlier jazz practice. The written arrangements provided a more reliable background against which soloists could improvise. At the same time, professionally trained musicians gave the music a more polished and sophisticated sound.

A Combo of Greats: *A number of great jazz musicians were brought together for the filming of the movie "A Song Is Born." The performers in the foreground are, from left to right, Louis Armstrong, Tommy Dorsey, Benny Goodman, Charlie Barnet, and Danny Kaye. Behind them, Lionel Hampton is shown at the vibraphone.*

The earliest of the big bands had eleven or twelve instruments, usually including three saxophones, two or three trumpets, one or two trombones, and four rhythm instruments—piano, tuba, banjo, and drums. In most bands the tuba was later replaced by the string bass, while the banjo was replaced by the guitar. By the 1950s, the typical big band included fifteen to eighteen players, with five saxophones, four or five trumpets, three to five trombones, piano, string bass, and drums.

Changes in Style

The big bands altered the elements of jazz in many ways. Melodic

AMERICAN POPULAR MUSIC

improvisation became "cooler" as musicians began to avoid the excitement of earlier styles and opted instead for variations and rhythms that were somewhat more restrained. Yet their melody, harmony, and rhythm often became more intricate, and novelties such as variations of the harmonic structure were introduced. Among these harmonic departures were the use of unusual chords and a much greater interest in chromaticism. The written arrangements led to a more controlled form and style. The thirty-two-bar, AABA structure of the popular song became the most common form, although the twelve-bar, AAB blues form was still in use.

Henderson: "King Porter Stomp"

Fletcher Henderson's arrangement of Jelly Roll Morton's "King Porter Stomp"—an arrangement made for clarinetist Benny Goodman—is an outstanding example of big band style. The music was intended for dancing, and the size of the band made it necessary to write out the arrangement for all instruments: three trumpets, two trombones, one clarinet, four saxophones, piano, guitar, bass, and drums. Based on the thirty-two-bar form and a repeating harmonic pattern, the piece presents solos in turn from trumpet, saxophones, clarinet, trumpet, and saxophones. Some degree of improvisation is apparent in all the solo sections. As in Armstrong's "West End Blues," the instruments join together to close the piece. All the ingredients of jazz are present to some degree but the style is controlled and refined.

Side 11, Band 5

Listening Guide for Henderson's "King Porter Stomp"

Timbre:	large band
Melody:	basic melody widely varied and replaced by other material
Rhythm:	duple meter; quick tempo
Harmony:	major mode; use of repeated harmonic pattern
Texture:	homophonic and contrapuntal
Form:	based on thirty-two-bar form

Bop

Parker

In the 1940s a number of jazz musicians began breaking away from big band swing and evolved a style called *bebop*, or more commonly *bop*. One of the key figures in the development of bop was Charlie Parker (1920–1955), an alto saxophonist, and, along with Louis Armstrong, one of the most brilliant improvisers in jazz history.

In bop, instrumentation was again reduced to small ensemble size. The group usually included a trumpet and a saxophone, while the rhythm section, which played a more important role than in the past, was made up of piano, guitar, bass, and drums.

The melody and harmony used in bop were more complex than that used in its predecessors. Improvisation came to be based increasingly on the harmonic structure of the music. In the 1950s a number of musicians made great use of ornamental tones, which often remained unresolved at the end of a phrase. The frequent occurrence of unusual chords also expanded the melodic possibilities. In effect, any note of the scale was potentially a part of any chord. Many bop artists, including Parker and Dizzy Gillespie, used the basic chords from standard popular songs and improvised upon them. In addition, the intricate phrasing that had become widespread in the 1940s was continued. No longer were phrases neatly organized into predictable lengths and patterns; they now varied quite extravagantly.

Use of the Rhythm Section

Bop was rife with rhythmic diversity and formal unpredictability. The rhythm section no longer functioned merely to set up a solid beat. Instead, each instrument was assigned a specific task in support of the solo melody and rhythm. The drummer might work for a legato effect, playing the beat lightly on the cymbal and concentrating elsewhere on the creation of counter-rhythms. The pianist might play single-note solos with the right hand and complement the basic harmonic structure with occasional chords in the left. Even the bass, though still concerned mainly with keeping time, sometimes forsook this role for a melodic role, playing more nimbly and contrapuntally. The addition of the electric guitar to the ensemble provided a new solo instrument. Furthermore, all the rhythm instruments now played solos. As a result of all these innovations, the bop structure became much less formalized, differing greatly from work to work and incorporating important elements from such differing musical traditions as symphonic music, popular music, and the blues.

Parker: "Ornithology"

An outstanding example of the bop style is found in "Ornithology," a variation on the popular song "How High the Moon." Parker on alto saxophone, Fats Navarro on trumpet, and Bud Powell on piano are supported by drums and bass. After a brief introduction by the piano, the tune that forms the basis for the piece is played by Parker. Heard first in the home key, the tune is soon clouded with chromaticism. The piece proceeds with lengthy, freely improved solos played by saxophone, trumpet, and piano in turn, leaving the basic tune far behind.

Side 11, Band 6

Listening Guide for Parker's "Ornithology"

Timbre:	small combo of alto saxophone, trumpet, piano, drums, and bass
Melody:	simple tune (with some chromaticism) widely varied and replaced with improvised material
Rhythm:	duple meter; quick tempo
Harmony:	major mode; basic chord pattern widely varied
Texture:	mainly homophonic
Form:	several sections of contrasting instrumentation

AMERICAN POPULAR MUSIC

Jazz in the Second Half of the Twentieth Century

Davis and Cool Jazz

In the late 1940s, Miles Davis (b. 1926) and a number of other young jazz musicians began to move into more experimental types of jazz. The "cool" style blended the rhythms and harmonies of bop with a more lyrical melodic approach. The arrangements were usually written down and were characterized by understated variations, relaxed rhythms, and contrapuntal style. Venturing beyond the basic bop ensemble, cool jazz experimented with the use of horn, flute, oboe, and cello, as well as Latin American and other more exotic instruments. Cool jazz harmonies were even more complex than those of bop, leading to protests from some critics that jazz was becoming cerebral and unemotional. Rhythm too became more complex, yet at the same time more relaxed. Among the innovators, Dave Brubeck is especially noted for having introduced bizarre time signatures such as $\frac{11}{4}$. Experiments with form were also made, with many jazz composers trying out early contrapuntal forms such as the fugue. Gerry Mulligan, Stan Getz, and the Modern Jazz Quartet were among the many important exponents of the cool jazz style.

Third Stream Jazz

In the late 1950s yet another important jazz style developed. Combining jazz and the traditional styles of serious music, it came to be known as "Third Stream" jazz. The music is well represented in the works of John Lewis and Gunther Schuller.

Recent Trends

While it is difficult to summarize all the many trends in jazz in the 1960s and 1970s, several distinct traits can be seen. One of the most basic and obvious characteristics of jazz in this period has been its eclectic nature. It has drawn from all the jazz styles of the past, as well as from rock, country and western music, electronic music, traditional serious music, and the music of other cultures. Miles Davis, who ushered in the cool style in the early 1950s, helped set the tone for the 1970s with his fusion of electronic and rock styles with jazz. Some of the most important innovators in recent years have been John Coltrane, Ornette Coleman, Herbie Hancock, Gary Burton, and the group known as Weather Report.

Broadway and Musical Comedy

Herbert and Romberg

In the late nineteenth century, light opera, or *operetta*, made its debut in the United States and quickly became very popular. A number of transplanted European composers—Victor Herbert (1859–1924) and Sigmund Romberg (1887–1951), in particular—captured Broadway audiences with works that combined sentimental plots, fast action, picturesque settings, and attractive tunes. Their operettas were patterned after the European comic operas of the time, but employed lighter melodies, spoken dialogue, and more frivolous plots. Herbert's were among the most popular, with such titles as *Babes in Toyland* (1903) and *Sweethearts* (1913), and songs such as "Because You're You" and "I'm Falling in Love with Someone."

Cohan

In the early 1900s, a fast-talking, aggressive Irish-American showman and producer named George M. Cohan (1878–1942) popularized a new art form, the *musical comedy*. Really a play with music, this was a combination of minstrelsy, burlesque, farce, pantomime, vaudeville, and operetta. Like jazz, musical comedy was an American invention. It differed most clearly from comic opera in that its music, dances, lyrics, and spoken dialogue more closely reflected the current moment. It differed from the early minstrel shows and vaudeville by its adherence to a plot and, as it matured, by the integration of all its parts into a unified, elaborately produced whole.

Cohan borrowed from a multitude of sources and added a kind of drive and ingenuity that have characterized American musicals ever since. He enchanted Broadway audiences with *Little Johnny Jones* (1904), *George Washington, Jr.* (1906), and other similar productions, highlighted by such catchy songs as "Yankee Doodle Boy" and the perhaps overly patriotic "Grand Old Flag."

Berlin

Irving Berlin (b. 1888) later took up the somewhat scattered threads of early musical comedy and tried to create more stylistically unified theatrical works. Berlin's first attempts included a "syncopated musical show" called *Watch Your Step* (1914), for which he wrote both music and lyrics. Its stars were the celebrated dancing team of Irene and Vernon Castle. Two of Berlin's most important contributions to American musical theater were *Face the Music* (1932) and *As Thousands Cheer* (1933). As in many other musicals of the 1920s and 1930s, the librettos were highly satirical, with numerous allusions to contemporary political and social events. Berlin climaxed his Broadway career with the enormously successful *Annie Get Your Gun* (1946).

Kern

Jerome Kern (1885–1945) was perhaps the first to truly integrate all the different elements of musical comedy: story, songs, dances, costumes, and sets. In the 1920s the typical show was a collection of good tunes and a passable plot, pieced together to form a rather loosely organized work. Kern's *Show Boat* (1927), with lyrics by Oscar Hammerstein II, did much to change this. It was an extraordinarily well-organized and successful production. Critical comments ranged from "almost a folk opera" to the accolade that "no other American piece of its vintage left so large a permanent musical legacy, and certainly no other surpassed it in quality." Other well-known musical comedies of the period were Vincent Youmans' *No! No! Nanette* (1925), George Gershwin's *Strike Up the Band* (1930), and Cole Porter's *Anything Goes* (1934).

Rodgers

Musical comedy reached its maturity in the 1940s and 1950s. The combined genius of composer Richard Rodgers (b. 1902) and writer-lyricist Hammerstein produced a number of strong and vividly memorable works. Their comedies were based on literary classics, deep-rooted folk themes, or contemporary events, with music both immediately attractive and of lasting worth. The songs frequently helped to advance the plot; there was thus a reason for their existence beyond the mere function of breaking up the dialogue at regular intervals. The show *Oklahoma!* (1943) marked one of the great moments in Broadway history. It had a genuinely American setting with all the standard American virtues: it was friendly, good-humored, colorful, clean, and fast-paced. In *Carousel* (1945) and *South Pacific* (1948), Rodgers and Hammerstein dealt with more serious themes and offered a more complex treatment of human character than had been customary in the average

Broadway show. *The Sound of Music* (1959) also dealt with a serious theme in the retelling of the saga of the singing Trapp family. Another masterpiece of the period, written very much in the tradition of Rodgers and Hammerstein, was *My Fair Lady* (1956) by Alan Jay Lerner and Frederick Loewe.

Bernstein

The production of *West Side Story* (1957) by Leonard Bernstein (b. 1918) ushered in a new kind of Broadway show, one in which the word "musical" was decisively severed from the word "comedy." There was nothing comic about Bernstein's theme: juvenile delinquency, gang warfare on New York City streets, and a love story based on *Romeo and Juliet*. The show had a dramatic impact with tragic overtones. Everything fit, with Jerome Robbins' balletlike choreography conveying what the unpolished, often inarticulate characters were unable to say in words. Bernstein's jazzy and musically sophisticated score quite effectively captured the wildness, ecstasy, and anguish of the dramatic situation.

Recent Trends

After the precedent set by *West Side Story*, the horizons of the musical were greatly broadened. A cross-fertilization seemed to take place between opera, musical theater, and the concert stage, yielding such varied works as the rock musical *Jesus Christ Superstar* (1970), Bernstein's *Mass* (1971), and Stephen Sondheim's *A Little Night Music* (1972). The American musical seems once again to be trying to do what it did at its beginning: pull together as many as possible of the recent developments in the various performing arts to create a form that reflects the current American spirit.

Country and Western Music

Today's country and western music is directly descended from the folk ballads brought to this country by the earliest settlers. The ballads long retained their original form and flavor in sparsely populated, ethnically homogeneous sections of colonial America. But eventually the southern Appalachian region became the last preserve for a strong heritage of these transplanted folk ballads.

Early Style

Even in Appalachia, the New World environment brought a number of changes in the original models. The music was played on different instruments—on the guitar and the banjo, for example—and it was sung in a distinctive high-pitched, nasal style. Moreover, new subjects were added. All ballads by their very nature deal with topical themes. The southern Appalachian ballads concentrated on typical American frontier themes—hard work, hard times, evangelical religion, migration, violent life and death, along with the usual love and loss themes. Religious emotionalism—one of the cornerstones of the poor white southerner's existence—spilled over into this secular music. And at the same time, southern blacks introduced their white neighbors to blues singing and guitar and banjo picking.

Until the coming of radio, country music remained isolated in the southern Appalachians, the deep South, the Mississippi Delta, and eastern Texas. However, by 1922 there were eighty-nine radio stations in the South, giving country musicians a new platform and a chance at a far wider audience.

Grand Ole Opry

In 1925, WSM radio in Nashville, Tennessee, inaugurated the Grand Ole Opry, now the oldest continuing radio show in the United States devoted to country music. The Opry featured fiddlers, guitarists, banjo players, singers, comedians, yodelers, and even barn dancers. Reigning over this scene was the Carter Family, the epitome of the traditional southern Appalachian singing family, and Jimmie Rodgers, the prototype of the country boy who makes it big singing about his kind of life.

Due largely to the influence of radio programs, country music found an audience in the North. During the Depression years, people found in the songs of the rural South expressions of the downtrodden hopelessness then spreading throughout the country.

Western Styles

Meanwhile, many southeasterners were migrating to the Southwest and to California, adapting their music to new influences they met along the way. A *western swing style* developed in Texas, where Mexican influence was strong. The music was heavy on the fiddles and made for dancing. From labor camps and oil fields came the loud sound of *honky-tonk*. In Hollywood, Gene Autry, Tex Ritter, and Roy Rogers glamorized the *singing cowboy*, with Dale Evans later adding the singing cowgirl. New instruments and new techniques for playing them were added. Country singers back in the East felt the effects of the new western branch of their music and began dressing in gaudy cowboy and cowgirl outfits. Eventually, the word "western" was grafted onto the designation "country" to produce country and western music.

Although country and western music had already infiltrated northern airwaves, many of the performers themselves moved north during World War II. At the height of the war, nearly two hundred out of the total of about six hundred recording artists in the United States were country performers. The big names were Roy Acuff, Ernest Tubb, and Bob Wills, and they were trying to win the war in their own way with country songs about patriotism and coming home.

Country Blues

In 1949 Hank Williams' "Lovesick Blues" helped to popularize a new variant style known as *country blues*. Williams' music was of a kind very popular in the early 1950s just before the advent of rock and roll. The singing was nasal, the accompaniment was a whining steel guitar, and the lyrics were straight from the heart.

Pop-Country Music and Bluegrass

In the mid-1950s, country and western music was almost eclipsed by the sudden emergence and enormous popularity of rock and roll. It did not make any sort of national comeback until the late 1960s. By then its styles were many and varied. *Pop-country* star Glen Campbell had considerable success with a song called "Wichita Lineman"; other popular figures were Chet Atkins and Roger Miller. The largely instrumental, virtuoso *bluegrass* style also came to the fore. But perhaps the biggest star of the early 1970s was Johnny Cash, many of whose songs seem to be drawn straight from the life of the poor dirt farmer in the southern hills.

Recent Trends

In recent years the Grand Ole Opry has continued to broadcast the many sounds of country and western music: George Jones' honky-tonk style from eastern Texas, Marty Robbins' gunfighter ballads from the Mexican border, Hank Williams, Jr.'s Cajun music from Louisiana, the mountain spirituals of Wilma Lee and Stoney Cooper, and Tex Ritter's cowboy tunes. Performance standards have become more professional than they were in the early days.

Guitars and fiddles, played with great expertise, are often augmented or replaced by an orchestra. Although the lyrics still deal with country themes, the music displays much greater sophistication.

Country and western music has also continued to make new inroads into the mainstream of American popular music. Singers such as John Denver and Kris Kristofferson have gained a nationwide audience while Kenny Rogers and Dolly Parton have become full-fledged media celebrities. Perhaps the single most important factor in attracting new audiences for the Nashville sound was the hit movie *Nashville*. While some would argue that the movie presented country and western music of a "sugar-coated" variety, no one would deny that the movie awakened new interest in the music and performers that Nashville has come to represent.

Rock Music

The appearance of *rock and roll* in the 1950s was as much a social phenomenon as a matter of musical expression. The astonishing popularity of rock and roll can scarcely be understood without reference to the unusual cultural context of its birth. The rapid population growth after World War II dramatically altered the age balance of the American people so that by 1960 about half the population was less than twenty-five years old. This major demographic shift gave young people unparalleled social and political importance. In addition, the almost uninterrupted prosperity of the postwar decades gave tremendous purchasing power to young Americans, making them an inviting market for consumer goods of all kinds.

One of the first indications of a youth movement was the popularity in the 1950s of cult figures, such as James Dean, who projected the image of the rebellious, cruising "hood." Simultaneously, a Bohemian revolt that had been gathering strength underground for many years began to emerge. Its adherents, the beatniks or "beat generation," loudly proclaimed their disenchantment with the values and goals of the prosperous American society. Instead they favored less materialistic philosophies and championed drug use and sexual freedom.

Early Style

Into this milieu of changing economic patterns and intermingling subcultures came "rockabilly" music. It was aimed at white audiences and began as a mixture of blues and country music. After acquiring a large urban following, it was rechristened rock and roll, a name taken from an old blues lyric, "My baby rocks me with a steady roll." Many black musicians became leaders in rock and roll, among them such important early stars as Little Richard, Fats Domino, Chuck Berry, Muddy Waters, B. B. King, and Bo Diddley.

Rock and roll was basically dance music. Its slangy lyrics usually described the pains and pleasures of young love or other trials of adolescence. Among its most important stylistic elements was the use of the electric guitar, which made possible certain startling experiments with timbre. Other instruments in the rock and roll combo were drums, a bass, possibly a saxophone, and occasionally a piano.

Julian Wasser

Rock Music Today: *The photo above shows the rock group Chicago just before its 1978 concert tour. Rock music has become such a large and well-paid industry that it is sometimes difficult to remember its roots in poverty and small town or rural settings.*

Melody was simple and repetitive, sometimes accompanied by a rhythmic series of nonsense syllables that came to be known as the "doo-wop" sound. The heavily accented four-beat measures took their basic rhythms from the blues. Harmony consisted mostly of elementary tonic-dominant chord progressions. The usual structure was an alternation of verse and chorus, the pattern and length of which changed somewhat from song to song.

At its outset, rock music was performed most often by males for a female audience. Among the groups that helped establish this pattern was Bill Haley and the Comets, whose jaunty "Rock Around the Clock" became one of the first hit rock songs. It was not Haley, however, who came to epitomize rock music. The king was Elvis Presley, who ruled popular music in the 1950s with a series of hits that began with "Heartbreak Hotel." Presley's simplicity, his intense energy, and his sexual suggestiveness enabled him to perfect the tough

Presley

"hood" image that so many rock singers later copied. This combination of brashness and lack of sophistication became standard for the rest of the decade.

Teen Rock

The time between Presley's peak in the late 1950s and the "British invasion" of the early 1960s was a transitional period. Most of the rock performers of the period showed no particular originality. Instead they preferred to continue the prevailing *teen rock* style found in the music of Pat Boone, Frankie Avalon, Fabian, Paul Anka, Bobby Darin, and Ricky Nelson. However, one group from those years was more adventurous and did exert some influence in the 1960s. This was the Everly Brothers, whose catchy lyrics and unusual harmonies were very much in evidence in the early Beatles' songs.

Beatles

The Beatles—Ringo Starr, John Lennon, Paul McCartney, and George Harrison—began the British invasion with a sensational impact in 1963. Together with the other English groups that followed, they reworked American country, rock, and blues, revived Presley's singing style and came up with a fresh, more sophisticated model of rock and roll. This synthesis came to be known simply as *rock*. The Beatles' first two hits, "Love Me, Do" and "I Wanna Hold Your Hand," evidence something of the simplicity, wholesomeness, and idealism that tended to characterize certain aspects of the youth rebellion of the 1960s. Like Presley and his contemporaries, the British rock composers of the 1960s were for the most part self-trained. Many were drawn from the lower classes of Liverpool and other English cities. Ironically, their music became the hallmark of prosperous American middle-class youth.

The Beatles' instrumental ensemble served as a model for most of the new rock groups. By the mid-1960s the standard rock combo consisted of three electric guitars—rhythm, bass, and lead—and drums. The music was generally characterized by I–IV–V chord harmony and an uncompromising beat. Elements of country and western music appeared regularly, while a number of groups borrowed extensively from the Mississippi Delta blues singers.

Rolling Stones

During the 1960s, a schism developed within rock music between the raunchy "bad guys," represented especially by the Rolling Stones, and such pointedly clean-cut "boys" as the Beatles. Divergent tendencies in their music paralleled the disparities in their public images. The Rolling Stones maintained an approach and style that was looser, rougher, less polished—in short, more hard-core than the Beatles' style. Around these two leading groups a host of lesser groups, such as the Yardbirds, the Kinks, and Eric Burdon and the Animals, soon arose.

It was also during the 1960s that the hippie movement began to affect rock music. With its slogans of "Flower Power" and "Tune in, turn on, drop out," this new offspring of the beat generation spread across the country from San Francisco. Hippies preached a mixed message of opposition to the Vietnam War, sexual freedom, togetherness, and mysticism. Rock music, fusing almost inevitably with the movement, carried the creed to the masses of middle-class youth. Rock groups on the West Coast and elsewhere retained the hard, rhythmic center of the music but experimented with new electronic techniques, more chromatic harmony, new instruments, and even new styles such as the orientally inspired *raga rock*.

Baroque Rock

The British invasion was to some extent continued when newer English groups, notably The Who, began to export Baroque rock and rock opera to America. *Baroque rock* sought to imitate the sound of instrumentation in the early eighteenth century. A Baroque rock combo might use any combination of orchestral string and wind instruments mixed with recorders, flute, oboe, horn, trumpet, and harpsichord. The style is largely contrapuntal. Procol Harum is one well-known group associated with this kind of rock.

Rock Operas

Rock operas, or rock musicals, made their first appearance on Broadway during the 1967–1968 season. *Hair,* subtitled "An American Tribal Love-Rock Musical," was among the first and remains perhaps the most famous. It featured music by Canadian rock-jazz composer Galt MacDermot and was built around a framework that permitted certain improvisations. Its favorable reception by major critics gave weight to rock's claim that it must be taken seriously as music.

Soul Music

Two other independent types of music—soul music and folk-protest songs—traded influences with rock throughout the 1960s. *Soul music,* based essentially on black folk music, had already contributed greatly to the development of early rock and roll. In the 1960s it formed a musical counterpart to the growth of black nationalism and black power and was enthusiastically received by a large part of the black community, not to mention white youths. James Brown, Aretha Franklin, Otis Redding, and Ray Charles headed the list of soul singers. Their music has a quality of frenzy, rhythmic drive, and intensity as well as an immediacy that sets it apart from mainstream rock music.

Folk-Protest Song

The *folk-protest song,* a survival from the Depression years, renewed its popularity during the 1960s, especially as the civil rights and antiwar movements grew. Its direct, personal style, pictorial imagery, and often plaintive tunes offered the singers particularly good means for delivering deeply felt, serious messages. Joan Baez's "Birmingham Sunday" is a haunting example. Later folk-protest songs were increasingly merged with rock. In the *folk-rock songs* of Bob Dylan, the poetic and musical voice of the youth counterculture was vividly expressed.

Recent Trends

In recent years rock music itself has moved in a variety of directions. Jefferson Airplane, the Doors, the Grateful Dead, and Country Joe and the Fish have pushed the West Coast sound to its limits. Others have experimented with various types of electronic equipment. There has also been a marked tendency for rock music to merge with other types of music. Bob Dylan's former group, The Band, has tried to forge a new union of country music and rock. Singers such as James Taylor and Carole King have once again linked rock and roll with popular ballads. Pink Floyd, Paul McCartney, and Stockhausen have mixed jazz, rock, and symphonic techniques.

For some, the death of Elvis Presley in 1977 seemed to represent the passing of an era. Despite early predictions, however, rock music has proven more than a momentary fad. Indeed it has outlived many of its founders and is still thriving. Times have seldom been better for talented vocalists such as Barry Manilow, Linda Ronstadt, and Billy Joel. The Beatles have gone their separate ways, but they remain a potent influence on today's music. Groups such as the Bee Gees owe much to the early British foursome. The Rolling Stones have also had their followers. Mixing hard rock with a great deal of showmanship, *acid rock* turned first to the *glitter rock* of the Alice Cooper variety and more recently to *punk rock* as represented by groups such as the Ramones. Rock, in all its varieties, is apparently here to stay. Whatever becomes of American popular music by the year 2000, it seems certain that rock will have been a major contributor.

Suggested Listening

Anglo-American Folk Music

Anglo-American Ballads [Folkways 2037]
Sea Shanties and Loggers' Songs [Folkways 2019]
Cowboy Songs [Folkways 2022]

Black Folk Music

Negro Folk Music, Vols. 1–5 [Folkways FE-4469/4473]
Singing the Blues [MCA 4064]
Mahalia Jackson's Greatest Hits [Columbia CS-8804]

Jazz

New Orleans, Vols. 1–5 [Folkways 2461/65]
The Big Band Era [RCA VPM-6043]
Milestones [Columbia PC-9428E]

Musical Comedy

Annie Get Your Gun [RCA LSO-1124]
Oklahoma! [Capitol SWAO-595]
West Side Story [Columbia OS-2001]

Country and Western

Country's Greatest Hits [Columbia CG-9]
Johnny Cash: Greatest Hits [Columbia CS-9478]
Bluegrass Hall of Fame [Starday 181]

Rock

Elvis Presley: Golden Records [RCA LSP-1707E, 2075E, 2765, 3921]
The Beatles: A Hard Day's Night [United Artists 6366]
Rolling Stones: Hot Rocks [London 606/7]

Listening Preview   Perhaps the most significant development in the music of the second half of the twentieth century has been the use of electronic equipment to generate sounds totally new to the human listening experience. Listen to Davidovsky's "Synchronisms No. 1," a work for flute and synthesizer (Side 12, Band 2, or a similar selection from the record library). In what ways do the sounds produced by the flute differ from the sounds traditionally associated with the instrument? How would you describe the sounds involved in the electronically synthesized part of the music?

30

Music in the Second Half of the Twentieth Century

The Early Postwar Years

The onset of World War II caused a reduction in musical activity, particularly in Europe. By the time the war had ended, the musical scene had changed considerably. Just before and during the war years, a number of composers, including Schoenberg, Bartók, Hindemith, and Stravinsky, had emigrated to the United States, where they were subsequently to exert great influence. The work of Schoenberg and Stravinsky has had an especially notable effect. In Europe, the development of twelve-tone music, censored during the war by the Nazis, was continued by a whole new generation of young composers.

Influence of Messiaen

Immediately after the war, Paris was once again the scene of lively musical activity. Many members of the European avant-garde were attracted to the harmony classes of Olivier Messiaen (b. 1908) at the Paris Conservatory. Work there included the analysis of the scores of such important modern composers as Debussy, Schoenberg, Berg, Webern, and Stravinsky. Messiaen himself was and has continued to be highly influential as both a composer and a teacher. His thorough study of the rhythms of Hindu music and Oriental music has had a major influence on his compositions. Some of his works contain rhythmic palindromes—that is, rhythmic patterns that are the same forward and backward—as well as rhythmic canons and a variety of other interesting rhythmic devices. Messiaen is also an expert ornithologist and has traveled all over the world notating various birdcalls. Some of his most exciting and colorful works are those that incorporate such calls. *Oiseaux exotiques* ("Exotic Birds"), written in 1956, offers a particularly fine example. The music is scored for piano, wind instruments, and percussion instruments, and makes use of forty different birdcalls. In the preface of the work, Messiaen has listed each bird and its native habitat.

The Expansion of Serialism

Some of Messiaen's young students were especially intrigued by the serialist works of Webern. They noted that while much of Schoenberg's music has an almost traditional structure in phrases and overall form, Webern's forms seemed to grow directly out of his use of the twelve-tone method. This they felt was the direction in which they should move. They were unsure, however, exactly how to proceed.

In 1949 Messiaen provided a possible answer in his *Modes de valeurs et d'intensités* ("Modes of Values and Intensities"), one of a group of piano pieces. In his use of the term "modes," Messiaen was referring specifically to a melodic mode of thirty-six pitches, a rhythmic mode of twenty-four durations, a "loudness" mode of seven intensities, and a performance mode of twelve different kinds of attacks, or ways in which a note may be struck. Within Messiaen's work the modes are organized so that a given pitch is always associated with the same duration, intensity, and manner of attack.

Total Serialization

The *Modes* introduced the idea of structuring each element of music—rhythm, dynamics, and so forth—in the same way that the twelve pitches are structured in the serialist, twelve-tone system. Thus, the concept of *total serialization* was born. The term "serial music," as it is used today, refers not merely to the use of a tone row but to any piece in which there is a systematic ordering of pitches and/or other musical elements. The ordering of these elements will determine various aspects of the composition according to what operations and transformations the composer chooses to apply to them. "Serial music" is thus nowaways a term of general description. A twelve-tone composition is just one specific type of serial music.

Boulez

One of Messiaen's students, Pierre Boulez (b. 1925), undertook the development of Messiaen's ideas in his *Structures*, a work for two pianos. Boulez serialized durations, intensities, and attacks as well as pitches in this composition. For the rhythm of his piece, he devised a sort of rhythmic row of twelve different durations, ranging from a single thirty-second note to the combined duration of twelve thirty-second notes (the equivalent of a dotted quarter note). The twelve values were ordered in a manner similar to that used for the twelve pitches of the chromatic scale. The two rows and their forms were then used independently in such a way that each note of the tone row was associated in turn with each value of the rhythmic row.

Boulez' system was at once more flexible and more varied than that of his teacher. In Messiaen's *Modes* each tone is associated with the same duration, intensity, and attack throughout. But in Boulez' *Structures*, the duration, intensity, and attack of every pitch are constantly and systematically changed.

In 1955 Boulez wrote *Le Marteau sans maître* ("The Hammer Without a Master"), a work that Stravinsky later hailed as a masterpiece. The work is a setting of three poems by René Char, a Surrealist poet much admired by Boulez. It is scored for flute, viola, guitar, alto voice, and a great number of percussion instruments, including a *vibraphone*, or electrified *marimba*. The music is divided into nine movements, five of which are purely instrumental. The other four are settings of the three poems, with one of the poems set in two different versions. The instrumental movements serve as preludes and postludes to, as well as commentaries on, the vocal movements.

Many influences can be seen in Boulez' *Le Marteau*, including that of Oriental music. Boulez became familiar with Oriental music when he traveled to Japan as the music director of a European theater company. *Le Marteau*

Performance Centers: *In cities around the world, beautiful new complexes are being built for the presentation of opera, ballet, and the music of symphony orchestras. New York City's Lincoln Center is shown above, with the State Theater (predominantly a theater for ballet) on the left, the Metropolitan Opera House in the center, and the New York Philharmonic's Avery Fisher Hall on the right.*

differs from Boulez' earlier *Structures* in that it does not make use of total serialism. Instead there are groups of intervals that appear in various permutations and transformations throughout. The work vacillates between a flowing lyricism and a stark abrasiveness—a contrast that is especially noticeable in the second movement.

Stockhausen

Another one of Messiaen's students, Karlheinz Stockhausen (b. 1928) has also made extensive use of serial techniques in his works, determining such things as density, register, and tempo changes by serial means. An example can be found in his *Zeitmasse* ("Time Block"), a piece for five woodwinds in which systematic changes in tempo are serially controlled. Many of the accelerations and decelerations in tempo are quite complicated. At a certain point, for instance, one instrument accelerates, another slows down, and a third maintains a steady tempo. The work is particularly interesting because it is in many ways typical of the thinking of mid-twentieth-century composers. Stockhausen was not trying to achieve a traditional ensemble of instruments. Rather, he sought to stress the independence of each instrument. Although the ensemble is in fact very strictly controlled in the part writing, the effect is one

MUSIC IN THE SECOND HALF OF THE TWENTIETH CENTURY

of great fluidity and freedom. The instruments move away from each other in the rubato sections, come together again at certain points, and move away again.

In his *Gruppen* ("Groups"), a work for three chamber orchestras written in the mid-1950s, Stockhausen explored some of these same ideas on a larger scale. In a performance of the work, the three orchestras led by three different conductors are often called upon to play in different tempos. As Stockhausen explained, in this work "sound-groups should be made to wander in space from one sounding body to another and at the same time split up similar sound-structures: each orchestra was supposed to call to the others and to give answer or echo."

Stockhausen has also explored electronic music. In 1953 he began experimenting with electronic sounds at the Cologne radio station. (In Europe, a number of government radio stations have installed facilities for electronic music.) At Cologne, Stockhausen produced his *Gesang der Jünglinge* ("Sound of the Youth"), one of the classics of electronic music. The work is essentially the combination of electronic sounds with the sound of a child's voice reading a biblical text.

In the United States, twelve-tone music has taken as many paths as there are composers writing it. Composers as different as Copland, Sessions, and Stravinsky have made use of twelve-tone methods in their works. The individuality seen in the many compositions is evidence that serialism can provide a framework large enough for the expression of a multitude of ideas.

Stravinsky's Serial Works

Stravinsky's development as a serialist composer has been one of the most discussed events of modern music. Serial techniques are found only in his late works, beginning with his *Cantata,** written in 1952. The work is a setting of some anonymous lyrics of the fifteenth and sixteenth centuries for soprano, tenor, female chorus, and a small instrumental ensemble. The instrumentation, some of the rhythmic motives and cadential harmonies, and the crossing of voices are all reminiscent of certain techniques found in late Medieval music.

The "Ricercar II" in Stravinsky's *Cantata* opens with a short phrase sung by the tenor:

Opening Phrase

The phrase, made up of eleven notes, many of which are repeated, is treated in serial fashion. The eleven notes are stated in retrograde, inversion, and retrograde inversion just as the notes of a twelve-tone row would have been.

In later works, Stravinsky developed his own very personal method of using the twelve-tone system. He commented in particular on his *Movements*

*Cantata by Igor Stravinsky. Copyright 1952 by Boosey & Hawkes, Inc. Excerpt reprinted by permission.

CONTEMPORARY MUSIC

for Piano and Orchestra, calling it "the most advanced music from the point of view of construction of anything I have composed."

Stravinsky: *Movements for Piano and Orchestra*

Stravinsky's *Movements for Piano and Orchestra** is very specifically scored for thirty-eight instruments, including woodwinds, brass, strings, piano, and celesta. The five movements are all quite brief, with frequent changes of meter. On the first page alone the following meters appear:

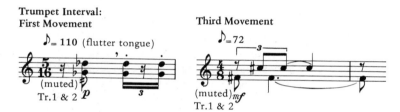

4	3	3	4	3	4	5	7	6	5
8	8	32	16	8	16	16	16	16	16

The music in Stravinsky's *Movements for Piano and Orchestra* is based on a twelve-tone row that is used to create myriad motivic features as well as an overall sense of unity. A number of the motivic features center on specific intervals. An interval of a fifth (of five notes), for example, is heard in the two trumpets at the beginning of the first movement and again in the third movement:

In other cases Stravinsky combined both pitch and rhythmic factors in motives that appear several times. The ascending leap in the first flute, heard at the beginning and end of the first movement and again at the opening of the fourth movement, is a typical example:

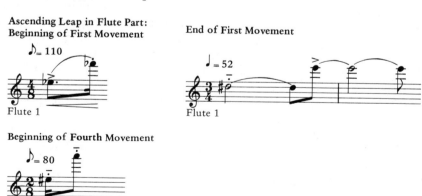

*Movements for Piano and Orchestra by Igor Stravinsky. Copyright 1960 by Hawkes and Son (London) Ltd. Excerpts reprinted by permission of Boosey & Hawkes, Inc.

Texture throughout the work is quite sparse, at times pointillistic. Melody and harmony seem merged into one, and form is very free, evolving as it does from the use of the tone row.

The fifth and final movement has a special function. Many of the motives heard earlier in fragmented form or in combination with other elements are now separated out and presented clearly, even insistently. The last movement thus provides both a climax and a clarification of the entire work.

Side 12, Band 1

Listening Guide for Stravinsky's *Movements for Piano and Orchestra*

Timbre:	piano and orchestra of string and wind instruments, harp, and celesta
Melody:	generally quite disjunct; seems to merge with harmony
Rhythm:	no repeated meter apparent to the listener; varying tempos
Harmony:	based on a twelve-tone row; tonality sometimes suggested by a repeated note or chord
Texture:	generally quite sparse; sometimes pointillistic
Form:	five movements; form of movements evolves freely from the use of the tone row

---

As many critics have noted, Stravinsky's serial music still has the "Stravinsky sound." One of the hallmarks of his style is the use of exact repetition, both on a small scale to generate rhythmic movement and on a larger scale as a unifying device. Schoenberg had devised the twelve-tone system partly to avoid the obvious use of repetition, but Stravinsky's twelve-tone music makes as effective use of repeated elements as his earlier music does. Stravinsky's adoption of the twelve-tone method thus showed that the polarity between tonal and atonal music was not an unbridgeable gap.

Babbitt

The American-born Milton Babbitt (b. 1916) has been outstanding both as a composer and as a theorist of twelve-tone music. His work has included the analysis of the serial procedures of Schoenberg and Webern and the exploration of a number of different ways of using the twelve-tone method to organize rhythm. His rhythmic theories are in many ways quite innovative. Drawing a parallel between two pitches in the tone row and the duration between two attacks—that is, the time between the beginning of one note and the beginning of the next—he has derived intervals of duration. A set of these intervals can then be used to structure the rhythmic elements of a composition. Babbitt has written a great variety of works, including *All Set* for jazz ensemble, *Composition for Four Instruments*, *Partitions* for piano, and four string quartets. Since his complex musical ideas call for very precise realization in performance, he has turned more and more in recent years to electronic music.

Electronic Music

The term *electronic music* generally refers to any music composed with the use of electronic equipment. As early as the first decade of this century, composers were envisioning the use of electronic instruments. By the early 1920s French composer Edgard Varèse (1883–1965) was urging the develop-

Varèse

ment of specific equipment by which he felt he could realize his musical ideas. But the technology was not yet sufficiently developed. The first concerts of electronic music in the United States were not held until after World War II. Today, however, there is wide interest in electronic music among both composers and listeners.

One of the reasons that so many composers have turned to electronic music is found in the limitations of traditional instruments. Most of the instruments now in use were perfected during the eighteenth and nineteenth centuries and are thus especially suitable for playing the music of that period. Many of them are largely restricted to the notes of the chromatic scale. Although new playing techniques are being developed, many composers find that only electronic instruments offer the completely new sounds they want.

A related problem found in nonelectronic music is the limited precision possible with live performers. Certain very rapid and complex rhythmic patterns that are perceptible to the human ear are, for example, virtually impossible for human performers to play. Such patterns can, however, be produced with ease by electronic means. In addition, an electronic work can be fully realized by the composer alone. The composer retains complete control of the final sound and does not have to rely on the interpretation of a performer. Not all electronic composers, though, wish to exercise such complete and invariable control. Some of the most effective electronic compositions combine live performance with taped sounds.

There has been great speculation about the potential resources made available to music by modern technology. After a century or more in which art was popularly regarded as more or less irrelevant to human progress, today's composers have been exhilarated by finding once more a point of contact between art and the front ranks of science.

At the present time, composers working in the electronic medium can proceed in one of two ways. On the one hand, they can record and modify instrumental sounds or sounds from the natural environment. Their other choice is to generate sounds directly by electronic means. The first method produces what French composers have called *musique concrète*, or, as it is often called in this country, *tape music*.

Musique Concrète

To modify sounds recorded on tape, composers can do a number of things. They may, for example, play the tapes backward, lower the pitch by slowing the speed of the tape recorder, fragment the tapes by splicing them, or form tape loops in order to create a repeating rhythmic ostinato. Most tape studios offer additional equipment for modifying sounds, including filters of various kinds that are similar in principle to those found on stereo preamplifiers but much more sophisticated.

Ussachevsky

An interesting example of tape music, or musique concrète, is found in *Of Wood and Brass* by Vladimir Ussachevsky (b. 1911). The work is composed almost entirely of instrumental sounds electronically modified. The original sounds were those of a trombone, a xylophone, and a gong. Ussachevsky, by modifying these few elements, was able to construct a work of great variety.

Musique concrète, the earliest form of electronic music, was soon followed by the development of equipment that could produce sound directly by electronic means. Oscillators and sound synthesizers of other kinds have made it possible for composers to obtain sounds of almost any timbre, intensity, and pitch, while maintaining direct control over the sounds produced. The exciting possibilities arising from this technology led, in the 1950s, to the establishment of several studios in the United States and Europe. Most of those in this country have been connected with universities. The first was the Columbia–Princeton Electronic Music Center, established at Columbia University in 1959. Since then other studios have been established at many universities throughout the country.

Composing electronic music is a laborious process. Each sound must be generated separately, and a great deal of editing and splicing is necessary to create even a short piece. The RCA Mark II synthesizer installed at the Columbia–Princeton Electronic Music Center was developed to speed up some of these operations. The machine combines all the equipment of an elaborate tape studio with sophisticated sound-generating devices.

Recently, many smaller sound synthesizers have been produced for purposes ranging from composition to the live performance of electronic music. Most of them have been designed with emphasis on particular features, so each has its own combination of advantages and disadvantages.

Use of Computers

Another important innovation in electronic music in recent years has been the use of computer programming. The computer calculates a series of numbers representing every sound in a composition and then converts these numbers into sound by means of a data translator coupled with a synthesizer. The composer, however, must still plan the composition and specify the sounds in it. The computer may be thought of as another kind of musical instrument, a means whereby a composer's work may be performed or realized repeatedly with precise accuracy.

The computer and, in fact, all the electronic devices discussed here demand more effort from the composer than writing for traditional instruments does. To produce the final tape of an electronic work, which is actually a performance of the work, the composer must determine dynamic values, tempo, phrasing, and all the other variables that are usually subject to some interpretation by a performer. In effect, composer and performer become one.

Davidovsky: *Synchronisms*

Davidovsky

Among the most interesting and virtuosic of electronic works is a series of six *Synchronisms* by Mario Davidovsky (b. 1934). Each of the six works combines electronically generated sounds, which are contained on tapes, and one or more instruments played live.

"Synchronisms No. 1"

In "Synchronisms No. 1"* the live instrument is a flute. The other sounds—the electronic sounds—are used particularly as extensions of the flute timbres. Several different timbres can be produced by the flute itself, depending on the

*Copyright © 1967 by Josef Marx, McGinnis & Marx Music Publishers, 201 West 86th St., NYC 10024. Used by permission.

fingering technique used and the way the flutist blows into the mouthpiece. A performer can, for example, control minute fluctuations in pitch very precisely, add noise elements to the sound, and attack sounds gently or percussively. By extending and enlarging upon these variations in the taped sounds, Davidovsky created a strong unity between the instrumental part and the electronic sounds. The example below shows the first part of the score:

Excerpt from "Synchronisms No.1"

The lower staff in each set of staves shows the flute part. The two upper staves provide necessary cues for the flutist and the person operating the tape

MUSIC IN THE SECOND HALF OF THE TWENTIETH CENTURY

Making Electronic Music: *In the last few decades, universities across the country installed electronic sound synthesizers and complex computers, giving their students and resident composers a chance to produce an incredibly varied range of sounds. The laboratory at the right is at the University of Michigan.*

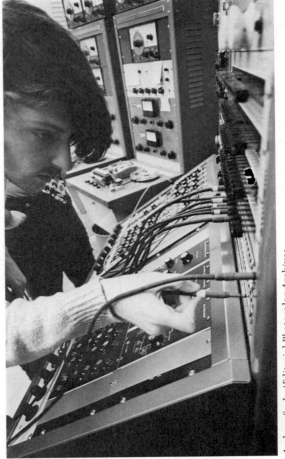

Andrew Sacks / Editorial Photocolor Archives

recorder. The extreme complexity of the electronic part precludes its being written out in traditional notation.

The flutist must maintain exact synchronization with the tape, which, unlike another live performer, is an inflexible element. The tape is stopped at certain points, both to provide sections of solo work for the flute and to keep the synchronization as precise as possible.

In addition to extending flute timbres, the electronic sounds also imitate some of the flute passages and motives. The motive shown at the beginning of Tape Cue 2 is, for example, quite similar to some of those found in the flute part. While flute and electronic sounds are sometimes heard as separate units in a kind of contrapuntal relationship, they are at other times heard as one combined whole.

"Synchronisms No. 1" is quite short, lasting only about three minutes. The music is divided into three main sections. Each of the first two sections finishes with a short part for tape alone; the third section is almost entirely for solo flute, with the electronic sounds entering very briefly at the end. In the first two sections, climaxes are achieved by accelerandos and crescendos in which flute and electronic parts seem to merge. At these moments, it is no longer possible to hear particular "notes" or the distinctions between the two parts. The total effect is quite spellbinding.

Side 12, Band 2

Listening Guide for "Synchronisms No. 1" from Davidovsky's *Synchronisms*

Timbre:	flute and electronically synthesized sounds
Melody:	often widely disjunct with unusual effects in the flute part; wide new spectrum of sounds of definite and indefinite pitch in the electronic part
Rhythm:	no repeated meter apparent to the listener; varying tempos
Harmony:	generally atonal in the flute part; no traditional concept of harmony in the electronic part
Texture:	monophonic and contrapuntal
Form:	three sections; form evolves freely

New Instrumental Techniques

The interest in electronic music has stimulated musical endeavor in many other areas as well. The repertoire for traditional instruments is being expanded rapidly, and even the techniques and styles of playing these instruments are changing. This is in part because electronic music has so greatly influenced what we might call the "sound ideal" of mid-twentieth-century music.

New Flute Techniques

The music written for the flute in Davidovsky's "Synchronisms No. 1" incorporates the use of a number of new techniques. The flute has especially fascinated modern composers because of its great range of sound. Although most flutists learn only about thirty or forty different fingerings, far more are possible. Even more sounds can be created by varying the way the flutist blows into the mouthpiece. A pioneering work for flute, *Density 21.5*, was written by Varèse in 1935. It is one of the earliest works to make use of new flute techniques, often requiring among other things that the keys be struck very hard to produce abrupt percussive sounds.

Penderecki

Other composers have emphasized the development of new techniques for different instruments. Polish composer Krzysztof Penderecki (b. 1933), in particular, has created striking new sounds for strings.

Penderecki: *Polymorphia*

New String Techniques

Written in 1961, Penderecki's *Polymorphia* is scored for twenty-four violins, eight violas, eight cellos, and eight double basses. The music contains numerous massive blocks of sound produced when the performers play glissandi, at any speed they wish, between two given pitches or between the highest note on each instrument and some indefinite low note. The score calls for a number of special effects, with strings played pizzicato as fast as possible to produce percussive sounds, fingertips used to tap the instruments, and the palm of the hand used to hit the strings. The results are often surprising and very unconventional.

Melody in *Polymorphia* is generally subsumed under the greater preoccupation with harmony. The texture is, not surprisingly, very dense. Form is very free and evolutionary.

Side 12, Band 3

Listening Guide for Penderecki's *Polymorphia*

Timbre:	orchestra of string instruments
Melody:	not present in traditional sense due to sliding pitches and tone clusters
Rhythm:	no clear meter; varying tempos; much rhythmic variety
Harmony:	dissonant and generally atonal until C major chord at end
Texture:	gradual change from sparse to dense to sparse; at times two or three layers of activity
Form:	quite free, evolving from use of harmonic material

New Use of Percussion

In addition to experimenting with string and wind instruments, modern composers have increasingly varied the use of percussion instruments, leading to some of the most attractive and exciting developments in contemporary music. Percussion instruments are no longer used merely for special emphasis or coloristic effects. Instead they have become an integral part of the whole, and there are now a large number of compositions for percussion only.

This development began early in the present century with the dazzling percussion parts Stravinsky wrote for *Les Noces* ("The Wedding") and *L'Histoire du soldat* ("The Soldier's Tale"). At about the same time, in Italy, the Futurists were proclaiming their allegiance to the noise-music of shipyards, steel foundries, and railroads.

Varèse played an important part in the development of the new percussion music. His *Ionisation* (1930–1933) was written for percussion alone. In this work and in others, he showed great sensitivity to the pitch level or register of the many percussion instruments of indefinite pitch.

Wen-chung

A student of Varèse's, Chou Wen-chung, has written a number of works that show the influence of his teacher, tempered by his own experience with Oriental music. His *Pien* (1966) is scored for piano, woodwinds, and percussion. Here the registers of percussion instruments form an important structural component. Sometimes the percussion instruments interact with the piano gap between high and low woodwinds.

The new role of percussion instruments points up a very important aspect of modern music. Dynamics, timbre, and rhythm are no longer subordinated to pitch. Today composers are treating them as important structural elements in their own right.

New Vocal Techniques

Innovations in vocal techniques are very much tied to the development of a sense of theater in contemporary music. This trend was apparent as early as Schoenberg's *Pierrot lunaire*. While making effective use of Sprechstimme, Schoenberg's work also requires that the singer have considerable histrionic ability. Today's singers may be asked to shout, whisper, groan, or murmur nonsense syllables, creating effects that range from the humorous to the macabre. Many singers, including Cathy Berberian and Jan de Gaetani, have chosen to specialize in new music, and some very interesting works have been written for them.

Berio

Circles, written by Luciano Berio (b. 1925) for Cathy Berberian, illustrates especially well a number of the demands made on singers by these contemporary scores. The work is a setting for voice, harp, and percussion of three poems by e.e. cummings. The singer must have a very wide range and must be able to execute a variety of vocal gymnastics in addition to singing. Timing must be perfect, both to sustain the dramatic tension and to maintain close coordination with the instruments. The sounds of syllables and even of letters are as important as the meaning of the words and are an integral part of the timbre. The percussion instruments are used to punctuate and emphasize the singer's line. A sibilant word in the text, for example, may be matched by a tingling buzz from a cymbal, or a sudden shout may be enhanced by an abrupt crash.

Crumb

A work similar in spirit to Berio's is *Ancient Voices of Children* by George Crumb (b. 1929). The work is a cycle of songs based on texts by Federico García Lorca. The music is set for mezzo-soprano, boy soprano, oboe, mandolin, harp, electric piano, and a large group of percussion instruments, including Tibetan prayer stones, Japanese temple bells, and tom-toms.

Crumb's *Ancient Voices of Children* achieves its dramatic impact mainly through the effective use of unusual vocal techniques. The second song, for instance, is whispered. Elsewhere a singer may shout or break up words into syllables. The vocal parts constantly cross the boundaries between speech and song until the two seem to merge. There are a number of references to Oriental and Spanish music and many special effects obtained through electronic amplification. At one point the mezzo-soprano sings into the amplified piano to produce what Crumb calls "a shimmering aura of echoes." A number of other unusual instrumental techniques are also found in the work, with the pianist at times called upon to apply a chisel to the piano strings to change their pitch.

New Principles of Structure

Cage

Another composer who has done much experimental work with instruments and, in fact, with almost every aspect of music is the American John Cage (b. 1912). Cage's ideas about music and the other arts have had considerable influence on artists in a number of fields. For him, art is not something separate from life; art is life and life is art. Thus part of his work as a composer has been to make people aware of all the sounds around them. "Wherever we are," he says, "what we hear is mostly noise. When we ignore it, it disturbs us. When we listen to it, we find it fascinating."

As a young composer in the 1930s, Cage followed the lead of Varèse in developing new forms of percussion music. His *First Construction in Metal* calls for the use of automobile brake drums, cowbells, and sheets of metal as well as more conventional percussion instruments. The work consists of a series of rhythmic units, combined and repeated in a systematic way, to form a symmetrical rhythmic structure. Cage's aim here was to devise a structure based not on melody or harmony but on rhythm alone.

Prepared Piano

In 1938 Cage invented the *prepared piano* for use in a modern dance score. His invention grew out of the work of another American composer, Henry Cowell, whose piano string technique was discussed in Chapter 28. In a prepared piano such as the one Cage created, the strings are muted at a number of points with pieces of wood, metal, rubber, or glass. This alters the timbre as well as the pitch of the strings. A piano must be prepared differently for each piece, in accordance with the specific directions of the composer. The work is then played from an ordinary score, resulting in completely unconventional sounds.

Cage has remarked that "Art should imitate Nature in her manner of operation." He has tried, as much as possible, to let things be themselves and to get beyond the usual ideas about self-expression. One critic has interpreted Cage's philosophy thus: "Only by getting out of the imprisoning circle of his own wishes and desires can the artist be free to enter into the miraculous new field of human awareness that is opening up, and thereby help others enter it as well."

In 1952 Cage tried to sharpen his listeners' awareness of all the sounds around them by means of his so-called "silent piece," a work entitled *4'33"*. When the work was first performed, the pianist sat at a piano in silence for precisely four minutes and thirty-three seconds, opening and closing the keyboard cover three times to indicate the beginning and end of the work's three movements. The "composition" was in actuality made up of all the sounds that occurred by chance in the auditorium during that time.

Aleatoric Music

"Letting things be themselves" has led Cage to abandon control over his works in many respects and to adopt methods that introduce the element of chance. The chance, or *aleatoric*, methods he has used vary greatly from work to work. In 1951 he composed *Music of Changes*, a work for piano, by using the *I Ching* ("Book of Changes"), an Oriental work that describes a method of throwing coins or marked sticks to obtain chance numbers. Almost every aspect of the composition is determined by this method. One coin toss might determine the duration of a note, another its pitch, and so on.

In recent years, Cage has used aleatoric methods less to determine the aspects of a composition and more as a means of leaving decisions up to the performers. Many of his latest works are made up of instructions to performers that may be interpreted in almost any way. *Variations II*, for example, is a work for any number of performers using any sound-producing means. The score consists of six transparent sheets, each containing a single straight line, and a seventh sheet containing points. The sheets are laid out in random order, and perpendiculars leading from the points to the lines are measured. These measurements serve as a free guide for the performers, to be interpreted into sound in any way the performers wish.

Of course these instructions give the performers such great freedom that

MUSIC OF CHANGES

John Cage

Score of Cage's *Music of Changes:* Cage's own notes about the performance of his Music of Changes *include the following directive: "It will be found in many places that the notation is irrational; in such instance the performer is to employ his own discretion."*

they virtually compose the piece, or rather a possible version of it, themselves. One recorded version of Cage's *Variations II* makes use of an amplified piano played by pianist David Tudor. Tudor produces rich and varied sounds, not only playing the keys but also stroking the strings with objects attached to contact microphones and phonograph cartridges.

Cage's attitude toward music and toward all the arts is an experimental one. He is interested more in the process than in the finished product. His concern is not so much with the operations by which people can manipulate their environment but with the fact that people and their environment together form a unity.

Cage's concept of art as a process that makes use of chance elements has definite parallels in the fine arts. In the works of the Abstract Expressionist or "action" painters such as Jackson Pollock, the fortuitous path taken by thrown or dripping paint is an important part of the work. One critic has commented, "By making art out of materials not usually familiar to art, Cage, along with his friend Marcel Duchamp, also provided . . . precedents for pop art, found objects, industrial sculpture, and much else."

During the late 1940s and early 1950s, Cage became well known in New York, and a group of composers and painters began to gather around him. **Brown** Notable among the composers was Earle Brown (b. 1926), who has since made much use of chance elements in his own music. Brown has been particularly interested in providing opportunities for spontaneous decisions during the performance of a work and the freedom to change the order of musical sections. He regards the performance of one of his works as "process rather than static and conclusive." His *25 Pages,** written for piano in 1953, was inspired by Alexander Calder's mobiles, in which, Brown has stated, "there are basic units subject to innumerable different relationships of form." The twenty-five pages of the work may be played in any order, and each staff may be read as either a bass or a treble clef. Each page may also be performed either side up: accidentals and dynamic markings are provided on both the left and right.

Use of Time The excerpt from Brown's *25 Pages* that appears below shows the **Notation** composer's use of *time notation*. To interpret the score, the performer must decide on a basic tempo and then determine how long to hold each note on the basis of its visual length.

Excerpt from *25 Pages*

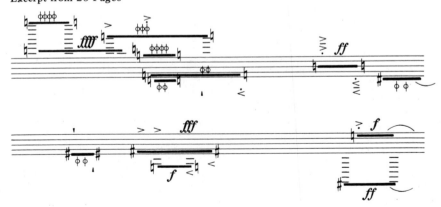

*Earle Brown, "25 Pages" (1953). Excerpt reprinted by permission: Universal Edition, London.

CONTEMPORARY MUSIC

A great many other composers have incorporated chance elements into their compositions to a greater or lesser extent. They include among others Boulez and Stockhausen.

Although chance methods offer one new possibility for structuring music, a number of composers have continued to search for yet other methods. Composer Elliott Carter (b. 1908), among others, has stressed the need young composers have for finding a new approach to structure. He believes that this need is much more important than the development of new styles of harmony or innovations in other musical elements. Problems of musical continuity, Carter feels, must be rethought today, just as ideas about harmony were revised and changed at the beginning of the twentieth century. Carter himself has developed a number of new ways of handling rhythmic and textural continuities—that is, the overall structure of rhythm and texture. Some of these new methods can be found in his *Double Concerto for Piano and Harpsichord.*

Carter: *Double Concerto for Piano and Harpsichord*

The structure of Carter's *Double Concerto* is essentially determined by the interplay of rhythm and texture. The texture is made up of several different layers, which often move at different speeds. The differentiation and interrelation of the various textural elements through rhythm is one of the hallmarks of Carter's style.

In a performance of the work, the two solo instruments, the piano and the harpsichord, are placed on either side of the stage, each with its own small orchestra of two percussion players and six other instrumentalists. Carter explained this arrangement in the following manner: "Primarily, both groups were chosen to suggest and reinforce the sonorities and character of the two soloists. . . . Each group . . . also contains elements of the opposing group to weld the entire sound into one." The harpsichord's percussion group, for example, contains wood blocks, triangles, and cymbals, while the piano's percussion group is made up of drums. The harpsichord is also supported by brass instruments to compensate for its smaller dynamic range.

Another important aspect of the *Double Concerto* is found in the way that instruments of indefinite pitch are used. A continuum is set up in which these instruments acquire a kind of pitch definition in relation to one another. A wood block, for example, sounds higher in pitch than a low snare drum but lower in pitch than cymbals. The pitched instruments also become more or less definite in pitch depending on how they are used in relation to one another. Musical statements are made by both sets of instruments, by those with definite pitch and by those with indefinite pitch. At the beginning of the composition, the percussion instruments state some of the basic rhythmic materials, materials that are only later played by the pitched instruments. At other times, a melodic phrase begun by a pitched instrument is continued by a percussion instrument.

Carter has often characterized his works in dramatic or poetic terms. Of his *Double Concerto* he has written: "The idea that there is always a large world going on from which items are picked out, brought into focus, and allowed to drop back, is one of the fundamental conceptions of the piece."

Carter's *Double Concerto* is divided into seven sections of contrasting character:

Introduction
Cadenza for Harpsichord
Allegro scherzando
Adagio
Presto
Cadenzas for Piano
Coda

The symmetrical structure of the work is striking. The slow middle section is surrounded by the two quickest sections. These in turn are surrounded by cadenzas, which are bracketed by an introduction and a coda. The overall structure thus depends in large part on changes of tempo and instrumentation.

First and Second Sections

The colorful use of percussion instruments is very apparent in the introduction. Melodic material is chiefly motivic, with the sonorities of the individual instruments nicely exploited in the presentation of the different motives.

The harpsichord cadenza is a virtuosic section that requires great skill from the player. Meter changes frequently in this section, as in the preceding section, giving the music a fluid and very free rhythmic feeling.

Side 12, Band 4

Listening Guide for Carter's *Double Concerto for Piano and Harpsichord*, First and Second Sections

Timbre:	harpsichord, piano, and two chamber orchestras of string, wind, and percussion instruments
Melody:	largely motivic
Rhythm:	no clear meter; slow to moderate tempos
Harmony:	disjunct, largely atonal
Texture:	generally sparse with frequent changes of instrumentation
Form:	evolves freely in each section as motives are repeated, developed, and extended

---

Music of the Present and the Future

The musical situation in the second half of the twentieth century is unique. There is an unprecedented variety of styles and a tremendous independence of outlook among composers. It is interesting that much of the emphasis in contemporary music is on aspects of construction, perhaps in part because traditional forms are no longer accepted as models. Each composition, to a large extent, must therefore create its own form; there are no conventional

Xenakis's Theories of Probability

solutions. Yannis Xenakis (b. 1922) is especially noted for his exploration of theories of probability concerning the recurrence of notes and rhythms. His work along with that of other composers may eventually lead to new conventions, but none of them have yet been widely accepted.

Even with all their independence, composers today have more of a chance to influence and be influenced by one another than ever before. The new music is notable for its internationalism. This, of course, is due partly to the development of the long-playing record, which can make any piece of music available all over the world. The phonograph record and stereophonic sound have had other effects as well. Several compositions have been commissioned especially for records and written to fit in one or two record sides.

Ironically, at a time in history when there are more media than ever before for the dissemination of new music, very little of this music has reached the public. The new developments have taken place, on the whole, outside of the symphony orchestras and other performance groups of the music establishment. The result is that the average concertgoer hears very little contemporary music. Such a situation is unprecedented. The public at the time of Mozart and Beethoven, for example, heard most new works almost as soon as they were written. There are, however, some encouraging signs that the audience for contemporary music is growing, and it is to be hoped that this trend will continue.

Increasing Role for Women

Another important aspect of modern music is the increasing participation and acceptance of women, not only as performers, but also as conductors and composers. While women have been active in the writing and performing of music for centuries, their role has grown enormously in the twentieth century. Women singers have enjoyed great prominence and prestige ever since the seventeenth century, but women composers and conductors have rarely enjoyed the success and popularity of their male counterparts. In recent decades, Margaret Hillis (b. 1921), conductor of the Chicago Symphony Chorus, and Sarah Caldwell (b. 1928), conductor of the Opera Company of Boston, have been acclaimed for their particular genius. Composers Thea Musgrave (b. 1928), Esther Williamson Ballou (1915–1973), and Pozzi Escot (1933) have all gained international repute. It will be especially interesting to see what future decades will bring to the role of women in music.

In the meantime, it is exciting to realize that this is an era of almost unparalleled possibilities for musical exploration. For the listener, the new music represents a challenge and an invitation to new musical experiences.

Suggested Listening

Expansion of Serialism

Boulez: *Le Marteau sans maître* ("The Hammer Without a Master") [Odyssey 32160154]. This cantata, written in 1955 and based on the poetry of René Char, is scored for alto voice and six instrumentalists. Many elements of the music—rhythm, dynamics, timbres, attacks, and pitches—are serialized. The setting provides a striking and sensitive interpretation of the strongly pictorial text.

Electronic Music

Xenakis: *Bohor I* [Nonesuch 71246]. This example of musique concrète, written in 1968, uses the electronically altered sounds of jewelry and a Laotian mouth organ. The evolution and contrasts of blocks of sound are strikingly executed. The work's premiere in Paris aroused great clamor among the audience, many acclaiming it and some denouncing it.

New Instrumental and Vocal Techniques

Penderecki: *Fonogrammi for Flute and Chamber Orchestra* [Angel S-36949]. This short piece is scored for flutes, strings, percussion, and harpsichord. In one notable passage for flutes, sounds are produced solely by striking the keys.

Berio: *Circles* [Mainstream 5005]. *Circles* is Berio's setting of poems by e. e. cummings, one of Berio's favorite poets. The work is written for soprano, harp, and two percussion instruments. Throughout, the instruments seem to punctuate the poetry rather than accompany it.

Aleatoric Music

Cage: *Concerto for Prepared Piano and Orchestra* [Nonesuch 71202]. Cage's concerto was written in 1951 for piano with various metal, wooden, and plastic objects attached. The orchestra consists of a string quintet, wind instruments, and percussion instruments. The three movements proceed without intervening pauses. The music is aleatoric, with pianist and orchestral players organizing the sounds and silences themselves, following general guidelines provided by Cage.

GLOSSARY

Accelerando   Gradual quickening of tempo.

Accent   Stress on a particular note.

Accidental   Sharp, flat, or natural sign before a note indicating that the pitch is not to be played as it normally would be in a given key, but is to be altered according to the sign.

Aerophone   Any instrument that produces sound by the vibration of a column of air in a tube.

Aleatoric Music   See Chance Music.

Alla Breve (Cut Time)   Meter in which a measure consists of two beats, and a half note has a value of one beat.

Allemande   Dance in duple meter and moderate tempo used in keyboard and ensemble music of the late Renaissance and Baroque periods.

Alto   See Contralto.

Aria   Elaborate solo song found primarily in opera, oratorios, and cantatas. Three important types: strophic-bass, with melody varied over a repeated bass line; ostinato, with lengthy melody over a short, constantly repeated bass line; da capo, in an ABA form.

Arioso   Vocal style found primarily in opera and oratorios; more melodic than the recitative but less rhythmically regular than the aria.

Arpeggio   Chord whose tones are played in succession rather than simultaneously.

Art Song   Elaborate solo song, usually with piano accompaniment.

Atonality   Tendency to avoid referring to or creating any specific tonal center in music.

Augmentation   Compositional technique for varying a theme in which the note values are lengthened in the repetition of the theme.

Ayre   Term used especially in the Renaissance and Baroque periods to denote a song or an instrumental composition of a songlike nature.

Ballad   In folk music, a narrative song dealing with topical themes.

Ballade   (1) Medieval French secular song based on a poetic form; (2) lyrical piano piece of the Romantic era.

Ballata   Medieval Italian secular song based on a poetic form.

Ballet   Artistic dance or series of dances.

Ballett   Renaissance part song, simpler than the madrigal, rhythmically regular, and usually with a "fa-la-la" refrain.

Bar Lines   Narrow vertical lines on a score, used to separate the measures.

Baritone   Male voice that lies between the tenor and bass in range.

Bass   Lowest male voice type.

Basso Continuo   Baroque practice in which the bass line in ensemble music is played by a low melodic instrument (cello, viol, or bassoon), while a keyboard instrument (organ or harpsichord) also plays the bass line and adds chords above it as indicated by figured bass. Also called thoroughbass.

Basso Ostinato   See Ostinato.

Beat   Pulse underlying most rhythmic patterns.

Bel Canto   Baroque Italian vocal style emphasizing beauty of sound.

Bimodality   Simultaneous use of the major and minor modes.

Binary Form   Two-part form in which the second part often seems to answer the first.

Bitonality   Simultaneous use of two different tonalities.

Blue Note Note of the major scale, generally the third or seventh tone, played with a slight slurring of the pitch.

Blues Style of American music with origins in rural black folk music, consisting of a twelve-measure unit divided into three lines of four measures each. The texts generally express sadness, longing, or complaint.

Bop Small-ensemble jazz style popular in the 1940s, requiring extensive knowledge of harmony and accomplished instrumental technique.

Break In jazz improvisation, a short, improvised cadenza.

Bridge Passage of secondary thematic importance played between two major themes, during which modulation usually takes place.

Caccia Canon for two upper parts, often supported by a lower part with notes of longer duration; popular in fourteenth-century Italy.

Cadence Harmonic formula that brings a musical idea to a close. Common types: authentic, with movement from the V chord to the I chord; plagal, with movement from the IV chord to the I chord.

Cadenza Elaborate passage for the soloist in a concerto, interpolated near the end of a movement, and often not written out by the composer but left to the performer to create.

Canon Composition for two or more voices in which one voice enters after another in exact imitation of the first melody. A round is the simplest and best-known type of canon.

Cantata Vocal composition developed in the Baroque period for chorus and/or solo voice(s), based on secular or religious texts, including several movements, and accompanied by an instrumental ensemble.

Canzona Italian instrumental work of the sixteenth and seventeenth centuries, derived from the vocal chanson.

Castrato Male soprano or alto, prominently used in Italian Baroque opera.

Cavatina Short, lyrical song.

Chamber Music Music for a small ensemble, usually with one performer to each part, and no conductor.

Chance Music Music into which the composer deliberately incorporates the effects of chance, either using chance methods to determine one or more elements of the composition or allowing the performers to introduce chance variations into the performance.

Chanson Literally "song"; term used for French secular song throughout the centuries.

Chant See Plainchant.

Chorale Hymn of the German Protestant church.

Chord Three or more tones played simultaneously.

Chordal Progression Movement from one chord to another in a logical manner.

Chordophone Any instrument that produces sound through the vibration of strings.

Chromatic Scale Scale made up of all twelve half steps of the ordinary octave.

Chromaticism Use of notes that do not belong to the basic scale of a composition.

Church Modes In plainchant and chant-derived music, four scale patterns, each of which spans an octave and occurs in two versions (authentic and plagal), resulting in eight modes. Four additional modes were added in the Renaissance. All of the modes differ from the major and minor scales in the location of the half steps.

Clef Sign at the beginning of a staff that indicates the pitches of the lines and spaces. Common clefs: treble (G), bass (F), alto and tenor (C).

Coda Closing section of a composition or movement, usually reinforcing the final cadence; in some nineteenth-century works in sonata form, the coda becomes long enough to be considered a contrasting section in its own right.

Color See Timbre.

Coloratura Elaborate style of singing, usually including fast scales, arpeggios, and intricate musical ornaments; often associated with a light, high soprano voice, particularly in opera.

Combo Jazz term for small ensemble.

Common Meter Hymn structure consisting of a four-line stanza with lines of eight, six, eight, and six syllables, respectively.

Common Time Meter in which a measure consists of four beats, and a quarter note has a value of one beat.

Concertato Style Baroque style emphasizing contrast, with performing groups playing or singing in alternation with one another.

Concertino The solo group (usually two violins and continuo) in a Baroque concerto grosso.

Concerto Work for solo instrument or instruments accompanied by orchestra, usually with three movements, the first of which often contains a cadenza.

Concerto Grosso Baroque concerto in which a small group of soloists (the concertino) plays against a small orchestra (the ripieno).

Conjunct Motion Melodic movement by small intervals.

Consonance Term used to refer to pleasing sounds, in contrast to dissonance.

Consort Renaissance term for family of instruments.

Continuo See Basso Continuo.

Continuo Madrigal Late Renaissance madrigal with relatively few voices, free dissonance, and basso-continuo accompaniment.

Contralto Lowest of the female voice types.

Counterpoint, Contrapuntal Texture in which two or more voices proceed relatively independently.

Countersubject Secondary melody in a fugue.

Courante Baroque dance, usually in triple meter and a fast tempo. Italian version called corrente.

Crescendo Gradual increase in volume.

Cut Time See Alla Breve.

Decrescendo Gradual decrease in volume. Also called diminuendo.

Development (1) Growth of a musical idea through change or transformation; (2) the second section in a sonata form.

Diatonic Scale Any major or minor scale, without chromaticism.

Diminuendo See Decrescendo.

Diminution Compositional technique for varying a theme, in which the note values are shortened in the repetition of the theme.

Discantus Medieval polyphonic style in which both tenor and duplum lines play a rhythmically active role.

Disjunct Motion Melodic movement by large intervals.

Dissonance Musical sounds that create a feeling of tension, often disagreeable to the ear.

Divertimento Late eighteenth-century composition in several movements for a small instrumental group, usually in a light, entertaining style and often including dance movements.

Dodecaphony See Serialism.

Dominant The fifth note of a major or minor scale.

Dotted Rhythm Uneven rhythm produced when notes are dotted and played half again as long as the original note value.

Double Stopping Playing two strings at a time on a violin or other string instrument.

Drone Note Tone held throughout a musical work.

Duplum Added line in Medieval polyphony.

Dynamics Intensity of sound; the various levels of loudness and softness in music. For specific dynamic markings, see chart on page 32.

Electronic Music Music in which sounds are created with an electronic synthesizer.

Embellishment See Ornament.

Empfindsamer Stil German transitional style, leading to the Classical style, in which the complexities of the Baroque era were rejected in an attempt to present emotions freely and subtly.

Ensemble Small group of performers, or a composition written for such a group.

Episode Passage of freely invented counterpoint separating statements of the subject in a fugue.

Equal Temperament See Temperament.

Étude Literally a "study"; composition stressing the development of technical performance skills; in the nineteenth century, a short piece for piano or other instruments.

Exposition The first section in a fugue or sonata form, in which the main melodic material is presented.

Fantasia Composition in free form, often including difficult passages for the performer.

Fasola Early American and English system of sight singing that depends primarily on the syllables *fa, sol,* and *la.*

Figured Bass Form of musical shorthand used in the Baroque period, in which the chordal accompaniment is indicated by numbers above or below the bass line, with some freedom of interpretation left to the performer.

Flat Sign indicating that a pitch is to be lowered by a half step.

Form Overall structure of a composition.

Frequency Rate of vibration of any medium, such as a violin string or a column of air, that determines the pitch of musical sounds.

Frottola Chordal, syllabic Italian part song of the Renaissance.

Fugal Having some characteristics of a fugue, usually involving imitation.

Fuging Tune Imitative psalm setting used particularly by some eighteenth-century American composers such as William Billings.

Fugue Contrapuntal composition originating in the Baroque period, based on a main melody, called a subject, that is presented in turn by each voice—usually three to five in number—and then repeated in different keys before ending in the original tonic.

Futurism Early twentieth-century movement favoring "noise music," especially the use of sounds derived from modern industrial society.

Gagliarda, Galliard Renaissance and Baroque dance, in triple meter and fast tempo.

Gebrauchsmusik Literally "music for use"; a style of twentieth-century music written principally for the use and pleasure of amateur performers.

Gigue Baroque dance, usually in a basically triple meter and a quick tempo.

Gliding Chords Chords repeated in parallel motion up or down the staff.

Glissando Very rapid scale, played on the piano by sliding the fingernail quickly over the keys.

Grace Note Very short added note used to embellish a principal note; often approaches the principal note by step just before the beat.

Grand Opera Nineteenth-century French opera style that placed great emphasis on elaborate spectacle.

Great Staff Combination of the treble and bass staves placed one above the other, with an empty space between for the ledger line of middle C. Most piano music is written on the great staff.

Gregorian Chant See Plainchant.

Ground Bass See Ostinato.

Harmony The sounding together of two or more tones.

Homophony, Homophonic Texture made up of a melodic line and chordal accompaniment.

Idée Fixe Literally "fixed idea"; a melody in the music of Berlioz, associated with a nonmusical idea and repeated throughout the work.

Idiophone Any instrument whose sound is produced through the vibrating of the whole body of the instrument.

Imitation The immediate repetition of a theme by different voices, either exactly or with small changes.

Imitative Counterpoint See Imitation.

Impressionism Artistic movement of the late nineteenth century characterized by an understated approach and designed to appeal to the senses rather than the intellect; represented musically by much of the music of Debussy and those whom he influenced.

Impromptu Short composition, usually for the piano, designed to sound like an improvisation; popular in the Romantic period.

Improvisation Composing music while performing it, either without a written score or by variations on a score.

Incidental Music Music incidental to the action in a play: e.g., a musical setting for a love song, or dance music for a ballroom scene; sometimes also overtures and music played between the acts of a play.

Instrumentation Parts assigned to particular instruments in an ensemble or orchestra.

Interval Musical and mathematical distance between two pitches.

Inversion Compositional technique in which a theme is repeated upside down.

Isorhythm Fourteenth-century technique in which a rhythmic pattern is repeated throughout, often with a repeated melodic pattern of the same or different length.

Jazz Indigenous American musical style of the twentieth century, distinguished by syncopated rhythm and highly improvisatory performance.

Key The basic scale of a composition, named for its tonic note and indicated on the score by a key signature.

Key Signature Sharps or flats placed at the beginning of each staff of music to indicate the key being used.

Klangfarbenmelodie Technique in which each note of a melody is given to a different instrument.

Lai Medieval French secular song based on a poetic form.

Lauda (pl. Laude) Italian devotional hymn, especially in the Middle Ages and the Renaissance, that influenced the development of the oratorio in the Baroque period.

Ledger Lines Short lines on which notes are placed when they fall above or below the lines of the staff.

Legato Smooth, connected manner of musical performance.

Leitmotiv Melodic, rhythmic, and/or harmonic motive associated with a person, thing, or idea in the operas of Richard Wagner.

Libretto Text of an opera or oratorio, often in poetic form.

Lied (pl. Lieder) Literally "song"; German art song, especially of the nineteenth century.

Lining Out Practice in which each line of a song or hymn is sung by a leader and immediately repeated by the group.

Lyric Opera Nineteenth-century French style of opera that was a compromise between grand opera and opéra comique.

Madrigal (1) Secular composition, usually for two or three voices, in fourteenth-century Italy; (2) secular composition for four or five voices in Italy and England in the sixteenth and early seventeenth centuries.

Major Scale Scale consisting of the following pattern of whole and half steps, beginning with the lowest pitch: whole–whole–half–whole–whole–whole–half.

March Music designed to accompany walking, in duple meter and a moderate tempo.

Mass In music, usually a polyphonic setting of the Ordinary: Kyrie, Gloria, Credo, Sanctus, Agnus Dei.

Mazurka Slavic dance in $\frac{3}{4}$ time, incorporating rhythmic touches of Eastern Europe; used especially by Chopin in the early nineteenth century as a basis for piano pieces.

Measure Rhythmic group of beats with an accent on the first beat in each group, and sometimes a secondary accent on a later beat; set off in written music by vertical lines called bar lines.

Melismatic Having many notes per syllable of text.

Melody Succession of tones that assumes a recognizable musical shape in conjunction with a rhythmic organization.

Membranophone Any instrument in which sound is produced through the vibrating of a membrane such as a drum head.

Meter Pattern of accented and unaccented beats. Common types: duple meter, with two beats, one accented and one unaccented; triple meter, with three beats, one accented and two unaccented.

Meter Signature See Time Signature.

Metronome Device invented in the early nineteenth century to indicate the proper tempo of a composition.

Mezzo-Soprano Female voice that lies between the soprano and contralto in range.

Microtonal Composition Music making use of an octave made up of more than twelve tones.

Minor Scale Scale consisting of the following pattern of whole and half steps, beginning with the lowest pitch: whole–half–whole–whole–half–whole–whole. The sixth and seventh degrees of the scale can be altered to create two additional forms of the minor scale, the harmonic and melodic.

Minuet Dance of the Baroque and Classical periods, in triple meter and moderate tempo; often used with trio in third movement of Classical symphony.

Missa See Mass.

Missa Brevis (1) In the Renaissance, a setting of the five parts of the Ordinary of the Mass in a simpler and shorter style; (2) in the Baroque period, a setting of the Kyrie and Gloria used in the Lutheran Church.

Mode (1) Scale such as the major or minor; (2) often used to refer to scales found in non-Western music. See also Church Modes.

Modified Strophic Form Form in vocal music in which all stanzas of a text are sung to music that is basically the same but with some changes in the repetitions.

Modulation Series of chords that changes the key or tonic note in a composition.

Monody, Monodic Style consisting of a melody and a simple accompaniment; used in early seventeenth-century Italian music, especially in opera.

Monophony, Monophonic Texture that is made up of a single line.

Motet (1) Prominent type of composition of the thirteenth century, usually for three voices, often combining religious and secular texts; (2) an unaccompanied choral composition of the fifteenth and sixteenth centuries, written in contrapuntal style, usually for four or five voices, generally with a religious text.

Motive Short melodic-rhythmic figure, generally consisting of from two to five notes, used as a unit in a composition.

Movement Relatively independent part of a large composition, usually having a clear beginning and ending.

Musique Concrète Twentieth-century style in which conventional sounds are altered electronically and recorded on tape to produce new effects.

Natural Sign indicating that a note is to be played without sharping or flatting; used only as an accidental, never in the key signature.

Neoclassicism Twentieth-century style that borrows certain characteristics of earlier periods—such as form, melody, instrumentation—and combines them with other elements used in a new way.

Neumatic Having several notes per syllable of text but not as many notes per syllable as in the melismatic style.

Neume Symbol used for note in Medieval notation.

Nocturne Literally "night piece"; a piano composition of the Romantic period.

Note Visual representation of musical sound.

Octave Eight-tone interval in which the higher pitch has twice as many vibrations per second as the lower.

Octave Displacement Technique in which the successive notes of a melody are placed in different octaves.

Office The form of daily common prayer in monastic and other religious communities, consisting mainly of psalms, hymns, and Scripture readings; usually divided into several sections distributed throughout the day.

Opera Drama expressed through music, with dialogue generally sung rather than spoken; developed first in Italy in the seventeenth century.

Opera Buffa Italian comic opera.

Opéra Comique French comic opera.

Opera Seria Literally "serious opera."

Operetta Light opera with spoken dialogue, often with frivolous plot.

Opus Literally "work"; used by composers to indicate the order in which their compositions were written, e.g., Opus 1, Opus 2.

Oratorio Religious or secular work for solo voices, chorus, and orchestra developed in the Baroque period; usually presented without staging or scenery.

Orchestration Arrangement of instrumental music to achieve a variety of effects.

Ordinary Those parts of the Mass in which the text always remains the same; principally the Kyrie, Gloria, Credo, Sanctus, Agnus Dei.

Ordre See Suite.

Organum The earliest Western polyphony, beginning in the ninth century, based on melodies borrowed from plainchant.

Ornament Note or group of notes added to a basic melody to embellish or decorate it.

Ostinato Melodic or rhythmic motive or phrase that is repeated persistently, often in the bass.

Overture Instrumental introduction to a vocal work or orchestral suite. Common Baroque types: French overture, with two sections, one slow and one fast; Italian overture, with three sections, fast—slow—fast. Common Romantic types: one-movement instrumental introduction to a vocal work; independent programmatic work written for concert performance. Latter type often called concert overture.

Pandiatonicism A diatonic tonal style without the restrictions of traditional chordal progressions.

Parallel Motion Harmonic technique in which voices produce a series of simultaneous notes that remain a steady, specific interval apart.

Paraphrase Technique Method that produces an elaboration of an existing melody.

Partita See Suite.

Pavane Slow, processional dance of the Renaissance and Baroque periods, in duple meter. Also called padouana.

Pentatonic Scale Scale of five tones.

Phrase Relatively short portion of a melodic line with a clear beginning and end, similar in length and function to a line of poetry.

Pitch Highness or lowness of a tone, determined by the number of vibrations per second.

Pizzicato Manner of playing a string instrument by plucking instead of bowing the strings.

Plainchant Monophonic church music of the Middle Ages, sometimes called Gregorian chant after Pope Gregory I. Also called chant.

Pointillistic Texture Sparse texture often made up of a single note or very short motive followed immediately by one in another part in a higher or lower register.

Polonaise Polish ceremonial dance in triple meter and moderate tempo; used by Chopin in the early nineteenth century for piano compositions.

Polychord Dense chord constructed as a composite of two or more triads.

Polyharmony Counterpoint, not of note against note, but of chord against chord.

Polyphony, Polyphonic Texture in which two or more voices proceed relatively independently.

Polyrhythm The use of several contrasting rhythms at the same time.

Polytonality Several tonalities occurring simultaneously.

Prelude (1) Free-form type of composition intended as an introduction; (2) in the nineteenth century, an independent short composition, usually for piano.

Prima Donna Italian for "first lady"; a female lead in an opera.

Program Music Instrumental music associated with nonmusical ideas that are often drawn from nature, art, or literature.

Program Symphony See Symphony.

Proper The parts of the Mass in which the texts change according to the particular rites of the day.

Raga Melodic formula in Indian music.

Ragtime Precursor of jazz, in duple meter, with liberal use of syncopation.

Realize To play a chordal accompaniment from a figured bass score.

Recapitulation (1) Section of thematic restatement; (2) the third section in a sonata form.

Recitative Declamatory type of singing developed in the Baroque period, used particularly in opera and oratorios. Emphasis is on free rhythm, uncomplicated melody, and clarity of text. Two types: secco ("dry"), accompanied only by continuo; accompagnato ("accompanied"), accompanied by ensemble or orchestra.

Relative Major and Minor Scales Major and minor scales that share the same key signature.

Requiem Mass Mass for the Dead in the Roman Catholic liturgy.

Resolution Movement from dissonant to more consonant sound.

Responsorial Singing Vocal technique in which a chorus answers phrases sung by a leader.

Rest (1) Period of silence in music; (2) sign used for notation of such silence.

Retrograde Compositional technique in which a theme is presented backward.

Rhapsody One-movement work in the style of a free fantasy; generally of heroic or romantic inspiration; popular in the nineteenth and twentieth centuries.

Rhythm Organization of sound in time, governed by such aspects as tempo and meter.

Rhythmic Polyphony Polyphonic texture created by interweaving of different rhythmic patterns.

Ricercar Imitative, contrapuntal instrumental piece of the sixteenth and seventeenth centuries, similar in style to the Renaissance motet.

Ring Shout In black religious music of the pre-Civil War South, a shuffling step with chanting and handclapping used in prayer meetings.

Ripieno Orchestral group in a Baroque concerto grosso.

Ritardando Gradual slowing down of tempo.

Ritornello Form Baroque form with alternating ripieno and solo passages, in which the ripieno returns to modified versions of the opening theme, while the soloist elaborates on the opening theme or contrasts with it in virtuoso fashion.

Rococo Style Highly ornamented style in music and the other arts in the early to middle eighteenth century.

Rondeau Medieval French secular song based on a poetic form.

Rondo Form Form prominent in the Classical period, in which a main theme, always in the tonic key, alternates with subordinate themes in contrasting keys.

Round See Canon.

Rubato Technique in which very small displacements in rhythm are introduced for expressive purposes. Literally, "robbing" time from one note and giving it to another.

Sarabande Baroque dance, in triple meter and a slow tempo.

Scale Arrangement of pitches, usually within an octave, on which tonal organization is based.

Scherzo Literally "joke." (1) A movement of a symphony, sonata, or quartet that replaced the minuet in the nineteenth century; (2) sometimes an independent composition. In both cases, usually written in a light and rapid style.

Section Discrete portion of a musical work.

Sequence (1) Repetition of a melodic motive or short phrase at different pitch levels; (2) a part of the Proper of the Mass.

Serialism Systematic ordering of pitches, and sometimes other musical elements, so that they always appear in a predetermined order; usually associated with the twelve-tone system.

Sforzando Sudden, sharp increase in loudness.

Shape-Note Notation Early American type of notation making use of four notes of different shapes—generally triangular, round, oblong, and diamond-shaped.

Sharp Sign indicating that a pitch is to be raised by a half step.

Sinfonia Instrumental work that developed into the Italian overture of the Baroque period.

Singspiel German comic opera of the eighteenth century, in which dialogue was usually spoken rather than sung in recitative as in Italian opera.

Sonata Instrumental composition of the Baroque, Classical, and Romantic periods; Baroque trio sonata for three melody instruments and continuo; Baroque solo sonata for one melody instrument and continuo; some Baroque sonatas and most later sonatas for single instrument.

Sonata-Allegro Form See Sonata Form.

Sonata Cycle Three- or four-movement structure of compositions such as the symphony, sonata, quartet, and concerto of the Classical and Romantic periods.

Sonata da Camera Baroque chamber sonata, usually comprised mainly of dance movements.

Sonata da Chiesa Baroque church sonata, usually including both contrapuntal material and homophonic dance-based forms; characteristically slow—fast—slow—fast in structure.

Sonata Form Form developed in the Classical period, consisting of an opening section called the exposition in which major themes are presented, a middle section called the development in which thematic material undergoes a variety of alterations, and a third section called the recapitulation in which the material of the exposition is restated.

Sonata-Rondo Form Form combining characteristics of both the sonata and the rondo forms.

Song Cycle Group of songs with a unifying theme.

Soprano Highest female voice type.

Spiritual American religious folk song, developed by blacks and southern rural whites.

Sprechstimme Literally "speaking voice"; vocal technique falling somewhere between speech and song, used frequently by Schoenberg and his contemporaries; in notation, an X is sometimes placed through the stem of a note, indicating that the pitch should not be sustained.

Staccato Literally "detached"; a manner of performance in which each note is made very short and clipped; indicated by a dot placed above or below the note.

Staff (pl. Staves) Series of horizontal lines (five in modern notation) on which musical notes are written.

Stanza One of several sections in a poem that are identical in length and structure.

Stile Rappresentativo Representative or theatrical style in the early Baroque era, based on the belief that music should be subordinated to the expression of ideas and emotions in the text.

String Quartet String ensemble made up of two violins, one viola, and one cello.

Strophe See Stanza.

Strophic Form Form of vocal music in which all stanzas of the text are sung to the same music.

Subdominant The fourth note of a major or minor scale.

Subject The primary melody in a fugue.

Suite Composition consisting of a number of dance movements, loosely linked. In Baroque period also called ordre or partita.

Syllabic Having one note per syllable of text.

Symphonic Poem Programmatic symphony in one movement. Also called a tone poem.

Symphony Orchestral composition, usually consisting of four movements, that originated in the Classical period. In the Romantic period, the abstract symphony generally retained the Classical emphasis on purely musical expression while the program symphony was meant to express nonmusical ideas as well.

Syncopation   Use of an accent on a beat that is not usually accented.

Synthesizer   Electronic instrument used to generate sounds.

Tala   Pattern of basic time units in Indian music.

Temperament   System of tuning. Equal temperament, devised in the seventeenth century, divides the octave into twelve equal intervals, enabling a keyboard instrument to play in tune in any key.

Tempo   Speed at which a composition is performed. For specific tempo markings see chart on page 13.

Tenor   (1) Highest of the ordinary male voice types; (2) in Medieval polyphony, original chant line with extended note values.

Ternary Form   Three-part form in which the third section is often a restatement of the material in the first.

Terraced Dynamics   Sudden changes in dynamic level, characteristic of Baroque music.

Text Painting   Direct association of musical ideas with words or a phrase in the text of a vocal work; e.g., a rising scale for the phrase "rise above us."

Texture   The number and relationship of musical lines in a composition. Types: monophonic, consisting of a single line; polyphonic or contrapuntal, with two or more lines, each relatively independent; homophonic, consisting of melody with chordal accompaniment.

Theme   Principal melody in a composition.

Theme and Variations Form   Form consisting of a theme followed by a number of variations on the theme.

Thoroughbass   See Basso Continuo.

Timbre   Tone color or specific quality of sound that distinguishes one instrument or voice from another.

Time Notation   Notation in which duration depends on the visual length of the notes as determined by the performer.

Time Signature   Pair of numbers placed at the beginning of a score: the upper number indicates the number of beats per measure; the lower number indicates the type of note that has a value of one beat.

Toccata   Virtuoso composition in free form, usually for keyboard.

Tonality   Aural effect of music centered around one note or based on a particular key.

Tone Cluster   Dissonant chord made up of several adjacent notes.

Tone Poem   See Symphonic Poem.

Tone Row   Basic melody in twelve-tone serial technique, using (in strict form) each note of the chromatic scale only once.

Tonic   Basic or home note of a scale, frequently called *do*.

Tremolo   Rapid repetition of a single note; also refers to a rapid alternation between two notes of a chord.

Tremolo   Rapid repetition of a single note.

Triad   Chord consisting of three tones with a specific intervallic relationship to one another.

Trill   Ornament, usually indicated by the abbreviation *tr* or a wavy-line symbol, in which the written note is played in rapid alternation with the note just above it.

Trio   (1) Composition for three performers; (2) the second section of a minuet or scherzo movement.

Triplet   Beat subdivided into three parts.

Turn   Ornament consisting of a group of four or five notes that "turn around" the note given in the notation.

Tutti   Literally "all." (1) Direction given in a composition when the entire group is to perform together; (2) term for the combined orchestral and solo groups in a Baroque concerto grosso.

Twelve-Tone System   Twentieth-century system of composition based on a tone row.

Variation   Compositional technique in which musical ideas are repeated with some changes.

Virelai   Medieval French secular song based on a poetic form.

Voice   (1) The human voice; (2) a part in an instrumental composition.

Waltz   Dance popular in the nineteenth century, in triple meter and a moderate tempo.

Whole-Tone Scale   Scale in which the octave is divided into six whole-step intervals.

SUGGESTED READINGS

General

BAINES, ANTHONY (Ed.). *Musical Instruments Through the Ages.* Baltimore: Penguin, 1961.

BORROFF, EDITH. *Music in Europe and the United States: A History.* Englewood Cliffs, N.J.: Prentice-Hall, 1971.

CROCKER, RICHARD. *A History of Musical Style.* New York: McGraw-Hill, 1966.

GROUT, DONALD J. *A History of Western Music,* Revised Edition. New York: Norton, 1973.

JANSON, H. W., and JOSEPH KERMAN. *A History of Art and Music.* Englewood Cliffs, N.J.: Prentice-Hall, 1969.

LANG, PAUL HENRY. *Music in Western Civilization.* New York: Norton, 1941.

Non-Western Music

BROWN, ROBERT. "Introduction to the Music of South India" in *Festival of Oriental Music and Related Arts.* Los Angeles: UCLA, 1960.

CHAO, MEI-PO. *The Yellow Bell: A Brief Sketch of the History of Chinese Music.* Baldwin, Md.: L. Elliott, 1934.

DENSMORE, FRANCES. *The American Indians and Their Music.* New York: The Woman's Press, 1936. Reissued by Finch Press Reprints, Ann Arbor, Mich.

DIETZ, BETTY WARNER, and MICHALE OLATUNJI. *Musical Instruments of Africa.* New York: John Day, 1965.

KISHIBE, SHIGEO. *Traditional Music of Japan.* Tokyo: Japan Cultural Society, 1969.

MALM, WILLIAM. *Japanese Music and Musical Instruments.* Rutland, Vt.: Charles E. Tuttle, 1959.

MALM, WILLIAM. *Music Cultures of the Pacific, the Near East, and Asia,* Second Edition. Englewood Cliffs, N.J.: Prentice-Hall, 1977.

NETTL, BRUNO. *North American Indian Musical Styles.* Austin, Tex.: University of Texas Press, 1954.

NKETIA, J. H. KWABENA. *The Music of Africa.* New York: Norton, 1974.

POPLEY, HERBERT A. *The Music of India.* New Delhi: Y.M.C.A. Publishing House, 1966.

WARREN, FRED, and L. WARREN. *The Music of Africa: An Introduction.* Englewood Cliffs, N.J.: Prentice-Hall, 1970.

WELLESZ, EGON (Ed.). *Ancient and Oriental Music.* (Vol. I of *The New Oxford History of Music.*) London: Oxford University Press, 1957.

WIANT, BLISS. *The Music of China.* Hong Kong: Chinese University of Hong Kong, 1965.

Early Music

ABRAHAM, GERALD (Ed.). *The Age of Humanism: 1540–1630.* (Vol. IV of *The New Oxford History of Music.*) London: Oxford University Press, 1968.

APEL, WILLI. *Gregorian Chant.* Bloomington, Ind.: Indiana University Press, 1958.

BLUME, FRIEDRICH. *Renaissance and Baroque Music.* New York: Norton, 1967.

BROWN, HOWARD M. *Music in the Renaissance.* Englewood Cliffs, N.J.: Prentice-Hall, 1976.

DAVISON, ARCHIBALD T., and WILLI APEL. *Historical Anthology of Music.* Cambridge, Mass.: Harvard University Press, 1966.

HOPPIN, RICHARD. *Medieval Music.* New York: Norton, 1978.

HUGHES, ANSELM (Ed.). *Early Medieval Music up to 1300*. (Vol. II of *The New Oxford History of Music*.) London: Oxford University Press, 1954.

HUGHES, ANSELM, and GERALD ABRAHAM (Eds.). *Ars Nova and the Renaissance: 1300–1540*. (Vol. III of *The New Oxford History of Music*.) London: Oxford University Press, 1960.

PARRISH, CARL, and JOHN F. OHL. *Masterpieces of Music Before 1750*. New York: Norton, 1941.

REESE, GUSTAVE. *Music in The Middle Ages*. New York: Norton, 1940.

REESE, GUSTAVE. *Music in the Renaissance*, Revised Edition. New York: Norton, 1959.

ROBERTSON, ALEC, and DENIS STEVENS (Eds.) *Ancient Forms to Polyphony*. (Vol. I of *The Pelican History of Music*.) Baltimore: Penguin, 1960.

ROBERTSON, ALEC, and DENIS STEVENS (Eds.). *Renaissance and Baroque*. (Vol. II of *The Pelican History of Music*.) Baltimore: Penguin, 1963.

SEAY, ALBERT. *Music in the Medieval World*, Second Edition. Englewood Cliffs, N.J.: Prentice-Hall, 1975.

Baroque Music

BLUME, FRIEDRICH. *Renaissance and Baroque Music*. New York: Norton, 1967.

BORROFF, EDITH. *The Music of the Baroque*. Dubuque, Iowa: William C. Brown, 1970.

BUKOFZER, MANFRED F. *Music in the Baroque Era*. New York: Norton, 1947.

DEAN, WINTON. *Handel's Dramatic Oratorios and Masques*. London: Oxford University Press, 1959.

DENT, EDWARD. *Opera*, Revised Edition. Baltimore: Penguin, 1966.

GEIRINGER, KARL, and IRENE GEIRINGER. *Johann Sebastian Bach: The Culmination of an Era*. New York: Oxford University Press, 1966.

GROUT, DONALD J. *A Short History of Opera*, Second Edition. New York: Columbia University Press, 1965.

HUTCHINGS, ARTHUR. *The Baroque Concerto*. New York: Norton, 1965.

NEWMAN, WILLIAM S. *The Sonata in the Baroque Era*, Revised Edition. Chapel Hill, N.C.: University of North Carolina Press, 1966.

PALISCA, CLAUDE V. *Baroque Music*. Englewood Cliffs, N.J.: Prentice-Hall, 1968.

ROBERTSON, ALEC, and DENIS STEVENS (Eds.). *Renaissance and Baroque*. (Vol. II of *The Pelican History of Music*.) Baltimore: Penguin, 1963.

ULRICH, HOMER. *A Survey of Choral Music*. New York: Harcourt Brace Jovanovich, 1973.

WHITTAKER, WILLIAM G. *The Cantatas of Johann Sebastian Bach*. London: Oxford University Press, 1959.

Classical Music

BLUME, FRIEDRICH. *Classic and Romantic Music*. New York: Norton, 1970.

BURK, JOHN. *Mozart and His Music*. New York: Random House, 1959.

CUYLER, LOUISE. *The Symphony*. New York: Harcourt Brace Jovanovich, 1973.

DENT, EDWARD. *Mozart's Operas: A Critical Study*, Revised Edition. London: Oxford University Press, 1947.

GEIRINGER, KARL. *Haydn: A Creative Life in Music*. New York: Doubleday, 1963.

GIRDLESTONE, C. M. *Mozart's Piano Concertos*. London: Cassell, 1948.

GROUT, DONALD J. *A Short History of Opera*, Second Edition. New York: Columbia University Press, 1965.

GROVE, GEORGE. *Beethoven and His Nine Symphonies*. London: Oxford University Press, 1948.

HUTCHINGS, ARTHUR. *A Companion to Mozart's Piano Concertos*. London: Oxford University Press, 1948.

LANDON, H. ROBBINS. *Haydn Symphonies*. Seattle: University of Washington Press, 1969.

MASON, DANIEL GREGORY. *The Quartets of Beethoven*. London: Oxford University Press, 1947.

PAULY, REINHARD. *Music in the Classic Period*, Second Edition. Englewood Cliffs, N.J.: Prentice-Hall, 1973.

ROSEN, CHARLES. *The Classical Style: Haydn, Mozart, Beethoven*. New York: Viking, 1971.

SIMPSON, ROBERT (Ed.). *The Symphony*, Vol. I: *Haydn to Dvořák*. Baltimore: Penguin, 1966.

SOLOMON, MAYNARD. *Beethoven*. New York: Schirmer, 1977.

TOVEY, DONALD F. *Beethoven*. London: Oxford University Press, 1945.

ULRICH, HOMER. *Chamber Music*, Second Edition. New York: Columbia University Press, 1966.

ULRICH, HOMER. *A Survey of Choral Music*. New York: Harcourt Brace Jovanovich, 1973.

YOUNG, PERCY M. *The Concerto*. Boston: Crescendo, 1957.

Romantic Music

ASAF'EV, B. V. *Russian Music from the Beginning of the Nineteenth Century*. Ann Arbor, Mich.: University of Michigan, 1953.

BARZUN, JACQUES. *Berlioz and the Romantic Century*, Third Edition. New York: Columbia University Press, 1969.

BLUME, FRIEDRICH. *Classic and Romantic Music*. New York: Norton, 1970.

BROWN, MAURICE J. E. *Schubert Songs*. Seattle: University of Washington Press, 1967.

CUYLER, LOUISE. *The Symphony*. New York: Harcourt Brace Jovanovich, 1973.

DALE, KATHLEEN. *Nineteenth-Century Piano Music*. London: Oxford University Press, 1954.

GILLESPIE, JOHN. *Five Centuries of Keyboard Music*. Dubuque, Iowa: William C. Brown, 1971.

GROUT, DONALD J. *A Short History of Opera*, Second Edition. New York: Columbia University Press, 1965.

HALL, JAMES H. *The Art Song*. Norman, Okla.: University of Oklahoma Press, 1953.

HORTON, JOHN. *Brahms Orchestral Music*. Seattle: University of Washington Press, 1968.

KIRBY, FRANK E. *A Short History of Keyboard Music*. New York: The Free Press, 1966.

LONGYEAR, REY M. *Nineteenth-Century Romanticism in Music*, Second Edition. Englewood Cliffs, N.J.: Prentice-Hall, 1973.

NEWMAN, ERNEST. *The Wagner Operas*. New York: Knopf, 1949.

NIECKS, F. *Programme Music in the Last Four Centuries*. London: Novella, 1907. Reprinted by Haskell House in New York, 1969.

PALMER, CHRISTOPHER. *Impressionism in Music*. London: Hutchinson, 1973.

SCHONBERG, HAROLD C. *The Great Pianists*. New York: Simon and Schuster, 1963.

SIMPSON, ROBERT (Ed.). *The Symphony*, Vol. I: *Haydn to Dvořák*. Baltimore: Penguin, 1966.

STEIN, JACK M. *Poem and Music in the German Lied from Gluck to Hugo Wolf*. Cambridge, Mass.: Harvard University Press, 1971.

ULRICH, HOMER. *A Survey of Choral Music*. New York: Harcourt Brace Jovanovich, 1973.

VALLAS, LÉON. *The Theories of Claude Debussy*. New York: Dover, 1967.

VAUGHAN WILLIAMS, RALPH. *National Music and Other Essays*. New York: Oxford University Press, 1963.

WARRACK, JOHN. *Tchaikovsky Symphonies and Concertos*. Seattle: University of Washington Press, 1969.

Early Twentieth-Century Music

AUSTIN, WILLIAM W. *Music in the Twentieth Century*. New York: Norton, 1966.

DERI, OTTO. *Exploring Twentieth-Century Music*. New York: Holt, Rinehart and Winston, 1968.

HANSEN, PETER S. *An Introduction to Twentieth-Century Music*, Second Edition. Boston: Allyn and Bacon, 1967.

LEIBOWITZ, RENE. *Schoenberg and His School*. New York: Philosophical Library, 1949.

PERLE, GEORGE. *Serial Composition and Atonality*. Berkeley, Cal.: University of California Press, 1963.

RETI, RUDOLPH. *Tonality, Atonality, Pantonality*. New York: Macmillan, 1958.

SALZMAN, ERIC. *Twentieth-Century Music: An Introduction*, Second Edition. Englewood Cliffs, N.J.: Prentice-Hall, 1974.

SCHOENBERG, ARNOLD. *Style and Idea*. New York: Philosophical Library, 1950.

SLONIMSKY, NICHOLAS. *Music Since 1900*, Fourth Edition. New York: Scribner, 1971.

STEVENS, HALSEY. *Life and Music of Béla Bartók*, Revised Edition. New York: Oxford University Press, 1967.

STRAVINSKY, IGOR. *An Autobiography*. New York: M. and J. Steuer, 1958.

STRAVINSKY, IGOR, and ROBERT CRAFT. *Expositions and Developments*. New York: Doubleday, 1962.

STROBEL, HEINRICH. *Paul Hindemith*. New York: Merlin, 1955.

TANSMAN, ALEXANDRE. *Igor Stravinsky*. New York: Putnam, 1949.

WHITE, ERIC W. *Stravinsky: The Composer and His*

Works. Berkeley, Cal.: University of California Press. 1966.

WITTLICH, GARY E. (Ed.). *Aspects of Twentieth-Century Music.* Englewood Cliffs, N.J.: Prentice-Hall, 1975.

American Music

BARZUN, JACQUES. *Music in American Life.* New York: Doubleday, 1956.

EDWARDS, ARTHUR C., and W. THOMAS MARROCCO. *Music in the United States.* Dubuque, Iowa: William C. Brown, 1968.

EISEN, J. *The Age of Rock.* New York: Random House, 1969.

GREEN, STANLEY. *The World of Musical Comedy.* New York: Ziff-Davis, 1960.

HITCHOCK, H. WILEY. *Music in the United States: A Historical Introduction,* Second Edition. Englewood Cliffs, N.J.: Prentice-Hall, 1974.

HODEIR, ANDRÉ. *Jazz: Its Evolution and Essence.* New York: Grove, 1956.

MARCUS, GREIL (Ed.). *Rock and Roll Will Stand.* Boston: Beacon, 1969.

NETTL, BRUNO. *Folk and Traditional Music of the Western Continents.* Englewood Cliffs, N.J.: Prentice-Hall, 1965.

ROACH, HILDRED. *Black American Music, Past and Present.* Boston: Crescendo Publications, Inc., 1973

SCHULLER, GUNTHER. *Early Jazz: Its Roots and Musical Development.* New York: Oxford University Press, 1968.

SHAW, ARNOLD. *The Rock Revolution.* New York: Macmillan, 1969.

SOUTHERN, EILEEN. *The Music of Black Americans: A History.* New York: Norton, 1971.

TIRRO, FRANK. *Jazz: A History.* New York: Norton, 1977.

Contemporary Music

BABBITT, MILTON. "An Introduction to the RCA Synthesizer" in the *Journal of Music Theory,* Vol. VIII, 1964.

CAGE, JOHN. *Silence: Lectures and Writings.* Middletown, Conn.: Wesleyan University Press, 1961.

COPE, DAVID. *New Directions in Music.* Dubuque, Iowa: William C. Brown, 1971.

DERI, OTTO. *Exploring Twentieth-Century Music.* New York: Holt, Rinehart and Winston, 1968.

HOWE, HUBERT S. *Electronic Music Synthesis.* New York: Norton, 1975.

JUDD, F. C. *Electronic Music and Musique Concrète.* Chester Springs, Pa.: Dufour, 1961.

RUSSCOL, HERBERT. *The Liberation of Sound: An Introduction to Electronic Music.* Englewood Cliffs, N.J.: Prentice-Hall, 1972.

SALZMAN, ERIC. *Twentieth-Century Music: An Introduction,* Second Edition. Englewood Cliffs, N.J.: Prentice-Hall, 1974.

TRYTHALL, GILBERT. *Principles and Practice of Electronic Music.* New York: Grosset and Dunlap, 1973.

WITTLICH, GARY E. (Ed.). *Aspects of Twentieth-Century Music.* Englewood Cliffs, N.J.: Prentice-Hall, 1975.

INDEX OF MUSICAL EXAMPLES

GENERAL INDEX

Baroque music (*continued*)
concerto, 111–118, 193
contrast in, 103–104
decline of, 147
fugue in, 118–120
harmony and texture in, 99–102
instrumental, 107–124
Mass, 139–142
melody and rhythm, 98–99,
149–151
opera, 127–132
oratorio, 136–139
orchestra, 108–109
origin of term "Baroque," 95
vs. Renaissance music, 104
rock, 427
sonata, 109-111
suite, 120–122
timbre, 102–103
types of compositions and form,
103
vocal music, 125–127
Bartók, Béla, 10, 342, 347, 350–353,
431
Basie, Count, 416
bass. *See also* Double bass
clef, 41
drum, 27
figured bass, 101
voice, 23, 217, 226
basso buffo, 226
basso continuo, 101, 109, 156
basso ostinato, 129
bassoon, 26, 103, 109, 155
beam, 43
beat, 10
Beatles, 426, 427–428
bebop. *See* Bop
Beckmann, Max, 362, 375
Bee Gees, 428
Beethoven, Ludwig van
bagatelles, 242
cadenzas, 194
chorus, use of, 314
in Classical-Romantic
continuum, 149
concertos, 193, 200, 201
deafness of, 181–182
and German nationalism, 317
and Haydn, 163, 179
improvisations, 239–240
incidental music, 292–293
influence on Romantic opera, 297
influence on Tchaikovsky, 275
life, 179
Masses, 225, 314
opera, 214, 219, 292
oratorio, 225
overtures, 292, 293
program music, 180–181, 283

Romantic symphony roots in, 265
Romantic tendencies in works,
267
sketchbook, 212 (illus.)
sonatas, 204–206, 213, 242
songs, 252
string quartets, 207–213
symphonies, 179–192
Beiderbecke, Bix, 415
bel canto, 99, 129
bells, 90
Bellini, Vincenzo, 301
Berberian, Cathy, 443
Berg, Alban, 382–384
Berio, Luciano, 443
Berlin, Irving, 421
Berlioz, Hector
choral works, 314
in Classical-Romantic
continuum, 149
idée fixe, 287
life and works, 284–285
and literature, 282
operas, 298
orchestration, 236
program music, 239, 266, 282, 296
songs, 263
Bernstein, Leonard, 422
Berry, Chuck, 424
Billings, William, 392
bimodality, 347
binary form
examples, 117, 122, 160, 161, 384
explanation of, 36
bitonality, 347
biwa, 57
Bizet, Georges, 292, 296
black music, 410–414, 427. *See also*
African music
bluegrass music, 423
blue note, 412
blues, 412, 413 (illus.)
Bohemia, music of. *See* Czech
music
Bolden, Buddy, 415
Boone, Pat, 426
bop, 418–419
Borodin, Alexander, 274, 319
*Boston Handel and Haydn Society
Collection of Church Music*
(Mason, compiler), 394
Boulanger, Nadia, 396, 397, 400
Boulez, Pierre, 432–433, 447
bow, bowed instrument, 25. *See
also* Instruments, string
Brahms, Johannes
in Classical-Romantic
continuum, 149
concertos, 276
importance as composer, 273

influence on other composers,
323, 374
Lieder, 262
life and works, 268–269
overtures, 292
piano works, 242
program music, 283
Requiem Mass, 315, 316
secular choral works, 314
symphonies, 266, 268–273
use of folk songs, 318
bridge, in sonata form, 159
Britten, Benjamin, 370
Brown, Earle, 446
Brown, James, 427
Brubeck, Dave, 420
Bruckner, Anton, 276, 315
Büchner, Georg, 382
bunraku, 57
Burton, Gary, 420
Buxtehude, Dietrich, 102, 110, 123,
133–134
Byrd, William, 84, 87, 90
Byron, Lord, 232

caccia, 73
Caccini, Giulio, 125
cadence, 17
cadenza, 194, 197, 245–246, 277
Cage, John, 443, 446
Calder, Alexander, 446
Caldwell, Sarah, 449
Calvin, John, 82
Camerata, the, 98, 125
Campbell, Glen, 423
canon, 79. *See also* Imitation
cantata, 38, 103, 132–136
canzona, 91
canzon da sonar, 109
Carissimi, Giacomo, 133
Carter, Elliott, 447–448
Carter Family, 423
Cash, Johnny, 423
castanet, 27
cavatina, 223
C clef, 41
celesta, 352
cello, 103, 108 (illus.), 109
chamber music
Classical, 157, 202–213
definition of, 202
ensemble for, 28, 235
experimentation in, 208
Romantic, 239
chance music. *See* Aleatoric music
chanson, 79, 84, 109
chant, Japanese, 56
chant, Gregorian. *See* Gregorian
chant
Char, René, 432, 449

Grateful Dead, the, 427
grave, 13
great staff, 41
Gregorian chant, 63–65, 77, 79, 345, 361–362
Gregory I, Pope, 63
Grieg, Edvard, 242–243, 276, 292, 318, 324–325
Griffes, Charles Tomlinson, 395
Grünwald, Matthias, 359–360
guitar, 25, 90, 249, 250, 323

Haley, Bill
half note, half rest, 43
half step, 153–154
Hammerstein, Oscar, II, 421, 422
Hampton, Lionel, 417 (illus.)
Hancock, Herbie, 420
Handel, Georg Friedrich
  concertos, 116–118, 193
  da capo aria, 129
  keyboard suites, 122
  life and works, 105–106
  operas, 132
  oratorios, 137–139
harmony
  in Bantu music, 48–49
  in Baroque, 99–102, 112; Baroque vs. Classical, 158
  Classical, 152–155; vs. Romantic, 238
  in Debussy's music, 330–331
  fundamentals of, 14–19
  in jazz, 417, 418–419
  major-minor, 99
  Medieval vs. Renaissance, 78
  in Monteverdi's Orfeo, 127–128
  in nationalistic music, 318
  Renaissance vs. Baroque, 104
  Romantic, 234–235; vs. early twentieth-century music, 348
  in twentieth-century music, 347, 352, 358–359, 397, 403–404
harp, 25, 236
harpsichord
  Baroque, 102–103, 108–111, 121, 122
  compared to piano, 28, 157, 203 (illus.)
  described, 27
  Renaissance, 91 (illus.)
Hartmann, Victor, 321
Hauptstimme, 384
Haydn, Franz Josef
  and Beethoven, 163, 179
  and Classical style, 148, 149, 161
  concertos, 200, 201
  and German nationalism, 317
  life, 162–163

modulation in, 154
and Mozart, 163, 171
operas, 214, 218, 219
oratorios, 225
piano sonatas, 204, 242
songs, 252
string quartets, 207, 208 (illus.), 213
symphonies, 161, 162–171
Haydn, Michael, 200, 201
Heine, Heinrich, 253
Henderson, Fletcher, 416, 418–419
Herbert, Victor, 420
Hillis, Margaret, 449
Hindemith, Paul
  and Gebrauchsmusik, 343, 356
  emigrates to U.S., 431
  and Neoclassicism, 344
  opera, 359
  philosophy of music, 356–357
  style, musical, 350, 358–359
homophony, 21, 22, 101–102, 155
Hopkinson, Francis, 392
horn, English, 26, 236
horn, French, 26, 103, 109, 156
humor in music, 343–344
hymn, 65, 315, 413–414. See also Chorale
Hypodorian mode, 64

Ibsen, Henrik, 324
I Ching, 444
idée fixe, 287
idiophone, 27
imitation
  in Bantu music, 48–49
  exact, 73
  in Renaissance polyphony, 77, 80
Impressionistic music, 328–335, 342
impromptu, 237
improvisation
  Baroque, 101, 123
  in concerto cadenza, 194
  in Indian music, 52–53
  Romantic, 239–240, 244, 250
incidental music, 239. See also Program music
Indian music, 52–53. See also American music, Indian
instruments. See also individual instruments
  American Indian, 50, 51, 52
  Baroque, 102–103, 108
  brass, 26–27, 30, 155–156, 237
  Chinese, 55
  early vs. modern 27–28
  electronic, 349. See also Electronic music
  Indian, 53

Japanese, 56–57
keyboard, 27
medieval, 71 (illus.)
percussion, 27, 30, 156, 236, 347–349, 352, 442
plucked, 25
reed, 25–26
Renaissance, 89–91
string, 24–25, 30, 108–109, 155, 156 (illus.), 441–442
twentieth-century techniques, 441–442
wind, 25–27, 116
woodwind, 25–26, 30, 155
instrumentation. See Orchestration; Timbre
interval, 14–15
inversion, 79, 379
Isaac, Heinrich, 81
isorhythm, 70–71
Italian music
  Baroque, 107, 133
  Florentine Baroque opera, 129
  fourteenth-century, 73–74
  nationalism in, 317
  Neapolitan Baroque opera, 130
  Renaissance, 84–87
  Romantic opera, 300–308
  Rome as center of, 83, 129
  in Venice, 83–84, 105, 129–130
Italian overture, 123
Ives, Charles, 402–404

Jackson, Mahalia, 414
Japanese music, 56–58
jazz, 344, 414–420
Jefferson, Thomas, 392, 393 (illus.)
Jefferson Airplane, 427
Joachim, Joseph, 268
Joel, Billy, 427
John XXII, Pope, 70
Jone, Hildegard, 388
Jones, George, 423
Joplin, Scott, 415
Josquin des Prez, 79–80

kabuki plays, 57
Kachina dance song, 51
Kalevala, 325
Kandinsky, Wassily, 375
Kansas City jazz, 416
Kaye, Danny, 417 (illus.)
Kern, Jerome, 421
kettledrum, 71 (illus.). See also Timpani
key, key signature, 42, 152–155. See also Chromaticism; Harmony; Modulation
keyboard, music for, 122, 206. See also individual keyboard instruments

King, B. B., 424
King, Carole, 427
Kinks, the, 426
Klangfarbenmelodie, 376
Köchel, Ludwig von, 173
Kokoschka, Oscar, 375
Kristofferson, Kris, 424
Kyrie eleison, 63

lai, 72
Landini, Francesco, 74
langue d'oc, 66
langue d'oïl, 67
largo, 13
Lassus, Roland de, 82
laude, 136
Lauds, 62
ledger line, 40
Lee, Wilma, 423
legato, 243
Leitmotiv, 310, 311
lento, 13
Leoncavallo, Ruggiero, 307
Leonin, 68–69, 70
Lerner, Alan Jay, 422
Lewis, John, 420
libretto, 218
Lieder, 38, 237, 252–263
lining out, 412
Liszt, Franz
    in Classical-Romantic
        continuum, 149
    concertos, 276
    life, 248–249
    and literature, 282
    Mass, 315
    Paganini's influence on, 249
    piano works, 248–250
    program music, 239, 266, 288, 296
    rhapsodies, 249–250
literature and music. See Music,
    and literature
Little Richard, 424
Loewe, Frederick, 422
Lorca, Federico García, 443
Lully, Jean-Baptiste, 108, 122–123,
    131–132
lute, 89–91, 109, 121
Luther, Martin, 81–82
Lutheran Church, 133, 139
lyric opera, 298–300

McCartney, Paul, 427. See also
    Beatles
MacDermot, Galt, 427
MacDowell, Edward, 327, 395
Machaut, Guillaume de, 71–73
madrigal
    continuo, 126
    as form, 37–38

fourteenth-century Italian, 73
Renaissance English, 87–88
Renaissance Italian, 85–87
Mahler, Gustav, 262–263, 276, 314,
    326, 403
major-minor harmony, 99
major scale, 15, 43
mandola, 71 (illus.)
Manilow, Barry, 427
Mannheim orchestra, 156
ma non troppo, 13
maracas, 27
march, 10, 38
Marenzio, Luca, 85
Marini, Biagio, 109–110
Mascagni, Pietro, 307
Mason, Lowell, 394
Mass, 38
    Baroque, 139–142
    Classical, 157, 225–226
    evolution of, 141
    fourteenth-century, 71, 79
    Medieval, 62–65
    Renaissance, 79–83
    Romantic, 239, 314–315
    secular songs in, 79
Massenet, Jules, 300
Matins, 62
mazurka, 246
measure, 10, 44
Medieval music, 61–74
    Church, 62–65
    fourteenth-century, 70–74
    growth of polyphony, 67–70
    Medieval period, 39, 61
    vs. Renaissance music, 78
    secular, 65–67
Meditations poétiques (Lamartine),
    288
melody
    in American Indian music, 50–52
    Baroque, 98–99; vs. Classical, 158
    Classical, 149–152; vs. Romantic,
        238
    conjunct, 7
    countermelody, 167
    Debussy's, 330
    definition of, 6–7
    disjunct, 6–7
    in early twentieth century, 345,
        358, 403
    in Gregorian chant, 64, 65
    in Indian music, 52–53
    Medieval vs. Renaissance, 78
    melismatic, 64
    in Monteverdi, 127–128
    Renaissance vs. Baroque, 104
    Romantic, 234, 267–268; vs.
        early twentieth-century, 348
    structure of, 7–9

syllabic, 64
and texture, 20–22
in Webern's music, 385
membranophone, 27
Mendelssohn, Felix
    incidental music, 239
    life and works, 293–294
    oratorios, 315, 316
    overtures, 292–295, 296
    piano works, 242
    symphonies, 266, 275–276
meno, 13
menuetto. See Minuet
Messiaen, Olivier, 431, 432, 433
meter, 10–12, 43–44, 151–152,
    345–346
Meyerbeer, Giacomo, 298
mezzo piano, mezzo forte, 32
mezzo-soprano, 23, 217
middle C, 40–41
Midsummer Night's Dream, A
    (Shakespeare), 239, 293
Miller, Roger, 423
Minnesinger, 67
minor scale, 154–155
minstrel show, 414
minuet, 12, 161
minuet and trio, 161, 169–170,
    176–177, 204
Missa brevis, 139
mode(s). See also Scale(s)
    Church, 64–65, 100–101, 331, 432
    Greek, 61, 100
    major, 43
    minor, 43
moderato, 13
Modern Jazz Quartet, 420
modulation
    in Baroque music, 99–100
    in Classical music, 153–155,
        159–160, 163
    definition of, 19
    in Romantic music, 234, 244, 245
molto, 13
monody, 98, 125–128
monophony, 20, 22
Monteverdi, Claudio
    instrumentation in, 28–30
    madrigals, 86–87, 125–126
    operas, 127–128, 130
    sinfonias, 122
Morley, Thomas, 87, 88
Morton, "Jelly Roll," 415
motet, 38, 70, 79
motive, 34–35, 180, 182–186,
    289–291, 353. See also
    Leitmotiv
movement, 38
    in Baroque works, 103, 112, 113
    in Classical works, 161, 194

Othello (Shakespeare), 307
overture, 38, 221, 239
    French, 121, 122–123, 131
    Italian, 130, 161

padouana. *See* Pavana
Paganini, Niccolò, 249, 251
painting and music. *See* Music, and painting
Palestrina, Giovanni Pierluigi da, 82–83
pandiatonicism, 347
parallel motion, 48–49
paraphrase technique, 80–81
Parker, Charlie, 418–419
partita, 121. *See also* Suite
Parton, Dolly, 424
part singing, 52. *See also* Polyphony
part writing, 77
pavana, 90, 121
Peer Gynt (Ibsen), 292
Peking opera, 55
Penderecki, Krzysztof, 441–442
Pergolesi, Giovanni Battista, 366–367
Peri, Jacopo, 125
Perotin, 70
Petrucci, Ottaviano dei, 84
phrase, 8, 35, 150
piano (instrument), 27, 156
    Classical-Romantic continuum in, 242
    Classical works for, 203, 242
    concertos, 195–201, 237–238
    Cowell's experiments with, 402
    vs. harpsichord, 28, 157, 203 (illus.)
    nineteenth-century improvements in, 252
    piano quartet, 202
    piano quintet, 202
    prepared, 444
    Romantic music for, 235, 237, 242–251
    and voice, in Lieder, 253
piano, pianissimo, 32
piccolo, 25, 236
Pink Floyd, 427
Piston, Walter, 400–401
pitch
    in Bantu music, 48
    in Chinese music, 54
    definition of, 6
    and dynamics, 32
    how voice produces, 23
    notation of, 40–43
più, 13
pizzicato, 115
plagal cadence, 17
plagal mode, 64

plainchant. *See* Gregorian chant
Plains Indians, music of, 50
poco, 13
Pointillism, 385
polka, 10
polonaise, 246
polychords, polyharmony, 359
polyphony. *See also* Counterpoint; Imitation; Texture
    Baroque, 101–102
    Council of Trent on, 82
    explanation of, 20–21, 22
    origins and growth of, 67–70
    in Reformation, 82
    Renaissance, 76–79
polyrhythm, 352
polytonality, 347
popular music, 344. *See also* American music, popular; Folk music
Porter, Cole, 421
Poulenc, Francis, 368
Powell, Bud, 419
prelude, 246
Presley, Elvis, 425–426, 427
presto, prestissimo, 13
prima donna, 216, 217
prima prattica, 98
Prime, 62
primitivism, 342
printing, music, 84
Procul Harum, 427
program music, 113–115, 180–181, 239, 282–296, 321–322
Progressivism (American), 401
Prokofiev, Sergei, 342, 344, 370–372
Proper, 63
psaltery, 71 (illus.)
Puccini, Giacomo, 307
Pueblo Indians, music of, 51
pulse, 151–152
Purcell, Henry, 110, 122, 129
Pushkin, Alexander, 319
Pythagoras, 52

quarter note, quarter rest, 43
quartet, 38. *See also individual types of quartets*
quintet, 38. *See also individual types of quintets*

Rachmaninoff, Sergei, 242–243, 327
raga, 52–53
ragtime, 415
Rainey, Gertrude "Ma," 412
Rameau, Jean-Philippe, 132
Ramones, 428
Ravel, Maurice, 263, 321–322, 335, 368–370
Razumovsky, Count, 209

recapitulation, 159–160. *See also* Sonata form
recitative
    Baroque, 99, 129
    in Classical opera, 217, 223, 224, 225
    in Eskimo music, 51
    recitativo accompagnato, 217
    recitativo secco, 129, 217
recorder, 28, 89
Redding, Otis, 427
reed, 25. *See also* Instruments, woodwind; *individual instruments*
Reformation, music of, 79, 81–82
relative major, 155
relative minor, 43, 155
religious music. *See also* Church, Catholic; Church, Lutheran; *individual cultures*
    in colonial America, 391
    in Renaissance, 79–84
Reményi, Eduard, 268
Renaissance music
    vs. Baroque music, 104
    general characteristics of, 75–76
    instruments in, 89–91
    late, 82–84
    vs. Medieval music, 78
    polyphony in, 76–78
    Renaissance period, 39, 75
    rhythm, twentieth-century use of, 345
    secular, 84–89
repeat sign, 159
repetition, 8, 34–35, 50, 244. *See also* Form
Requiem Mass. *See* Mass
resolution, harmonic, 17
Respighi, Ottorino, 335
responsorial singing, 48–49
rest, 44
retrograde, 38, 250
rhapsody, 38, 250
rhythm
    in ars nova, 70–71
    in American Indian music, 50–52
    in Bantu music, 49
    in Baroque music, 98–99, 122, 140; vs. Classical, 158
    Classical, 149–152; vs. Romantic, 238
    in Debussy, 330
    dotted, 168
    in early twentieth century, 345–346, 352, 358, 364–366
    in Indian music, 52–53
    in Japanese music, 57
    in jazz, 414, 419
    Medieval vs. Renaissance, 78

in nationalistic music, 318
palindromes, 431
in Renaissance, 77; vs. Baroque, 104
rhythmic motion, 12
Romantic, 234; vs. early twentieth-century, 348
as structural element, 9–13
in American music, 397, 403, 436
ricercar, 91, 118, 123. *See also* Fantasia
Rimsky-Korsakov, Nikolai, 274, 319, 320, 362–363
ring shout, 411
ripieno, 112
ritardando, 12
ritornello, 37–38, 112, 114–115, 116, 160
Ritter, Tex, 423
Robbins, Marty, 423
rock music, 424–428
Rococo, 148
Rodgers, Jimmie, 423
Rodgers, Richard, 421–422
Rogers, Kenny, 424
Rogers, Roy, 423
Roi s'amuse, Le (Hugo), 302
Rolling Stones, the, 426, 428
Romantic music
    Classical influences of, 173, 233, 240–241
    vs. Classical music, 238
    vs. early twentieth-century music, 348
    emotion in, 233
    form in, 239–241
    harmony and texture in, 234–235
    late Romantic music, 326–328
    melody and rhythm in, 234, 235
    orchestra in, 236–237
    for piano, 242–251
    Romantic period, 39, 229, 233
    "Romantic" vs. "Classical," 148–149
    songs, 252–264
    twentieth-century reaction against, 341–342
    types of compositions, 237–239
Romberg, Sigmund, 420
Romeo and Juliet (Shakespeare), 422
rondeau, 72
rondo form, 38
    in Bartók, 355–356
    in Classical music, 160, 194, 197, 204, 205–206
    in Romantic music, 279–280, 289–291
Ronstadt, Linda, 427
Rossi, Luigi, 133

Rossi, Salomone, 109, 122
Rossini, Gioacchino, 301, 315
round. *See* Imitation, exact
rubato, 99, 243–244
Rubenstein, Anton, 274, 319
Rückert, Friedrich, 260
"Russian Five, The," 319
Russian music, 274, 318–322, 327, 370
Russolo, Luigi, 342

sackbut, 89
Saint Mark's Basilica (Venice), 83–84, 105
Saint Martial (monastery), 67
Saint Peter's (Rome), 82
Saint-Saëns, Camille, 300
Salomon, Johann Peter, 163
samisen, 57
Sanctus, 63
Sand, George. *See* Dudevant, Aurore
sarabande, 121, 122
Satie, Erik, 343–344, 368
saxophone, 26
scale(s). *See also* Modes
    chromatic, 15, 42
    major, 15, 16, 43, 153–154
    minor, 15, 16, 43, 155
    pentatonic, 54, 331
    twentieth-century use of various, 345, 351
    whole-note, 330
Scandinavian music, 324–325, 327
Scarlatti, Alessandro, 123, 129, 130, 133
Scarlatti, Domenico, 110–111
Schaeffer, Pierre, 345
Schein, Johann Hermann, 121
scherzo, 180, 246–247
Schiller, Friedrich von, 253, 306
Schoenberg, Arnold
    atonal works, 375–378
    and Berg, 382
    emigrates to U.S., 431
    and Expressionist painting, 375
    influence of Brahms and Wagner on, 374
    late Romantic works, 327
    melody in, 345
    and serialism, 344–345, 378–381
    and Sprechstimme, 442–443
    and Webern, 385
Schubert, Franz
    chamber music, 213
    in Classical-Romantic continuum, 149
    influence on Brahms, 268
    late works, 255
    and Lieder, 237, 252, 253–258

life of, 253
piano sonatas, 204
secular choral works, 314
symphonies, 265–266
Schuller, Gunther, 420
Schumann, Clara, 259–260, 262, 268
Schumann, Robert
    and Brahms, 268
    on Classical works, 147, 181
    concertos, 276
    Lieder, 237, 258–262
    life and works, 258–262
    piano works, 242
    symphonies, 266, 275–276
    as writer, 282
Schütz, Heinrich, 133
Scott, Sir Walter, 301
Scriabin, Alexander, 327, 335
Scribe, Eugène, 298
section, as formal device, 35
secunda prattica, 98
Seeger, Pete, 410
sequence, 114
serial music
    as new art form 381–382
    Berg's, 382
    examples of, 380–381, 383–384, 385–388, 435–436
    origins of, 344–345
    post-World War II, 431–436
    Schoenberg's, 378–381
    total serialization, 432
    Webern's, 385–388
Sessions, Roger, 401
Sext, 62
sforzando, 32
sharp, 42, 154
shawm, 71 (illus.), 89
Shostakovich, Dmitri, 342, 370
Sibelius, Jean, 325, 327
Sills, Beverly, 23, 217
sinfonia, 122–123
singing school, 391–392
singspiel, 218–219, 226
sitar, 53
"Six, The," 343–344
sixteenth note, sixteenth rest, 43
sixty-fourth note, sixty-fourth rest, 43
Smetana, Bedřich, 322–323
Smith, Bessie, 412, 413 (illus.)
Smithson, Harriet, 284–285
solo
    concerto, 112
    performer in Classical concerto, 194
    sonata, Baroque, 109–111
    voices, in opera, 216–217
sona, 55

sonata, 55
  Baroque, 103, 109, 111
  Classical, 157, 202, 203–206
  Romantic piano sonata, 242,
    246–247
sonata-allegro form. See Sonata
  form
sonata cycle
  in Classical music, 157, 194, 204,
    207
  in Romantic music, 237, 239–241
sonata da camera, 109–110
sonata da chiesa, 109–110
sonata form
  in Beethoven, examples of,
    182–186, 190–192, 204–205,
    209–213
  in Classical concerto, 194
  description of, 159–160
  in Haydn, example of, 164–165
  in Mozart, examples of, 173–175,
    175–176, 177–178, 195–197
  in Romantic music, examples of,
    269–270, 272–273, 277–278
  in twentieth-century music,
    examples of, 354–355,
    360–361, 368–370, 372
sonata-rondo form, 170–171
Sóndheim, Stephen, 422
song, 38. See also Ayre; Folk music;
    Lieder
  art song, Romantic, 252–264
  Classical, 157
  cycle, 237
  group work, 411
  modified strophic, examples of,
    256–258, 263. See also
    Strophic form
  occupational, 409
  orchestral, 262–263
  role of piano in, 252–253
  secular Medieval, 79
  secular Renaissance, 89, 90
  shout song, 411
  song sermon, 412
  troubadour, 66–67
Song Is Born, A (film), 417 (illus.)
soprano, 23, 216–217
Sorrows of Young Werther, The
    (Goethe), 229, 231
sound, origin of, 5
Sousa, John Philip, 395
Spanish music, 323–324
spiritual, 412–413
Sprechstimme, 376, 442–443
staccato, 210
staff, 6, 40
Stamitz, Johann, 156
stanza, 36
stile rappresentativo, 98

Stockhausen, Karlheinz, 427,
    433–434, 447
Stradivarius, Antonius, 113 (illus.)
Strauss, Richard
  Lieder, 262
  operas, 326–327
  program music, 239, 283,
    288–291, 296
Stravinsky, Igor
  on Boulez, 432
  early works, 362–366
  emigrates to U.S., 431
  harmony and texture in, 364–365
  influence on American
    composers, 396
  melody, 345
  on music, 5, 19
  as nationalist composer, 342
  and Neoclassicism, 344, 366–367
  rhythm and meter in, 345,
    364–365, 366
  serial works, 434–436
  and tonal music, 350
  and twentieth-century percussion
    techniques, 442
string ensembles, 202.
string quartet, 157, 202, 207–213,
    239
strophic form
  explanation of, 35–36
  in Lieder, 253
  strophic aria, 300
  strophic-bass aria, 129
structure. See Form, musical;
    individual musical elements
style brisé, 121
stylistic periods, Western music,
    38–39
subdominant chord, 17, 152–153
subject, of fugue, 118–119
suite, 38, 103, 120–122, 161
Sutherland, Joan, 217
su-yueh music, 54
"swing." See Jazz
symphonic poem, 38, 239, 283–284,
    288–291
symphony, 38
  Classical, 157, 161–192, 207,
    266–268
  origins in Baroque sonata, 111
  program, 239, 266, 283, 284–287.
    See also Program music
  Romantic, 237, 265–276
symphony orchestra. See Orchestra
syncopation, 11
synthesizer, sound, 28

tabla, 53 (illus.)
tala, 52–53
tall tales, 410

tambura, 53 (illus.)
tape music. See Musique concrète,
    437
Taylor, James, 427
Tchaikovsky, Peter Ilyich
  concertos, 276–280
  life and works, 273–275
  meter in, 10
  program music, 239, 283
  symphonies, 266, 273–275
  and Western style, 319
Tebaldi, Renata, 217
temperament, equal, 100–101
tempo, 12, 13, 32
tempus perfectum, 70
tenor
  clef, 41
  in organum, 67
  voice, 23, 217
Terce, 62
ternary form
  in Baroque music, example of, 117
  in Classical music, examples of,
    160, 169–170, 176–177,
    187–189, 204
  explained, 36
  in modern music, examples of,
    361, 369
  in Romantic music, examples of,
    260–261, 270–272, 278
text painting, 77, 85–87, 128. See
    also Program music
texture
  Baroque, 99–102; vs. Classical,
    158
  Classical, 152–155; vs. Romantic,
    238
  explanation of, 20–22
  Medieval vs. Renaissance, 78
  Renaissance vs. Baroque, 104
  Romantic, 235; vs. early
    twentieth-century, 348
  in twentieth-century music, 347,
    352, 404
theme, 159–160, 163, 195–200
theme and variations
  in Classical works, 160, 165–169,
    186–187, 194, 198–200, 204
  explanation of, 36–37
  in jazz, 414–415
  in Webern's music, 386–388
thirty-second note, thirty-second
    rest, 42
Thomas, Ambroise, 299
Thomas, Theodore, 394
tie, 44
timbre. See also Orchestration;
    individual instruments
  Baroque, 102–103, 108–109; vs.
    Classical, 158

	Medieval and Renaissance Periods	**Baroque Period**
	c. 500–c. 1600	c. 1600–c. 1750

Major Composers	Ventadorn (12th cent.)	Monteverdi (1567–1643)
	Leonin (12th cent.)	Frescobaldi (1583–1643)
	Vitry (1290–1361)	Schütz (1585–1672)
	Machaut (c. 1300–1377)	Lully (1632–1687)
	Landini (1325–1397)	Buxtehude (c. 1637–1707)
	Ockeghem (c. 1340–c. 1495)	Corelli (1653–1713)
	Dufay (c. 1400–1474)	Purcell (c. 1659–1695)
	Isaac (c. 1450–c. 1517)	A. Scarlatti (1660–1725)
	Josquin (c. 1450–1521)	Couperin (1668–1733)
	Palestrina (c. 1524–1594)	Vivaldi (c. 1675–1741)
	Morley (1557–1602)	Rameau (1683–1764)
	G. Gabrieli (c. 1557–1612)	J. S. Bach (1685–1750)
	Gesualdo (1560–1613)	D. Scarlatti (1685–1757)
	Monteverdi (1567–1643)	Handel (1685–1759)

Major Political, Social, and Cultural Figures	Pope Gregory I (c. 540–604)	Donne (1573–1631)
	Charlemagne (742–814)	Rubens (1577–1640)
	Eleanor of Aquitaine (c. 1122–1204)	Bernini (1598–1680)
	Dante (1265–1321)	Rembrandt (1606–1669)
	Chaucer (c. 1340–1400)	Milton (1608–1674)
	Da Vinci (1452–1519)	Molière (1622–1673)
	Machiavelli (1469–1527)	Spinoza (1632–1677)
	Michelangelo (1475–1564)	Locke (1632–1704)
	Raphael (1483–1520)	Wren (1632–1723)
	Luther (1483–1546)	Louis XIV (1638–1715)
	Henry VIII of England (1491–1547)	Racine (1639–1699)
	Elizabeth I of England (1533–1603)	Newton (1642–1727)
	Cervantes (1547–1616)	Defoe (c. 1659–1731)
	Shakespeare (1564–1616)	Swift (1667–1745)
		Watteau (1684–1721)